MATERIALS FOR THE STUDY OF BUSINESS

EDUCATION FOR BUSINESS

THE UNIVERSITY OF CHICAGO PRESS
CHICAGO, ILLINOIS

THE BAKER & TAYLOR COMPANY
NEW YORK

THE CAMBRIDGE UNIVERSITY PRESS
LONDON

THE MARUZEN-KABUSHIKI-KAISHA
TOKYO, OSAKA, KYOTO, FUKUOKA, SENDAI

THE MISSION BOOK COMPANY
SHANGHAI

EDUCATION FOR BUSINESS

BY

LEVERETT S. LYON

PROFESSOR OF POLITICAL ECONOMY AND DEAN OF
THE SCHOOL OF COMMERCE AND FINANCE
WASHINGTON UNIVERSITY

THE UNIVERSITY OF CHICAGO PRESS
CHICAGO, ILLINOIS

Published September 1922
Second Edition August 1923

Composed and Printed By
The University of Chicago Press
Chicago, Illinois, U.S.A.

TO
L. N. L.

PREFACE TO THE FIRST EDITION

Business education in America is unique in its vigor and in its lack of guidance. It has exhibited a remarkable growth and aroused an unusual interest in the general mind, but it has received a minimum of thoughtful attention from those institutions which are professionally concerned with education.

Business education has never been subjected to an "overview." As a result no one type of business education institution has been able clearly to outline its program in relation to the work of other types. With this disability, institutions have multiplied, not to supplement one another, but largely to compete in doing similar work.

Without a clear sense of purpose and relationships the organization of a rational curriculum in any type of school has been difficult. As a result the many capable persons planning business courses and teaching business subjects have planned and taught often in terms of tradition, custom, or, at best, immediate goals.

But to any who will pause to take a detached point of view, it will appear at once that nothing is to be gained when concerned with a problem of curriculum by accepting traditional studies and attempting to juggle them into some defensible arrangement. It will be obvious that courses in business education should be built up in terms of purposes, and it will be quite as clear that different forms of institutions may well serve different ends. To determine the general objectives of business education, to indicate the important agencies concerned and to suggest the place of each is the purpose of this work. It is, therefore, not a discussion of the curriculum for a *particular* type of school, but an approach and point of departure for a study of the curriculum of *any* type of business course.

The book should thus have a use as an introductory text in that increasing number of institutions which are training teachers of business subjects and where there is a growing realization that no narrow approach to a study of business education will prove permanently satisfactory. For such schools it should make possible a foundation course upon which more specialized courses can be built with an understanding of the business educational structure as a whole. The volume should also render a service to those general readers who have a serious interest in the whole field of business education and to those persons who have already made a professional connection with any special phase of it. For the former it will be a survey more or less complete in itself; for the latter it is a method of approach to their special problems.

The emphasis given the public secondary school needs a word of explanation. First of all, the general extent of business education in such schools is so great as to warrant a more elaborate discussion of the high school than that given to other institutions. Moreover, the varied forms in which the secondary schools' relation to commercial education appears causes a somewhat extended treatment. Related to these considerations is the fact that normal schools' interest in commercial education will center in high-school problems. Finally, there is no doubt that the high school has been farther astray in the work it has attempted than have most of the other institutions participating in giving business education. At the same time, its proper rôle is so important and so certain not to be performed save by the public high school that almost any extent of emphasis could be justified.

The book has its origins in specific problems of curriculum-making. For several years the writer was responsible for certain phases of the business curriculum in a large high school. In the effort to deal with the problem presented there, most of the ideas expressed in this volume had their beginning. The School of Commerce and Administration of the University of Chicago later furnished a congenial atmosphere for the development of these ideas and an opportunity to discuss them with mature students engaged in teaching and school administration.

Obligations, especially to authors and publishers for permission to quote material, are many. A careful effort has been made to give specific acknowledgment for these quotations where they appear, as well as for the kindness of several individuals who have prepared statements. From E. W. Barnhart, chief of the Commercial Division of the Federal Board for Vocational Education, there have come a number of valuable suggestions. Through his kindness, and through the courtesy of F. G. Nichols, the writer was given early access to the results of the Federal Board's occupational surveys. William Bachrach, supervisor of commercial education in the Chicago high schools, has had the temerity to experiment with the material in the classes of the Chicago Normal School while it was still in proof, and has made contributions as a result.

Among my colleagues, L. C. Marshall read the entire manuscript and offered many invaluable suggestions, while Professors Emery Filbey, Franklin Bobbitt, and C. O. Hardy have given helpful criticisms on particular chapters. A special obligation is due Miss May R. Freedman for help in the collection and arrangement of material and the preparation of the Index. In no small way has the physical burden been lightened by the secretarial and stenographic aid of the Misses Sigrid M. Johnson, A. M. Tillotson, Nira Cowan, and D. Mulloy.

LEVERETT S. LYON

UNIVERSITY OF CHICAGO
August 1, 1922

PREFACE TO THE SECOND EDITION

This volume was prepared with the hope, expressed in the preface to the first edition, that it might be of service to general readers and to students in institutions giving teacher training. If the general reader had been the only reader contemplated, the clear expression of a point of view would have been the only matter of primary importance. But to make the book valuable to students, the evidence was laid out in some detail, conflicting attitudes were expressed, questions interpolated, and material otherwise introduced for the constant discussion and reaction of class work.

These introductions into the skeleton of thought make it possible for the student to develop a view through his own thinking, but they constitute something of an interference to the reader who wishes to see quickly approach and conclusions only. There has therefore been added in this edition a final chapter which is something of a sketch of the book as a whole. It is hoped that this chapter may serve the general reader as a certification of viewpoint and the student as a summary as well. As the title of the chapter indicates, there is also the belief that this summarized viewpoint may aid educators in applying the ideas of the book to practical situations.

The development of certain material has made possible in this edition a new proposal on page 600, and one rather significant point has been emphasized by italics on page 577.

LEVERETT S. LYON

CHICAGO
June 26, 1923

TABLE OF CONTENTS

PART I. A STATEMENT OF THE CASE

PART II. THE OBJECTIVES OF EDUCATION FOR BUSINESS

PART III. MODERN AGENCIES OF EDUCATION FOR BUSINESS

A. THE OUTSTANDING INSTITUTIONS. CHAPTERS X–XV

B. MODERN EXTENSIONS OF THE HIGH-SCHOOL COMMERCIAL COURSE. CHAPTERS XVI–XX

PART IV. HIGH-SCHOOL COMMERCIAL-CURRICULUM REFORM

PART I

A STATEMENT OF THE CASE

CHAPTER I

THE GROWTH AND POSITION OF BUSINESS EDUCATION

The growth of education for business has been a matter of common observation and interest for some years past. To such an extent has this been the case that figures are hardly necessary to demonstrate the fact.

But the growth of business education, though vigorous almost beyond precedent, has not been a wholly regular nor a wholly uniform growth. Certain phases of its development have outstripped others, certain aspects which have at times expanded rapidly at other times have been retarded. New types of institutions aiding business education have from time to time sprung into existence, and almost without exception have shown remarkable vitality. Figures can therefore clarify much that is vague in the common knowledge: they can give tangibility to impressions and establish a sense of relativity.

Because of chronological precedence, if for no other reason, certain statistics concerning the private commercial school may well be put first and may furnish a sort of basis by which changes may be judged.

TABLE I

INCREASE IN NUMBER OF STUDENTS IN PRIVATE COMMERCIAL SCHOOLS FROM 1893 TO 1918*

	Year		Percentage Increase
	1893	1918	
Students in private commercial schools	115,748	289,579	150.18

* U.S. Bureau of Education, *Education Report*, 1893–94, II, 2170; *Biennial Survey of Education*, Bulletin No. 47, 1919, p. 5.

The year 1918 is the latest for which figures are shown in biennial reports of the Bureau of Education. A period of twenty-five years is sufficiently long to do justice to the facts to be considered. The figures in Table I show the growth in number of students in private commercial schools for a period of twenty-five years including and preceding 1918. The figures show an increase in the number of students in private commercial schools between 1893 and 1918 of 189, 579, or a percentage increase of 150.18. The growth has not been entirely uniform, if the statistics of the Bureau of Education may be trusted. According to the enumeration of the Bureau the number of students in these schools declined steadily from 1893 to 1898. At the latter date there were approximately 70,000 enrolled. From 1898 there was a sharp increase until 1901, when there were approximately 135,000 such students. From that time there were fluctuations both up a id down until 1911, after which there came a steady rise to the present number. (The details of this growth may be seen in Fig. 1, p. 6.)

GROWTH OF BUSINESS EDUCATION IN SECONDARY SCHOOLS

If we turn to education for business as represented by the secondary schools we find a very marked growth indicated in a number of ways.

TABLE II

INCREASE IN NUMBER OF HIGH SCHOOLS TEACHING COMMERCIAL WORK*

	Year		Percentage Increase
	1911	1918	
Number of high schools........	1,752	2,953	68.55

* U.S. Bureau of Education, *Biennial Survey of Education*, Bulletin No. 19, 1920, p. 13. The data for the last year include those for the junior high schools.

Table II shows that the number of high schools teaching commercial work is rapidly increasing. From 1911 to 1918 the increase was 68.55 per cent. (Figures are not available prior to 1911.)

The past twenty-five years have been the period of great growth of high schools and of high-school students. Table III presents certain pertinent data concerning this growth.

TABLE III

INCREASE IN NUMBER OF PUBLIC HIGH SCHOOL STUDENTS AND PUBLIC HIGH SCHOOL COMMERCIAL STUDENTS FROM 1893 TO 1918*

Number of Students	Year		Percentage Increase
	1893	1918	
High-school students..........	289,274	1,925,473	565.62
High-school commercial students	15,220	278,275	1,728.35

* U.S. Bureau of Education, *Education Report*, 1893–94, II, 217; 1907, II, 1045; and advance sheets from the *Biennial Survey of Education*, Bulletin No. 31, 1920, p. 4, and Bulletin No. 19, 1920, p. 138.

The number of students shows an increase from something over a quarter of a million to well toward two million—a striking gain. The percentage of increase is 565.62 per cent. But this growth looks meager when compared to the growth in the number of commercial students among these high-school students. Here the percentage increase is 1,728.35 per cent.

TABLE IV

INCREASE IN NUMBER OF STUDENTS IN COMMERCIAL AND BUSINESS COURSES IN PRIVATE HIGH SCHOOLS AND ACADEMIES, IN PUBLIC HIGH SCHOOLS, AND IN COMMERCIAL AND BUSINESS SCHOOLS FROM 1893 TO 1918*

Type of School	Students Enrolled		Percentage Increase
	1893	1918	
Private high schools...........	4,466	23,801	432.93
Commercial and business schools	115,748	289,579	150.18
Public high schools............	15,220	278,275	1,728.35

* U.S. Bureau of Education, *Education Report*, 1900–1901, II, 2268; *Biennial Survey of Education*, Bulletin No. 3, 1920, p. 44; Bulletin No. 19, 1920, p. 13; Bulletin No 47. 1919, p. 5.

Table IV makes possible some comparisons between the increase of numbers in several types of institutions giving business courses of a somewhat similar kind.

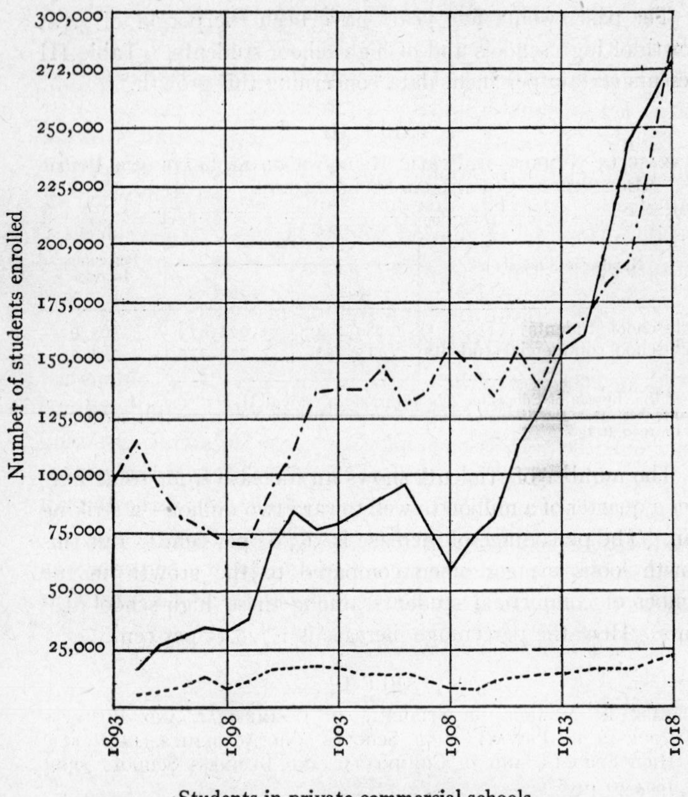

Students in private commercial schools
Students in commercial courses in public high schools
Students in commercial courses in private high schools

Compiled from *Reports of U.S. Commissioner of Education* and *Bienniel Survey of Education*
1902, II, 2003; *1906*, II, 1095;
1907, II, 1117; *1910*, II, 1249.
Bulletin No. 47, 1919, p. 5;
" No. 19, 1920, p. 13;
" No. 3, 1920, p. 5.

Figures for public and private high schools are unavailable for 1893 and 1907 and for all types in 1917.

FIG. 1.—Number of students enrolled in private commercial schools, and in commercial courses in public high schools and private high schools from 1893–1918.

The outstanding gain has been in the public high school, although the more than 400 per cent increase of the private high school is striking. The private business school shows a relative lag, in spite of its large actual gains.

Figure 1 presents the same data in some detail showing actual and relative positions of these three institutions year by year since 1893. The diagram shows clearly the period of growth, of loss, of stagnation, and of keenest rivalry of these institutions.

PERCENTAGE OF HIGH-SCHOOL STUDENTS IN COMMERCIAL COURSES

A consideration of the relatively rapid growth of commercial students in secondary schools leads naturally to an inquiry concerning the proportion of high-school students which is taking commercial work. There are presented in Table V the general facts as they are indicated by the data collected by the Bureau of Education. This table shows that while in 1893 the percentage of students in commercial work was 5.26, the percentage in 1918 was 14.45. In other words, the percentage has somewhat less than trebled.

TABLE V

PERCENTAGE OF STUDENTS IN COMMERCIAL COURSES IN PUBLIC HIGH SCHOOLS IN 1893 AND 1918*

Year	Students in Commercial Courses	All Students	Percentage in Commercial Work
1893	15,220	289,274	5.26
1918	278,275	1,925,473	14.45

* U.S. Bureau of Education, *Education Report*, 1893–94, II, 217; 1907, II, 1045; the *Biennial Survey of Education*, Bulletin No. 31, 1920, p. 4, and Bulletin No. 19, 1920, p. 138.

The situation is perhaps better shown by the results secured from a private survey made with a questionnaire in 1917–18. This questionnaire covered each state in the Union and was addressed to all high schools having over two hundred pupils in commercial courses, as shown by the latest report of the Commissioner of Education then available. In addition, the

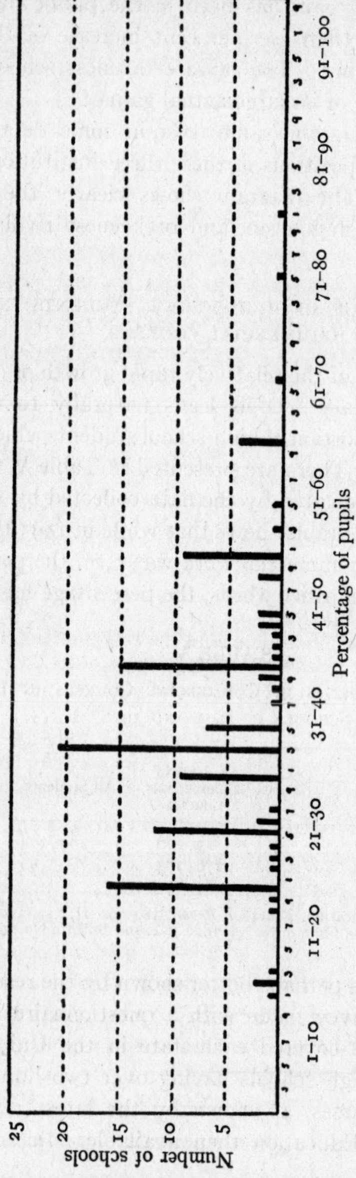

FIG. 2.—Number of schools reporting various percentages of pupils in commercial courses, as reported by 123 high schools*

* Adapted from L. S. Lyon, *A Survey of Commercial Education in the Public High Schools of the United States*, University of Chicago, 1919.

questionnaire covered a considerable number of high schools having a smaller number of students.

A summary of the data dealing with the percentage of pupils in commercial courses indicates that, of the 136 schools replying to the questionnaire, 123, or 90.5 per cent, gave the percentage of students in commercial work. An examination of Figure 2 will indicate the distribution reported. Vertical bars in this diagram show the number of schools reporting various percentages of pupils in commercial work. It will be suspected after a moment's study of this diagram that the percentages stated by school officials are not absolutely accurate. Clearly, these officials sent in their reports in convenient numbers that only approximated the percentages of their students that are in commercial work. There is no reason, however, why this fact should invalidate the use of the figures for forming general conclusions.

A more accurate picture of the situation is given in Figure 3. In this diagram the percentages 11–20, 21–30, etc., have been grouped together, and we thus secure a basis for representation in groups of percentages.

Sixteen schools, 13 per cent of those answering this question, reported 20 per cent of their students in commercial courses. Twenty-one schools, 17.9 per cent of those reporting, estimated one-third of their students to be in commercial work, and fifteen schools, 12.3 per cent, indicated that 40 per cent of their students were in commercial courses. No school reported less than 10 per cent of their pupils in commercial courses, nine reported 50 per cent, and four reported 60 per cent. Three schools reported more than 60 per cent of their students in this type of work. Plainly the mode is in the neighborhood of 33⅓ per cent. Figure 2 shows that a larger number of schools reported 20 per cent of their students in commercial courses than reported 25 per cent, 30 per cent, or any other per cent until 33⅓ is reached. The question may fairly be raised whether there are actually fewer schools that have 25 per cent than have 20 per cent. One of two answers must be given: Either there are fewer schools in the 25 per cent class than in the

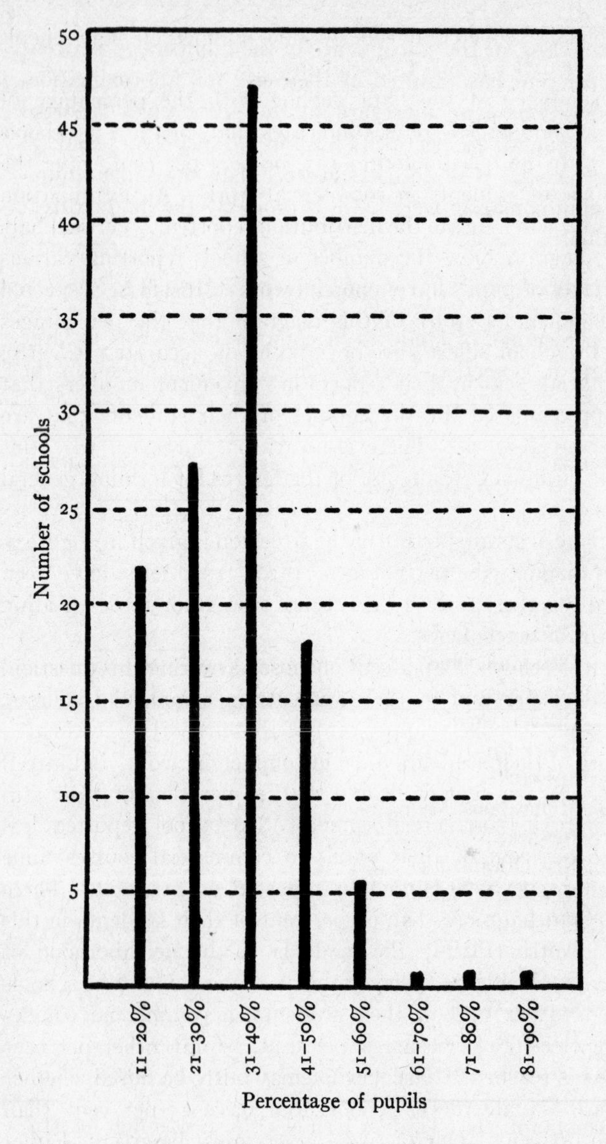

FIG. 3.—Number of schools reporting indicated percentages of pupils in commercial courses, as reported by 123 high schools.

20 per cent class, or the convenience of the numbers 20 per cent and $33\frac{1}{3}$ per cent has resulted in their use for approximation. Similar questions arise in regard to the percentages reported between $33\frac{1}{3}$ and 40 per cent, 40 and 50 per cent, and 50 and 60 per cent. The second answer, that convenient numbers for approximation were used, is probably the more correct explanation.

LARGE AND SMALL COMMUNITIES COMPARED

The percentage of students in commercial courses in large cities seems in general to average somewhat higher than in the

TABLE VI

PERCENTAGE OF STUDENTS IN COMMERCIAL COURSES IN THE HIGH SCHOOLS OF CERTAIN LARGE CITIES IN 1917-18*

City	Percentage
Boston, Mass	50-60
Brooklyn, N.Y	29
Chicago, Ill.	30
Cincinnati, Ohio	26
Cleveland, Ohio	11
Columbus, Ohio	25
Denver, Colo	50
Jersey City, N.J	31.7
Milwaukee, Wis.	45
Minneapolis, Minn.	28
Newark, N.J	25
New Orleans La	25
New York, N.Y	29
Pittsburgh, Pa.	25
Portland, Me	37.5
San Francisco, Cal.	27.6
Seattle, Wash	70
Hartford, Conn.	45

* From answers to a questionnaire.

smaller communities. Table VI shows the percentage of students in commercial courses in the high schools of certain large cities of the United States.

It will be seen that in only one case (that of Cleveland, Ohio) does the percentage run below 25. It is perhaps interesting that a community thought to be as academic in its interests as Boston shows from 50 to 60 per cent of its high-school students in commercial work, and that this proportion is surpassed only on the western coast, where Seattle has 70 per cent of its students in such courses.

In a discussion of commercial work in high schools the statement is often made that it is in the cities only that commercial work has taken any hold. An effort has been made to present the facts of the case in Table VII. In this connection, it may be well to quote from the Bureau's report the definitions of these types of schools and the basis of the classification used:[1]

This classification has been made on the basis of support, it being generally agreed that *rural* support will look toward rural interests, and *city* support toward city interests. The following definition of a rural high school has been used in grouping the reports: A rural high school is one supported by a state, a county, a township, or a district, or by an independent village which had a population less than 2,500 in 1910. Union high schools are considered as rural. A city high school is one supported by a city having a population of 2,500 and over in 1910. Many of the rural high schools are located in cities having a population of 2,500 or over, and in many instances serve as city high schools as well, but are supported by a rural taxing unit, i.e., by a unit larger than that determined by the corporate limits of the city proper. In case the city had a population of 10,000 or over, such a dual high school has been considered as a city high school, it being thought that such a large municipality would more generally determine the curriculum of the high school and would contribute very largely to its support. These city high schools have been divided into two groups, the first including all of those high schools supported by cities which had a population of 5,000 or over, and the second those supported by cities having a population from 2,500 to 4,999 in 1910. There are about as many cities in the first group as in the second, but about twice as many high schools. . . . If some are inclined to question the practice of considering as cities

[1] From U.S. Bureau of Education, *Biennial Survey of Education, 1916–1918*, Bulletin No. 19, 1920, p. 9.

TABLE VII

PERCENTAGE OF HIGH-SCHOOL STUDENTS IN RURAL, VILLAGE, AND CITY COMMUNITIES TAKING COMMERCIAL WORK*

States	City			Village			Rural		
	Students	Commercial Students	%	Students	Commercial Students	%	Students	Commercial Students	%
United States	848,545	212,853	25.0	121,887	14,622	11.9	673,174	50,780	7.5
Alabama	7,297	932	12.8	921	49	5.3	10,314	237	2.2
Arizona	2,447	444	18.1	118	2	1.6	1,204	407	33.8
Arkansas	3,899	665	17.0	1,850	25	1.3	5,977	733	12.2
California	54,666	11,401	20.8	3,569	313	8.7	25,965	1,971	7.5
Colorado	9,879	1,987	20.1	2,575	290	11.2	6,120	550	8.8
Connecticut	16,284	5,985	36.7	......	......	....	6,068	2,484	4.9
Delaware	1,251	345	27.5	210	......	....	1,105	76	6.8
District of Columbia	6,926	1,892	27.3	......	......	....	......	......	...
Florida	1,802	......	...	470	85	18.0	5,888	195	3.0
Georgia	8,906	355	3.9	2,238	101	4.5	12,595	149	1.1
Idaho	1,666	81	4.8	1,816	120	6.6	6,077	704	11.5
Illinois	54,536	12,742	23.3	4,515	844	18.6	45,782	4,401	9.5
Indiana	26,302	3,936	14.9	6,284	374	5.9	33,438	352	1.0
Iowa	13,329	2,506	18.8	7,478	736	9.8	34,561	1,073	3.1
Kansas	13,507	1,700	12.5	5,636	649	11.5	30,617	2,016	6.5
Kentucky	8,750	1,724	19.7	1,704	4	0.2	9,921	44	0.4
Louisiana	5,075	1,459	28.7	1,418	231	16.2	8,788	403	4.5
Maine	6,829	2,315	34.0	588	152	25.8	10,481	1,790	17.0
Maryland	3,949	1,680	42.5	......	......	....	18,608	803	4.3
Massachusetts	61,896	25,835	41.7	......	......	....	17,797	6,211	34.8
Michigan	33,039	6,172	18.6	5,112	653	12.7	25,795	1,520	5.5
Minnesota	22,124	5,329	24.0	4,144	326	7.8	21,818	1,735	7.9
Mississippi	3,642	226	6.2	962	101	10.8	8,030	115	1.4
Missouri	26,494	5,738	21.6	4,286	346	8.0	25,897	828	2.1
Montana	3,178	607	19.1	185	45	24.3	7,073	1,089	15.4
Nebraska	6,905	1,173	16.9	2,002	432	21.6	20,111	1,016	5.1
Nevada	400	......	...	170	8	4.7	960	713	74.2
New Hampshire	4,918	1,650	33.5	343	58	16.9	3,110	806	25.9
New Jersey	47,382	11,875	25.0	3,809	907	23.8	9,549	2,946	30.8
New Mexico	851	32	3.7	374	45	12.0	2,215	231	10.4
New York	124,515	40,055	32.1	8,121	1,089	13.4	30,181	1,473	4.8
North Carolina	4,434	666	14.9	1,543	206	13.3	11,875	149	1.2
North Dakota	1,864	222	11.9	811	119	14.6	8,945	578	6.4
Ohio	60,634	12,917	21.3	6,894	903	13.0	37,673	2,541	6.7
Oklahoma	7,943	2,040	25.6	5,510	235	4.2	18,172	604	3.3
Oregon	8,124	1,010	12.4	1,837	174	9.4	7,991	907	11.3
Pennsylvania	81,757	24,381	29.8	12,860	2,128	16.5	32,996	2,007	6.0
Rhode Island	7,010	2,496	35.5	......	......	....	1,288	436	33.8
South Carolina	2,867	174	6.0	929	......	....	4,974	17	0.3
South Dakota	2,360	396	16.7	1,436	298	20.7	8,182	358	4.3
Tennessee	5,555	479	8.6	985	74	7.5	11,090	552	4.9
Texas	26,829	3,746	13.9	5,660	373	6.5	29,254	346	1.1
Utah	4,010	748	18.6	1,330	158	11.8	3,834	208	5.8
Vermont	2,487	582	23.4	791	174	21.9	4,647	1,009	21.7
Virginia	11,596	2,219	10.5	1,515	58	3.8	13,529	257	1.8
Washington	17,896	3,183	17.7	2,899	356	12.2	13,512	1,354	10.5
West Virginia	6,487	1,116	17.2	1,621	173	10.6	8,236	614	7.6
Wisconsin	22,484	5,449	24.2	5,620	1,128	20.0	20,844	2,209	10.0
Wyoming	908	208	22.9	213	80	37.5	1,883	163	8.4

* Compiled from U.S. Bureau of Education, *Biennial Survey of Education*, Bulletin No. 19, 1920, Tables 29, 30, 31, 57.

municipalities having a population from 2,500 to 4,999, the statistics of the high schools located in such places may be combined with those of rural high schools. To facilitate reference to these two classes of cities in the following pages the larger municipalities are denominated "cities" and the smaller ones, "villages."

A study of Table VII will show that although commercial work as indicated by the percentage of students in high schools in commercial courses has taken a stronger hold in the cities, the growth of such work has been impressive in village and rural communities. Connecticut, Arizona, Massachusetts, Nevada, and Rhode Island all show that more than one-third of the high-school students in rural communities are in commercial courses, and there are one or two striking instances, such as that of Nevada (which, however, is possibly explainable on grounds of school organization), where the commercial students are a very large proportion of the high-school students in rural communities. In villages also the percentage of commercial students is high in a great many states, the highest percentage being in Wyoming, where 37.5 of village high-school students are commercial students.

RECENT GROWTH OF COLLEGE TRAINING FOR BUSINESS

The first school of commerce in the United States which could be properly spoken of as of collegiate grade was the Wharton School at the University of Pennsylvania, founded in May, 1881. No other one was organized until 1898, when the University of California and the University of Chicago inaugurated such schools. In 1900 the University of Wisconsin, Dartmouth College, and New York University opened schools of business. The University of Michigan followed in 1901. No other school of commerce was founded until 1908. In the field of collegiate education for business, the really striking growth has been very recent. A study based on a survey of the colleges which are members of the Association of Collegiate Schools of Business gives the facts presented in Figures 4 and 5.[1]

[1] The data used in these diagrams includes only collegiate schools of business which are members of the association.

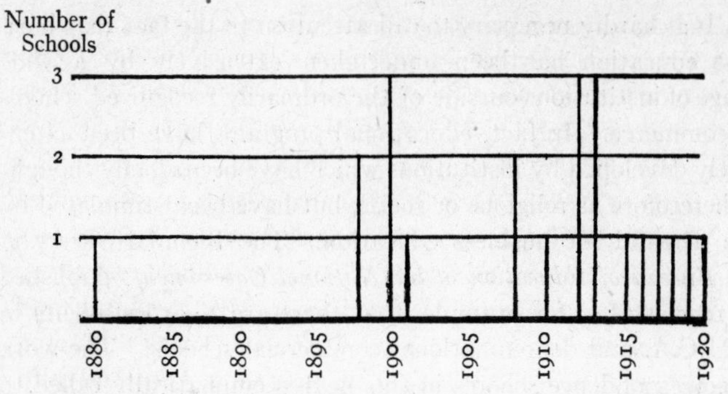

FIG. 4.—Number of collegiate schools of business ‿ounded in each of indicated years.

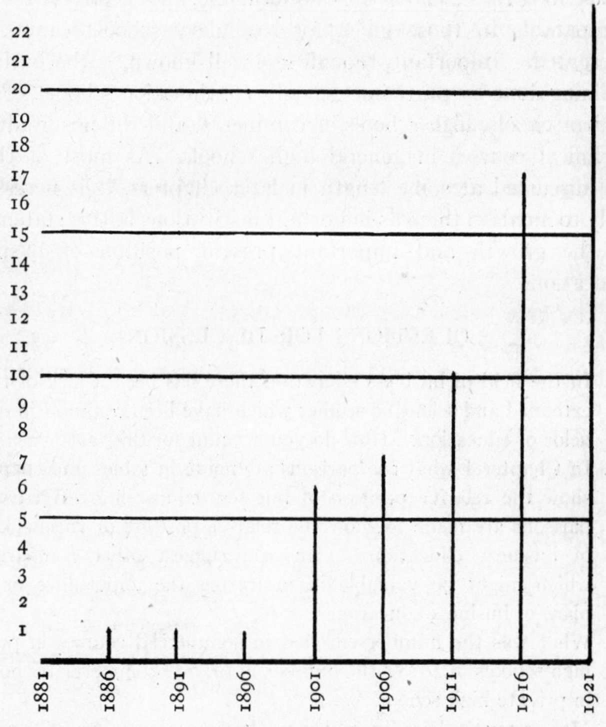

FIG. 5.—Number of collegiate schools of business in existence at beginning of each indicated year.

It is hardly necessary to call attention to the fact that business education has been undertaken extensively by a wide range of institutions outside of the ordinarily recognized schools of commerce. In fact, educational programs have been extensively developed by institutions which have been chiefly thought of heretofore as religious or social, but have been stimulated by the demand for business education. The Biennial *Survey of the Bureau of Education of the National Government*, published in 1920, states, for example, that there are 19,056 students in Y.M.C.A. and denominational commercial schools. The work of correspondence schools in this field is emphatically called to general attention through advertisements. Accurate statistics concerning these schools are unobtainable, and records of growth comparable to those given for secondary schools cannot be presented. Important, though less well known, is the business training done by part-time schools, continuation schools, corporation schools, high schools of commerce, and the postgraduate technical courses in general high schools. As most of these are discussed at some length in later chapters, it is necessary only to mention them as important institutions in this statement of the growth and important present position of business education.

QUESTIONS FOR DISCUSSION

1. In the field of business education there has been a lack of those extended and scientific studies which have been common in other fields of education. How do you account for this fact?
2. In Chapter I what comparisons are made in tables and charts to show the relative position of business education? What comparisons are made to show the relative position of various kinds of business education? Can you suggest other comparisons which might be valuable in indicating the importance or the place of business education?
3. What was the number enrolled in commercial courses in public high schools in 1918? the number in private commercial schools? in private high schools?
4. Make a rough chart (merely heavy horizontal lines drawn approximately to scale) showing; (*a*) the number of high-school students

in 1918, (*b*) the number of high-school students in commercial courses in the same year, (*c*) the average number of commercial students per high school, (*d*) the number of students in private commercial schools.

5. How do you account for the relative lag in the growth of private commercial schools between 1908 and 1913? How do you account for the spurt in business-college enrolment between 1916 and 1918?
6. Table V shows the percentage of high-school students in commercial courses to be 13.35 per cent. In a study of the high schools of certain large cities, published in 1915, Superintendent F. V. Thompson found that "on an average about a third of all pupils in the cities are in commercial courses." How do you account for the differences in these two reckonings?
7. Figure 2 shows the number of schools reporting various percentages of pupils in commercial courses. How do you account for the irregularity of the ordinates in this diagram?
8. What facts are disclosed by examination and comparison of Tables VI and VII? How do you account for the fact that the percentages of students in commercial courses in large cities average higher than in smaller communities?
9. What explanation can be given for the fact that no collegiate school of business appeared in the United States before 1881? How do you account for the rapid increase of collegiate schools of commerce from 1908 to the present time?
10. Although private commercial schools, high-school commercial courses, and collegiate schools of business have attracted attention, there is a long list of other institutions participating in business education. Make as long a list as possible of types of institutions which are participating.
11. On the basis of the data presented in Chapter I formulate a statement or series of statements which seem to you adequately to express (*a*) the position and (*b*) the importance of business education. Formulate a second series of statements which seem to you to present adequately the position and importance of secondary-school commercial courses.

CHAPTER II

AN APPROACH TO CURRICULUM-MAKING

All useful study of content in education must lead toward curriculum-making. The curriculum is the goal. It is the outward expression of the educational philosophy. It is the device by which educational thought is given reality and made of use in accomplishing purposes. Beyond the curriculum, of course, lies educational method, which may find expression in texts or classroom practice. But the content of classroom instruction is largely presupposed in the organization of the curriculum. Therefore in a study concerned with content the important question is, How shall we approach curriculum-making?

Several methods have been used in the formulation of the curriculum. One of the most common has been mere imitation. A curriculum was needed for a given school; it was obtained by copying what was done elsewhere with little consideration of its origin or its applicability. This has been done even by the best educational minds working under the most auspicious circumstances.

Soon after the American occupation of the Philippine Islands, the writer was a member of a committee of seven appointed to draw up an elementary-school curriculum for the islands. The members had all taught or supervised within the islands for two or three years and were reasonably familiar with their peculiar conditions. It was a virgin field in which we were free to recommend almost anything by way of meeting the needs of the population. We had an opportunity to do a magnificent and original constructive piece of work.

And what did we do? We assembled upon a table in the committee-room copies of the American textbooks in reading, arithmetic, geography, United States history, and the other subjects with which we had been familiar in American schools. We also assembled such American courses of study as we could find; and without being conscious of it, we mobilized our American prejudices and preconceptions as to what an elementary-school course ought to be. On the basis of these things we made out a course of study for the traditional eight elementary-school grades. We provided the traditional amount of each subject for each grade, distributed them as in American schools, and recommended American textbooks for the work.

The thing was not adapted to the conditions within the islands. As a matter of fact, we did not try to adapt it to those conditions—though we honestly thought that we were doing the thing needed. The difficulty was that our minds ran so completely in the grooves of traditional thought that we did not realize the possibility of anything else. We greatly needed something to shatter our self-complacency and bring us to see education in terms of the society that was to be educated. We needed principles of curriculum-making.[1]

The business courses in the high schools of the United States furnish any number of instances of imitation of one another. Likewise they furnish many examples of pure imitation of the business college. Colleges and universities, in many cases, are no exception. They have copied one another; they have copied the secondary schools; they have copied the business colleges; and they have copied the correspondence schools.

Where a more thoughtful procedure has been employed in curriculum-making, it has been common to combine a number of studies to each of which certain values have been ascribed.

The idea is prevalent that different studies represent separate kinds of values, and that the curriculum should, therefore, be constituted by gathering together various studies till a sufficient variety of independent values have been cared for. The following quotation does not use the value, but it contains the notion of a curriculum constructed on the idea that there are a number of separate ends to be reached and that various studies may be evaluated by referring each study to its respective end. "Memory is trained by most studies, but best by languages and history, taste is trained by the more advanced study of languages, and still better by English literature; imagination by all higher language teaching, but chiefly

[1] Adapted by permission from Franklin Bobbitt, *The Curriculum*, pp. 282–83. Houghton Mifflin Co., 1918.

by Greek and Latin poetry; observation by science work in the laboratory, though some training is to be got from the earlier stages of Latin and Greek; for expression, Greek and Latin composition come first and English composition next; for abstract reasoning, mathematics stands almost alone; for concrete reasoning, the Greek and Roman historians and orators come first, and general history next. Hence the narrowest education which can claim to be at all complete includes Latin, one modern language, some history, some English literature and one science."

There is much in the wording of this passage which is irrelevant to our point, and which must be discounted to make it clear. The phraseology betrays the particular provincial tradition within which the author is writing. There is the unquestioned assumption of "faculties" to be trained, and a dominant interest in the ancient languages; there is a comparative disregard of the earth on which men happen to live and the bodies they happen to carry around with them. But with allowances made for these matters (even with their complete abandonment) we find much in contemporary educational philosophy which parallels the fundamental notion of parceling out special values to segregated studies. Even when some one end is set up as a standard of value, like social efficiency or culture, it will often be found to be but a verbal heading under which a variety of disconnected factors are comprised. And although the general tendency is to allow a greater variety of values to a given study than does the passage quoted, yet the attempt to inventory a number of values attaching to each study and to state the amount of each value which the given study possesses emphasizes an implied educational disintegration.[1]

This method of curriculum construction has long been an underlying assumption in the minds of many educators. Once we hold it up for inspection its vigor lessens. It is thus criticized by Dewey:

We cannot establish a hierarchy of values among studies. It is futile to attempt to arrange them in an order beginning with one having least worth and going on to that of maximum value. . . . .

It also follows that the attempt to distribute distinct sorts of value among different studies is a misguided one, in spite of the

[1] Adapted by permission from John Dewey, *Democracy and Education*, pp. 286–87. Macmillan Co., 1916.

amount of time recently devoted to the undertaking. Science for example may have any kind of value, depending upon the situation into which it enters as a means. To some the value of science may be military; it may be an instrument in strengthening means of offense or defense; it may be technological, a tool for engineering; or it may be commercial—and aid in the successful conduct of business; under other conditions, its worth may be philanthropic—the service it renders in relieving human suffering; or again it may be quite conventional—of value in establishing one's social status as an "educated" person. As a matter of fact, science serves all these purposes, and it would be an arbitrary task to try to fix upon one of them as its "real" end. All that we can be sure of educationally is that science should be taught so as to be an end in itself in the lives of students—something worth while on account of its own unique intrinsic contribution to the experience of life. Primarily it must have "appreciation value." It we take something which seems to be at the opposite pole, like poetry, the same sort of statement applies. It may be that, at the present time, its chief value is the contribution it makes to the enjoyment of leisure. But that may represent a degenerate condition rather than anything necessary. Poetry has historically been allied with religion and morals; it has served the purpose of penetrating the mysterious depths of things. It has had an enormous patriotic value. Homer to the Greeks was a Bible, a textbook of morals, a history, and a national inspiration. In any case, it may be said that an education which does not succeed in making poetry a resource in the business of life as well as in its leisure, has something the matter with it—or else the poetry is artificial poetry.

The same considerations apply to the value of a study or a topic of a study with reference to its motivating force. Those responsible for planning and teaching the course of study should have grounds for thinking that the studies and topics included furnish both direct increments to the enriching of lives of the pupils and also materials which they can put to use in other concerns of direct interest. Since the curriculum is always getting loaded down with purely inherited traditional matter and with subjects which represent mainly the energy of some influential person or group of persons in behalf of something dear to them, it requires constant inspection, criticism, and revision to make sure it is accomplishing its purpose. Then there is always the probability that it represents the values of adults rather than those of children and youth, or those of pupils a generation ago rather than those of the present day. Hence a further need for a critical outlook and survey. But these considerations do not mean that for a subject to have motivating value to a pupil (whether intrinsic or instrumental) is the same thing as for him to be aware of the value, or to be able to tell what the study is good for. . . . .

As a matter of fact, such schemes of values of studies are largely, but unconsciously justifications of the curriculum with which one is familiar. One accepts, for the most part, the studies of the existing course and then assigns values to them as a sufficient reason for their being taught. Mathematics is said to have, for example, disciplinary value in habituating the pupil to accuracy of statement and closeness of reasoning, it has utilitarian value, in giving command of the arts of calculation involved in trade and the arts; culture value in its enlargement of the imagination in dealing with the most general relation of things; even religious value in its concept of the infinite and allied ideas. But clearly mathematics does not accomplish such results, because it is endowed with miraculous potencies called values; it has these values if and when it accomplishes these results and not otherwise. The statements may help a teacher to a larger vision of the possible results to be effected by instruction in mathematical topics. But unfortunately, the tendency is to treat the statement as indicating powers inherently residing in the subject, whether they operate or not, and thus to give it a rigid justification. If they do not operate, the blame is not put on the subject as taught, but on the indifference and recalcitrancy of pupils.[1]

A third method of curriculum-making might be called the "interests theory." This method is somewhat similar to the second. It is a method of which much has been heard in these days when a great variety of new subjects has arisen for which their advocates are seeking a philosophical justification. This scheme, however, appears to be as open to objection as the preceding one.

Life presents a diversity of interests. Left to themselves, they tend to encroach on one another. The ideal is to prescribe a special territory for each till the whole ground of experience is covered, and

[1] *Op. cit.*, pp. 281–82, 287–88.

then see to it each remains within its own boundaries. Politics, business, recreation, art, science, the learned professions, polite intercourse, leisure, represent such interests. Each of these ramifies into many branches: business into manual occupations, executive positions, bookkeeping, railroading, banking, agriculture, trade and commerce, etc., and so with each of the others. An ideal education would then supply the means of meeting these separate and pigeon-holed interests. And when we look at the schools, it is easy to get the impression that they accept this view of the nature of adult life, and set for themselves the task of meeting its demands. Each interest is acknowledged as a kind of fixed institution to which something in the course of study must correspond. The course of study must then have some civics and history politically and patriotically viewed; some utilitarian studies; some science; some art (mainly literature of course); some provision for recreation; some moral education, and so on. And it will be found that a large part of current agitation about schools is concerned with clamor and controversy about the due need of recognition to be given to each of these interests, and with struggles to secure for each its due share in the course of study; or, if this does not seem feasible in the existing school system, then to secure a new and separate kind of schooling to meet the need. In the multitude of educations education is forgotten.

The obvious outcome is congestion of the course of study, over-pressure, and distraction of pupils, and a narrow specialization fatal to the very idea of education. But these bad results usually lead to more of the same sort of thing as a remedy. When it is perceived that after all the requirements of a full life experience are not met, the deficiency is not laid to the isolation and narrowness of the teaching of the existing subjects, and this recognition made the basis of reorganization and the system. . . . .

The situation has, of course, its historic explanation. Various epochs of the past have had their own characteristic struggles and interests. Each of these great epochs has left behind itself a kind of cultural deposit, like a geologic stratum. These deposits have found their way into educational institutions in the form of studies, distinct courses of study, distinct types of schools. With the rapid change of political, scientific, and economic interests in the last century provision had to be made for new values. Though the older courses resisted, they have had at least in this country to retire their pretensions to a monopoly. They have not, however, been reorganized in content and aim, they have only been reduced in amount. The new studies, representing the new interests, have not been used to transform the method and aim of all instruction, they have been injected and added on. The result is a conglomerate, the cement of which consists in the mechanics of the school program or time table.[1]

Less definite, but still, to some persons, important principles to be followed in organizing the curriculum are the notions of moral and mental discipline and the matter of the students' tastes. These must be cared for, it is asserted. And if these are cared for the curriculum is satisfactory. Caring for taste and, perhaps even more, caring for discipline have at times gone to great lengths. But this basis for curriculum-making, like those that have preceded, finds its strength questioned and even ridiculed in this day of more liberal and more careful thought.

It is, indeed, absurd to invent formal difficulties for the professed purpose of discipline, when, within the limits of science, industry, literature, and politics, real problems abound. Method can be best acquired, and stands the best chance of being acquired, if real issues are presented. Are problems any the less problems because a boy attacks them with intelligence and zest? He does not attack them because they are easy, nor does he shrink from them because they are hard. He attacks them, if he has been wisely trained, because they challenge his powers. And in this attack he gets what the conventional school so generally fails to give—the energizing of his faculties, and a directive clue as to where he will find a congenial and effective object in life.[2]

Anyone who has taught courses dealing with the curriculum has found firmly fixed in the minds of his students an adherence to one or more of the schemes of curriculum-making discussed above. All of us perhaps have been at one time or another under the spell of some of them. But in attempting to formulate a curriculum for business education the writer has found all

[1] *Op. cit.*, pp. 288–90.

[2] Adapted by permission from Abraham Flexner, *A Modern School*, p. 21. General Education Board, 1916.

these plans almost futile. They seem to lead nowhere, to make the student satisfied with the most conventional imitation, to repress vigorous thinking, as to either the purposes or the results of an organized course of study.

What follows is, then, an effort to apply a new point of view to the study of education for business and to the formulation of curricula for that purpose. Some special emphasis will be placed on commercial education in the secondary schools.

An adequate approach to education for business involves a careful examination of two matters: First, we must determine the purpose of business education. We must ascertain objectives, ends. We must ask and answer, What is the task or function of education for business in society as it now exists? Later we may organize appropriate studies as *means*. But to try to plan a curriculum before we know its purpose is unavailing. It is as useless as to set architects to work to design a building without stating the use to which the structure is to be put.

When we are as clear as possible as to purposes, we may sensibly go about planning methods. But even then we cannot immediately plan the curriculum for the high-school commercial course, the collegiate school of business, the business college, or any other one type of business-training institution. *For no one type of institution does the job alone.* As our second task, we must examine all of those agencies which play a part in business education and attempt to divide among them the total task of educating for business. Modern social organization is an organization of specialists, and to nothing does this statement apply more than to educational institutions. We can conclude as to the objectives of any one institution only when we have examined all of them and estimated their possibilities. It is only, then, when we assign duty to *each*, that we can intelligently assign duty to *any*.

If we are interested, for example, in how to organize the curriculum of the high-school commercial course we cannot think of that alone. We must think of it as one of a battery of institutions. Its proper work is the work which must be done, but which other pieces of social machinery cannot do better. The same statement holds good for the business college, the corporation school, or any other device for business education which we may consider. When we have seen the purpose of the whole and have defined the part which is to be played by the institution in which we are interested, then, and only then, are we ready to consider curriculum.

What has been said above may be presented diagrammatically:

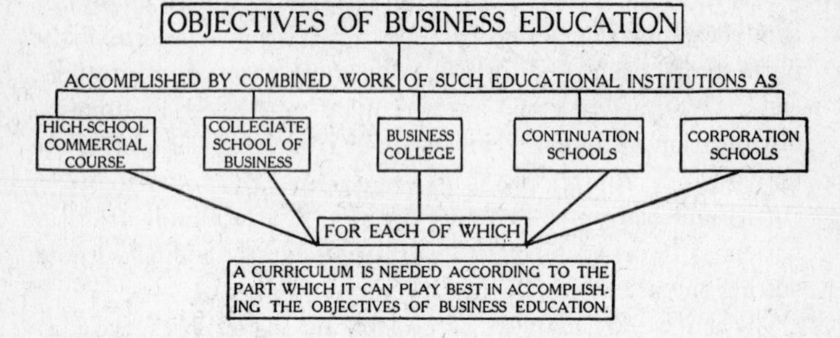

The task, thus, for anyone who is interested in business education can be divided into three stages.

1. He must determine the purposes, or task, or function of education for business in modern society.

2. He must examine the several institutions which, in our specialized society, can well participate in accomplishing those purposes and determine the part which can properly be played by the institution in which he is interested.

3. He must plan the organization of work (the curriculum) which will best achieve that specialized part which this institution undertakes.

QUESTIONS FOR DISCUSSION

1. "All useful studies of content in education must lead toward curriculum-making." Is this statement justified?
2. "All branches of human activity have risen above the stage of empiricism and rule of thumb only as they have been able to build upon the accumulated facts of experience and accurate conclusions drawn therefrom." Explain and comment on the truth or untruth of this statement.

3. The quotation in Question 2 is used to introduce a discussion of "scientific management or organization in business." Has it any pertinence in a study of an educational problem?
4. What is your idea of the "rule of thumb" in business? Is there any of it in school work? If so, make a list of some of the factors that tend to keep it in control. What factors, if any, tend to make control more rational—tend toward a more "scientific management"?
5. "It is a splendid exercise for every man, at least once in his life, to throw himself unreservedly and with enthusiasm into some study and for a time 'go the limit' in thoroughness, accuracy, caution and open-mindedness. Such an experience will exert a lasting and beneficial influence upon his thinking." Can this be done in a study of curriculum making? Does it necessitate the "scientific attitude"?
6. "The school teacher is 'an old fogy' says the business man; the business man has little culture and questionable motives says the pedagogue." Have these been somewhat common views? If so, why? What factors are at work to intensify or modify these attitudes?
7. If examination and imitation of other courses is not to be made the basis for formulating curricula, what other methods might be used?
8. "Different studies represent different kinds of values. The curriculum should, therefore, be constituted by gathering together various studies until a sufficient variety of independent values has been cared for." Support or criticize this statement. Upon what concepts is it based?
9. "We cannot establish a hierarchy of values among studies." Explain. If not, how choose at all?
10. What is your understanding of the "interests theory" of curriculum-making?
11. "Since the curriculum is always getting loaded down with purely inherited traditional matter and with subjects which represent mainly the energy of some influential person or group of persons in behalf of something dear to them, it requires constant inspection, criticism and revision to make sure it is accomplishing its purpose." Is there any such traditional matter in the usual high-school or college business curriculum? What subjects might be open to this charge? If any, attempt to explain how they "arrived" and "stayed" in the form in which they exist.

12. "One accepts, for the most part, the studies of the existing courses and assumes from the fact that they are there, that there is sufficient reason for their being taught." Is there truth in this statement? Is there a tendency to blame the pupil rather than the subjects if curricula so justified fail?
13. What would you understand to be meant by the expression the "check and balance theory" of curriculum construction?
14. "In the multitude of educations, education is forgotten." Explain.
15. "The present commercial course in secondary schools is a hodgepodge of miscellaneous and ill assorted fragments." Does this overstate or understate the situation as you see it?
16. Students of business subjects are pointing out that nothing is more valuable than a systematic approach to a problem from a new point of view. Can such an approach "from the outside" be of any use in a study of commercial curricula?
17. "The commercial curriculum may be a problem, but in the secondary schools, at least, it can never be improved by outsiders. Such persons have nothing to offer but impractical theories." Comment on this statement.
18. "The most practical thing in the world is theory." Comment.
19. What reasons can you list for believing that a new point of view in commercial training might prove fertile; wherein lies the "fertility of a new point of view"?
20. What could you list under the caption "Enemies of Originality and Advance in Commercial Education"?
21. An attitude of friendly but complete skepticism is needed in approaching a problem of curriculum. No study in the business course of high school or college has proved its right to a place. Can you take this attitude?
22. Outline the plan for an approach to business education suggested in Chapter II. How would you suggest determining the purpose or task of education for business?

PART II

THE OBJECTIVES OF EDUCATION FOR BUSINESS

CHAPTER III

WHAT IS BUSINESS?

INTRODUCTORY STATEMENT

In attempting to arrive at the objectives of education for business, it is proposed that certain evidence be examined. In part the evidence is the evidence of circumstances; in part it is personal testimony and opinion.

It seems reasonable to believe that in arriving at the objectives of education for business one should consider very carefully what this thing "business" is. In our study of "what business is" we shall be concerned in part with the way in which business is conducted and in part with the social implications of business. Both of these viewpoints will have suggestion for our purposes.

A second field of evidence which we shall examine in our effort to determine the objectives of education for business may be designated "what business says it wants." That is, we shall turn to business itself in our inquiry of what education is needed for business. In studying what business says it wants, however, there are two quite different methods of securing information. One method is to take the direct statements of business men when they have been thinking definitely about the question. Such statements appear in their public addresses, printed papers, and occasional books. A second method is to study the occupations of persons in business, to analyze these occupations, and to conclude concerning the education necessary for performance in them. The amount of such indirect evidence is fortunately considerable: it appears in replies to questionnaires which have been circulated a nong business houses, in educational surveys, and in the studies and occupational analyses of various governmental agencies.

Finally, in arriving at the objectives of education for business, we may find help in a consideration of the purposes of all education. There is not, and perhaps can never be, any real objective proof of what these properly are. All that can be done is to survey the statements of those persons whose views have won them attention and respect. We should notice, however, that the students who have given most thought to such general purposes have not been concerned primarily with education for business. A study of the general purposes of education, therefore, is not significant in arriving at the objectives of business education excepting when it is carried on as part of public-school work. But when such is the case, a departure from accepted principles of public education would seem to require an explanation.

A VIEW OF WHAT BUSINESS IS

Many people, when they think of business, bring to mind a somewhat inchoate lot of images concerned with buying and selling, price-making, profit-seeking, and overwork, blended with ideas of efficient competition and unfair practices. It goes without saying that such a collection of notions gives no view of business in a large sense and gives no notion of the social importance or significance of business as a whole. It is the purpose of this section to set forth an idea of what business is, and of the social work which business performs. It is purposed to do this that we may, from an examination of what business is, see more clearly the form of education which will prepare people for engaging in commercial and industrial enterprises.

An understanding of what business is, requires an examination of some facts which are of basic importance. These facts are elementary enough to the student of economics, though they are sometimes overlooked even by him in certain aspects of his work.

Humankind has found itself in this world confronted by two matters of elementary significance: One of these is the fact of wants. We want things, and, as the economist has pointed out over and over again, these wants seem to be capable of limitless multiplication. New wants grow apace. "The more we have the more we want" may not be literally true, but it is true certainly that we have never yet had a stage of society in which all persons had everything they wanted. We have then the basic fact of wants.

If we can think of society as a group of persons interested in gratifying its wants, it is pertinent next to notice the materials from which want-gratifying goods may be made. Society has on hand a supply of such materials—social resources they may well be called. Although the total amount of these resources is considerable, they can be put into only a few classes. It is worth while to put first the *natural resources*. These are of varied kinds, such as fertile land, minerals, water-power, timber supplies, and the many factors which make up climatic conditions. So important are these resources that persons who are interested in geographic study are likely to express man's dependence upon them in such terms as these:

All these materials for a living come directly or indirectly out of the soil or crust of the earth. The man in a ship at sea or in a steel sky-scraper in a modern city gets his sustenance from the soil just as surely as does the farmer who takes potatoes from the furrow. Each particular method by which a man gets some useful commodity leads to an industry often of world-wide distribution. To understand the way the human race turns the earth into its home, we have but to study the various industries by which groups of men achieve their living.

While ultimately depending upon the contents of the earth's crust, most of our living comes indirectly through the intermediate stages of plant and animal life, the crust itself supplying directly but a small part of our wants. In and upon the earth is the indispensable water, without which we would promptly perish. While the more solid substances of the earth's crust are also directly available and of great value, as salt, building stones, and metals, we depend chiefly upon vegetation for our support. The plants grow from the soil. We eat them or clothe ourselves with their fibres, cut them into pieces, shape them into tools, and build our houses and barns, extract their juices and dig their roots for drugs and medicines. We burn them for fuel, shape them into articles of luxury, and thus make them help in the supply of some of the wants of each of the six classes. The animals in turn eat the plants and each other, and furnish us their meat and milk as nourishment; their wool and furs become our clothing, their tougher hides make our shoe leather, the tents of the nomad, and the belts of the engine wheel, while the cultural services are hinted by the soft leather bindings of our choicest books.[1]

A second type of raw material or social resource of which society has a considerable, but limited supply, is its labor power. Definitions of labor power are many. One writer defines labor as "The application of human faculties to the production of wealth." Says another writer, "Labor is the voluntary exertion of bodily or mental faculties for the purpose of production." But whatever the differences of detail in the definitions of labor, most of them bring us back to the thought that labor is simply the physical or mental effort which may be used for the creation of those goods which gratify human wants.

Fortunately we are not compelled to turn natural resources into want-gratifying goods with our bare-handed labor power. During the past we have accumulated, viewing us as a social group, a very considerable number of implements, and these implements may be thought of as a third material, or social resource. These implements are all about us in innumerable forms. Not only tools and machinery, but factory buildings, railroads, sidewalks, office buildings, drainage systems, are all examples of mechanical devices which we have created for use in the task of want-gratifying. The economist calls this class of goods capital, and the economist defines capital as the goods which we have produced with past effort, which we do not consume directly in gratifying wants, but which we use to help to produce other goods. Although when our attention is centered upon natural resources as a production resource, or upon labor, it is easy to make us feel its importance almost to the exclusion of everything else, still it will be seen with a moment's thought how largely we depend upon our resources of capital. Almost every task is aided by some mechanical contrivance, large or small. In many cases the machine has almost, if not entirely, eliminated the necessity of human effort.

A final form of social resource may be designated as acquired knowledge, or possibly better by some such composite term

[1] Adapted by permission from J. Russell Smith, *Industrial and Commercial Geography*, p. 3. H. Holt & Co., 1913.

as acquired knowledge and institutions. Perhaps under this heading should go the acquirements of society in fields of learning, perhaps our accumulated knowledge of mathematics, chemistry, physics, and the like. It is only fair to observe, however, that these can be thought of as characteristics of labor power, that is, phases of an individual's knowledge, or else they are in books and may therefore be considered as capital. On the other hand there are certain qualities and characteristics of individuals which apparently are not their possession alone. Such ethical attributes as honesty, morality, respectability, courtesy, and fairness are not, and cannot be, the acquirements of individuals. By their very nature they imply a social situation. There cannot be such a thing as honesty excepting in terms of certain social standards. Society in its development has built up a great mass of possessions of this character. Conceive of carrying on the work of the everyday world as we know it without our social standards of honesty, truthfulness, good faith, reliability, punctuality, or any of a dozen other such virtues, and one senses the significance of this form of resources in the work of creating want-gratifying goods. Perhaps in this same class of resources should be thrown language and writing, as these communicating devices, somewhat like those traits which have been discussed above, are meaningless excepting in a social sense.

Society has then at hand, in its effort to produce whatever it can produce of want-gratifying goods, a certain stock of materials. These materials we may speak of as society's social resources. This stock includes our supply of natural resources, of labor power, of capital, and of acquired knowledge and institutions. Diagrammatically, this notion may be presented as follows:

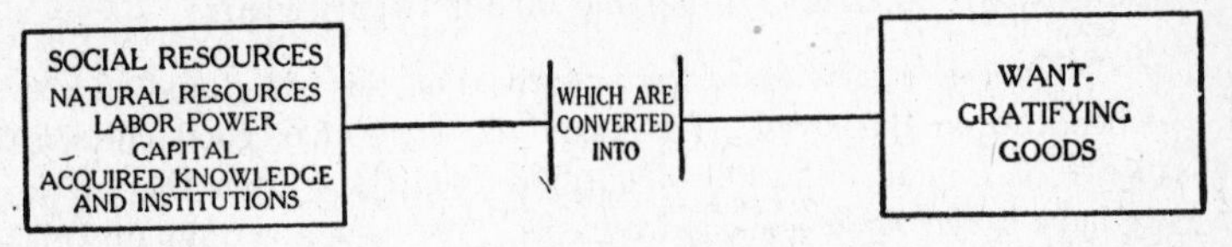

There is at least one rather gratifying fact about this view of society's activities; it is applicable at any time from the beginning until the present. Whether one thinks of society in the Garden of Eden, at the time of Abraham, in the Middle Ages, on a colonial farm, or at the present time, the situation is the same. Society always has been and always will be concerned with the task which has been suggested. Social resources exist and wants exist. Social effort is to change the social resources into the goods which gratify wants.

But the supply of any one kind of social resource or the particular character of that kind has by no means been the same continuously. If we think of the time when American Indians occupied the North American continent, we might be justified in saying that their natural resources were more extensive than ours. The supply of labor power was much smaller. Capital was almost negligible, and acquired knowledge and institutions were likewise meager. We should observe, too, that at any given time and for any social group the supply of resources has definite limitations. Although, compared with earlier ages, we have a vast supply of capital, we have not so much as we might wish. We have unlocked great stores of natural resources, but no argument is needed to prove that we should be grateful if more of these were available. So also our other types of social resources are limited at any one time.

Since any social group is, then, confronted with the task of securing whatever it can secure of want-gratifying goods from a limited amount of social resources, we may face the task of how the work shall be done. This is equivalent to saying that some form of organization, an economic system, must be devised. A simple explanation of some possible types of economic organization has been expressed, making use of the notion that a group of people are supposedly shipwrecked on some fertile island, with no chance of getting off for twenty years:

> No one else is living or has ever lived on this island and we are dependent on ourselves. The island is fertile, has good climate, plenty of rainfall, all sorts of natural resources. From the wreck we have saved some tools and utensils. We have a certain amount of acquired knowledge. Under such conditions how would we undertake the task of gratifying wants?

There are, of course, several ways in which we might do it:

1. Each person might go apart from the others and set about the task alone. He would attempt to find or produce all of the things he wanted to eat and wear or use in any other way to gratify his wants. If it were done in this way, no person would be co-operating with any of the others. Each would be in somewhat the same situation as a family on the frontier—*self-dependent* and *self-sufficing*.

2. On the other hand, a council might be called and it might be agreed that all should co-operate in producing economic goods. The form of co-operation might be such that all would work at every job. All would work together in hunting, then in fishing, and then in helping to raise crops.

3. A different form of co-operation might be decided upon. A central committee might be appointed to determine what *specialized* work each one should do. This committee might have power to require certain ones to fish, others to hunt, others to work in the fields. All the finished products might be turned into a common fund or reservoir. A common dining-room might take care of the wants of all for food. Clothes might be distributed from the central storehouse. The governing committee would be required to be careful to have enough on hand to supply the necessities before luxuries were considered. Such a community would be called a communistic society. It would be very much like the one which was used at one time by the colonists who settled in Virginia. All of the activities of the members of the colony were under the control of authorities. Whatever the settlers produced went to the common stock, while they were fed and clothed from the company's store house.

4. A fourth plan might be to allow each person to produce anything he thought was needed and to trade or barter with the others for things which they had produced. Under such an arrangement, the person who fished might barter fish for game, the hunter might barter game for fish and grain, while the ones who had raised crops would be anxious to exchange their crops for meat and fish. Would not such a plan be somewhat like the one we use at present?

These are only a few of the possible forms or methods of economic organization. No matter what form may be in use, the situation may be illustrated by the diagram shown at top of next page.

The economic organization or economic system which is used in our society today might be very sensibly spoken of as our want-gratifying machine. If we tried to name its parts, we should no doubt think of laws, banks, factories, labor unions, contracts, schools, transportation systems, private property, competition, employers'

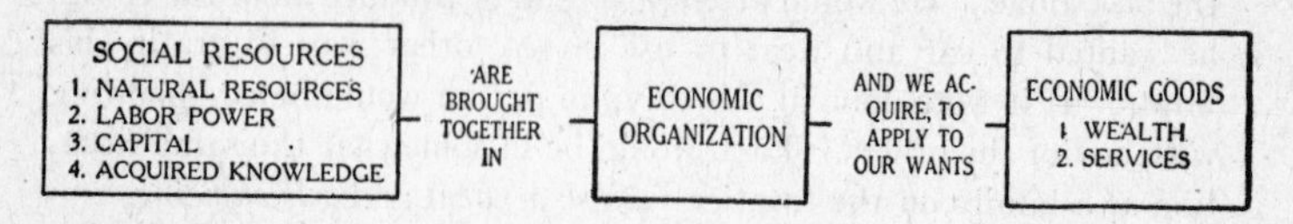

associations, chambers of commerce, specialization, insurance companies, inheritance, wages, interest, profits, and many other institutions.[1]

We have seen then that the economic organization, the method of turning social resources into want-gratifying goods, may be one of a number of different kinds. For our purposes, we must see that our existing organization is not the first or the second or the third suggested in the quotation above. It is not one which can be called socialistic, nor one of individual self-sufficiency. It is one which has certain peculiar characteristics. Some of these are so different from what have preceded that they have led us to give it a name, and that name is *Business*. We might then in the diagram just above substitute for the phrase "Economic Organization" the word *Business* or, perhaps better, label our particular kind of economic organization *Business*.[2] It thus becomes apparent that business is that scheme of economic organization which is at present largely responsible for gratifying human wants. Business is that system of economic organization to which in great measure we have intrusted the all-important social task of utilizing our social resources, to secure for society whatever society secures. While it is an exaggeration to state that business occupies all economic activities (for some portion of it is in the hands of government and other non-business schemes of organization), it is not too much to say that so far as most of our wants are concerned,

[1] Adapted by permission from Marshall and Lyon, *Our Economic Organization*, pp. 17–19. Macmillan Co., 1921.

[2] This statement must be taken in a general sense here. A more detailed explanation, as well as certain modifications of the statement, appears in the chapters that follow.

their gratification depends very largely upon the efficiency of business. *Business, thus, as society is now arranged, is as socially significant as want-gratification.* And since want-gratification is concerned, not only with those many wants which enrich the standard of living, but with those which are concerned with the existence of life itself, the function of business, in the present order, is vital.

Such being the case, it is not too early to observe that in approaching a study of education for business we are approaching something larger than the routine of the office or the higgling of the market. We are concerned with an activity than which there are few more fundamental and far-reaching in our civilization.

QUESTIONS FOR DISCUSSION

1. The introduction to Chapter III proposes the examination of certain evidences tending to show the proper objectives of education for business. Just what is this evidence? Do you think the evidence proposed is pertinent and relevant?
2. Is the evidence proposed adequate? Can you suggest other evidence which you think would be useful in indicating the proper objectives of education for business?
3. The fact of wants and the fact of social resources are basic in a study of business. Explain this statement.
4. What types of social resources has society at its command? Be prepared to define each type.
5. Have human wants existed as long as human beings? Were social resources in existence a thousand years ago? ten thousand years ago? Has the same amount of each type of social resource always been in existence as exists now? What forms of social resources seem to you to have increased most rapidly in the past fifty years? Have any forms decreased?
6. Society's supply of social resources is like the family cupboard. It is the source from which all want-gratifying goods must be drawn. Unfortunately, the supply of social resources at any given time is limited. Is this statement true? Can the supply be increased? If so, how?
7. Ever since people have lived upon the earth it has been necessary to have some form of economic organization. Explain. What is

the general task of our economic organization? In what ways was the economic organization of the American Indians different from ours? In what ways was the economic organization of the Virginia colonists different from ours?

8. When a man or boy hunts for a job, is he trying to find his place in the economic organization?
9. All persons who are engaged in economic activity are trying to make a living. Are all these persons playing a part in our economic organization? Are they all in business? Is the farmer in business? the teacher? the actor? the doctor? the banker? the author? the preacher?

CHAPTER IV

INDIVIDUAL ENTERPRISE AND THE SPECIALIZATION OF BUSINESS UNITS

The conclusion that business is the great social project of utilizing social resources to gratify human wants, though perhaps suggestive and stimulating, is not a sufficiently detailed notion to give the most aid in determining how to educate for business. We must examine in more detail some of the characteristics of business.

It has been suggested in the preceding chapter that our modern economic organization is one in which the responsibility of organization is thrown upon the individual. The social resources upon which our social group is dependent are not used for the most part by social action. *Individuals* are permitted to take these social resources and to attempt to convert them into want-gratifying goods. In large part they attempt to use social resources in the way that they believe will prove most profitable. It is this characteristic of freedom of individual enterprise, of individuals attempting to gratify human wants at a profit to themselves, that is ordinarily called business. It is thus seen that going into business simply means that an individual sets himself up to take part in the social enterprise of want-gratification. In our modern system, then, there rests upon the shoulders of business men a great responsibility—a responsibility to get as much for all of us as it is possible to get from our existing supply of social resources. But each individual business man is interested not so much in doing the most for society as in doing the best he can for himself. Therefore we may think of the situation as though society had found it necessary to make use of some device which would compel the individual enterpriser to consider society's needs. The device which is in use is competition. No one business man is permitted to have control of all social resources. Anyone has some opportunity to compete in gratifying wants. What society secures from its supply of social materials depends upon the intelligence and efficiency of business management and the reality of the competition among individual business enterprises.

Competition, to give us the best, must be both real and intelligent. Five men may run a hundred-yard dash. Someone is sure to win, even though the fastest of the lot may run with the assistance of crutches. This will be competition, but there will be little quality in it. So it is with the competition of business. Someone, under our system of permitting anyone to try, is sure to succeed, and the fact that we see him succeed may easily lead us to think of him as efficient. Success and efficiency, if one is thinking of efficiency in some absolute sense, are not at all identical. Success merely means that one has proved himself superior to his competitors, but if his competitors are more or less lame, halt, and blind in a business way, the winner himself may be much less efficient in his use of social resources than society might wish. It is the need of society, then, not only to permit competition to be as unrestricted as possible, but to give it as much quality as possible. Both of these considerations make demands upon business education. They demand that there shall be many competitors in the business race and that each of these shall be as well trained as possible.

But in considering these demands it is well to have in mind the extent to which business education gives opportunity to compete. Some persons who are born the sons of men connected with large business houses can obtain much of a managerial viewpoint and a managerial education merely from association. Others must rely entirely upon what the schools (meaning no particular type of school) may offer. And what the schools must offer if they are to give society the desirable supply of high-quality competitors is education for management. It must be education which fits individuals to go into business; it must be education which enables young persons to assume, with real hope of success, control of social resources with the purpose of converting them into want-gratifying goods.

Closely related to individual enterprise as a characteristic of modern business is a second characteristic which we may call the specialization *of* business units. There is also a specialization *within* business units to which we must later give attention, but this must not be confused with the specialization *of* business units and what it suggests in education for business. This we shall now consider.

To understand the significance of specialization and appreciate the probable permanence of its character, it is necessary to see that it is a method of production. Desirous of producing goods which gratify wants, society, quite without realizing it, has hit upon the device of specialization. As Clay, the English economist, says, "Specialization is fundamental in economic organization because it is the means by which man increases the return to a given amount of work. It brings about this result in two ways: by subdivision of tasks and by repetition of tasks. Subdivision results in operations easier in themselves, repetition enables operations to be performed with greater ease."

The specialization *of* business units, which is our consideration here, has been, perhaps, less emphasized than the specialization within business units. Such specialization arises rather from the subdivision of *processes* than from the subdivision of tasks. There are special business units that carry on specialized parts in the creation of every kind of goods or services of which one can think. Farms and ranches do not supply us with food, but are merely specialized parts of a long process of food-supplying. Automobile factories do not furnish us with automobiles, but are one specialized unit in a long series of units, which together furnish us with those vehicles. Mines, railroads, sawmills, churches, offices, schools, and theaters are all separate units specializing in special tasks and each contributing to the production of many types of want-gratifying goods.

The specialization of business units which furnishes us with such a commodity as the breakfast egg has been thus described:

A useful way of seeing the advantage of specialization of economic units is to follow through the work that must be done in bringing us some such product of daily consumption as eggs. We shall see that the egg on our breakfast table is the result of the specialized services of a great many economic units. The farmer whose poultry yard has furnished him with eggs could sell these in a number of ways. He might send them directly to consumers in the cities, but ordinarily he does not know just who wants eggs at any particular time or does he know how many could be used by any household and what price it would be willing to pay. Before he could sell eggs in this direct "producer to consumer" fashion, it would also be necessary for him to grade the eggs very carefully so that there could be no dissatisfaction on the part of the purchasers, to pack them for shipment, and to arrange for the collection of money due him. Instead of selling his eggs this way, a more common method is to take them to a neighboring country town and dispose of them to the storekeeper. A village storekeeper thus acts as a first centralizing depot where the eggs from the entire neighborhood are collected. In some cases the storekeeper runs the eggs over his "candling machine" and discards those that are spoiled. If he does this, he is performing a second task, that of grading, which must be done before people in the cities care to purchase eggs.

The storekeeper in the country town is in hardly a better position to sell eggs directly to the consumers in the cities than was the farmer. No more than the farmer does he know how many eggs are desired by any particular family nor just what families wish such goods. In other words, he has no "market connections" with consumers in the city. He might, of course, make such market connections, but experience has shown him that it is simpler to pass the eggs on, a large quantity at a time, to someone in the city, and let him perform this function of finding consumers.

In the height of the egg-laying season, the storekeeper of a fairly large town may collect a half carload or even a carload of eggs in the period of a week. He now ships these to a buyer of eggs in quantity in the city. Such a quantity buyer is sometimes called a "wholesale receiver" or "large dealer" or "centralizer." The wholesaler usually grades the eggs carefully into "selects," "seconds," "spots," and other classes according to their quality. This wholesaler, like those who have handled the eggs ahead of him, might possibly sell them directly to consumers. But he is hardly in a position to know the wishes of all the people in every locality of a city (and he is very busy with these other tasks). As we might expect, therefore, still other specialized middlemen come in to take care of this function. The centralizer or large dealer could sell to the grocery stores, the hotels and restaurants, and the bakers which are the principal channels through which eggs pass to consumers. But even of these there are so many in a city of any size that it is difficult for him to keep in touch with all of them and know the market needs and desires of each. In some cases he does sell directly to these buyers. In other cases, he relies on men called "jobbers" to keep in constant touch with the

CO-OPERATING SPECIALIZED BUSINESS UNITS IN EGG PRODUCTION

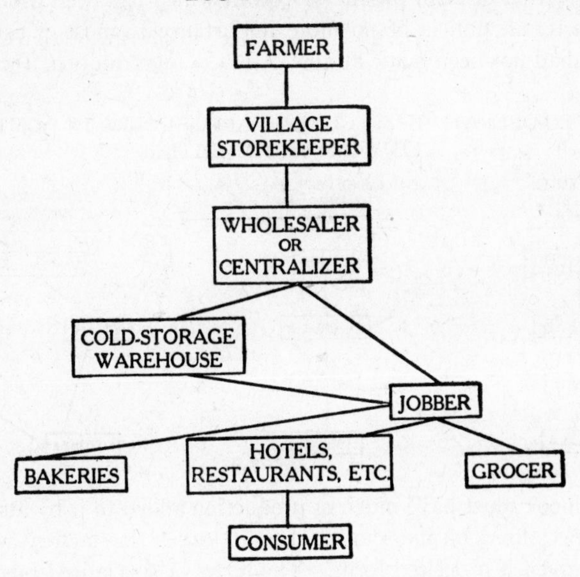

needs of all the bakers, grocers, hotels, restaurants, and other retail outlets and to sell them the number and quality of eggs demanded.

The jobbers who find a market for the eggs received by the wholesaler are not the only persons to whom the stock might be disposed of. Eggs are laid in largest numbers during the months of March, April, May, and June. The supply which pours into the cities during the "laying months" must, if we are to be provided during the winter, be so conserved as to last throughout the year. Therefore, certain individuals who believe it will be profitable to store and preserve eggs purchase them from the wholesale receiver and place them in cold storage warehouses. Here they are kept until winter, when, during the scarce season, they are sold, usually through the jobbers, to the bakers, grocers, hotels, and restaurants.

We must not imagine that there are never any variations in this line of specialists. Sometimes eggs are shipped directly from farms to city residences; sometimes other middlemen than those we have mentioned take part in the work of marketing eggs.[1]

Such series of specialists are not, of course, confined to production of farm products. Cloth which has been produced by a textile mill is of no more importance to most of us than if it had not been made at all. A hat, a fountain pen, a watch,

CO-OPERATIVE SPECIALIZED PRODUCERS IN SOME COMMON COMMODITIES

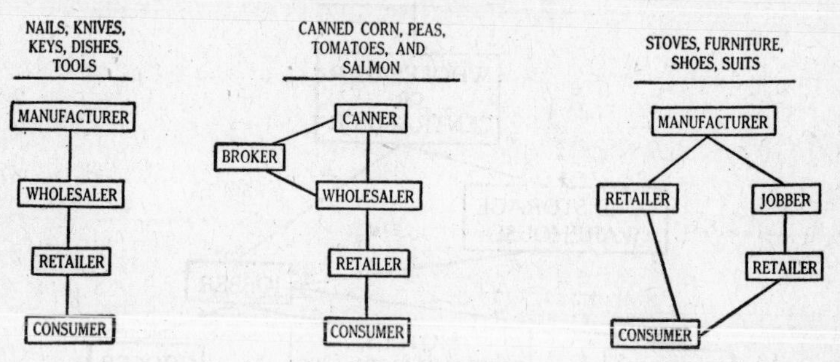

or a book must have much of production added to it by a series of specialized business units after it leaves the factory which has given it a desired form. The series of specialized business units which co-operate in the production of some common types of goods may be shown diagrammatically.

Diagrams will show that it is not only in the creation of tangible, material goods that specialization of business units is used. Specialized business units are quite as useful in making available services which gratify human wants.

These diagrams tell at best only part of the story of specialization of business units. There is not only a line of consecutive

[1] Adapted by permission from Marshall and Lyon, *Our Economic Organization*, pp. 129–31. Macmillan Co., 1921.

specialized business units in each of the operations indicated, but each one of these specialized units is related to a number of other specialized agencies. Thus, for example, we have the

SPECIALIZED PRODUCTION OF CERTAIN SERVICES[1]

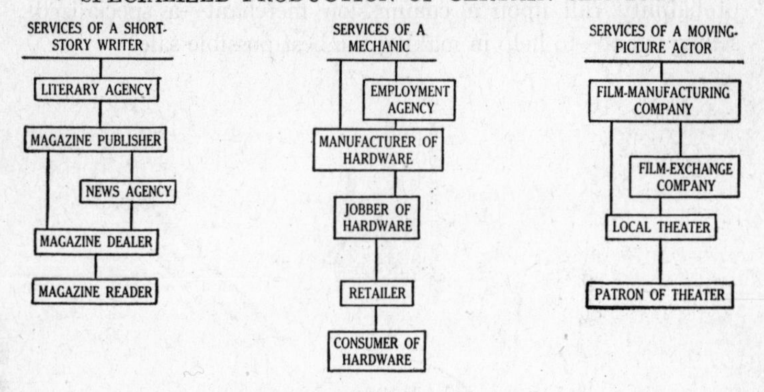

CO-OPERATING SPECIALIZED BUSINESS UNITS IN WHEAT-FLOUR PRODUCTION[2]

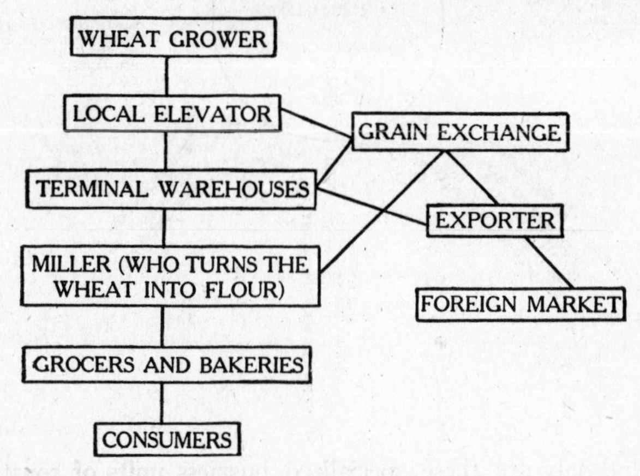

local elevators and the terminal warehouses, both of which are specialists in the production of bread. Each of these makes use of specialized transportation agencies; each relies on banks to furnish it with funds, thus calling in the aid of other special-

[1] *Op. cit.*, p. 134.

[2] *Ibid.*, pp. 132–33.

ists; each calls upon insurance companies and the hedging markets of the organized grain exchanges to aid it in carrying the risks which are incident to ownership; each of these concerns also, when it wishes to dispose of the grain, will in all probability call upon a commission merchant—a specialized selling agent—to help in making the best possible sale.

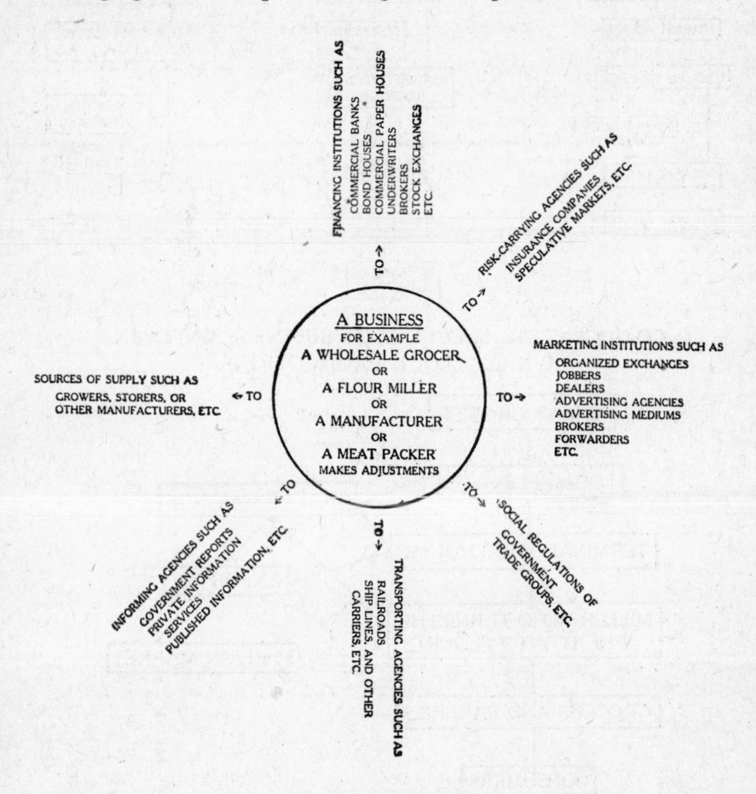

Not only are these specialized business units of constant service, but the government and perhaps private agencies as well are specializing in giving protection from theft or violence, while a score of agencies are gathering information about crops, demand, and prices, all of which are of the greatest use in the production of bread.

If we should give our attention to almost any of the other specialized units in the production of any type of goods, we should find the case much the same. Whether it is the manufacturer of groceries, the wholesaler of hardware, or the retailer of shoes, we should find him dependent upon a great variety of other specialists—specialists from whom he bought, specialists to whom he sells, specialists who aid him in one phase or another of his activities.

The significance to education for business of this specialization of business units is not far to see. Operating a business appears from this view not to be operating a series of activities confined by the four walls of a unit. Operating a business is rather making an adjustment—an adjustment of one specialized unit to the activities of a great number of other specialized units. The degree of success which accompanies a business enterprise depends upon the skill with which such an adjustment is made.

A study of business, therefore, at least a study of business which is to give any consideration to the managerial aspects of business, must include a study of relationships. Since the relationships of which any individual business unit is one part are almost without number, and extend in bewildering fashion in each direction, an overextensive knowledge of relationships is impossible. Anything approaching an adequate knowledge of relationships is difficult and demands, of those who are interested in understanding business, a study of the make-up and structure of society much more far-reaching than anything which has been customary in most so-called business courses.

At first blush it will seem to many of those who are most interested in business education, and especially to those who from long acquaintance with business education have come to think of the task as a training in technique alone, that it is beside the point to suggest a broad training in relationships. The fact of specialization of business units, however, carries with it one great implication: *there is no training for a managerial point of view excepting a training in relationships.*

But why train for a managerial point of view? If there are some whose long familiarity with the customary commercial courses makes them feel such a purpose to be undesirable, let them consider that even the commercial student is entitled to an opportunity to seek success in business. And although there are many who may not wish to direct businesses of their own, or who may never have the financial opportunity to do so, it is worth while to remember that promotion within a business depends largely upon one's ability to aid the management. Any notion of how to aid the management, and any success in so doing, depends entirely upon an appreciation of managerial problems. It should also be realized that it is only with a knowledge of the specialized character of business units that a student who is preparing to enter business has any real basis for a vocational choice. It is from such a knowledge that he sees what businesses really do, and from such a knowledge he may be able to direct himself to that type of specialization for which he is best fitted.

Finally, we must recall the thought expressed in the opening half of the chapter, that society needs, if it is to get the most from its resources, well-trained competitors. A large number of such competitors is possible only if students are trained for the management of business. In any society, therefore, in which individual enterprise and specialization of business units are underlying facts, education for business which neglects a broad instruction in the relationships to which every business must adjust itself belies its name, and is, at best, education for business in an incomplete, narrow, and partial sense.

QUESTIONS FOR DISCUSSION

1. Specialization is said to be a method of production; a method of converting social resources into want-gratifying goods. Can you think of it in this way? Can you think of any methods, other than specialization, which we use?
2. It has been said that a society, no matter how it is organized, must necessarily carry on production; it must convert its social resources into want-gratifying goods. It is only the methods of

production which differ. If this statement seems to you true, give illustrations of methods of production formerly used by society which are in contrast to the methods we use.

3. In modern society who decides what specialized part each person shall play? Can you imagine a society in which some authoritative head assigned each worker to his specialized task?
4. Is there specialization in an army unit? Is the specialization a matter of free choice, of individual enterprise, or is it a specialization by authority?
5. When boys or girls decide upon an occupation, are they determining a specialized task which they shall perform in society's work of production? If an adult shifts from one type of work to another, is he redirecting his specialized effort?
6. Make a list of the forces which you think influence a person in deciding what specialized work he shall undertake. How strong do you think is the motive of pay or pecuniary reward?
7. Society makes use of specialization and relies upon the hope of gain to guide the specialists into those tasks where they will be most useful. Does this seem to you a statement which is in general true? What are some of the factors which might make a person take a job in which he could earn more, but in which you think he would be less useful to society than in some other occupation?
8. When a man goes into business, is it desirable from society's point of view that he shall be efficient in the work which he undertakes?
9. "If business men are efficient, it may result in more gain for those individuals, but there is no assurance that there will be any gain for society through their increased skill." Does this seem to you true? Why, or why not?
10. What devices does society use to attempt to secure for everyone the increased production resulting from increased efficiency?
11. "Competition to give the best results must be both real and intelligent." Illustrate the meaning of this with specific examples drawn from business.
12. Why is it that sons of men connected with large business houses are more likely to become managers of large businesses than the sons of men who work at trades? Do you think it desirable that it should be so? Do you think the school has any responsibility in the situation?

13. What studies in the commercial courses with which you are most familiar tend to train students to understand the management of businesses? What proportion of the total of these courses do such studies constitute?
14. Explain with illustrations what is meant by the "specialization *of* business units."
15. Are middlemen producers? Are producers middlemen?
16. The bank is sometimes called a financial middleman. Explain what this statement might mean.
17. "If the 'middleman' secures too much profit it is because he has not enough competition." Is this true? Is it socially desirable that there should be competition among middlemen? Have business courses any responsibility in this connection?
18. Operating a business consists largely of making adjustments. Adjustments of what? Are the factors to which adjustment must be made largely "within" the business or "without"?
19. If success in business depends largely upon the skill with which adjustments are made, what general type of instruction should be given to students who are preparing for business?
20. Give an example of the way in which a wholesale grocer makes use of financial institutions, risk-carrying agencies, marketing institutions, government, transporting agencies, information agencies, sources of raw materials. Do the same for a manufacturer of automobiles.
21. Suggest a course which might give a student who was preparing for business some knowledge of each of the phases of relationship in which he will operate.
22. "But after all, not everyone can be thought of as needing education in the problems of business management. Most of the students in the commercial department are predestined to routine clerical tasks. For them several years of stenography, typewriting, and bookkeeping are sufficient. To talk of anything else is nonsense." Comment.
23. "To talk of any training in the problems of business management for high school commercial pupils is undemocratic. It is an effort to give an education adapted to the few rather than the needs of the many." Comment.
24. Try to formulate a general statement or statements which summarize the ideas and suggestions for business education which come to you from a study of Chapter IV.

CHAPTER V

SPECIALIZATION WITHIN BUSINESS UNITS

The second form of specialization is specialization within business units. This is a no less important method in the business of producing want-gratifying goods than the specialization *of* business units. A realization of the nature and extent of this form of specialization is quite as pregnant with suggestions for business education as the form previously studied, but the suggestions are of a very different character. Before drawing conclusions, however, it is well to be sure that we understand specialization within business units with some clearness.

The classic expression of specialization within an industry is the oft-quoted statement of Adam Smith:

> To take an example, therefore, from a very trifling manufacture, but one in which the division of labor has been very often taken notice of, the trade of the pin-maker; a workman not educated to this business (which the division of labor has rendered a distinct trade), nor acquainted with the use of the machinery employed in it (to the invention of which the same division of labor has probably given occasion), could scarce, perhaps, with his utmost industry, make one pin in a day and certainly could not make twenty. But in the way in which this business is now carried on, not only the whole work is a peculiar trade, but it is divided into a number of branches of which the greater part are likewise peculiar trades. One man draws out the wire, another straights it, a third cuts it, a fourth points it, a fifth grinds it at the top for receiving the head; to make the head requires two or three distinct operations; to put it on is a peculiar business, to whiten the pins is another; it is even a trade by itself to put them into the paper; and the important business of making a pin is, in this manner, divided into about eighteen distinct operations, which, in some manufactories, are all performed by distinct hands, though in others the same man will sometimes perform two or three of them. I have seen a small manufactory of this kind where ten men only were employed, and where some of them consequently

performed two or three distinct operations. But though they were very poor, and therefore but indifferently accommodated with the necessary machinery, they could, when they exerted themselves, make among them about twelve pounds of pins in a day. There are in a pound upward of four thousand pins of a middling size. Those ten persons, therefore, could make among them upward of forty-eight thousand pins in a day. Each person, therefore, making a tenth part of forty-eight thousand pins, might be considered as making four thousand eight hundred pins in a day. But if they had all wrought separately and independently, and without any of them having been educated to this peculiar business, they certainly could not each of them have made twenty, perhaps not one pin in a day; that is, certainly, not the two hundred and fortieth, perhaps not the four thousand eight hundredth part of what they are at present capable of performing, in consequence of a proper division and combination of their different operations.[1]

But what seemed to Adam Smith as the marvelous specialization of his day appears elementary in our time. More and more have jobs been divided. This division in manufacturing is thus illustrated in shoemaking:

In the cutting-room the parts which form the upper are cut out. For the best goods this is done with a hand knife. For the less expensive classes of leather, and for linings and gussets—which are usually cut from cloth—a die is used. The die-cutters are also block-hands, dinkers, and clickers. A skiver works in the fitting- or stitching-room, and skives or cuts to a bevel in a skiving machine the edges of the pieces for the uppers. Cementers or pasters put cement on the skived surfaces which folders fold over and stick together by pressure either in a machine or by hand, thus producing a finished instead of a raw edge. Upper-stitchers include all workers on sewing-machines in the fitting-room, whether on leather or linings. An eyelet-row stitcher puts stitching on the quarter, just outside the place where the row of hooks and eyelets will be. A closer stitches or closes the quarters together at the back, and a seam-rubber or seam-pounder smooths this seam by rubbing or pressing it out as flat as possible on a machine. A gore- or gusset-stitcher stitches in gores or gussets such as appear in congress boots. A lining-stitcher, lining-maker, or liner sews together the different pieces of the lining,

[1] From Adam Smith, *The Wealth of Nations*, Book I, chap. i.

and a closer-on or in-seamer stitches the lining into the quarters. When the vamps are lined separately a vamp-liner does the work. On fine work a lacing-stitcher binds the lining with a facing of leather. A beader operates a machine of the same name which presses together the seam made around the top of the quarters by closing on. A top-stitcher or corder runs stitching around the quarters just below this seam, through the quarter and lining. A buttonhole-machine operator puts the quarters for button shoes through her machine, which makes a cut, lays a heavy cord around the edge, and stitches over the cord and through the edge, making a buttonhole. The buttonhole-finisher's machine sews down that part of the heavy cord which passes from buttonhole to buttonhole. The buttons are sewed on by hand or by machine, or are fastened on with wire staples. A gang-punch operator punches the holes for eyelets in laced shoes. An eyeleter or fastener-setter sets in the eyelets with an eyeleting machine. A hooker puts in the hooks with a hooking machine. A marker or tip-marker marks on the vamp the place where the tip is to go, and a tipper or tip-stitcher stitches it on; sometimes a tip-paster pastes or gums the tips onto the vamps before they are stitched. A perforator perforates the edges, and a tip-fixer glues down or otherwise adjusts them. A vamp-closer stitches the two ends of the vamp together behind. A vamper sews together the quarters and vamps. A barrer or stayer stitches back and forth through the edges of the two quarters. A heel-stay stitcher and an eyelet-stay stitcher put on heel stays and eyelet stays, respectively, after the lining has been closed on. A fancy stitcher is employed on some work to do stitching, which serves merely as decoration. A foxing stitcher sews to the back of the vamp of some shoes a piece of leather called a foxing. On fine work, a tongue-binder binds the edges of the tongues with cloth or leather; the tongues are stitched into place by tongue-stitchers. A strap-maker makes leather straps for ladies' slippers, or straps by which shoes are pulled onto the foot. Table workers are unskilled operatives who do such work as gumming or pasting, tip marking, and sewing on buttons, by hand, at tables in the stitching-room.[1]

The specialization in the large meat-packing plants was once vividly impressed upon the writer by a young Russian

[1] Adapted from the *U.S. Census Special Report on Employees and Wages*, 1903, pp. 1199–1201.

student who described his first job in America. "I was taken," said he, "into a room where, on a table, were a pile of paper sheets and innumerable cattle livers. My guide seized a liver in one hand and a sheet of paper in the other and wrapped the first in the second. He told me to do the same. I did. 'Keep on doing it,' said my instructor. I did. I was now educated for industry. For over a year I stood at that table and wrapped livers with no notion of the whence, the why, or the wherefore. But I became an expert liver wrapper."

Although specialization in manufacturing has often been pointed out, the prevalence of specializing in office work has been much less realized. The specialization in some of these units is of the greatest importance to persons engaged in educating for business. Office work for example has become highly specialized. The possibilities of such specialization may be realized from the following description of differentiations in occupations in a prominent metropolitan bank:

The same division of labor exists in a bank, to be reckoned, however, by departments rather than individual "jobs."

For instance, John Smith & Co., a prosperous concern, is approached by the New Business Department, and its account solicited. The company agrees to open an account, and makes an initial deposit of cash and checks. Taken in by the Receiving Teller, the credit is charged through to the City Books Department, where it is entered on the books by one of a large force of bookkeepers. The checks are separated by the teller, and those on local banks are charged to, and handled by, the Clearings Department; those on other cities by the Transit Department, which sends these items to the bank's country correspondents. The letters enclosing these items are handled by the Mail Department, which finally sends them on their way. Under special arrangements, the items are often charged on the Country Books on the day of their receipt at destination.

Meanwhile the Signature Department has filed specimen signatures of the officers authorized to sign for the account, and the name of the company has been given to the Addressograph Department, where a plate is made in anticipation of the many times the name must be used.

The officers of the company now find that its business necessitates a loan, and come with a request for $100,000. The Bank Officers discuss the matter, have the Credit Department investigate the company's reputation for prompt payment (the letters of inquiry being actually run off in the Stenographic Department), and at the close of the investigation, the Executive Committee agrees to a loan of $50,000 unsecured, and a further loan of $50,000 secured by acceptable collateral. For this, there are brought to the bank some good bonds which have been in the assets of the company, and after the Collateral Department has checked them over and O.K.'d them, the loan is put through at the Discount Department, which makes out a credit to the company's account of the amount of the loan less discount.

After the account has been on the books for awhile, the Analysis Department analyzes its value to the bank by crediting it with the proper profit, and charging it with its fair share of "overhead," etc. The Average Cards Department records on a large card the average balances month by month, together with the maximum and minimum loans. At the end of each month, the Cancelled Vouchers Department returns to the company all the checks drawn that month.

John Smith & Co. has a branch in San Francisco handling a petty cash account with a San Francisco bank. This account being drawn low, the Wire Transfer Department is called upon to telegraph funds to the San Francisco bank.

Drafts drawn against the customer are handled by the City Collection Department, and presently some notes receivable are brought in for the bank to collect. Those payable out of town are handled by the Country Collection Department, those within the city by the Note Teller. The Paying Tellers of course cash the customer's checks. When the company wishes to invest part of its surplus funds, it buys some stocks through the Special Securities Department. Any difference in figures which arises in handling the account is adjusted by the Audit Department.

Having received such good service at the bank, Mr. Smith, the president of the company, now suggests that his wife open an account in the affiliated Savings Department. As she accumulates a little ready money, she wishes to invest it in some trustworthy bond, and the Bond Department takes care of this for her. Having a friend in Japan to whom she wishes to send a Christmas gift of money, she turns again to the bank, and the Foreign Department sells her a foreign draft, with due allowance for exchange.

Mr. Smith now being called upon to undertake a journey which he feels may possibly be somewhat hazardous, he decides to let the Trust Department create a living trust, whereby his family will be safely provided for in any eventuality.

Mrs. Smith's sister, who has managed a small business since her husband's death, is now induced to transfer her account to this "family" bank, and is satisfactorily taken care of by the Women's Department; wishing to buy a small home, the Real Estate Department sends a man out to make an appraisal of the desired property. She decides to take a box in the Safety Deposit Vaults for her securities, and as the coupons on her bonds fall due, takes them to the Coupon Department to be cashed or deposited.

In addition to these departments, there are others not dealing directly with the individual customer; for instance, all general information goes to the General Files, and the accounts of the bank with other banks are kept in the General Books. Shipments of currency to the bank's correspondents are handled by the Currency Department.

There are also a group of departments related only indirectly to the customer, known as "internal service" departments, including the Chief Clerk's Department, the Guards, the Interest, Telegraph, Telephone, Printing, and Supply Departments.[1]

The following analysis of 2,306 positions held by 1,000 men and boys brings out the characteristic of specialization in office work by showing the wide range of positions held.

TABLE VIII

2,306 POSITIONS HELD BY 1,000 MEN AND BOYS*

Position	Number
Officials, Managers, Supervisors:	
Executives	40
Department managers, agents	30
Credit men	16
Secretaries, treasurers, assistant secretaries	11
Advertising men	5
Supervisors	5
Efficiency engineers	2
Total	109

*Adapted by permission from Bertha M. Stevens, *Boys and Girls in Commercial Work.* p. 24. The Survey Committee of the Cleveland Foundation, 1916.

[1] A statement prepared by Miss A. L. Batchelder, Continental and Commercial Bank, Chicago, March, 1922.

TABLE VIII—*Continued*

Special:	
Salesmen, solicitors	139
Distributors, demonstrators, canvassers, collectors	84
Inspectors	12
Storekeepers	4
Buyers	2
Estimator	1
Total	242
Bookkeepers, etc.:	
Bookkeepers, assistants	151
Cashiers	37
Paymasters, assistants	14
Accountants, assistants	10
Statistical workers	5
Auditors, assistants	4
Tellers	2
Total	223
Stenographers:	
Stenographers	174
Private secretaries	3
Total	177
Clerks:	
Shipping	85
Cost production	63
Receiving, stock	59
Sales order	48
Time	47
Record entry	20
Mail	15
Bill	12
Railway	12
Claim	7
File, index	7
Inventory	7
Invoice	6
Sale	4
Pricing	3
Routing	2
Voucher	2
Unspecified	927
Total	1,326

TABLE VIII—*Continued*

Machine Workers:	
Billers	13
Multigraph operators	3
Typists	3
Total	19
General Clerical Workers:	
Office boys, messengers	166
Checkers and general office workers	44
Total	210
Grand Total	2,306

TABLE IX

2,816 POSITIONS HELD BY WOMEN AND GIRLS*

Officials, Managers, Supervisors:	
Supervisors	23
Executives	14
Department managers	13
Secretaries and treasurers, assistant treasurers	4
Total	54
Special:	
Copywriters, proofreaders	14
Research worker	1
Total	15
Bookkeepers, etc.:	
Bookkeeping and cashier assistants	324
Auditing assistants	196
Statistical workers	35
Bookkeepers	7
Auditors	2
Cashiers	2
Total	566
Stenographers:	
Stenographers	948
Stenographers and billers	20
Private secretaries	19
Stenographers and dictating-machine operators	4
Managers, stenography bureau	2
Stenography and translator	1
Stenography and bookkeeper	1
Total	995

* Bertha M. Stevens, *op. cit.*, p. 25.

TABLE IX—*Continued*

Clerks:	
Credit	18
Information	6
Claim	4
Record	3
Insurance	2
Employment	1
File	1
Mail	1
Order	1
Stock	1
Total	38
Machine Workers:	
Typists	399
Billers	130
Tabulating-machine operators	32
Comptometer operators	28
Multigraph operators	19
Billing and comptometer operators	18
Machine operators, not requiring training	16
Total	642
General Clerical Workers:	
Filing and general clerical	155
Recording, entering, cataloguing	132
Checking, counting, sorting	127
Long-hand writing	71
Information desk, telephone	21
Total	506
Grand total	2,816

The committee making the survey just quoted indicated that the following were "typical work and positions in large office organizations":[1]

[1] *Ibid.*, p. 35.

ADMINISTRATIVE	CLERICAL
Types of work	Types of work
Financiering	Accounting and bookkeeping
Organization and administration	Credit work
Merchandising and advertising	Handling of funds
Development and experimentation	Correspondence
Efficiency engineering	Filing and records
Workers	Workers
Officials	Auditors
Managers	Accountants
Salesmen and advertising men	Bookkeepers
Other specialists	Credit men
Assistants to above	Cashiers
	Clerks
	Stenographers
	Machine operators
	Telephone operators
	Messengers
	Office boys

What conclusions regarding education for business are to be drawn from the fact of specialization within business units? Two, at least, impress themselves. First, *if people are to do specialized work they must be trained for specialized performance.* Specialized techniques must be taught. This is only saying that people must be taught to do what they are to do. The tendency in business education has been to appreciate this fact readily enough, though, as will appear, there has been on the part of educators a strange lack of awareness of the changes in the performance requirements of industry.

A second conclusion, arising from a realization of the specialized tasks of business, is that *performance in a business will go but little toward teaching the business as a whole.* Time was, of course, when experience in a business was the recognized method of learning the business. To many it is still the recognized way. But such recognition is largely a mistaken recognition. The reason is the specialization within business units. The lining stitcher and the eyeleter are not learning even shoe manufacturing, to say nothing of how to direct such a business, nor is the successful liver wrapper on the logical route to the directorate of a packing-plant. Though it has been true for a shorter period, the same conclusions hold good in office work. Specialized technique is required in office work, specialized technique can be sold to employers, and specialized technique must be taught. But specialized work in the office does not, with very few exceptions, give a knowledge of the business as a whole. The opportunity of the billing clerk, the file clerk, the ledger poster, the invoice clerk, the storekeeper, the teller, the machine operator, to learn of those relationship adjustments which constitute the real conduct of the business is negligible. Unless the business is small, bookkeepers, cashiers, timekeepers, and so-called accountants have little more chance. As business tends to become larger, specialization deprives the specialists of the chance to learn from their daily work even the relationships within the unit itself. Examples are everywhere. Ask the typical salesperson, even one of several years' experience, what his daily work has taught him of the organization and administration of the department store. Ask him what his work has shown him of the considerations which underlie the policies of the house. Ask the clerk (in any one of a dozen capacities) in a large bank or general office what he has learned in one or two years about the relationships of his department to other departments and the integration of all. Or ask what has been made clear to him concerning the policies of the institution. Ask any of these questions and it will be seen quickly enough that specialization within a business unit has made experience of very doubtful service as a teacher of business. It has made it of almost no value if we consider its utility in teaching the general relationships in the organization and administration of which business consists.

Sensing, then, the intense specialization of all large-scale modern business, we may conclude, first, that specialized techniques must be taught. We need not yet conclude *where* they should be taught. That question must wait until we consider the various institutions which offer their services for the task. Second, we may decide that specialization has made "learning by experience" of doubtful value so far as the broader phases of business are concerned. The task of teaching these relationships, then, must be taught somewhere outside business itself. The assignment of that duty, too, may well wait for later discussion.

QUESTIONS FOR DISCUSSION

1. Is specialization *within* business units also a "method of production"? Does it result in more rapid production than non-specialization? Make out as long a list as possible of the ways in which specialization *within* business units increases production as compared with non-specialization.
2. Is there specialization of the teaching staff within the school unit with which you are most familiar? What seems to you the advantages and disadvantages of such specialization?
3. Think of any business (several if possible) with which you are familiar. Is specialization used? Does the amount of specialization seem to vary to any degree with the size of the business?
4. Does it seem to you that specialization is increasingly common in teaching commercial courses? What evidence have you noticed?
5. Suppose that a boy graduating from the commercial course of a high school takes a job in a large bank, or in the general office of a railroad company, large wholesale house, or manufacturing plant, what are his chances of "learning the business"?
6. "The specialists in a modern office or factory are separate, individual, unrelated units. They know little of the work of one another. They care less. There is no co-operation." How much truth is there in these statements?
7. "Specialization within business units leads to a feeling of futility in the minds of the specialists. One cannot be interested where he has no sense of his contribution to the whole." Do you think this statement is sound? Why is there so little sense of contribution to the whole result when one is specializing? What might be done to make a realization of the specialist's contribution more clear to the specialist?
8. A study of modern business units makes it clear that specialization within those units prevails. Thus it follows: (1) specialized training must be given; (2) the public schools must teach it; (3) commercial courses must be devoted to it. With what ones of these statements, if any, do you agree?
9. Formulate a series of statements that seem to you to summarize the suggestions for business education that come from a study of this chapter.

CHAPTER VI

SCIENCE IN BUSINESS AND LARGE-SCALE PRODUCTION

There are at least two other characteristics of the modern method of want-gratification to which we must give some attention if we would have an adequate notion of what business is. These are the scientific or technological character of business and the large scale of operations. As with specialization, so with the application of science to industry and the large scale of modern operations. Both can be thought of as methods of producing goods. Large-scale operations and the use of natural forces, machine industry, as it is often called, have proved themselves such powerful instruments of increasing production that there is every reason to believe that they will become more and more typical of business. The fact that these methods are prevalent, like the fact of specialization of and within business units, has much to suggest to anyone who is interested in education for business. Let us consider them in turn.

Early industry was hand, tool, human-power industry. Everyone is familiar with the methods of household manufacture in colonial days in America. Manufacture was thought of in terms of craftsmanship rather than factory production. Natural forces were not extensively employed. Human energy was the source of power, and the contributions of physics and chemistry to production had not yet been made. But the application of these and other sciences to industry came, and came with great suddenness.

The change from hand industry to power industry in England, sudden, decisive and bringing with it innumerable results in almost every phase of life, is called the Industrial Revolution. One may think of the Industrial Revolution as beginning in 1750, or he may think of it as beginning some centuries before that time. One may think of its continuing for fifty years or sixty years, or he may quite sensibly think of it as still going on, as we are steadily making more and more use of science in our work of gratifying wants. Certain it is that some of the most striking and most sudden applications of science to business were made in the years immediately following 1750. The textile industry was of great importance in England at that time, and to aid manufacture one invention pressed upon another. In 1738 the flying shuttle gave a new speed to weaving, which had been the "neck of the bottle" in the process of making cloth. In 1764 a new spinning device, the spinning jenny, and in 1779 the spinning mule were devised. The year 1789 saw a machine constructed which could be operated by water or steam power; in 1792 Eli Whitney introduced the cotton gin. The importance of these machines becomes apparent when we realize that in this same period the use of steam in manufacture was begun, the manufacture of steam engines being started in 1781. Consonant with these great changes came new uses of science in coal mining and in smelting ore. More gradually, but as certainly, science pervaded other industries. All of us are familiar with some of its achievements in transportation and communication which we witness in the railroad, the airplane, the steamship, the telephone, the telegraph, and the wireless.

These changes, for many reasons into which we cannot go here, were much retarded in America. In some ways and in some sections the United States was little more advanced in its use of science in industry in 1850 than England was in 1750. But when the change came, it came rapidly. During the past fifty years America has led in the extent and daring with which science has been applied to many phases of business. At present there is probably no country in which science plays a larger part in everyday affairs.

The result of the application of science to industry is a changed world—a world which has changed so markedly and so suddenly that even our fathers often think of it in old-fashioned terms. Science is now everywhere.

The knowledge and control of chemical facts and processes are involved in the manufacture of most common necessities of modern life, such as steel, glass, copper, lead, aluminum, illuminating gas, hydrocarbons, cotton, wool and silk textiles, paper, soap, and glycerin, in preparing sugar, starch, etc., and also in many operations concerned with building and construction. It is important in the industry of the household as well as in the industries of the world. Chemistry has contributed greatly to human comfort and welfare in the past; but this is only an earnest of what it will contribute in the future. One can hardly overestimate the importance of the study of chemistry in any field in which one is likely to labor.[1]

The contributions of physics are innumerable. Whether we think of transportation by rail, on water, or in the air, whether we think of manufacturing in almost any of its varied forms, lighting, heating, or refrigeration, we find that physics underlies the industry concerned. What the scientist, the explorer for the industrial world, discovers is almost invariably put to practical use.

Other sciences pervade industry in general perhaps less insistently, but in particular industries they are of basic importance and in many significant. Metallurgy, geology, biology, and botany need only to be mentioned to call to our minds their importance in everyday affairs. There is hardly a moment of our lives unaffected by "engineers" of electricity, architecture, sanitation, heating, ventilation, hydraulics, gas, transportation, or mechanics. Each of these makes application of one or a dozen sciences.

But what has this invasion of industry by science meant for business education? In its simplest terms, it has meant that business education, if it is to embody the characteristics of modern business, must provide some training in the sciences as well as in social relations. This does not mean that to be equipped for engaging in any general business activity one must become a master of all the sciences, or an expert in any one branch. But there are many types of business where

[1] Adapted by permission from Smith and Jewett, *Introduction to the Study of Science*, pp. 418–19. Macmillan Co., 1918.

executive control demands at least intelligence concerning technological considerations. In the direction of industrial processes, for example, which call for the application of various phases of science, those in charge should be sufficiently informed about their technological aspects to be able to engage the right engineers, to understand their work, and to make decisions regarding the results.

An understanding of science at first glance may appear necessary only in the case of engineering projects or of industries engaged in changing the physical composition or appearance of certain materials, as in the manufacture of steel or the dyeing of fabrics. The extent of the use of scientific knowledge, however, goes far beyond such direct applications into the field of commercial activity. Cost accounting, which is not generally regarded as a branch of the exact sciences, must consider, for example, power requirements, the relative efficiency of various processes, and the relation of any one of these processes to the costs of the business. Even when the advice of engineering specialists is employed, the accountant must be able to understand their terminology and viewpoint. Banking, to use a case in another field, is essentially concerned with the intelligent placing of loans. The intelligent placing of loans depends for its success not upon a knowledge of the matters of routine detail within the bank, but upon a knowledge of the probable achievements of those firms to whom accommodation is extended. It then becomes evident that accuracy by the banker in estimating such achievements calls at least for a sensitiveness to the conditions of plant, equipment, methods, and processes as they affect production. As in the case of the accountant, the assistance of a scientific expert does not relieve the banker from the necessity of being able to appreciate various technological considerations. Finally, in merchandising, which may not appear to be anything more than a means of exchanging goods, a knowledge of the physical make-up of the goods to be bought and the adaptability to various uses of the goods to be sold is required. The most direct example of this particular use occurs in the sale of goods for the technical processes of public

TABLE X

RELATIVE INCREASE OF CAPITAL AND EMPLOYEES IN MANUFACTURING*

	1850	1860	1870	1880	1890	1900	1910	Percentage Increase in 1910 over 1850
	All Manufacturers in the United States							
Average per establishment:								
Product	$8,280	$13,420	$13,420	$21,100	$28,070	$25,418	$76,993	830
Capital	4,330	7,190	6,720	10,960	19,020	19,269	68,638	1,485
Number of employees	7.7	9.3	8.1	10.6	13.8	10.4	25.0	225
	Iron and Steel							
Number of establishments	468	542	726	699	699	668	654	40
Average product	$43,600	$97,000	$275,000	$419,000	$683,000	$1,203,500	$2,119,000	4,760
Average capital	46,700	82,000	161,000	295,000	591,000	858,000	2,282,000	4,787
Average number of employees	53	65	103	107	250	333	426	704

*From Marshall, Wright, and Field, *Materials for the Study of Elementary Economics*, p. 170. University of Chicago Press, 1913.

utilities, factories, railroads, and the like, where a knowledge of the scientific principles which underlie the technique is a prerequisite to effective merchandising. These immediate values of some study of science are quickly reflected from a study of the technological aspects of modern business. Its deeper use to the business administrator, as to others, lies in its fundamentally educative character.

The second characteristic of modern business which has been indicated for discussion in this chapter is its tendency to large size. Certain phases of this tendency toward large-scale operations are brought out in a mere enumeration of factual data.

It will be worth while to notice in examining Table X the fact that corporations rather than the individuals or other forms of business enterprise manufactured more than 83 per cent of the total value of products; that the average per establishment for corporations for 1914 was more than $258,000, as contrasted with something over $13,000, the average per establishment of individual concerns.

The tendency toward large-scale production appears to be on the increase. This tendency lies, of course, in the fact that there are a number of underlying advantages in this form of production as applied to many types of goods. These advantages are stated by one writer as follows:

> What are the economic advantages of manufacturing in a large plant and doing business on a large scale, and how important are they? Different industries differ among themselves very greatly in these respects, and any general statement will need modification when applied to a particular case. What is said will be more applicable to those groups of industries which are better adapted for concentration.
>
> 1. *The handling of material.*—The handling of material on a large scale in itself gives great economy.
>
> 2. *The use of machinery and departments.*—In the large manufactory it is possible to use machinery to an extent not possible in the small establishment. The introduction of labor-saving machines is well known to be one of the greatest causes of economic efficiency.
>
> 3. *Subdivision of labor.*—In most manufactories an article must go through many processes before it is completed. Specialization of

labor is only possible in the large manufactory, and it is generally agreed that such specialization gives increased efficiency.

4. *Integration.*—A further step in the development of concentration of industry is its integration; that is, a corporation handles, not one stage of manufacture only, but a number or even all of the stages from the raw material to the finished product. This again gives increased economy and efficiency, because all the different units of the integrated industry are in harmony, one with reference to the other.

5. *Parallel consolidation and specialization.*—Under these conditions it is possible to make the same product at the different plants, or to specialize the different manufactories under the same organization so that one shall handle one line of work, and another another. Further, the work of any one branch may become standardized and require comparatively little shifting or changing of machines.

Cross freights are avoided to a large extent when the manufactories of one district supply the markets of that district. For articles which are heavy as compared with their cost, for instance, salt and steel rails, this factor may be one of controlling importance.

6. *Saving by-products.*—A further advantage of magnitude is the use of by-products. The small manufactory cannot spend much money in such utilization, although the coarser of them may be saved.

7. *Consolidation of allied industries.*—The final stage in consolidation is the union of allied and connected industries. This frequently goes beyond integration, in that the lines of manufacture are absorbed which use as raw material the by-product of the central organization.

8. *Keeping establishments up to date.*—The large company uses only the most modern manufactories which have complete and highly efficient machinery and practices, including the latest labor-saving devices and the best technical improvements.

9. *Investigating departments.*—The large organization is able to have an investigating department in order that discoveries may be made for still further improvements.

10. *Business advantages of concentration.*—Thus far the industrial advantages of concentration only have been given. Upon the business side there are also great economies. Some of the most important of these are as follows:

a) Big organizations are able to buy in large quantities and thus gain the advantages of the lowest rates of purchase.

b) Big organizations are able to sell in large quantities and most advantageously. A large part of the cost of business under new conditions is the marketing of products. In the marketing there are great costs in commercial travelers, in advertisements, etc. With the large concentration the advertising cost per unit of sale is much lower than with the small industry.

c) When there is a single great federated establishment, orders can be received at a central office and from that office distributed to the different plants as best required by efficiency in manufacture, taking into account the expense of transportation.

d) Also the mere size of an establishment, so that it may be able to take a large order at a time and fill it promptly, gives a great advantage over smaller concerns.

e) For entering foreign trade the business economies of concentration are undoubtedly very great. Sending to foreign countries to build up a trade for an industry is an expensive undertaking.

f) The losses through poor debts are less with large organizations than with small ones. Frequently where there are many organizations having keen competition with a large number of traveling salesmen, sales are made without careful reference to the ability of the purchaser to pay.

g) One of the greatest advantages of concentration with co-operation of the independent units is the regulation of production. The great losses are avoided which result from investments of capital in manufactories which run only a portion of the time and before they shut down produce more goods than can be sold at a profit.

h) A less amount of capital is necessary in order to handle a combined business than would be necessary if a great organization were subdivided. If a concern be fairly independent of the banks and the necessity to pay excessive rates of interest, it must keep a considerable amount of ready cash on hand to handle its business. A very large concern, in which the variations in the demands for the different products compensate for one another to some extent at least, is able to handle its business with a relatively small cash reserve.

11. *Opportunity for high order of ability.*—It may be that a final advantage of concentration will be the opportunity for the display of ability of the highest order.

12. *Other advantages of concentration.*—Other advantages of concentration are frequently claimed. Among these are: steady employment of labor, better wages, better protection against industrial accidents, the maintenance of superior quality, etc. These

points are not here introduced as advantages of concentration, since in reference to them there is a marked difference of opinion.[1]

But the social and managerial advantages of large-scale production we cannot stop here to discuss at length. Its importance for our purposes lies in certain ways in which it affects the knowledge needed by one who takes part in industry.

In the first place the increasing scale of business (coupled with science in industry and with specialization) has brought new methods of management into business.

It was found that the very structure of a large business, the relation of one part to another, and the assignment of duties and responsibilities could be kept clear only with such mechanical aids as charts and diagrams. The organization plan and devolution of duties even in departments have often become so large that detailed chartings are useful.

Ideas of the most efficient relations between executives, subexecutives, advisers, and subordinates often find expression in such terms as line organization, staff organization, and functional organization These relations may be expressed in "Control Manuals" or illustrated by the use of charts.[2]

LINE AND STAFF ORGANIZATION

(THE GENERAL MANAGER IS ADVISED AND GUIDED BY A STAFF OF EXPERTS)

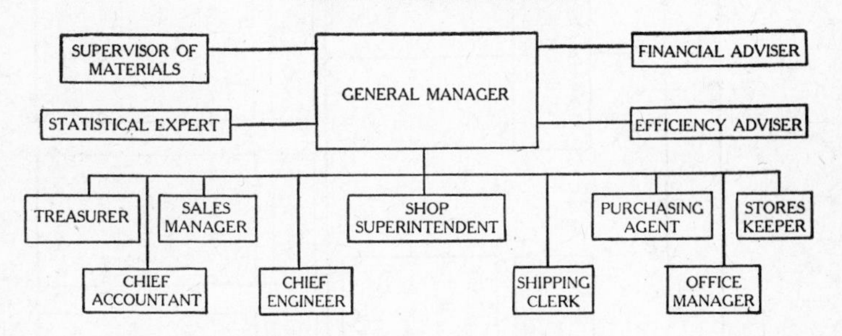

[1] Adapted by permission from C. R. Van Hise, *Concentration and Control*, pp. 8–19. Macmillan Co., 1914.

[2] Taken by permission from Alexander Hamilton Institute, *Report No. 102*, Organization Charts, p. 9.

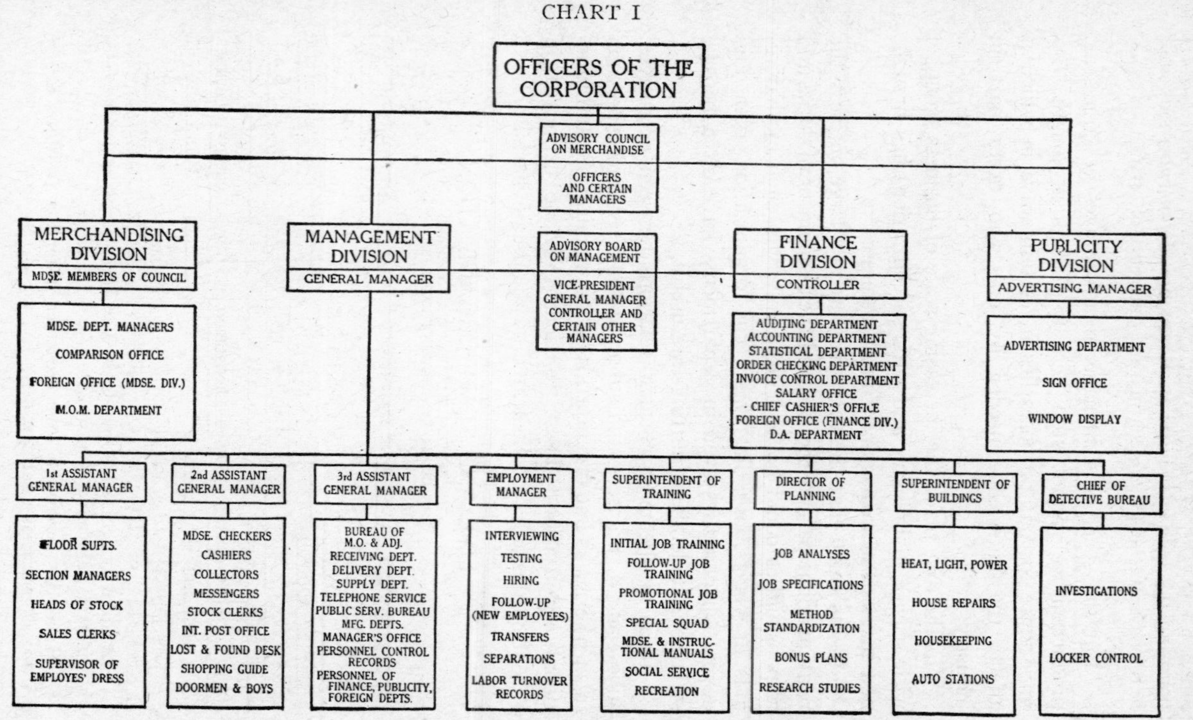

CHART OF A DEPARTMENT STORE

CHART II

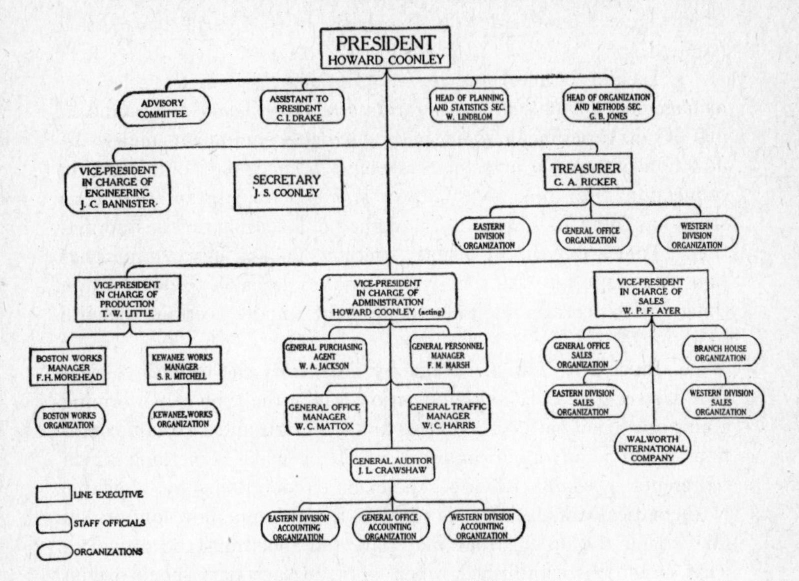

CHART OF A MANUFACTURING PLANT[1]

The new spirit and method in the organization and control of industry had its origin in manufacturing. More than any one other person Frederick Taylor stirred thinking in this field. One student of Mr. Taylor's methods thus points out some of the requirements in the scientific control of modern large-scale business:

As I analyze it, there are three principal aims in it: (1) seeking of more precise information through investigation, experiment, etc.; (2) as great an amount of prediction of what is going to happen in business operation as is possible on the basis of the unusual amount of exact information acquired; (3) precise control of the processes of conducting the business by various functionalized people in such

[1] Chart II taken by permission from J. O. McKinsey, "The Walworth Manufacturing Company," Pamphlet No. 3, Cases and Problems, *Materials for the Study of Business.* University of Chicago Press, 1922.

wise as to bring about as precisely as possible the predictions which have been made on the basis of the exact information required.

1. Seeking of more precise information. It is in the scientific-management plant that investigation and experiment—the establishing of an experiment room with adequate equipment under the direction of capable investigators—have been worked out. It is in connection with this investigation and experimentation that time study has come in. I cite it as a method of acquiring precise information. Time study simply means a method of acquiring exact information with respect to the time which it takes a person to do a certain thing, with certain definite equipment, under certain definite conditions.

2. Precise prediction. If one by time study and other investigation has secured and filed information telling the time of performing a unit operation with certain tools and materials under certain conditions, then if an order comes in to do or make something which represents a combination of these unit operations, by a simple mathematical calculation it is possible to determine how long it will take to fill the order, what materials and tools must be provided, what conditions established, when work on each part should begin, when and how they should be assembled, etc. In other words, an accurate layout of work on the job becomes possible. In most plants layout is by guess. Guess involves waste. An accurate layout of separate jobs means accurate layout and dovetailing of all jobs, and economical and efficient operation of materials, equipment and labor; in other words, more precise control.

3. Precise control. This means that to each of a number of persons shall be assigned, with authority, the responsibility of maintaining one or more of the standard conditions on the basis of which the prediction or layout of a job is made. The principal standard conditions to be maintained are:

a) Standard materials.

b) Standard storing and issuing of materials.

c) Standard conditions under which work is performed.

d) Standard methods of performing operations.

Through what machinery are the three primary aims of scientific management (investigation, prediction, precise control) accomplished? This machinery is described in the words *functional organization.*

Functional organization is carried out to an unusual degree in manufacturing plants by scientific management. First, there is functional organization in large; planning is separated entirely from doing. Now, in an ordinary manufacturing plant an order is received to make something. That is sent down to the foreman with an order to "make twenty-five of these by the 25th of June." The foreman turns to the workman and says, "start on these day after tomorrow." There your foreman has planned who is to do it; how long it will take; how it is to be done; and so on. Under scientific management, on the other hand, in a room called the planning room, where is kept on file all the information which has been gathered regarding all phases of operation, the planning is done. First, a list is made of the operations involved in filling this order, and of the materials and equipment required; second, an estimate is made of the time it takes to do each one of the operations with due allowance for uncertainties; third, a day is determined when work on the order is to start in order to meet the date of promised delivery. All planning of that sort is done, and proper orders are made out. On the proper date these orders are issued to the man who has charge of the material, telling him to send it to such and such a machine; and to the workman at that machine telling him to start the work. Accompanying the order issued him is the analysis of the job and definite instructions for its performance.[1]

It is with the implications of large-scale industry for education that we are most concerned. We may set down three as important:

1. It is the large-scale character of business quite as much as it is specialization and the pervasiveness of science that makes it impossible to learn business rapidly by being in it. It is the overwhelming size of the factory, the volume of the large bank and the great store, that staggers the attempt of the novice to comprehend.

2. Comprehension becomes possible only in terms of the techniques which have been devised for depicting large and impersonal relations. This means not only familiarity with

[1] Adapted by permission from H. S. Person, "Scientific Management," *Proceedings of Tuck School Conference* (1912), pp. 4–5; and "Scientific Management," *Bulletin of the Taylor Society*, II (1916), pp. 17–19.

organization schemes and charting methods, but a knowledge of the "laws" and principles of management, of "measuring and communicating aids of control," of budgets, records, time study, quotas, business indices, and barometers. Thus the student of business needs a knowledge of these matters. If his position is small and insignificant, he needs it to relate himself to his surroundings. If he attains a position of authority, such knowledge is a necessary part of his executive equipment. Therefore the devices of large-scale organization must be taught.

3. Finally, the large-scale character of business (again coupled with specialization and science in industry) has made business so impersonal in nature that it is imperative that an understanding of this quality be gained by all who are entering business life. Strong is the man who, tutored to the notion that our co-operative life is personal, that service is rewarded in the observation of its own results, can come to realize the realities of the situation without rancor and resentment. One who has early sensed clearly the scale of modern production, the concealment of human effort in the "transfer of thought to the machine," and the ramifying nature of specialization, has a strong support. He has the basis for realizing that his contribution is certain, though unseen, and important, though unknown.

QUESTIONS FOR DISCUSSION

1. Can you think of machine industry, like specialization, as a method of production? Just how is machine industry more productive than industry without machines?
2. "Machines may be used instead of physical labor, but they can never take the place of mental labor except of the most routine kinds." Is this true? Have commercial courses ever trained students in such a way that they found themselves engaged in a competition with a machine?
3. What does the term "Industrial Revolution" bring to your mind? What is the point of saying that the Industrial Revolution is still going on? Can you see any point to the statement "the Industrial Revolution had its beginnings in the explorations of the fifteenth century"?

4. Machine industry, science applied to production, will become more extensive as goods are sold over wider markets. What factors are at work to make markets increasingly wide?
5. The suddenness with which the Industrial Revolution came makes it difficult for us to realize the significance and the pervasiveness of science in industry. Comment.
6. Think of the first five articles upon which your eye rests. Has chemistry played an important part in their construction? Has physics? Have any other of the natural sciences?
7. Is it not really nonsense to say that an accountant needs any knowledge of science and its applications to industry?
8. How do you explain the fact that the term "efficiency" in business is associated in the minds of many people with the engineer? What kind of training has the engineer had? What is your notion of the work done by an efficiency expert in a manufacturing plant? Is such an expert likely to be an accountant? With what fields of knowledge should he be familiar?
9. "I have known good bankers who not only did not know anything of technology, but did not know much of anything excepting the characters of the men with whom they dealt. It is all foolishness to talk of the need of such outside matters for a banker." Is honesty a sufficient guaranty of payment by a business borrower? Is a knowledge of the honesty of the borrower a sufficient quality in the man who lends other people's money?
10. The buyer for an investment bank is considering the purchase of a million-dollar issue of bonds of a manufacturing concern. These bonds are to run for forty years. If they are purchased, they will be sold to a large number of investors, large and small. As one of the investors, you are told that the bond house has investigated the good intentions of the company and believes that they are entirely satisfactory. Are you willing to invest your money on this investigation? List the other facts which you would like to have looked into. List the fields of knowledge in which the investigator would need training.
11. Make a rough diagram (heavy horizontal lines drawn approximately to scale are enough) showing the average number of employees in manufacturing plants in the United States in 1850 and in 1910. Do the same for the average capital invested; for the average product per plant. What does this indicate as to the scale of business operations?

12. What are the alleged advantages of large-scale operations?
13. Has large-scale production had any effect on overhead costs in business? Have overhead costs affected the work of the accountant?
14. Why has the increasing scale of business made necessary new methods of management? In what way has the application of science to industry increased the need for better management? In that way has specialization increased the need for more careful management?
15. How could an organization chart be of aid in the control of a business? Why was it that business organization charts were heard of little, if at all, fifty years ago?
16. Draw up a chart which indicates the lines of authority and responsibility for the educational institution with which you are most familiar.
17. Look through the statements on page 77 concerning some of the requirements of scientific control of a large business. What courses, if any, now given in the high-school commercial course would be of great value in such control of a business? What courses in collegiate schools of business? What types of courses would you suggest might be introduced to give some understanding of such control?
18. Set down a list of statements which seem to you to present (*a*) the suggestions which you find for business education in a realization of the large-scale character of business; (*b*) the types of study which a student would need to make to understand large-scale business and its management; (*c*) the effects on the individual worker of specialization, machine industry, and large-scale production; (*d*) the value to specialized workers of a knowledge of the nature of modern business.
19. As a result of our study of what business is, set down a tentative list of the objectives of business education.

CHAPTER VII

WHAT BUSINESS SAYS IT WANTS: DIRECT EXPRESSIONS

No evidence concerning what should be the make-up of the commercial curriculum appears to carry more weight than what business says it wants. But, as has been indicated in the introductory statement to Chaper III, it is easy to misinterpret and misjudge what business says it wants. What business wants from education is expressed to some degree directly in statements, books, and answers to questionnaires. The examination of such evidence will occupy us in the present chapter. In the following chapter we shall examine the indirect statements of business.

In attempting to state what business says it wants it appears altogether desirable to let business make the statement. In this chapter and the next, therefore, the "evidence" is given without more interpretation than is involved in the process of selection. As a result, the form used is a series of selections or readings rather than a continued statement.

The direct statements of what business wants are of a rather miscellaneous sort. There are first presented here some of the types of general statements which are very common, and which unfortunately often pass as being more valuable than they are. Statements 3 and 4 consist of evidence of rather thoughtful types, of more interest to those concerned with collegiate business education than for persons training younger pupils. Statement 5 is particularly pertinent to special types of students. The two final statements are expressions of labor leaders. It has seemed proper to include such views in a section on what business says it wants. For the most part, however, the readings are selected because they are expressions of general views of what formal education as a whole should do in training for business.

STATEMENT 1

An Argument against Education for Business[1]

I do not employ college men in my banking office, none need apply. I don't want them, for I think they have been spoiled for a business life. The college man is not willing to begin at the bottom. He looks down on the humble places, which he is fitted to fill. And, indeed, he looks down on all business as dull and unattractive. . . . . His thoughts are not with his business, but with his books, literature, philosophy, Latin. Now no man can approach the exacting business life in that half-hearted way. Business requires the undivided mind.

I think that a man has just so many niches in his brain. In each niche so many facts . . . . as it were, fit, and then the niche is full. Now, at college a man is busy filling up the niches, and if he goes through college in the right way, his niches are all full. No, ... the college man is not the successful man in money affairs. It is the man who has started in as an office boy and who gets the education of keenness and practical knowledge that comes from early contact with business men.

He has his natural sharpness and originality, and the edge of it is not dulled by ideas and theories of life entirely out of harmony with his occupation.

STATEMENT 2

The Few and Simple Demands of the Business World[2]

Every commercial student wants a position as soon as he finishes his course. He is in training for business. When his course is finished and he starts out to look for a position, what is it that is going to enable him to get one? Upon what qualities will business men judge him or her? Two very important qualities are personal appearance and personality.

The careful employer watches the applicant's movements. He gets the tone of voice. He notes the choice of words. He

[1] Adapted from *Great Britain Special Report on Educational Subjects*, Vol. II, Part 2, pp. 287–88. Board of Education, 1902.

[2] Adapted from the *Business Journal* (June, 1916), pp. 451–52.

notices the affected or unaffected manner and he observes the applicant's self-confidence. The qualities that good employers desire and appreciate are clean habits, willingness, untiring energy, loyalty, alertness, initiative, and originality, the ability to use good judgment, painstaking thoroughness and enthusiasm.

STATEMENT 3

The Questionnaire of the Illinois Manufacturers' Association on College Courses in Business Education[1]

The questionnaire which the Committee on Education of the Illinois Manufacturers' Association circulated among the members of the Association was designed to determine the attitude of the membership toward university courses in business administration and to secure suggestions concerning the nature of the courses to be offered.

Of the eighty-two firms making reply the addresses of but seventy-two can now be determined. Three answers were received from outside the state. Of the remaining sixty-nine houses, sixty are located in Chicago and three in Peoria, while replies were received from one firm in each of the following cities: Aurora, Clyde, Decatur, East St. Louis, Harvey, and Quincy.

The types of business engaged in by those making reply are diverse, including automobile, milling, electric, packing, soap, and tack companies. The sizes range from small to large, the latter having the larger proportionate representation.

Five questions were proposed in the questionnaire. The number of definite answers to the first and second questions is seventy, to the third, sixty, to the fourth, forty-three, to the fifth, forty-five.

The first question is as follows: What education do we want young men to have to whom we may look in time to improve the organization of our office staff, increase the efficiency, and reduce its cost? The replies to this question show the follow-

[1] Adapted by permission from The Committee on Education, Report of the Illinois University Conference (1913), pp. 92–98.

ing distribution of views as to the educational needs of the office force:

No educational requirement	1
Grammar or common school	15
Continuation school	1
High school, without mention of business courses	13
High school, with emphasis on business courses	7
High school, supplemented by business college	3
Business college	1
General university course, without mention of courses in business administration	5
Special university courses along business lines	24

A number of those favoring scanty education show a more or less rabid prejudice against higher education, while those favoring secondary education frequently refer to the desirability of still higher training. It will be seen that the number favoring special university training along the lines of business administration out-number any other single class and constitute 34 per cent of the number giving specific answers as compared with 24 per cent who favor nothing above the common schools, 28 per cent who emphasize general high-school training, scarcely 6 per cent requiring business-college training, and 7 per cent who insist on a broad, cultural college course.

The returns seem to indicate the comparative failure of the business college to equip men for the larger needs of business offices. They show, further, the employers' insistence on the ability to write legibly and to use good English. The evidence implies a strong expectation that the university business-administration courses will produce more expert office help.

Question number two is as follows: What kind of training should young men have whom we may expect to improve our accounting systems, perhaps introduce systems of cost accounting that will make it easier to apportion costs and profits, and to determine what parts of our organization pay and what do not? So far as could be determined the distribution of views as to the training needed for this work is as follows:

Business college	5
High school or business college	1
High school, without mention of specific courses	2
High school, with emphasis on manual and mechanical training	2
General university course	3
Engineering, without mention of business courses	2
Engineering, with mention of business courses	2
Special university training, without mention of business courses	15
Special university training, with mention of business courses	12
University or apprenticeship	1
Practical experience, without mention of any educational requirement	14
Practical experience, with apprenticeship or special investigations	3
Practical experience, with mention of education but no specification as to kind	2
Practical experience, with common-school education	3
Practical experience, with high-school course	3

There is considerable scattering of opinion due to the diversity of industries and the small extent to which cost accounting systems have as yet been applied to the problems of administration in most lines of business.

The feeling seems to prevail that much depends on common sense, thinking power and experience. Seven per cent of the houses demand business-college training, 7 per cent high-school training, and 49 per cent make some kind of university study a minimum requirement. Although 36 per cent emphasize practical experience, one-third of these expressly favor education of some kind, and no one of the others expresses opposition to education, although making no specific requirements.

Thus, in the case of expert accountants as in the case of men in other lines, the business college appears to be discounted in its ability to give adequate training. Doubtless the greater degree of expertness felt to be necessary in the case of accountants is the chief explanation for the emphasis laid upon technical university training. The fact that an accounting system must be adjusted to the needs of the individual concern as well as to the special type of business probably makes the call for practical experience more insistent.

The replies, then, show the majority to be strongly in favor of specialized university accounting course, while the emphasis upon experience surely demands the most perfect laboratory development and a large amount of "field work."

Question number three relates to advertising and was stated as follows: What kind of education will give us young men who can make our advertising more efficient? The returns from the sixty houses making specific replies give the following as the proper method of training for advertising work:

No educational requirement	1
High school and practical experience	2
Business college	1
Practical experience	12
General college training, supplemented by business experience	3
General college training, supplemented by special business training	5
General college training, without further specifications	14
Engineering, without mention of business courses	1
Special university courses bearing on advertising	21

The table of replies shows that 20 per cent insist on practical experience, while 37 per cent favor general cultural education, nearly a fourth adding, however, that it be supplemented by specialized business knowledge. Thirty-five per cent maintain that special university courses should be followed by the prospective advertising expert, one-third of these specify one or more lines of study which they think deserve special attention. Of the latter, three name salesmanship courses, two psychology, one expression, and one statistics.

In the replies considerable mention is made of advertising "genius," "publicity sense," and intuition. There is an evident feeling that there is a large element in the advertiser's business that cannot be supplied by mere scientific training However, in so far as educational training enables the advertiser to know more completely the needs of the purchasers, and to give better expression to his printed statements or appeals of other kinds, the consensus of opinion among those making reply favors education for prospective advertising specialists.

Question number four relates to salesmanship and is as follows: What training will give us better salesmen?

The amount of indefiniteness to the replies to this question is especially great. Of the sixty-six who ventured answers at all, twenty-three were not specific enough to be classified. That is, they did not give expression to any opinion as to the particular kind of preparation to which the prospective salesman should subject himself. Most of them left off with giving a nebulous statement relating to the genius, integrity, the religious or social qualities of the salesman. It appears in the case of salesmen even more prominently than in the case of advertising specialists that personal qualities appeal to many business houses as the prime requisite to successful salesmanship rather than a particular course of scientific training through which the candidate may have passed.

Of the forty-three replies subject to classification the following distribution of methods of preparation for salesmanship was made:

Practical experience	18
General cultural training	12
Special salesmanship courses	13

Nearly 42 per cent laid the emphasis on practical experience, 28 per cent on general cultural training, and 30 per cent on special training for which the university is fitted.

It appears that the business houses are not yet convinced of the efficacy of scientific salesmanship, and that the burden of proof rests with the universities. Some of those answering seem to be extremely skeptical of the value of a scientific study of salesmanship, and few, if any, consider it more than an adjunct whose promise of usefulness is moderate.

Question number five is stated as follows: Can we get young men who can aid our business by thorough knowledge and study of transportation routes and rates, the development of new markets and new uses for our products?

Among the forty-five definite replies received, the diversity of opinion is shown in the table on following page:

No, without further comment	10
No, with a slight concession	2
Yes, without further comment	25
Yes, specifying "in practical field"	6
Yes, specifying technical university study	2

Twenty-seven per cent of those making definite replies gave negative answers. Some of them may have misunderstood the question, thinking that it related to a present supply rather than a possible future supply of men having the knowledge indicated. At any rate, fully 73 per cent believe in the possibility of securing men whose studies in transportation and market conditions will enable them to render important commercial service. Six of those answering in the affirmative stated that the knowledge should be gained "in practical field" or "with some commercial house." While only two specified that they thought that this knowledge should be derived from technical university study, yet the statement in the questionnaire, that its object was "to enable the University of Illinois to shape and organize its course," justifies us in regarding an affirmative answer as favorable to university courses along the designated lines. Practically all who insist that the university cannot do this work successfully have doubtless seen the necessity of specifying that the training should be received "in the practical field." If this be granted, we may gather from the replies that approximately 60 per cent of the houses answering are in favor of special university study as a preparation for expert commercial work in transportation, the opening of new markets, and the discovery of new uses for products.

The percentage of those giving definite answers in favor of special university courses as shown by the returns on the five questions is as follows:

Question	Subject	Percentage Favoring University Training
1	Office assistants	34
2	Cost accountants	49
3	Advertising specialists	35
4	Salesmen	30
5	Experts on transportation, new markets, and products	60

It is difficult to determine beyond doubt to what degree the above figures represent the views of all the members of the Illinois Manufacturers' Association. The fact that fewer than one out of ten of those receiving the questionnaires took the trouble to mail their replies should not be overlooked. It may easily be true that a larger proportion of those holding views extremely favorable or extremely unfavorable sent their replies than those holding less decided views. This being the case the replies may be taken to be fairly representative of the opinions prevailing among the members of the Association generally, although no more than a fair degree of representativeness should be claimed for them.

Taking the returns as they stand, the demand for university-trained office assistants is voiced by one-third of the houses answering the questionnaire. Special university training for accountants is requested by practically one-half the concerns. Although personality and talent figure greatly in the success of advertising experts and salesmen, about one-third of those making reply favor university courses to qualify men more completely for this work. The conduct of transportation, the opening of new markets, and the better disposal of products, 60 per cent of the answering houses are in favor of placing in the hands of men trained in special university courses.

STATEMENT 4

What the Exporter Needs That the Educator Can Supply[1]

In order to reach the highest degree of business efficiency there must be a groundwork of theory supplemented by experience and practice. We recognize this truth by insisting that one of the schemes of our national life shall be compulsory school education. As to the point to which school education should be carried in order to fit one properly to take up the duties of commercial life, there is some controversy, but there is no

[1] Adapted by permission from a pamphlet by E. H. Huxley, president of the United States Rubber Export Company.

question as to the necessity of at least some theoretical education and probably no serious dispute that this should be carried at least through the grades of the ordinary high school. . . . . The highest degree of efficiency cannot be obtained wholly by practical experience nor wholly by theoretical education. If entire reliance is placed on practical experience the result will be the same as with a man who commits to memory certain problems so that he can solve them, but does not understand the underlying theories which enable him to solve other problems similar in principle but different as to detail. From practical experience a man may be able to conduct certain branches of an export business, such for example as the accounting or traffic, and become reasonably proficient up to the point where some new phase presents itself or some new condition arises hitherto not present; at that point the man with a clear understanding of the underlying theories will be able to apply them practically to the changed conditions, while he who has only carried out and been concerned in the ordinary routine will probably be at sea and wholly unable to cope with the situation. We start therefore with the admission that the combination of a theoretical education in the principles and underlying bases of certain subjects, with a later practical experience in their application, is essential to produce the best results.

The question then is, Exactly what is wanted from the educator? Evidently we do not want an attempt to produce a finished product, because we have admitted that practical experience is a necessary supplement; therefore, what we do want is the theory. The subjects which might be covered are many, but of relative importance, and the necessary subjects would be determined by the completeness desired and the point to which it is desired to carry the education. There are some subjects which are essential and others which are desirable to a greater or less degree, but not essential. A table might be prepared indicating the subjects to be considered, somewhat as follows:

1. Ocean Transportation and Rates, including the various documents, invoices and papers
2. Insurance, war and marine

3. Foreign Exchange and international banking
4. Foreign Credits
5. Tariff Laws and Regulations
6. Packing, Shipping and Marking with especial reference to the needs of individual countries
7. Foreign Correspondence
8. Commercial Geography
9. Languages
10. Advertising
11. Commercial and Political History
12. Social and Political Economy
13. Racial Characteristics and Conditions
14. Statistics and Reports
15. Political Science and Psychology

This list is not intended to be considered as necessarily complete but at least covers the main essentials and some of, what might be termed, the luxuries of education. Some of the subjects present singly in themselves the possibilities of a life study and it is of course presupposed that their study is not to be carried beyond reason. The general subject of insurance, for example, may in itself become a profession and it is obviously not intended that a requisite for the proper handling of insurance matters in an export business should undertake a professional knowledge such as might be acquired by an expert in devoting his life to that particular subject. The insurance department of the average exporter need not necessarily be handled by a professional expert, neither would the general accounting department require the services of one whose knowledge extended to the point required or desirable in an international banker. In order, however, to take advantage of every possibility to make money and in order to conduct the various departments with the greatest economy and the highest efficiency, a theoretical knowledge of the underlying principles of these various subjects seems to me to be essential; this knowledge to be supplemented by practical experience.

The first eight subjects appear to be the most important and to be really essential; the others to be undertaken only by him who desires to become unusually proficient, more so perhaps than might be considered absolutely necessary. The courses should, I think, consist mainly of lectures; laboratory work or practical examples might be included to a very small extent but practical application should come in the practical experience in business. It is not intended to fix any particular limit to the extent to which the subjects should be studied, other than possibly the fixing of a reasonable amount of time which it should be necessary to expend on the part of the student. . . . . It is a common practice to enlist the services of business men as instructors; this is all right, provided those men have grounded themselves thoroughly in the theory of the subject, but the object would be defeated if the lectures by such men should be only a history of their own practical experience, and personally I should favor the choice of educators who have made the theory of the various subjects a study, rather than business men who had been concerned only, or largely, in their own occupation.

STATEMENT 5

A Statement of Department Store Needs[1]

Phase 1—*Appearance*

Cleanliness of hands, hair, face, nails, shoes, dress, etc.
Manners—courtesy.
Approach—Now and later, self-reliance, decision.
Speech—"I ain't done it"—"it don't."

Phase 2—*Application*

Writing } Accuracy
Spelling }
Truthfulness, age, salary, experience.
Complete in detail—give test blanks of questions often.
Cigarettes—slang, gum.

[1] By Charles P. Avery, of Marshall Field & Co. Notes sent the author as the "skeleton of an address" given on December 27, 1917, before the National Commercial Teachers Federation.

Phase 3—*Employee*

Loyalty

Personality—develop pleasing smile that wins friends.

Fractions—percentage, mechanical speed, fundamental only.

Dependable—listens—"Message to Garcia." No hesitation nor miscarrying. Discipline.

Patience—realization business is a continuation of school.

STATEMENT 6

WHAT INDUSTRY WANTS FROM THE SCHOOLS[1]

The question was asked three times this morning and this afternoon as to what industry wanted from the schools, and I am going to try to answer that question. I think you will anticipate what my answers are to be from what I have already said. Our industries—our company, at any rate—wants from the public schools, from the colleges, and from the high schools just one thing, and that is native or trained ability to solve new problems right the first time they are presented. Ability to think. If I might split that up a little bit, we will call it originality, initiative and judgment. When I say that, I am presuming that you all know full well that we want good character. I do not believe we need to discuss that point. By character, we mean it in its very broadest sense, a fellow who is courteous, who is considerate, who is tolerant, who will work five minutes overtime in order to save an hour the next day, or will work for the love of his work, and does not quit exactly when the whistle blows. I have called that co-operation. I do not think there is anything more important than that, and I am sure that we all recognize it so clearly it is hardly worth while to discuss it.

Then we want just a very little bit of fundamental information. We would not put a boy who had been taught machine

[1] Adapted by permission from C. R. Dooley in *Fifth Annual Proceedings of the National Association of Corporation Schools* (1917), pp. 192–93. The National Association of Corporation Schools was succeeded by the National Association of Corporation Training which has since been succeeded by the National Personnel Association. Reference to the literature will be according to the name of the association at the time of publication.

tool operation and nothing else into a portrait painter's shop; he would not know the difference between a screwdriver and a paint palette, so he does need a little bit of fundamental information, but that is on the end of the list, and so I will repeat that we want initiative, originality and judgment along with the highest type of character in its fullest sense. I would even go so far as to say if he has these three things, which may be grouped under one heading, namely, the capacity to go ahead and solve new problems, I do not care very much whether he has a large amount of specific information. If a girl comes into the office as a stenographer, it is of little importance to us whether she can write sixty words a minute on the typewriter, and take down her notes at one hundred words per minute and transcribe everything you dictate, and transcribe it exactly as you dictate it. It is far more important if she has a capacity for quick comprehension about our business, gathering the essential elements of our business, and whether she has good judgment of the construction of a letter, so that by and by, as she gets worked into the organization and some man dictates a letter hurriedly, she can at the right time suggest that the letter is not clear and should be rephrased in certain particulars. The other day I turned a letter over to a new girl in our office, who had not been there very long, and asked her what she thought of the letter, a letter some other firm had turned out, and she said that the letter looked neat, and was a very nice letter. I said: "I don't care how it looks, is it clear, do you understand it, is it a good forcible letter?" That is the idea which is typical of the capacity which we want in all kinds of people.

STATEMENT 7

What Public Educational Institutions Should Not Attempt[1]

Personally, I believe that the matter of vocational education is in danger of being carried too far, and that we may lose sight of the broad general purpose and aims of education.

[1] Adapted by permission from L. E. Barringer, General Electric Co., in *Sixth Annual Proceedings of the National Association of Corporation Schools* (1918), pp. 261–62.

Applying vocational education to young men and women to render them efficient and competent workmen does not necessarily educate them for all the needs of life, nor will the best vocational training make the most efficient and competent workmen.

Vocational education may become too subdivided, special and narrow. In this city I have personally opposed the extension of the manual training course to the fifth and sixth grades as a step too far.

It is not enough that a young man should be taught to manipulate his hands skilfully in order to become a good mechanic or carpenter, nor is this necessarily sufficient for the employer of such a man. He should be alert and possess a full realization of the meaning of his work and of the broader opportunities for himself in the entire field of which his job is a part.

We need more inspirational teaching, more education of the young for the broad essential needs of life. They should be impressed with the value of health, vigor, co-operation, energy, and with the need of continued acquisition of knowledge and skill after school days have been finished. For herein lie the foundations of "efficient, capable workmen," just as much, if not more so, than in the highly specialized knowledge imparted in the training for the mechanical arts.

STATEMENT 8

What Business Wants from the Schools[1]

The work of the committee on public education has been based more on agreed facts than on newly gathered data. We have found sufficient agreement as to lack of effective work on the part of the public schools and enough misunderstanding on the part of employers so that we have deemed it wise to begin work on the following basis:

a) The public schools are burdened with subjects for instruction which have accumulated from year to year and which, no

[1] Adapted by permission from "Report of Committee on Public Education," *Fourth Annual Proceedings of the National Association of Corporation Schools* (1916), pp. 233–34, and the *Ninth Annual Proceedings* (1921), pp. 134–36.

matter how desirable singly, have demanded so much time and attention that they have diminished the time and drill formerly given to more fundamental subjects.

b) The demands of the world on educational systems have steadily grown. A higher type of intelligence is needed each successive year in all vocations, and yet industrial growth has made necessary the employment of men farther and farther down the social scale.

c) The demands of industry and commerce for trained employees have never been logically classified.

d) The duty of the public school is to train young people in whatever subjects are of general importance to large groups of people.

e) The duty of the so-called corporation school is to train specific workers for the diversified tasks which they must meet.

f) Temporarily it appears necessary in many instances for the corporation schools to parallel the work of the public schools and to repeat work which has not been done effectively by them.

A discussion of the subject has brought out the following classifications of the activities of the public schools:

a) Those subjects which will probably be useful to help the graduate earn a living.

b) Those which teach the appreciation of things which are not necessities.

c) Recreation, preferably spelled "re-creation."

Many subjects overlap two or all of these classifications, as, for example, music, which may be taught as a probable future means of livelihood through execution, as a means of appreciation of the masters, or as a purely re-creative respite from the daily round of work.

The first step in considering possible changes in public education is to determine the relative value of the various subjects of public school instruction with the pupils' future as a citizen, a member of society, and a producer in mind.

His value as a member of society depends, of course, in a large measure on his ability to produce enough to make him independent of his fellow-men, to house and clothe him in comfort, and to feed him well enough so that he can take real satisfaction in the appreciation of the artistic things with which our modern life surrounds him.

The pressure of the forward march of inventive science has made necessary for producers a training which could not have been predicted a few years ago. It is entirely possible that much of the discontent which has been expressed both by laymen and professional instructors with regard to the present state of public schools is due to the fact that the strides which business has made have not been matched by those of the schools which, in many instances, have not found themselves with money enough to take care of the increased number of pupils, to say nothing of making progress in the science of education.

As a basis for discussion before the Association, the following rough classification of the studies which are most commonly included in the grammar school curriculum has been prepared. No amount of preparation of data or other statistical study can possibly accomplish so much in determining the value of this division as an open discussion, so this matter is presented with the distinct desire to provoke discussion and not as a finding of this committee.

a) The following are of value to the very great majority of all pupils for their practical use in everyday and business life:

Reading
Mathematics (especially arithmetic)
Penmanship
English, spoken and written

This list is practically the three R's, if writing is held to include correct writing of the language as well as penmanship. It is a very brief list, but it is presented as covering the subjects which employers of our boys and girls agree on as necessities.

b) The following subjects are of large value because they tend to enlarge the appreciative powers of the pupils and because they have a re-creative effect:

History
Music
Freehand Drawing

Physiology
Nature Study
Science (bearing in mind this is for grammar schools only)
Chemistry (bearing in mind this is for grammar schools only)

c) Certain other subjects including:

Civics
Geography
Physical Culture
Mechanical Drawing
Manual Training

appear to offer possibilities in the way of training that combines something of the function of both of the above.

The teaching of a certain portion of civics which is usually given rather little consideration, that of the future relation of the pupil himself to society, is or should be of intense value to the nation and especially to its industries and commerce. Instead of that, our children are taught much about the higher functions of government, and the machinery of courts and legislatures with which most of them have little later opportunity to come in contact.

Geography, especially that of the immediate locality, city and county, has a great value. It is desirable that he should be initiated into the use of maps, so that he can trace means of travel and freight routes from one point to another.

Physical culture, in the sense of bringing up a rugged lot of children in place of spindly, flat-chested youths, lacking in endurance, is something much to be desired. It is hardly a part of the classroom instruction, however, but rather a part of the recreation, which now too often consists in hanging over a schoolyard fence, surreptitiously smoking cigarettes. Its value is incalculable, but it is best taught by recreation, as witness the work of the Boy Scouts and other outdoor organizations.

The above statements appear to be borne out by the results of a questionnaire, which was sent to the members of the Association, a copy of which is annexed to this report. This brought out between 5,000 and 6,000 individual replies to specific questions, so that it may be presumed to represent as a whole the well-thought-out opinion of large employers of labor.

It appears that we are unanimous in thinking that the following subjects are of prime necessity:

Addition. Whole numbers
Subtraction. Common fractions
Multiplication of decimal fractions
Division
Percentage
Simple interest
Reading
Penmanship
English composition
Business English
Spelling usual words

These in themselves form a pretty well-rounded education, but to this 60 per cent of our answers would add for certain parts of their organization:

Proportion
Compound interest
Spelling of technical words
Geography (Physical and Commercial)
U.S. History (Political)
Physiology
Civics (intimate relations of people with their government)

The following subjects are apparently considered of little or no value by 70 per cent of the members who answered these questions:

Cube root
Music (vocal and reading)
Science
Chemistry
Principles of Government
Foreign languages

When the above statements are discussed, we expect to hear decided exceptions taken to the apparent relegation of subjects like history, music, and freehand drawing to the position of re-creative or appreciative subjects. On the other hand, it seems as if the present taste of the American people for ragtime music might be a protest against the school methods of teaching music and the abominable taste that is shown in what might equally well be artistic millinery, a protest against the method of teaching drawing. In other words, has the teaching of these subjects for many years past had an uplifting effect on the American people? History, too, if studied merely as a chronicle of the dead past, possibly has not had the effect for which we have been seeking. Should not history be studied in search for the inspiration and encouragement which it may give us, rather than for the memorizing of facts, many of them most lamentable?

The classification which we have offered of the different forms of drawing may also arouse discussion, as may also our entire omission of manual training from among the subjects of earning value. It may, however, be argued that every form of drawing and every principle taught in manual training is an underlying principle of some trade or profession, which is of vital commercial importance to those who make their living by its practice, and as such they become subjects of special training which may very well be the work of a corporation school.

If, however, these matters are made a part of the curriculum of the public schools, the time which can be allotted to them is so small and the number of pupils who can see a future value in them is so limited, that little of value can be expected, except as they may create ability to appreciate the work of others, or may be a means of re-creation.

The boy who makes a piece of furniture by old and laborious methods which would not be tolerated in modern manufacture, has not taken any appreciable steps toward becoming an expert workman, but he may have discovered that the expert workman is a man possessed of skill which he should and can appreciate. He has also, in the course of his work, had a combination of mental and manual exercise, which is valuable from the re-creative standpoint, if no other.

STATEMENT 9

Some Evidence from New York and Pittsburgh[1]

The evidence of the business world is against the assumption that clerical training is the main objective of commercial education. Business men in particular do not assert that this conception is sound. Through the courtesy of the New York Chamber of Commerce some evidence bearing upon this point was secured during February and March of the current year (1912). A circular letter was sent to about a hundred of the largest commercial houses of New York City.

A few quotations from typical replies from New York business men may be given here: "We employ no male stenographers. Occasionally we can use a business school graduate in our bookkeeping department. The study of business principles ought to be of value." "For the majority of positions in our employ we should prefer that he had a knowledge of the other subjects named by you." "A knowledge of stenography and typewriting would be necessary in filling certain positions where a male stenographer was desired. In our particular business a knowledge of bookkeeping as it is generally taught in high schools might in some cases be helpful, but hardly ever absolutely necessary. A study of the fundamental principles of business, such as merchandising, advertising, salesmanship, and business organization would in general seem to be more valuable to young men than specialization upon clerical subjects."

This same study was made in Pittsburgh with somewhat similar results respecting the relative importance of fundamental and clerical subjects. Of those replying, 32 per cent think that bookkeeping alone is essential; 28 per cent state that all three are necessary; 19 per cent think that none of the three subjects is essential; 15 per cent think that penmanship is essential; 11 per cent think that mathematics is necessary; 11 per cent consider a knowledge of good English indispensable; 8 per cent

[1] Adapted by permission from F. V. Thompson, *Commercial Education in Public Secondary Schools*, pp. 106–8. World Book Co. 1915.

think that arithmetic is valuable; 4 per cent state that typewriting and bookkeeping are necessary; 3 per cent think that designing and advertising are valuable.

STATEMENT 10

What Is Commercial Education?[1]

Not long ago, in an educational paper of some standing, I noticed that the business college was merely a clerk factory to turn out business assistants, but that the aim of the high school was to turn out business men. I suppose the writer should have said, to carry out his thought, successful business men. This statement, with some variation, has been repeated frequently and has been made a great deal of. But to me it is an expression without definite meaning. What is a business man? Is he a wholesale or retail merchant? A banker? An exporter? A railroad manager? A manufacturer? A clerk? A bookkeeper? A commercial traveller? It seems to me that anyone who is engaged in any occupation arising from the exchange of commodities is essentially a business man, and if he succeeds he is a successful business man. The successful business man owes his success sometimes to his education, but more often to his tact and special knowledge of the business in which he is engaged. All that the commercial high school can do for its pupils is to teach them to use the tools of business, in order that the natural gifts in a business way which they all possess in some measure may be developed and their value increased. A competent business man, as such, cannot be made in a school. Many men who have the best instruction possible do not succeed in business because so many things besides education are necessary to insure success. Business ability is inherited. Some families—nay, some races—seem to be endowed with the commercial instinct.

What is a commercial education? I well know a successful bank president and financier who cannot keep a simple set of books; a prominent business man of my acquaintance received

[1] Adapted from *Great Britain Special Reports on Education*, Vol. II, Part 2, pp. 327–28. Board of Education, 1902.

all the business training he ever had as a journalist; another, in the classical course of a university; another received a liberal high-school course; another, an elementary-school education; and another—a most successful business man—had no school education at all. There were successful business men in former generations; there are splendid business men today who never had the special training the commercial high-school course proposes to give, though some of them have had the advantages of a business-college course. It seems to me, therefore, that any education which a business man has, and which makes him a better business man, is for him a business education, no matter whether it was obtained in the walls of a school or not.

Now, it seems to me there is nothing mysterious in this question, and there has been no great discovery lately as to what constitutes a business education. We are merely beginning to realize its value and necessity today, and the great danger of failure in our commercial courses lies in our desire to do so much for our pupils that we over-estimate the value of some parts of the courses we would offer, and by endeavoring to accomplish too much fail to provide a sensible, practical and workable curriculum. Our laudable desire to have a great school should not obscure the need of having a good school.

STATEMENT 11

The Demands of Modern Business[1]

The mental equipment of a business man needs to be greater to-day than was ever before necessary. Just as the sphere of a business man's actions has broadened with the advent of rapid transportation, telegraphs, cables, and telephones, so has the need for broad understanding of sound principles increased. It was steam processes of transportation and production that really made technical education necessary. The electric dynamo created the demand for technically educated electrical engineers. So the railroad, the fast steamship, the electric

[1] Adapted by permission from F. A. Vanderlip, *Business and Education*, pp. 15–19. Duffield Co., 1907.

current in the telephone and cable, and the great economic fact of gigantic and far-reaching business combinations, are making the science of business a different thing for any conception of commerce which could have been had when Girard was the most successful of American business men. The enlarged scope of business is demanding better trained men—men who understand principles. New forces have made possible large scale production, and we need men who can comprehend the relation of that production to the world's markets. There has been introduced such complexity into modern business, and such a high degree of specialization, that the young man who begins without the foundation of an exceptional training is in danger of remaining a mere clerk or bookkeeper. Commercial and industrial affairs are conducted on so large a scale that the neophyte has little chance to learn broadly either by observation or experience. He is put at a single task. The more expert he becomes at it, the more likely it is that he will be kept at it unless he has had a training in his youth which has fitted him to comprehend in some measure the relation of his task to those which others are doing.

Conditions have vastly changed. A new order of equipment is demanded. The staunchness of character, the same intrepid will, today will play their part as they played it then, but in addition there is now demanded a breadth of technical knowledge, a fund of specialized information, a comprehension of intricate relations, and an understanding of broad principles which the conditions of a century or even a generation ago did not make imperative.

STATEMENT 12

A Plea for a Larger Vision of Commercial Education[1]

In the last analysis commerce and industry are vast social forces originating and being maintained and made possible in and by collective human activity gathered together in communi-

[1] Adapted by permission from Dr. Paul Kreuzpointner, Pennsylvania Railroad Company, in the *Sixth Annual Proceedings of the National Association of Corporation Schools* (1918), pp. 293–95.

ties and united into the nation. The reaction of these vast collective enterprises upon communities changes the habits, customs, and usages of the people. It raises or lowers the moral, political, intellectual, educational, aesthetic and physical standard of populations according to the greater or less skill and knowledge required to carry on these enterprises or the intellectual standard favored and maintained among the millions of industrial workers in shop, factory, store and office. . . . .

High-grade as the New York commercial course of study is, it nowhere articulates or co-ordinates business interests and their human agents with the silent, slow-working but all-powerful social, economical, cultural and ethical forces outside of the store, and which forces are the basis of the prosperity or adversity of all business transactions in the struggle for existence. Thus, by the irony of fate and a short-sighted conception of the relation of commercial and industrial enterprises to society, community and national welfare, these enterprises contribute to keep our schools upon a lower standard than they would be if business and industry were not satisfied with a purely utilitarian educational product. Thus, we have the anomalous condition that individually and as citizens the managers of business enterprises clamor for educational progress but in their official capacity they retard and hinder that progress by rejecting anything in the line of educational product as useless and impractical that does not contribute in the shortest way to utilitarian ends. In this attempt to separate the educational business interests from the educational, social and civic interests we may find the source of much of the prevailing misunderstanding, suspicion, lack of confidence, and retardation, between school and industrial and commercial enterprises.

Moreover, the traditional American high school was destined and organized as a preparatory school for college and is still considered in that light. Hence, commercial education, vocational education, and domestic science are simply annexes and are treated as such and therefore not accorded the time, the teachers, the laboratories and financial support needed to give them the constructive value which they ought to have.

Are there no culturizing, civilizing elements in our vast commercial and industrial enterprises worth cultivating in addition to methods for training clerks and mechanics and semi-skilled workers?

Society, which is represented by national organization and institutions, cannot maintain its orderly government and standard of civilization for any length of time with only vocationally trained workers, clerks, salesmen and women, etc., without any, or at best only a narrow conception of the workings of the larger, broader social and civic forces with rights, attendant duties and responsibilities. And contrariwise an ever so highly cultured and socially trained society cannot exist without a thorough vocational and commercial training for occupational efficiency.

The late Dr. W. T. Harris, United States Commissioner of Education, once defined civilization as follows: "A people is civilized when it has formed institutions for itself, which enable each individual to profit by the industry of all his fellow-citizens; when it enables each individual to profit by the experience and wisdom, the observations and the thoughts of his fellow-citizens; when it encourages each individual into a rational self-activity by which he contributes, either through his industry or through his observations and thoughts, to the benefit of the people with whom he lives." Is an education, vocational or commercial, which serves utilitarian ends exclusively, able to maintain such a standard of civilization?

STATEMENT 13

The Attitude of the American Federation of Labor toward Industrial Education[1]

Do I know what industrial education is, and what are its purposes and ideals? But since my personal knowledge is of very little consequence to anyone, except as a sort of reflex of the knowledge of the millions of workers, the question is, in fact, *Does organized labor understand what industrial education*

[1] Adapted by permission from Samuel Gompers, president of the American Federation of Labor, in *Bulletin of the National Society for Promotion of Industrial Education*, 1914, No. 20, pp. 107–13.

is, and what are its purposes and ideals? Finally, if it does understand these purposes and ideals, *Does it approve of them* and will it co-operate sincerely in the development of tried and proven rational schemes of industrial education?

You should know that *organized labor does not oppose the development of industrial education in the public schools.* Indeed that would not at all fairly indicate the attitude of organized labor. I say to you that the organization constituting the American Federation of Labor have been for years engaged in the work of systematically providing industrial education to their members. This instruction has been given through the medium of the trade union journals and schools established and maintained by them. Organized labor, I repeat, is not opposed to industrial education. It is eager to co-operate actively in instituting industrial education in our public schools. The working man has too little time, and can therefore take but little interest in any other sort of education.

Organized labor cannot favor any scheme of industrial education which is lop-sided—any scheme, that is to say, which will bring trained men into any given trade without regard to the demands for labor in that trade. *Industrial education must maintain a fair and proper apportionment of the supply of labor power to the demand for labor power* in every line of work. Otherwise its advantages will be entirely neutralized. If, for example, the result of industrial education is to produce in any community a greater number of trained machinists than are needed in the community, those machinists which have been trained cannot derive any benefit from their training, since they will not be able to find employment except at economic disadvantages. Under these conditions industrial education is of no advantage to those who have received it, and it is a distinct injury to the journeymen working at the trade who are subjected to a keen competition artificially produced. Industrial education must meet the needs of the worker as well as the requirements of the employer.

Organized labor has always opposed and will continue to oppose sham industrial education, whether at public or private expense. It has opposed and will continue to oppose that superficial training which confers no substantial benefit upon the worker, which does not make him a craftsman, but only an interloper, which may be available in times of crisis, perhaps, as a strike breaker, but not as a trained artisan for industrial service at other times. Industrial education must train men for work, not for private and sinister corporation purposes.

STATEMENT 14

What Labor Wants from Education[1]

Hitherto the working class has never been seriously consulted as to what it wants from education or what it believes ought to be the true aims of education. Governments, contending parties, education institutions, and influential sections of the community having definite views as to the place of the working class in their scheme of life have conceded to it a minimum of what they conceived to be for its good.

As a natural result, the education provided for working people has been very limited in quantity, while the system has been so permeated by an atmosphere of commercialism as seriously to vitiate the quality.

The same spirit can be discerned in many of the utterances of those who are now demanding educational reform. Their dominating idea is still that of increasing our industrial efficiency. The working class is still to fit in with preconceived notions as to its proper place in a generally accepted scheme of things, and educational reform is only to concern itself with equipping the workers to become more efficient bees in the industrial hive. This is a positive danger which the W.E.A. must be prepared to encounter.

For thirteen years our Association has been steadily preparing the ground for the time when working people themselves should say, and with no uncertain voice, what they want from education and what they conceive ought to be its true aim and

[1] Adapted by permission from J. M. Mactavish, *What Labor Wants from Education*, pp. 1–8. The Workers Educational Association, 14, Red Lion Square, Holborn, W.C., 1916.

purpose. Only by having clear ideas on these matters can we hope to counter the aims of the commercialists.

Within the limits of inherent capacity, education can give us what we want. Viewed broadly, all that man is, apart from heredity, is due to education. *It is therefore necessary that labour should have an educational ideal.* That ideal must take into consideration the needs of the individual, the needs of the class, the needs of the nation, and the needs of the race. In a perfect society it would be possible for education to harmonise fully all these conflicting needs. But in the world as it is to-day, it is necessary, in order to arrive at an ideal, that is a reasonable induction from established facts, to consider the special needs of each. A Tutorial Class syllabus would be an absurdity in Crusoe's curriculum when teaching his man Friday. The free development of the individual is as inconsistent with the Eastern ideal of fitting a man to occupy his predestined place in a caste bound society as a purely vocational education is in a democratic state.

Let us now examine these needs more closely.

The need of the individual.—The need of the individual is the development of those inherent qualities with which heredity endowed him and which, when fully developed, make personality.

The needs of the class.—The working class has its own peculiar educational needs. The material prizes of life are limited, and only a few can win them. After all the prizes have been won there still remains the great mass for whom under existing conditions there are not material prizes other than work and wages. These form the working class, and as such have educational needs peculiarly their own.

Since, under the existing state of society, the vast majority are wage-earners, education must give them a knowledge and a clearer understanding of the social and economic forces that mould and mar their lives. Only through a fuller knowledge and a clearer understanding of these can the workers attain to economic and social freedom. Further, since the experiences of the past ages are embodied in history, science, art and literature, education must equip the working class to share in its racial heritage.

The needs of the nation.—Our educational ideal must fit in with our national ideal. Our national ideal is that of a democratic self-governing community which aims at giving the fullest possible scope to the expression of individuality. But the world is divided into nations whose interests are to some extent conflicting, and most of whom are not living under democratic institutions. Hence our Educational Ideal must provide for a people who are efficient in national competition, strong in national defense, yet free in thought, speech, action, and government, having initiative, intelligence, self-reliance, self-discipline, respecting others as they respect themselves.

The need of the race.—Just as the great need in the national development of the individual is freedom to become one's self, so the great need in the development of the human race is the freedom of each people to work out its own destiny without undue interference from others. For this reason, our educational ideal must include the making of good-will.

Having summarised the educational needs of the working class, we can, with more or less accuracy, state our educational ideal.

Labour wants from Education health and full development for the body, knowledge and truth for the mind, fineness for the feelings, good-will towards its kind, and, coupled with this liberal education, such a training as will make its members efficient, self-supporting citizens of a free self-governing community. Such an education, and only such an education, will meet the needs of the individual, the class, the nation and the race.

When should vocational training begin?—It is here we must consider at what age a vocational education can begin without injury to the free full development of the individual. There is a general agreement amongst educationalists that specialisation under the age of sixteen checks all-round growth and tends to stereotype the mind. From this there follow two conclusions: (1) Since the all-round development of the child ought not to suffer check under sixteen, children ought not to leave school under that age. (2) Any technical education given under that age should avoid anything in the nature of mechanical specialisation, and for that reason should only be given by a fully qualified teacher.

If it were possible, it might be desirable that vocational instruction should be confined to the workshop. By this means the danger of confusing it with education would be avoided. But this is no longer possible. Changed industrial conditions will impose on the community the task of providing, in its own interest, facilities for vocational and professional training for all. Both individual and national interests demand that every member of the community, irrespective of class or sex, should be efficient workers. If this is done, no doubt new problems will arise. The community must devise ways and means of utilising the skill it has trained. To train skill without using it is waste. Fresh safeguards must be devised for the maintenance and improvement of Labour's Standard of Life. These are matters of vital importance. But, difficult as they may be to attain, they ought not to be used as a denial of the individual's right and duty to become an efficient self-supporting member of the community, or the community's right and duty to get the best out of its citizens.

But the instruction that fits men and women to play their part in industry ought to be secondary to the liberal education that gives health and vigour to the body, knowledge and wisdom to the mind, enabling men and women "to see life steadily and to see it whole." Is this what Labour wants, or will it still remain content with an education that does little more for hundreds of thousands of children than fit them to earn wages? Let Labour give its answer clear and emphatic. But let it remember that the future of its children will be helped or hindered by its decision.

QUESTIONS FOR DISCUSSION

1. Have you ever heard an argument comparable to that expressed in Statement 1?
2. Note the qualities desired for business as expressed in Statement 2. These few and simple demands ought easily to be met, ought they not? How should the proper training be given?
3. The Illinois Manufacturers' Association reached what conclusion concerning the type of men desired to improve their office organization? Why should so large a number believe that university business training was necessary for the organization of office work?
4. In indicating the training which should count in "improving" accounting systems, introducing cost accounting, fifteen employers of the Illinois Manufacturers' Association indicated that special university training without mention of business courses was desirable; twelve, the same training with mention of business; fourteen, practical experience without mention of any educational requirement. How would you account for the fact that these three qualifications were considered as of about equal importance? This questionnaire was answered in 1913. Would it be your guess that a questionnaire taken today would show the same proportion of approval for these types of training?
5. How do you account for the fact that in no case was the high school commercial course mentioned as the proper training for men who could improve accounting systems? How do you account for the fact that in no case was the high-school commercial course mentioned as the proper training for young men to make advertising more effective? How do you account for the fact that special university courses on advertising were favorably viewed by so large a percentage of the Illinois manufacturers and that general college training and practical experience rank second and third, respectively?
6. The compilers of the Illinois Manufacturers' Association questionnaire state that "the amount of indefiniteness to the replies of this question [the question asked what training will give better salesmen] is especially great." How do you account for the fact that there was more indefiniteness in replying to this question than to the others?
7. Taking the "exporters' needs" as outlined in Statement 4 as satisfactory objectives, how would you organize a four-year

curriculum for a high-school commercial course to give the training which is asked for? how a collegiate course?

8. Reorganize the statement of qualifications desired by the department store as indicated in Statement 5. For how many of these qualifications should a secondary-school commercial course be responsible? How many of them are taught in the educational institution with which you are most familiar? How many of them appear to you to be any more applicable to department-store work than they would be in practicing medicine? school teaching? working as paying teller?
9. "I will repeat that we want initiative and originality. I would go so far as to say that if he [the boy] has the capacity to go ahead and solve new problems I do not care whether he has any specific information or not." Can initiative and originality and character be taught? If so, by what courses? Can the capacity to solve new business problems be taught? Are they taught by the bookkeeping courses, the typewriting courses? What is a business problem?
10. "If a girl comes into our office . . . . it is of little importance to us whether she can write sixty words a minute on the typewriter . . . . it is far more important if she has a quick capacity for comprehension about our business." What training can be given which will give pupils a capacity for quick comprehension?
11. "Nor will the best vocational training make the most efficient and competent workman. He should possess a sure realization of the meaning of his work." What does this statement mean? Do you think there is any truth in it? What is the meaning of the work of a bookkeeper?
12. Be prepared to summarize the general conclusions reached by the National Association of Corporation Schools as they are presented in Statement 8.
13. What conclusions regarding the high-school commercial course would you draw from the evidence gathered by Superintendent Thompson in Pittsburgh and New York?
14. The writer of Statement 10 asks, What is a business man? Does he answer the question? Can you answer it?
15. What is Vanderlip's view of the demands of modern business? What observations do you think have led him to this view?
16. "In this attempt to separate the educational business interests from the educational social and civic interests, we may find the

source of much of the prevailing misunderstanding and suspicion between school and industrial and commercial enterprise." Can you give meaning to this statement?

17. What is Mr. Gompers' view of the proper objective for vocational education as viewed by labor?
18. If the needs of the individual, the needs of the class, the needs of the nation, and the needs of the race are the proper aims for education, what are each of these needs?
19. Formulate in a series of statements the suggestions for business education that you secure from Chapter VII.

CHAPTER VIII

WHAT BUSINESS SAYS IT WANTS: INDIRECT EXPRESSIONS

In this chapter we shall be studying some of the indirect statements of business. These indirect expressions are those which are found upon analyzing employments. It is quite likely that the indirect expressions of business are more accurate than the direct expressions. This is one of the cases in which action speaks more dependably than words. When the business man is called upon to analyze the educational needs of workers and to express these for public consumption, he, like any of us, when we find ourselves thinking in an unaccustomed field, is likely to be influenced by what he thinks will appear well. When occupations or jobs are analyzed, we get a definite picture of the work at which the business man puts his employees. By analyzing these occupations, therefore, one may find what is desired. In studying occupations for the purpose of learning how to educate for them, one matter, however, must be kept in mind. It is possible that, if employees had a different educational equipment, the tasks at which they are placed would be different. That is, actual vocations do reflect what business wants, but they also reflect what business is able to do with such material as it is receiving. To the extent that this latter consideration is important, a study of vocations reveals the educational acquirements of those employed as well as the wishes of employers.

EVIDENCE OF TYPE 1. THE BUSINESS DEMANDS OF CERTAIN CITIES

A. Opinion in Minneapolis[1]

In all conferences held by the survey with employers and employees from the business world, there was, of course, a

[1] Adapted from *Minneapolis Vocational Education Survey*. Bulletin of United States Bureau of Labor, No. 199, 1916, p. 81.

recognition of the very great need for the proper technical training of the commercial worker. In practically every instance, however, there was an agreement upon the statement that there was at least equal need, if not even greater need, in business today of certain habits of work and mental attitudes toward work which are as necessary as technical training, if not even more so, for the success and advancement of office employees.

Many persons possessing admirable technical knowledge fail to apply this knowledge in their daily work to the greatest advantage to themselves and to their employers, because they have not acquired habits of expressing themselves in terms of painstaking attention, system, order, neatness, punctuality, and accuracy. It is perhaps even more true that many fail to make anticipated progress because they do not bring to their tasks certain mental attitudes which express themselves in terms of ambition, loyalty, initiative, self-confidence, and willingness to assume responsibility.

Much as the business world realizes the need of these habits and mental attitudes, the large majority of business concerns have few, if any, suggestions to make as to the way in which these habits and attitudes are to be developed. Most of them have failed to inaugurate in their own establishments any plan for insuring them, although a few have been conspicuously successful in so doing.

B. The Demands of Employers in Des Moines[1]

Clay D. Slinker, Director Business Education, Des Moines, Iowa, makes the following statements:

A remarkable thing brought out by the survey is the number of young workers who feel the need of a better general business education. About 45 per cent of the whole number listed this as their principal training need.

One of our largest employers said the other day that no one should undertake office work who does not have a high

[1] Adapted by permission from *Survey of Junior Commercial Occupations in Sixteen States*. The Federal Board for Vocational Education, June, 1920, p. 38. This survey was prepared under the direction of F. G. Nichols.

school education. This opinion seems to be held by many who call upon us for assistance in securing office help. The invariable call is for thoroughly efficient help for which the employer is willing to pay a wage corresponding to ability shown. In the larger offices the work is narrowly specialized, but even these offices demand mature workers. Our leading stores do not care to employ salespeople under eighteen years of age.

C. The Survey of Rochester, New York[1]

Purposes of the survey.—

1. That the requirements of business with reference to commercial employees may be better understood by the local educational authorities.

2. That the commercial courses now being offered by the schools of Rochester may be more thoroughly understood by the business men who are in a position to pass intelligent judgment of their merit.

3. That such changes in the present course of study as may seem necessary after careful consideration, may be made upon the recommendation of this committee.

4. That in business training as in industrial training, the educational authorities and business men may continue to co-operate with each other to the end that more efficiently trained young people may be available when clerical help is required.

Kinds of positions included.—The survey includes 1303 commercial workers divided among twenty-one positions as shown in table on page 118.

Typewriting.—Quite a large proportion of the employers stated that any office worker would be much more valuable with a knowledge of typewriting even though he was not able to write shorthand.

Bookkeeping.—About 60 per cent of the employers canvassed stated that an assistant bookkeeper does not need to be familiar with the principles of double-entry bookkeeping, as the modern set of books is highly sectionalized and much of

[1] Adapted by permission from *Survey of Needs in Commercial Education*, pp. 3–12. Rochester Chamber of Commerce, 1915.

the bookkeeping work is mere routine; 40 per cent of those canvassed seem to feel, however, that any office worker is much more valuable and also much more certain of promotion if he is well grounded in the fundamental principles of double-entry bookkeeping.

TABLE XI

SURVEY OF 1,303 COMMERCIAL WORKERS

Kind of Work	Female	Male
1. Advertising Clerks	1	1
2. Auditors	14	0
3. Bookkeepers	30	58
4. Clerical—factory	10	3
5. Clerical—general office	259	195
6. Cost clerks	3	0
7. Cashiers	67	2
8. Collectors	0	1
9. Credit Clerks	2	0
10. Mail Order Clerks	1	0
11. Messengers	7	20
12. Order and Billing Clerks	39	28
13. Pay Roll Clerks	21	1
14. Sales and Record Clerks	58	2
15. Salespeople	210	40
16. Stenographers	83	8
17. Shipping and Receiving Clerks	0	92
18. Stock Clerks	5	4
19. Timekeepers	1	3
20. Typists	29	2
21. Tag Writers	3	0
Totals	843	460
Grand Total	1303	

Advertising and salesmanship.—All the employers agreed that fundamental principles of advertising and salesmanship should be taught in connection with commercial courses.

Adding machines.—Ninety per cent of the employers canvassed used adding machines and 60 per cent stated that it would be very desirable to have instruction given on the adding machine in connection with commercial courses.

Dictating machines.—Dictating machines are used by $33\frac{1}{3}$ per cent of the employers included in our canvass and it was suggested that graduates of commercial courses should have some facility in the art of transcribing from the dictating machine.

Male stenographers.—Ninety per cent of the employers do not use male stenographers and yet the 10 per cent who do use such stenographers have some exceptionally good positions open to young men.

Cuttings from recommendations of the committee to the school authorities.—From the survey it would appear that general business training should receive more attention in addition to the technical instruction in bookkeeping. Every commercial course graduate should be familiar with the principles of double-entry bookkeeping, but he does not need to be an expert bookkeeper. Only $6\frac{1}{2}$ per cent of the 1303 commercial workers are bookkeepers and the majority of these are routine clerks on a highly specialized and sectionalized set of books.

One hundred per cent of the firms replied that advertising should be taught in the schools. It is therefore recommended that this matter be presented to the schools with the request that such courses be given to all day commercial students as well as to evening classes.

In view of the fact that adding machines are used by 90 per cent of the firms canvassed, it is recommended that operators be trained in the commercial courses.

It is strongly recommended that such business habits as obedience, courtesy, industry, thoughtfulness, promptness, loyalty, etc., be made the subjects of definite and conscious instruction in all commercial courses. Frequent talks by those who know their value should be given to commercial students. No teacher can handle these subjects as effectively as the man in business can.

It is also recommended that pupils be taught the very great advantage of sticking to one job long enough to thoroughly test its advantages before seeking another position and that future prospects are better than immediate gain.

General education, maturity, thorough knowledge of English, good vocabulary, clean personal habits, etc., are necessary to success in stenographic work. Only those who have reasonable assurance of success should be encouraged to enter this field..

Since 78 per cent of the firms canvassed have no definite plan of promotion, and the remaining 22 per cent have a plan only with reference to their selling force, it is recommended that all firms be urged to devise some plan whereby every worthy employee will be made to understand that promotion will automatically and surely follow success on his part. It is believed that this is the best way to make the floater a permanent link in any business organization. The number of employees under twenty-six years of age in this survey who have been promoted to their present positions is only $33\frac{1}{3}$ per cent of the total. The statistics bear out the complaint that employees of this type do not remain in one place long enough. A promotion plan might remedy this situation to some extent.

D. A Survey in Milwaukee[1]

An experimental survey was made in Milwaukee in June, 1919. The report on this survey was not made in exactly the same form as were those received from other cities, therefore, it was not possible to tabulate the results with the others in this final report. However, the figures given in the summary on page 121 indicate that the situation in Milwaukee is exactly the same as it is elsewhere.

The following important statements are quoted from the Milwaukee report and bear out the general conclusion reached as a result of this survey:

General, as well as technical educational requirements for entrance into commercial positions, are reaching higher standards. Applicants for such positions are confronted by the question: "What can you do? What education and prepara-

[1] Adapted by permission from *Survey of Junior Commercial Occupations in Sixteen States*, pp. 35–36. The Federal Board for Vocational Education, June, 1920. This survey was prepared under the direction of F. G. Nichols.

tion have you had?" In Milwaukee, employers of office help favor young people who are seventeen or more years of age, and who have had a full, or at least part, high school education. Unfortunately there are not enough secondary school graduates to supply the demands of business. Economic reasons compel thousands of worthy and ambitious boys and girls to leave the elementary schools to find employment.

TABLE XII

COMMERCIAL OCCUPATIONS OF 1,067 BOYS AND GIRLS UNDER SEVENTEEN YEARS OF AGE IN THE CITY OF MILWAUKEE, WIS.

Kind of Work Done	Number	Per Cent
1. Bookkeeping exclusively	12	1
2. Bookkeeping in part only	48	4½
3. Shorthand exclusively	42	4
4. Shorthand in part only	72	7
5. Billing	31	3
6. Calculating machine operating	38	3½
7. Dictaphone operating	5	½
8. Bookkeeping machine operating	2	..
9. Typewriting	98	9
10. Messengers	68	6⅓
11. Retail selling	48	4½
12. Shipping clerk work	24	2⅓
13. Time keeping	17	1⅔
14. Cost clerk work	15	1½
15. Multigraph operating	11	1
16. Addressograph	29	2¾
17. Filing	102	9½
18. Telephone operating	161	15
19. Miscellaneous clerical work	244	23
	1067	100

In Milwaukee there are approximately 1067 boys and girls between the ages of fourteen and seventeen who are doing office work (mostly in small offices). Only a very small number have had some high school training. About 200 have taken business courses, either in high schools, continuation or private business schools. All of these boys and girls are attending the part-time continuation school. Fully 90 per cent of them are following courses of study intended to advance them in their commercial work.

It will be noticed that only about 5½ per cent are doing actual bookkeeping work, and only 11 per cent are doing stenographic work, proving that, as a rule, young boys and girls are not employed for such work.

In reply to the question, "What must you know, learn or do to advance yourself in your position?" 951 boys and girls under seventeen, who are now commercially employed, responded. The replies are grouped as follows:

Bookkeeping	158	Calculating Machine	44
Billing Machine Operating	12	Addressograph Operating	1
Multigraph Operating	1	Telegraphy	5
Dictaphone Operating	2	Bookkeeping Machine Operating	3
Filing	12	Selling	40
Telephone Operating	6	Time Keeping	8
Shipping Clerk Work	3	Mail Clerk Work	4
Cost Clerk Work	15	Buying	4
Advertising	3	Banking	5
Business Law	3	Checker	4
Cashier	3	English	99
General Clerical	25	Spelling	44
Penmanship	86	Correspondence	15
Arithmetic	44		
Stenography	302		

The fact that about 50 per cent call for bookkeeping and stenography may be due to a lack of opportunity to pursue other courses; to a lack of knowledge that other kinds of office work offer as much pay and advancement as bookkeeping and shorthand, or because the false notion prevails among many young folks (old folks too) that bookkeeping and stenography lend more dignity, refinement and respect to a position. They look with disdain upon general clerical work, machine operating, retail selling, etc.

English in some form is called for by about 30 per cent. This is significant. In a general way it may be stated that more time can profitably be given to the teaching of the essentials of English, arithmetic, penmanship, general clerical work, filing and machine operating, rather than to technical bookkeeping and stenography, especially when the educational background does not equal at least a high school education.

E. Conclusions from the Cleveland Survey[1]

The range of a boy's possible future in commercial occupations is as wide as the field of business. He cannot at first be trained specifically as a girl can be because he does not know

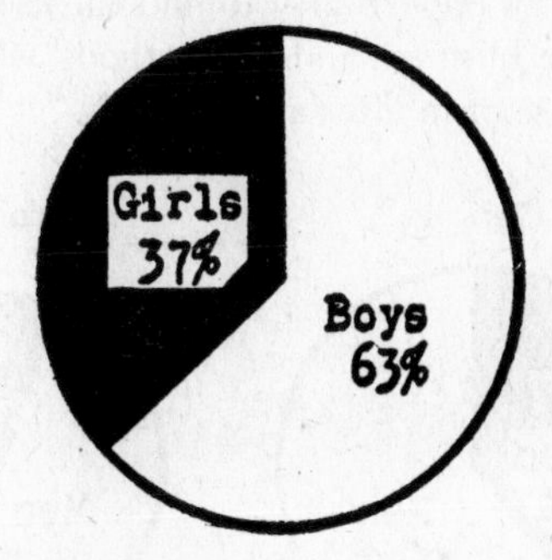

Fig. 6.—Boys and girls under 18 years of age in office work in Cleveland. Data from report of Ohio Industrial Commission, 1915.

what business will do with him or what he wants to do with business. The girl's choice is limited by custom. She can prepare herself definitely for stenography, bookkeeping, or machine operating and be sure that she is preparing for just the opportunity—and the whole opportunity—that business offers to her. Her very limitation of opportunity makes preliminary choice and training definitely possible things.

The difference between boys' work and girls' begins at the beginning. Boys are given the larger share of the positions which the youngest workers can fill. Figure 6 illustrates this and the figures of the United States Census for 1910 clearly cor-

[1] Adapted by permission from Bertha M. Stevens, *Boys and Girls in Commercial Work*, pp. 15–27. Survey Committee of the Cleveland Foundation, 1916.

roborate it. Boys are taken for such work and taken younger than girls, not merely because the law permits them to go to work at an earlier age, but also because business itself intends to round out their training. Girls, on the contrary, are expected to enter completely trained for definite positions, and this fact alone would in most cases require that they be older than boys when they begin work. Furthermore, because boys in first positions are looked upon as potential clerks, miscellaneous jobs about the office have, for them, a two-fold value. They give the employer a chance to weed out unpromising material; and they give boys an opportunity to find themselves and to gather ideas about the business and its methods which they may be able to make use of in later adjustments.

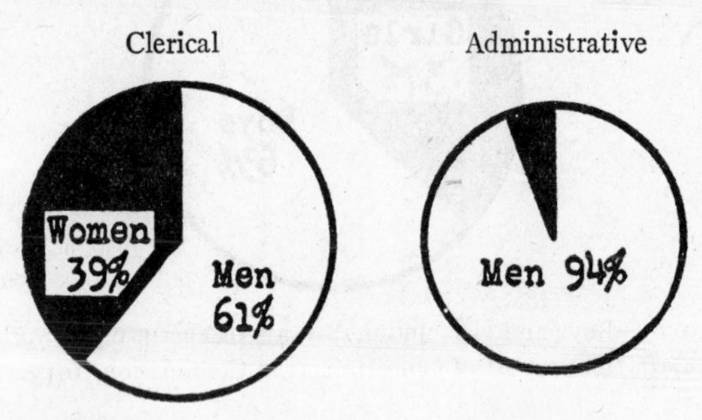

FIG. 7.—Men and women 18 years of age and over in clerical and administrative work in offices in Cleveland. U.S. Census, 1910.

A comparison of the opportunities held out to each sex is shown in several ways in diagrams and tables. Figure 7 shows that girls' training, if it is to meet the present situation, must prepare for a future in specialized clerical work; boys' futures must apparently be thought of as in both the clerical and administrative fields. The term "clerical" as here used covers bookkeepers, cashiers, and accountants, stenographers, typists, and unspecialized clerks, and a miscellaneous group of younger workers, such as messengers, office boys, etc. "Administrative" covers proprietors, officials, managers, supervisors and agents, but it does not include salespeople.

It is far from the intention of this report to overlook or to discredit the advances which women in this day are making toward a responsible part in business. And, while the present practical training of the mass of girls for commercial work must be based upon the kind of positions the mass of women now hold, there is no ground for interpreting such a program of training as an attempt to limit the opportunities of women. The limitation is, by custom, already set. It is, largely, the part

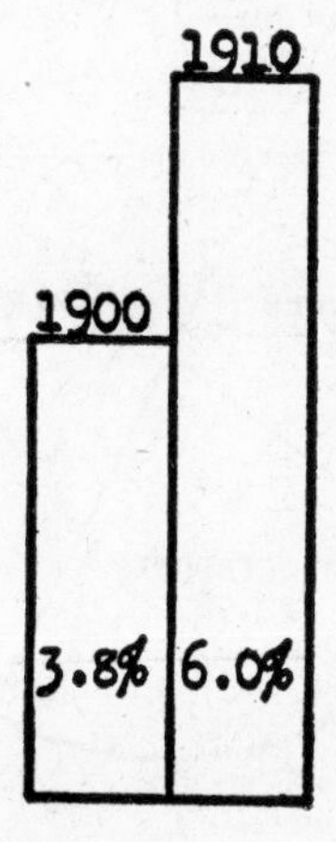

FIG. 8.—Increase in the percentage of women in administrative positions in office work in Cleveland from 1900 to 1910. U.S. Census.

of women themselves to surpass it, if the wider field is the thing they really desire. It is known that women are demonstrating, in many individual instances, their capacity to step beyond the bounds of clerical occupations; and there is evidence, in the trend of the figures of the United States Census, that women in the future will have an increasing share in creative and administrative work. Figure 8 shows that in the 10 year period between 1900 and 1910 the proportion of Cleveland women in administrative positions in office work increased more than one-half.

The total number of persons in clerical work in Cleveland—men and women, boys and girls—is, according to the United

States Census, approximately 22,000. Figure 9 shows the distribution of these workers on the basis of occupation. Clerks make up by far the largest number.

Stenographers and the bookkeeping groups are about equal, but the sum of these is not much greater than the number of the clerks alone. The junior workers, including messengers, office boys, etc., are, as may be expected, a tiny minority.

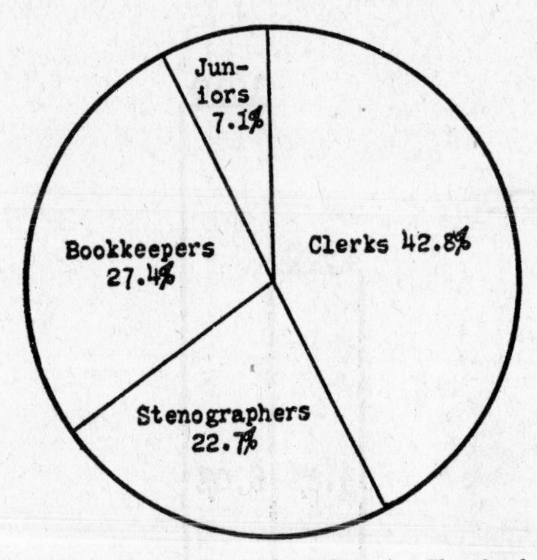

FIG. 9.—Distribution of clerical workers in Cleveland according to positions. U.S. Census, 1910.

The distribution of the various kinds of clerical workers, on the basis of sex, is illustrated by Figure 10. It will be noted that, of the men, it is the clerks that make up by far the largest portion. Among the women, it is the stenographers. The numbers of men stenographers and women clerks are correspondingly few. In the bookkeeping groups the proportions of men and women are most nearly alike, and, for both men and women, these groups are the second largest. Later in this chapter reference is made to a difference in the kinds of bookkeeping work which men and women commonly do. The larger proportion of boys among the youngest workers has already been explained.

Two tables have been prepared showing again, for both sexes, the contrast in the number and kinds of positions they hold. The table for men and boys is a classification of 2,306 clerical and administrative positions; for women and girls, 2,816. The information had to be obtained from differing sources. The positions for men and boys are those held by

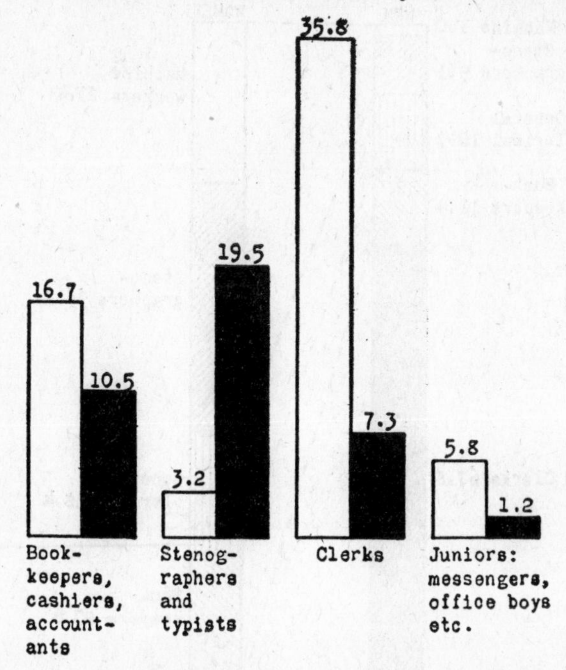

FIG. 10.—Percentage distribution of men and women in office work in Cleveland. Columns in outline represent men and boys; those in black, women and girls. U.S. Census, 1910.

1,000 applicants for office work at the Employment Bureau of the Cleveland Young Men's Christian Association, 1912–1915.

The records of this Bureau are kept with great care and completeness and they have proved a valuable source of information about work, wages, and training.

Figure 11 shows in graphic form the distribution of the non-administrative positions. This diagram presents in more detail the same kinds of facts that have already been brought out in Figure 5. Excluding for both men and women the workers in administrative positions, we have left those doing general office work of a clerical nature. Among the men and boys these positions number 1,955 as compared with 2,747

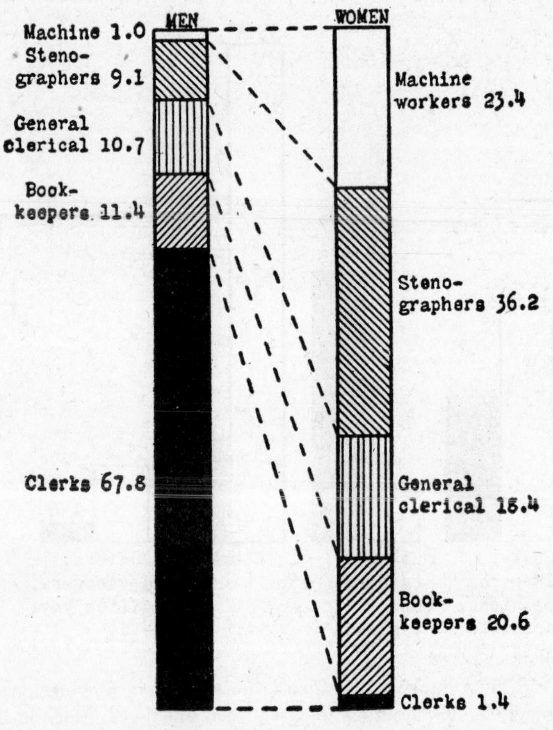

FIG. 11.—Percentage distribution of non-administrative positions in office work held by men and women in Cleveland 1912–15; 1,955 positions for men and 2,747 for women.

positions for the women and girls. Clerks make up the largest groups of men, and machine workers the smallest; stenographers make up the largest group of women, and clerks the smallest. The diagram shows that among each 100 men 68 are clerks, while among each 100 women, only one is a clerk. On the other hand, among each 100 men, only one is a machine operator, while of each 100 women, 23 are machine operators.

F. What Business Does with Boys and Girls in New York[1]

TABLE XIII

Occupations of Boys

Business	Kind of Work	Wage	Age
	Bookkeepers 4	Wage Range $5–$9	Age Range 16
Furniture and fixture	Assistant bookkeeper, typewrites all bills and takes care of ledger	$9.00	16
Embroidery and lace	Assistant bookkeeper, enters orders received and checks deliveries	8.00	16
Clothing—outer	Bookkeeper	7.00	16
Furniture and fixture	Assistant bookkeeper	5.00	16
	Clerks 95	Wage Range $3–$16	Age Range 14–18
Railroad	Billing clerk	$16.00	17
Railroad	Receives all freight shipped to New York and collected by wagon	12.00	17
Banking and brokerage	Weighing and in charge of testing coffee	11.00	18
Clothing—outer	Helper, shipping department	11.00	17
Civil service	Clerk	10.00	18
Stationery	General office-worker	10.00	18
Banking and brokerage	Junior clerk, statistical work	10.00	18
Toilet articles	Shipper, makes out bills and directs drivers	10.00	18
Shirtwaists—ladies'	Assistant buyer and receiving clerk	10.00	17
Advertising	Junior clerk. Secretary to member of firm	9.25	17
Real estate	Office assistant. File clerk and general office-worker	9.00	18
Department store	Newspaper clipping. General office work	9.00	18
Dry goods and notions	Assistant receiving clerk	9.00	17
Groceries	Enters bills and checks orders	9.00	17
Wall paper	Order clerk	9.00	17
Butcher	Shipping clerk	9.00	17
Dry goods and notions	Bill clerk	8.50	17
Dry goods and notions	Clerical worker and salesman	8.00	18
Clothing—outer	Replaces orders for shipment	8.00	18
Clothing—outer	Makes out tickets. Charges goods	8.00	17
Department store	Assistant advertising manager. Attends to transferring and correcting	8.00	17
Printing and publishing	Fills orders. Order clerk	8.00	17
Printing and publishing	Keeps account of manuscripts	8.00	17
Banking and brokerage	Clerical worker	8.00	17
Banking and brokerage	General office worker. Does filing and errands	8.00	17
Advertising	Office worker	8.00	17
Motor supplies	Shipping clerk	8.00	16
Hardware	Assistant shipping clerk. Ships goods	8.00	16
Feathers	Helper on shipping	8.00	16
Newspaper	Attendant, in charge of four boys	7.50	16
Cement and stone	Salesman's clerk	7.50	16
Novelties	Prepares orders for shipment	7.50	16
Confectionery	Ships orders	7.00	18
Rubber products	Mail clerk and office assistant	7.00	18
Jewelry	Assistant shipping clerk. Prepares orders for shipment	7.00	17
Banking and brokerage	Stock boy. Fills stock cards	7.00	17
Dressmaking	Assistant shipping clerk	7.00	17

[1] Adapted by permission from Bertha M. Stevens, *Private Commercial Schools, Manhattan and the Bronx*, pp. 135–43. Public Education Association of the City of New York, 1918.

TABLE XIII—*Continued*

Business	Kind of Work	Wage	Age
	Clerks—*Continued*	Wage Range $3–16	Age Range 14–18
Insurance	Changes names of beneficiaries in policies	$ 7.00	17
Groceries	Assistant to secretary. General office work	7.00	17
Jewelry	Office and clerical work	7.00	17
Furniture and fixture	File clerk	7.00	17
Insurance	Policy checker	7.00	17
Dental supplies	Shipping clerk. Ships goods	7.00	17
Automobile	Junior clerk. General office worker	7.00	16
Drugs and medicines	Records charges or overcharges and errors	7.00	16
Dressmaking	Shipping clerk, packer, etc.	7.00	16
Mail order house	File clerk. Delivers packages to chutes	7.00	16
Bottle cap making	Does clerical work for superintendent	7.00	15
Glassware and china	Receives goods and checks them	7.00	14
Insurance	Mail clerk. Stamps and seals envelopes	7.00	14
Banking and brokerage	Clerical and general office worker	6.25	17
Civil service	First grade clerk. Does filing and indexing	6.25	17
Steamship	Does bookkeeping and filing. Keeps records	6.25	16
Department store	Sends out letters and catalogs	6.00	18
Department store	Sample clerk	6.00	18
Art work	Clerical worker	6.00	17
Photography	Information boy. Gives information, takes orders	6.00	17
Woolens	Files correspondence, etc.	6.00	17
Dressmaking	Packs orders for shipment	6.00	17
Tobacco	Prepares orders for shipment	6.00	17
Clothing—outer	Ships goods, makes out labor tickets, gives out goods to cut	6.00	17
Dry goods and notions	Receipt clerk	6.00	17
Advertising	Does all office work and filing	6.00	17
Printing and publishing	Keeps time. Typist	6.00	16
Automobiles	Ships goods	6.00	16
Banking and brokerage	Stock boy—clerical work and errands	6.00	16
Printing and publishing	Filing clerk	6.00	16
Clothing—outer	Assistant shipping clerk	6.00	16
Clothing—outer	Files letters and bills. Opens mail	6.00	15
Printing and publishing	Files letters	5.50	16
Stationery	Sample clerk. Shows stock	5.50	16
Hat, cap, bonnet	Assistant shipping clerk	5.00	18
Law and collections	Law clerk. Answers cases on calendar. Does office work	5.00	17
Stationery	Shipping clerk	5.00	17
Butcher	Files receipts and claims	5.00	17
Novelties	Packs, ships, and delivers goods	5.00	17
	Packs, ships, and does general work	5.00	17
Banking and brokerage	Board boy. Puts up quotations on stock board	5.00	17
Dry goods and notions	Shipping clerk	5.00	17
Button making	Ships goods. Attends to stock	5.00	17
Real estate	General office worker. Care of receipts, collecting rents, etc.	5.00	16
Clothing—outer	Helper. General office worker	5.00	16
Tobacco	Packs, stamps, and does errands	5.00	16
Printing and publishing	Stamps mails. Deposits same in post-office	5.00	16
Printing and publishing	Filing clerk	5.00	15
Clothing—outer	Helper in shipping department	5.00	15
Jewelry	General utility worker: Office work and errands	5.00	15
Department store	Collects goods from different departments	4.00	16
Clothing—outer	Helper in shipping department	4.00	16
Clothing—outer	Assistant shipping clerk	4.00	16
Painting	Assistant clerk. Answers bell	4.00	15
Glassware and china	Billing clerk	3.00	16
Not reported	Receiving clerk	....	16

TABLE XIII—*Continued*

Business	Kind of Work	Wage	Age
	Errand-Messengers 3	Wage Range $4–$5	Age Range 14–16
Hotel and restaurant	Office work and messenger	$5.00	16
Silk making	Stock book and errands	4.50	16
Dressing	Helps bookkeeper. Does errands	4.00	14
	Office Boys 47	Wage Range $2–$8	Age Range 14–18
Building and contracting	Office boy. Switchboard operator	$8.00	16
Banking and brokerage	Clerical worker	8.00	16
Expressing and trucking	Helper in office	8.00	16
Produce	Office boy	7.50	16
Printing and publishing	Sub-clerical worker	7.00	17
Leather and skin	Typist	7.00	16
Advertising	Office boy. Does errands	7.00	15
Advertising	Office boy. Mail clerk	6.00	17
Building and contracting	Office boy. Answers telephone	6.00	17
Furniture and fixture	Office boy. Telephone work and mailing	6.00	16
Buttons	Office boy. Runs errands	6.00	16
Metal, steel, iron	Office clerk	6.00	16
Department store	Office boy. Does filing and general office work	6.00	16
Hardware	Office boy	6.00	16
Banking and brokerage	Clerical worker and errand boy	6.00	16
Steamship	Office boy. Telephone work and mailing	6.00	16
Dry goods and notions	Does errands and filing	6.00	15
Building and contracting	Sub-clerical worker	5.50	16
Clothing—outer	Office boy	5.00	18
Neckwear	Office and errand boy	5.00	17
Feathers	Office and errand boy	5.00	17
Painting	Office and telephone boy. Receives and announces visitors	5.00	17
Musical instruments	Office boy. Marks price of goods on sales slips	5.00	17
Metal, steel, iron	Does telephone work and mailing. Errand boy	5.00	17
Lighting fixtures	Office, errand, and telephone boy. Addresses letters	5.00	16
Liquors	Office, switchboard, and errand boy	5.00	16
Butcher	Office, mail, and errand boy	5.00	16
Express and trucking	Office and errand boy	5.00	16
Telephone	Messenger and office boy. Files papers	5.00	15
Clothing—outer	Takes care of mail books	5.00	15
Lithographing	Directs callers. Does errands	5.00	15
Furniture and fixtures	Office, errand, and telephone boy	5.00	15
Electrical appliances	Office, errand, and telephone boy. Receives goods	5.00	15
Law and collections	Office boy. Answers bells and telephone calls	5.00	14
Hardware	Office boy	4.50	16
Machinery	Office boy. Cleans office, does errands	4.50	14
Groceries	Office, telephone, and errand boy	4.00	16
Glassware and china	Office, telephone, and mail boy	4.00	16
Painting	Errand and telephone boy. Does typing and takes care of samples	4.00	16
Oil products	Watch-office boy	4.00	15
Novelties	Office boy	4.00	15
Real estate	Office, mail, and telephone boy	4.00	15
Religion	Does light bookkeeping and switchboard work	4.00	15
Hardware	Addresses envelopes. Does errands	4.00	14
Drugs and medicines	Office boy. Answers bells	4.00	14
Doctor	Office boy, during summer and after school	2.00	15
Woolens	Office boy	....	15

TABLE XIV

OFFICE POSITIONS HELD BY UNTRAINED GIRLS FOURTEEN TO EIGHTEEN YEARS OF AGE, INCLUSIVE*

Business	Kind of Work	Wage	Age
	Addressers 3	Wage Range $6	Age Range 16–17
Mail order house	Addresses mail	$6.00	17
Mail order house	Addresses envelopes	6.00	16
Printing and publishing	Addresses envelopes	6.00	16
	Bookkeepers 7	Wage Range $5–$9	Age Range 14–17
Dressmaking	Answers letters and keeps books	$9.00	17
Hat, cap, bonnet	Does all bookkeeping for firm	7.00	16
Machinery	Makes entries. Takes dictation, copies letters	5.00	15
Express and trucking	Takes charge of books for father	5.00	15
Furniture and fixtures	Answers telephone; correspondence work. Keeps the books	5.00	15
Dressmaking	Enters orders	5.00	14
Steamship	Balances accounts for father	....	17
	Cashiers 8	Wage Range $2.50–$9	Age Range 14–17
Clothing—outer	Cashier. Does some bookkeeping	$9.00	15
Department store	Takes cash, checks parcels	8.00	17
Butcher	Cashier	8.00	17
Department store	Tallies time of employees. Receives money for sales	7.00	16
Groceries	Sits at register and makes change	6.00	14
Hotel and restaurant	Takes charge of cash	5.00	16
Department store	Cashier and packer	5.00	17
Butcher	Cashier and bookkeeper	5.00	16
	Clerks 45	Wage Range $3.50–$10	Age Range 14–18
Tobacco	Factory pay-roll clerk	$10.00	18
Department store	Keeps records of correspondence	10.00	18
Dressmaking	Keeps track of material given out	10.00	17
Advertising	Graphotype operator	10.00	15
Department store	Files orders	....	14
Printing and publishing	Does posting and billing. Assistant bookkeeper	9.00	18
Printing and publishing	Files letters. Assistant bookkeeper	8.00	18
Department store	Addressograph machine operator	8.00	17
Dry goods and notions	Shipping clerk	8.00	17
Printing and publishing	Makes out bills	8.00	17
Banking and brokerage	Keeps track of money received and files bills	8.00	16
Embroidery and lace	Marks goods	7.50	18
Printing and publishing	Files bills	7.00	18
Department store	Writes call checks	7.00	17
Religion	Does typing	7.00	17
Department store	Files and addresses letters	7.00	16
Photographing	Does general office work	7.00	16
Shirtwaists—ladies'	Assistant bookkeeper	7.00	17
Tobacco	Tabulates sheets. Does filing	6.50	16

* *Bureau of Attendance Records*, 1915.

TABLE XIV—*Continued*

Business	Kind of Work	Wage	Age
	Clerks—*Continued*	Wage Range $3.50–$10	Age Range 14–18
Stationery	Files letters. Assistant bookkeeper	$6.00	17
Mail order house	Fills out blanks for customers	6.00	17
Clothing—outer	Keeps account of received goods	6.00	16
Clothing—outer	Cuts tickets	6.00	16
Agricultural	Printer. Works at stenciling and estimates	6.00	16
Mail order house	Writes letters	6.00	16
Department store	Attends to mail, makes out bills and keeps books	6.00	15
Department store	Attends to mail orders	5.00	15
Feathers	Charges accounts	6.00	15
Medical instruments	Does general office work	5.50	16
Department store	Audits due bills	5.00	18
Department store	Enters sales. Turns in amounts to cashier at end of month	5.00	18
Department store	Sorts bills. Looks up orders	5.00	17
Department store	Answers telephone. Looks up orders	5.00	17
Printing and publishing	Files bills	5.00	16
Pattern making	Files order cards	5.00	16
Clothing—outer	Does clerical work	5.00	16
Department store	Entry clerk. Puts checks on boxes	5.00	16
Printing and publishing	Addresses envelopes. Files cards	5.00	15
Department store	Clerk in mail order department	4.50	17
Department store	Checks up commission of clerks	4.50	16
Department store	Keeps track of appointments in alteration department	4.00	16
Department store	Enters bills in books	4.00	17
Department store	Files letters. Answers telephone	4.00	16
Department store	Does general office work	4.00	17
	News Clipper 1	Wage Range $5	Age Range 17
Newspaper	Cuts clippings from papers and pastes them	$5.00	17
	Telephone Operator 1	Wage Range $5	Age Range 17
Department store	Calls up self charges	$5.00	17

TABLE XV

OFFICE POSITIONS HELD BY BOYS FOURTEEN TO EIGHTEEN YEARS OF AGE WHO HAVE HAD COMMERCIAL TRAINING*

Business	Kind of Work	Wage	Age
	Bookkeepers 2	Wage Range $8–$10	Age Range 17
Roofing	Keeps accounts	$10.00	17
Leather and skins	Assistant bookkeeper	8.00	17
	Clerks 12	Wage Range $4.50–$10	Age Range 15–18
Instruction	Shipping clerk	$10.00	17
Electrical appliances	Shipping clerk. Gets orders ready and ships them. Also receives goods	8.50	17
Embroidery and lace	Does filing, indexing, and typing	8.00	16
Railroads	Filing clerk	6.25	17
Law and collections	Does typing and filing	6.00	18
Machinery	General office worker	6.00	17
Plumbing	Keeps charges and letter books	6.00	16
Stationery	Packs orders for delivery	6.00	16
Tobacco	Sends out letters. Does stamping	5.50	16
Engineering and motor supplies	Does filing and order work	5.00	16
Steamship lines	Mail clerk. Folds and inserts circulars	5.00	16
Mail order house	Checks invoices. Does billing and mailing	4.50	15
	Copy Holder 1	Wage Range $5	Age Range 17
Printing and publishing	Copy holder for proof reader	$5.00	17
	Office Boys 7	Wage Range $4–$6	Age Range 14–17
Furniture and fixtures	Office and mail boy. Does errands	$6.00	16
Amusement	Office boy	5.00	17
Architecture	Office boy. Files Drawings	5.00	16
Department store	Office boy. Does clerical and telephone work	5.00	15
Law and collections	Does minor clerical work and errands	5.00	15
Real estate	Does general office work and errands	4.50	17
Drugs and medicines	Office boy	4.00	14
	Stenographers and Typists 4	Wage Range $9–$12	Age Range 15–18
Electricity and gas	Stenographer and typist	$12.00	18
Railroad	Correspondence. Enters freight cards	10.00	18
Automobile	Stenographer and typist	10.00	17
Printing and publishing	Typist	9.00	15

* *Bureau of Attendance Records*, 1915.

TABLE XVI

OFFICE POSITIONS HELD BY GIRLS FOURTEEN TO EIGHTEEN YEARS OF AGE WHO HAVE HAD COMMERCIAL TRAINING*

Business	Kind of Work	Wage	Age
	Bookkeepers 6	Wage Range $6–$8	Age Range 15–17
Automobile	Assistant bookkeeper. Does general office work. Enters charges in books	$8.00	17
Department store	Does billing. Answers telephone. Looks up charges	7.00	17
Dental supplies	Enters charges. Assists in bookkeeping	6.00	17
Printing and publishing	Keeps book and accounts	6.00	15
Plumbing	Makes out bills	....	17
Funeral—Undertaking	Bookkeeper and stenographer for father	....	17
	Cashier 1	Wage Range $6	Age Range 17
Groceries	Does bookkeeping and makes change	$6.00	17
	Clerks 15	Wage Range $3.50–$9	Age Range 14–18
Glove making	Does general office work	$9.00	18
Furniture and fixture	Comptometer operator	8.00	17
Printing and publishing	Files letters. Assistant bookkeeper	8.00	18
Printing and publishing	Files bills	7.00	18
Drugs and medicines	Operates adding machine	7.00	17
Printing and publishing	Addresses envelopes	7.00	17
Tobacco	Assistant bookkeeper	6.50	16
Instruction	Does typing	6.00	18
Stationery	Files letters. Assistant bookkeeper	6.00	17
Mail order house	Enters orders in books. Keeps monthly totals	5.50	17
Mail order house	Writes and keeps account of mail	5.00	17
Medical instruments	Answers telephone and takes orders	5.00	17
Mail order house	Sends out requisitions	5.00	16
Glassware and china	Does clerical work, filing, etc.	5.00	15
Box making	Answers telephone and enters bills	5.00	15
Drugs and medicines	Makes out bills and transfers	5.00	14
Feathers	Addresses mail	3.50	14
	Telephone Operators 2	Wage Range $6–$8	Age Range 16–18
Clothing—outer	Correspondence and billing. Does typing	$8.00	18
Furniture and fixtures	Does filing and writing	6.00	16
	Stenographers and Typists 27	Wage Range $5.50–$12	Age Range 16–19
Law and collections	Law clerk	$12.00	19
Advertising	Does secretarial work	12.00	19
Dressmaking	Does bookkeeping and stenography	12.00	18
Automobiles	Works on pay-roll, books, letters, etc.	12.00	17
Liquors	Keeps track of orders and letters	12.00	17
Tobacco	Takes dictation	10.00	18
Civil service	Keeps records	10.00	16

* *Bureau of Attendance Records*, 1915.

TABLE XVI—*Continued*

Business	Kind of Work	Wage	Age
	Stenographers and Typists—*Continued*	Wage Range $5.50–$12	Age Range 16–19
Box making	Stenography and bookkeeping	$9.00	16
Printing and publishing	Dictation of letters	8.75	16
Mining and mining products	Takes dictation. Does copying	8.00	18
Real estate	Has entire charge of office dictation	7.00	19
Embroidery and lace	Does office work	7.00	17
Department store	Files bills. Does typing	7.00	17
Express and trucking	Does bookkeeping. Receives and answers mail	7.00	17
Printing and publishing	Takes dictation. Does office work	7.00	16
Dressmaking	Switchboard work and correspondence	7.00	16
Law and collections	Copies and addresses envelopes	6.25	17
Law and collections	Types all legal work	6.00	19
Hotel and restaurants	Does typing and stenography	6.00	17
Law—collections	Types letters	6.00	17
Funeral—undertaking	Keeps accounts of books. Types charges	6.00	17
Department store	Fills in circular letters	6.00	17
Mail order house	Does typing	6.00	17
Real estate	Types and files letters	6.00	16
Printing and publishing	Types letters to subscribers	6.00	16
Department store	Makes out bills	5.50	17
Drugs and medicines	Does typing	....	18

TABLE XVII

A Comparative Summary of Opportunities and Wages for Boys and Girls Trained in Commercial Work in New York City—1915 Record

	Boys		Girls	
	Number of Jobs	Wages	Number of Jobs	Wages
Bookkeeping	2	$8–$10	6	$6–$8
Clerks	12	4.50–$10.00	15	$3.50–$9.00
Cashier	....	....	1	$6
Copy holder	1	$3	....	....
Office boys	7	$4–$6	....	....
Telephone operators	....	....	2	$6–$8
Stenographers and typists	4	$9–$12	27	$5.50–$12.00

EVIDENCE OF TYPE 2. THE EMPLOYMENT DEMANDS OF CERTAIN TYPES OF BUSINESS

A. An Insurance Company[1]

Our study of all the office positions of the Metropolitan Life Insurance Company held by young people under twenty-

[1] Adapted by permission from Bertha M. Stevens, *Private Commercial Schools*, pp. 111–13. Public Education Association of the City of New York, 1918.

one years of age cannot, we know, be accepted as a study of the conditions in business as a whole. It can represent only the conditions likely to be met in a large, standardized business. But standardization exists on so extensive a scale in New York City, and its tendency to spread is so great, that the number of workers involved and likely to be involved is sufficient to make standardization a matter to be reckoned with in questions of training. Everyone who has contact with the business world must be aware of the hordes of office employees to be found in railroad and other transportation offices, in public utilities offices such as the telegraph and telephone, in wholesale houses of the sort which maintain establishments in several cities, in the offices of large insurance corporations and many other kinds of already standardized business. Our information concerning the positions at the Metropolitan Life Insurance Company, 733 in number, includes, for each position, the workers' definite statement regarding the use of stenography and bookkeeping; and, in the case of those workers who have had commercial training, an additional statement regarding the general value of their training to the position in question. As Figure 12 shows, more than three-fourths of the boys' positions and nearly all the girls' find neither stenography nor bookkeeping useful, as such; not one position finds specific use for stenography and bookkeeping combined; less than one-fifth of the boys' positions, and a negligible portion of the girls', use bookkeeping alone; and the use of stenography alone is for both sexes negligible. We should emphasize the point that the information here submitted came as direct answers to definite questions, and there is no room for conjecture, in so far as the workers' opinion is concerned. The representative of the company points out, in this connection, that the trained boys and girls are likely to prove more desirable than the untrained ones. Yet, he was willing to concede that, for those not specifically employed at stenographic or bookkeeping work, something might be taught which would be more applicable to their work than the ordinary stenography and bookkeeping training which commercial schools generally give.

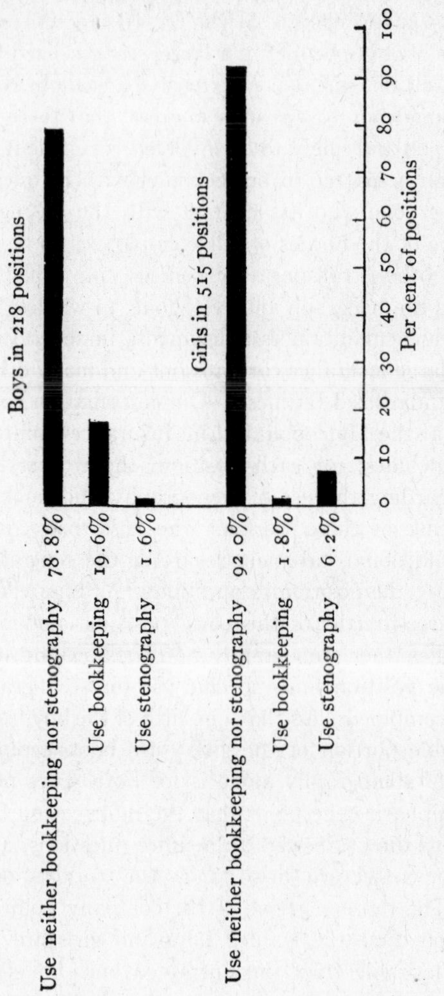

FIG. 12.—Use of stenography and typewriting in all office positions held by employees of the Metropolitan Life Insurance Company, under 21 years of age. September, 1916.

B. An Analysis of Clerical Employees in One Large Financial Corporation[1]

TABLE XVIII

Number	Position	Age	Education	Experience	Salary
	Male Employees				
50	Office boys	15–16	P. S. graduate	3 mos.–2 yrs.	$ 8–12
40	Messengers	16–18	1 yr. H. S.	6 mos.–2 yrs.	10–15
50	Junior clerks	17–18	2–3 yrs. H. S.	3 mos.–1 yr.	15–18
75	Senior clerks	18–22	H. S. graduates	3 mos.–2 yrs.	18–25
	Female Employees				
50	Clerical	17–19	P. S. graduates	6 mos.–1 yr.	$10–13
50	Typists	19–24	1–2 yrs. H. S.	6 mos.–2 yrs.	13–15
85	Dictaphone Stenographers	22–28	H. S. graduates Coll. graduates	2 yrs.–5 yrs.	18–25
30	Secretaries Semi-executive	25–35	H. S. graduates Coll. graduates	5 yrs.–10 yrs.	25–50

C. The Demands of a Mail Order House[2]

Among the employees of Montgomery Ward & Co., Chicago, there is a definite distinction between the work of boys and girls.

Boys of sixteen are used in merchandising and clerical work. Under clerical work are classified all kinds of messenger service between departments, which is considered an important branch of the work. Boys are assistants in the stock rooms. They are not employed in any division of bookkeeping, but several of the head accountants are men. As the business is conducted entirely by mail, the correspondents are important factors. The majority of them are men and they are called "high-priced," being paid from $25 per week upwards. Ninety per cent of the clerical force are women and girls.

File clerks are required to have finished the eighth grade, but they are not expected to have any preparation for business. The first step in teaching them filing is practice in sorting.

[1] Adapted by permission from Gertrude B. Thayer, Educational Director, Jones and Baker, in the *Sixth Annual Proceedings of the National Association of Corporation Schools* (1918), p. 104.

[2] A statement prepared by Mary B. Shelley, 1918.

Stenographers who have finished the four-year high-school course are preferred and such stenographers are paid $12 a week to start, but stenographers who have had only one year in high school and who have learned shorthand at a business college are employed at $9. The two-year high-school course has sent almost no candidates here.

Typists must be sixteen years of age and are required to have completed the eighth grade. Typists who show unusual ability and who are especially good in English are given an opportunity to become dictaphone operators. Dictaphone operators are graded about the same as stenographers. About twenty stenotypists and one shortwriter are employed on the same basis as stenographers.

The accounting work is done entirely by girls and women, with the exception of a few head accountants who are men. The comptometer is used in large numbers in the accounting department.

A minimum wage of $8 per week is paid in all departments and advancement is regular, but not automatic. If employees do not merit advancement, they are discharged. This policy is of recent development. Formerly mediocre people were retained and advanced slowly, with the result that many are still employed who are below average ability and who are retained solely because of long service. Stenographers are advanced as rapidly as possible and may become private secretaries. They are chosen for these positions because of executive ability as well as proficiency as stenographers. The salary is "large." Because of the tendency of women to get married, comparatively few of them are made correspondents. Some of the best correspondents they had were lost in this manner and the management became discouraged, but they may be obliged to employ more women correspondents because of war conditions.

EVIDENCE OF TYPE 3. NATIONAL SURVEYS OF COMMERCIAL EMPLOYMENTS

A. The Census Enumeration[1]

TABLE XIX

Occupation	Total	Male	Female
Trade	4,242,979	3,575,187	667,792
Bankers, brokers, and money lenders	161,613	156,309	5,304
Bankers and bank officials	82,375	78,149	4,226
Commercial brokers and commission men	27,552	27,358	194
Loan brokers and loan company officials	4,385	4,255	130
Pawnbrokers	1,088	1,066	22
Stockbrokers	29,609	29,233	376
Brokers not specified, and promotors	16,604	16,248	356
Clerks in stores	413,918	243,521	170,397
Commercial travelers	179,320	176,514	2,806
Decorators, drapers, and window dressers	8,853	7,698	1,155
Deliverymen	170,235	170,039	196
Bakeries and laundries	20,888	20,858	30
Stores	149,347	149,181	166
Floorwalkers, foremen, overseers	26,437	22,367	4,070
Floorwalkers and foremen in stores	20,604	16,565	4,039
Foremen (warehouses, stockyards, etc.)	5,833	5,802	31
Inspectors, gaugers, and samplers	13,714	12,683	1,031
Insurance agents and officials	134,978	129,589	5,389
Insurance agents	119,918	114,835	5,083
Officials of insurance companies	15,060	14,754	306
Laborers in coal and lumber yards, warehouses, etc.	125,609	124,713	896
Coal yards	25,192	25,157	35
Elevators	11,312	11,244	68
Lumberyards	43,351	43,279	54
Stockyards	22,888	22,859	29
Warehouses	22,866	22,156	710
Laborers, porters, and helpers in stores	125,007	116,602	8,405
Newsboys	27,961	27,635	326
Proprietors, officials, and managers	34,776	33,715	1,061
Employment office keepers	3,026	2,357	669
Proprietors, etc., elevators	8,858	8,836	22
Proprietors, etc., warehouses	6,353	6,310	43
Other proprietors, officials, and managers	16,539	16,212	327
Real estate agents and officials	149,135	139,927	9,208
Retail dealers	1,328,275	1,249,295	78,980
Salesmen and saleswomen	1,177,494	816,352	361,142
Auctioneers	5,048	5,045	3
Demonstrators	4,823	1,639	3,184
Sales agents	41,841	40,207	1,634
Salesmen and saleswomen (stores)	1,125,782	769,461	356,321
Undertakers	24,469	23,342	1,127
Wholesale dealers, importers, and exporters	73,574	72,780	794
Other pursuits (semi-skilled)	67,611	52,106	15,505
Fruit graders and packers	8,074	4,988	3,086
Meat cutters	22,884	22,804	80
Other occupations	16,952	10,711	6,241
Clerical Occupations	3,126,541	1,700,425	1,426,116
Agents, canvassers, and collectors	175,772	159,941	15,831
Agents	130,338	121,428	8,910
Canvassers	14,705	10,514	4,191
Collectors	30,729	27,999	2,730
Bookkeepers, cashiers, and accountants	734,688	375,564	359,124
Clerks (except clerks in stores)	1,487,905	1,015,742	472,163
Shipping clerks	123,684	118,944	4,740
Other clerks	1,347,992	882,068	465,924
Messenger, bundle, and office boys and girls	113,022	98,768	14,254
Bundle and cash boys and girls	6,973	2,506	4,467
Messenger, errand, and office boys and girls	106,049	96,262	9,787
Stenographers and typewriters	615,154	50,410	564,744

[1] Adapted from the *Fourteenth Census of the United States*, 1920. Population—Occupation Statistics, pp. 9–11.

B. A Private Survey in 1917–18[1]

The questionnaire asked school officers to report on the percentage of their students that found work as stenographers, bookkeepers, and clerks, respectively. The following table summarizes the reports on this question:[2]

TABLE XX

Distribution of Commercial Students into the Various Types of Office Work in Which They Find Initial Employment

Distribution of Commercial Students into Various Percentage Groups	Percentage of Schools Reporting Stenography (94 Schools Reporting)	Percentage of Schools Reporting Bookkeeping (87 Schools Reporting)	Percentage of Schools Reporting Clerical Work (62 Schools Reporting)
Per Cent			
1–25	17	81.6	82.3
26–50	46.8	16.1	11.3
Over 50	36.1	2.3	6.4

According to this table stenography is very commonly the first occupation of commercial students. Thirty-six per cent of the schools reporting on the number of their students who take positions in stenography declared that they place over 50 per cent of their students in such work. Only 2.3 per cent of the schools reporting on bookkeeping asserted that over 50 per cent of their students find work as bookkeepers, while 6.4 per cent of those reporting on clerical employment stated that over 50 per cent of their students enter business life as clerks.

These figures are in rather sharp contrast to those shown for the city of Cleveland. General census figures, furthermore, show a large proportion of office employees to be in clerical positions. Undoubtedly the terms of this question of the questionnaire were given different interpretations by different persons making reports. In general, it would appear, however, that stenography is a very substantial stepping-stone to other

[1] This material is reprinted from a monograph by the author. *A Survey of Commercial Education in the Public High Schools of the United States*, pp. 47–49. University of Chicago, 1919.

[2] Where the word "few" was used on a report it was taken to mean less than 25 per cent.

office work, and is with great frequency the type of employment first secured.

A further study of the preceding table shows that of the schools reporting on the percentage of their students beginning work as stenographers 46.8 per cent state that from 26 to 50 per cent find such work; 17 per cent report 25 per cent or less of their students beginning in the stenographic field. It also appears from an examination of the table that of the schools reporting on the percentage of their pupils who take positions as bookkeepers, 16.1 per cent state that from 26 to 50 per cent of their pupils begin work as bookkeepers; 81.6 per cent of these schools reported 25 per cent or less of their students taking employment as bookkeepers. Of the 62 schools that reported concerning their pupils becoming clerks, 11.3 per cent stated that 26 to 50 per cent take such positions and 82.3 per cent reported 25 per cent or less of their students taking places as clerks.

C. A National Survey of Junior Commercial Occupations[1]

It is important to remember that this survey includes only commercial workers, i.e., boys and girls holding office and store positions. Furthermore, only workers under eighteen years of age are included, i.e., from fourteen to seventeen years inclusive. It was the intention to limit the scope of the study to young employees, who are eligible to receive continuation school instruction.

It is perhaps rather significant that 67 per cent of those included in this study have had a full grammar school education or better, while 84 per cent have completed the seventh grade or more. This would seem to indicate that those who get less than a grammar school training do not find their way into the business office. Since only 33 per cent of the younger office

[1] Adapted by permission from *A Survey of Junior Commercial Occupations in Sixteen States*, pp. 15, 17, 19–22, 24. The Federal Board for Vocational Education, June, 1920. This survey was prepared under the direction of F. G. Nichols.

workers left school before they completed the eighth grade, it is safe to conclude that specialized vocational commercial training cannot be justified below the eighth grade. A larger number had received one or more years of high school training than had received less than a full grammar school course. Of those who entered high school 53 per cent finished only one year; 28 per cent left at the end of the second year; 12 per cent remained through the third year; and 7 per cent finished the high school course.

It is evident that the 7 per cent who finished the high school course at seventeen years of age were above the average. These figures represent fairly normal conditions. About 40 per cent of those who enter high school leave at the end of the first year in most cities. An additional 25 per cent are gone at the end of the second year. The mortality at the end of the third year is always small, representing those who withdraw because of sickness, unexpected economic pressure in the home, removal to another city, etc. The failures are, for the most part, weeded out by the beginning of the third year.

Of the number of junior workers who had received some business training, 36 per cent were trained in high schools; 13 per cent in private business schools; 20 per cent in continuation schools; and the remainder in the junior high school, evening school, and corporation school. These facts are of no special significance when taken alone. They may become highly important, however, when considered in connection with the positions held by these workers, and the kind of training they had received. Of those who had received business training, 37 per cent had studied bookkeeping three months or more; 37 per cent had studied business arithmetic for that period of time or longer; 46 per cent were enrolled in the business writing class three or more months; 29 per cent of this group studied business English at least three months; 27½ per cent were enrolled in the shorthand classes for a like period; and 41 per cent had received at least three months' instruction on the typewriter. A negligible number had been instructed for this length of time in office practice, office machine work, salesman-

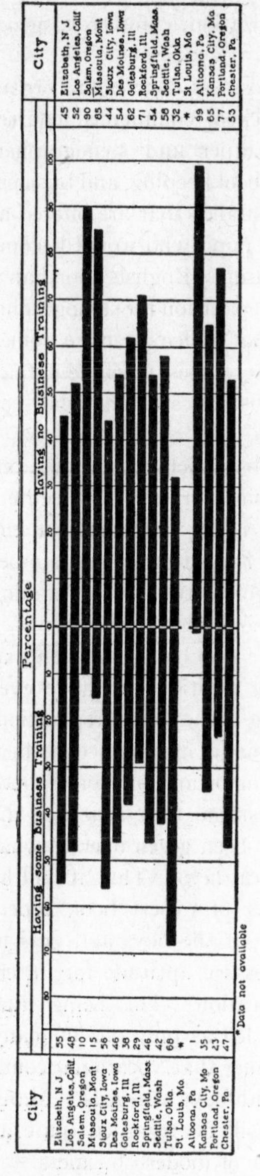

FIG. 13.—Special business training of young workers

FIG. 14.—Business training young workers have received

ship, commercial law, business organization, commercial geography, and junior clerical work.

It is apparent that elementary business courses are organized like the more advanced high school commercial courses with two positions in mind—bookkeeper and stenographer. Business writing, business arithmetic, bookkeeping, and business English make up the usual group of studies that are offered as an adequate training for the younger pupil who would become a bookkeeper or clerical assistant. Business English, shorthand, and typewriting represent the usual preparation for stenographic work. It is, perhaps, significant that office practice, office machine, and commercial geography courses reach less than 5 per cent of our younger group of business students who seek employment at an early age.

A careful study of the list of jobs which these boys and girls now have reveals the fact that business training that centers around bookkeeping and stenography is not functioning in the cases of young office workers. Again it is apparent that a number of common office employments afford opportunities for training comparable with bookkeeping and stenographic employments.

Only a very small number of those who have had the usual type of business training are holding positions, or have ever held positions, for which such training is the best preparation. The real full-fledged bookkeeper is but one of many office workers and his work has become really more important and correspondingly difficult and exacting. At the same time much of the detail or routine part of his work has been given over to what may be called general or special clerical help. Thus it will be seen that a relatively smaller number of expert bookkeepers are required and that only a fraction of the boys and girls in our commercial classes have the necessary aptitude for, interest in, or desire to train for this vocation. This being true, bookkeeping will henceforth be regarded as only one of many very much worth while types of training that vocational counselors must have in mind in dealing with boys and girls. Many other types of commercial training will be regarded quite as important in meeting the requirements of modern business.

Again, the stenographer, too, must be regarded as but one type of office employee. The prevalent idea that to be trained for office work one must have the ability to write shorthand

TABLE XXI

Distribution of Junior Workers by Positions and Businesses

Positions	Retail	Wholesale	Commission	Manufacturing	Transportation and Telegraph	Public Utilities	Government	Financial and Insurance	Professional	Theatrical	Publishing and Printing	Hotel	Foreign Trade	Totals
Messenger	236	51	9	134	115	145	30	100	34	0	14	0	2	870
General clerk	163	36	9	82	47	27	5	58	12	0	6	0	2	447
Cashier	50	6	0	1	0	1	9	1	1	2	0	0	0	71
Timekeeper	1	3	0	16	2	2	0	0	0	0	1	0	0	25
Shipping clerk	27	18	0	9	1	0	0	0	0	0	1	0	0	56
Receiving clerk	7	4	0	3	0	1	0	0	0	0	0	0	0	15
Stock clerk	106	31	0	27	11	6	0	1	0	0	0	0	0	182
Switchboard operator	9	0	0	10	4	218	0	2	1	0	2	0	0	246
File clerk	53	43	3	30	63	17	3	16	2	0	4	0	0	234
Mail clerk	32	29	2	13	12	10	50	16	2	0	5	0	0	171
Bundle wrapper	152	23	0	16	0	2	0	0	0	0	1	0	0	194
Delivery-wagon driver	85	11	0	6	0	3	5	0	0	0	1	0	0	111
Typist	9	8	2	13	3	17	3	1	11	0	6	0	0	73
Stenographer	22	16	1	19	4	3	1	3	16	0	3	0	0	88
Dictaphone operator	1	1	0	1	0	0	0	0	0	0	0	0	0	3
Bookkeeper	10	2	0	6	0	7	0	5	3	0	0	0	0	33
Entry clerk	6	1	1	0	2	0	0	2	0	0	4	0	0	16
Ledger clerk	3	2	0	9	2	0	0	0	1	0	0	0	0	17
Cost clerk	0	1	0	1	0	0	0	0	0	0	0	0	0	2
Billing clerk	11	5	0	4	1	7	0	1	0	0	0	0	0	29
Salesman (retail store)	342	1	0	1	0	0	0	0	0	0	0	0	0	344
Bookkeeping-machine operator	0	0	0	1	0	0	0	1	0	0	0	0	0	2
Calculating-machine operator	10	1	0	6	3	0	1	7	0	0	0	0	0	28
Duplicating-machine operator	1	2	0	9	2	6	0	0	2	0	0	0	0	22
Addressograph operator	2	3	1	3	1	0	0	1	1	0	0	0	0	12
Miscellaneous machine operator	15	0	0	4	0	0	4	0	0	0	0	0	0	23
Statement clerk	0	0	0	0	0	0	0	1	0	0	0	0	0	1
Collector	4	0	0	0	0	3	0	0	0	0	0	0	0	7
Miscellaneous	87	26	31	42	1	25	1	3	6	0	13	10	0	245
Totals	1,444	324	59	466	274	500	112	219	92	2	61	10	4	3,567

must be put aside. That business schools receive calls for stenographers or bookkeepers only does not alter the situation. The training of these two types of office workers is their specialty and business men think of them only in this connection. Frequently they camouflage their calls because a call for a clerical worker, a file clerk, a cashier, a cost clerk, etc., would get but little consideration. How often the statement is made, "Technical skill in bookkeeping doesn't count; what I want is a girl or boy with a head." It would pay any private or public business school to ascertain just what the members of its 1915 class are doing now and compare their present occupations with the office records of their placement to see what has happened. This refers especially to the younger students whose placements are within the restricted range of this survey.

It may be significant that of the number of boys and girls included in this part of the inquiry, only 13.6 per cent of those who had received instruction in bookkeeping had ever been employed in bookkeeping work. Only 12 per cent of those who were trained in shorthand had enjoyed the distinction of being employed as a stenographer. These facts may prove nothing, but they surely furnish food for thought and challenge business educators to dig a little deeper into their problem in the hope of discovering even greater opportunities of service than have hitherto manifested themselves.

D. Some Challenging Statements[1]

1. Not more than 2 per cent of commercial workers under eighteen years of age are stenographers and yet the majority of such young people who take business courses study shorthand.

2. Only about 1 per cent of such workers are properly classified as bookkeepers, while practically all business course students devote much of their time to bookkeeping. We are not getting all we should out of this subject and the time devoted to it should be shortened, or the teaching method should be revised.

3. There are at least three dozen commercial occupations that are worthy of serious consideration in any comprehensive

[1] Adapted from a pamphlet by F. G. Nichols, based on findings of the Special Committee on Commercial Education, 1920. Later published as part of *Survey of Junior Commercial Occupations in Sixteen States*.

plan for giving business training. Commercial teachers are not for the most part concerned about more than a bare half dozen subjects in their thinking. Three of these dominate all elementary commercial education plans to the positive detriment of many boys and girls.

4. General clerical positions bring young office employees into contact with more people, reveal a wider range of aptitudes, offer better opportunities for advancement, and furnish employment to a larger proportion of our commercially trained young men and women than do stenographic and bookkeeping positions. Special office practice, however, is usually reserved for the few who survive to the end of the long four year course.

5. In some cities at least a third of the commercial occupations listed offer salary returns quite equal to those made in shorthand and bookkeeping positions. Such jobs are not to be sneered at by those who would offer commercial training programs that will meet the vocational needs of all who are entitled to consideration.

6. Timekeepers, receiving clerks, and entry clerks frequently earn more money than assistant bookkeepers among such younger office workers.

7. Office machine operating requires brains and training, public opinion to the contrary notwithstanding. To be a good calculating machine operator one should be fairly well trained in the accurate manipulation of figures. So far we have been quite content to "demonstrate the machine," rather than to teach picked boys and girls to operate it.

8. "Telephone girls" require training, get good wages, have good conditions under which to work, and are not without promotional possibilities. In numbers employed this occupation is not far behind the other better known business employments. Some girls are especially qualified for this type of service.

9. The retail store not only claims a very large proportion of our very young people, but offers exceptional opportunities for future advancement. However only a small fraction of young store workers actually sell goods. Furthermore only a small fraction stay long enough to become salespeople.

10. The file clerk has an opportunity to render exceptional service for which a high salary may be expected. Contrary to popular belief it is not a "blind alley" job. In our commercial courses we fail to do more than expose our boys and girls to this important subject which is especially well adapted to certain types of young people.

11. In at least one city twelve of the occupations listed offer "special opportunities for advancement." All vocational training should have this feature definitely in mind.

12. Most young people sense the need for more of what may be called a "general business training," as distinguished from "special training."

13. By enabling those who have dropped out of school to make up what they have lost, the continuation school is sending many back to the all-day school. What does this suggest in the way of training?

14. A modified type of business education must be provided for boys and girls between fourteen and seventeen years of age if their vocational needs are to be met.

15. General training, motivated by commercial applications, must be furnished along with any specialized business training.

16. The demand for traditional types of business training by young people who can not profit by receiving such training must be converted into a demand for more suitable types of business training by educating both the boys and girls and their parents in the real vocational needs that have been established by ample evidence.

E. A Senior Commercial Occupations Survey[1]

The data summarized in the report were collected by survey committees in the following cities: Baltimore, Md.; Battle

[1] Adapted from a *Preliminary Report on the Senior Occupations Survey.* The Federal Board for Vocational Education, April, 1922. These advance sheets were made available through the courtesy of E. W. Barnhart, chief of the Commercial Service, Federal Board for Vocational Education.

The tables referred to in this statement appear in the original, but are so extended as to make their inclusion here inadvisable.—Author.

Creek, Mich.; Boston, Mass.; Dallas, Texas.; Los Angeles, Cal.; Meriden, Conn.; Springfield, Mass.; Tacoma, Wash.

These cities include three of our very largest, three of intermediate size and two of the small (35,000). So the figures are truly representative of commercial occupations throughout a wide range of city conditions.

A CLASSIFICATION OF GENERAL OFFICE POSITIONS*

EXECUTIVE

- General
  - General Manager
  - Office Manager
- Department Executives and Assistants
  - Accountant
    - Auditor
    - Comptroller
    - Cost Accountant
  - Advertising Manager
  - Credit Manager
  - Employment Manager
  - Personnel Director
  - Sales Manager
  - Traffic Manager
  - Purchasing Agent
- Minor Executives and Executive Assistants
  - Chief Clerk
  - Head Bookkeeper
  - Head Stenographer
  - Head, Mail Room
  - Division Head
  - Chief File Clerk
  - Supervisor, etc.

CLERICAL†

- Stenographic
  - Stenographer
  - Dictaphone Operator
  - Ediphone Operator
  - Stenotypist
  - Secretary
- Bookkeeping
  - Accountant
  - Bookkeeper
  - Bookkeeping-Cashier
  - Entry Clerk
  - Ledger Clerk
  - Journal Clerk
- Recording Clerks
  - Bill Clerk
  - Collector
  - Cost Clerk
  - Invoice Clerk
  - Order Clerk
  - Price Clerk
  - Payroll Clerk
  - Statistical
  - Stores
  - Time Clerk
  - Voucher
  - General Clerk

MACHINE OPERATORS

- Addressing Machine
  - Addressograph
  - Bellknap
  - Elliott
- Billing Machine
  - Elliott-Fisher
  - Remington-Wahl
  - Underwood
- Bookkeeping Machine
  - Burroughs
  - Elliott-Fisher
  - Ellis
  - Remington-Wahl
  - Underwood
- Calculating Machine
  - Burroughs Calculator
  - Comptometer
  - Marchant
  - Monroe
- Card Punching Machine
- Duplicators
- Graphotype
- Multigraph
- Mimeograph
- Photostat
- Telephone Switchboard

* Special types of business not included in this list.

† Special clerical positions in particular businesses not included.

EXECUTIVE	CLERICAL†	MACHINE OPERATORS
PROFESSIONAL AND SEMI-PROFESSIONAL‡	Non-recording Clerks	Tabulating Machine
Certified Public Accountant	Cashier (Coin)	Typewriter
Senior Accountant	Errand boy	
Junior Accountant	File	
Business Service Experts	Mail	
Advertising	Messenger	
Systematizing	Office boy	
Traffic	Page	
Employment	Receiving	
Correspondence	Shipping	
Translating	Stock	
Commercial Engineer		

† Special clerical positions in particular businesses not included.

‡ Called upon to render special services occasionally in the general office.

LESSONS FROM THE SURVEY FOR COMMERCIAL EDUCATION

The most striking characteristic of the facts thus far collected is the overwhelming predominance of the general recording group of office workers: at all ages for men, from eighteen to thirty, this group contains more than half, at times five-eighths, of the men office workers; at all ages for the senior women this group leads, though never in so great a preponderance as with the men.

The general clerk is the foundation of this group. What he does is a composite of all the occupations listed in the recording and non-recording groups with perhaps an occasional bit of the bookkeeping group also. On the whole schooling for the general clerk is schooling for this group. The general clerk must have a knowledge of all kinds of office work and the best methods for doing the great range of tasks which falls to the all-round office worker. The general clerk is not buried in a highly specialized field; he helps everywhere in the office so if his preparation is broad enough, he has the greatest opportunity to rise, to become a supervisor, an office manager, or, in time perhaps, an even higher executive. Obviously then the commercial course should definitely include and train for the range of work and promotion which the general clerk has before him.

The training of a general clerk should be that which gives the widest possible knowledge of business and the highest attainable degree of skill in certain kinds of office work. The general clerk should know what services are available from every business organization—telephone, telegraph, express, post office, railroad, bank, insurance, credit bureau and similar business service companies—and more important still, know exactly how to use each service with all the common precautions observed by careful business men. Such a clerk must know how to use office reference books, guides, directories, rating books and should know how to read the daily financial and market reports. For his work as a mail clerk, a cashier, a file clerk, the general office worker must be skilled in folding and handling large volumes of mail; know how to count, stack, and handle coin and currency; as well as know how to file and find the papers entrusted to him. His training must give him familiarity with all the usual or unusual business papers, orders, invoices, statements, bills of lading, domestic and foreign, and prepare him for all the everyday problems associated with making out and handling these papers. A properly prepared clerk will have a penmanship flexible enough to permit him to write a heavy hand on checks, a minute hand on 3×5 record cards, a legible hand in pencil on duplicating forms whether he is sitting down or standing up; he must have also a knowledge of arithmetic extending from the work of a billing clerk to that of a payroll or statistical clerk. In order to do all this work such a clerk must be familiar with the tools of the office, the typewriter, adding machines, numbering machines, stamp affixer; kinds of papers, of pens, or ink, and the whole world of common office appliances. For his success as a worker as well as for possible promotion, he should be acquainted with some of the problems in managing and conducting an office—especially those centering about directing workers and fixing wages and developing incentives for increased efficiency. A limited knowledge of elementary bookkeeping, enough to have him understand the use of the cash book, the ledgers and how to post could be included.

An analysis of the bookkeeping texts now in general use and a study of the usual methods of teaching bookkeeping show that the bookkeeping courses commonly given do not prepare for the work of the general clerk. The bookkeeping as customarily presented is too narrow; it has too strictly in mind the actual keeper of the ledger. The texts make no provision for teaching the extent or use of common general business services—the telephone, the railroad, or even the bank—nor are the transactions of any one kind sufficient to afford the variety of problems necessary. For example: to teach all that a general clerk should know about filling out railroad bills of lading, negotiable and non-negotiable bills, covering shipments of all kinds to all points, is not the purpose of the bookkeeping text; hence the three or four now required to be filled out by the average text do not give sufficient, nor varied enough training in using so common a form. The bookkeeping course as now organized requires too much time for financial statements and the theory of debit and credit and does not devote enough time or attention to giving accurate, general business information or to developing definite office skill. Counting college currency does not develop a knowledge of how to handle money, taking inventory of cans of corn in the shape of tiny pieces of paper does not prepare a pupil for a real inventory.

The bookkeeping may have a place in our commercial education but its place is after the general office training; not in place of it. The bookkeeping should be viewed as a specialized kind of office work which to be intelligently done should be based upon a wide knowledge of business services and subsidiary office work. It may be a proper field for specialization in the high schools. It is not now, and the present teaching materials—texts, incoming and outgoing papers, etc.—do not permit it to be an introductory business course fitting for general office work which the sixteen to twenty year boy and girl are called upon to do when employed as messengers, file, stock, or other clerical workers such as those listed under the recording and non-recording groups, though summed up in the work of the general clerk.

The changes in the high school commercial course needed to give the general office training outlined are not extensive. In place of the present bookkeeping course in the first two years of the high school there might be:

FIRST YEAR

1. An elementary course in Business Procedure and Practices.

2. An Elementary Office Practice and Information course one-half year on a double period basis.

SECOND YEAR

3. An Advanced Office Practice and Information course one-half year on a double period basis.

4. An Elementary Office and Commercial Organization course one-half year on a double period basis.

Along with these unit courses should go the penmanship, arithmetic, English and economic geography usually taught but each should be modified in order to contribute to the utmost to the preparation for general office work which business demands. Typewriting would be a desirable elective here.

General clerical training will be far more valuable for the large number of pupils who drop out of the eighth, ninth, and tenth grades than the smattering of unassimilated bookkeeping which now furnishes their equipment for earning a living. The Introduction to Business Procedure and the Elementary Office Practices and Information are far more suitable to the junior high school pupils than the bookkeeping or shorthand now being introduced. For either the junior or senior high schools the courses as outlined are constructed on a unit basis each unit of which is valuable for the boy or girl who must drop out when it is completed and each advanced unit of which tends to attract the children in the lower classes and so to hold them in school.

STENOGRAPHY FOR GIRLS

A study of the percentage of each age-group in the stenographic group shows rather conclusively that there is little place in business for the stenographer who is less than eighteen, and that the greatest number employed are between twenty and twenty-four. As eighteen is approximately the average age of graduation from the high school, it is evident that there is little vocational value in giving shorthand instruction below the third year of the high school course. The first two years can be used to far better advantage in giving a broad knowledge of business practices and office work which will give the immature and unexperienced high school girls some background of general business information on which to place the shorthand with its constant assumption of an accurate knowledge of the business situations presented in the dictation given. The occupational figures afford small consolation for those who want to have stenography taught in the first two years of the high school course or in the junior high school so as to turn out stenographers at sixteen or less for whom the business man has little use, and then only because they are cheap workers.

STENOGRAPHY FOR BOYS

The percentage of the total number of men between eighteen and thirty employed as stenographers would seem to indicate that there was some justification for teaching shorthand to boys. However, the comparatively small number of men included in the table raises a doubt about the relative position of stenography as a man's job especially when occupational figures from other sources indicate that men constitute less than 5 per cent of all the stenographers and that only a very small percentage of men commercial workers are found in stenographic positions. In general it seems safe to say that stenography is of real vocational value to a boy in two cases only: First, to follow as a profession—as a public or court reporter; second, to use in obtaining a position close to an important executive who will recognize the superior abilities of his stenographer by a rapid promotion to a supervisory or executive position. This last justification is based upon two rather slender assumptions: first, that the boy is of such extraordinarily superior ability that he will be reasonably certain of promotion once he finds the right office; second, that this marvel will find a position near an executive ready and willing to promote him to the awaiting vacancy. In either case only the unusual boy should be admitted to the shorthand class.

THE COMBINATION COURSE

Curiously enough among the returns from 2600 commercial workers all of whom were canvassed by commercial teachers, there has been found but one stenographer-bookkeeper. Evidently the commercial teachers who had advised or required boys and girls to take bookkeeping and shorthand found but little to justify their recommendations. Combination courses for boys are, with the exception of the boy who takes shorthand as an extra subject, entirely unjustified as preparation for modern business positions. A few girls may find employment in small offices where a combination training is needed, but a good general office training will suffice for all the bookkeeping work to be done in so small an office. Stenography in the cities included in this survey is one field; bookkeeping is another; and there is small justification for requiring either boys or girls to prepare for two distinct fields.

BOOKKEEPING

The ages at which the bookkeeping group employs a considerable percentage of workers—20–27 for men, 22–27 for women—seems to indicate that bookkeeping is viewed by business men as a very responsible task to be given only to experienced workers, preferably to those who have had experience in their own office and who have had an opportunity of learning the system and routine developed in that office.

The absence of any large number, or percentage, of bookkeepers below the age of twenty would seem to point still further to the fact that technical vocational bookkeeping should be given in the last years of the high school course only. The schoolmen who teach all the boys and girls of fourteen bookkeeping, that only a small number will use vocationally, and then only after six to eight years, certainly are optimists in the value of cold storage education.

RETAIL STORE SELLING

Retail store selling and related positions hold third place for the senior group of commercial workers, second place for the juniors and second place for both groups combined. If the financial returns in store work are equal to those from shorthand, bookkeeping or general office work for women, this field is evidently worth entering.

Training courses for retail store service as generally organized in the high schools have been confined to the last two years.

The largest field for commercial workers in this country is found in the retail trade. Store work for men holds in this survey a comparatively small place, but this is largely because few stores employing men were included in the survey.

MACHINE OPERATING

Machine operating seems to be pre-eminently a woman's field. The modern office uses typewriters, calculating, duplicating and bookkeeping machines to a very large extent.

Queerly enough in the development of commercial education in this country, the demand for short course instruction in the public schools has never been met by the development of machine operating courses. The operation of some of the more complex office machines, such as the typewriter-bookkeeping machines, should be considered as distinct vocations and, if training is given in the public schools for these fields, they should be treated as separate occupations.

TRAINING FOR SUPERVISORY AND EXECUTIVE POSITIONS

There is an interesting difference in the field of executive positions so far as relative number of men and women employed are concerned. Only a very small percentage of the women seem to rise to executive positions and then rather late. Men are found in executive positions in larger numbers and at much earlier ages. The reasons for this are not worth while discussing, but the schools should recognize this fact in the type of training given the boy.

A large number of high school students—many not in the commercial department—expect to enter business upon graduation and then, through family connections, in a short time to rise to supervisory or executive positions and eventually become independent business managers. The number of students who have this program in mind can be readily ascertained in any school by checking the number of academic graduates who enter business without having had more than a course or so in the commercial department. For many of these students the commercial department with its routine clerical bookkeeping work, is unattractive and often belittled by family and business associates. These boys will not go to college and they will enter business with no understanding of the fundamental principles which underlie our present business structure. Their equipment in this respect is but little inferior to that of the graduates from the commercial department, for no place in our secondary schools has been found where the social-economic subjects which give an insight into the organization and structure of our social and economic life are taught.

The need for subjects from this field becomes all the more striking when one seeks to find out what becomes of our high school graduates after a business apprenticeship of from five to ten years. Those who are still found in the field of commerce after this time are scattered throughout the whole field, but only those whose training and aptitudes have fitted them for promotion have risen to the higher positions. Only those who have gained, either through schooling or experience, an insight into the principles which underlie the structure and functioning of our modern business organization will be able to take an intelligent part in business, civic and social life and become intelligent and constructive critics of the faults they find.

Considering the need for a broader preparation in this field of economics, of business and social life, there is undoubtedly urgent need for the development of a general business course in the commercial department of the high school which will offer as electives, during the third and fourth years, half-year courses suited to high school students in the following fields: finance and financial organization of modern society, marketing and market organization, labor and personnel problems and relations, elementary business management problems, elementary economics, elementary psychology stressing individual relationships.

Of course these new subjects will accompany, not supersede, any specialized vocational courses in bookkeeping, stenography or retail selling which may be offered in the third and fourth years of the high school. These are to be the related commercial subjects which will furnish the background for the technical commercial courses. They may crowd out some of the college preparatory courses for the pupils in the commercial department, but if they do it will be because their intrinsic worth for those who will not go to college justifies the change. Certainly their holding power for commercial department students will exceed that of the college preparatory subjects which they replace. In the program of the general high school student who does not take the commercial course these subjects will function as social science subjects and should replace some of the non-usable college preparatory subjects ordinarily taken. The teaching of these subjects in the secondary schools has been demonstrated to be entirely within the range of high school pupils by schools which have been experimenting with some of these subjects and a program for the development of these social science subjects in the secondary schools, including the teaching of these subjects, has been recommended by several committees of prominent educators who are studying the expansion of the social science subjects in the high school.

The purpose of these subjects is not found in their deferred values but in their possibilities for immediate realization. These subjects will function at once in giving the students an understanding of the business world in which they work. Beginners who have a knowledge of these fields will be better employees, more sympathetic and willing co-operators, more discriminating in absorbing and interpreting their daily experiences, more intelligent citizens when passing upon the social and economic issues, and finally somewhat prepared for the problems to be solved by the independent business manager.

EVIDENCE OF TYPE 4. DIFFERENT DEMANDS FOR THE SEXES IN COMMERCIAL OCCUPATIONS

A. The Evidence of a Private Survey in 1917–18 on Different Demands for Boys and Girls[1]

The following table shows that high-school principals have observed business men's requirements to be quite different for boys and girls. As this table indicates, nearly two-thirds of the schools reporting on this question indicated that a difference has been noted between the requirements in business for the sexes. In spite of this fact, the commercial course has persisted in giving the same work for both boys and girls.

TABLE XXII

Observations of Principals Concerning Business Men's Requirements of Boys and Girls (66 Schools Reporting)

Noting Different Requirements of Boys and Girls		Noting No Different Requirements of Boys and Girls	
Number	Percentage	Number	Percentage
42	63.4	24	36.6

Some of the replies indicating the differences which have been noticed in business requirements are interesting and instructive and are quoted below: "Girls are wanted mostly as stenographers and bookkeepers and are expected to merely follow directions. Boys are expected to learn to exercise judgment and initiative and advance in the business." "Boys are expected to grow up with the business; girls are expected to remain in same position until they drop off into the troubled sea of matrimony; otherwise requirements alike."

[1] This material is reprinted from a monograph by the author. *A Survey of Commercial Education in the Public High Schools of the United States*, pp. 46–47. University of Chicago, 1919.

It is interesting to notice how definitely these comments fit into the conclusions made in the Cleveland survey, where one of the summaries on business education for boys reads as follows: "Boys' training looks forward to both clerical work and business administration; but as clerical work is a preparation for business and is likely to occupy the first few years of wage-earning, training should aim especially to meet the needs of clerical positions."

This same view of the need of training for administration for boys is expressed in other phrasing in replies received: "Boys, initiative; girls, routine." "Business men do not require stenography of boys so generally as of girls." "Find little difference; but Miss C—— says they will take a worse boy than girl for the same job." "Most business men want boys who can eventually become salesmen." "Girls for stenographic positions. Boys for other positions." "Greater initiative demanded of boys." "Looking for possible salesmen or executives in hiring boys." "Business men would make the central aim of commercial training of boys the fitting of them for managerial and executive positions, while they think of girls as only worthy of high-grade office positions as stenographers and bookkeepers."

Such a statement as that employers are "more lenient with girls" and the impression that "business men seem to be more severe regarding punctuality and accuracy with boys than with girls" remind one of Miss Stevens' quotation from *Potash and Perlmutter:* "Some lady bookkeepers come to the store so late and goes home so early that they hardly allow themselves enough time downtown to go out and eat lunch at all." "If most lady bookkeepers would spend half so much time over their books as they do over their hair we would get a trial balance once in a while without calling in one of them satisfied public accountants."

One school principal seems to summarize the case very well with the statement: "Generally if you can say a boy has pep and a girl is quiet, you have satisfied the business man."

B. THE EVIDENCE OF THE FEDERAL BOARD'S SURVEY[1]

About 56 per cent of the total number of workers canvassed are boys, and 44 per cent are girls.

It is interesting to note that only 8.9 per cent of the total number of boys and girls included are fourteen years of age. Of the boys only 11.8 per cent are in the fourteen year old group, while but 5 per cent of the girls are in this group.

Of the total number only 22 per cent are in the fifteen year group; 26.6 per cent of the boys and 16.3 per cent of the girls are but fifteen years of age.

Of the entire number 33 per cent are sixteen years of age; 32.7 per cent of the boys and 32.9 per cent of the girls are in this age group.

The remainder of the entire group, or 36.1 per cent are in the seventeen year age group; 28.7 per cent of the boys and 45.7 per cent of the girls are seventeen years of age.

From the analysis of the figures given on page 164 it is evident that fewer girls than boys enter commercial employments at fourteen years of age. The same is true of the fifteen year age. There are more sixteen year old boys than there are sixteen year old girls in business positions. This is reversed, however, in the seventeen year age group.

In the future it is quite likely that differentiated business training will be given to boys and girls. While boys and girls are employed for similar work at the outset, later promotions tend to draw them apart. Their ultimate job objectives may suggest specially adapted courses for either group. At any rate, special vocational training for boys is needed earlier in the curriculum than it is for girls. In states where the continuation school law takes effect gradually, those who are making plans for the fourteen year old group next year, the fifteen year old group the following year, and so on, will find in these figures some evidence as to the probable size of their classes and

[1] Adapted from *Survey of Junior Commercial Occupations in Sixteen States*, pp. 35-37. The Federal Board for Vocational Education, June, 1920. This survey was prepared under the direction of F. G. Nichols.

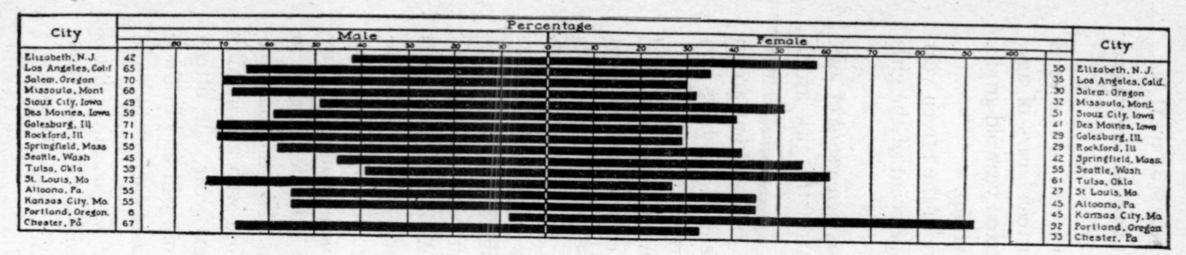

FIG. 15.—Percentage distribution according to sex of junior workers in indicated cities

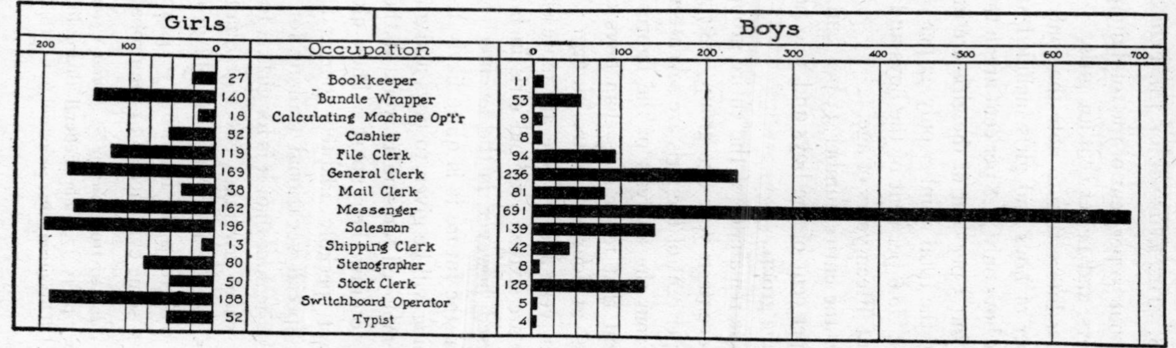

FIG. 16.—Relative importance of fourteen positions

the division of the enrollment by sexes. Wherever the numbers enrolled and the work they perform seems to justify it, boys and girls should be enrolled in separate classes. For example, girls will not be interested in the Shipping Clerk Course and boys can scarcely be expected to require the Dictaphone Course. Every attempt should be made to meet the individual as well as the group needs of all continuation school boys and girls.

TABLE XXIII

Distribution of Junior Workers by Age and Sex

Positions Held by Boys and Girls from 14 to 18 Years of Age	Boys				Girls				Positions Paying as Well as Bookkeeper and Stenographer Marked X*	Positions Offering Special Opportunity for Advancement Marked A*
	14	15	16	17	14	15	16	17		
Messenger	110	229	228	124	16	32	69	45	XXXX	AAAAAA
General clerk	21	56	74	85	8	34	50	77	XXXXXXX	AAAAAAAA
Cashier	0	1	0	7	3	14	18	17	XXX	AAA
Timekeeper	0	2	5	6	0	2	2	2	XX	AA
Shipping clerk	4	7	18	13	0	0	0	13	XXXX	AAA
Receiving clerk	1	0	2	7	0	0	1	4	XX	....
Stock clerk	2	37	42	47	3	16	10	21	XXX	AAAAAA
Switchboard operator	0	1	2	2	0	11	67	110	XXX	AA
File clerk	2	18	39	35	4	18	40	57	XXXXX	AAAAA
Mail clerk	4	18	30	29	2	8	13	15	XX	AA
Bundle wrapper	7	15	17	14	3	31	55	51	X	A
Delivery wagon driver	14	26	36	22	0	0	0	0	XX	A
Typist	0	1	0	3	0	4	15	33	X	AA
Stenographer	0	1	1	6	0	8	24	48	....	AAA
Dictaphone operator	1	2	0	0	0	0	1	0	....	A
Bookkeeper	0	1	1	9	0	0	8	19	....	AAA
Entry clerk	1	1	2	6	1	1	1	6	XX	A
Ledger clerk	0	0	2	2	0	2	3	0	X	A
Cost clerk	0	0	0	0	0	0	1	0	....	....
Billing clerk	0	0	4	7	0	3	8	7	XX	AAAA
Salesman (retail store)	14	25	51	49	14	28	61	93	XXXX	AAAAA
Bookkeeping machine operator	0	0	0	1	0	0	1	0	X	....
Calculating machine operator	1	4	2	2	1	1	3	13	X	A
Duplicating machine operator	1	3	4	5	0	0	4	5	XX	....
Addressograph operator	0	1	4	1	0	2	2	2	X	....
Miscellaneous machine operator	0	0	0	2	0	3	5	10	....	....
Statement clerk	0	0	0	1	0	0	0	0	....	....
Collector	0	2	0	5	0	0	0	0	....	....
Miscellaneous	36	40	44	38	18	22	20	22	....	....
Totals	219	491	608	528	73	240	482	670	3,311	....

* Each *X* indicates that a city reported the indicated position as paying quite as well as bookkeeper or stenographer. Thus, four cities checked "messenger." Each *A* indicates that one city specified the indicated job as having exceptional promotional possibilities. Thus six cities so marked "messenger."

EVIDENCE OF TYPE 5. ANALYSIS OF JOBS IN COMMERCIAL OCCUPATIONS

A. The Purpose of Job Analysis and an Example[1]

The first element in the selection of applicants for given jobs is the determination of the human qualifications necessary for their successful performance. This is predicated upon thorough study of a job content. . . . . Often job analysis reveals that certain qualifications which have long been regarded as necessary in applicants for given jobs are not essential; and vice versa, it is often discovered that qualifications necessary to the successful performance of certain work have been entirely overlooked. In making job specifications care should be taken to distinguish between the essential and the desirable qualifications for jobs.

It is interesting to compare the human qualifications looked for in applicants for the same job by different employment managers, and then to check these against the qualifications determined upon by job analysis. The following list shows the variety of qualifications desired and indicates which of them seems, as a result of job analysis, really essential for the jobs in question:

Position	Qualifications Desired by Five Employment Managers		Qualifications Determined by Careful Job Analysis
File Clerk	Accuracy	4	Alertness
	Neatness	2	Accuracy
	Industry	1	Love of Monotony
	Intelligence	1	Loyalty to Work
	Concentration	1	Good Memory
	Carefulness	1	
	Judgment	1	
	Speed	1	
	Orderliness	1	
	Appearance	1	
	Character	1	
	Experience	1	
	Training	1	

[1] Adapted by permission from the *Ninth Annual Proceedings of the National Association of Corporation Schools* (1921), pp. 216–18.

Position	Qualifications Desired by Five Employment Managers		Qualifications Determined by Careful Job Analysis
Hand Bookkeeper (Bank)	Speed	4	Accuracy
	Experience	4	Penmanship
	Accuracy	3	Neatness
	Penmanship	3	Reliability
	Neatness	2	Knowledge of Principles of Bookkeeping
	Character	2	
	Intelligence	1	
	Dependability	1	
	Industry	1	
	Concentration	1	
	Reliability	1	
	High School Education	1	
Money Counter	Accuracy	4	Accuracy
	Speed	3	Speed
	Integrity	3	Patience
	Concentration	2	Trustworthiness
	Patience	1	
	Vigilance	1	
	Neatness	1	
	Industry	1	
	Appearance	1	
	Health	1	
	Experience	1	
Typist	Accuracy	5	Accuracy
	Speed	4	Speed
	Neatness	3	Neatness
	Experience	3	Good Memory
	Character	2	
	Intelligence	1	
	Dexterity	1	
	Education	1	
	Appearance	1	
	Industry	1	

TABLE XXIV

An Analysis of Clerical and Office Positions

General Nature of the Position	Education Required	Experience Required	Personal Qualities	Intelligence	Age	Examples
Executive	Graduation from a recognized college or university. Lack of education may in some cases be compensated for by high intelligence or skill as shown in previous experience	Four or more years' experience in the general line in which he is to be employed or in a closely allied line	Executive ability, initiative, originality, co-operativeness, ability to develop men, reliability	Superior	26–45	Sub-division managers and up
Minor executive clerical—A position involving executive supervision of a non-routine section where employee must in addition to having executive ability be experienced in the work of his section and position as administrative assistant to higher officers	*a*) Graduation from a recognized college or university *b*) Two years college or equivalent	*a*) Three or more years' experience in the general line in which he is to be employed or in a closely allied line *b*) Four or more years' experience	Executive ability, initiative, reliability, co-operativeness, ability to develop men	High average	35–40	Section heads, administrative assistants, assistant division and sub-division managers
Special and supervisory—A position involving (*a*) supervision of routine or clerical work where work is extensive enough so that supervision is the main feature of the position, (*b*) work on special assignments of a varied nature, (*c*) work requiring training or experience of an unusual nature, (*d*) work involving unusual responsibility	*a*) Graduation from a recognized college or university *b*) High school education	*a*) One or more years' experience *b*) Three or more years' experience	Reliability, accuracy, initiative, co-operativeness	High average	24–35	Heads of sections where work is purely clerical and routine, confidential clerks, clerks of special assignments, first class secretaries, accountants
Senior clerical—A clerical position of trust and responsibility involving (*a*) knowledge of bookkeeping, accounting or statistics, (*b*) supervision of junior clerks, (*c*) expert stenography	*a*) Graduation from a recognized college or university *b*) High school education plus one year of business education or equivalent	*a*) Little or no experience *b*) One or more years' experience	Reliability, accuracy, neatness, speed, initiative	Average	21–30	Bookkeepers, ledger clerks, statistician, pricing and summary clerks, cost clerks, expert stenographers and secretaries

TABLE XXIV—*Continued*

General Nature of the Position	Education Required	Experience Required	Personal Qualities	Intelligence	Age	Examples
Junior clerk (A grade)—An office position requiring a skilled operator or an experienced clerk	Four years high school or two years high school and six months business school or equivalent	Six months or more experience in the same general line	Reliability, accuracy, neatness, speed	Low average	18–24	Experienced stenographers, Ediphone operators, stencil cutters, posting clerks
Junior clerk (B grade)—An office position of a semi-skilled nature requiring that the employee have mastered either through experience or special training the operation he is to perform	Two years high school and three months business school or equivalent	Enough experience to insure familiarity with the work done and rapid learning, except in the case of business course graduates specifically prepared for the positions they are to occupy	Reliability, accuracy, neatness, speed	Low average	18–22	Inexperienced stenographers, experienced typists, general clerks, subject classification
Novice clerical (A grade)—An office position of a simple routine nature which can be learned very readily by those who have passed through the grade below or have had some experience or schooling in machine operation and typing	Grammar school plus comptometry school or typist school	None if trained in comptometry school or typist school—otherwise same experience in the grade below	Reliability, accuracy, neatness	Low average	18–21	Comptometrist, inexperienced typist, experienced machine operators, first and second rater, clerk, proofreaders
Novice clerical (B grade)—An office position of a simple routine nature that can be satisfactorily learned by a minor in one or two weeks—position consisting mainly of one or more of the following: (*a*) alphabetical or numerical filing, (*b*) simple machine operation (adding, hectograph, mimeograph, addressograph, etc.), (*c*) simple checking, inspecting or sorting	Grammar school	None	Reliability, accuracy	Low average	16–19	Sorting clerks, inexperienced adding machine operators, deduction entry clerk, clock card checker, inexperienced file clerk
Messenger and office boys	Sixth grade	None	Reliability	Low	16 15 with age and school certificate	Messengers, office boys

B. Job Analysis of Junior Commercial Occupations of the Federal Board for Vocational Education[1]

In the job analysis charts which follow an attempt has been made to describe briefly the duties of each position and to indicate the training, both commercial and general, which junior commercial workers should receive. Promotion is more a matter of the quality of work done than it is of the kind of position in which the work is done. Promotional lines are not very well marked for junior commercial workers. There are, however, certain general directions in which boys and girls with special aptitudes may be expected to advance. Since these promotional lines are not very well defined for workers under eighteen years of age, the suggestions concerning advancement and promotional training are given in a separate part of each chart, under the heading "More remote objectives and training." This indicates that such promotional training as is suggested should be given to commercial workers over eighteen years of age in the evening school and other types of extension courses.

It is not claimed that the charts which follow are complete, nor do they represent an intensive piece of research work. They are intended to be suggestive to those who are concerned with the continuation-school problem and to stimulate continuation-school commercial teachers to such further investigation as may be required to develop necessary instruction material.

It should be emphasized again at this point that these charts are all based upon the data furnished in connection with commercial workers between the ages of fourteen and seventeen inclusive. Positions under the same name held by older commercial workers will show greater variety of duties and the need for more advanced training.

[1] Adapted by permission from *A Survey of Junior Commercial Occupations in Sixteen States*, pp. 42–52. The Federal Board for Vocational Education, June, 1920. This survey was made under the direction of F. G. Nichols.

TABLE XXV

Junior Commercial Occupations—Open to Boys and Girls under Eighteen Years of Age

Group 1—Clerical Type

No.	Job	Duties	Training Required		More Remote Objectives and Training	
			Commercial	Related	Promotional Line	Later Promotional Training
1	General clerk	(*a*) Answering telephone (*b*) Sorting and arranging vouchers (*c*) Prepare deposits and make them (*d*) Copy contracts (*e*) Filing (*f*) Typewrite from copy (*g*) Trace way-bills (R.R.) (*h*) Handle mail—in and out (*i*) Open and arrange mail (*j*) Meet callers and learn wants (*k*) Make notes and memoranda (*l*) Check orders (*m*) Make out bills	(*a*) Office practice (*b*) Business writing (*c*) Business arithmetic (*d*) Typewriting (*e*) Elementary business organization	(*a*) English (*b*) Physical education (*c*) Citizenship	(*a*) Supervisor of a group (*b*) Head file clerk (*c*) Office manager (*d*) Correspondent	(*a*) Business correspondence (*b*) Filing and systematizing (*c*) Employment management (*d*) Office management
2	Shipping clerk	(*a*) Prepare goods for shipping (*b*) Checking orders against invoices and shipping receipts (*c*) Check goods to see that all goods called for are in the shipment	(*a*) Business writing, including marking alphabet (*b*) Wrapping, boxing, and crating (*c*) Shipping practice	(*a*) English (*b*) Physical education (*c*) Geography—commercial	(*a*) Superintendent of shipping department (*b*) Salesman (*c*) Buyer	(*a*) Transportation; rail, truck, and water (*b*) Commercial law (*c*) Packing for shipment (for export) (*d*) Salesmanship (*e*) Foreman training (*f*) Employment management

TABLE XXV—*Continued*

No.	Job	Duties	Training Required		More Remote Objectives and Training	
			Commercial	Related	Promotional Line	Later Promotional Training
2–*Cont.*	Shipping clerk—*Cont.*	(*d*) Marking goods for shipment (*e*) Weighing shipments (*f*) Preparing freight bills (*g*) Looking up routes (*h*) Recording shipments made (*i*) Mailing shipment papers				
3	Receiving clerk	(*a*) Unpack goods received (*b*) Check merchandise received against invoice (*c*) Note condition of shipment when received (*d*) Checking up returned goods and notifying proper department (*e*) Be responsible for goods until removed from receiving room to storeroom or departments (*f*) Receipt for freight and express received	(*a*) Business writing (*b*) Business organization (*c*) Transportation (*d*) Merchandise	(*a*) English (*b*) Physical education (*c*) Geography — commercial (*d*) Citizenship	(*a*) Superintendent of receiving department (*b*) Salesman (*c*) Buyer	(*a*) Textiles and other merchandise (*b*) Commercial law (*c*) Salesmanship (*d*) Foreman training (*e*) Employment management

TABLE XXV—*Continued*

No.	Job	Duties	Training Required		More Remote Objectives and Training	
			Commercial	Related	Promotional Line	Later Promotional Training
4	Stock clerk	(*a*) Receiving merchandise and storing it until required (*b*) Checking it with buyer's order and invoices (*c*) Keeping stock records (*d*) Delivering new stock to departments as needed upon requisitions of department heads (*e*) Marking goods for identification (*f*) Filling orders for shipment direct from stock (*g*) Issue sample merchandise to salesman upon requisition and keep record of such items for the bookkeeping department (*h*) Keep record of returned goods when restored to stock (*i*) Prepare inventory from stock records and check with merchandise as required	(*a*) Business writing (*b*) Business organization (*c*) Merchandise (*d*) Business practice	(*a*) English (*b*) Physical education (*c*) Citizenship	See "Stock clericals"	See "Stock clericals"

TABLE XXV—*Continued*

No.	Job	Duties	Training Required		More Remote Objectives and Training	
			Commercial	Related	Promotional Line	Later Promotional Training
4–*Cont.*	Stock clerk—*Cont.*	(*j*) Keep stock room files (*k*) Notify buyers or department heads when stock needs replenishing				
5	File clerk	(*a*) Filing letters, vouchers, reports, etc., for future reference (*b*) Preparing folders for special use (*c*) Planning filing systems for special purposes (*d*) Getting from files material required (*e*) Classifying all material to be filed for easy reference (*f*) Keeping index card file and cross reference files (*g*) Transferring old material to "dead files"	(*a*) Filing systems (*b*) Card systems (*c*) Business organization (*d*) Lettering (*e*) Typewriting	(*a*) English (*b*) Physical education (*c*) Citizenship (*d*) Business correspondence	(*a*) Chief file clerk (*b*) Superintendent of files (*c*) Correspondent (*d*) Office manager	(*a*) Advanced filing courses (*b*) Efficiency course (*c*) Advanced business correspondence (*d*) Office management (*e*) Commercial law
6	Mail clerk	(*a*) Sorting incoming mail (*b*) Distributing it (*c*) Collecting outgoing mail (*d*) Preparing it for mailing	(*a*) Office machine course (*b*) Office practice (*c*) Postoffice regulations	(*a*) English (*b*) Physical education (*c*) Citizenship (*d*) Geography	(*a*) File clerk (*b*) Chief file clerk (*c*) Office assistant (*d*) Office manager	(*a*) Office management (*b*) Advanced filing systems (*c*) Business correspondence (*d*) Economics

TABLE XXV—*Continued*

No.	Job	Duties	Training Required		More Remote Objectives and Training	
			Commercial	Related	Promotional Line	Later Promotional Training
6—*Cont.*	Mail clerk—*Cont.*	(*e*) Handling special delivery mail in and out (*f*) Handling registered mail in and out (*g*) Dispatching outgoing mail (*h*) Delivering carbons and originals to file department				

GROUP II—OFFICE MACHINE OPERATING

No.	Job	Duties	Training Required		More Remote Objectives and Training	
			Commercial	Related	Promotional Line	Later Promotional Training
7	Typist	(*a*) Copying form letters (*b*) Typing circulars, advertisements, and other material for printer's copy (*c*) Typewriting card records (*d*) Typing bills and statements (*e*) Cutting stencils (*f*) Typing specifications, etc. (*g*) Typing contracts (*h*) Addressing envelopes (*i*) Typing order forms	(*a*) Typewriting (*b*) Business forms (*c*) Office practice	(*a*) English (*b*) Physical education (*c*) Citizenship	(*a*) Dictaphone operator (*b*) Stenographer (*c*) Secretary (*d*) Office manager	(*a*) Typewriting speed practice (*b*) Shorthand (*c*) Secretarial practice (*d*) Office management (*e*) Business organization

TABLE XXV—*Continued*

No.	Job	Duties	Training Required		More Remote Objectives and Training	
			Commercial	Related	Promotional Line	Later Promotional Training
8	Billing clerk	(*a*) Billing on the typewriter or special billing machine (*b*) Verifying invoices prepared (*c*) Routing bills for mailing or entry	(*a*) Business forms (*b*) Commercial arithmetic (*c*) Typewriting	(*a*) English (*b*) Physical education (*c*) Citizenship	(*a*) Typist (*b*) Dictaphone operator (*c*) Stenographer (*d*) Bookkeeper	(*a*) Advanced typewriting, speed practice (*b*) Dictaphone practice (*c*) Shorthand (*d*) Bookkeeping
9	Duplicating machine operator and addressograph machine operator	(*a*) Operate the mimeograph (*b*) Operate the multigraph (*c*) Operate other duplicators according to local requirements (*d*) Keep record of material run, file stencils and copies of all material duplicated (*e*) Operate addressograph, seal and stamp envelopes	(*a*) Office duplicator practice (*b*) Office practice (*c*) Addressograph practice (*d*) Practice on sealing and stamping machine	(*a*) English (*b*) Physical education (*c*) Citizenship	Difficult to suggest direct and natural lines. Promotion will depend upon quality of work done and natural abilities which are revealed	
10	Calculating machine operator	(*a*) Figuring and checking invoices, outgoing and incoming (*b*) Figuring and checking payrolls (*c*) Figuring and checking inventories (*d*) Figuring and checking books in the auditing department	(*a*) Machine theory and practice (*b*) Typewriting (*c*) Elementary bookkeeping	(*a*) English (*b*) Physical education (*c*) Citizenship	(*a*) Retail store 1. Special operator 2. Head calculating machine department (*b*) Manufacturing office 1. Head of department 2. Assistant bookkeeper 3. Bookkeeper	(*a*) Bookkeeping (*b*) Accounting (*c*) Economics (*d*) Business administration (*e*) Commercial law

TABLE XXV—*Continued*

No.	Job	Duties	Training Required		More Remote Objectives and Training	
			Commercial	Related	Promotional Line	Later Promotional Training
10—*Cont.*	Calculating machine operator—*Cont.*	(*e*) Figuring profits and losses (*f*) Figuring discounts and interest (*g*) Income tax reports			4. Auditor	

GROUP III—MISCELLANEOUS

No.	Job	Duties	Training Required		More Remote Objectives and Training	
			Commercial	Related	Promotional Line	Later Promotional Training
11	Messenger or office boy	(*a*) Deliver messages (*b*) Run errands of various kinds (*c*) Fill ink wells and look after other details around the office (*d*) Answer telephone (*e*) Run office machines (*f*) Make himself generally useful in assisting other members of the office staff	(*a*) Business English (*b*) Business writing (*c*) Office practice (*d*) Business arithmetic (*e*) Local geography	(*a*) Physical education (*b*) Citizenship	(*a*) General clerk (*b*) Bookkeeper (*c*) Stenographer (*d*) Salesman (*e*) Office manager NOTE.—The office boy or messenger has an opportunity to gain useful knowledge about all the above lines. He may choose the one for which he seems best adapted and make special preparation accordingly.	To be determined by promotional lines selected

TABLE XXV—*Continued*

No.	Job	Duties	Training Required		More Remote Objectives and Training	
			Commercial	Related	Promotional Line.	Later Promotional Training
12	Collector	(*a*) Call on customers to collect accounts (*b*) Receive cash and deliver receipted bills (*c*) Report collections to the office (*d*) Report on those who fail to pay	(*a*) Business arithmetic (*b*) Business writing (*c*) Business practice	(*a*) English (*b*) Physical education (*c*) Citizenship	(*a*) Cashier (*b*) Auditor (*c*) Head collections department (*d*) Credit man	(*a*) Practical auditing (*b*) Credits and collections (*c*) Advanced business correspondence (*d*) Commercial law

GROUP IV—RECORDING

No.	Job	Duties	Training Required		More Remote Objectives and Training	
			Commercial	Related	Promotional Line	Later Promotional Training
13	Assistant bookkeeper	(*a*) Make routine records in connection with a complete set of books under direction (*b*) Keep a simple set of office records for a small business (*c*) Record work in retail store such as grocery or market (*d*) Recording and posting sales	(*a*) Business arithmetic (*b*) Elementary bookkeeping (*c*) Business forms (*d*) Business writing	(*a*) English (*b*) Physical education	(*a*) Bookkeeper (*b*) Head bookkeeper (*c*) Auditor (*d*) Junior accountant (*e*) Accountant (*f*) Certified public accountant	(*a*) Advanced bookkeeping (*b*) Advanced business mathematics (*c*) Accounting (*d*) Auditing (*e*) Economics (*f*) Commercial law

TABLE XXV—*Continued*

No.	Job	Duties	Training Required		More Remote Objectives and Training	
			Commercial	Related	Promotional Line	Later Promotional Training
14	Entry clerk	(*a*) Enter orders on bill heads (*b*) Prepare credit memoranda (*c*) Enter and check car numbers (*d*) Make entries in bank books (*e*) Enter charges in day book	(*a*) Business writing (*b*) Business arithmetic	(*a*) English (*b*) Physical education	(*a*) Assistant bookkeeper (*b*) Bookkeeper (*c*) Head bookkeeper (*d*) Accountant (*e*) Teller (bank) (*f*) Cashier (bank)	(*a*) Bookkeeping (*b*) Advanced business mathematics (*c*) Accounting (*d*) Banking and finance (bank) (*e*) Economics (*f*) Commercial law
15	Ledger clerk	Post entries in the ledger	Same as 13	Same as 13	Same as 13	Same as 13
16	Cost clerk	Make production records and assist in figuring costs	Same as 13	Same as 13	(*a*) Assistant bookkeeper (*b*) Bookkeeper (*c*) Cost accountant	(*a*) Bookkeeping (*b*) Accounting (*c*) Cost accounting (*d*) Advanced business mathematics (*e*) Economics
17	Bookkeeping machine operator	(*a*) Bank work 1. Check teller work 2. Statement work (*b*) Commercial office 1. Posting sales ledger 2. Posting purchase ledger	(*a*) Bookkeeping (*b*) Machine practice (*c*) Typewriting	(*a*) English (*b*) Physical education (*c*) Citizenship	(*a*) In a bank 1. Ledger clerk 2. Bookkeeper 3. Head bookkeeper to 4. Auditor or 5. Receiving teller 6. Paying teller 7. Assistant cashier 8. Cashier	

TABLE XXV—*Continued*

No.	Job	Duties	Training Required		More Remote Objectives and Training	
			Commercial	Related	Promotional Line	Later Promotional Training
17—*Cont.*	Bookkeeping machine operator—*Cont.*				(*b*) In a commercial office 1. Bookkeeper 2. Head bookkeeper 3. Department head to 4. Assistant manager 5. Manager or 6. Assistant auditor 7. Auditor	
18	Timekeeper	(*a*) Keep time record of employees (*b*) Make out payroll (*c*) Check absences of employees	Same as 13	Same as 13	Same as 13	Same as 13
19	Statement clerk	Prepare and mail statements of personal accounts	Same as 13	Same as 13	Same as 13	Same as 13

TABLE XXV—*Continued*

GROUP V—STENOGRAPHIC

No.	Job	Duties	Training Required		More Remote Objectives and Training	
			Commercial	Related	Promotional Line	Later Promotional Training
20	Stenographer	(a) Take dictation (b) Transcribe it (c) Make carbon copies (d) File correspondence or prepare for files (e) Look after all details connected with getting out the daily mail	(a) Shorthand (b) Typewriting (c) Business correspondence (d) Business English (e) Office practice	(a) Physical education (b) Citizenship	(a) Head stenographer (b) Correspondent (c) Reporter	(a) Advanced dictation (b) Advanced business correspondence (c) Business organization and management (d) Economics (e) Commercial law
21	Dictating machine operator	(a) Transcribe from the dictaphone or ediphone (b) Handle details connected with getting out the daily mail	(a) Typewriting (b) Business correspondence (c) Business English (d) Office practice	(a) Physical education (b) Citizenship	(a) Correspondent (b) Supervisor of stenographic department	(a) Advanced business correspondence (b) Office management (c) Economics (d) Commercial law

TABLE XXV—*Continued*

GROUP VI—RETAIL STORE SERVICE

No.	Job	Duties	Training Required		More Remote Objectives and Training	
			Commercial	Related	Promotional Line	Later Promotional Training
22	Salesperson (Junior)	(*a*) Sell merchandise of various kinds—novelties, dry goods, groceries, drugs, 5 and 10 cent articles, etc. (*b*) Arrange and display stock (*c*) Keep stock in salable condition (*d*) Make out sales checks and other store forms, etc. (*e*) Use cash register, also O.K. telephone (*f*) Take orders by telephone and through mail (*g*) Give information and direct customers (*h*) Occasionally mark goods—take inventory, figure discounts (*i*) Wrap packages (*j*) Give *service* to customers	(*a*) English (*b*) Spelling (*c*) Arithmetic (*d*) Use of cash register (*e*) Use of O.K. telephone (*f*) Use of tube system (*g*) System (*h*) Salesmanship (*i*) Service (*j*) Store policy and rules (*k*) Store directory and merchandise location (*l*) Store organization (*m*) Personal hygiene (*n*) Merchandise (*o*) Advertising (*p*) Legible handwriting	(*a*) Citizenship (*b*) Industrial history as related to manufacture of merchandise (*c*) Color and design (*d*) Recreation and use of leisure time (*e*) Books and reading (*f*) Writing (*g*) Hygiene	(*a*) Head of stock (*b*) Assistant buyer (*c*) Buyer (*d*) Merchandise manager or Sales manager or 1. Head of stock 2. Divisional superintendent 3. Floor manager 4. Superintendent of floor 5. Assistant superintendent 6. Superintendent or Employment manager or Personnel manager or General manager	(*a*) Care of stock (*b*) Stock arrangement—showcases, window display (*c*) Advertising writing and sketching (*d*) Supervised trips to factories and markets (*e*) Arithmetic 1. Mark up 2. Mark down 3. Inventory 4. Stock plans (*f*) Sales promotion (*g*) Merchandise study (*h*) How to deal with people (*i*) Business forms (*j*) Store rules and policies (*k*) Floor manager's rules (*l*) Service (*m*) Sales promotion (*n*) Expense reduction (*o*) Store organization (*p*) Employment and management

TABLE XXV—*Continued*

No.	Job	Duties	Training Required		More Remote Objectives and Training	
			Commercial	Related	Promotional Line	Later Promotional Training
23	Messengers, including minor office boys and girls, mail clerks, special deliveries, etc., millinery mfg., alteration room, shoppers	(*a*) Run errands (*b*) Collect time cards (*c*) Distribute mail and interdepartmental messages (*d*) Deliver telegrams and special deliveries (*e*) Buy railroad tickets (*f*) Carry cash, bundles, transfers, etc. (*g*) Trace orders or packages (*h*) Take advertising to departments (*i*) Errands for service desks where refunds and exchanges are cared for (*j*) Collect sales checks vouchers, tissue books, etc. (*k*) Distribute supplies	(*a*) Department location (*b*) Store directory (*c*) Local geography—streets, public buildings, railroad station (*d*) Store rules (*e*) System (*f*) Store organization (*g*) Accuracy (*h*) Arithmetic (*i*) English and spelling (*j*) Personal appearance (*k*) Promotional possibilities (*l*) Thoughtfulness and service (*m*) Legible writing, including figure making	(*a*) English (*b*) Personal and public hygiene (*c*) Citizenship (*d*) Economics—wages, spending, thrift (*e*) Commercial geography	(*a*) Inspector wrapper (*b*) Head of floor boys or girls (*c*) Cashier (*d*) Office positions (*e*) General clerical (*f*) Stock Note.—Any of the above may lead to selling or to other semi-executive positions. (*g*) Salesperson	(*a*) Wrapping bundles (*b*) Tying knots (*c*) Supplies — their care and requisition (*d*) Responsibilities of use of rubber stamp (*e*) Arithmetic—counting back change, etc. (*f*) Use of cash register (*g*) Care of stock (*h*) Stock clerical duties
24	General clerical	(*a*) Merchandise and service clerical work for buyers and floor managers (*b*) Help on payroll, time records, etc.	Same as Course 1 (general clerical) plus additional work to suit needs of special group or individual.			

TABLE XXV—*Continued*

No.	Job	Duties	Training Required		More Remote Objectives and Training	
			Commercial	Related	Promotional Line	Later Promotional Training
24—*Cont.*	General clerical—*Cont.*	(*c*) Write letters, make out rate cards, file records, some copying and typing (*d*) Help manager care for new employees (*e*) Address envelopes, distribute bulletins, advertising copy, superintendent's orders, etc. (*f*) Answer telephone (*g*) Look up charges, etc. (*h*) Sort checks, make records of sales (*i*) Check up merchandise in receiving and stock rooms (*j*) C.O.D. and other delivery records Example: *Floor manager's clerical assistant*—Assists floor managers in duties of lighting, ventilation, elevators, inspectors' desks, O.K. telephone, telephones, appearance of sections, signs, supplies, emergencies, time records, lunch periods, attendance records, pay	(*a*) Store organization (*b*) Public hygiene (*c*) Service (*d*) Merchandise location (*e*) Knowledge of merchandise (*f*) Attention to detail (*g*) Secretarial duties (*h*) Use of cash register (*i*) Arithmetic (*j*) Spelling (*k*) Local geography (*l*) English (*m*) Personal appearance	(*a*) Citizenship (*b*) English (*c*) Commercial geography (*d*) Textiles	(*a*) Merchandise clerical (*b*) Salesperson (*c*) Assistant buyer (*d*) Buyer (*e*) Merchandise manager or Assistant floor manager (*f*) Aisle supervisor (*g*) Store manager (*h*) Service manager	(*a*) Principles of merchandising (*b*) Salesmanship (*c*) Trips to markets (*d*) Arithmetic (*e*) English (*f*) Expense and control (*g*) Employment management (*h*) Sales promotion

TABLE XXV—*Continued*

No.	Job	Duties	Training Required		More Remote Objectives and Training	
			Commercial	Related	Promotional Line	Later Promotional Training
24—*Cont.*	General clerical—*Cont.*	envelopes, employment requisitions, after hour permits, shopping permits, store system, shipping instructions, cash register, delivery schedules, etc., adjustments, meetings, notices and services.				
25	Bundle wrappers, cashiers, examiners	(*a*) Examination of sales checks for form, items, legibility, agreement as to kind, number, price and total, correct address, floor manager's O.K. (*b*) Stamping of checks with rubber stamp, folding check to insure care of merchandise (*c*) Care of wrapping, desk dusting, ordering supplies, paste, paper, twine, etc. (*d*) Wrapping bundles (*e*) Receiving money, counting back change	(*a*) Store rules (*b*) Knowledge and use of supplies, grades of paper, twine, etc. (*c*) Writing (*d*) Store rules, policies (*e*) Arithmetic (*f*) Personal hygiene, dress, and appearance (*g*) Accuracy, responsibility, and alertness (*h*) Error system (*i*) Store system (*j*) Accounting (cross balance) (*k*) Store organization (*l*) Promotional possibilities	(*a*) Commercial law (*b*) Bookkeeping (*c*) Auditing (*d*) English (*e*) Commercial geography (*f*) Hygiene (*g*) Citizenship	(*a*) Salesperson (*b*) Head cashier (*c*) Head of tube room (*d*) Head inspector (*e*) Junior auditor work Note. — Experience as an inspector or cashier is best background to insure promotion to selling or any other position.	(*a*) Salesmanship (*b*) Merchandise location (*c*) Knowledge of merchandise (*d*) Employment (*e*) How to deal with people (*f*) Auditing (*g*) Financial records and operations

TABLE XXV—*Continued*

No.	Job	Duties	Training Required		More Remote Objectives and Training	
			Commercial	Related	Promotional Line	Later Promotional Training
25—*Cont.*	Bundle wrappers, etc.,—*Cont.*	(*f*) Checking up errors, etc. (*g*) Work on tubes in desk or in tube room (*h*) File orders on which part payment has been made				
26	Stock, including stock clericals	(*a*) Care of stock (varies in different departments and types of stores) (*b*) Putting on tags—marking (*c*) Keeping stock records (*d*) Assist salespeople, head of stock, assistant buyer and buyer (*e*) Care of returned merchandise, exchanges, etc. (*f*) Occasionally sell merchandise (*g*) Arrange show cases and department display (*h*) Assist in taking inventory (*i*) Write letters and orders	(*a*) Arithmetic (*b*) Writing (*c*) Use of ticketing machine (*d*) Tag and marking merchandise (*e*) Accuracy (*f*) Order (*g*) Color and design related and display (*h*) Sewing (buttons, hooks and eyes, etc.) (*i*) Hand work, including bead work, typing ribbons, etc. (*j*) Personal appearance	(*a*) Citizenship (*b*) Commercial geography (*c*) English (*d*) Hygiene (*e*) Spelling	(*a*) Head of stock or Merchandise clerical (assistant to the assistant buyer) (*b*) Assistant buyer (*c*) Buyer, etc., or Position in merchandise office, or Salesperson	(*a*) Arithmetic (*b*) Simple policies of mark up, mark down, inventory, stock turnover (*c*) Stock plans (*d*) Merchandising (*e*) Market location and buying (*f*) Resources (*g*) English (*h*) Foreign language, if interested in foreign buying (*i*) Salesmanship

TABLE XXV—*Continued*

No.	Job	Duties	Training Required		More Remote Objectives and Training	
			Commercial	Related	Promotional Line	Later Promotional Training
26—*Cont.*	Stock, etc.—*Cont.*	(*j*) Answer telephone, make appointments, etc. (*k*) Disburse merchandise and supplies				
27	Miscellaneous	(*a*) Delivery room assistant. Making route sheets and sorting packages (*b*) File clerk—filing, looking up papers when called for, etc. (*c*) Office workers—on billing machines, calculating machine, duplicating machines, typists, check sorters in auditing room (*d*) Switchboard operator caring for all incoming and outgoing calls, receiving telegrams, etc., operating signal system for executives and protective officers (*e*) Elevator operator, call floors, merchandise location, answer customers' questions	(*a*) Store organization, promotional possibilities (*b*) System (*c*) Store directory (*d*) Store policies (*e*) English (*f*) Use of telephone (*g*) Spelling (*h*) Writing (*i*) Personal appearance (*j*) Service (*k*) Salesmanship Special or individual work to suit needs of each worker, such as color and design for window trimmers' assistant	(*a*) English (*b*) Citizenship (*c*) Hygiene (*d*) Recreation	(*a*) Head of delivery (*b*) Head of filing room (*c*) Head biller (*d*) Head bookkeeper (*e*) Chief operator on telephone board (*f*) Elevator starter in charge of operators (*g*) Machinist (*h*) Timekeeper or assistant in superintendent's office (*i*) Window trimmer (*j*) Head of mail order section (*k*) Salesperson Note. — Promotion from the miscellaneous group may lead in a variety of directions.	(*a*) Postal regulations (*b*) Traffic regulations (*c*) Filing (*d*) Billing machine operating; also principles of supervision (*e*) Employment supervision — uniforms, dress, and conduct (*f*) Store mechanics (*g*) Store system and service (*h*) Display, advertising (*i*) Knowledge of merchandise (*j*) Salesmanship (*k*) Service (*l*) Store policy (*m*) Store directory

TABLE XXV—*Continued*

No.	Job	Duties	Training Required		More Remote Objectives and Training	
			Commercial	Related	Promotional Line	Later Promotional Training
27—*Cont.*	Miscellaneous—*Cont.*	(*f*) Machinist's assistant—helping chief engineer or electrician (*g*) Timekeeper's assistant — collects time cards, makes out reports, etc. (*h*) Window trimmer's assistant—gets out merchandise, forms, fixtures, cleans, polishes, etc. (*i*) Mail order shopper—fills orders, sends out packages, etc. (*j*) All positions which are not in first five groups				

C. An Analysis of the Work of Certain Commercial People[1]

A. THE STENOGRAPHER

The Survey census report shows twenty-six men and eighty-seven women stenographers. This occupation was especially analyzed in those establishments where type studies were made. Of the twenty retail stores, only four employ stenographers, of whom one is also a bookkeeper. One of the three factory offices especially studied and the telephone company office had no stenographer and the two factory offices each employed two.

What the worker does: regular duties.—The stenographer, by means of abbreviations, letters and word symbols, records verbal statements, after which she transcribes them on the typewriter. To master the work involves the knowledge of an alphabet of characters used to express words phonetically. In addition to phonetic spelling, short cuts are made by the use of "word signs," which may represent whole phrases. Some systems of shorthand also vary the position of the symbol in relation to the line, and shade the pencil stroke, while others use neither position nor shading. Technique involves rapid writing of symbols and accurate transcription of notes.

In addition to writing letters, which usually requires the greater portion of the time of the stenographer, the work of nine stenographers studied, two of whom are men, involves answering the telephone, receiving visitors, and assisting the bookkeeper and cashier.

Special knowledge required.—The special knowledge required involves thorough mastery of a system of shorthand, the ability to transcribe notes rapidly and accurately; the fundamentals of bookkeeping; and general office procedure, including receiving visitors, answering the telephone, weighing packages, and correctly stamping them, and correctly using filing devices and card catalog systems.

What the worker does: special duties.—One of the stenographers, in addition to the duties already described, is also a

[1] Adapted from the *Report of the Richmond, Indiana, Survey for Vocational Education.* Bulletin of the Indiana State Board of Education, Indiana Survey Series No. 3, 1916, pp. 388–98.

bookkeeper keeping summaries of receipts and expenditures, records of charge accounts with a tickler system, and all mailing lists. Another stenographer, employed in a retail store, keeps the cost book, makes out on the typewriter the monthly bills of all customers, takes charge of the c.o.d. money returned on delivered packages and keeps the daily ledger. Another attends to mail order business and helps typewrite customer's monthly bills. In two of the factories the stenographer was required to do billing and filing and in the other, to accurately copy and record all specifications and contracts.

Special skill required.—In stenography, skill consists of making clear outlines in taking notes, and of using the typewriter with accuracy and speed. The latter is analogous to the mechanics of playing the piano and requires the same dexterity of each finger acting separately and the proper position of the hand above the keyboard. The stenographer should also understand the mechanics of her tool, the typewriter, so that she may quickly change ribbons and make minor adjustments. Considering the wide range of the stenographer's work in Richmond, she should be able to operate adding and posting machines.

General education required.—The relation between education and success in stenography is positive. The Richmond High School course is so organized that none can be considered a commercial graduate who is not also a high school graduate. The school considers this a selective occupation which only mature and well-educated boys and girls should enter. There are many gradations in stenographic work from tabulating or typing envelopes to the intricate technique of stenography in banks and railroads. Success in the former type of position does not demand high school training, but for promotion to more responsible work and for a high degree of success in such work, a high school education is essential.

Promotion.—The most significant aspect of promotion is the differentiation between opportunities for boys and girls. In Richmond no comparative figures are available, but from the table, heading this chapter, it may be seen that 157 men as compared to eleven women are employed in positions of shipping, cost, bill and ledger clerks, which are positions of responsibility and well paid. All the six male stenographers, whose work was studied in detail, have opportunity to advance to more responsible positions, such as cost clerk, traffic man and rate clerk. For the one woman, whose position was studied, no promotion was possible save increase in salary. It may be safely said that women usually continue to be stenographers and promotion consists of increased wages usually obtained by changing positions. For young men, the stenographic position may be a stepping stone, leading to continuous advancement, the exact character of which depends upon the type of establishment.

B. THE BOOKKEEPER

According to the census returns of the Survey, there were on March 1, 1916, forty-seven male and thirty-seven female bookkeepers in Richmond, in addition to seven males and thirteen females who were cashiers and bookkeepers. This study is based upon a careful analysis of ten bookkeepers, seven of whom were employed in six store offices and three in three factories. These ten bookkeepers, unlike the stenographers, have no general office duties aside from answering the telephone.

What the worker does.—The bookkeeper keeps a systematic record of business transactions in order to show their relation to each other, and the state of the business in which they occur. In its simple aspects, bookkeeping involves the use of the day book, the cash book and ledger. In its more highly developed aspects, it involves the use of specialized types of all sorts of record books and forms. Naturally, the work varies with the size and system of the company. Even within the limited scope of this study it was found to range from a simple journal of entries to a highly organized system of accounts for every department of a complicated business. The simpler methods are largely used by the proprietors themselves in the retail stores, where no office worker is employed. The more complex systems are used in large factories and in large stores.

A typical schedule of the bookkeeper's work in a retail store involves keeping the store ledger, journal, day book for charge sales, general cash book, ledger and ledger auxiliaries, and syncopated journal. The syncopated journal groups numerical facts which would otherwise have to be recorded in several different journals and involves nine groups: Merchandise, cash, expense, interest and discount, freight and express, stock accounts, and bills payable and receivable. In addition, the bookkeeper makes out statements to customers each month, and directs the collection of unpaid bills; makes monthly summaries of receipts by departments, pays firm bills (manager signs all checks), takes charge of letters and filing, considers questions of credit, if the manager and assistant are absent; receives payment of bills at cash window and makes change; receives and adjusts complaints about charges, banks cash and checks, and keeps the bank books.

A schedule of bookkeeping work in a factory includes keeping ledger, synoptic ledger and cash book; entering all shipments; and summarizing statements from pay-roll. The work requires the adding machine in obtaining totals. The detailed work of factory accounting is described in the discussion of the cost clerk.

Special knowledge required.—Aside from a thorough working knowledge of all types of bookkeeping, the bookkeeper must know the commodities of the company which are sold or manufactured, as well as the business details of office procedure in municipal and institutional offices. A knowledge of transportation and how to obtain accurate information about mercantile rates should be a part of the equipment of every bookkeeper who pays bills on freight and express. How to bank, how to compute interest and discount, and all the multitudinous details of office technique must be known by the bookkeeper.

Special skill required.—Success in bookkeeping and accounting depends upon mental rather than manual skill, but the mental equipment is worthless without skill in penmanship and in operating an adding machine.

General education required.—What has been written concerning the general education needed by the stenographer, applies to the bookkeeper with the reservation that the stenographer, in order to advance to highly paid positions, must have an accurate knowledge of English and general information. The bookkeeper is more of a specialist, having less general contact with the public than the stenographer, and if highly expert in accounting, can fill a position whether a high school graduate or not. On the other hand, difficult problems in bookkeeping require a trained mind which higher education develops. Such advanced positions as treasurer, purchasing agent, or secretary could not be filled by an average person without more than eighth grade education.

Mental and physical requirements.—Practically no attempt has been made to discover the qualifications for success in this work. Ability to analyze a problem and invent solutions for new problems are certainly essential for success. The steadiness and reliability of character needed by this worker, who handles large sums of money often with very little supervision, cannot be overestimated. They are distinguishing features of this position.

Promotion.—The position of bookkeeper is sometimes filled by promoting the assistant bookkeeper or cashier. "Once a bookkeeper, always a bookkeeper," is a slogan whose truth is attested by the fact that all the ten bookkeepers found in these type studies have held their positions for many years and do not expect to change them. The position of treasurer or secretary of the company is sometimes filled by promoting the bookkeeper and there is more possibility of such advancement for men than for women.

Source and selection of workers.—The responsible post of bookkeeper is seldom filled in any establishment by taking a new worker from a school. The subordinate positions of ledger clerk or assistant bookkeepers may be filled by inexperienced graduates of business courses but advanced positions or general bookkeepers require experience as well as special training.

C. THE CASHIER

According to the Survey census returns, there were twenty-seven male and fifteen female cashiers in Richmond in March, 1916. Type studies were made of seven cashiers, two of whom had bookkeeping duties, also.

Type of work.—The term "cashier" applies to two entirely different kinds of work: taking in money direct on sales, making change and keeping a simple record of the transactions; and the issuing of money for the pay-roll, and paying company bills. The cashier in the retail store often has some general duties to perform, such as helping the bookkeeper in the dry-goods store and making sales in the grocery store. The cashier of the large establishment may be responsible for seeing that the books are correctly kept.

What the worker does.—As the work of each of the seven cashiers is distinctive in some respect, the detailed schedule of the day's work of each will be reported.

1. The worker collects the money from the cash register, totals it and checks it against the amount of sales which are cashed up on the register during the day. She does the banking, makes out invoices, and keeps a record of incoming merchandise.

2. The cashier checks sales slips, foots extensions and totals, and makes change, which is sent back by the carrier to the sales girl. Every morning she receives money from the bookkeeper, for which she accounts. Every evening she totals the cash and checks it with cash sales slips and the original sum received. She also keeps a cash book.

3. The cashier sits at a desk on the first floor and makes change for the salesmen, ringing up the cash in the register according to the number of each salesman. By this means she keeps a record of individual sales. She receives the charge sales slips from the clerks on the floor, which she enters to the customer's account, adding the total of the sale on the face of the envelope within which is placed the sales slip. At the end of each week or month, according to the custom of the customer's payments, on charge accounts she obtains totals by the adding machine, with the bill and the sale slip. She type-

writes invoices for individual customer's bills; fills out the regular form for cash sales at the end of the day, which, in turn, are collected for statement at the end of the week; answers telephones and if not engaged, and all salespersons are busy, she waits on customers. She also does the banking.

4. The cashier is the head of the tube system, making change for all sales. This tube system is also used for shooting messages to any part of the building or the warehouse. All the messages go to the cashier, who re-routes them when necessary. She keeps the index file of individual customers and records bill payments; and keeps the cash book and records amounts of sales by departments. For "fill in work" at odd moments, she does typing.

5 and 6. They inspect sales slips and make change in the cash balcony; record charge sales, entering them in cash book according to departments; file sales slips by the clerk's number, total each clerk's cash and charge sales, and enter them in record books by clerks and departments. The assistant cashier does odd jobs in the office and assists in writing letters.

7. The head bookkeeper or cashier has full charge of general ledgers and all cash. He banks, pays bills of the house, and makes out all checks. He also makes out order cards for machines and sends "manifest" to the repair man.

General education required.—Some high school training is required for cashiers. Of these studied the majority of workers had more than eighth grade education. Knowledge of arithmetic and banking is needed, and in the higher positions which bring the worker in contact with the public, advanced general education is essential.

How special knowledge and skill are obtained.—Employers interviewed for this study stated that most cashiers of the less expert type can get what special knowledge they need on the job, provided they have a thorough knowledge of commercial arithmetic and bookkeeping. The necessary training in these two fields must be obtained in school.

Mental and physical requirements.—Accuracy and rapidity in counting and computing change is necessary for success as a cashier. The qualifications of the expert cashier are practically the same as for the bookkeeper.

Promotion.—The cashier may become bookkeeper, since part of the required duties are to prepare statements for the bookkeeper.

Source and selection of workers.—Workers are taken from the outside or from the sales force. In the latter case they are chosen because of their alertness and knowledge of the business.

Seasonableness and overtime.—The cashier in the retail store has the same hours as the salesperson. In order to get the day's balance, some overtime is occasionally required. Their work is not seasonable.

Hazards and inherent character of work.—The work is confining and responsible in character, involving all the mental and physical strains of a confining, sedentary life.

Wages.—Of three schedules received for retail cashiers, two quoted wages at six and one thirty dollars per week.

D. THE CLERK

The term clerk has been used to designate a group of workers which could not be classified elsewhere. The range includes clerical workers, bill clerks, stock, shipping, and receiving clerks, file clerks, timekeepers, and cost and statistical clerks. Clerical work, except in the railroad office, usually is the most subordinate form of office work. Statistical and cost clerks, at the other end of the scale, are the most expert positions requiring specialists who are well remunerated.

Number employed.—In Richmond there were 217 males and 36 females designated as clerks working in various offices. It will be noted in the opening of this chapter, that the majority of clerks were employed in railroad and express offices, and the offices of shops and factories.

Definitions of various types of clerks.—The clerical worker keeps records, opens and distributes mail, writes tags and slips and does checking and posting. In the railroad office, however, the term is more loosely used and includes such experts as the rate clerk and the chief clerk, whose work is not only highly specialized but executive.

The bill clerk prepares invoices, usually on a typewriter or billing machine. There are very few bill clerks in Richmond, except in railroad offices. This work sometimes involves rechecking figures.

Stock clerks keep records of all materials in the stock room and records of all materials issued. Stock is usually issued in accordance with signed requisitions which are checked against the department.

The shipping clerk works in the office and warehouse, checking and supervising outgoing material. The receiving clerk is in charge of incoming material, checking it against the invoice for quality, quantity and condition.

The file clerk is employed to correctly file away all correspondence, orders, contracts and papers of the firm. The order is generally alphabetical, with folders for correspondence and cards for reference tabulation. It is the file clerk's duty to keep the orders correctly filed and find such material as is needed for reference by the other clerks.

The timekeeper summarizes the time for all departments, computing the wage for each worker. In one factory the cost clerk is also timekeeper. Frequently the foreman of the department keeps the time of the employees under him. If the work is on a piece basis, the time put in by the men is important only as a record of efficiency. One employer stated that the wage received by this clerk was about seventy-five dollars a month.

Statistical and cost clerks are experts engaged in analyzing the production costs of all departments in order to determine the parts of the business which are most and least profitable, the proportionate cost of labor, raw materials and overhead expense. It is on the basis of these computations that prices are fixed, that charges on output are made, that wages are cut or raised, and that sales are directed.

D. A Job Analysis of Retail Selling[1]

The girl who sells handkerchiefs must have a knowledge of linen, lawn, cotton, mercerized cotton, shamrock, and light

[1] Adapted from *Minneapolis Vocational Education Survey*, pp. 408–17. Bulletin of United States Bureau of Labor, No. 199, 1916.

silks. She should know the combination of fibers used and be able to tell from the appearance and feeling just what is the combination in a particular handkerchief. For example, she should know that in certain high-priced handkerchiefs the thread running one way is linen and that running the other shamrock. She should know that this makes a more sheer and a softer-looking handkerchief than pure linen, but is not so durable, she should know that French linens, because of their greater brilliancy, are more desirable than Irish linens. She should know the difference between domestic and foreign goods, between hand and machine embroidering, between punched and pulled hems, between real and Armenian lace, and between either of these and imitations. She should know which colors are fast and which are likely to fade so that she can tell the customer about the care needed in laundering.

Most persons are not in a hurry when buying handkerchiefs, so the girl must have the skill to give many points as to value in beauty and wearing qualities, and to show goods in detail. She should like details and be perfectly familiar with the workmanship on handkerchiefs. The work does not require measuring or estimating fractional parts, so computations are easy.

The sales person who sells hosiery may sell knitted underwear. Though usually sold in different departments, these goods have many points in common. The same methods of manufacture and the same materials are used to a great extent. The sales person should know sizes, full-fashion, seamless, and outsize hosiery; pure dye silks, thread silk, loaded or plated silk; the various grades of cotton, lisle, mercerized, and wool mixtures, and weights used; and be able to use this knowledge in selling the various kinds of stock. It is desirable that the different kinds of knitting used should be understood. She is frequently called upon to estimate the size the customer needs, especially in children's wear; so should be able to judge from the size of the shoe or the age of the child.

The sales person who sells gloves should know the leathers and fabrics used, care of gloves, and how to fit all kinds. The knowledge of fabrics should cover silk, cotton, lisle, and chamoisettes, that of leathers should cover lamb leathers such as capeskins, mochas, chamois, and dogskins, and kid leathers such as suede.

A saleswoman's interest in her work should be increased by knowing that the softness and durability of glove leather depends on the age of the animal and the place where it was raised; that leather from skins taken from the young of hardy, mountain-climbing sheep is stronger than that from the young of animals which browse in lowlands and on plains, and that the best gloves are made from skins of kids found in the southeastern part of France.

She should know enough about gloves to make the customer understand that care must be exercised in washing a doeskin glove because it is the process of manufacture and not the leather itself which has made it washable. She should know the various parts of a glove; the different stitchings—spear, plain, filet, and three-row; and the different methods of seaming, such as Prix seam, pique, and round seam, and the customary usages and peculiar merits of each. If she understands the manufacture of gloves she can explain the difference in durability, softness, and purpose of each style of glove and can give the customer much acceptable information about their proper care.

A saleswoman must know how to use the stretcher and powder. She must be able to fit gloves and to judge by looking at a woman's hand what size glove to try. She should know the best position for the customer to assume while being fitted and how to stand so as to avoid unnecessary strain of the muscles of the back.

The reshaping of the glove after fitting demands skill. A machine has been invented for this purpose, but it is not used so extensively as to eliminate the hand reshaping of the glove. This must be so skillfully done that the glove will not show that it has been fitted. Mending of gloves is important. A sales person may be trained to look after mending as part of her work, or it may be done in a special department.

The sales person who sells jewelry should have a knowledge of silver, because much jewelry is made of silver. She must know what is meant by gold-filled, gold-rolled, and gold-front jewelry. She should be able to show interesting things about different pieces of jewelry, as, for example, the desirability of a chain composed of soldered links as compared with one having unsoldered links. She should have accurate knowledge of the materials used in buckles, pins, bracelets, hair ornaments, fancy purses, and beads. Jewelry is a part of dress and so is affected by style, to which the sales person should give attention.

E. A Job Analysis for Selling[1]

VARIABLE FACTORS IN BUSINESS WORK—SALESMANSHIP AS AN EXAMPLE

Inherent differences in qualifications of salespersons.—This study of salesmanship in the retail stores of Richmond, has indicated the whole range of work required of men and women of widely varying mental and physical endowments, and educational qualifications. A few examples cited from this report will but serve to illustrate this point. The hardware salesman must possess mechanical ability in order to set up and adjust machines and implements. The dexterous hands of the jewelry salesman are not needed for success in the grocery store, nor is the girl selling notions required to have the keen color discrimination and the artistic taste of the salesperson at the silk counter. Good looks are of more importance to the girls at the neckwear counter than to the one who sells hosiery. Artistic taste is not so essential to the man who sells leather goods as to the clerk in a florist's shop.

Inherent differences in commodities sold.—For salespersons in book stores, a college education is an asset; for furniture salesmen, a general education rich in historical content about manners and customs of various people and periods and their homes and furnishings is valuable; and the demonstrator of a complicated agricultural implement is greatly profited by a

[1] Adapted from *Report of the Richmond, Indiana, Survey for Vocational Education*, pp. 388–97. Bulletin of Indiana State Board of Education, Indiana Survey Series No. 3, 1916.

technical education. On the other hand, it can scarcely be honestly contended that a general education beyond the sixth grade is needed for selling in the five and ten cent store, or that an education beyond the ninth grade is a marketable asset for the grocery clerk.

CONSTANT FACTORS IN SALESMANSHIP

Fundamentals underlying study of merchandise.—While actual differences in stock knowledge required of salespersons handling various commodities are vital and oftentimes great, there are certain fundamental basic elements underlying the study of merchandise; knowledge of the industries of the United States and Europe; centers of production of commodities of various types; source and composition of raw materials into finished products, including study of color, pattern and design.

Economics of mercantile trade.—The content, of the economics of mercantile trade about which all salespersons should be informed regardless of the commodity sold, includes the following: The world's producing, buying and selling markets; rudiments about traffic and transportation; basic reasons for variations in market prices; the relation between wholesale and retail trade; the basis of fixing selling prices; and methods of displaying and advertising goods.

Technique of meeting customers.—The types of customers with whom salespersons have to deal are constant, regardless of the purchase the customer seeks to make. The classification reported in the Minneapolis Survey is suggestive: "The customer looking for a definite thing; the one not knowing just what to buy; the customer who is just curious about what is for sale. The first type of customer must be convinced that the salesperson can show either the very object desired or something better; the second type is open to persuasion; and the third must be attracted and won."

SUGGESTIONS CONCERNING TRAINING FOR SALESMANSHIP

Salesmanship, a splendid field for men.—The widespread public attention focused upon schemes for training young girls for department store positions, has had a tendency to create the impression in the minds of young men that the field of selling is of most worth and promise to young women. The Richmond Survey shows that men predominate in the field, at the ratio of three to one, and that in only two types of stores, the dry goods and five and ten cent stores, are women in the majority. Practically all positions of major responsibility in the Richmond stores are held by men. Probably this condition will continue to exist. Nor is Richmond peculiar in this respect. According to the report of 1910 census of occupations of residents of Indiana, there were about 90,000 salespersons in the State, 70 per cent of whom were males. The following census figures about numbers employed in this field in the State are illuminative:

TABLE XXVI

	Males	Females
Salespersons in stores	26,639	10,647
Retail dealers	32,093	1,237
Brokers and agents	8,338	1,210
Commercial travelers and demonstrators	6,854	361
Total	73,924	13,455

Schemes for training for salesmen must be broad enough to adequately throw open the possibilities of selling to promising young men, and teach, in so far as possible, the basic aspects of merchandising necessary for entrance, proficiency and promotion.

The schools' responsibility.—Classes in salesmanship for youths who have not yet entered the field as wage-earners and for those who are salespersons but who seek organized instruction, must be organized on an entirely different basis. Classes for the former must include the fundamental common elements of mercantile salesmanship, and, for the latter, the distinctive problem peculiar to commodities sold and store organization. There is no question but that the public schools have a direct responsibility in offering preparatory courses for those who seek this type of employment. Although this Survey has revealed some of the constant as well as variable factors involved, the study was neither broad nor intensive enough to submit a complete bill of particulars which might be accepted without challenge. A detailed and intensive study to determine the solid, common ground underlying all sales work, should be made at once, since the field is so promising and public interest is so great. No texts are yet available which touch the real problem, since practically all works on salesmanship discuss only such common requisites as reliability of character, ambition, patience and tact, all of which underlie a salesman's success no more than that of a doctor, a mechanic or a nurse. A reliable text cannot be written until the intensive study suggested is made.

The course of the future for those preparing for salesmanship.— To understand the composition and manufacturing of stuffs, textiles, silverware, rugs, etc., a salesman must have a knowledge of applied chemistry; to appreciate and explain patterns in textiles and jewelry, fashion of hats and costumes as well as to arrange displays on counters and in windows, a salesman must have training in design, color and harmony of line and space. English, penmanship and arithmetic are necessary for sales records, and practical economics.

A study of applied economics, including mercantile traffic and transportation, is necessary in marking goods and setting prices. Commercial geography and industrial studies are necessary in obtaining a knowledge of the world's producing, buying and selling markets and manufacturing processes. The course of the future must contain at least all these basic elements.

These suggestions constitute an hypothesis, that there might be worked out for salesmanship a course in a way analogous to a general course in pedagogy, psychology, sociology, and history, now required of all who enter the teacher's profession. No such courses at present are available for salesmanship. The vague and vaporous books on personality, conduct and advertising, which are current in schools of salesmanship and correspondence courses, at present offer a mere starting point for the salesmanship course of the future, which will take such generalities for granted and begin with specific studies.

QUESTIONS FOR DISCUSSION

1. The persons making the Minneapolis Survey concluded that even where "ample technical knowledge" existed, certain qualities were often lacking. What were these qualities? Does it seem probable that high skill in bookkeeping, for example, could leave one devoid of these qualities?
2. How could large employers, as in Des Moines, justify the belief that office work should not be undertaken by anyone who does not have a high-school education?
3. From an examination of the survey of Rochester, New York, what conclusions do you reach on the following matters: (*a*) specialization in office work, (*b*) the value of general bookkeeping courses, (*c*) the value of special clerical courses, such as machine operation, (*d*) the value of attempting to train in advertising and selling, (*e*) the weaknesses and strength of the high school or business college commercial curriculum as you are familiar with it.
4. Examine the survey in Milwaukee and make conclusions concerning all of the issues raised in the preceding question, so far as the data are applicable.
5. Follow the same procedure for the evidence presented in the Cleveland survey.
6. Follow the same procedure for the evidence presented in the survey of occupations in New York.
7. Would data such as those given in the statements of Type 1 be valuable for purposes of vocational guidance if presented to Freshmen in high-school commercial courses?
8. Does an examination of the demands in specific types of business bear out in general the conclusions which you reached from the study of the surveys made in various cities?
9. Do studies of specific businesses indicate a greater or less use of the conventional bookkeeping, stenography, and typewriting than was found in the city surveys?
10. To what extent, if at all, are your conclusions of what business says it wants modified by A, B, and C of evidence of Type 3?
11. Under evidence of Type 3, Section B shows that 36 per cent of the reporting schools state that over 50 per cent of their commercial students find initial employment in stenography. The Cleveland survey indicates that only 22 per cent of the clerical

workers in Cleveland are stenographers. How do you account for this difference?

12. Examine evidence of Type 3, C and D. Are the conclusions which are there reached concerning the type of work done by commercial workers and the training which they receive a criticism of the commercial course in high schools as you know it?
13. Does the evidence indicate that stenography, typewriting, and bookkeeping are worth while as stepping-stones and should, therefore, be taught? If this is true, is it likely that a greatly disproportionate amount of time is given them in the secondary schools? Is it conceivable that they might with propriety be dropped entirely from the secondary schools?
14. From your study of the evidence of what business wants, are we justified in the tentative conclusion reached earlier that there must be training for specialized technique?
15. If the quantity of typewriting, stenography, and bookkeeping in the secondary commercial courses were greatly reduced, what could be substituted "to fill up the time?"
16. Why has there not been differentiation in the commercial training given boys and girls? Does the evidence justify the belief that the demands are different for the sexes?
17. What explanations can be given for the different occupations in which boys and girls take their initial positions? What explanation can be given for the different occupations in which boys and girls are found after a period of years? Are the reasons which you give reasons which are likely to continue to be true?
18. What do you understand to be the meaning of the term job analysis?
19. Of what value is job analysis for one who is interested in business education?
20. Was our study of what business is, part of a job analysis? Is our whole undertaking to reach conclusions concerning the objectives of business education merely a job analysis? If so, a job analysis of what job?
21. Work through the junior commercial-occupations job analyses made by the Federal Board. Concerning it, what would be your answer to these questions: (*a*) Would such an analysis be valuable to boys and girls beginning the high-school commercial course? (*b*) What value has it for teachers of commercial work? (*c*) Are you led to the belief that the way to train for commercial

occupations is to give courses in each of these jobs, training in each instance for the particular requirements as the job analysis indicates them to exist?

22. What is wrong with conventional commercial courses if the conclusions of the Junior Commercial Survey are sound?
23. Since stenography, typewriting, and bookkeeping are the courses given high-school commercial students, why did the Federal Board find it necessary to make so many items in their classification of positions?
24. What is a "general clerk"? What training is proposed for him in the Board's report? Should the high school train for this position?
25. What is the Board's criticism of existing bookkeeping texts? Does the criticism seem justified? What, if anything, should be substituted?
26. Attempt to work out a brief outline of the courses proposed by the Board in Section E of evidence of Type 3.
27. In what ways do the conclusions on stenography agree and disagree with the conclusions of the "Junior Survey"?
28. On the basis of the Board's report what do you believe the secondary school should do regarding machine-operating courses? Regarding retail-selling courses?
29. What are the "supervisory and executive positions" mentioned in "the Senior Survey"? Who will obtain these positions? Try to put content into the courses suggested for training for these positions.
30. Does the job analysis made in the Richmond, Indiana, survey bear out the conclusions reached by the Federal Board?
31. The Minneapolis survey puts special emphasis upon job analysis of retail selling. What were the conclusions reached as to the requirements for such work? Judging from the requirements for retail selling as indicated by Sections D and E of Evidence of Type 5, how much to the point has been the typical "course" in salesmanship?
32. Various surveys bring out the fact that a large number of high-school commercial graduates find their way into retail selling. Studies such as the Minneapolis and Richmond surveys indicate that the most important training for retail selling is a detailed knowledge of the goods sold. Since the high-school student can never be sure of the type of goods which he will eventually be

selling, it follows, does it not, that courses should be given which would make commercial students intimately familiar with *all* goods?

33. If we do not follow the suggestion given in the preceding question, what shall we do about this matter of training for retail salesmanship?
34. Formulate a series of statements which summarize the suggestions for business education obtained from Chapter VIII.

CHAPTER IX

THE FUNCTIONS OF EDUCATION IN A DEMOCRACY

All education given by the public schools must be in sympathy with the best-known ends of public education. This statement holds true regardless of the course to which it may be applied. No course of study in the American public school, however vocational its character, can, if it omits education of the kind needed in a democracy, be anything but a misappropriation of public funds. In seeking the ends or objectives of business, therefore, so far as we are thinking in terms of the secondary school, we shall need to give consideration to the needs and purposes of all education in a democracy such as ours. In doing this, as in the two preceding chapters, the best method seems to be to submit such evidence as is available. A consideration of the evidence, rather than a consideration of an interpretation, is the useful procedure. There are, then, presented here a series of statements, for the most part statements of persons whose opinion is well recognized as of value, regarding objectives of public education. It is necessary to draw from such evidence a conclusion and to combine that with our conclusions drawn from the study of what business is and what business says it wants, in arriving at a tentative working statement of the objectives of education for business.[1]

STATEMENT 1. THE MEANING AND AIM OF EDUCATION

A. Some Objectives of Public Education[2]

The administrative awakening to the need of determining with definiteness the goals of public education is coming sur-

[1] Although the classic statement of Herbert Spencer has been omitted to give place to more modern views, chap. i, at least, of *Education* might well be read.

[2] Adapted by permission from Franklin Bobbitt, "The Objectives of Secondary Education," *School Review*, XXVIII, December, 1920, 738–48.

prisingly late. In the world of economic production it is axiomatic that nothing can be done until it is decided what products are to be turned out; but in the field of public education we have in large measure been building and organizing our huge plants and operating them full blast without having definitely predetermined the kinds of products which we are going to turn out. Exceptions, of course, must be made in the case of a few things, such as the ability to read, to write, to spell, to compute, to read maps, to express one's self in clear and correct English, and a few others. These matters are mainly taken care of upon the elementary level. The high schools for the most part have not particularized their objectives in terms of human activities or human well-being. The situation is well stated by Dr. Snedden:

The great problems of secondary education today are, of course, problems of aim. The concrete, immediate aims which control the large majority of our administrative and pedagogic procedures in the American high school (and how very concrete and definite and exacting many of them are) are of quite unknown value. We have not defined them in terms of human good; we seem unable to estimate the value of the results achieved in our efforts to realize them. We teach our prescribed algebra strenuously and with some very definite objectives, but we flounder pitfully when we try to prove that these objectives are really worth while. We have refined and standardized our immediate objectives in teaching physics and chemistry, but what we actually attain by it all in terms of human well-being remains concealed in the obscurity of vague phrase and inadequate generalization. We drive our boys and girls hard up the steeps of Latin, French, and German, but we are forced to fall back on mystical and uncertain faiths in the endeavor to justify our driving of particular youths up these particular steeps.

We have in reserve, of course, large, splendid aims which are alleged, finally, to guide the evolution and destinies of our secondary schools. Do we not freely use such terms as "character formation," "mental discipline," "self-realization," "social efficiency," "culture," "citizenship," "leadership," "intellectual power," and a score of other unanalyzed general phrases, as expressive of our ultimate goals? And in these are there not summed up most of the purposes that really count in this life? It must be admitted that we do still live largely in a maze of faith (and fable) as regards education. . . . . For, after all, our great fine aims in secondary education, expressed in tenuous even though aspiring phrase, are in reality only faith aims; in practice they rarely actually guide us in choice of ways and means; and we seldom stop to measure the tangible results of our teaching against the shadowy and ever-varying interpretations of these aims as set forth in books and journal articles.

During the five years since Dr. Snedden's statement appeared, much, very much, has been done. The National Education Association Commission on the Reorganization of Secondary Education in its "Cardinal Principles of Secondary Education" has presented seven groups of educational objectives. Such an official pronouncement, even though tentative and merely a basis of further effort, is now greatly needed. The present writer would suggest consideration of a somewhat more inclusive series, as follows:

1. Education for general physical efficiency. Play-level and work-level.

2. Education for general mental efficiency. Play-level and work-level.

3. Education for unspecialized activities of production, distribution, conservation, and consumption. Play-level and work-level.

4. Education for one's specialized calling.

5. Education for citizenship.

6. Education for general social relationships and contacts. Play-level and work-level.

7. Education for social intercommunication. (Languages and other modes of intercommunication.) Play-level and work-level.

8. Education for religious attitudes and activities.

9. Education for parental responsibilities.

B. ARE THERE EDUCATIONAL AIMS?[1]

There is nothing peculiar about educational aims. They are just like aims in any directed occupation. The educator,

[1] Adapted by permission from John Dewey, *Democracy and Eduction*, pp. 124–26. Macmillan Co., 1916.

like the farmer, has certain things to do, certain resources with which to do, and certain obstacles with which to contend. The conditions with which the farmer deals, whether as obstacles or resources, have their own structure and operation independently of any purpose of his. Seeds sprout, rain falls, the sun shines, insects devour, blight comes, the seasons change. His aim is simply to utilize these various conditions; to make his activities and their energies work together, instead of against one another. It would be absurd if the farmer set up a purpose of farming, without any reference to these conditions of soil, climate, characteristic of plant growth, etc. His purpose is simply a foresight of the consequences of his energies connected with those of the things about him, a foresight used to direct his movements from day to day. Foresight of possible consequences leads to more careful and extensive observation of the nature and performances of the things he has to do with, and to laying out a plan—that is, of a certain order in the acts to be performed. And it is well to remind ourselves that education as such has no aims. Only persons, parents, and teachers, etc., have aims, not an abstract idea like education. And consequently their purposes are indefinitely varied, differing with different children, changing as children grow and with the growth of experience on the part of the one who teaches. Even the most valid aims which can be put in words will, as words, do more harm than good unless one recognizes that they are not aims, but rather suggestions to educators as to how to observe, how to look ahead, and how to choose in liberating and directing the energies of the concrete situations in which they find themselves. As a recent writer has said: "To lead this boy to read Scott's novels instead of old Sleuth's stories; to teach this girl to sew; to root out the habit of bullying from John's make up; to prepare this class to study medicine,—these are samples of the millions of aims we have actually before us in the concrete work of education."

C. The Social Aim of Education[1]

The problem of education is, therefore, reduced to this: whether the members of society shall continue to pass through life surrounded only by the natural and unorganized influences which everywhere exist, by which they are indeed constantly acquiring knowledge, such as it is, and many conceptions which are not knowledge because they consist of erroneous inferences; whether they shall thus be left to form all kinds of undigested and unsystematized ideas, half of which are objectively unreal, and most of the remainder too narrow to be of any value, yet to which their conduct will rigidly correspond, producing its legitimate effect upon themselves and upon society; or, whether they shall be required to pass a portion of their early lives under a system of artificial circumstances, so regulated that the bulk of the influences which appeal to the senses and produce ideas will be both reliable and important, and from which, under no other than the normal operations of the mind, reliable and valuable knowledge must necessarily result, solid character be formed, and the highest ethical and dynamic actions be induced, exerting rigidly corresponding effects upon themselves and upon society. It is, in short, the question whether the social system shall always be left to nature, always be genetic and spontaneous, and be allowed to drift listlessly on, intrusted to the by no means always progressive influences which have developed it and brought it to its present condition, or whether it shall be regarded as a proper subject of art, treated as other natural products have been treated by human intelligence, and made as much superior to nature, in this only proper sense of the word, as other artificial productions are superior to natural ones.

As the ultimate end which every feeling organism, every individual man, and society collectively, both morally should and physically must directly or indirectly pursue, is the increase of happiness, so the highest achievement of the developed

[1] Adapted by permission from Lester F. Ward, *Dynamic Sociology*, II, 632–33, 541. D. Appleton & Co., 1897.

intellect and social consciousness of man is the substitution for the unsuccessful or partially successful and costly direct efforts to attain that end, of a systematic, predetermined, and successful scheme for the organization of happiness. Such a scheme must have for its primary object the equal distribution of the extant knowledge of the world.

D. Education as an Agency of Social Control[1]

The art of education like the art of agriculture deals with growing things. Though agriculture has been practiced and discussed for so many ages, and enlists the imperious bread-and-butter interests, yet it is only now becoming scientific. We have already observed that in the opinion of the agronomists the yield of American corn lands could be doubled by the application of the lessons of science, and that it is equally within the truth to say that the harvest of life for the people of America could be doubled if the possibilities with which they are endowed by nature were brought to approximate realization. For this it is not enough to make the benefits of present methods in education more nearly universal, as Ward so impressively advocated, important as that is. It is essential to introduce into our education guiding principles which have been only dimly apprehended and applied. Heredity sets the limits within which individual development can vary. By all means let us do what we can by the program of eugenics, by selective regulation of immigration, and by promotion of public health, to improve the biological quality of population. But after all is done we shall have the problem of making the most of the latent possibility of each rising generation just as the farmer has the problem of securing the largest yield and highest conservation of his land. And as the same land may yield little or much and that which it yields may be corn, alfalfa, or weeds, so the same population may yield Periclean achievement and levels of character which we know only by rare but blessed instances, or futility and deviltry.

[1] Adapted by permission from Edward C. Hayes, *Introduction to the Study of Sociology*, pp. 660–61, 665–66. D. Appleton & Co., 1915.

Within the limits set by birth, individuality is a social product. Without education by social contacts there would be no such thing as individuality as we understand that term. Social contacts begin to be educative among the higher animals. Social relations not only determine that there shall be self-consciousness, but even more certainly they determine what the nature of the self-thought shall be. We inherit contrasting instincts, instincts of competition and of co-operation, of self-assertion and of loyal self-subordination. Social contacts have power to determine whether the self-thought, to which both spontaneously and voluntarily a man's acts conform, shall be one of swaggering self-assertion, of more refined self-aggrandizement, or predominantly one of service. The self-thought is complex; social contacts determine the nature of the elements which it contains. And the future development of personality is largely a reaction between the self-thought already established and the subsequent stream of social suggestion.

Education the chief agency of social control.—The direction of ambition is socially determined. We want to be winners at the game that is being played. The small boy's springtime obsession for marbles is gone long before fall, because "the boys aren't playing marbles any more." The Indian who dreamed and longed and risked his life to hang scalps at his belt, or the Filipino who measures his success by the number of skulls over his door, or the Kafir or Thibetan whose standard of greatness and mainspring of endeavor is the size of his herd, or the American toiling to make a high score at the dollar-piling game and to support his wife in competitive ostentation, have not selected these goals as an expression of their own independent individuality. The operation of the same principle of the molding of personal ambition by social radiation caused the Spartans to despise money. The swift advance of Germany from the foot to the head of great European powers has been due largely to the fact that achievement in science has been a goal of ambition of her most gifted sons, so that by her application of science to industry and government she has been able to redemonstrate the truth that knowledge is power. A traveler in Florence asked one of the curly-headed, great-eyed urchins of its streets what he would like to be when he grew up, and the boy replied, "A sculptor." Now, Florence has sculptors, though not all of her sculptors are great. A street boy in an American city would not have answered so; he might have said that he wanted to become pitcher for the White Sox, or boss of the ward. Jane Addams says that in a ward chiefly inhabited by workingmen there was difficulty in replacing a corrupt boss by an honest workingman as its aldermanic representative, because the people wanted to vote for a man who was a success. Where the soubrette, the boss, the money-maker, represent success, soubrettes, bosses and money-makers will be produced. Why did the Spartan boy let the fox gnaw his vitals without giving a sign, and why did Spartan soldiers commit suicide because they had not perished with their comrades on the battlefield? What was it that made Spartans out of Greeks whose name elsewhere became a synonym for self-indulgence? Grit was the social ideal in Sparta. Whatever society adequately appreciates, society will get, up to the very limits of human possibility, whether it be prizefighters, money kings, scientists, or constructive statesmen. No other reform is so fundamental as a shifting of emphasis in social valuations. Ambition in a given population or in a given individual may be drawn out in any one of various directions. Its direction and its power are not fixed by "human nature," but are matters of education.

Society must impart to its members tastes, interests, ambitions, and a set of moral detestations and moral enthusiasm strong enough to inhibit instincts and to elicit zeals—detestations and enthusiasms that are not inborn and that embody the lessons of race experience respecting the conduct of life. Nature does not give us a conscience any more than it gives us a language, but only the capacity to acquire one; social evolution and education must do the rest. The task of order and progress is not only to erect the towering structure of social organization out of individual units, but also to make the bricks of which alone such a structure can be built.

E. Education Should Guide Human Wants[1]

The aims of education should then be: to make men want the right things, and to make them better able so to control all the forces of nature and themselves that they can satisfy these wants. We have to make use of nature, to co-operate with each other, and to improve ourselves.

The first great element in making human wants better is to increase the good will—the disposition to care for others' welfare as well as for one's own—the desire to see the good wants of others satisfied. To wish the welfare of all men is one of the best of wants, for it is a want which every satisfier of all will satisfy.

The second great means of making human wants better is to cultivate the impersonal pleasures. Some satisfactions, such as the enjoyment of productive labor, health, good reading and study, are impersonal in the sense that for one to have the pleasure does not prevent anybody else from having it. They are unlike the pleasure of eating or owning or wearing things, where the pleasure of one man usually uses up a possible means of satisfying some other man. One of the most nearly perfect of all impulses is the impulse to advance knowledge of ourselves and the world in which we are to live. For this impulse is impersonal—all men may profit by the truth. It enriches everybody else's possibilities of satisfying the same want—the more knowledge man has, the easier it is to get more. It predisposes men against unsatisfiable wants—to know what the world really is prevents us from wanting what it cannot give. It leads to the satisfaction of all good wants—knowledge is power.

The third great means of making human wants better is the elimination of wants which must in the nature of things bring about a surplus of dissatisfaction. Such, for instance, are the wants represented by superstition.

[1] Adapted by permission from Edward L. Thorndike, *Psychology*, pp. 11–13. Macmillan Co., 1912.

F. The View of a Labor Leader[1]

Most important among the opportunities that are the rights of children are educational opportunities. Education is vital not only to the welfare of the individual, but to that of the whole nation. It is the only *foundation* and the hope of *ideals of democracy*. It enables the possessor to understand and to measure his powers and to use his ability most effectively. . . . .

There have come ideals of an education that teaches out of life and work: that deals with the concrete materials of environment and the duties and activities of life. This education seeks to put into the lives of all that understand, appreciation of the significance of service performed in all the relations of life—an appreciation that shall illuminate all of work and life.

G. The Modern View of Education[2]

The Meaning of Education, as conceived in the present, is found in this harmonization of interest and effort. This is but another attempt to solve the problem of the individual and of society, which, as we have seen, has been the educational problem as it has been the ethical problem, from the beginning of human life. How is the individual to be educated so as to secure the full development of personality and at the same time preserve the stability of institutional life and assist in its evolution to a higher state? It is the old problem of securing both individual liberty and social justice. Interest and effort give in modern form Aristotle's problem of well-being and well-doing. Interest, representing the emphasis or the factor of individualism, is an outgrowth of the naturalistic movement of the eighteenth century. The education of effort is the survival in conservative circles of the old education of authority expressive of the religious and social views prevalent since the Reformation period. These views have survived longest in educa-

[1] Adapted by permission from Samuel Gompers, in *American Federationist*, XXIII (February, 1916), 126.

[2] Adapted by permission from Paul Monroe, *Brief Course in the History of Education*, pp. 405–6. Macmillan Co., 1911.

tional institutions that are controlled by religious denominations or by certain dominant classes in society, as in the English public schools and universities.

The meaning of education, as at present conceived, is found in the attempt to combine and to balance these two elements of individual rights and social duties, or personal development and social service. The meaning of education in the present finds its whole significance in this very process of relating the individual to society, so as to secure both development of personality and social welfare. It is true that for the last two decades the tendency in thought, in reaction to the extreme emphasis on interest and on individualism, has been to stress the social factor. Education has been defined as preparation for citizenship, as adjustment to society, as preparation for life in institutions, as the acquisition of the racial inheritance.

But definitions more acceptable to present thought seek to combine both factors and to find a harmonization of them in the nature of the educational process. . . . . From whatever line of investigation the problem of education is now approached, its meaning is given in some terms of this harmonization of social and individual factors. It is the process of conforming the individual to the given social standard or type in such a manner that his inherent capacities are developed, his greatest usefulness and happiness obtained, and, at the same time, the highest welfare of society is conserved.

STATEMENT 2. EDUCATION A NECESSITY[1]

Society exists through a process of transmission quite as much as biological life. This transmission occurs by means of communication of habits of doing, thinking and feeling from the older to the younger. Without this communication of ideals, hopes, expectations, standards, opinions, from those members of society who are passing out of a group life to those who are coming into it, social life could not survive. If the members who compose a society lived on continuously, they

[1] Adapted by permission from John Dewey, *Democracy and Education*, pp. 1–11. Macmillan Co., 1916.

might educate the newborn members, but it would be a task directed by personal interest rather than social need. Now it is a work of necessity.

Individuals do not even compose a social group because they all work for a common end. The parts of a machine work with a maximum of co-operativeness for a common result, but they do not form a community. If, however, they were all cognizant of the common end and all interested in it so that they regulated their specific activity in view of it, then they would form a community. But this would involve communication. Each would have to know what the other was about and would have to have some way of keeping the other informed as to his own purpose and progress. Consensus demands communication.

We are thus compelled to recognize that within even the most social group there are many relations which are not as yet social. A large number of human relationships in any social group are still upon the machine-like plane. Individuals use one another so as to get desired results, without reference to the emotional and intellectual disposition and consent of those used. Such uses express physical superiority, or superiority of position, skill, technical ability, and command of tools, mechanical or fiscal. So far as the relations of parent and child, teacher and pupil, employer and employee, governor and governed, remain upon this level, they form no true social group, no matter how closely their respective activities touch one another. Giving and taking of orders modifies action and results, but does not of itself effect a sharing of purposes, a communication of interests.

The inequality of achievement between the mature and the immature not only necessitates teaching the young, but the necessity of this teaching gives an immense stimulus to reducing experience to that order and form which will render it most easily communicable and hence most usable.

We are thus led to distinguish, within the broad educational process which we have been so far considering, a more formal kind of education—that of direct tuition or schooling. In undeveloped social groups we find very little formal teaching and training. Savage groups mainly rely for instilling needed dispositions into the young upon the same sort of association which keeps adults loyal to their group. They have no special devices, material, or institutions for teaching save in connection with initiation ceremonies by which the youth are inducted into full social membership. For the most part, they depend upon children learning the customs of the adults, acquiring their emotional set and stock of ideas, by sharing in what the elders are doing. In part, this sharing is direct, taking part in the occupations of adults and thus serving an apprenticeship; in part, it is indirect, through the dramatic plays in which children reproduce the actions of grown-ups and thus learn to know what they are like. To savages it would seem preposterous to seek out a place where nothing but learning was going on in order that one might learn.

But as civilization advances, the gap between the capacities of the young and the concerns of adults widens. Learning by direct sharing in the pursuits of grown-ups becomes increasingly difficult except in the case of the less advanced occupations. Much of what adults do is so remote in space and in meaning that playful imitation is less and less adequate to reproduce its spirit. Ability to share effectively in adult activities thus depends upon a prior training given with this end in view. Intentional agencies—schools—and explicit material—studies—are devised. The task of teaching certain things is delegated to a special group of persons.

Without such formal education, it is not possible to transmit all the resources and achievements of a complex society. It also opens a way to a kind of experience which would not be accessible to the young, if they were left to pick up their training in informal association with others, since books and the symbols of knowledge are mastered.

But there are conspicuous dangers attendant upon the transition from indirect to formal education. Sharing in actual pursuit, whether directly or vicariously in play, is at least personal and vital. These qualities compensate, in some measure, for the narrowness of available opportunities. Formal instruction, on the contrary, easily becomes remote and dead—abstract and bookish, to use the ordinary words of depreciation. What accumulated knowledge exists in low grade societies is at least put into practice; it is transmuted into character; it exists with the depth of meaning that attaches to its coming within urgent daily interests.

But in an advanced culture much which has to be learned is stored in symbols. It is far from translation into familiar acts and objects. Such material is relatively technical and superficial. Taking the ordinary standard of reality as a measure, it is artificial. For this measure is connection with practical concerns. Such material exists in a world by itself, unassimilated to ordinary customs of thought and expression. There is the standing danger that the material of formal instruction will be merely the subject matter of the schools, isolated from the subject matter of life-experience. The permanent social interests are likely to be lost from view. Those which have not been carried over into the structure of social life, but which remain largely matters of technical information expressed in symbols, are made conspicuous in schools. Thus we reach the ordinary notion of education: the notion which ignores its social necessity and its identity with all human association that affects conscious life, and which identifies it with imparting information about remote matters and the conveying of learning through verbal signs: the acquisition of literacy.

Hence one of the weightiest problems with which the philosophy of education has to cope is the method of keeping a proper balance between the informal and the formal, the incidental and the intentional, modes of education. When the acquiring of information and of technical intellectual skill do not influence the formation of a social disposition, ordinary vital experience fails to gain in meaning, while schooling, in so far, creates only "sharps" in learning—that is, egoistic specialists. To avoid a split between what men consciously know because they are aware of having learned it by a specific job of learning, and what they unconsciously know because they have absorbed it in the formation of their characters by intercourse with others, becomes an increasingly delicate task with every development of special schooling.

Communication is a process of sharing experience till it becomes a common possession.

STATEMENT 3. THE EVOLUTION OF THE CONCEPT OF EDUCATION[1]

The history of education is the history of mankind. In the epoch of primitive civilization the manner of life was so simple as to preclude all idea of formal knowledge. Necessity for food and shelter taught the primitive man the means and method of supplying his natural wants. Repetitions of his successful attempts established habits which became to him the ideal of life.

These ideals varied greatly in their content, with different people in different climes. The necessities of one race were superfluities in another, but in each and all, certain essential factors in the struggle for material existence became the elements of an educational ideal.

In order to comprehend the development of education among any people it is necessary to understand the process and progress of civilization, for education and civilization are inseparably connected.

That education should fit the individual to be a citizen has been a persistent motive from time immemorial. No matter how varying the conditions, or how unlike the standards of life, this element has been common to the educational ideals of all countries.

As the State came to be independent of the Church, and passed under the influence of philosophy, science, and sociology, the idea of what constitutes citizenship was constantly changing in the minds of educators. So that in later times education has come to mean the fitting of an individual not only to discharge his duty to the State, but also to fulfill his obligation to society.

[1] Adapted by permission from Mabel Irene Emerson, *The Evolution of the Educational Ideal*, pp. 1–3, 154–64. Houghton Mifflin Co., 1914.

With the beginning of the twentieth century there came a marvelous development in commerce and in the industries. Great wealth has been amassed both by nations and by individuals, and a spirit of competition has tended to emphasize the importance of productive power. The spirit of the age is commercialism. A citizen, to be of value to the State, must have the power to produce something of value in the industrial world. The importance of a nation now depends on its industrial activities, and on the number of its skilled individual producers. So great is the rivalry among nations that it has become a matter of necessity to modify the methods of education in order to have a greater number of productive citizens. Consequently society has demanded that some provision be made in the school curriculum for instruction along eminently practical lines.

It is now seen that education for citizenship must include something more than mere culture; that while it must not exclude what is essential to the proper development of the individual, it must also include that which shall be of direct and immediate value to society.

Germany was one of the first to recognize that industrial development and political advancement of nations depend entirely on the kind of education given to children. Hence Germany has, for a long time, had industrial, trade, and technical schools. France and England have also responded to the general demand. America, because of her great natural resources, has been slow to realize the necessity of establishing industrial schools.

For certain intellectual vocations, such as law, medicine, the ministry, and teaching, professional schools have long been established. But the vast majority of children, upon leaving the elementary or secondary schools, enter a trade or business. For this reason wise educators are today attempting to enlarge the horizon of such children by giving them an intellectual grasp of their chosen vocation as a whole, and a practical experience of the work in detail. It is with the hope of making children something more than automatic machines in a highly specialized business that the effort is being made to fit them for positions that require intelligence as well as manual skill. To this end vocational and industrial schools are now being established in which the cultural value of education is not neglected, but rather subordinated to the practical needs of the child's environment. This is bringing about a new sense of values and a consequent readjustment in the curricula of schools.

There are practically five divisions of vocational education: professional; agricultural; commercial or business; industrial; and household arts. Because of the fact that industry has become the chief factor in determining conditions of living and working in the world, vocational education pertaining to the industries is, at the present time, receiving the greatest emphasis.

Since the latter part of the nineteenth century manual training has been taught in over seven hundred American cities. But this work has been academic in character and cultural in its results. With the great changes that have taken place in the world, America has become essentially an industrial nation. Manual training has done good work in its place, but it has not been able to produce that efficiency which is needed in the industrial world.

STATEMENT 4. A PRIMARY CULTURE FOR DEMOCRACY[1]

One who looks even a little beneath the surface of things may see that there is no question more timely than that of culture, and none which has more need of fresh and fundamental conceptions. It is by no means a question merely of the decoration of life, or of personal enjoyment; it involves the whole matter of developing large-minded members for that strong and good democracy which we hope we are building up. Without such members such a democracy can never exist, and culture is essential to the power and efficiency, as well as to the beauty, of the social whole.

[1] Adapted by permission from Charles H. Cooley, "A Primary Culture for Democracy," *Publications of the American Sociological Society*, XIII (1918), 1–3, 8–10.

We may all agree, I imagine, that culture means the development of the human and social, as distinct from the technical, side of life. Our recent growth, so far at least as it is realized in our institutions, has been mainly technical, the creation of an abundant economic system and a marvelous body of natural science, neither of them achievements of a sort to center attention upon what is broadly human.

It is true that along with these has come a growth of humane sentiment and aspiration, of a spirit Christian and democratic in the largest sense of those words; but this remains in great part vague and ineffectual. To give it clearness and power is one of the aims of the culture we need.

There is also, I am sure, a growing demand for culture. In the course of the greatest struggle of history, which is also a struggle for righteous ideals, the people everywhere have learned that the social order needs reconstruction, and that the popular will has power to transform it, as has actually been seen in molding nations to efficiency in war. All this gives rise, especially in the young, to large and radical thinking, which permeates the armies, the press, the labor unions, and other popular associations; and among the first results of this thinking is a demand for a new sort of liberal education, through which all members of the coming order shall get a wider outlook, a higher and clearer idealism, and so be prepared to create that free, righteous, and joyful system of life to which they aspire.

Indeed our democracy, in spite of its supposed materialism, has long had at heart the ideal of culture. Culture has been a god that we somewhat ignorantly worshiped. We are not satisfied with beholding the multiplication of material things, nor even with the hope of greater justice in their distribution; we want joy, beauty, hope, higher thoughts, a larger life, a fuller participation in the great human and divine whole in which we find ourselves. Even those popular movements which formulate their aims in material terms are not really materialistic but get their strongest appeal from the belief that these aims are the condition of a fuller spiritual life.

Another reason for turning our thoughts to culture is that the economic outlook demands it. We are apparently entering upon a period of cheap, standardized production upon an enormous scale, which will multiply commodities and perhaps increase leisure but will make little demand upon the intelligence of the majority of producers and offer no scope for mental discipline. Work is becoming less than ever competent to educate the worker, and if we are to escape the torpor, frivolity, and social irresponsibility engendered by this condition, we must offset it by a social and moral culture acquired in the schools and in the community life.

Our culture must be a function of our situation as a whole. Just as the arts, like literature, painting, and sculpture, can not be merely traditional but must spring fresh and creative from the living spirit of the time, so also must culture, which is likewise an expression of the general life. It may be contrasted with, perhaps opposed to, the apparent trend of things; but if so it is only because it is rooted in a deeper trend. If it does not function in the whole it is nothing.

I am in sympathy with those who cling to the great humanistic traditions of the past. There can be no real culture that is altogether new; it can only be a fresh growth out of old stems; but it must be that; it must be new in the sense that it is wholly reanimated by the spirit of our own time. Any attempt to impose an old culture upon us merely because the educated class cherish it, or because it can be supported by general arguments having no reference to our actual needs, must fail. Through control of institutions the classicist, or the scientist, or the religionist may for a time force the forms of an old learning upon a new generation; but before long all that does not vigorously function in the life of the day will slough off and be forgotten.

Certainly no culture can be real for us that is not democratic. This does not mean, however, that it must be superficial, or commonplace, or uniform. These are traits which the enemies of democracy have endeavored to fix upon it, but which do not belong to its essence. Democracy is at the bottom a more humane, inclusive, and liberal organization of life, and certainly a democratic culture will be one based on large and kindly conceptions, meeting the needs of the plain people as well as of the privileged classes, and worked out largely through the schools and other popular institutions. Because culture has in the past been inaccessible to the masses and still is so in great part, we must make it our very special business to bring it within their reach; but the idea that such a culture must lack refinement and distinction has no basis in sound theory and will be refuted as fast as we make democracy what it can and should be.

The studies, the teachers, the social activities of the schools and the community, are all expressions of an underlying current of life which molds their character for better or worse and can only gradually be changed. It would be fatuous not to see that this current is largely unfavorable to the development of any real culture, either primary or secondary. The influence in our society which is organized and dominant is commercialism; the elements of culture are for the most part scattered, demobilized, and impotent. The very idea and spirit of it are starved and crowded out.

If we divide the sources of culture into two parts, those that derive from tradition and those that come to us more directly from participation in life, we shall find that the former especially are deficient. Perhaps the first requisite of progress is to face the fact that we are, as a people, in a state of semi-barbarism as regards participation in that heritage which comes only by familiarity with literature and arts. And since this is lacking in the people at large, including the bulk of the educated classes, our schools, which are nothing if not an expression of the people, do not readily supply it. The wealthy and energetic men who have general control of education mean well, but their whole life-history, in most cases, has been such that words like culture, art, and literature can be little more to them than empty sounds, and whatever provision they make for them can hardly fail to be somewhat perfunctory and superficial.

I do not mean that culture is irreconcilable with commercial activities or with technical training in the schools. On the contrary, periods of commercial expansion have usually been those when arts and literature flourished most; and technical training, if moderate in its demands and enlarged by a constant sense of the social whole to which it contributes, may itself involve a most essential kind of culture. But our commercialism has been exorbitant and exclusive; and our technical training is rarely of a sort which makes the student feel his membership in the larger whole. Both must be transformed by a social spirit and philosophy before they can join hands with culture.

These are the underlying reasons for the unsatisfactory state of our schools and for the extreme difficulty of introducing any culture spirit into them. American education, on the culture side, is deadened by formalism from the first grade in the primary schools to and including the graduate departments of our universities. In spite of much sound theory and honest effort on the part of teachers the stifling gases of commercialism have passed from the general atmosphere into academic halls and devitalized almost everything having no obvious economic purpose. I doubt if there has on the whole been any progress in this way, perhaps rather a retrogression, during my own time.

When I contemplate the state of culture in our colleges I cannot wonder that it does not flourish in the elementary schools. Thus, to take only one indication, I have reason to think that serious spontaneous reading is far less common among university students than it was forty years ago. This is my own observation, confirmed by others and corroborated by the evidence of a veteran bookseller, who told me that he sold fewer books of general literature to, say, 5,000 students at the time of our conservation than he did to one-fourth of that number in the Victorian era.

I find the outlook somewhat more cheerful as regards that sort of culture which we get as a by-product of a co-operation with our fellows. This is a plant which grows untended in a free and friendly life; and I think that democracy is giving our feelings, our manners, and our social perceptions an enlargement which is truly, in its way, a kind of culture. That consideration, helpfulness, and ready sociability which, it appears, have endeared our soldiers to the villages of France are a part of our civilization and may well prove to be the first fruits of a new sort of culture. Let us cherish and diffuse this spirit in every possible way, especially through that school and community organization of which I have spoken. It is not only a fine thing in itself but will help us to appreciate and acquire that transmitted culture, akin to it in essence, which we now so sadly lack.

On the whole, our present condition as regards a popular culture, though unsatisfactory, is not unpromising. We have energy, good-will, and a sincere though vague idealism. We may expect these to work gradually upon all departments of life, our schools, our communities, our economic institutions, and the general atmosphere of the country, slowly bringing to pass a culture which will certainly be fresh, democratic, and human, and need not be deficient in those things that have to be learned from the past. . . . . In the way of culture, as in technical training, our higher schools should offer the best that the world has achieved, and should also foster specialized culture groups to kindle and support the individual in his struggle for a larger life.

STATEMENT 5. EDUCATION AND THE NATIONAL IDEAL[1]

Our nation has hardly yet passed out of its early adolescence. Indeed only with the present war has there been any widespread thought as to our national destiny nor any clear-cut attempt to formulate a philosophy of our social life. . . . . And yet we have had in this country from the very beginning of our history some fairly clear-cut ideals, and these have exerted a profound influence on our educational system. The ideals of liberty, equality, justice, the separation of church and state, and self-government which, however rudimentary, found expression or

[1] Adapted by permission from L. M. Bristol, "Education and the National Ideal," *Publications of the American Sociological Society*, XIII (1918), 166–76.

are implicit in the Declaration of Independence and the Constitution, have been the very foundation stones of our system of free public schools; indeed some of these ideals and their educational correlate go back to early Colonial days.

Not only have the ideals of liberty, equality, justice, and self-government, however uncritically held, been prominent in this country from Colonial times, but since the Declaration of Independence and the formation of our national government there has been a more or less conscious widespread feeling that we were working out here an experiment in democracy which would be an example to other nations. . . . The equality boasted of in our Declaration of Independence is seen to be a very vague and shadowy thing, for we know all too well now that men are not born equal in physical, mental, or moral capacity, and that the actual conditions of life are not such as to bring about equality of opportunity nor at all times even equality before the law. Indeed though our President has said we were fighting to make the world safe for democracy, some have been led to ask seriously whether or not democracy as it actually exists in this country is really worth saving. Moreover we are led to raise the question as to what we mean by democracy and find, upon reflection, that the democracy for whose safety we offered our all is not so much a form of government as a condition of social life.

Liberty, equality, justice! It is for us to make these ideals factual in every department of our social life; a liberty, however, that is consonant with social strength; an equality that with normal human beings means primarily equality of opportunity for self-development, self-expression, self-enlargement and service, and a justice which includes a recognition of individual limitations and imperfections, but also of social responsibility and one that is based primarily on an estimate of the long-run well-being of the social group and of all humanity. And then that ideal of democracy! This, too, must be translated from the realm of the abstract and ideal to the reality of actual, intelligent participation in associated living and in social control whether through diffused public opinion or through public opinion crystallized in legislative enactment. But the one comprehensive national ideal to which all others are subordinate may well be this—and I suggest it as the next logical step in the development of our national ideal: to work out here in America a form of associational life, both as a national whole and in subordinate social groups, so manifestly good that it shall challenge the admiration of other peoples to the degree that they shall desire to adapt our ideals and institutions to their own peculiar conditions and needs. This ideal, too, has the advantage of affording an objective test of the good so insisted upon today in science.

To make this effective as a national ideal requires that it be the ideal in subordinate groups. States should consciously vie with states in the excellence of their system of government, in their treatment of the abnormal classes, in methods of taxation, and other matters pertaining to social welfare. Cities should vie with cities in the development of civic consciousness, in the effectiveness of municipal government in its various departments and activities, and in the manifest excellence of its social organizations—educational, fraternal, philanthropic, and religious. No higher compliment can be paid to a city than that some "plan" it has devised should prove so effective that it would spread to other cities by reflective imitation, as the Galveston plan of government by commission, or the Cleveland plan of budget system for united philanthropies, or the Gary system of schools.

The educational system of the democracy that is worthy of imitation must discover the mechanic and train the mechanic, but its chief function will be to help the boy with a mechanical bent to find himself and his place in the world and give him every opportunity to become as efficient as possible not only as a mechanic but as a member of society. So, too, it must discover the chemist and train the chemist. It must discover the doctor, the lawyer, the artist, the industrial organizer, the political and the religious leader, and train each for effective participation in the life of the social group and of humanity, each doing his task supremely well, each inspired with a purpose to add something to the sum total of human achievement, each with an enlarged self-consciousness so that he thinks and feels not only in terms of the empirical self, but increasingly in terms of family, community, church, industry, nation, humanity.

Three subordinate aims may well be kept in mind, yet all, as above indicated, are included in that of rational participation: the acquirement of useful knowledge and moral judgment, or critical assimilation, the development of power and initiative, or cultivation, and the motivation of a life-purpose with a social outlook, or inspiration. Each is to "enter into the spiritual possessions of the race," according to President Butler, but chiefly to the degree necessary for effective participation in the life of the group. Each is to acquire power over self, over nature, and over his fellow-man, not, however, for narrow personal ends, but for largeness of life and social service. And to hold our youth steady in the task of splendid achievement there is needed the motive of a great purpose. All too much of our school work today is a deadening routine and a spiritless grind. The teacher who can inspire his pupils with a purpose to be in order to do and to toil in order to serve is rare indeed. But never did life offer such a challenge to red-blooded youth as today. The call for the heroic will by no means end with the signing of the treaty of peace. The work of reorganizing American democracy and reconstructing the war-cursed regions of Europe furnishes the basis for an all-compelling appeal to the idealism and enthusiasm of youth which no educator can afford to overlook.

STATEMENT 6. THE POSSIBLE CREATIVE EXPERIENCE IN MODERN INDUSTRY[1]

As I have said before there is a common supposition among people who are not employers of labor, that such features of industry as the mechanical devices of modern technology and the division of labor in factory organization, are in their nature

[1] Adapted by permission from Helen Marot, *Creative Impulse in Industry*, pp. 134–45. E. P. Dutton & Co., 1918.

opposed to the expansive development of the people involved; that these features of apparent intrinsic importance to mass production are antagonistic to individual growth and to the interest of workers in productive effort.

Without question, it is the business of educators to determine whether such features of industry as machinery and the division of labor are fundamentally opposed to growth or whether they are opposed only in the way in which they have been put to use and directed. We can discover whether or not these features are opposed only as the people concerned have the chance to master them and undertake, through their experience, to turn them to account.

Because industry has been impersonalized and the mechanics of associated effort in industry worked out in such large measure, it is today possible to conceive of spiritual as well as physical association in productive enterprise. A difficulty in the way of this conception, aside from the business complex, is our habit of thinking exclusively of creative effort as an individual expression. In describing the individual expression we would say that a man may create a machine but that when men jointly produce one they work. The creative act is in the conception of the machine in conjunction with its construction, and the conception, after our habit of thinking, is an individual and isolated achievement. As a matter of fact it frequently is. A man may create a machine if he conceives it and constructs it or if he conceives and directs its construction. Those he directs, those who do the work of construction alone, do not participate in the creative act, as the creative act is the concentrated intellectual and emotional expression and effort to produce an article or idea. The creative impulse is concerned with the transforming of a concept or some material into an expanded concept or a new object. The creative impulse itself finds its satisfaction in the process of completion and loses its force when the concept or object is produced. The use of the concept or object created is not a characteristic of the creative but of the social impulse. A man who is interested in the use or application of a product, the value it has for others, possesses the social impulse as well as the creative. One impulse is intensive and the other extensive.

But the creative effort is not *necessarily* an individual matter. It may be possible for a group of people to associate cordially and freely together with a single creative purpose and endeavor. It may be possible for each worker to experience the joy of creative work as he takes part with others in the planning of the work along with the labor of fabrication. It is a creative experience or dull labor as his association with others in the solution of the problem is freely pursued and genuine, or as it is forced and perfunctory.

Industry offers opportunities for creative experience which is social in its processes as well as in its destination. The imaginative end of production does not terminate with the possession of an article; it does not center in the product or in the skill of this or that man, but in the development of commerce and technological processes and the evolution of world acquaintanceship and understanding. Modern machinery, the division of labor, the banking system, methods of communication, *make possible* real association. But they are real and possible only as the processes are open for the common participation, understanding and judgment of those engaged in industrial enterprise; they are real and possible as the animus of industry changes from exploitation to a common and associated desire to create; they are real and possible as the individual character of industry gives way before the evolution of social effort.

While our institutional life is an acknowledgment that interdependence is a necessary factor in modern wealth production, we still measure the strength of a man, or a society, or a nation, and say of all that they are strong or weak as they are able apparently to stand alone. We have not yet discovered that a desire to stand alone in an enterprise where people are of necessity dependent is a weakness and that our ability to co-operate with others in such an enterprise is a measure of our strength. "From a social standpoint dependence denotes a power rather than a weakness; it involves interdependence. There is always danger that increased personal independence will decrease the social capacity of an individual. In making him more self-reliant, it makes him more self-sufficient; it may lead to aloofness and indifference. It often makes an individual so insensitive in his relation to others as to develop an illusion of being really able to stand and act alone, an unnamed form of inanity which is responsible for a large part of the remediable suffering of the world." As industry through the ages has changed from the isolated business of provisioning a family to the associated work of provisioning the world, it blazed a pathway for relationships which are socially creative. But art in social relationships will not be realized until a passionate desire for the unlimited expression of creative effort overcomes inordinate desires of individuals for self-expression. Art in living together is possible where the intensive interest of individuals in their personal affairs and attainments, in their social group, in their vocation, in their political state, is deeply tempered by a wide interest and sympathetic regard for the life of other groups and people. Art in social relationships is contingent as well on ability to work for social ends while remaining in large measure disregardful of the personal stakes involved. Because of our inability to lose our personal attachment for our own work, because of what it may yield us in personal ways, the world never yet has experienced the joy and creative possibility of associated effort. And because it has not we have still to experience art in social contact.

STATEMENT 7. PUBLIC AND PRIVATE ASPECTS OF VOCATIONAL EDUCATION[1]

The rapid extension of public education to include the so-called "vocational" interests and activities raises important problems concerning the social aspect of such education. These problems are well illustrated by commercial education.

There are two independent and often contradictory conceptions of commercial education. We may call one the private view, and the other the public view.

[1] Adapted by permission from Benjamin C. Gruenberg, "Commercial Education," *School and Society*, XII (1920), 300–330.

The former of these is much the older; it had a vogue long before any of the public schools attempted to supply commercial education. The fundamental postulates of this view, those that differentiate it from the public view, are as follows:

1. As to society, life is a competitive struggle for individual advantage; success is for the few who attain the advantage.

2. As to commerce, business is carried on for profits; success is measured by the amount of profit.

3. As to education, training prepares for success, and it is therefore worth getting, even at a temporary sacrifice.

4. As to the individual, he who is prepared, wins; he who is not, loses.

Under this view the private dispenser of education may offer to train for success, by inculcating habits, technique, information, power, and so on—all values that give advantage (over those who have not these habits, powers, etc.) and thus lead to success.

The fundamental postulates of the public view of commercial education may be stated as follows:

1. As to society, life is an organized enterprise to overcome obstacles to human welfare, and to promote the common advantage wherever possible.

2. As to commerce, business is service organized for the more effective and more economical distribution of goods and services over an ever enlarging area of the earth, and of human interest.

3. As to education, training prepares for better service, and so for more satisfactory living.

4. As to the individual, those who are prepared serve better, in proportion to their preparation (native differences being beyond control and accepted without prejudices).

Under this view the public school may offer to train only for types of service that are recognized as of public or general use, by inculcating habits, technique, information, power and ideals that make for proficiency, adaptability and satisfaction in service.

Educators generally accept the situation (economic, political, social) in which they find themselves, and assume responsibility only for the elaboration of technique that will most effectively accomplish the task assigned to them by others. Or they undertake to "rationalize" what they find—perhaps to justify themselves in evading more serious responsibility. It is proper to inquire, however, whether educators, as "servants of the public," have not a still greater responsibility in the direction of discovering and formulating forms and purposes of education, even at the risk of coming in conflict with traditional school purposes.

For example, we have accepted the competitive relationship for the most part without question. We have organized and conducted our schools on the assumption that this relationship is basic, essential and permanent. We have not only directed our "training" of children toward competitive ends, we have both justified further education because of its ability to make every child excel every other child (*vide* vast literature of the last two decades purporting to evaluate higher, and especially commercial, education in terms of dollars and cents and in terms of relative "success"), and we have conducted our pedagogy upon a competitive psychology.

The welfare of the individual, no less than the welfare of the community, requires that significant superiorities be cultivated and that irremediable inferiorities be disregarded. It means that in the case of Socrates, for example, his inferiority as a sculptor or merchant shall not stand in the way of exploiting his superiority as a propounder of impertinent and embarrassing questions.

To have the schools turn out the kind of boys and girls that the business man wants means not only training for the kind of workmanship that business experience shows to be needed or desirable, but it means further the inculcation of certain attitudes toward property and government, of certain theories concerning relations between employers and workers, a certain scheme of values—in short, it means indoctrinating the rising generation with a whole philosophy of a special class.

The community is interested in having each individual trained for his optimum productiveness, in terms of socially desirable values. It is not interested either in encouraging its least scrupulous or in handicapping its least businesslike children.

So long as our commercial education remains in private control we can at most undertake to regulate the "morals" or "standards" of the instruction. But the moment the public itself takes a hand in commercial education, it becomes incumbent upon the agents of the public—commissioners, instructors, educators, professors—to justify their work in terms of social service.

STATEMENT 8. THE DEMOCRATIC CONCEPT AND VOCATIONAL ASPECTS OF EDUCATION[1]

The implications of human association.—Society is one word, but many things. Men associate together in all kinds of ways and for all kinds of purposes. One man is concerned in a multitude of diverse groups, in which his associates may be quite different. It often seems as if they had nothing in common except that they are modes of associated life. Within every larger social organization there are numerous minor groups: not only political subdivisions, but industrial, scientific, religious, associations. There are political parties with differing aims, social sets, cliques, gangs, corporations, partnerships, groups bound closely together by ties of blood, and so in endless variety.

Hence, once more, the need of a measure for the worth of any given mode of social life. In seeking this measure, we have to avoid two extremes. We cannot set up, out of our heads, something we regard as an ideal society. We must base our conception upon societies which actually exist, in order to have any assurance that our ideal is a practicable one. But the ideal cannot simply repeat the traits which are actually found. The problem is to extract the desirable traits of forms of community life which actually exist, and employ them to criticize undesirable features and suggest improvement. Now in any

[1] Adapted by permission from John Dewey, *Democracy and Education*, pp. 94–101, 358–70. Macmillan Co., 1916.

social group whatever, even in a gang of thieves, we find a certain amount of interaction and co-operative intercourse with other groups. From these two traits we derive our standard. How numerous and varied are the interests which are consciously shared, how full and free is the interplay with other forms of association? If we apply these considerations to, say, a criminal band, we find that the ties which consciously hold the members together are few in number, reducible almost to a common interest in plunder; and that they are of such a nature as to isolate the group from other groups with respect to give and take of the values of life. Hence, the education such a society gives is partial and distorted. If we take, on the other hand, family life, we find that there are material, intellectual, aesthetic interests in which all participate and that the progress of one member has worth for the experience of all other members—it is readily communicable—and that the family is not an isolated whole, but enters intimately into relationships with business groups, with schools, with all the agencies of culture, as well as with other similar groups, and that it plays a due part in the political organization and in return receives support from it. In short, there are many interests consciously communicated and shared; and there are varied and free points of contact with other modes of association.

The democratic ideal.—The two elements in our criterion both point to democracy. The first signifies not only more numerous and more varied points of shared common interest, but greater reliance upon the recognition of mutual interests as a factor in social control. The second means not only freer interaction between social groups (once isolated so far as intention could keep up a separation) but change in social habits—its continuous readjustment through meeting the new situations produced by varied intercourse. And these two traits are precisely what characterize the democratically constituted society.

Upon the educational side, we note first that the realization of a form of social life in which interests are mutually interpenetrating, and where progress, or readjustment, is an important consideration, makes a democratic community more interested than other communities have cause to be in deliberate and systematic education. The devotion of democracy to education is a familiar fact. The superficial explanation is that a government resting upon popular suffrage cannot be successful unless those who elect and who obey their governors are educated. Since a democratic society repudiates the principle of external authority, it must find a substitute in voluntary disposition and interest; these can be created only by education. But there is a deeper explanation. A democracy is more than a form of government; it is primarily a mode of associated living, of conjoint communicated experience. The extension of space of the number of individuals who participate in an interest so that each has to refer his own action to that of others, and to consider the action of others to give point and direction to his own, is equivalent to the breaking down of those barriers of class, race, and national territory which kept men from perceiving the full import of their activity.

The meaning of vocation.—At the present time the conflict of philosophic theories focuses in discussion of the proper place and function of vocational factors in education. The bald statement that significant differences in fundamental philosophical conceptions find their chief issue in connection with this point may arouse incredulity: there seems to be too great a gap between the remote and general terms in which philosophic ideas are formulated and the practical and concrete details of vocational education. But a mental review of the intellectual presuppositions underlying the oppositions in education of labor and leisure, theory and practice, body and mind, mental states and the world, will show that they culminate in the antithesis of vocational and cultural education. Traditionally, liberal culture has been linked to the notions of leisure, purely contemplative knowledge and a spiritual activity not involving the active use of bodily organs. Culture has also tended, latterly, to be associated with a purely private refinement, a cultivation of certain states and attitudes of consciousness, separate from either social direction or service. It has been an escape from the former, and a solace for the necessity of the latter.

So deeply entangled are these philosophic dualisms with the whole subject of vocational education, that it is necessary to define the meaning of vocation with some fullness in order to avoid the impression that an education which centers about it is narrowly practical, if not merely pecuniary. A vocation means nothing but such a direction of life activities as renders them perceptibly significant to a person, because of the consequences they accomplish, and also useful to his associates. The opposite of a career is neither leisure nor culture, but aimlessness, capriciousness, the absence of cumulative achievement in experience, on the personal side, and idle display, parasitic dependence upon the others, on the social side. Occupation is a concrete term for continuity. It includes the development of artistic capacity of any kind, of special scientific ability, of effective citizenship, as well as professional and business occupations, to say nothing of mechanical labor or engagement in gainful pursuits.

We must avoid not only limitation of conception of vocation to the occupations where immediately tangible commodities are produced, but also the notion that vocations are distributed in an exclusive way, one and only one to each person. Such restricted specialism is impossible; nothing could be more absurd than to try to educate individuals with an eye to only one line of activity. In the first place, each individual has of necessity a variety of callings, in each of which he should be intelligently effective; and in the second place any one occupation loses its meaning and becomes a routine keeping busy at something in the degree in which it is isolated from other interests.

The place of vocational aims in education.—Bearing in mind the varied and connected content of the vocation, and the broad background upon which a particular calling is projected, we shall now consider education for the more distinctive activity of an individual. An occupation is the only thing which balances the distinctive capacity of an individual with his social service. To find out what one is fitted to do and to secure an opportunity to do it is the key to happiness. Nothing is more tragic than failure to discover one's true business in life, or to find that one has drifted or been forced by circumstance into an uncongenial calling. A right occupation means simply that the aptitudes of a person are in adequate play, working with the minimum of friction and the maximum of satisfaction. With reference to other members of a community, this adequacy of action signifies, of course, that they are getting the best service the person can render.

The dominant vocation of all human beings at all times is living—intellectual and moral growth. In childhood and youth, with their relative freedom from economic stress, this fact is naked and unconcealed. To predetermine some future occupation for which education is to be a strict preparation is to injure the possibilities of present development and thereby to reduce the adequacy of preparation for a future right employment. To repeat the principle we have had occasion to appeal to so often such training may develop a machine-like skill in routine lines (it is far from being sure to do so, since it may develop distaste, aversion, and carelessness), but it will be at the expense of those qualities of alert observation and coherent and ingenious planning which make an occupation intellectually rewarding. Moreover, the discovery of capacity and aptitude will be a constant process as long as growth continues. It is a conventional and arbitrary view which assumes that discovery of the work to be chosen for adult life is made once for all at some particular date. One has discovered in himself, say, an interest, intellectual and social, in the things which have to do with engineering and has decided to make that his calling. At most, this only blocks out in outline the field in which further growth is to be directed. It is a sort of rough sketch map for use in direction of further activities. It is the discovery of a profession in the sense in which Columbus discovered America when he touched its shores. Future explorations of an indefinitely more detailed and extensive sort remain to be made. When educators conceive vocational guidance as something which leads up to a definitive, irretrievable, and complete choice, both education and the chosen vocation are likely to be rigid, hampering further growth. In so far, the calling chosen will be such as to leave the person concerned in a permanently subordinate position, executing the intelligence of others who have a calling which permits more flexible play and readjustment. And while ordinary usages of language may not justify terming a flexible attitude of readjustment a choice of a new and further calling, it is such in effect. If even adults have to be on the lookout to see that their calling does not shut down on them and fossilize them, educators must certainly be careful that the vocational preparation of youth is such as to engage them in a continuous reorganization of aims and methods.

Present opportunities and dangers.—In the past, education has been much more vocational in fact than in name. The education of the masses was distinctly utilitarian. It was called apprenticeship rather than education or else just learning from experience. The schools devoted themselves to the three R's in the degree in which ability to go through the forms of reading, writing, and figuring were common elements in all kinds of labor. Taking part in some special line of work, under the direction of others, was the out-of-school phase of this education. The two supplemented each other; the school work in its narrow and formal character was as much a part of apprenticeship to a calling as that explicitly so termed.

To a considerable extent, the education of the dominant classes was essentially vocational—it only happened that their pursuits of ruling and of enjoying were not called professions. For only those things were named vocations or employments which involved manual labor, laboring for a reward in keep, or its commuted money equivalent, or the rendering of personal services to specific persons. For a long time, for example, the profession of the surgeon and physician ranked almost with that of the valet or barber—partly because it had so much to do with the body, and partly because it involved rendering direct service for pay to some definite person. But if we go behind words, the business of directing social concerns, whether politically or economically, whether in war or peace, is as much a calling as anything else; and where education has not been completely under the thumb of tradition, higher schools in the past have been upon the whole calculated to give preparation for this business. Moreover, display, the adornment of person, the kinds of social companionship and entertainment which give prestige, and the spending of money, have been made into definite callings. Unconsciously to themselves the higher institutions of learning have been made to contribute to preparation for these employments. Even at present, what is called higher education is for a certain class (much smaller than it once was) mainly preparation for engaging effectively in these pursuits. In other respects, it is largely, especially in the most advanced work, training for the calling of teaching and special research. There are, however, obvious causes for the present conscious emphasis upon vocational education—for the disposition to make explicit and deliberate vocational implications previously tacit. In the first place, there is an increased esteem, in democratic communities, of whatever has to do with manual labor, commercial occupations, and the rendering of tangible services to society. In theory, men and women are now expected to do something in return for their support—intellectual and economic—by society. Labor is extolled; service is a much-lauded moral ideal. While there is still much admiration and envy of those who can pursue lives of idle conspicuous display, better moral sentiment condemns such lives. Social responsibility for the use of time and personal capacity is more generally recognized than it used to be.

In the second place, those vocations which are specifically industrial have gained tremendously in inheritance in the last century and a half. Manufacturing and commerce are no longer domestic and local, and consequently more or less incidental, but are world-wide. They engage the best energies of an increasingly large number of persons. The manufacturer, banker, and captain of industry have practically displaced a hereditary landed gentry as the immediate directors of social affairs. The problem of social readjustment is openly industrial, having to do with the relations of capital and labor. The great increase in the social importance of conspicuous industrial processes has inevitably brought to the front questions having to do with the relationship of schooling to industrial life. No such vast social readjustment could occur without offering a challenge to an education inherited from different social conditions, and without putting up to education new problems.

In the third place, there is the fact already repeatedly mentioned: Industry has ceased to be essentially an empirical, rule-of-thumb procedure, handed down by custom. Its technique is now technological; that is to say, based upon machinery resulting from discoveries in mathematics, physics, chemistry, bacteriology, etc. The economic revolution has stimulated science by setting problems for solution, by producing greater intellectual respect for mechanical appliances. An industry received back payment from science with compound interest. As a consequence, industrial occupations have infinitely greater intellectual content and infinitely larger cultural possibilities than they used to possess. The demand for such education as will acquaint workers with the scientific and social bases and bearings of their pursuits becomes imperative, since those who are without it inevitably sink to the rôle of appendages to the machines they operate. Under the old régime all workers in a craft were approximately equal in their knowledge and outlook. Personal knowledge and ingenuity were developed within at least a narrow range, because work was done with tools under the direct command of the worker. Now the operator has to adjust himself to his machine, instead of his tool to his own purposes. While the intellectual possibilities of industry have multiplied, industrial conditions tend to make industry, for great masses, less of an educative resource than it was in the days of hand production for local markets. The burden of realizing the intellectual possibilities inhering in work is thus thrown back on the school.

In the fourth place, the pursuit of knowledge has become, in science, more experimental, less dependent upon literary tradition, and less associated with dialectical methods of reasoning, and with symbols. As a result, the subject matter of industrial occupation presents not only more of the content of science than it used to, but greater opportunity for familiarity with the method by which knowledge is made. The ordinary worker in the factory is of course under too immediate economic pressure to have a chance to produce a knowledge like that of the worker in the laboratory. But in schools, association with machines and industrial processes may be had under conditions where the chief conscious concern of the students is in sight. The separation of shop and laboratory, where these conditions are fulfilled, is largely conventional, the laboratory having the advantage of permitting the following up of any intellectual interest a problem may suggest; the shop with advantage of emphasizing the social bearings of the scientific principle, as well as, with many pupils, of stimulating a livelier interest.

Finally, the advances which have been made in the psychology of learning in general and of childhood in particular fall into line with the increased importance of industry in life. For modern psychology emphasizes the radical importance of primitive unlearned instincts of exploring, experimentation, and "trying on." It reveals that learning is not the work of something ready-made called mind, but that mind itself is an organization of original capacities into activities having significance.

Both practically and philosophically, the key to the present educational situation lies in a gradual reconstruction of school materials and methods so as to utilize various forms of occupation typifying social callings, and to bring out their intellectual and moral content. This reconstruction must relegate purely literary methods—including textbooks—and dialectical methods to the position of necessary auxiliary tools in the intelligent development of consecutive and cumulative activities. But our discussion has emphasized the fact that this educational reorganization cannot be accomplished by merely trying to give a technical preparation for industries and professions as they now operate, much less by merely reproducing existing industrial conditions in the school. Put in concrete terms, there is danger that vocational education will be interpreted in theory and practice as trade education: as a means of securing technical efficiency in specialized future pursuits.

Education would then become an instrument of perpetuating unchanged the existing industrial order of society, instead of operating as a means of its transformation. The desired transformation is not difficult to define in a formal way. It signifies a society in which every person shall be occupied in something which makes the lives of others better worth living, and which accordingly makes the ties which bind persons together more perceptible—which breaks down the barriers of distance between them. It denotes a state of affairs in which the interest of each in his work is uncoerced and intelligent: based upon its congeniality to his own aptitudes. It goes without saying that we are far from such a social state; in a literal and quantitative sense, we may never arrive at it. But in principle, the quality of social changes already accomplished lies in this direction. There are more ample resources for its achievement now than ever there have been before. No insuperable obstacles, given the intelligent will for its realization, stand in the way.

QUESTIONS FOR DISCUSSION

1. How may we justify a study of the purposes of public education in general when our chief interest is the purposes of business education? Could it be justified if our effort was to discover the purposes of the private commercial school alone?
2. "The aims of education should then be to make men want the right things." How shall we determine what the right things are? What does Thorndike think are the right things?
3. "The purpose of education for business is to provide the largest possible number of human beings with that genuine culture which will enable them to understand the meaning of progress and their contribution to it." Comment.
4. "That democracy alone will be triumphant which has both intelligence and character." Could intelligence mean different things at different times? Could character?
5. If approximately only 12 per cent of high-school students graduate, what is the duty of the secondary school in the matter of educating for citizenship?

6. "A society marked off into classes need be specially attentive only to the education of its ruling elements." Why? Who are the ruling elements of our society if we are a democracy?
7. "Society exists through a process of transmission quite as much as biological life. This transmission occurs by means of communication of habits of doing, thinking and feeling from the older to the younger." What does this mean regarding education as a social task?
8. "As civilization advances, learning by direct sharing in the policies of the grown-ups becomes increasingly difficult." What do we do as a result?
9. "To savages it would seem preposterous to seek out a place where nothing but learning was going on in order that one might learn." How do they do it? How was it done in the Middle Ages? Make a list of the devices we use. What does this point of view indicate as to the origin of schools? What as to the responsibility of the teaching profession? As to development of new type of schools as American academies, business colleges, commercial courses, and corporation schools?
10. "There is the standing danger that the material of formal instruction will be merely the subject matter of the schools, isolated from the subject matter of life-experience. The permanent social interests are likely to be lost from view." Can you suggest any subjects of which you think this is true? What are some of these permanent social interests? Why should school matter thus become isolated?
11. "If even adults have to be on the outlook to see that their calling does not shut down on them and fossilize them, educators must certainly be careful that the vocational preparation of youth is such as to engage them in a continuous reorganization of aims and methods." Is this statement pertinent to business educators? Does it suggest anything as to how this volume should end? If we conclude with the definite statement of the one best commercial course, are we consistent with or opposed to philosophy?
12. "The larger number of human relationships in any social group are still upon the machine-like plan. Individuals use one another so as to get desired results without reference to the emotional and intellectual disposition and consent of this use." Give examples. What are some of the difficulties which stand in the way of organizing a society in which all interested are shared?

13. "We might as well try to imagine a business man doing business, buying and selling, all by himself, as to conceive it possible to define the activities of an individual in terms of his isolated actions." Is our high-school commercial curriculum planned carefully to relate the individual to his social environment? Can we teach business ethics without an understanding of this environment?
14. "For this reason wise educators are today attempting to enlarge the horizon of children by giving them an intellectual grasp of their chosen vocation as a whole." For what reason do you suppose? What types of courses would seem to you necessary to give this grasp?
15. "It is today possible to conserve the spiritual as well as the physical association in productive enterprise." What do you understand this to mean? Is it more difficult today than it was when society was simpler? Can there be spiritual association in an army corps? What are some of the difficulties in the way of this association in the present order of society? Is such association desirable?
16. The author of Statement 6 used the phrase "art in social relationships." What do you understand this phrase to mean? Can there be art in business relationships?
17. What are the conceptions of commercial education expressed in Statement 7? Are the two compatible?
18. Suppose that you believed these two things to be true: (*a*) Modern business is a very effective way of producing economic goods. (*b*) There are many features of modern business which are unsatisfactory. As a person responsible for business education what do you think should be done about it?
19. "In many cases—too many cases—the activity of the immature being is simply played upon to secure habits which are useful. He is trained like an animal rather than educated like a human being." Explain. Do we ever do this? If so, give instances. How can we avoid it? Is the typical high-school business course as you know it a course which favors the few or the many?
20. A Chicago manufacturer declares that "the thing the school must do is to train people who can work well at such jobs as business men have to offer and who are not too proud or too ambitious to work in minor positions." What agreement or disagreement have you with this?

21. "It is the office of the school to balance the various elements in the social environment, and to see to it that each individual gets an opportunity to escape from the limitations of the social group in which he was born." Explain.
22. "Traditionally, liberal culture has been linked to the notions of leisure, and a spiritual activity not involving the use of bodily organs." Does this inspire you as an educational aim?
23. "More fundamental is the fact that the great majority of workers have no insight into the social aims of their pursuits, and no direct personal interest in them. The results actually achieved are not the ends of their actions, but only of their employers. It is this fact that makes the action illiberal." With this as a basis, suggest a few of the liberal subjects in the high-school commercial curriculum—a few of the illiberal ones.
24. What is culture? What is liberal education? What should education in a democracy undertake to do?

PART III

MODERN AGENCIES OF EDUCATION FOR BUSINESS

A. The Outstanding Institutions
Chapters X–XV

B. Modern Extensions of the High-School Commercial Course
Chapters XVI–XX

CHAPTER X

SOME EARLIER FORMS OF BUSINESS EDUCATION AND THE DEVELOPMENT OF SPECIALIZED AGENCIES

In the preceding section we have attempted to determine at least tentatively, what the function of business education is. We are now ready to examine those agencies or institutions which co-operate in performing this function. In an age as changing as ours no complete survey of such agencies can be made. New divisions spring up with such frequency that their coming is unnoticed, and their growth is often undiscovered until they become of consequence.

This chapter undertakes to give something of the story of the development of education for business. Development is, perhaps, the wrong word, since the chapter does not attempt to follow a wholly logical procedure. We are interested in seeing that education for business has always existed in some form or other. We are interested in seeing that, while the form is simple and unorganized under elementary conditions, it has changed with the changing order of society into a highly differentiated and highly organized scheme. We shall not attempt to trace each step of the change, but rather to look at education for the business of living in a simple society; then to examine more closely the well-organized plan which existed at the time when Anglo-American business may be thought of as beginning; then to shift our view to modern business education in America as it responded to a changing economic system.

If we look, then, at education in a primitive group, we will find that its aims can be conceived as not dissimilar from those which occupy us in the present time. The methods and devices for accomplishing these ends were, however, very different.[1]

[1] This statement is adapted by permission from Arthur James Todd, *The Primitive Family as an Educational Agency.* G. P. Putnam's Sons, New York, 1913, pp. 147–48 and pp. 178–80.

The curriculum of savage education includes two general groups of "subjects," vocational and moral, the latter including custom, tradition, and religion. Yet in practice the two groups are constantly associated. Tradition or taboo may rigidly prescribe the technique of industry, and religion constantly breaks over into the economic régime, not only to determine the forms of industry, but even to proscribe and interrupt their normal course of operation; as, for example, where mortuary customs require the destruction of property or suspension of labor or the lying fallow of land. Among the lowest nature-peoples, where the range of ideas is narrowest, the arts few and simple, social organization the loosest, the curriculum reduces to its lowest terms. Yet even here learning is not an easy process; for under such conditions each generation must go back to the beginning, as there is no storing up of capital or tools or even of methods. On the contrary, the practice of destroying the property of the dead left to the survivors the difficult task of creating *above* their means of production. Only with the rise of intelligence, the settlement in a more or less permanent abode, the accumulation of property, the division of labor, the formation and transmission of tradition, and the organization of conscious education, could there be any short cut, any recapitulation in brief of racial experience. This stage once reached, the "course of studies" becomes immediately more varied and more precise. The development of trade and political organization, together with the increasing complexity of social and religious concepts, brings a corresponding extension and depth to the content of education. Ordeals, drill, initiatory rites, instruction in tribal traditions, religious beliefs, laws, and customs, begin to occupy the larger part of the curriculum, which still includes occasional definite lessons in the tribal arts of self-maintenance. But, far from being delivered *en bloc* by some primitive educational expert, their whole system of instruction was developed out of the very heart of savagery itself by the slow zigzag method of trial and failure in the struggle for existence.

It remains only to mention briefly a few other elements in the savage course of study. Language required considerable attention. Games, mimetic plays, and dancing had vast significance both as subject and method. Certain tribes, notably the Iroquois, gave particular attention to training for political life. The Cherokees had a regular school for magicians. Nature lore is handed down through legends and traditions both gay and sober by the Indians of the South-west. Especially the rabbit, coyote, bear, antelope, mouse, rattlesnake, magpie, woodpecker, eagle, horned toad and their kindred form the heroes of these tales. Such primitive "nature study" was of course closely connected with totemism in some form or other, but at the same time furnished a real literature of wit, wisdom, and morals. The art of story-telling was often highly cultivated. Some Indian tribes had special *raconteurs*, who regaled their little audiences around the family hearth or in the men's house. Among the Yukis there were men who dressed and acted like women, and "devoted themselves to the instruction of the young by the narration of legends and moral tales. The Chippeways had regular bards. With the Pueblos the old men are the story-tellers and cast their tales in a sort of blank verse. Similar story-telling by shamans and elders exists in the Andaman Islands. It is unnecessary to go into enumerative details, for the fiction habit is universal, and scarce a tribe but has its Homer or its Celtic Bard. With us fiction is light weight in matter and function; but not so in savagery; there it not only serves to while the passing hour, but also becomes a tremendously effective pedagogic aid.

"In the long winter evenings, while the fire burns brightly in the centre of the lodge, and the men are gathered in to smoke, he (the boy) hears the folklore and legends of his people from the lips of the older men. He learns to sing the love songs and the war songs of the generations gone by. There is no new path for him to tread, but he follows in the old ways. He becomes a Dakota of the Dakota."

EDUCATION IN MEDIEVAL ENGLAND

If, without giving any attention to the educational scheme of the ancients, we let our minds leap to the dawning of modern enterprise, we find in the apprenticeship system of medieval England a thoroughly organized educational system with well-recognized aims and carefully worked-out methods. It is worth our while to make a rather careful examination of that system, partly because medieval apprenticeship has been often misunderstood; partly because it depicts an economic organization whose differences from and similarities to our present society provide valuable study; partly because it gives us a picture of an educational scheme which can be usefully examined in comparison with our own.

We have done medieval apprenticeship an injustice in conceiving it to be primarily a training in technical skill. Medieval apprenticeship attempted technical training in craft skill, but it also attempted much more. It was the institution relied upon to give candidates for membership in the guilds the ability to conduct a business in a difficult economic and social environment. It was even more. It was the institution relied upon to effect a complete social adjustment for the youths who were to become influential in town life.[1]

The coming of modern business may have brought us large-scale production, machine technique, and the wide market, but it certainly did not introduce a complicated problem for the director of a business. Complexity was already old. The master-guildsman was confronted with a large number of problems. He had need to be versatile indeed to administer them successfully. Within his shop and store he dealt with his customers if they bought wares or if they brought materials upon which he was to work, as was frequently the case with the bakers. If men sold him raw materials from which he was to fashion articles for trade, as might be the case if he were one of the tapicers who were required by their ordinances to buy "good wool of England or Spain," he might likewise meet them in his own shop.

The master-craftsman was the chief factor in the technical work in his shop. He not only directed the work of his employees, the journeymen, and guided the efforts of the apprentice, but he performed a large part of the work himself. As master, he organized the work of the others and administered questions of wages, discipline, and hours and conditions of work. Even where the broad policies in these matters were laid down by the brotherhood, their administration was in his hands.[2]

[1] This statement concerning medieval apprenticeship is adapted and reprinted by the courtesy of the publishers from an article by the author in the *School Review*, XXVIII, No. 8, October, 1920.

[2] "It was no uncommon thing for the wardens to distrain his workshop and his working tools for non-payment of wages or the king's ferme." Joshua Toulmin Smith, *English Gilds* [London: N. Trubner & Co., 1870], IV, cxxvii.

To the degree necessary the guildsman was a capitalist. He furnished the shop and the implements of production. An inventory of the instruments of a brewer of London in 1335 showed the following: "two leaden vessels, one old chest, and one *masshfat* (mash-vat), value 18d; one rarynfat (fining-vat), value 6d; one *heyr* (highstand) for tuns, value 12d; three sets of handmills, value 4s; one piece of lead, value 2d; one tun, and one half-tun, value 8d; one *yelfat* (ale-vat), value 18d; 5 *kemelynes* (tubs for brewing), value 10d; one *clensingbecche* (Qy. as to this), value 4d; also, one *alegist* ("gist," or stand for small casks), value 2d."[1]

The master-craftsman was a teacher, charged with the tremendously important duty of teaching others to perform the many duties which he himself faced. He was bound under the clauses of indentures to instruct his apprentices well and fully in all the arts of his trade and he was subject to penalties if he should fail in his duties as an educator. He agreed that he would keep his apprentice "as an apprentice should be, that is to say meat and drink, hose and shoes, linen, woolen, and his craft to be taught him and nothing hid from him thereof."

The "internal problems" of business administration could not be allowed to occupy the entire attention of the guildsman. Even more numerous and perplexing were a set of matters which may be regarded as "external problems."

The craftsman manager directed his business unit in a complex social environment. An analysis of this social environment indicates that there were some three spheres that need consideration. One was the market, the "trade" of the craftsman. The proper treatment of the problems in this field must have taxed then, as it does now, the best thought of the "manager." Second was the guild itself. This brotherhood of business men of a common calling, organized as it was for mutual aid and protection and for eliminating the wastes of competition, brought with it all the responsibilities and problems of associated

[1] Henry Thomas Riley, *Memorials of London and London Life in the Thirteenth, Fourteenth, and Fifteenth Centuries.* London: Longmans, Green & Co., 1868, I, 194.

action. Finally, the guildsman was a citizen and a public officer. Membership in the guild was frequently coincident with citizenship and the guilds were semi-public bodies. They were the recognized devices used by municipality, or central government, or both, for the regulation and control of industry, for "the gild under the master and wardens became a better unit for civic administration than the ward under the alderman."[1]

In considering the perplexities of the guildsman in all this, it is well to keep in mind that the demands of the social environment of the business were then, as now, tangled and interlaced. "In actual practice, state, borough, and gild presented frequently the appearance of a three-fold combination of almost equal forces working together for a common end. It is therefore not always easy to consider the gilds apart as distinct organs with their own special purposes and functions." Especially is this obvious when we note that guildsmen themselves were often magistrates, as in 1241 when a member of the mercers' guild became mayor of London and later members of the vintners' company frequently held that office. In the same way in Durham "the twenty-four," two of whom were elected from each of the twelve "misteries" of the town, constituted, with twelve aldermen, the common council; and in York the common council consisted of members chosen from the crafts.[2]

The not easy task, then, of the master-craftsman in dealing with external relations of his business was to harmonize the social demands of the guild, the city, and perhaps the state with the acquisitive possibilities of the market.

Specific illustrations of the clash of business interest with one or more of the agencies of control will show more clearly the difficult position of the master-craftsman and will serve to make more vivid the difficult situation for which the guilds used apprenticeship as a preparation.

[1] Charles M. Clode, *The Early History of the Guild of Merchant Taylors of the Fraternity of St. John the Baptist, London, with Notices of the Lives of Some of Its Eminent Members* (London: Harrison & Sons, 1875), I, 55.

[2] Stella Kramer, *English Craft Gilds and the Government* (New York: Columbia University Press, 1905), I, 3.

One task of the guildsman as a business man was to secure demand for his goods. This led to a display of wares and other simple forms of advertising. But here the craftsman met with social regulations, and, it should be noted, social regulations for which he himself was in part responsible. The ordinances of the Spurriers of London ordered that "no one of the trade shall hang his spurs out on Sunday, or any other days that are double feasts; but only a sign indicating his business; and such spurs as they do sell they are to show and sell within their shops, without exposing them without or opening the doors or windows of their shops, on the pain aforesaid."[1]

As to the quality of product that would be most profitably marketed there was again place for a clash between the individual guildsman and the agencies of control. The desire individually to profit by adulteration and the sale of inferior goods must have been strong, but social agencies controlled. For example, the ordinances of the Pelterers of London required that "no one of the trade shall mingle bellies of calabre with furs of puree, or of minever of bisshes" (*calabre*, a poor fur; *puree*, a superior fur; *bisshes*, some part of the skin of the hind).[2] And when one acted against these ordinances he forfeited his furs to the guild in which the default was found, and, in addition, was imprisoned and fined upon his release. The Wax-chandlers of London forbade, on pain of confiscation, imprisonment, and fine, the use of cobbler's wax, rosin, fat, "or other manner of refuse," or the use of old wax and worse within and new wax without.[3] The Pepperers of Soperlane had a list of forbidden acts that reflects a recognition more of deceitful ingenuity, and so profit-seeking, than of pious honesty among that "worshipful brotherhood," and the White-tawyers demanded an amercement and a forfeit from all who falsely wrought skins.[4]

[1] Henry Thomas Riley, *Memorials of London and London Life in the Thirteenth, Fourteenth, and Fifteenth Centuries* (London: Longmans, Green & Co., 1868), I, 321–22.

[2] *Ibid.*, p. 329.

[3] *Ibid.*, p. 300.

[4] A. E. Bland, P. A. Brown, and R. H. Tawney, *English Economic History; Select Documents* (London: G. Bell & Sons, Ltd., 1914), p. 23.

The question of working hours and the conditions of work were likewise matters on which the craftsman must have found himself of one opinion in his own shop and of another in the guild hall. The exercise of self-interest, however, brought him into conflict with social regulation. The Spurriers of London found that "many persons of the said trade had compassed how to practice deception by working by night rather than by day." "And then they introduce false iron, and iron that has been cracked, for tin, and also they put gild on false copper and cracked." Further than this, these night workers spent the day in wandering about and then "having become drunk and frantic, they take to their work." Annoyance to the sick, and broils with the neighbors were the inevitable results, as well as danger to the whole city, from the sparks "which so vigorously issue forth in all directions from the mouths of chimneys in their forges."

Wages as well as hours and conditions of work were part of the guildsman's labor problem. It would be only less erroneous to assume that each individual craftsman and journeyman was habituated to and satisfied with prevailing rates than to assume that the modern manager is happily acquiescent with the minimum-wage and child-labor laws or that trade unions are always content with the findings of arbitration boards. The whole organization of apprenticeship was, of course, in one sense the setting up of machinery to administer certain labor matters, but we find that questions of wages of journeymen were often to be met.[1] Wage appeals were made[2] and in certain towns what we would think of as crude labor exchanges were established to provide for the best adjustment of the supply of labor to the demand.[3]

We are sometimes inclined to assert that the craft guilds were monopolistic and thus lead ourselves to the thought that

[1] *York Memorandum Book* (Durham: Andrews & Co., 1912), Vol. CXX of the Publications of the Surtees Society, p. 107.

[2] Henry Thomas Riley, *op. cit.*, p. 307.

[3] See E. Lipson, *An Introduction to the Economic History of England* (London: A. and C. Black, Ltd., 1915), I, 309–10, for a more extended discussion.

the craftsman escaped the problems of competition. A more careful analysis shows this to be an error. Among the merchant guilds the "common fund" of profits may have been sometimes known, but such an agreement was not consistent with craft-guild organization. The craft guilds were examples of association rather than amalgamation or merger. Each individual felt the pressure of his own pecuniary interests as well as the interests of the whole. In so far as comparisons are possible with modern monopolistic organizations the guilds are better compared to wholesalers' or retailers' trade associations than to the United States Steel Corporation or the Northern Securities Company. They were associations rather than combinations, and there must have been a constant pressure by the individual to override the ruling of the association just as in the early industrial pools the members were with difficulty kept in line.

All of the regulations regarding quality of work which were so carefully supervised by the wardens are indications that the market interests of one individual were at odds with those of another in the same craft.

But not only within the guild was there a tendency to compete. Ever urgent was the problem of competition between guilds. Thus in London, in 1395, a dispute arose between the cobblers and the cordwainers, in which the cobblers alleged that they could no longer make a living as formerly, because of the encroachments of the cordwainers on their trade.

In adjusting his individual business, therefore, to its social environment the master-craftsman manager faced a number of problems of peculiar difficulty and complexity. Coloring all of them and confusing all of them was the fact that he must consider them from several points of view at the same time. Whether he considered his problem of wages, labor, hours and conditions of work, advertising, the quality of goods, or the proper nature of competition, his was not a single eye. He was at once employer, worker, legislator, public citizen, and, perhaps, municipal official. He made guild regulations to restrain what he himself wished to do. He was the object of his own legislation. In a position of such difficulty and complexity he held company with his fellow-guildsman and into that company he admitted new members. But he admitted them only by the road which he helped to build—the road of apprenticeship.

Such a view of the craftsman's problems indicates something of the real purpose of the institution of apprenticeship. It brought the novice into real competition with his fellow-guildsmen but it brought him also into a social partnership. It qualified him not only to work but to vote on all the social questions that were of business importance. Its ideal was not unlike the ideal which we hold for education in a democracy—an instrument qualifying for equal participation in activities of social, business, and political life. With such an ideal it would be strange if apprenticeship was not molded to bring satisfactorily trained members into the brotherhood. And, in such a training, right attitudes and accepted points of view were as important results as technical skill. There was need that the guild bring the new members to the common mind quite as much as a primitive tribe, a trade union or a modern nation, finds a need for training novitiates to the general attitudes of the group.

There is a great deal of direct evidence indicating that apprenticeship was purposed to adjust the apprentice to his social environment. First of all it is worth while to wonder if a guild membership bought by many years of service would not go farther toward giving the new guildsman the desired point of view concerning the admission of new members than any amount of direct propaganda could have done. Moreover, this long training made the guildsman competent to teach the technical work which was necessary to continue the circle of guild life. That the pedagogical duties of the master were taken seriously by the guild becomes evident when it is noted that the guilds, in certain towns, did not allow everyone to assume the duties of instruction. Thus at Chester it was forbidden by the goldsmiths that the graduate apprentice should be allowed to take apprentices of his own, until he had served three years as a journeyman.[1]

[1] Rupert H. Morris, *Chester in the Plantagenet and Tudor Reigns* (Chester: Printed for the author, 1893), p. 443. Regulations having the

But there were in the organization of apprenticeship other elements which were definitely planned to guide the conduct of the apprentice, to regulate his morals, and to form his character in such a way that he would be fitted for his complicated task. The apprentice, apparently, was as strictly bound by regulations pertaining to his behavior as he was by those pertaining to his work. If the guilds admitted undesirable characters to the brotherhood, it was not due to failure to attempt to exclude them. The apprentice was "bound" to behave. The master exercised a superintendence over his moral well-being, and this superintendence could be enforced with proper discipline. Even the apparel of the apprentice was regulated in a way purposed to be good for the cultivation of a spirit proper to his position. He was forbidden to gamble and even to enter gambling houses or other places of moral danger. In some cases an examination or a proof of moral qualities was required of the apprentice before admission to the guild was permitted. The apprentice was frequently forbidden to marry until he had become one of the craft, or if allowed to marry the permission of the master was necessary.[1]

The master also who contracted to teach his trade to an apprentice was required by the guild regulations to pay strict attention to his moral and social education. The Ordinances of the Cappers of Coventry are perhaps typical in their provision that the wardens might admonish a master of whose treatment an apprentice complained and could remove the apprentice for better instruction to a different master. They tested the efficiency of instruction by yearly examinations of apprentices.

---

same effect were in vogue at Leicester where the journeyman was required to work for wages for three years before setting up shop (*Records of Leicester*, III, 28). Similar rules prevailed for the carpenters and paviors of London.

[1] Instances of close supervision of conduct are shown in Joshua Toulmin Smith's "English Gilds, CXXIX," in *The Records of the City of Norwich* (Norwich: Jarrold & Sons, Ltd., 1906–10), II, 28; in Mary Dormer Harris, *Life in an Old English Town* (London: Sonnenschein & Co., Ltd., 1898) p. 274; and in extracts from the *Records of the Merchant Adventurers of Newcastle-upon-Tyne* (Durham: Andrews & Co., 1895–99), Vol. XCIII of the Publications of the Surtees Society, II, 20.

Finally, there was, as the most important element in the social education of the apprentice, his close, personal, and continuous relation to the master-craftsman. From the standpoint of training in the management of business, both in internal and external relations, the effect of this was all-important. The apprentice was associated with the master every day in the shop. He met those who came to sell and those who came to buy. Every attack upon the problems of internal administration was under his observation, and no contact with the social environment was so far removed that he was unaware of it. Daily he must have heard the master discuss the social situation with fellow-craftsmen of the same interests, and doubtlessly the apprentice, as he grew in skill and the confidence of the master, must have entered into the discussion of business problems.

The relationship of master and apprentice outside of the shop was of such a character as to effect the most desirable education for the apprentice, both in business and in all those important social contacts which have been described. The master was bound to feed, clothe, and house the apprentice. The younger man ate at his master's table, slept under his roof, aided the wife and family of the guildsman in their home, and was in a very full sense "one of the family." Social differences were small, and the future of the apprentice of such certainty, if he took advantage of circumstances, as to give no reason for a feeling of caste.

With such features, it is evident that the institution of apprenticeship was well planned to train for business in that broad sense which involves an adaptation to the social environment by which a business is limited and conditioned quite as much as in the technical processes of craft skill.

As such a training it might have lasted indefinitely had the economic conditions remained unchanged. But the discoveries and explorations of the fifteenth century opened the world to the possibility of exchange. The rapid growth of banking, transportation, and communication devices aided this possibility. Political changes too were important in giving England a new centralized national strength. These changes undermined the strength of the locally organized town and guild. Finally there came the application of steam to industry. The machine became more important than the artisan. For both guild and craftsman the curtain was drawn.

AMERCANTILIST'S VIEW OF EDUCATION FOR BUSINESS

Thus the firmly knit medieval organization for manufacture did not endure. Even by the seventeenth century it had given place to a vastly different form of organization and one in which the scheme of apprenticeship could not operate effectively. In the meantime the attention of enterprising Englishmen was centering more and more on foreign trade, in the development of which England had begun to see her future greatness. No scheme of education for business comparable to that thoroughgoing training through apprenticeship developed in this period, but it is interesting to notice in passing the statement of a famous mercantilist of the period regarding "the qualities which are required in a perfect merchant of foreign trade."[1]

My son, in a former discourse I have endeavoured after my manner briefly to teach thee two things: The first is Piety, how to fear God aright, according to his Works and Word: The second is Policy, how to love and serve thy Country, by instructing thee in the duties and proceedings of sundry Vocations, which either order, or else act the affairs of the Common-wealth; In which as some things do especially tend to preserve and others are more apt to enlarge the same: So am I to speak of Money, which doth indifferently serve to both those happy ends. Wherein I will observe this order, First, to show the general means whereby a Kingdom may be enriched; and then proceed to those particular courses by which Princes are accustomed to be supplied with Treasure. But first of all I will say something of the Merchant, because he must be a Principal Agent in this great business.

The love and service of our Country consisteth not so much in the knowledge of those duties which are to be performed by others, as in the skilful practice of that which is done by ourselves; and there-

[1] This statement is adapted from Thomas Mun, "Early Tracts on Commerce."

fore, my Son, it is now fit that I say something of the Merchant, which I hope in due time shall be thy Vocation; Yet herein are my thoughts free from all Ambition, although I rank thee in a place of so high estimation; for the Merchant is worthily called The Steward of the Kingdoms Stock, by way of Commerce with other nations; a work of no less reputation than trust, which ought to be performed with great skill and conscience, that the private gain may ever accompany the publique good. And because the nobleness of this Profession may the better still up thy desires and endeavors to obtain those abilities which may effect it worthily, I will briefly set down the excellent qualities which are required in a perfect Merchant.

1. He ought to be a good penman, a good arithmetician, and a good accomptant, by that nobler order of Debtor and Creditor, which is used onely amongst Merchants; also to be expert in the order and form of Charter-parties, Bills of Lading, Invoices, Contracts, Bills of Exchange, and Policies of Ensurance.

2. He ought to know the measures, weights, and monies of all foreign countries especially where we have trade, and the monies not only by their several denominations, but also by their intrinsique values in weight and fineness, compared with the Standard of this Kingdom, without which he cannot well direct his affairs.

3. He ought to know the Customs, Tolls, Taxes, Impositions, Conducts and other charges upon all manner of Merchandize exported or imported to and from the said foreign countries.

4. He ought to know in what several commodities each Countrey abounds, and what be the wares which they want, and how and from whence they are furnished with the same.

5. He ought to understand, and to be a diligent observer of the rates of Exchanges by Bills, from one State to another, whereby he may the better direct his affairs, and remit over and receive home his Monies to the most advantage possible.

6. He ought to know what goods are prohibited to be exported or imported in the said foreign countreys, lest otherwise he should incur great danger and loss in the ordering of his affairs.

7. He ought to know upon what rates and conditions to fraight his Ships, and ensure his adventures from one Countrey to another, and to be well acquainted with the laws, orders and customes of the Ensurance office bothe here and beyond the Seas, in the many accidents which may happen upon the damage or loss of Ships or goods, or both these.

8. He ought to have knowledge in the goodness and in the prices of all the several materials which are required for the building and repairing of Ships, and the divers workmanships of the same, as also for the Masts, Tackling, Cordage, Ordnance, Victuals, Munition, and Provisions of many kinds; together with the ordinary wages of Commanders, Officers and Mariners, all which concern the Merchant as he is an Owner of Ships.

9. He ought (by the divers occasions which happen sometime in the buying and selling of one commodity and sometimes in another) to have indifferent if not perfect knowledge in all manner of Merchandize or Wares, which is to be as it were a man of all occupations and trades.

10. He ought by his voyaging on the Seas to become skilful in the art of Navigation.

11. He ought, as he is a Traveller, and sometimes abiding in Foreign Countreys to attain to the speaking of divers languages, and to be a diligent observer of the ordinary Revenues and expenses of foreign princes, together with their strength both by Sea and Land, their laws, customes, policies, manners, religions, arts, and the like; to be able to give account thereof in all occasions for the good of his Countrey.

12. Lastly, although there be no necessity that such a Merchant should be a great Scholar; yet is it (at least) required that in his youth he learn the Latin tongue, which will the better enable him in all the rest of his endeavours.

BUSINESS EDUCATION IN THE UNITED STATES

With these snapshots of education for business in mind we may turn to the development of education for business in America. The earliest form was apprenticeship, surviving to some extent, but by no means extensive or highly organized. The public elementary schools, too, must be kept in mind, since reading and writing are clearly enough vocational subjects. We are more concerned, however, in following the growth of those institutions which may be thought of as technical agencies in the field of business training. The development of these institutions depends for its explanation upon the development of American industry.

The original territory of the Colonies was doubled by the Louisiana Purchase. By 1853, Florida, Texas, the Oregon

Claim, the Mexican Cession, and the Gadsden Purchase had again doubled the area of the United States. Into this newly acquired territory poured population from the East. Between 1820 and 1850 the population of nine new western states in the Mississippi Valley had increased more than 300 per cent and continued to increase. The westward movement of population created for eastern manufacturers a market possibility which had been undreamed of before. The institutional devices for reaching this lucrative western market came on apace. Primitive river traffic in flatboats was supplemented by the steamboats. River freight-traffic charges fell from $140 to $20 a ton. By 1856 more than a thousand steamboats plied the Mississippi and its tributaries. Lake commerce was also being developed, and by 1840, 500 miles of canals had been completed, connecting the lakes with the Ohio River. In 1860 there was already a network of railroad systems as far west as the Missouri. Supplementing these facilities had come the telegraph in 1844. Gradually there developed in various lines of trade the increasing use of the sales agent and the wholesaler-retailer type of market distribution by means of which the needs of the West for manufactured goods might be supplied. Concomitant with these there came a growth of commercial agencies, of market news reports, of newspapers and other media for carrying information. In summarizing this development Clark says:[1]

> By 1825 American manufacturers had facilities for placing their products conveniently in all parts of the country. Domestic goods were quoted regularly in prices current from Boston to New Orleans and were standardized sufficiently to be ordered by conventional descriptions. Thereafter, the development of home markets was extensive rather than intensive. Its course was controlled by improved communication and growth or settlement rather than by fundamental changes of organization. A single generation had witnessed this advance from a dispersed and unorganized national market to systematic methods of distribution, controlled by adequate commercial machinery.

[1] Victor S. Clark: *History of Manufactures in the United States, 1607–1806*, p. 358–59.

Factory production, a wide market, and the large volume of business transacted with distant customers, gave rise to a demand for a vast amount of what A. W. Shaw has called the facilitating processes of business. Transactions must be recorded, letters must be written, reports of business too large for personal observation must be given as a means of control to the business organizer, calculations of diverse sorts and varieties must be made, estimates and proposals computed and presented for the judgment of the director of the large business. In other words, the increased size of business, coupled with a distant impersonal market and the variety of specialized functionaries who aided in the distribution of goods, called upon accounting and communication to function as they had not functioned before. The work which was called for did not need a great amount of intelligence, enterprise or initiative; it required accuracy, exactness, and painstaking care in the performance of specialized clerical tasks. For such training apprenticeship was at best a clumsy and extravagant instrument. To replace it there now appeared, at first in primitive form and later in a highly organized way, the institution which we know as the American business college.

Students of the early history of the private commercial schools in America agree as to the pioneers in the movement but disagree as to the individual who is to be classed as first. R. M. Bartlett, first of Philadelphia, then of Pittsburgh, and finally of Cincinnati, is claimed by some writers to be the first in the business-college field. His position is disputed respectively by the champions of Peter Duff, of Pittsburgh, of G. N. Comer, of Boston, and Jonathan Jones, of St. Louis, all of whom offered private commercial education in the early days of the movement. Dolbear, who opened a school in New York in 1835, is also named by some as the leader in the field. Unquestionably among the first of the private schools was that of James Gordon Bennett, who is said to have started a school in New York in 1824 which he heralded with the following announcement:

The subscriber, encouraged by several gentlemen, intends opening in Ann, near Nassau Street, an English classical and mathematical school for the instruction of young gentlemen intended for merchantile pursuits. Instruction will be given in the following branches:—

Reading, elocution, penmanship, and arithmetic; algebra, astronomy, history, and geography; moral philosophy, commercial law, and political economy; English grammar and composition; and also if required, the French and Spanish languages by natives of these countries.

Bookkeeping and merchants' accounts will be taught in the most approved and scientific forms.

The school will be conducted, in all the principal branches, according to the inductive method of instruction, and particularly so in arithmetic, geography, and English grammar.

It will commence about the first of November.

References: J. S. Bartlett, M.D., Albion Office; Messrs. Smith and Hyslop, Pearl Street; Mr. Henry T. Margarey, Broadway; Mr. P. Whitin, Jr., Maiden Lane.

J. GORDON BENNETT

N.B.—Application may be made to J. G. B. at 148 Fulton Street.[1]

Bartlett's statement of his experience in seeking employment illustrates at once the failure of the old apprenticeship system to train for the new commercial demands and the demand which was growing up for workers in the clerical side of business.

He says that when he became of age he wished to know more of bookkeeping, but could find no instruction. He offered to enter business houses and learn, but was told that proprietors did not want to be bothered. The predicament in which he was placed was of not being taken into an office unless he knew bookkeeping, and yet having no place to go and learn.[2]

The early business colleges and the early efforts toward education by penmen were for the most part the individual

[1] This announcement is from a paper read by Mr. E. M. Barber before the Eastern Commercial Teachers' Association in 1903.

[2] Herrick, *Meaning and Practice of Commercial Education*, p. 180.

efforts of men who saw a need and attempted personally to fill it. The year 1853 marks a new epoch in the history of the type of business training which we are here considering. In that year H. B. Bryant and H. D. Stratton, both of whom had been students in a Cleveland business college, formed a partnership with James W. Lusk and established the first Bryant and Stratton School. The entrance of Bryant and Stratton into the field marks the institutionalizing of the ideal of Bartlett, Packard, and others. Bryant and Stratton set about to make their business college a national institution which should give training for business to the population of every part of the country. They proposed to establish one of their schools in every city of over 10,000 population. Each of these schools was to use uniform textbooks. Instruction was to be given in penmanship, bookkeeping, commercial arithmetic, and commercial law. They devised a system of interchangeable scholarships which enabled students to transfer to schools in various cities at will, and to obtain the work offered at such periods throughout their lives as were most convenient. Their usual scheme of organization in a new city was to establish a "local partner" who took charge of the school and received a commission ranging from 30 to 50 per cent of the income.

The early development of the business college was in response to the developing economic organization. The second stage, in which it became nation wide in scope and carefully organized, shows a similar relationship. The following quotations, one dealing with industrial development after 1850, and one with the development of the business college after 1850, indicate how closely the educational institution was following economic changes.

In England the big factory came in late in the eighteenth century, beginning in the cotton industry; but its rise was retarded in America.

Although one must be extremely careful not to imagine that any establishments just like the average are actually to be found, and not to forget the great variety of sizes and kinds of businesses that exist, still it is of some significance to note the change in the size of the average manufacturing establishment. . . . .

One may form a rough picture of the average manufacturing establishment of 1850 having a capital of $4300, employing 7 wage earners, and turning out products valued at $8200. Over against this may be put the establishment of 1910 with its capital of $64,800, its labor force of 25 men, and its output valued at over $76,000. In contrast with Hamilton's characterization one may put the words of a living economist:

"The typical unit of production is no longer a single family or a small group of persons working with a few cheap, simple tools upon small quantities of material, but a compact and closely organized mass of labor composed of hundreds of individuals co-operating with large quantities of expensive and intricate machinery, through which passes a continuous and mighty volume of raw material on its journey to the hands of the consuming public."[1]

Against this view of changing industry place this statement concerning the growth of the business college:

About the middle of the fifties there were not more than a dozen commercial schools scattered in the large cities from Boston and Philadelphia to Chicago and St. Louis. They had arisen with the idea of facilitating the entrance of young men into minor positions as clerks and bookkeepers. The instruction offered was very meagre,—some so-called commercial arithmetic, a little practice in keeping accounts and a certain amount of ornamental penmanship made up the total. A school of this kind did not require a large force of teachers, in many cases the entire instruction was given by one man. . . . .

In those days there were no text books for the "commercial colleges"; and arithmetic and bookkeeping were taught by manuscripts prepared by actual accountants engaged in business. As with the text-book authors, or rather manuscript authors, so with the students. These came primarily from the ranks of those already employed at the time in business houses, a fact which necessitated the institution of evening classes. The average time spent in a business college was not more than three months, so that equipment, instruction, fees, time and grade of work were all pretty much on a par. Poor as such education must have been, it evidently filled a need, for commercial colleges throve and multiplied and with success became still more successful. Increased popularity led to higher

[1] Haney, *Business Organization and Combination*, p. 18.

fees, longer courses, to the preparation of printed texts; life and interchangeable scholarships were abolished; the teaching force was increased; students were no longer adults wearied by daily labor; the commercial school began to draw young men and boys looking forward to employment; day classes largely took the place of evening instruction; school equipment improved and gradually these institutions grew into the apparently permanent place in public favor which they enjoy today. Official statistics of the bureau of education report 341 of these schools with 1,764 instructors and 77,746 students, 82 per cent being in day classes. Contrast this with the record of forty years ago, when there were fewer than a dozen schools of this kind, with say thirty teachers and a thousand pupils, and the figures become sufficiently impressive.[1]

Whatever may have been the limitations of the business college, it must be credited with giving rise to a supplementary institution which has developed into importance; this is the convention of commercial teachers. Bryant and Stratton in 1863–64 called the first convention of "local partners." It is alleged that this first convention served chiefly as a rendezvous at which the local partners discussed their grievances against the organization for which they worked, and that as a result this and later meetings were fatal to the continuance of the Bryant-Stratton system. Be that as it may, the convention held in Cleveland in 1866 was considered of enough educational importance to receive publicity in *Harper's Weekly* and to be attended by such a personage as James A. Garfield. *Harper's Weekly* for October 13, 1866, in commenting on the meeting, makes the statement that "through individual institutions and admirable textbooks the sphere and limit of business education have been as clearly defined as those of law, medical, and theological schools."[2]

[1] James, *Monograph on Commercial Education in the United States.* James was writing about 1899. The *Bureau of Education Report* for 1916 states that there are at least 1,300 independent commercial schools in the United States. Of these, 843 schools reported 183,286 students. In 1918, 890 schools reported 289,579 students.

[2] For the names and dates and specific facts in business-college history, the writer has drawn freely upon Herrick's *Meaning and Practice of Com-*

About the same time there was formed the National Union of Business Colleges, an organization opposed to the Bryant-Stratton chain. The chain eventually fell victim to the forces opposed to it, and the various local partnerships were sold out to individuals or to smaller local chains of schools. Conventions of commercial-school directors continued to be held almost every year, until in 1890 agitation was begun for connection with the National Education Association. In 1893 the Business Education Section was first recognized by the National Association, and the report of the National Education Association for that year contains the first pages devoted exclusively to business training. The Commercial Section in the National Education Association appears, from reports of its proceedings, to have passed more and more under the influences of secondary commercial teachers, normal schools, and high schools of commerce. Two institutions, the Commercial Teachers' Federation and the Eastern Commercial Teachers' Association, are still influenced largely by private commercial-college interests.

It is not strange that the rapidly developing secondary schools, tax supported, should be called upon, once the possibility was seen, to perform the work which was being done by the private business colleges. Nor is it more strange that there should be a demand for modifications of the classical education with which the high school began, and that the demand should be for such "practical training" as the business college was supposed to offer. It is said that commercial education in public schools was first considered in Boston in the fifties, and that it had its beginning in New York Free Academy in that decade. In 1863 shorthand (and perhaps bookkeeping) was made a part of the course of study in Central High School, Philadelphia, and the St. Louis High School. The introduction of this work is supposed to be the origin of clearly defined commercial education at public expense in the United States.

---

mercial Education, James's *Monograph on Commercial Education in the United States*, reports of the Business Education Section of the National Education Association, and reports of the National Commercial Teachers' Federation.

In 1875 came the typewriter. Patents for "typographers" and similar machines were taken out in considerable numbers between 1829 and 1870, but in 1875 C. L. Sholes and C. Glidden, having effected various improvements in previous mechanisms, placed the manufacture of their typewriter in the hands of E. Remington & Sons. The significance of the typewriter as a technical instrument aiding business communication needs no discussion. Shorthand, the handmaiden of typewriting, was already developed when the typewriter appeared. Since the time of the Greeks various systems of stenography had been in use and in England, and even in America, shorthand had gained a considerable prevalence in legal, court, and literary work before the coming of the typewriter. The Isaac Pitman system, appearing in different forms in 1830 and 1840 in England and said to have been widely copied and disseminated in America by Ben Pitman, Graham, and Munson, was supplemented in 1888 by the method of Gregg, another Englishman, who introduced his work in America in 1893. These developments, like that of the steel pen, were stimulated by the communication necessities of wide market exchange. Training in the use of stenography and the typewriter were and are phases of training in business communication.

The early courses in commercial work in high schools were modeled closely after those of private business colleges. Teachers were for the most part drawn from business-college faculties or from business-college graduates. During recent years there is evidence of some change, however.

OTHER INSTITUTIONS MULTIPLIED

In the meantime there have been growing, as we have seen in Chapter I, a number of other institutions. The business colleges, later supplemented by the secondary schools, were not allowed to monopolize the field of business education. Correspondence schools and other private colleges of a more advanced character than the business college did not overlook this lucrative market for their wares. The developing western market, which at first offered a great opportunity to eastern manufacturers, began in time to furnish a less easy field for profitable exchange.[1] This fact made it necessary for manufacturers to utilize salesmanship and advertising in a fashion undreamed of in the days of easier distribution. To some extent courses dealing with such subjects appeared in the secondary schools. But their development in these schools was slow and fragmentary. The secondary school was bound by its tradition of technical training, and had, furthermore, pupils of too young an age for proper work of the sort needed. The collegiate school of business, therefore, with an initial interest chiefly in marketing problems, came into existence. (The production side of the matter had been well taken care of by engineering schools.) Here courses in salesmanship, advertising, marketing, as well as in accounting and related subjects, were developed. These schools broadened their field of operations and furnished places for developing and gathering the knowledge needed to make organized courses of study possible.

The high school also began to extend in a number of ways. Experiments of various forms were tried, the high school of commerce, the co-operative school, the evening school, the post-graduate course being among them. Corporations also, either dissatisfied with the work of the public or private schools, or feeling that such work should be supplemented, established a great variety of training courses of their own. The corporation school has thus become one of the important educational agencies. In the meantime a demand arose for an opportunity to continue public education after the regular course of instruction had been completed or dropped. This was supplemented by a demand that the years of required school attendance should be extended. These forces brought into existence and nurtured the continuation school.

Thus we find ourselves in a vastly different situation from that of an earlier age. No more is vocation merely the simple and direct, even though difficult task, of taking from nature immediate subsistence. No longer is the group with which one

[1] A somewhat more extended discussion of this matter is given in the chapter dealing with collegiate schools of business.

co-operates in this activity small and of comparative simplicity in organization, and no longer are such simple devices as imitation and association adequate for training. The task of making a modern citizen is more difficult than making "a Dakota of the Dakota." For our more complicated tasks we make use of many specialized educational institutions. As in all specialization, a central problem is to secure a proper division of the labor to be done and to maintain an organization of our specialization which gives it a maximum of productivity. Since there is no central authority to assign duty, nothing can be of more aid to those who must define the task of an institution than an understanding of the agencies involved. It is with helping to such an understanding that the following chapters are concerned.

QUESTIONS FOR DISCUSSION

1. Has business in some form or other always existed? Has education for business in some form always existed? In answering this question, in what sense are you using the term business?
2. What were the chief methods of education in a primitive group? Why would these same methods be unsatisfactory today?
3. Young people no longer absorb ideas from those about them. The family has lost its influence; changes in the economic system which made imitation futile. It is the large scale of industry which makes formal education necessary. It is specialization which made necessary the building of a schoolhouse. Examine these statements. How much truth do you think there is in each one?
4. What was medieval apprenticeship?
5. In what ways can the medieval guildsman be compared to the manager of a business today?
6. "The guildsman was worker, citizen, public officer, teacher, capitalist, and manager, all in one." Explain.
7. What were the internal business problems of the guildsman?
8. What were some of the important external business problems of the guildsman?
9. "In actual practice, state, borough, and guild presented, frequently, the appearance of a threefold combination of almost equal forces working together for a common end." Show how each of these forces was operating in guild life.

10. Work out a statement showing how apprenticeship trained for each of these various aspects of guild life.
11. Give a list of reasons showing why other educational agencies came to supplement apprenticeship.
12. What were the qualities which Thomas Mun believed a "perfect merchant" should have? Should a perfect exporter of today have all of these qualities?
13. "The extensive development of business teaching in America depends for its explanation upon the westward movement of American industry." Put as much meaning into this statement as you can.
14. What do you understand by the "facilitating processes of business"?
15. Prior to 1850 the development of the business college was retarded. What economic conditions were the cause of its slow growth up to this time? After 1850 the business college expanded rapidly. What were the economic conditions upon which this growth was based?
16. The increasing size of business put a premium on communication and control. The development of certain techniques made possible an increased amount of training in these fields. Explain.
17. What are some of the important facts in the development of accounting, stenography, and the typewriter?
18. What are some of the economic facts lying behind the growth of interest in advertising and salesmanship? Is there a relation between this interest and the collegiate school of business?

CHAPTER XI

THE BUSINESS COLLEGE

In the opening chapter we have noticed certain statistics relating to the private commercial school or business college. In the chapter immediately preceding this one the growth of the business college was pictured in relation to the changing economic situation. Something may be gained by a glance at those chapters if the perspective suggested is not in mind. We are now to make a more careful examination of the business college, chiefly as a contemporary institution, with a view to determining its proper rôle on the stage of educational activity.

There are three main matters to be considered. First, a concept of the business college in quantitative terms should be gained. What is the modern business college merely in numbers and enrolment? How important a thing is it physically? Second, qualitative features of the business college should be examined. What is the modern business college? What types of work does it offer? What is the distribution of students among courses? What kinds of business colleges are there? What administrative methods are typical? These considerations are clearly of great importance in guiding us toward a conclusion as to the work it can best do.

In examining these features of the business college it will be worth while to note some earlier appraisals of its character. Such a view will aid in determining whether the business college has been a flexible and changing institution or whether it has tended and still tends to run true to its earlier forms.

Finally there is the assignment of a place or task. What work can the business college best do? This assignment should be made with possible devices for improvement in mind. A consideration of such devices is therefore pertinent.

THE EXTENT OF BUSINESS-COLLEGE EDUCATION

What, then, of the present-day business college in physical terms? Figure 17 presents a graphic answer so far as numbers are concerned. In observing this figure, however, it must be borne in mind that the figures used are those of "schools reporting." The Bureau of Education maintains a mailing list of 1,329 private commercial schools which is believed to contain a large percentage of such schools in the United States. The figure above shows only 890 schools. This is about 67 per

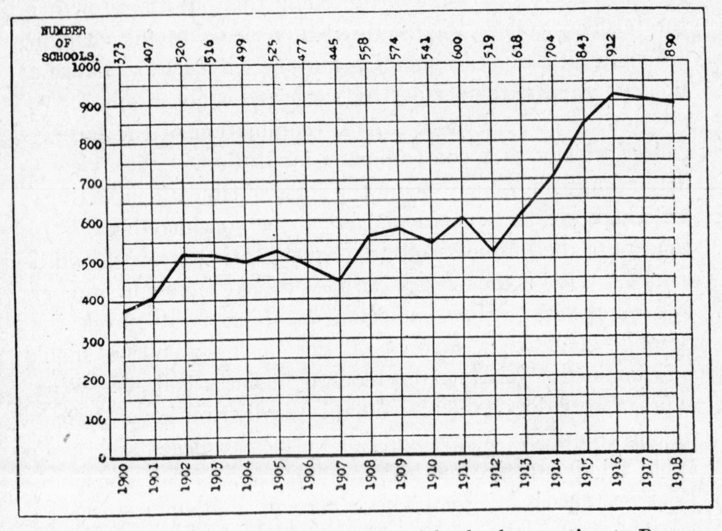

FIG. 17.—Number of private commercial schools reporting to Bureau of Education for indicated years.*

* Adapted by permission from *Private Commercial and Business Schools, 1917–18*, p. 4. *U.S. Bureau of Education Bulletin, No. 47, 1919.*

cent of the actual number in the country. Similar considerations should be kept in mind in viewing other points in the chart.

The number of students in private commercial schools is indicated in Figure 18. The figure shows the number of men and of women as well as totals.

It will be observed that a decided increase in enrollment has taken place since 1916. This increase of 97,191 students, or over 50 per cent, has not been due to an increase in the number of schools reporting, since it has been shown above that there was an actual decrease of twenty-two schools reporting. Assuming that there are 1,329 private commercial schools in the United States, one can readily see that the 912 schools reporting in 1916 and the 890 reporting in 1918 constitute fair samples of the total number. It is unlikely, also,

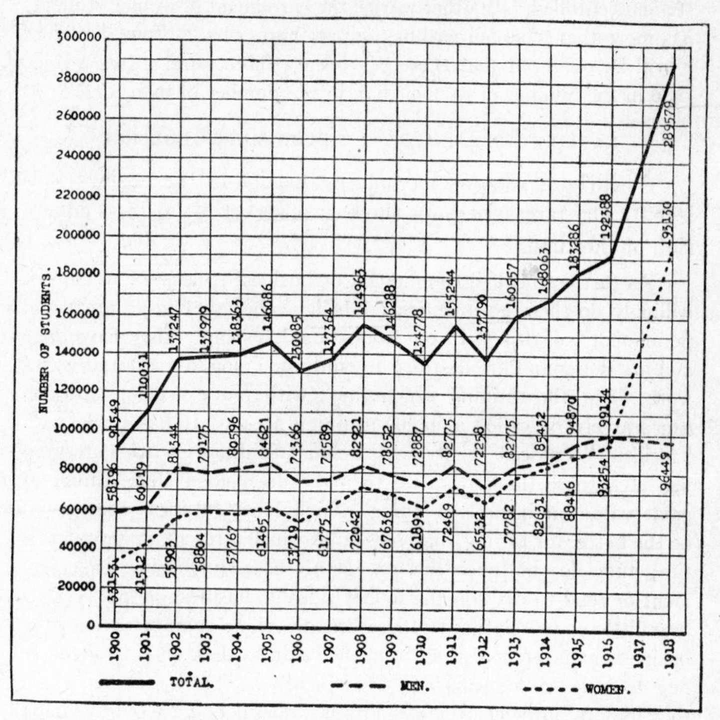

FIG. 18.—Number of students in private commercial schools reporting for indicated years.*

* Adapted from *Private Commercial and Business Schools, 1917–18*, p. 9. *Bureau of Education Bulletin, No. 47, 1919.*

that larger schools reported in 1918 than did in 1916. The increase of 50 per cent in enrollment within the past two years (before 1918) has undoubtedly been due to war demands. The call for clerks, stenographers, bookkeepers, and telegraph operators has caused many students to enter private commercial schools where the necessary training could be secured in the shortest time.

This conclusion is further warranted by the fact that the large increment in enrollment is due wholly to the increase in the number of women students. It will be noted that there has been a decrease of 2,685, or 27 per cent, in the number of men students enrolled and an increase of 99,876, or 107 per cent, in the number of women students enrolled. In other words, the enrollment of women students has more than doubled within the past two years. From the figure it will be observed that there has been a more rapid increase since 1900 in the number of women than in the number of men.[1]

EARLIER APPRAISALS OF THE BUSINESS COLLEGE

As early as 1890 we have an evaluation of the business college by Dr. James, perhaps the best observer of business education of the time.[2]

As to the so-called commercial or business colleges, I would not willingly do them an injustice. I believe that they are a great and permanent constituent of our educational system. They have done and are doing and are destined to continue doing, a great and useful work. But the training which they, with few exceptions, furnish can scarcely be called a higher training at all. It has to do with "facilities"—indeed chiefly with manual facilities—writing, reckoning, etc., those things that go to make up a good clerk, things of great value in themselves, things which every business man would be the better for having, and yet things which after all are only facilities; they do not touch the essence of successful business management or tend to develop the higher sides of business activity; they bear little or no relation to those broader views characteristic of the business manager as distinct from the business clerk and are of course next to useless as a means of liberal education. The knowledge which they impart, however valuable in itself, "does not suffice to fit a young man for the struggle of commercial life, for wise management of a private estate or for efficient public service."

In 1904 Dr. James carried the picture of the business college into the present century, and gives a basis for judgment as

[1] Adapted by permission from *Private Commercial and Business Schools, 1917–18*, pp. 9–10. U.S. Bureau of Education, Bulletin No. 47, 1919.

[2] From an address by Edmund J. James, "Schools of Finance and Economy," before the American Bankers' Association at Saratoga, September 3, 1890.

to the progress, or lack of progress, being made by these institutions, as well as a basis for considering their essential utility:[1]

Before leaving this subject of the "Commercial College," i.e., the private, elementary, unendowed, unassisted and uninspected educational undertaking, it is desired to emphasize again how important a function it has performed in our American educational system. It set out to give the girl or boy, man or woman, who desired to secure a position as clerk or bookkeeper just such assistance as was needed to prepare for such work. No matter how young or how old, how educated or how ignorant the candidate, the commercial college undertakes to give him an immediate and definite training in bookkeeping, commercial arithmetic, penmanship, stenography and typewriting, or such portion thereof as is desired. It made of each student a special case; did not hold him back to work along with a class, gave him every assistance in its power, made entrance to the school as easy as possible, rarely requiring any other condition than paying the fee; facilitated the leaving and helped the pupil in finding work.

That it did this work well, at least to the satisfaction of its pupils, is sufficiently attested by the hundreds of thousands of people who have attended the schools in the last fifty years. Pupils were required to pay fees and in many cases high fees for instruction. The annual tuition fee varies in the better schools from $50 to $150 and even $200 for a school year of ten months. The payment of such fees by men and women who have to earn their own living at comparatively low salaries testifies eloquently to the value which they themselves set upon the instruction which they receive.

It is perfectly safe to say that in the quality of the work which they do, and in the equipment for this particular work, the American commercial colleges have no rivals. They are as much superior to anything of the sort to be found elsewhere in the world as are the American schools of dentistry to their counterparts—and for very much the same reason, viz., that they are engaged largely, one may say chiefly, in the mechanical work in which Americans excel the rest of the world. They are not educational institutions in any broad sense of the term at all. They are trade schools pure and simple, and that in a very narrow sense. They train for facilities. Of course all training has intellectual results, even that of the prize

[1] Adapted by permission from Edmund J. James, *Commercial Education*, pp. 16–18. Louisiana Purchase Exposition Co., St. Louis, 1904.

fighter. But the commercial college aims not to train the best bookkeepers, or stenographers, for, to such, a high degree of education is necessary, but to take the boy or man as he is, with or without education, stupid or bright, and make as good a bookkeeper or stenographer out of him as is possible by simply superadding a brief technical training. The limitations of such a school are perfectly evident to every educationist. It trains the clerk, the routinist, the amanuensis, not the manager or director of business enterprises. That hundreds of the students of the colleges have become successful business men of initiative and independent enterprise simply proves that they had native ability for that sort of thing; not that this sort of training was especially helpful, though it is only fair to say that many of these men trace their start in business to the technical skill in bookkeeping, etc., which they acquired in the schools.

THE BUSINESS COLLEGE IN 1912

In 1912 the City Club of Chicago made an extensive study of vocational training in its city and included a thorough investigation of the business college of that date and place. The evidence which they submitted is important in showing the further development of these private agencies for business education. The facts found as well as the conclusions drawn are worth examination:[1]

Some general facts.—The forty or more commercial colleges, on the other hand, offer apparently exactly what the students desire, a commercial education only. The average commercial college presents an air of business; the equipment is quite adequate and the plan of work, especially on the technical side, seems at first desirable. The students are offered a course in business theory and practice, which seems suited to fit them for the ends desired.

Criticisms may, however, be made upon the work of the private business college. Only a few of them are really efficient, and in every case the course is too short. The whole attempt is to drive the student through in as short a time as possible, this being, of course, an attractive feature in the case of the student who must be a wage-earner immediately after he graduates; from his point of view the

[1] Adapted by permission from *A Report on Vocational Training in Chicago and in Other Cities*, pp. 240–42 and 252–56. By a committee of the City Club of Chicago, 1912.

sooner he graduates the better. The business colleges will take students ordinarily without regard to age, though several maintain they take no one under fifteen years. They pay little attention to previous training and do not take into account the natural adaptability or ability on the part of the student, i.e., no attempt is made to inquire whether the prospective student is fitted to become a business man either in a directive or directed position. All is grist that comes to the business college mill.

A further criticism is that business colleges feel that they are under the necessity of keeping their attendance, to pay dividends on their capital, and therefore conduct a vigorous campaign of solicitation which extends even to the pupils in the grammar schools. It is estimated that 25 per cent to 35 per cent of their gross receipts are paid out to solicitors. It is, perhaps, pertinent to inquire if this money could not be more profitably expended by the business colleges themselves in equipment or teaching staff.

They also need public supervision. They are not open to inspection by the public officers and are not regulated by the school board or other school authorities.

The typical commercial course in commercial colleges includes bookkeeping, commercial arithmetic, commercial law, penmanship, business correspondence, shorthand and typewriting, and what is called English, including reading, writing, spelling, grammar and, in some cases, history, geography, arithmetic, etc. The average time for such a course is about eight months, and the average tuition is about $11 per month.

The commercial colleges themselves insist that their methods are the correct ones, that their course is arranged to give the maximum of practical work in the minimum of time, that the course is conducted by teachers especially trained for business work who make it a practice to keep in touch with the latest business methods, and that, therefore, their courses are much more efficient than can be given in the public high schools at present. It is true, however, that the greater number of students turned out by the commercial colleges, as well as by the high schools, are inefficient, except possibly in a mechanical way; and they still require detailed instruction in that which they are supposed to have learned in school. The business training of the public schools and of the commercial colleges does not fit their graduates to take up business work with the expectation of working themselves into positions of responsibility.

What the solicitors were doing in Chicago in 1912.—Most of the solicitors for these schools are working on a commission basis and tend, therefore, to be more interested in securing the students than they are in telling the truth; in the amount of business they secure than in the maturity or fitness of the pupils they solicit. In very many cases the pupils, even from the fifth grade and up, are induced to leave the public schools for the purpose of taking a course in some business college. Pupils are solicited who have no adaptability for commercial training.

Many students are secured by means of what must be regarded as misrepresentation on the part of the solicitor. They promise the prospective student a job at the end of his short term of study. They draw attention to the fact that certain students have completed courses of study in a short period of time and are now holding good positions. Some of them who enroll have sufficient native ability or have received such previous training that they are enabled to complete the work in the promised time and hold a job when secured. The solicitor uses these examples as a bait to catch others who have not these qualifications. No guarantee is given that the student will be able to hold a position, and many take places only to lose them because they are incompetent.

When the standard of those who seek clerical and office work is as low as that to which our business men testify, it is not difficult to promise some sort of a place to the graduate of a six months' course. This superficial training, especially when it has been added to an incomplete elementary schooling, does not lead to later success, but condemns the boy or girl to the low wages and drudgery which are the necessary lot of the inefficient.

Thus the guarantee of a position after a short term of study in a business college becomes a source of positive injury to the children whom it attracts, and is at the same time ruining excellent material. For the same children might, after the completion of the elementary period with adequate business training, become efficient clerks and stenographers, able to gain a higher wage and take higher positions.

That such children are being solicited and enticed from the public schools in all parts of our city is a fact that is affirmed by every public-school principal whose opinion was sought in the investigation of this problem.

A high-school teacher states: "As the most evident reason why pupils from the grammar schools go to the private business schools rather than to the public high school, may be given the work done among grammar-school pupils of the upper grades and their parents by the solicitors of the business schools."

A high-school teacher of stenography says: "The business colleges are indefatigable in their efforts to secure the pupils as low down as the fourth grade."

In ten high schools located in various sections of the city, 862 pupils in the first year of the high school were asked to write a theme on "Why do not more pupils enter the high schools of our city?" The number of reasons in these themes varies from two or three to a dozen. But it is an interesting fact that 565 of these pupils give, as a leading reason, the work of the business college agents.

One proprietor says: "Business-college training in Chicago is in large measure a failure, because of soliciting children, and employing teachers who lack training. Poor foundation, poor teachers and text-books which produce the largest cash dividend are not conducive to efficient office help.

"Many of the proprietors care more for the dollars received as tuition than the kind of training they are giving; because of solicitation, we are getting our pupils too young and immature; the high cost of solicitation renders it impossible to provide high-class instructors."

Still another says: "We will get just as much business if we let the students alone until they are two or three years older. We would have more students if we would abolish soliciting and apply that large drain to the building up of our schools, making our rooms more attractive, securing more efficient instruction. I would abolish soliciting tomorrow if I could."

THE MOST RECENT STUDY OF THE BUSINESS COLLEGE

In 1918, a study of private commercial schools in New York City was undertaken by the Public Education Committee of that city. It brings our examination of the qualitative features of these schools approximately down to date:[1]

[1] Adapted by permission from Bertha Stevens, *Private Commercial Schools in New York City*, pp. 18–21, 33–41, 82, 92, 96. Report of the Committee to Investigate Private Commercial Schools, Public Education Association, of the City of New York, 1918.

TYPES OF SCHOOLS

From the sixty-seven private commercial schools of Manhattan and the Bronx, we have selected thirty-one for special investigation. Group 1, made up of schools superior in their equipment and in the calibre of their teaching force and students; Group 2, representing competent schools which have good equipment and good teachers but students of varied types, less discriminatingly selected than in the case of the foregoing group; Group 3, schools cheap in equipment, personnel and methods of advertising, and caring more for speed and numbers than for individual excellence; Group 4, made up of schools of low standard, whose meagre equipment and dirty, neglected classrooms cannot expect to do more than prepare students to enter low grade positions; Grade 5, representing schools which are unscrupulous in their dealings with their students or the public. In educational facilities the schools of Group 5 are similar to the schools of Group 3 or 4.

An example of Group 1.—This school is as impressive in its dignity and beauty as many private academic schools are. . . . . One has a feeling that educational purpose and high business ideals are as important to the school as the success of its commercial enterprise. It gives the impression of being, if not keenly alive to changing demands in business, at least well deserving of its established reputation for thoroughness and quality.

The distinction of this school seems to be its careful training of pupils, its high minimum wage and the confident assurance of success which lifts it above the level of unscrupulous or undignified competition. It impressed the visitor as a good, wide-awake business school wherein students could find efficient, specialized training; but there was no discernible atmosphere of idealism or general educational interest.

An example of Group 2.—The chief asset of the school is the personality of the principal and the shorthand teacher. This was shown in their wholesome, dignified appearance, their earnestness in dealing with the pupils, and their direct and intelligent discussion of school matters with the visitor. The place was clean and honest, and one would not be afraid to recommend it to a poor young person in search of specific training.

The proprietor, a scholarly looking man, said he had heard of this investigation and proceeded to ask a few direct and very reasonable questions regarding its method and purpose. He is a man of intelligence and culture, and well informed in matters relating to education generally. The admirable organization and equipment of his own school are evidence of his standards. One wondered why, with all this, so few students of maturity or more than elementary education were attracted to it.

An example of Group 3.—This is a small makeshift sort of a school crowded into a few rooms on the second floor of a store building. Two distinct impressions came to the visitor at once: the cheap character of the school and the plausible, intelligent discussion of the principal, who is quick-minded and very alert to the investigator's point of view. If the principal practised his ideas, the school ought to be a fine thing—which it does not appear to be. The whole enterprise seemed shoddy, as if undercapitalized.

The school in general gives the impression of living by its wits and of being "up to the minute" in new methods and new ideas in commercial education and in its policy of adaptability to conditions;

TABLE XXVII

THE REQUIREMENTS AND OFFERINGS OF 31 SELECTED SCHOOLS IN NEW YORK CITY

Group	Age of Majority of Pupils	Academic Preparation of Majority of Pupils	Range of Usual Period of Instruction	Cost Range for Usual Course of Instruction	No. of Schools Which Guarantee Positions
1......	16–20 years	Some H. S. ed.	6–10 mos.	\$60–\$180	None
2......	15–17 years	8th grade	3– 8 mos.	55– 65	None
3......	15–17 years	8th grade	3– 7 mos.	45– 65	5
4......	15–16 years	8th grade	6– Indefinite	48– 55	2
5......		(Information included by Groups 3 and 4)			

Courses Offered	No. of Schools
Stenography, bookkeeping, "secretarial" course..............	19
Stenography, bookkeeping, typing........................	1
Stenography, bookkeeping..............................	4
Stenography, bookkeeping, typing, accounting..............	1
Stenography, "secretarial" course........................	1
Stenography, telegraphy................................	1
Shorthand, typing......................................	1
Shorthand, advanced shorthand...........................	1
Secretarial course......................................	1
Filing..	1

TABLE XXVIII

Physical Conditions in 31 Schools of Manhattan and the Bronx

	Type of Building	Appearance of Classroom	Light	Ventilation	Cleanliness
Group 1 (6 schools)	Remodelled clubhouse. Specially constructed building. Modern brick building. Bank building	All schools of this group have ample space and give an impression of dignity, suitability and general attractiveness. One school achieves beauty as well as practicability	Good. One school so planned in all rooms that light comes from back and left	Good	Good
Group 2 (9 schools)	Remodelled residence. Office building. Bank building. Newspaper building. Over store. Over moving picture theater	For the most part, well kept and well furnished in a plain, sensible way. Several have fine, large rooms with high ceilings. One school is particularly well adapted and equipped	Good in every school except one and this school has adequate daylight in some of its rooms	Adequate in every school except one	All schools clean One school somewhat untidy
Group 3 (8 schools)	Modern office building. Old office building. Newspaper building. Over store	Two schools are spacious. One school is crowded and one has objectionably narrow stairs and hall. Most are simple, inexpensive, business-like, and modern, and have a minimum amount of equipment	Good in four schools. Insufficient in two schools and poorly arranged in one school	Excellent in one school. Adequate in five schools. Insufficient in two schools	Six schools clean. Two schools fairly clean
Group 4 (4 schools)	Remodelled clubhouse. Remodelled residence. Over moving picture theater	Classrooms are dingy and neglected looking although the reception office may be presentable. Stairways dirty in all and in two schools too narrow	Two schools dark. Light good in one school and fair in the other	Insufficient in all. Two schools are practically unventilated in some of their rooms	No schools of this group are clean. Class rooms and stairs especially dirty
Group 5 (4 schools)	Remodelled residence. Old office building. Modern office building	One school crowded in small rooms. Others have adequate space.	Adequate in three schools. Fair in one school.	Adequate	Adequate

but it seemed to spread itself too thin. We did think, however, that the purpose of the school is to be frankly honest in all its representations.

An example of Group 4.—The first reaction was that nothing good could be said of the school. It seemed to be making its money by fitting low grade pupils for low grade positions, and to be doing this in the kindly guise of working for the good of the young and for the promotion of efficiency. The manager had an air of fatherly kindness and showed a certain subtlety in giving all the right answers. But, before the visit was over, the investigator was impressed with the relation of good will existing between teachers and pupils; and also, she felt that the degree of attention the teachers secured was a thing to be commended.

The emphasis of the school's advertising and the remarks of the principal lead one to suppose that this school considers itself a sort of social center or settlement for its foreign neighbors. In conversation the principal seemed intelligent, very much in earnest and alert to general questions of commercial education; but the dark, dingy classrooms and the untidy children who filled them seemed to tell a different story.

MODERN COMMERCIAL COLLEGE SOLICITATION

Private commercial school solicitation of eighth grade pupils about to be graduated from public schools is general. Of 1,952 such children, in twenty-four school districts, 1,288 were reached by agents or through the mails. This soliciting was done by forty-six different private commercial schools.

As many as twelve private commercial schools have operated at the same time in a single school district. There is more solicitation of girls than of boys.

Names and addresses of pupils about to be graduated are secured from school children, from name brokers, or by disguised advertising.

Most solicitors work on commission and have no other connection with the school which employs them. They can make verbal contracts which the school later may not uphold.

Arguments used most effectively by agents are the shortness of the course, the futility of high school education or training, the undesirability of doing factory work, and the guarantee of a position.

Some business schools have sent directly to the principal's office supplies of blotters, rulers and other useful trifles carrying the advertising of the school, and have asked to have these distributed. So far as we know, such permission is not given. In other cases, representatives have placed these things in piles on a teacher's desk in the classroom at noon without permission, hoping that they will be distributed during the afternoon session. A few elementary school papers have carried a commercial school's advertisement.

Various forms of advertisements were left at homes by agents, or sent to the children by mail. Among these forms were rulers, blotters, buttons, "dope" capsules, picture postals, graduation congratulations, invitations to dances, application forms on postal cards addressed to the school, illustrated booklets, lists and pictures of graduates. Two schools gave dances to the children of elementary graduation classes. A little girl of fourteen gave this report of the dance: "Many kids were there, all 8-B girls, I think, except a few of them that go to that school already. There were many more girls than boys. It was very hot and crowded and they were screaming from the tops of their voices but it was nice decorated. Nine o'clock I went home, but I heard they had later refreshments. I knew girls who went to the dances and did not come home until two o'clock in the morning, alone. They said they had a good time."

In its statement of purpose, the character of its claims, its use of English, and in the quality of taste shown in the material and make-up of the printing, a school reveals itself; and it does this with special effectiveness if its publications are considered in contrast with those of other schools. But reliable judgment of schools on this basis is possible only for persons of some education and maturity. The children for whom this propaganda is designed are not capable of rating it. Extravagant claims, cartoons picturing high success by way of the business school, or even irrelevant color prints of sunsets, are the means which we have found most likely to win their approval and choice.

It would be unfair to close a discussion of the advertising in New York's private commercial schools without some recognition of the honest, intelligent and attractive propaganda of the better schools. A number of such schools put emphasis upon the qualifications of their teachers and show, with dates, the educational institutions attended and the experience of the teachers prior to employment at the school.

The spirit of rivalry.—Competition is a matter of serious concern to most private commercial schools. It is a kind of competition that is not so likely to be the life of the commercial education trade as it is to be its death or disabling. It is very hard for new or small schools to keep from "going to the wall"; and especially among schools of Group 4 the effect of competition is too often to concentrate all the energy and ingenuity upon methods of outwitting a rival, instead of using this energy and ingenuity in building up a better school and thus winning fairly by offering to students a better thing for their money. The hottest rivalry is to be found in the relations of the private schools with each other. This is to be expected because it is the private schools, only, which offer similar subjects within a somewhat similar time range. The public school curriculum is widely different from that of the private school and the time required is much longer. School A, Group 3, is the active rival of School B of Group 2 and vice versa. School C, Group 4, concentrates its energies largely upon School D of the same group; but School C is so much the smaller institution that D does not reciprocate actively. Rivals are fought with all disregard of truth and fairness. Tales of rivals' misdoings were recounted to us enthusiastically in the course of the investigation. An incident which occasioned some unpleasant publicity for a New York private commercial school a number of years ago is talked of as if it had happened yesterday; and yet the thing which occurred was an accident which might, with equal chance, have befallen almost any school in the city. To illustrate methods used in competition, we cite the case of a school which obtained the names of its rival's enrolled students and sent them communications offering to secure positions for them. We have seen evidence, which to us is conclusive, that last summer this same school sent, to the students of its rival, postcards which read, "Do not come to school. Infantile paralysis," and signed them with the typewritten name of the rival's school-manager.

Sudden closing.—"Going out of business" is common enough, in the case of New York's schools of commercial training, to warrant careful watching whether the closing be the result of competition, under-capitalization or deliberate unscrupulousness. The investigation has learned of three schools which closed suddenly during the last year:

The "E" school. "It was always Mr. E's custom," students said, "to keep everyone paid up right to the very minute. If you hadn't paid you couldn't come in class. When the school closed there were about one hundred girls there and some were cheated out of months of schooling and a good deal of money. The day before the school failed Mr. E. went around to the pupils and collected money."

Another girl in school "H," who said she had paid $30 and had received only one month's instruction when the school closed, corroborated in detail the events noted in the foregoing record. She said she did not get any of her money back and thought about fifteen students suffered a loss similar to hers.

INDIVIDUAL INSTRUCTION

"Individual instruction" is the only method adaptable to a group of students uneven in their attainments and capacity. It is true that the greater number of New York City schools show homogeneity in the general character of their students, the age being fifteen or sixteen and the preparation, as a rule, eighth grade; but these students do not enter or leave together. With the exception of the best schools, registration, dropping out and graduation go on all through the year. There are, as a rule, no set dates for beginning and ending. Under such conditions strict grading is impossible and students must have their lessons assigned and explained individually or in very small groups. Class work, which is so rarely possible, has the advantage of general discussion; it gives to students the chance to profit by each other's mistakes and to teachers an opportunity to find out what the students do not know or understand. In the poorer schools, where individual instruction is the only kind given, students may drift along in a vague, unintelligent way. They have little or no home work; and the written work done in class does not, students say, receive a teacher's careful correction.

THE SIZE OF BUSINESS COLLEGES[1]

The Chicago study in 1912, and the New York study in 1918, although of interest and value as intensive investigations, may well be supplemented by the examination of some of the qualitative features stated as a result of broader service. The Bureau of Education, in certain recent publications, presents

[1] Adapted by permission from *Private Commercial and Business Schools*, pp. 6–8. U.S. Bureau of Education, Bulletin No. 47, 1919.

some worth-while data concerning the variation in size of business colleges:

By reference to Figure 19 it will be noted that many schools are very small, 248 having an enrollment of less than 100 for the year, and 227 having an enrollment of from 100 to 199, inclusive. Only three schools have an enrollment exceeding 2,500. The median enrollment of the 890 schools falls between 186 and 187. This means

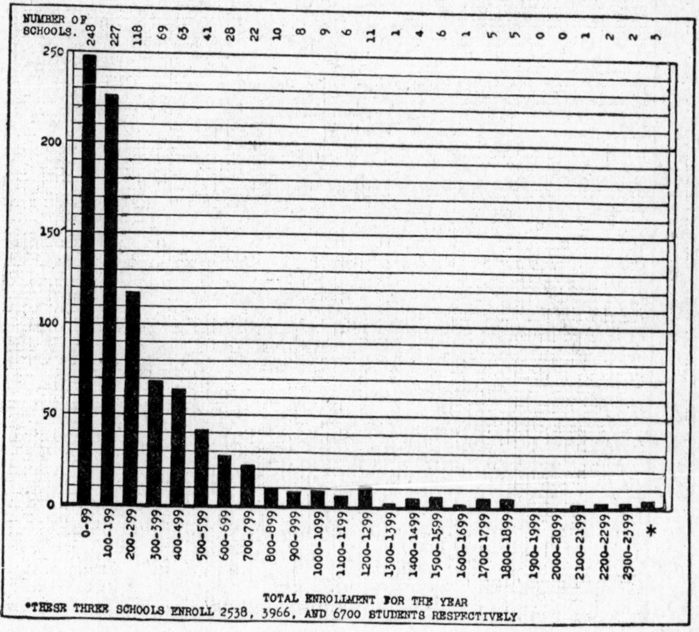

FIG. 19.—Number of schools with indicated enrollment

that 445 schools have an enrollment of 187 or over and 445 schools have an enrollment of 186 or less. The median, therefore, falls in the second bar in Figure 19 in the group having an enrollment of between 100 and 199, inclusive. If the enrollment in all schools is arranged in order of magnitude, and the array is divided into four nearly equal groups of 222, 223, 222, and 223 schools, respectively, it is found that the first group contains schools having an enrollment of 90 students or fewer; the second an enrollment of from 90 to 186; the third an enrollment of between 187 and 400; and the highest group, an enrollment of 400 and over. In other words, half the commercial schools have an enrollment of between 90 and 400, inclusive. The average enrollment is 325 students.

The curve in Figure 20 enables the reader to determine readily the percentage of students in any desired percentage of schools, or

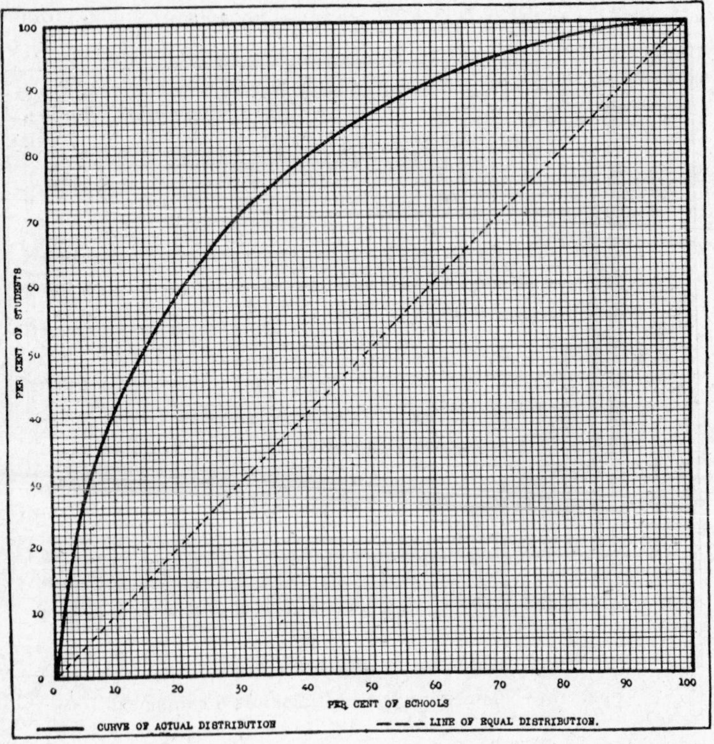

FIG. 20.—Proportion of students to proportionate number of schools

vice versa. Reading from the vertical scale, one will observe that 60 per cent of the students are enrolled in about 22 per cent of the schools, and 90 per cent of the students in about 59 per cent of the schools. Reading from the base line, one may see that 50 per cent of the schools enroll 85.5 per cent of the students, and 30 per cent of the schools enroll 70.4 per cent of the students. If the enrollment were equally distributed in all schools, the curve would follow the "line of equal distribution" in such a way that 50 per cent of the schools would enroll 50 per cent of the students, and 70 per cent of the students would be enrolled in 70 per cent of the schools. The "bowing" of the curve away from the line of equal distribution indicates the dispersion in the distribution. The further the curve recedes from the line of equal distribution the greater the dispersion. The nearer the curve comes to the vertical and horizontal axes of the graph, the nearer the maximum dispersion is reached. For a large group of measures the two axes represent for all practical purposes the greatest inequality possible between the largest and the smallest schools.

TYPES OF WORK IN BUSINESS COLLEGES

Not all students in private commercial schools take the same course. There is a considerable amount of specialization even within the rather limited offering of these schools. The telegraphic course, for example, has in recent years attracted students in considerable numbers, while the bookkeeping and stenographic courses, as individual subjects of study, have each at one time or another held the lead. Night-school work is also an important phase of the private commercial school's offerings, and this appears to have been particularly significant in recent years. The investigation of the Bureau of Education follows:[1]

Enrollment in day and night courses.—This year 716 private commercial schools reported night courses. This means that over 80 per cent of such schools maintained night courses. It is of interest to note the very rapid rise in enrollment in night courses. The increase has been very pronounced since 1912, and especially so within the past two years. In the day courses there has been a corresponding increase for the same periods, but the rate of increase has not been so great. This is very apparent in Figure 21, in which the enrollment for each year has been reduced to index numbers. By means of these index numbers the two curves are brought nearer each other in such a way that comparisons showing the rates of increase may be made. The relative steepness of the slopes of the

[1] Adapted by permission from *Private Commercial and Business Schools*, 1917–18, pp. 11–16. U.S. Bureau of Education, Bulletin No. 47, 1919.

two curves between any two consecutive points indicates the rate of change. Thus between 1916 and 1918 the curve for the night school enrollment shows a steeper slope than the curve for the day schools. Consequently a more rapid change in night school enrollment within this period has taken place.

The moving average of index numbers.—In both curves certain irregularities will be observed. Undoubtedly these low points are

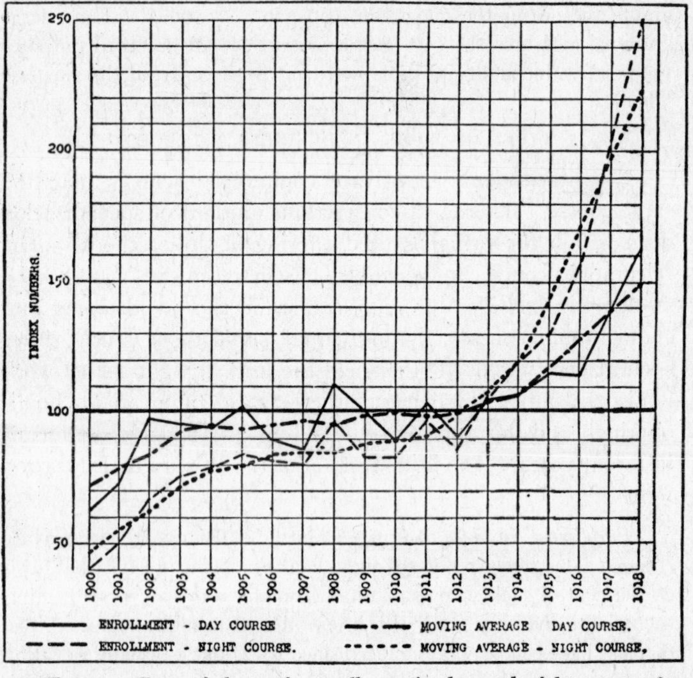

FIG. 21.—Rate of change in enrollment in day and night courses for indicated years.

due more to the failure of commercial schools to submit reports than to any other factor. If all schools had reported each year presumably a more gradual rise would have appeared in the curves. To eliminate these fluctuations in the index curves, moving averages have been applied. The enrollment in night schools since 1900 has increased 560 per cent, while the enrollment in day schools has increased only 157 per cent. Without doubt these percentages would not have been so large had not the war demands for commercial school graduates been so great.

Enrollment by course of study.—It will be observed in Figure 22 that a decided increase in the number of students enrolled in stenographic courses is shown in 1918. The number increased from 70,554 in 1916 to 152,402 in 1918, or 116 per cent. This abnormal increase has presumably been caused by the demand for stenographers on

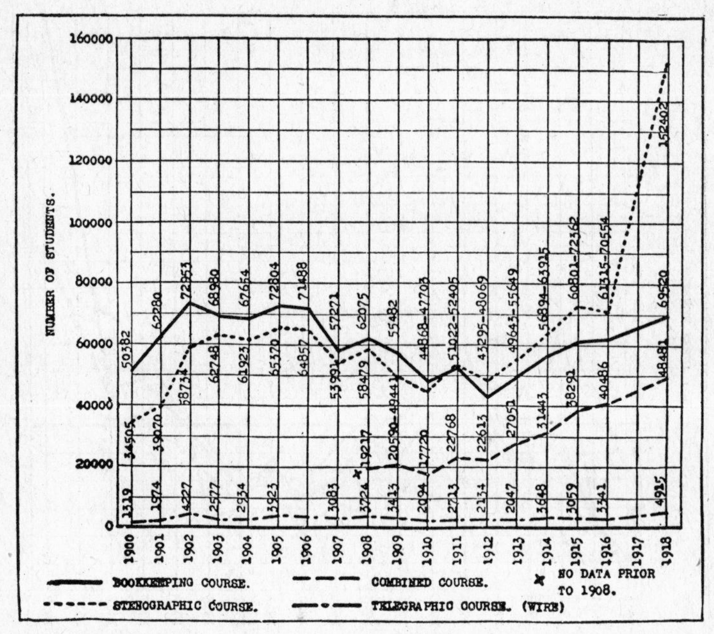

FIG. 22.—Number of students enrolled in indicated courses of study for indicated years.

account of the war. The enrollment in the combined course which includes a study of shorthand also shows a gradual rise since 1910, but no very pronounced increase is evident in 1918. Evidently the demand for stenographers in 1918 was so insistent that few students would resist it long enough to complete both a stenographic and a bookkeeping course. The bookkeeping or commercial course shows in general a decrease from 1902 to 1912, and a gradual increase since that time. This course evidently did not receive a very great impetus on account of war conditions. The bookkeeping course in 1900 apparently was more popular than the other courses offered in private commercial schools. It continued to lead until 1911. Since 1911 the stenographic course has been decidedly the most popular.

Since the curves in Figure 22 are so far apart, it is difficult to compare the increases in enrollment in the various courses offered.

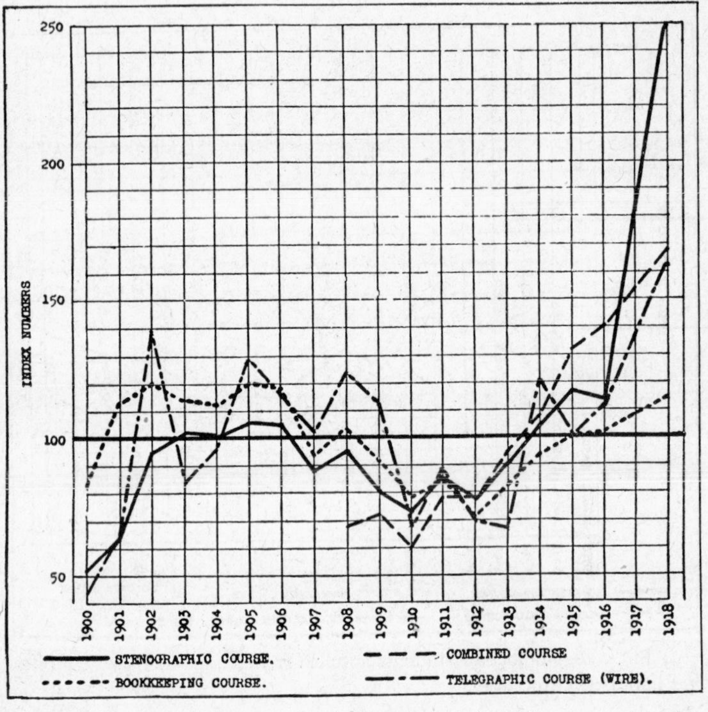

FIG. 23.—Rate of change in enrollment in principal courses of study for indicated years.

For example, was the increase in enrollment in the course in telegraphy (wire), from 1916 to 1918, proportionally as great as the corresponding increase in the combined or in the bookkeeping course? To answer such questions the enrollments given in Figure 22 have been reduced to index numbers which are plotted in Figure 23. From this graph it will be noted that the slope of the curve for the course in telegraphy (wire) is steeper between 1916 and 1918 than either of the curves for the bookkeeping or the combined course. The relative rate of increase has, therefore, been greater. However, for the same interval the curve for the stenographic course is steeper even than that for the course in the telegraphy wire. In the rate of increase in enrollment, therefore, between 1916 and 1918, the stenographic ranks first; the telegraphic, second; the combined, third; and the bookkeeping, fourth. Similar comparisons might be made between any other two consecutive intervals. It must be borne in mind that the relative positions of the curves do not indicate rates of increase. For example, between 1916 and 1918 the curve for the combined course stands above the "telegraphic" curve, but the latter shows the greater increase during this period.

TUITION RATES IN PRIVATE COMMERCIAL SCHOOLS

The tuition rates in private commercial schools were made a subject of study by the Bureau of Education. They show considerable variation:[1]

Altogether, 454 schools reported the tuition rate charged for the commercial or bookkeeping course. Of this number, 217 schools, or 48 per cent, offer a course extending from 3½ to 6 months; and 85 of these, or 39 per cent, charge a fee ranging from $60 to $69. Again, 175 schools, or 39 per cent of the total number reporting, maintain a 6½ to 9 months' course; and 48 of these, or 27 per cent, charge a fee of $70 to $79. Only 44 schools, or less than 10 per cent of the total number, offer a 9½ to 12 months' course, and the charge for tuition in most instances is over $100.

Figure 25 contains two very symmetrical distributions similar to the corresponding ones in Figure 24. In other words, groups 2 and 3 in this graph have almost the same number of schools charging lower or higher tuition fees than the rate indicated by the longest bar in the group. In the 3½ to 6 months' group the most common rate is $60 to $69, 88 schools charging this fee. In all, 64 schools charge a lower and 70 schools a higher rate than this. In the 6½ to 9 months' group 49 schools charge a tuition fee of from $70 to $79. Altogether, in this group 53 schools charge a lower and 95 a higher rate than this. Greater variation from the central tendency is shown in this group

[1] Adapted by permission from *Private Commercial and Business Schools*, 1917–18, pp. 25–28. U.S. Bureau of Education, Bulletin No. 47, 1919.

than in Group 2. In other words, the distribution is slightly skewed in the direction of higher tuition rates. Any school falling in this group and charging $110 or more for the course should be able to justify its action. The single-hatched bars representing Group 4 in this graph show the same irregularity as the corresponding bars did in the next preceding graph. Likewise, groups 1 and 5 are small and consequently show no marked central tendency.

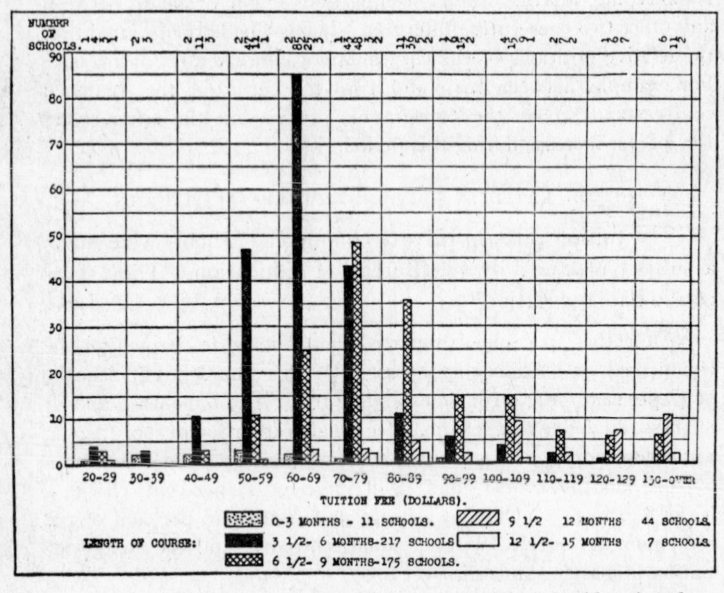

FIG. 24.—Tuition fee for the entire commercial or bookkeeping day course.

Altogether the tuition rates for the stenographic course in 463 schools are represented in this figure. Of this total, 222 schools, or 48 per cent, offer courses requiring from $3\frac{1}{2}$ to 6 months for completion; and 197 schools, or 43 per cent, offer courses requiring from $6\frac{1}{2}$ to 9 months for completion. In other words, 91 per cent of the schools represented in this graph fall in these two groups. This tendency to centralize around a 6 months' course further supports the statement made above that the "average" graduate from a private commercial school has had only six months of training.

Tuition rates for the entire combined day course.—As it takes about twice as long to complete the combined course as either the bookkeeping or the stenographic course, a higher scholarship fee is necessarily charged. In Figure 26 it will be observed that no schools undertake to give this course in three months or less, consequently Group 1 is not represented. There are relatively fewer schools in groups 2 and 3 than in the two graphs next preceding. The majority of the

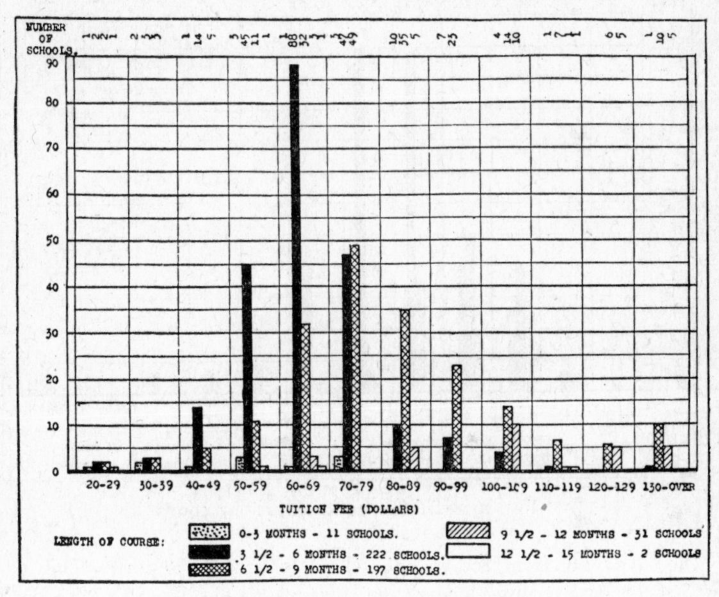

FIG. 25.—Tuition fee for entire stenographic day course

schools are found in Group 4; that is they require from 9½ to 12 months for the completion of the course. Altogether, 321 schools reported the scholarship fee charged for the combined course. Of this number, 172 schools, or 54 per cent, fall in Group 4. The customary fee charged students in schools of this type for this course is from $100 to $139, inclusive. Only 30 schools charge a higher rate, while 33 charge a lower rate. In the schools in Group 5, that is in schools offering a course requiring from 12½ to 15 months for completion, the largest group of schools charge from $140 to $149. Two other groups almost as large, consisting of 12 schools each, charge

\$100 to \$119 and \$120 to \$139, respectively. It will be noticed that remarkable symmetry is evident for the single-hatched, double-hatched, and black bars. A tendency for a few schools to charge an unusually high fee is shown in the isolated bars at the right.

In addition to the schools listed in Figure 26, 12 schools offer a combined course extending from 16 to 42 months and charge tuition

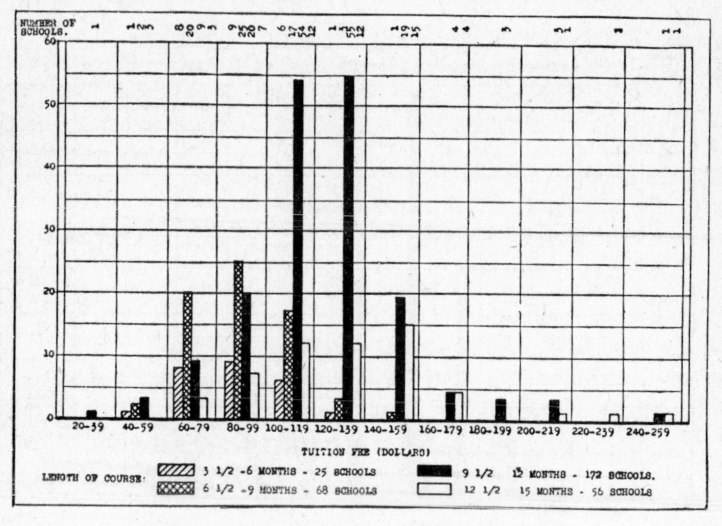

FIG. 26.—Tuition fee for entire day course

fees varying from \$60 in one school to \$270 in another. Only 3 schools have a course longer than 18 months, and 5 offer an 18 months' course. The usual charge for the course ranges from \$110 to \$180.

CONTROL OF THE BUSINESS COLLEGE NEEDED

Most careful observers of the business college have been inclined to agree that it has performed for American business and for the community at large, a useful piece of work. Most of the observers are also inclined to agree that the business college, speaking now generically, has been guilty of a very large amount of bad practice. It is an institution whose activities often furnish a striking example of the lack of incidence between private gain and social welfare. The urge for a rectifying of business-college practice, with the retention of its useful function, has been frequent.

The state of New York makes a rather unavailing effort to control the business college through its State Department of Education:[1]

> At the present time the State Department of Education has no legal authority to inspect the private business schools in operation in this state. Under the Regents' regulations private business schools may be registered by the State Department of Education. When a school of this type makes application for registration a very careful inspection is made of the institution to determine its fitness to offer commercial courses. This inspection includes a careful study of the qualifications of teachers, courses of study, housing facilities and equipment. No school is approved unless it meets the best of the standards in the field of commercial education.

While such approval and registration make it possible for the school to make an added appeal for patronage, this seems to be an insufficient if not a feeble control method. Stronger methods are needed.

Miss Bertha Stevens, who compiled the report of the New York Committee to Investigate Private Commercial Schools, says:[2]

> To make private schools safe, in New York City, there is need for:
>
> The issuing of a State license, without which it should be illegal to open or maintain any sort of private educational institution.
>
> Annual registration of all private educational institutions with the State Department of Education. Registration should be compulsory upon these institutions.
>
> State censorship of advertising material. It should be required of the schools to file with the State Department of Education, samples of all forms used.

[1] The quotation is a statement by L. A. Wilson, director of the Division of Vocational and Extension Education of New York state, April, 1922.

[2] Adapted by permission from Bertha Stevens, *Private Commercial Schools, Manhattan and the Bronx*, pp. 133–34. Report of the Committee to Investigate Private Commercial Schools, the Public Education Association of the City of New York, 1918.

Official standardization of course of study, entrance requirements, preparation of teachers, and equipment. Also, schools should furnish to the State evidence of solvency and sufficient capitalization.

Regular official inspection and supervision, with power to revoke licenses.

A published official list of schools which are legally entitled to exist.

To keep unfit pupils from entering private commercial schools, there is need for:

Enforcement of the compulsory education law. Schools enrolling pupils who are under the law, should be required to report the names of such pupils to the Bureau of Attendance. The Bureau of Attendance would then determine whether the pupils are being instructed in conformity to law; and if necessary, could compel their return to the public schools.

Popular propaganda, directed to parents and public school children, which will inform them convincingly that the average eighth-grade pupil is not ready to study stenography; that success in any kind of office position is likely to depend upon good academic preparation; and that the alternative of factory work need not be shunned, since such work may be both dignified and profitable.

Public school competition, whereby the public schools offer, like the private schools, a brief vocational extension course for office training. Such a course, however, should not include stenography and it should be refused to unsuitable candidates. Parents of children thus refused should be informed of the fact and the reason.

Publicity with regard to the proportionate number of pupils who leave private commercial schools before graduation. Schools should be required to send to the State Department of Education, lists of names of persons entered and graduated within the year.

The better type of business college manager, although slow, perhaps, to recognize the necessity for regulation and improvement, has not been entirely lacking in such thinking. An organization which has in it the possibility of great good in this connection, if it conscientiously carries out a program of improvement, is the National Association of Accredited Commercial Schools.

This Association was formed December 12, 1912, in Chicago with a charter list of twenty-one schools. Regular meetings have been held annually since, and a number of special meetings have been called to consider matters of immediate importance. Early in 1920 its membership numbered over two hundred private business schools in the United States and Canada:[1]

The fundamental purpose of the National Association of Accredited Commercial Schools is the development and maintenance of better educational standards, first, among its own membership, and second, in commercial schools of every class. Better educational standards will mean greater efficiency on the part of our graduates, and a stronger demand for their services, an increased attendance in commercial schools, and more satisfactory standing among educational institutions of all classes. Incidentally, every school in the Association will be benefited in a financial way and will thus be able to offer more to its patrons.

This Association is seeking to educate the general public, and especially the business community, to an understanding of the fact that a business education means a definite amount of training along definite lines for definite purposes. This is being accomplished through the standardization of courses of study.

The fixing of definite standards for graduation means the lengthening of the average term of enrollment on account of the premium that will be placed upon graduation, and further means the better preparation of the student for the duties that he will assume after leaving the schoolroom.

The Education Committee offers a list of Accredited texts, to which list have been admitted only those books that are modern, practical, teachable, scholarly and fully in keeping with the spirit of progress.

Tuition is made transferable upon an equitable basis which will be explained to anyone interested.

The Association conducts every summer a training school for commercial teachers. Special attention is paid to the psychology and pedagogy of the commercial subjects. Teachers in this training school are available first to members of the Association and afterwards to anyone who may wish to employ them.

A Universal Employment Department is maintained in which a graduate of any Accredited school is entitled to membership. That

[1] The statements here quoted are from pamphlets issued by the authority of the Board of Governors of the National Association of Accredited Commercial Schools.

is to say, the graduate of a school in Denver would receive free the best services of the employment department of a school in New York, should he desire it.

The members of the Association are required to maintain the highest possible business standards in their relation with the general public, and with their students, and every school is required to subscribe definitely to the standards of practice herein set forth.

Each member of the Association is entitled to use the Association emblem upon his advertising matter, stationery, diplomas, etc.

This Association is definitely pledged to use its best efforts to eliminate from the school field irresponsible institutions that have neither educational ideals nor moral standards, and are organized merely to prey upon the credulity of the people. This Association condemns the indiscriminate guaranteeing of positions, inadequate tuition rates, short, incomplete courses, and misleading representations, whether in direct solicitation or in general advertising.

This Association will actively prosecute whenever possible under the Fraudulent Advertising Act, schools that can be shown to be using fraudulent, misleading advertising, or advertising methods that are condemned by the Fraudulent Advertising Act.

The National Association of Accredited Commercial Schools extends to every school in the United States that is willing to assist in the consummation of the purposes herein set out, and will measure up to the requirements for membership, a cordial invitation to ally itself with this movement for better conditions in the field of business education.

"STANDARDS OF PRACTICE"

The following "Standards of Practice" were adapted at the 1914 annual meeting of the National Association of Accredited Commercial Schools, and is submitted as the creed to which every applicant for membership in the organization must definitely subscribe before the institution can be favorably considered for membership:

The members of this association are definitely committed to the general policy of effecting an immediate betterment of the individual schools of the Association, to the end that the whole system of private commercial education in the United States may be improved, and may be placed in a more favorable light as a necessary part of the educational machinery of our country.

For the purpose of accomplishing the objects herein set out, each member of this organization will:

1. Maintain in his own institution such policies and practices as will in his community and elsewhere reflect credit upon the cause of business education.

2. Pay his legitimate debts promptly and in a business-like manner.

3. Follow in his business relations with his students and with the general public those standards of business procedure and honor that prevail in the best business houses.

4. Provide the very best quarters and equipment for his school that his income will allow, or that the Education Committee of this Association may recommend.

5. Install and support the standard courses of study as promulgated by this Association.

6. Select and teach texts that are included in the accredited list of the Association.

7. Avoid exaggeration of every kind in every form of advertising.

8. Make no misleading statements or misrepresentations of any kind, either in person or through any agency.

9. Deal fairly and in a dignified manner with all classes of competition.

10. Cultivate within the school itself and in its community the highest possible moral standards.

11. Refuse either directly or indirectly to guarantee positions to prospective students and to make no statements regarding prospective employment that are not fully corroborated by the experience of the school.

12. Report promptly to the proper officer of the Association any violation of the ethics of the profession, as understood by this Association, whether these violations occur within or without the membership of the Association.

13. Each member agrees to submit to a board of arbitrators to be appointed by the president any difficulty or disagreement that may arise as between himself and any other member of the Association, and further agrees to abide by such decision and to carry into effect such provisions or requirements as may by said board be prescribed.

14. Each member of this Association shall be one whose character and reputation are above reproach, and who shall so order his

general conduct as to entitle him to be regarded as a suitable person to direct the education and moral development of the young people in his institution.

THE MERITS OF THE MODERN BUSINESS COLLEGE

The values to be found in private commercial schools of better grade and the advantages which they offer for certain forms of work are thus set forth by the proprietor of a progressive school:[1]

Many factors have contributed to the changes which have taken place or are now occurring in private business schools. A most important factor is the breakdown of the social prejudice which for so long kept the better-educated, better-bred women from the business office. The war dealt a smashing blow at this prejudice, but there had been a steady, if gradual, change in sentiment in this regard for a long time previous to that. Also the demands of business men have become more and more exacting, and with the advent of competition in the form of free public-school commercial courses, the private school proprietor has had to raise his requirements and improve the quality of his output.

It is, then, this modern type of business school whose existence I am justifying. For the inefficient school I hold no brief; the sooner such schools fail and disappear (as they will fail and disappear) the better for everyone.

In the first place, the private business school has real value as a stimulus to the work of the public school. Just as much of the inefficiency of the old time business college can be traced to the lack of public school competition, so would the public school commercial course lose much of its efficiency if private school competition were entirely removed.

In the next place, I believe that there is a keener personal interest in the student in the private business school. That this may be from a selfish motive does not lessen the value to the student, particularly the somewhat backward student, of this keener interest. The private business college cannot afford to have failures; its success depends upon the success of its students, because it could not exist and make a profit if it did not get the majority of its students through voluntary recommendations of its graduates. This means that there cannot be

[1] This statement was prepared by Paul Moser, of the Moser Shorthand College of Chicago.

a certain percentage of failures as in the public school, but that each student whose tuition has been accepted and retained must be made capable of holding a position, and that the teacher must devote the time to each student that will make this possible.

The private business school is more responsive to the demands of the business man and is more closely in touch with the actual requirements of business. This contact comes through the placement bureau of the business college. Even though the reputable business college will not "guarantee a position," the fact remains that the graduate looks to the school for a position and that the well-placed graduate is the school's most loyal advertiser. The business college manager soon hears either from the business man himself or from the graduate who has failed to make good in what respect the student was deficient and can take effective measures to bolster up the weak spots in his curriculum. In the public school, on the other hand, even where placement work is done, there is no obligation to place the student. It is simply something extra that may or may not be done, and in many cases the placement work is done in a central office which may never have been in contact with the student and knows nothing of his fitness for a particular position.

The well-run business college has more of the practical atmosphere of the office than the high school, and this has a marked influence to give the student a businesslike viewpoint and poise.

There are minor practical advantages that the business college has over the public schools. Its work is more individually planned, permitting enrolment at frequent intervals, whereas the public-school curriculum is on the semester basis. The brighter, more ambitious student has more opportunity to forge ahead in the business college because classes are not as rigidly kept together as in public-school courses.

Personally I believe that it is worthy of consideration as to whether high-school commercial courses have not been growing too rapidly. There is a grave danger that such work will be started too soon in the student's high-school course; that the foundation and cultural courses will be neglected, and that in consequence the student's educational background will be insufficient.

THE RÔLE OF THE BUSINESS COLLEGE

The private commercial school remains largely as it began, an institution concerned with doing the immediate thing. The interests of business-college managers do not, and probably cannot ever, lie in education of a fundamental sort. This is no criticism of the business college. The business college should not undertake training of a fundamental sort. The relation between the student's gain and his expenditure is remote when he buys fundamental education. Therefore the private school with a commercial-college tradition cannot supply such education successfully. That task must be undertaken by other institutions. The business college, however, has an important and useful part to play in the general scheme of education.

As a training-school in the technique of office practice, where its pupils have had a proper educational basis, it is doubtful if the business college has ever been surpassed or even equaled. If these institutions could be so regulated that they did not draw to themselves a great number of persons at an age when there is no justification for their being trained in technique, and if the general features of building and equipment could be publicly supervised, it seems that they might safely be trusted with a very large part of the technical office-work training which is now done in other institutions.

The proper rôle of these schools may vary somewhat with the size of the community. They have a real place as specialists in the offering of technical training, and they have there a large place.

QUESTIONS FOR DISCUSSION

1. Trace the growth in number of business colleges over the eighteen years indicated in the charts. Try to account for sharp changes in number of schools. Do the same for the numbers of students in business colleges.
2. How would you account for the sharp rise in the number of women taking business-college training between 1916 and 1918 and the falling off of men?
3. Even since 1900 the number of women in business colleges has increased more rapidly than the number of men. How would you account for this fact?
4. What was President James's appraisal of the business college in 1890? How much had President James's opinion changed by 1904?

5. List the characteristics of the business college which were pointed out by the Chicago City Club. How far do these fit in with your experience with business colleges? List under the headings "Favorable," "Adverse," the characteristics of the business college as given by the Chicago City Club.
6. Why should the Chicago City Club object to business-college solicitation of pupils? Isn't this merely "going after business"?
7. List under two headings, "Favorable" and "Adverse," the characteristics of the business college brought out in the New York survey.
8. What is the median enrolment of the 890 private commercial schools discussed by the Bureau of Education in the report quoted? What is the average enrolment?
9. What types of work are offered in the modern business college? How do numbers in evening courses compare with numbers in day courses in the modern business college?
10. What courses are offered in the modern business college? How does the enrolment compare in each? What ones show the most growth in recent years?
11. From a study of the charges made by business colleges, what would you say is the principle that underlies their rates? Are the charges fairly uniform? How would you account for the variations? How do charges vary for different types of courses? What is your judgment of the fairness of these charges?
12. How might registration by the State Board of Education of certain business colleges as "approved" tend to raise the standards of this type of education? What is the weakness of this form of control? What are Miss Stevens' ideas of what is needed "to make private schools safe"? Comment on each of them.
13. What is the National Association of Accredited Commercial Schools? What advantages might accrue to a school from joining this Association? What steps has this organization apparently taken to improve the standards of the private commercial school?
14. Will the forces which Moser believes have brought about "the modern business college" destroy the undesirable ones and compel high standards from those that survive?
15. Would you favor a law forbidding business colleges to register students who were not eighth-grade graduates? High-school graduates?
16. What seems to you the rôle or place of the business college in a planned scheme of education for business?

CHAPTER XII

PRIVATE COLLEGIATE SCHOOLS OF COMMERCE AND CORRESPONDENCE SCHOOLS

In general, private business schools other than the business college are of two classes: the correspondence school and the private school which offers business training of a more or less advanced character. The second of these has been, perhaps entirely, an outgrowth of the collegiate school of business movement. Individuals have set up schools to imitate the work done by collegiate schools of business and have offered in many cases a semblance and, in some instances probably, a reality of collegiate business training.

Semi-charitable organizations such as the Y.M.C.A. have reached into this field. They have not limited their activities to college type of training, but have offered business training of almost every grade and kind. In many ways these schools are quite comparable to the better type of private school, and one example, Y.M.C.A. schools, therefore, will be given some attention here as an illustration of this form of school in general.

The correspondence school is an older institution and had developed in one or two cases a fairly advanced form of training for business before the collegiate school of business movement came into full flower. On the other hand, once the collegiate school of business did develop, the growth of correspondence schools was stimulated by the opening of this new field of education and the organization of new material through the energy of the universities.

Although no attempt will be made in this chapter to make an exhaustive treatment either of private business schools or of correspondence schools, enough data will be presented to give the reader a picture of these institutions and a basis for judgment in attempting to place them in a specialized scheme of education.

ORIGIN OF Y.M.C.A. EDUCATION

As recently as 1909 the United States Bureau of Education made an investigation of the work of the Y.M.C.A. in the educational field:[1]

At the time when the first Young Men's Christian Associations in North America were organized in 1851, at Montreal and Boston, there appears to have been little thought of including a definite educational program in the work of these associations.

In 1889, the International Convention, for the first time, indorsed educational work as a function of the association. The subject had also been discussed for several years previously at state conventions. In 1893, the International Committee established a department of education with George B. Hodge as senior secretary. This department was made responsible for the studying of the fundamental principles of the work and for gathering data from the various associations on which suggestions for development could be made.

In 1900 there began a period of expansion and extension. Instead of the class work being limited to the winter time, such instruction was continued throughout the spring. Day work was also introduced, and summer schools for boys were organized to supplement the work of the public schools. Special schools, such as automobile, salesmanship, advertising, insurance, real estate, textile designing, plumbing, fruit culture, and many others were established. The educational program of the association was also extended into fields outside the building.

There was a steady increase in the number of associations employing educational secretaries. To some extent, supervision from state committees was inaugurated. Higher standards of instruction were established. The years from 1900 to 1915 witnessed a remarkable growth of the association educational work, as exhibited by the statistical data shown on page 316.

Since 1916, the educational work of the associations has continued along lines that have become recognized as standard.

The particular function of the association, through its educational service, has been to furnish and to make easily accessible to men and boys, mainly those in industry, such courses of instruction as would

[1] Adapted by permission from William Orr, senior educational secretary of the International Committee, *Educational Work of the Young Men's Christian Associations, 1916–1918*, pp. 3–6. U.S. Bureau of Education, Bulletin No. 53, 1919.

enable them to become better citizens and workmen. It is significant that even at the very outset of the educational work, this purpose appears in the courses in ancient languages intended to aid men preparing for the ministry. While such subjects as these no longer appear in the programs of instruction, the vocational aim has continued to dominate.

TABLE XXIX

	1901	1915
Number of lectures and talks	3,041	14,819
Educational club members	4,618	26,700
Number of associations with educational secretaries	21	84
Number of paid teachers	901	2,592
Total different students, day and evening	26,906	83,771
Number of international certificates won	1,532	2,240
Students in association day courses	560	8,031
Students outside building	350	22,653
Expense of advertising	$12,607	$81,772
Tuition receipts	$48,000	$814,024

In business education, especially, has the Y.M.C.A. developed of recent years, and in the larger cities it now offers a course quite comparable to that of many collegiate schools of business. The work of such a school in the business educational scheme is thus described by the Chicago director.[1]

The national headquarters of the United Y.M.C.A. Schools, representing a federation of the local Y.M.C.A. Schools, announced a total enrollment for the school year 1920–21 of over 120,000 students in day and evening classes and over 20,000 students in extension or home study courses. Of this number it is estimated that 50 per cent of these students were enrolled in business courses of various kinds.

In the development of the program of strictly business education most of the Y.M.C.A. Schools have followed the usual classification of secondary and collegiate grade courses. In the secondary field an attempt has been made to design courses especially to fit the needs of boys and young men which is in contrast with the business courses in most of our high schools and business colleges which have been adapted to a considerable degree to the needs of young women.

In the field of collegiate business education the trend has been toward the development of standard Schools of Commerce of recog-

[1] A statement prepared by H. C. Daines, director, Central Y.M.C.A. Schools, Chicago, May, 1922.

nized standing. The courses which have been offered have been announced to meet the general and specialized needs of the employed man. While the courses have been designed on the assumption that a man has had at least a high school education, registration has been open to mature business men, not high school graduates, who show evidence of being able to profitably pursue the course. This is in accordance with the precedent of well established universities.

A program of business education approved by the Board of Governors of the United Y.M.C.A. Schools provides for the development of five four-year standard curricula in Production, Accountancy, Banking and Finance, Marketing, and Business Administration. Special commissions have been working on each of these curricula and many of the Schools of Commerce in our larger cities have very elaborate courses of study set up paralleling that of the well established evening university schools of commerce. Two year certificate courses are offered in Real Estate, Credit Management, Foreign Trade, Employment Management, Insurance, Traffic Management, and Purchasing.

These various curricula are made up of one semester and two semester unit courses which may be entered by men who are unable to take the more complete courses. Many of our Schools of Commerce are granting the degrees of Bachelor of Commercial Science and Master of Commercial Science. Some of these schools have distinctive university and collegiate names. The aim in all of these schools is to offer exceptionally practical training adapted to the need of the employed man. Many of the instructors in these schools are prominent business men who are willing to teach one or two evenings a week but who could not be induced to accept a regular full time teaching position in a university.

Through the headquarters of the United Y.M.C.A. Schools in New York City a number of texts have been published especially adapted to the needs of the mature student and to night school methods of instruction.

CORRESPONDENCE SCHOOLS

The beginnings of correspondence schools, and something of the relation between the correspondence-school movement and the universities, are well stated in the following paragraphs:[1]

[1] Adapted by permission from Frank H. Palmer, "Correspondence Schools," *Education*, XXXI (September, 1910), 47–48. The Palmer Company, Publishers.

Instruction by correspondence is an outgrowth of the university extension movement which originated in England in 1868. Societies were formed in that country for the encouragement of home study, and plans or outlines were prepared to guide the reading of those who became interested. In 1873 the idea crossed the water and a similar society was formed in Boston which added correspondence with its members as an integral part of its plan. Ten years later a "Correspondence University" was formed in New York state with headquarters at Ithaca, with a board of instructors from different colleges and universities. It offered at low cost helpful instruction by correspondence to such persons as could not leave their homes for attendance at established institutions of learning. The Chautauqua movement soon followed and became very popular throughout the country. The late Dr. William R. Harper, on assuming the presidency of the University of Chicago at its establishment in 1892, endorsed the method and made it a part of the work of the University as a Correspondence Division of the University Extension Department. From the first the movement has had the co-operation and support of the colleges and universities, many of the professors in which have been the instructors in the various courses offered by the correspondence schools. There are said to be now over two hundred such schools in the United States. One of the largest of these, the International Correspondence Schools of Scranton, Penn., claims to have enrolled in the twenty years of its existence 1,281,800 names. It has about five hundred instructors and furnishes instruction in 203 subjects.

The modern correspondence school.—The modern correspondence school is a thing of almost infinite variety. A description of its varied forms, as well as an attempt to classify the various forms, has thus been made:[1]

The courses [of modern correspondence schools] cover nearly every known human activity ranging from raising poultry to training engineers. They include instruction in accounting, law, electrical engineering, meter engineering, signal engineering, wireless operating, automobile driving and repairing, lettering and designing, drawing and cartooning, drafting, advertising and selling, public-speaking,

[1] Adapted by permission from Lee Galloway, "Correspondence School Instruction by Non-Academic Institutions," *Annals of the American Academy*, LXVII (September, 1916, *New Possibilities in Education*), pp. 202–9.

watch repairing, executive management, English and even ventriloquism. A person may be made into a traffic inspector, a detective or a musician—all by mail.

EXTENT OF INFLUENCE

The best measure of the influence of these schools is the number of students enrolled and the amount of money spent in preparing the courses of instruction as well as in advertising them. One school offering four main courses—accounting, law, traffic management and business administration—has enrolled 90,000 students. A correspondence law school has put 40,000 enrollments upon its records within the last five years, while another school offering a general business course for executives has enrolled over 40,000 within approximately the same time. Even those schools which appeal to the narrower fields of highly specialized activities such as music, credits and collections and so on, show a wide influence. Over 260,000 persons have received instruction from one school teaching music by mail since its establishment twenty years ago, while the active list that follows the weekly lessons never falls below 10,000 students.

In the same length of time, a school of design and lettering has enrolled 9,455 students, and a correspondence collection school has enrolled 7,236 in about ten years. Even a highly specialized field, that of investments, has enabled one school to keep up an average yearly enrollment of 120. Within the first five years of its history the Alexander Hamilton Institute enrolled over 40,000 men whose average age is thirty-two years and whose average income is over $2,700 a year.

VARIETIES OF CORRESPONDENCE SCHOOLS

Classified according to the nature of instruction offered, correspondence schools fall into three groups:

1. Schools offering general training in fundamental subjects such as the Home Correspondence School.

2. Schools offering specialized technical training, such as the Blackstone Institute for law, Pace and Pace for accounting and the American Collection Service.

3. Schools offering general commercial training, such as the Alexander Hamilton Institute, the American School of Correspondence and the La Salle Institute.

Perhaps a more significant classification is one based on the character of the ownership and control. Here again we find three types as follows:

1. Public correspondence schools—those connected with universities (Wisconsin, Minnesota, Chicago).

2. Private—such as described above.

3. Quasi-public—such as the National Commercial Gas Association and the American Institute of Banking.

The text and lesson material varies from school to school. The larger and more prominent ones put out texts of real educational merit. They differ from the regular school or college texts in that the diction is extremely simple, explanations are very elaborate and truisms are never omitted.

Can an institution which is in the field for profit be relied upon to give proper attention to those phases of education which do not yield a profit in dollars and cents?

Good business policy demands that the interests of the consumer stand first. In the case of the correspondence schools a violation of this principle has brought about more than one recent failure just as it did in the case of many large merchandizing establishments of recent memory. It is not a question of inherent differences between the commercial and educational elements in the composition of a correspondence school, but the universal problem which faces every enterprise—the problem of deciding between the long run and the short run policies of a business. There is plenty of internal evidence both in the material of instruction and in the organization of the better schools to prove that the commercial character of the work does not necessarily interfere with a broad and liberal treatment of the subjects.

However, one phase of correspondence school activities shows a tardy development. This is an element which creeps into the advertising of even the best schools. An examination of the advertisements and circular letters reveals many objectionable features. They bristle with special scholarships, reduced prices for limited periods, free offers and the like. It is not that the schools play up their best and strongest features but the fact that they use the quack's methods of appealing to men's weaknesses rather than to their strength and that their innumerable special offers of scholarships, reduced prices, etc., are as a matter of fact practically perpetual in one form or another.

A correspondence school need not be tied to an academic institution in order to be endowed with high ideals, pure motives and professional methods, but there is still a strong prejudice against these institutions which is based on the practices of the weak and fraudulent schools which deliberately cater to the delusions of the simple-minded and by misleading advertisements exploit the gullible public. Correspondence schools like the common public schools will grow in number and influence as the demand, not only for popular education, increases, but also for a continuous education which lasts far beyond the "school days" of the active man whether he be mechanic, professional or business man.

Appraisals of the correspondence school.—The correspondence school, at least the privately managed one, has its friends and its foes. There are, as well, those persons who believe that many of the correspondence schools are doing a useful work, believing at the same time that many are guilty of every type of malpractice and bad advertising conceivable. The more pessimistic attitude toward the performance of the private correspondence school is thus expressed.[1]

Though a great deal of incidental good is done in furnishing instruction to ambitious young men, the private correspondence schools constitute, in the main, a vicious and inefficient system of education for the following reasons:

(1) Many of them are fraudulent. It is difficult for the post-office authorities to detect whether or not a concern is doing a legitimate business. By liberal advertising, it is possible for a company to reap a harvest before a fraud order can be issued. It is possible, moreover, for a concern to stay within the letter of the law and yet exploit its patrons.

(2) The degree of efficiency, even among the technically honest firms, is not high. A staff of ill-paid clerks is generally employed at answering letters and replying to questions. Even though the work is standardized, these people cannot furnish complete and accurate information or high-grade instruction.

(3) The charges for tuition are too high. The fees per course vary from $20 upwards, the average charge by the International

[1] Adapted by permission from Paul H. Douglas, *American Apprenticeship and Industrial Education*, pp. 2410. New York: Longmans, Green & Co., 1921.

Correspondence Schools being $75. This constitutes a severe drain upon a poor man's resources, and their collection is only possible because they are paid in installments rather than in a lump sum. Were the tuition fees actually invested in the educational side of the business, no complaint could of course be made, but such is not the case.

(4) An enormous amount is wasted in competitive advertising and canvassing. Most of the expenses of a modern correspondence school are indeed in the sales and not in the educational department. One large school claiming an enrollment of 350,000 pupils had twenty branch offices each with its quota of salesmen and employed in all over 2,500 people. Only 370 of these were, however, connected with the educational work! Fifteen per cent of the force was devoted to the actual instruction itself, while 85 was employed in the administration and sales side of the business. This indicates a shocking disproportion of energy and resources, and is one that would not exist under a publicly operated system with the wastes of competition eliminated.

(5) A further criticism of private correspondence schools is that only a small percentage ever finish the courses that they begin. Veiled in secrecy as the records are, only estimates are possible. The Minnesota Department of Labor Statistics found that less than one-third of those who began courses in Minneapolis, finished them. The percentage, for the country, as a whole, of those who complete their course is probably even less. The Canadian Commission on Technical Education declared it to be as low as 5 or 10 per cent.

(6) Finally, correspondence school courses, even at their best, are a decidedly unsatisfactory means of education and should be used only as a last resort. The instruction lacks personal touch, there is an inevitable delay in replying to questions which is generally at least as long as a week, and sometimes a fortnight or a month. This robs the study of much of its interest and the student soon loses heart and generally drops out. These schools cannot be called a solution, in any real sense, of the problem of industrial education.

The huge numbers who have sought further technical education at their hands is, however, adequate proof of the fact that the present educational system of the country has failed to meet the need of the times. Because of the lack of a better system, men have turned to privately managed schools both at long and short range to secure the training that they have needed.

A more optimistic view of the performance, as well as the possibilities of the correspondence school, is the following statement of Mr. A. M. Simons.[1]

The most prominent characteristic of correspondence school work, to the outsider at least and especially to the person who has been accustomed to the atmosphere of the conventional school, is its frank, commercial outlook.

A correspondence school teaches to make money. This fact carries with it a large number of handicaps, as its managers are continuously reminded. It has some advantages, however. Its appeal speaks a language that is understood in every field of industry. The person who has had a long experience in business grows suspicious of anyone who wishes to do anything for him for nothing. He always fears that before they have finished, they are not only going to "do him good," but also "plenty." When the correspondence school makes its appeal on the ground that it can make money by teaching someone else how to increase his income, it is speaking the most familiar language in the business world today.

It gets its students by familiar business methods. The fact that it spends a large percentage of the money received from a student in advertising, is urged as proof that its methods are wasteful. The defenders of advertising have long ago furnished with it a reply which it seems is more justifiable as applying to the correspondence school than to almost any other field.

The sums spent in advertising education are, in part at least, spent in educating people to the need of education. Selling education to the general public is not an easy task. Teaching a person that he needs a certain line of training may be as essential a part of his education as the training which he purchases, and there is certainly some justice in making the student pay for his education all along the line.

When the correspondence school enters the field of business, it has certain peculiar advantages in competing for the favor of those seeking education. Whether these advantages are all desirable or not, I shall not argue, because I am not either defending, indicting, or praising correspondence schools, but only describing the reasons why, in a nation filled with free educational institutions, they are able

[1] A statement prepared by A. M. Simons, director of Foremanship Training, American School, April, 1922.

to find a place and secure the patronage of hundreds of thousands of the brightest young people in industry.

The correspondence school has few or no traditions. There are some who would say it has no standards. But many times it will be found that the same thing is meant in both cases, and the indictment is not so strong as it sounds.

The residence school, especially if supported by public money, by endowments, or through public solicitation of funds, must maintain scholastic traditions often running back through centuries. It cannot afford to experiment. It must always think of its traditions.

Now business, and especially mechanical industry, is a field in which the greatest rewards frequently go to those most willing and able to break traditions. Industry grows by discovery, invention, and the hunting out of new ways to do things.

The correspondence school can keep pace with this. If a new occupation, like employment management, wireless operation, or automobile construction appears, it can at once adjust its curriculum to meet the emergency. For, while it is constantly trying to sell education to new customers, it is equally diligent to find out what those customers want. It can move into a new field instantly. Its test of whether the new field is educationally desirable (it must be frankly admitted) is the business test: "does it pay?" Are there enough persons who desire training in the new field to support the educational facilities? It can expand instantly to meet a new demand and contract its forces almost as quickly.

The correspondence school is always in session. It is ready to offer facilities whenever a period of idleness, a sudden impulse and desire for change, a hope of promotion, or any of the other multitude of motives that impel people in the industrial world to seek an education, chance to arise in the individual. It fits into odd spells, into vacant places in educational equipment, into all ordinary relations of life, without seriously disturbing any of them. It is especially suitable to the industrial worker, in that it adjusts itself to his existing knowledge and methods of education. He has learned something by experience on the job. He is learning more as he works. He has, perhaps, developed trade skills to a high degree, but he is still lacking in the intellectual background and wider relations which are coming more and more to be considered as essential to promotion. The correspondence school comes forward supplementing all of his existing knowledge and duplicating none of it, since he is perfectly at liberty to move as swiftly as he wishes over that which he already knows and to dally as long as he pleases over the portions which suit his purposes.

A further reason of great importance, which is seldom realized, is the privacy furnished. Most of the students of correspondence schools are adults, or approaching that stage. They are usually seeking to fill in a gap in their knowledge which they have only discovered when confronted with its need. Frequently the discovery of this gap by someone else might cost them financial loss and personal discomfort. To attend a residence school is to confess their ignorance and to advertise it, perhaps, to the very people from whom they wish to conceal it.

A great many preachers and grade school principals are taking a high school course with a school with which I am familiar. The preacher naturally feels that if his congregation knew that he were taking such a course, their respect for him would fall. He may be mistaken, and if right the congregation may be blamed, but he prefers to acquire the knowledge quietly rather than test their opinion.

The teacher who is keeping ahead of his class by correspondence work has the same feeling in an even more intensive degree.

In industry perhaps the most frequent reason for taking a correspondence course is to be in line for promotion to some position already fixed upon. It requires very little knowledge of office politics to know that there are plenty of instances in which, if a superior knew that a subordinate had picked upon the very job held by the said superior, there would be trouble.

Of course, these things may all be wrong, but I think no one will deny that they exist and are a part of the things that must be considered in planning a practical educational program.

It is indeed difficult to assign a place to the correspondence school alongside of a group of other specialized institutions, each striving to do its part in a program. If all of the other institutions now in existence did their job thoroughly, the correspondence school would probably have little place. Its success is rather the outgrowth of the defects and limitations of the public and private educational system. Its greatest usefulness is to fit into those chinks left in the building done by other institutions. Add to the fact that its infinite variety of offerings make possible some filling for almost any chink, the fact that the filling can be done at almost any time, and there is much to be said for the usefulness of the honest and well-managed correspondence school.

On the other hand, there is in the correspondence-school situation every possibility for exploitation which is to be found in the position of the private business college. It has in it all of those possibilities, aggravated by the fact that it deals impersonally and at long range, and with many who are less informed even than the youthful clients of the business college.

There seems no doubt that the sale of education is a proper field for an increased amount of public regulation. Unregulated exchange is based on the assumption that the parties deal on something approximating equality. In the sale of education, however, there is, in the very essence of the situation, a frank admission that there is no such parity. One is informed, the other is uninformed, and few situations can give a greater opportunity for exploitation than this. In the circumstances it is quite in keeping with the legal theory of fiduciary relationships to throw upon correspondence schools and other private educational institutions a degree of responsibility which does not now exist and to surround them with an amount of legal regulation which will smother those taking advantage of an innocent patronage.

QUESTIONS FOR DISCUSSION

1. The business college has its counterpart in the field of collegiate business work. Give a number of examples of private schools which illustrate this statement.
2. The correspondence schools are much older than the private collegiate school of business. How would you explain this fact?
3. In very few instances, perhaps in none, have business colleges grown into private business schools of collegiate grade. How would you explain this fact?
4. The Y.M.C.A. school of commerce may be studied as an example of the private school of business of collegiate grade. In what ways is this illustration satisfactory? In what ways unsatisfactory?
5. Private business schools of collegiate grade have reason to keep their courses of a more practical and a more immediately useful nature than do university schools of business. Why is this true?

6. Private collegiate business schools have the double problem of developing an organized curriculum extending over a period of years, and also of planning short unit courses. What object have they in each of these types of courses? Give an example of each type of work.
7. Trace briefly the history of correspondence work. What criticisms or comments can you make on the classification of the correspondence schools given in the text? Make an appraisal of each of the appraisals of the correspondence schools given in the text.
8. Is there a justifiable place for such schools as that illustrated by the Y.M.C.A. school of commerce? If so, make out a statement or series of statements indicating what you believe that place to be.
9. Is there a place in business education for the correspondence school? If so, work out a statement or series of statements of what you believe to be the place of such schools.

CHAPTER XIII

THE CORPORATION SCHOOL[1]

A corporation school is a school operated by a business enterprise (usually by a corporation) to train people for its own uses and as a part of its business operations. There is little to be gained by attempting to relate the corporation school to medieval apprenticeship or even to the industrial technical school movement. The corporation school is the offspring of large-scale industry and concentrated control rather than of educational forbears.

It appears to be generally believed that the earliest corporation school in America was that founded by the R. Hoe Printing Press Company of New York in the early seventies.[2] Not before 1905 did the movement attain any swing, but since that time it has been rapid and of an increasingly substantial character.[3] The corporation school movement was so well developed and so clearly recognized by 1913 that on January 24 of that year the representatives of forty-eight establishments maintaining corporation schools met in New York City and organized the National Association of Corporation Schools. By vote of the Executive Committee, August 17, 1920, the name of the organization was changed to the National Association of Corporation Training.[4] The latest *Proceedings* available (June,

[1] This chapter is for the most part adapted from an article by the author, "The Corporation School and Its Place in a Scheme of Business Education," *Journal of Political Economy*, November, 1921. The chief sources of the data are the *Proceedings of the Annual Conventions* and the *Bulletins of the National Association of Corporation Training.*

[2] The opinion that the first apprenticeship school maintained by a business corporation was that established by the Chaix Printing Company of Paris, in 1863, is expressed by A. J. Beatty in his *Corporation Schools* (Public School Publishing Co., Bloomington, Ill., 1918), pp. 42–43.

[3] No doubt some of the impetus given by the war will prove unlasting.

[4] *Bulletin of the National Association of Corporation Training*, September, 1920, p. 391. The National Association of Corporation Schools has recently been succeeded by the National Personnel Association.

1921) reports 131 Class A members. The year preceding there were 147 such members. Since that first meeting this organization has held conventions annually. At these meetings the various problems connected with corporation schools have been discussed at length.

The purposes of this association are set forth in each report of the annual conventions to be the following: (1) to develop the efficiency of the individual employee; (2) to increase efficiency in industry; (3) to influence courses of established educational institutions more favorably toward industry.

The National Association of Corporation Training has grown in size with succeeding years, has organized committees dealing with the various phases of corporation school work, and has made the varied and scattered facts concerning corporation schools of the United States fairly available. Monthly bulletins are issued by the association and the proceedings of its annual conventions are published.

TYPES OF CORPORATION SCHOOLS

While corporation schools differ infinitely in detail there are six definite and distinct types which are recognized by the literature of the National Association of Corporation Training. These are: (1) special training schools, (2) trade apprenticeship schools; (3) office-work schools; (4) advertising, selling, and distribution schools; (5) retail salesmanship schools; (6) schools for unskilled labor; some of these types have important subdivisions. Concerning the special training schools, for instance, the National Association's committee, which undertook a classification, reported:[1]

Each school has an individuality which reflects the individuality of the business and the officials controlling it. By overlooking minor details of organization and retaining only the most general character-

[1] The classification and illustrations of special training schools which follow are collected and adapted from the *Proceedings of the Fourth Annual Convention of the National Association of Corporation Schools*, pp. 88–128. In many cases, as in the quotation, the exact phrasing of the report is used. The names of firms listed as using one or another of the types of training courses are taken from the same sources.

istics as the basis of classification we are able to crowd all the various special training schools into five fairly well defined groups or types of schools.

There is probably no single school which can be said to fit perfectly into the group to which it is assigned. Broadly speaking, the various types of special training schools may be fairly well characterized as follows:

TYPE I. Company Business—Study Courses (non-productive)
- Plan No. 1—For new employees
- Plan No. 2—For old employees

TYPE II. Company Business—Study and Practice Courses (partly productive)
- Plan No. 3—For new employees
- Plan No. 4—For old employees

TYPE III. Company Business—Work Courses (productive)
- Plan No. 5—For new employees
- Plan No. 6—For old employees

TYPE IV. Company Continuation Schools
- Plan No. 7—Day continuation courses (partly productive, partly general study classes; on company time; for new or old employees)
- Plan No. 8—Evening continuation courses (general and special study classes; on student's time; any employee)
- Plan No. 9—Correspondence continuation courses (general and specific subjects; on student's time)

TYPE V. Public or Private Continuation Schools—Co-operative
- Plan No. 10—Co-operative plan (part work and part school course)

A. TYPE I. COMPANY BUSINESS—STUDY COURSES

The distinguishing feature is the fact that the student employee spends all of his time in studying, not being expected to do any productive work during the period of training. It is designed to get definite results and get them quickly.

PLAN NO. I. FOR NEW EMPLOYEES

Purpose.—(*a*) to teach specific duties; or (*b*) to give a broad knowledge of the business—that is, its organization, policies, products, methods, plant, and personnel.

Characteristic features.—Student's time entirely non-productive; students are selected by the company; attendance is compulsory; attendance is on company time; students receive pay while taking the course; length of course comparatively short, usually a few weeks; students are grouped at or sent to the most convenient place for instruction; small groups, intensive instruction.

Students.—Plan is adaptable to students whose previous education varies from uncompleted grammar school to high school, technical school, or college, or their equivalent.

Educational methods.—Definite plan and outline for entire course common.

PLAN NO. 2. FOR OLD EMPLOYEES

Purpose.—Usually to broaden knowledge of a business as a whole. (Methods similar to Plan 1.) Among other companies which have sometime reported using this type of special training school are: the Addressograph Company, the American Steel and Wire Company, the American Telephone & Telegraph Company, the Pennsylvania Railroad and the United Cigar Stores.

B. TYPE II. COMPANY BUSINESS—STUDY AND PRACTICE COURSES

In this type of training there is less emphasis on study and more on experience in working departments. The proportion varies a great deal. In some the time on study-work is but a small percentage of the total time, while in others as much as half is spent on the study and instruction work. The student is expected to do some productive work, which is a factor in keeping down the cost of giving the training. In general, these courses are longer than those of the first type. The ultimate purpose is properly to prepare students of marked ability for responsible positions on the executive or technical staff of the company.

PLAN NO. 3. STUDY AND PRACTICE COURSE—FOR NEW EMPLOYEES

Purpose.—To give an insight into a business as a whole.

Students.—Under this plan most of the new employees are college-trained men, or men of equivalent maturity and training, selected because of their capacity for accepting responsibility after they have gotten well established in the business.

Educational methods.—Definite plans for entire course; training department shifts men to give a variety of experience; work assignments chosen on account of their value as experience; talks and conferences with instructors and company officials; specially prepared work scheduled with notes relating work experience with study material.

PLAN NO. 4. STUDY AND PRACTICE COURSES—FOR OLD EMPLOYEES

[This plan varies from Plan No. 3 primarily in the fact that the employee's fitness for certain work is discovered before he is assigned to the training course, which is intended as an aid in developing the employee for more responsible work. No emphasis is placed on previous education—rather on previous success in the company's work.] Among other companies which have sometime reported using this type of special training school are: the American Locomotive Company, the Burroughs Adding Machine Company, the Commonwealth Edison Company, the Carnegie Steel Company, the General Electric Company, and the Goodyear Tire and Rubber Company.

C. TYPE III. COMPANY BUSINESS—WORK COURSES

This type of course omits practically all of the study features of Type I and emphasizes the varied work feature of Type II. In general, the training covers a longer time. The demands of the productive work are the controlling factors.

PLAN NO. 5. WORK COURSES FOR NEW EMPLOYEES

Purposes.—Opportunity for practical experience; to maintain a group of trained men from which some may be selected for more responsible work; to train employees for more versatility in the company's business.

Characteristic features.—Employees' time is expected to be entirely productive; no time is given at company's expense for related instruction; students are selected by the company; students' work entirely similar to other employees; students are assigned to several departments; no special supervision is given; student may continue indefinitely in a department if the production needs demand it.

Students.—New employees; previous education varied.

Educational methods.—Variety of experience; observation of related work.

PLAN NO. 6. WORK COURSES—FOR OLD EMPLOYEES

[Essentially the same as Plan No. 5, except for modifications to fit the needs of employees who have already had some experience. The employee may return to the work which he was doing at the time of entering the course, or be used as an aid in preparing an old employee for a new position.] Companies which have sometime reported using this type of special training include: the American Optical Company, the Atchison, Topeka & Santa Fe Railroad, the Cadillac Motor Company, the Consolidated Gas and Electric Light and Power Company of Baltimore, R. R. Donnelley & Sons, the Fore River Shipbuilding Company, and the Norton & Norton Grinding Company.

D. TYPE IV. COMPANY CONTINUATION SCHOOLS—DAY, EVENING, AND CORRESPONDENCE

This type of school is marked by a somewhat broader educational outlook than are some of the other types, providing that a very considerable share of the student's time be given to general education instead of confining him to such work as promises greater immediate efficiency in a particular position.

Accordingly, we find classes in English, mathematics, history, civics, geography, spelling, hygiene, typewriting, shorthand, sewing, and dressmaking. These are all in addition to a multitude of subjects directly connected with or related to specific occupations, such as engineering, drafting, machine operation, printing, office work, telephone operation, and salesmanship.

PLAN NO. 7. COMPANY DAY CONTINUATION SCHOOLS

Purposes.—To aid employees to fit themselves for advancement; to continue their general education; to increase interest or efficiency in present work; to discover employees for various lines of work.

Characteristic features.—Students are not selected by company; attendance is voluntary.

Students.—Any employee who meets the educational requirements for the particular subject or grade of work.

Educational methods.—Day classes on company time; or day classes part on company and part on employee's time; supervised by company educational department or by employees' organization of committee; classes meet from one to four times a week; courses vary from a few weeks to progressive assignments covering several years; usually held on company premises; company usually furnishes all necessary facilities.

PLAN NO. 8. COMPANY EVENING CONTINUATION SCHOOL

[Similar to Plan No. 7, except the classes are generally held on employee's time with no pay for time so spent. Courses partly self-supporting; enrolment fee required as guarantee of good faith.]

PLAN NO. 9. COMPANY CORRESPONDENCE CONTINUATION SCHOOL

[Similar to plans No. 7 and No. 8, except that it is designed primarily to reach by correspondence employees who for one reason or another cannot be reached through plans No. 7 and No. 8. A new departure in this field is the organization of courses by associations of employers and employees.] A list of companies which have sometime reported using special training course, Type IV, would include: the American Bridge Company, the American Tobacco Company the Curtis Publishing Company, the International Harvester Company, and the Metropolitan Life Insurance Company.

E. TYPE V. PUBLIC OR PRIVATE CONTINUATION SCHOOLS—CO-OPERATIVE PLAN

PLAN NO. 10. PART WORK—PART SCHOOL COURSE

[This type is similar to Type II (Study and Practice plans), except that the study work is done and the administration of the plan is carried on under the direction of public-school authorities instead of within the company.

As these features put this class of school in the realm of public education, it is not taken up here, except to point out that the plan is depended upon by some companies to take care of the special educational work which other companies are doing within their own organizations.

The expense of instructors is borne by the public while the company pays the employee for the time spent on productive work and in some instances, as at the plant of Swift & Company, in Chicago, furnishes a schoolroom and equipment.

This type of school is not a corporation school in the strict sense.]

The table on page 336 fairly well summarizes the general features described on page 334.[1]

It may be worth while to illustrate the foregoing general statements with specific cases. Such illustrations follow.[2]

TYPE I. COMPANY'S BUSINESS—STUDY COURSES (NON-PRODUCTIVE)

ADDRESSOGRAPH COMPANY

The training work of the Addressograph Company is confined to the training of salesmen. There are three classes of this service, sales correspondents, advertising men, and branch manager.

Average number of college men employed each year: thirty (not exclusively college men).

Nature of work after finishing company training: salesmanship.

Training courses given at: home office in Chicago.

Total length of training course: six weeks.

Salary during training: no salary, but expenses may be advanced upon request up to $15 to $20 per week.

Principal features of training course: first, a thorough mastery of the Addressograph: second, a scientific course in salesmanship; and third, introduction into actual selling under the guidance of an expert salesman.

Previous education preferred: business administration from recognized colleges.

TYPE II. STUDY AND PRACTICE COURSE (PARTLY PRODUCTIVE)

MONTGOMERY WARD AND COMPANY

Average number of college men employed each year: fifteen.

Nature of work after finishing company training: executive, or managerial positions, or accounting, according to ability.

Training courses given at: Chicago and Kansas City.

Total length of training course: six months.

[1] *Op. cit.* Types I, II, III train directly only for the company's own business, teaching either the business as a whole or specific duties; Types IV and V give also general education. A variety of methods for allocating expense for corporation schools is also suggested but is too varied for reproduction here.

[2] The illustrations of Types I, II, and III are taken from *Proceedings of the Fifth Annual Convention of the National Association of Corporation Schools*, pp. 480–85.

TABLE XXX

Types of Special Training Schools*

Type	Plan	Characteristic Features							Method of Instruction							
		Attendance Compulsory	Day or Evening	Work productive	For New or Old Employees	Entrance Requirements	Do Students Receive Pay?	Whose Time	Study and Recitation	Supervised Study	Lectures	Laboratory	Shopwork	Correspondence	Observation Trips	No. of Schools
I	1	Yes	Day	No	New	Varies	Yes	Company	X	X	X	X	....	....	X	12
	2	Yes	Day	No	Old	Satisfactory Service	Yes	Company	X	X	X	X	....	....	X	6
II	3	Yes	Day	Part	New	Varies	Yes	Company	X	X	X	X	X	X	X	8
	4	Yes	Day	Part	Old	Satisfactory Service	Yes	Company	X	X	X	X	X	....	X	11
III	5	Yes	Day	Yes	New	Varies	Yes	Company	....	....	....	....	X	....	....	15
	6	Yes	Day	Yes	Old	Efficient Service	Yes	Company	....	....	....	....	X	....	....	10
IV	7	No	Day	No	Varies	None	Yes	Company	X	....	....	X	X	....	X	14
	8	No	Evening	No	Any Employee	None	No	Student's or Half and Half	X	X	....	....	....	....	X	19
V	9	No	....	No	....	None	No	Student's	....	....	....	....	....	X	....	5
	10	No	Day and Evening	Part	Any Employee	None	Half time	Half and Half	X	....	....	X	X	....	....	18

* Member companies maintaining special training schools, 62.

Salary during training: initial, $15 to $18 per week, depending upon ability.

Principal feature of training course: a thorough textbook study of scientific business management, and practical experience in the various branches of the business following orders "through" the house from receipt of the order to the shipment of goods.

Previous education preferred: university graduation or equivalent training; evidence of leadership is highly valued.

TYPE III. COMPANY BUSINESS—WORK COURSE (PRODUCTIVE)

AMERICAN BRIDGE COMPANY

This company, which engages in bridge building, barge, and other steel construction, operates plants in New York City and Elmira, New York; Philadelphia, Pittsburgh, and Ambridge, Pennsylvania; Trenton, New Jersey; Edgemoore, Delaware; Canton and Toledo, Ohio; Gary, Indiana; Chicago, Illinois; Detroit, Michigan; Minneapolis, Minnesota; and St. Louis, Missouri.

Average number of college men employed each year: sixty.

Nature of work after finishing company training: operating, mechanical engineering, erecting, or construction department work.

Training courses given at: Ambridge and Gary.

Total length of training course: one to two years.

Salary during training: initial, $60 per month; $70 per month after three to six months.

Principal features of training course: It is preferred that the graduate students enter the operating department. This shop experience gives an acquaintance with materials essential for any employee in any department.

Previous education preferred: civil, mechanical, electrical, or chemical engineering.

TYPE IV: PLAN NO. 7. COMPANY CONTINUATION DAY SCHOOL[1]

R. H. MACY AND COMPANY

The primary school of R. H. Macy and Company is its continuation school where a rather fundamental knowledge of arithmetic, spelling, reading, local geography, and hygiene is given. These subjects are presented in a manner which shows their applicability to business.

[1] From the *National Association of Corporation Schools Bulletin*, October, 1918, pp. 460–62.

This school is located one-half block from the store. Here students of both sexes from fifteen to twenty years of age spend two hours each morning, from nine to eleven o'clock, except on Mondays. The duration of the course is three and one-half months, giving each student about 150 hours of instruction. Two hours each morning are allowed for study on store time and at store expense.

This course includes several bus trips about town to give the students a working idea of the city; also it includes talks by store executives and instructors on current political and business subjects.

Graduation exercises are held at the completion of the course at which time diplomas, class pins, and prizes for exceptional standing are awarded by members of the Board of Education and store officials. After graduation these students are urged to join the Alumni Association of the Continuation School which holds monthly meetings for business and recreational activities.

TYPE IV: PLAN NO. 8. CORPORATION EVENING CONTINUATION SCHOOLS[1]

THE BROOKLYN EDISON COMPANY

This Brooklyn Edison Company has had in vogue for about seven years now the practice of giving the students the choice of any night school in greater New York which he may desire to attend. The student pays the tuition fee. If he finishes the course with a grading of two-thirds, the Brooklyn Edison Company refunds his fee. About five years ago the company started their own classes, giving lectures on electricity and system practice. Now we have five different courses in electricity to which any member or employee of the company is admitted on the payment of $10; and if he passes, this money is refunded. To make sure that any man can get his money back, we give him 25 per cent for attendance, 25 per cent for his notebook, and graduate him if he gets 67 per cent. He cannot fail to get his money back if he keeps on the job. In addition to our classes there is another feature. We have Pratt Institute, Columbia University, and any number of classes in private schools which our employees can enter if they believe that a course in those schools will help them with their work. If there are those desiring to enter these classes, the matter is referred to our educational committee composed of five department heads, and this committee receives

[1] *Proceedings of the National Association of Corporation Schools, Fifth Annual Convention*, pp. 203–4.

recommendations from the man's immediate bureau head as to whether such course of instruction will help him in his work or not.

The work has been carried on for three years now and we are finishing the students in the public schools; and in our own work, 71 per cent of the people who apply, men and women, get their money back. The money is taken out weekly, 50 cents to $1 a week, or higher. I remember that last year we had one man who applied for $170 worth of tuition. He took some fixed courses, requiring him to give five nights a week, besides his eight hours a day in the drafting-room, and he got away with it.

THE AMERICAN INSTITUTE OF BANKING[1]

[The American Institute of Banking, described here, is of special interest as an elaborate plan, one undertaken by an association and centrally directed, and one which has been in successful operation since 1900. The A. I. B. is a section of the American Bankers' Association.][2]

The most successful part of Institute work thus far has been done in city chapters. Classwork in the Institute study courses should be conducted during the same period under the direction of a suitable instructor employed by the chapter and approved by the Institute. Each class member is supplied with textbooks and instructors are expected to conduct examinations prescribed in connection with each textbook. . . . . The following articles of association are recommended for any new city chapters that may be organized.

1. Knowledge City Chapter is hereby organized for the purpose of co-operating with the American Institute of Banking section of the American Bankers' Association in (*a*) the education of bankers in banking and such principles of law and economics as pertain to the banking business; (*b*) the establishment and maintenance of a recognized standard of education by means of official examinations and the issuance of certificates of graduation.

[1] Adapted from George E. Allen, *History of the American Institute of Banking*, a pamphlet published by the A. I. B.

[2] An excellent example of a similar organization is the Chicago Central Station Institute which was founded in 1912 as the Bureau of Education for the following companies: Commonwealth Edison Company, Federal Sign System (Electric), Illinois Northern Utilities Company, Middle West Utilities Company, Public Service Company of Northern Illinois. It was founded for the purpose of organizing and conducting special educational courses for present and prospective employees of the supporting companies.

2. Any employee, or officer, or director of a bank or other financial institution in Knowledge City or vicinity may be an active member of this chapter upon election and payment of annual dues of $4 in quarterly instalments in advance. Such dues include individual subscription to the *Bulletin of the American Institute of Banking* at the rate of 50 cents a year, payable in quarterly instalments in advance, etc.

Outside of study classes in city chapters, equally effective instruction is provided by the Correspondence Chapter. In correspondence instruction each student is supplied with the serial textbooks including exercises. The exercises in connection with each textbook are to be submitted to instructors whenever done. The work of students thus produced is corrected and returned with such criticisms and suggestions as may be helpful in each case. . . . .

The membership of the Correspondence Chapter, in addition to its incorporators, shall be limited to bank officers and other employees who reside outside of the jurisdiction of city chapters and state chapters and are not members of any city chapter or any state chapter. . . . .

In suitable states students of banking are organized in state chapters for the purpose of pursuing the Institute courses of study in classes or by correspondence according to circumstances. State chapters thus far organized are affiliated with respective state bankers' associations. The idea of a state chapter is simply to localize and popularize Institute instruction. Correspondence instruction in state chapters is identical in character with the work of the Correspondence Chapter. Classwork in state chapters is identical in character with classwork in city chapters.

TYPE IV: PLAN NO. 9.[1] A CORPORATION CORRESPONDENCE CONTINUATION SCHOOL

We have had a salesman's correspondence course for some time.

That does not say that we have not used the material which is available from textbooks, and from courses which have been prepared in various ways by educational institutions on salesmanship. We have used the bulk of that material, but we have used it by applying it to our own business. We have avoided general terms, scientific terms, technical terms in connection with the work. We have

[1] Adapted from statements by "a delegate" in the *Proceedings of the Third Annual Convention of the National Association of Corporation Schools*, pp. 581–84.

changed these courses and applied illustrations that the salesman can pick up—that he runs up against in his daily talks with customers; actual illustrations that he has experienced—that his fellow salesman has experienced in the same district There are certain courses that are established for general use, but with these courses we have a great deal less interest displayed.

We have used most of the scientific information that has been produced in textbooks of other courses, but the salesman did not see the application of that scientific principle to his own business until we applied it to his own daily work.

We do not have to require it—the salesman likes it—for without it he himself feels that he has not definitely gotten over the ground.

We do require written replies to examinations that we send to our agents, and we have been well satisfied and pleased with the results we have been getting.

We send out a paper with ten questions that require originality in the answers. There, of course, we give full play to the man, and the replies are really instructive; they show the value of the course.

We likewise have been deeply impressed by the treatment of the ethics of the profession. It opens up a new field which a man started for but which he has overlooked. The correspondence courses show a man that what he has been doing as a matter of daily habit is really amenable to scientific principles.

But the written replies are very good and we have a staff of examiners who examine these papers and show the agent his weak points.

CORPORATION SCHOOLS OTHER THAN SPECIAL TRAINING SCHOOLS

Thus far we have given a rather detailed consideration to "special training schools." There remain to be considered the five other distinctive forms of corporation schools outlined on page 329.

THE TRADE APPRENTICESHIP SCHOOL

One of the best illustrations of a well-organized trade apprenticeship school (although there are many others) is that of the Lakeside Press. The school for apprentices of the Lakeside Press was established in July, 1908. The school is organized to meet the demands both of the employer and of the apprentice.[1]

A special room is provided for the school, one part being equipped as a modern schoolroom and the other part as a model composing-room. In the school the boys are under the direction of instructors who devote their entire time to the school. They are the supervisor, who teaches a part of the academic work and has general oversight of the boys in the factory; the instructor, who has direct charge of the academic work and assists the supervisor; the instructor in printing, who has charge of the trade instruction in the school; and the instructor in presswork, who has charge of the apprentices in the pressrooms.

The course of apprenticeship is divided into two periods: first, that of pre-apprenticeship, for the first two years, during which time the boys spend half time in the school and half time in the factory, and second, that of apprenticeship, when the boys spend full time in the factory, with the exception of several hours each week when they attend the school.

The students are in school three and one-half hours daily, during the pre-apprenticeship course, and are divided into two classes graded according to their standings. They also work four and one-half hours daily in the shop, or at work connected with the factory or the counting-room.

The boys are paid for the time actually spent in the factory during the two years. In the school the instruction and all materials used are furnished free.

The amounts actually earned by the boys are shown in the following table:

TABLE XXXI

	Rate Per Week	Total	Bonus for Efficiency
First year, 52 weeks	$2.40	$124.80	$25.00
Second year, 52 weeks	3.00	156.00	25.00
First half third year, 26 weeks	5.00	130.00	....
Second half third year	6.00	156.00	....

Arithmetic is reviewed from the factory side. An applied arithmetic has been prepared to be used in connection with the review

[1] The Lakeside Press is the printing establishment of R. R. Donnelley & Sons Company of Chicago. The statement here given is adapted from the *Bulletin of the National Association of Corporation Schools*, November, 1916, pp. 33–37.

work. Elementary bookkeeping is taught by means of lessons especially arranged for the printing office. The elements of algebra and geometry are taught, and whenever possible the problems are applied to the trade. Every apprentice is required to read and review at least six books of standard literature each year.

The pre-apprentices spend one and three-quarters hours daily doing academic work. This time is divided into two periods, and the lessons given are in design, English, and mathematics, alternating with history and elementary science. The lessons in design are applied in the written as well as the printed work, in all the different subjects. Every exercise is a lesson in English. The rules laid down for good book-work are followed in all written work. Proof marks are used in correcting all exercises, and the marks are definite and easily understood.

When the pre-apprenticeship course is completed, at the end of two years, the boys, then sixteen years of age, enter the factory as regular apprentices to learn some one of the trades in the different branches of the printing business. During their pre-apprenticeship course they become acquainted with the various departments, and with this knowledge are able to select the line of work for which they are best fitted. The boys are under supervision during the apprentice period, and are scheduled for a definite time to each of the different lines of work in the trade selected, and are given every opportunity to learn the trade as a whole.

The academic training, begun during the pre-apprenticeship course, is continued during the apprenticeship; the boys attend school for several hours each week during the entire course and receive regular pay. The courses of instruction advance, and new subjects are added as the apprentices master the work. Much attention is given to designing; layouts for jobs are made, and when carried out in type are carefully criticized. Mechanics, industrial history, English, hygiene, and economics are given.

THE OFFICE-WORK SCHOOL

The corporation school to train for "office work" has become important. What it is and what it can do has been expressed as follows:[1]

It is of some importance to know exactly what is meant by the term "office-work school." Any definite, systematic method of

[1] This is a condensation of a statement made by W. William Schulze of the Alexander Hamilton Institute, *Proceedings of the Second Annual*

training employees so that they will perform their assigned office duties correctly and intelligently is an office-work school.

The office-work school, if properly conducted, will: (1) insure the proper instruction of each individual employee; (2) enable you to train your office employee much more cheaply than by the old haphazard method; (3) enable you to eliminate useless motion; (4) serve as a distinct aid in standardizing office methods; (5) help you train understudies; (6) be of valuable assistance in preparing and issuing office instruction manuals; (7) stimulate loyalty to the concern; (8) help you build good will by training office employees to be more attentive and courteous in their dealings with outsiders; (9) enable you to standardize output and establish salaries upon a more scientific basis; (10) enable you to select applicants for positions more effectively.

The significance and pertinence of the office-work school, even for persons well prepared generally, is indicated by J. W. Dietz, who as educational director of the Western Electric Company has had a long and successful experience.[1]

In the manufacture of our product we have a great deal of detail to contend with, and the terms that are used are extremely special. We have a lot of stenographers who, when they come to us and hear the terms "dish wheel," "cup wheel," and different mechanical terms, do not know what they mean. We found that our correspondence and office work suffered materially from lack of that knowledge. To bring about a better understanding, we divide the clerks from the correspondence, bookkeeping, and other departments into small groups, and periodically guide them through the shops, not so that they are required to observe all the operations in a comparatively short time, but to show them enough to enable them to understand the operation of each department. When that is complete, having had ocular evidence of what they saw on paper, we bring them into the lecture-room and explain by means of lantern

---

Convention of the National Association of Corporation Schools, pp. 500, 515–16. Among the companies conducting office-work schools are the Western Electric Co., the Burroughs Adding Machine Co., and the National Cloak and Suit Co.

[1] The statement in *Proceedings of the First Annual Convention of the National Association of Corporation Schools*, pp. 219–20.

slides the operations they have actually witnessed, and explain to them why certain operations must take place, and why a certain product is called a certain thing. We found the intelligence in handling the office work materially improved. We are getting up a special dictionary of a series of terms as applied to our particular business, and a very complete definition of each term is given. We use words that are ordinarily used in English, but they have a quite different meaning, and we find it improves matters very materially to give special instruction as to their use.

In the summertime, usually in July, the various agents throughout the country send in their salesmen who have directly to do with our product, and they are for the time-being guests at the shop. The sessions begin in the morning and last until evening, including a certain amount of shopwork. In this the office employees take part. To be sure that nothing goes out that is not perfect in the way of diction and grammatical construction, we have all our correspondence censored by people well educated and specially trained along the lines of English construction, and in that way the censor of the correspondence has an opportunity to select and watch those who appear to be weakest in that direction. Those are taken aside for special instruction and told the method they should adopt for study to produce the most desirable results.

ADVERTISING, SELLING, AND DISTRIBUTION SCHOOLS

To a considerable extent selling and distribution schools have been illustrated above in our discussion of special training schools. The Addressograph Company, the American Steel and Wire Company, the Atlantic Refining Company, and the Carnegie Steel Company have all reported to the National Association of Corporation Schools that they use Type I of the special training schools for training salesmen. The Yale & Towne Manufacturing Company makes use of Type II; Graton & Knight and the Norton & Norton Grinding Company use Type III for developing salesmen's ability.

Devices which can be hardly classified as corporation schools, but which are used extensively by many firms, are the brief, but intensive, courses given in connection with salesmen's conventions and the sales manuals which are at times elaborate in their instructions to salesmen.

Selling schools have in some instances been developed to such an extent that specific illustrations will be well worth while. A manufacturer's school for salesmen is well illustrated in the following description of the plan used by the Ford Motor Company:

THE COURSE IN DISTRIBUTION OF THE FORD MOTOR COMPANY[1]

The producer should always consider the problem of distribution as that of distribution to the ultimate consumer.

The study of distribution is the study of placing what you have where it is wanted, but also the study of what is wanted and of where and when wants can be created so as to place what you *will* have—often not so much to find as to make or wake a market.

Distribution

Making the market (getting orders)	Meeting the market (filling orders)
1. Planning a) What amounts of orders are desired and when b) How to get them there	1. Packing
2. Representing by advertisements and salesmen	2. Routing
3. Closing sales by salesmen	3. Following through to arrival by traffic men
	4. After-service (to insure permanent satisfaction)

Four factors in distribution:

1. What is to be moved
2. Whither it is to be moved
3. How it is to be moved
4. Guarantee of future

1. Goods
   a) Quality
   b) Bulk
   c) Perishability (by marring or spoiling)
2. Demand
   a) Existing and to be increased or regulated
      Advertising (paid, or publicity, or premiums)
      Salesmen (orderseekers, visiting salesmen)

[1] Taken from the *Proceedings of the National Association of Corporation Schools, Fifth Annual Convention*, pp. 649–51.

b) To be created
   Where can need of it best be roused?
   Advertising and salesmen of type to create the special demand desired due to plan of production and to need product can fill

c) By what kind of people?
   Where and in what numbers do they live?
   What classes and territories shall be selected as most profitable? (those in big cities or small or in country?)

d) Affected by competition, how
   By service given, or attention to delivery

e) Seasonal
   Frequency (single or repeated orders)
   How elastic (can be built up—sensitive to trade conditions)

3. Methods of moving these goods to meet this demand

a) Sell to whom

(1) Direct to consumer—Mail orders
   Canvassers
   Salesmen

(2) Through middlemen—Wholesaler
   Broker or brokerage association
   Jobber
   Retailer
   Producers' association
   Chain stores
   Subsidiary companies
   Agents

(3) Combination of (1) and (2)

b) Deliver by means of

(1) Existing methods—as to quality and speed and cost

Carriers	Routes	Handling
Horses	Paved roads	Number of times handled
Trucks	Country roads	Handlers in whose employ
Freight—railroad	Railroads	
Freight—boat	Lakes	
Express	Rivers	
Parcel post	Canals	
Messenger boys		
Merchants' del.		

(2) Individual methods to be evolved

(*a*) Special devices, as Standard Oil Co.'s pipe lines or Ford Motor Co.'s assembly plants

(*b*) Private carriers'—chain of traffic men along railroad lines—boats owned by company—own delivery system rather than merchants' delivery

(*c*) By leasing right to use product—as shoe machinery or victrola or slot machine

By paying for license and power to operate, as Pullman Co. with its sleepers

4. Guarantee of future, namely, service, during and after the sale.

[Definition: Service is everything, outside of the product itself, which the distributor does to increase the purchaser's satisfaction in obtaining and in using the product, such as special accommodation, reliability and courtesy in all dealings with purchaser, clear instruction as to how to derive greatest use, handy depots for obtaining replenishment, or repair parts and service, for middle men, assistance toward disposal of product]

The school for salesmen of a concern making a great variety of technical products and selling them to dealers is described as follows by one of its representatives:

THE SALESMEN'S SCHOOL COURSE OF THE ELI-LILLY CO.[1]

The Lilly organization.—Before outlining the work of the Lilly Salesmen's School, I feel that it would be in order to give you a few hints regarding the business of this concern.

In the first place, we have no direct accounts with retail druggists, physicians or anyone excepting manufacturers and wholesale druggists. Our total number of charge accounts, therefore, amounts to less than 300. We believe that it is the province of the manufacturer to make, the jobber to job, the retailer to dispense, the physician to prescribe and the public to consume. That, in a nutshell, is the business policy of Eli-Lilly Co.

We feel that all parties connected with the marketing of pharmaceutical and biological products are entitled to their fair and just

[1] Adapted from the *National Association of Corporation Schools, Fifth Annual Convention*, pp. 657–66. Copyright, 1917, by the National Association of Corporation Schools.

compensation for handling or dealing in these products, and in view of this Lilly policy was adopted in 1894.

Fundamental qualifications of prospective salesmen.—A man to become a member of our sales or retail staff must have a technical education, must be either a graduate or registered pharmacist or a graduate physician, must be high grade, of splendid moral character, a man who stands well in his community, bears a good reputation for past record and is able to take several rather strong tests for intellect, decision and ability.

OUTLINE SHOWING CHARACTER OF INSTRUCTION

Section 1

Introductory. Policy by President, General Manager, *et al.*
Ordering Supplies
Preliminary Talk on Price List
Botanical Inspection Crude Drug Materials
Chemical Control of Materials and Manufacturing Processes
View of the Indianapolis Laboratories and System Study
Pharmaceutical Development and Certain Lilly Products
The Older Lilly Specialties

Section 2

Special Formulas
Labeling and Packaging Finished Products
Stockkeeping and Shipping
Advertising
Credits and Expenses
Physiological Testing and Experimental Medicine
Lilly Quality
Orders, Communications and Reports

Section 3

New Items and Future Specialties
The Newer Lilly Specialties
Complaints and Returned Goods
Lilly Policy
Demonstration Sale: Selling a Nice Lilly Order to a 40 per cent and 10 per cent Preferred Retail Customer of Our Competitors (time limit 20 minutes)
Demonstration Detail Interview on Lilly Biologicals (time limit 20 minutes)

Why It Pays to Call on Every Drug Store, Large and Small
What I Am Doing to Educate My Customers on the Wisdom of Buying through the Jobber
What I Have Accomplished with Jobbing Salesmen
How I Persuaded a Large 40 per cent and 10 per cent Direct-Buying Retailer to Buy Lilly Products through the Jobber at 40 per cent Discount
A List of Large Retailers Who Were Buying from Direct-Selling Competitors at 40 per cent and 10 per cent Discount Whom I Changed to Buying Lilly Products at 40 per cent through the Jobber; Arguments I Used to Switch Them.
How the Advertising Department Co-operates with Salesmen in Detail Work.
How I Detail Alcresta Tablets of Ipecac to Physicians
How I Detail Liquid Blaud
How I Detail Ampoules
How I Detail Dental Lotion
Talking Points on Dental Line

Section 4

Laboratory Organization and Efficiency
New Packages
Dental Line
Prices
Selling Points on Dental Line

Section 5

General Inspection Smallpox Vaccine Building
Manufacturing Smallpox Vaccine—Demonstration
Inspection of Animal Building
Harvesting Ripe Vaccine—Demonstration
General Inspection of Antitoxin Building
Preparation of Horses
Inoculation of Diphtheria and Tetanus Horses—Demonstration
Inspection of Tuberculin and Testing Laboratories
Bleeding Horses—Demonstration
Concentration and Purification of Antitoxins
Drug Plant Cultivation

Section 6

Selling Points on Antitoxins and Serums
Detail Talking Points on Antitoxins and Serums

Section 7

Preparation of Bacterial Vaccine
Preparation of Rabies Virus, Lilly
Inspection of Laboratories Demonstrating the Filling and Packaging of Bacterial Vaccines, Serums and Antitoxins
Our Biological Line—Advantageous Talking Points for Jobber, Retailer and Physician during Epidemics
Vaccines—How I Detail Them—How I Sell Druggists
Issuing Equipment

It will be noted that the crude product is followed from the beginning, taking it through each process of manufacture down to the finished product. The course then takes up the business policy of the concern and devotes considerable time to that. The demonstration sale and the demonstration detail interview immediately following the demonstration sale should be especially noted.

Purpose of school.—One of the fundamentals of the school is to give every Lilly salesman and detail representative all the information there is to be had about the products of this house. It tries to thoroughly familiarize the men with every product that the firm makes. The salesman is expected to know his products simply inside out, and to be able to weave a wonderful story about their source and follow each step of their manufacture right down through to the finished product. This, as I see it, is one of the greatest aids to efficient salesmanship—know your line and this will beget enthusiasm.

An example of an extensive, successful, and in some of its features, unique sales school is that of the Curtis Publishing Company. It is thus described by M. E. Douglas, sales manager of the company.[1]

Today our sales division is conducting what we believe to be the world's greatest school in salesmanship for boys. This school, consisting in the beginning of one instructor, now includes forty highly trained correspondents, fifty roadmen, two thousand district agents, and fifty thousand to fifty-five thousand parents who, upon suggestions from us, are co-operating in training the boys. The pay-roll of our sales division, which is maintained solely to handle the business promoted by our sales agents, approaches $400,000 a year.

[1] From the *Proceedings of the Second Annual Convention of the National Association of Corporation Schools*, pp. 177–81.

At the time of their appointment, boy agents and their parents are given personal instructions by the roadmen. Three or four times a year the roadmen revisit each district agent and give additional instructions, according to our changing plans and methods.

Our district agents and our branch managers personally instruct the boy agents whom they supply.

Conferences of our branch managers, conventions of our roadmen, conventions of our district agents by states and by sections are frequently held.

Our expert correspondents, whose helpful letters to the boys have been the means of developing this highly trained force, in rotation spend a part of their time with agents in the field each year.

For the training of the boys, personal instruction is supplemented by printed matter suited to the age and experience of the boys and of their parents. Some of this printed matter is sent out from the home office, some from the branch offices, some from the offices of the district agents.

This printed matter includes both manuals of an educational nature and booklets intended to have an inspirational effect.

Our manual for the boys themselves is a 100-page booklet entitled *How to Sell 100 Copies Weekly*. When a boy's first paid order is received at the home office, at the branch, or at the district agency, this manual is given to the beginner. In language adapted to the boy's age and experience, the manual tells him how to get his first list of steady customers among his friends and neighbors, and by easy stages leads him, if he has it in him, up to rank among our champion boys. We have printed and distributed 100,000 copies of this manual.

For parents we have the 56-page manual entitled *What Shall I Do with My Boy?* After reading this manual the interested parent helps the boy to master the selling plans described in the booklet *How to Sell 100 Copies Weekly.*

For district agents we have the manual entitled *The District Agent as a Sales Promoter*, 291 pages. This booklet contains a full discussion of such subjects as the relation between promotion and distribution, the relation of the Curtis boy to promotion and distribution, how to get boys, how to train green boys for salesmanship, how to hold boys that have made good, etc.

Our sales division publishes each month the house organ called *Our Boys*, one copy of which is mailed to each boy regular agent, sub-agent and special agent throughout the country. Announcements of interest to our boys, new selling plans, stories of the selling achievements of various boys—all this is given entirely without cost to the boys. The "Parents' Personal Page" is a special feature.

We have a second house organ called *Our District Agents*, printed monthly and mailed to district agents only. Inspirational and educational matter with reference to promoting sales through boys appears in each issue.

Constant effort is made to train the boys to sell the article rather than the publication. This involves arousing the boy's interest in the article, helping him to understand it, so that he can talk about its good points. Interested parents are helping their boys to identify the feature articles and to learn what to say about them to their prospects. Among other plans for training the boys to sell the article or story of special local interest are these two:

Each week we send to a selected large list of boys printed forecasts of the contents of coming issues. These forecasts tell the boys what to say about the special features of the issue.

Another and a most potent factor in the training of our boys is the personal letter. The correspondents in the home office and at the branch offices participate in the boys' hopes, in the boys' imaginings, in the boys' desires; they give of themselves to the boys; they interest themselves in the boys' undertakings, so they know how to write letters that reach beneath the vests of the boys, are able to direct the boys' desires, to help the boys to substitute real selling methods in place of the personal or sympathetic appeal for trade.

RETAIL SALESMANSHIP SCHOOLS

Retail salesmanship schools are, in so many instances, conducted by corporations in co-operation with the public-school systems,[1] that one is likely to confuse such undertakings with the strictly corporation school. Many of the larger department stores furnish examples of the latter, however. The work of the retail selling school of one of the largest of the "chains" is thus described by one of those responsible for its conduct.[2]

[1] As in Boston and Cincinnati.

[2] Adapted from a statement by H. G. Petermann of the United Cigar Stores Co., *Proceedings of the Third Annual Convention of the National Association of Corporation Schools*, pp. 557–58.

All new salesmen are required to pass through this training course, which covers a period of fourteen to twenty-one days. Our method of buying and selling, also our rules relative to the handling of customers are made plain to the new man.

All departments of our business are covered in talks and textbooks. Lectures are given on the culture and manufacture of tobacco grown in different countries. Talking points are taught them on Amber, Meerschaum, Briar, Calabash. Good service talks, salesmanship, customs duties, internal revenue, etc., etc. In fact, the history of tobacco from the time the seed is planted in the ground until the internal revenue stamp is placed on the box that contains the finished product is explained—we get right down to the how and why, so that even a child may be able to understand it.

Written examinations are given to make men think and work to determine their progress. A quiz upon the sales manual. Written notes on previous days' work, etc., etc. All of the men sent by the employment department to our training department do not reach a store. While in school they are on probation. Those who show a lack of interest in our proposition, or after a fair trial, do not measure up to the required "United" standards, are weeded out.

SCHOOLS FOR UNSKILLED LABOR

Corporation schools for unskilled labor are for the most part concerned with the teaching of English, the prevention of accidents, and "Americanization." Such schools present unusual difficulties of organization and the persons who are directing such schools speak as often in terms of these difficulties as in terms of accomplishment. More detailed discussion of them may be omitted at this place.

THE ORGANIZATION AND ADMINISTRATION OF CORPORATION SCHOOLS

One of the most interesting things about the corporation-school movement is the thoroughly professional attitude which is taken, by its best representatives at least, toward the technical phases of their work. Proper means of organization and administration have been given a great deal of attention and the relation of the corporation school to certain other forms of training has been made the subject of a special investigation.

The statements which follow are largely drawn from the reports, suggestions, and recommendations made by special committees and individuals in corporation school work.[1]

The superintendent of the corporation school performs duties somewhat similar to those performed by the same official for the Board of Education, although they are likely to be much more specific in character since the corporation school is usually restricted in its purpose to a few well-defined lines of procedure.

In corporation schools there cannot be the same close adherence to types that is found in public-school systems. As a rule, each corporation school is distinctive in its organization and administration even when intended for the same general purpose as some other similar school.

Perhaps no other feature of corporation school organization presents more difficulties than the finding of properly qualified teachers. The ideal teacher for a corporation school is one who has a thorough knowledge of his subject with a practical experience in it and the ability to impart instruction intelligently. He is one who can work well in the thing he teaches and who can teach well the thing in which he has worked. He must be of commanding and forceful personality because with few exceptions the conditions he has to contend with in the training of young people in industry are not the normal conditions that are suited to secure the best results from the student. The student who has spent part of his day in physical labor is apt to be sluggish in his studies and indifferent in his mental efforts. Such teachers are difficult to find and they command salaries much above the average.

The selection of good textbooks is of first importance and is of unusual difficulty for a corporation school owing to the great diversity in the subject-matter of instruction desired and the somewhat limited supply of texts that are prepared to meet the peculiar requirements of the corporation school.

[1] The *Proceedings of the Fifth Annual Convention of the National Association of Corporation Schools* contains a discussion of "Organization and Administration." The *Proceedings of the Sixth Annual Convention*, pp. 97–127, contains a section on the same subject. *Ibid.*, pp. 57–82, contains an excellent plan for viewing the same problems. An appraisal of corporation school pedagogy is attempted by A. J. Beatty in *Corporation Schools.*

In a type of education to which general systems are so ill adapted, the importance of the educational director is obvious. A number of university and college teachers have been drawn into this form of work. The duties of this executive have been described by a corporation-school committee to be:[1]

(*a*) To organize the various curriculums and courses of study; (*b*) To select the instructors for the various departments; (*c*) To supervise and criticize the methods of instruction; (*d*) To aid the instructors in developing text books and lesson-sheets; (*e*) To adopt a suitable system of records for students' work which should show their industry, their progress, and attainment; (*f*) To select the students for the various courses and keep in touch with the sources of supply; (*g*) To keep the higher officials of the company informed as to the needs, the efficiency, the results, and the expense of the work; (*h*) To supervise the records of the department in such a manner as to show the costs of the various courses, and the various items of increased efficiency in the concern which may be attributed to the work of the department.

The report continues:

Such a program as this demands a man of no small caliber and his selection is a task which demands the most careful consideration. Unfortunately the supply of such high-grade men is not equal to the demand and many corporations have been compelled to place their educational work in charge of men who have not had sufficient technical training in school administration to guarantee the highest efficiency.

Most of the men who are in charge of educational departments are graduates of technical schools and in the majority of cases they are men who have been exceptionally efficient in some executive capacity. These qualifications are highly essential and no one who has not had such technical training and such shop experience should be placed in charge of an expensive educational plant, but technical and theoretical training in school administration as viewed from the standpoint of professional educators is an invaluable asset in such a position.

The importance of the educational director and the need of granting him real power is repeatedly expressed as the basis

[1] *Proceedings of the Fourth Annual Convention of the National Association of Corporation Schools*, pp. 100–102.

of solid success in corporation-school administration. An official of the Norton Grinding Company, for example, states that their educational department "consists of a supervisor directly responsible to the general manager, an assistant, and an advisory board consisting of nine men from the management of the two companies."

Mr. F. H. Yoder, of the Pennsylvania Railroad, expresses the same view, declaring:

> The first step is to establish responsibility in a higher official; a man with vision and foresight; a man who would not have to consider the question of dollars and cents and immediate return for all money invested. Minor officials must of necessity keep down expenses in their departments, and naturally educational work under them cannot be expanded. If a business depression arises, all work not bringing immediate returns will have to be curtailed in order to reduce expenses. For this reason, it is necessary to resort to a higher official who can look to the future and see the future benefits of the educational work to the company, irrespective of the immediate conditions. It therefore seems that the first step in the matter of administration and supervision is to establish your responsibility in a higher official.

The chart on page 358 shows one possible integration of training in the organization of a large business.

THE RÔLE OF THE CORPORATION SCHOOL

What then is the rôle of this modern form of education by business? What is the proper specialized task of the corporation school in a coherent program of education for business?

The corporation school is chiefly concerned and may be expected to continue to be concerned with those forms of instruction which are calculated to bring a profit to the company involved. Although many corporation-school directors have been actuated by broader motives, the corporation school is by nature part of a business enterprise and in so far as the school cannot indicate a financial gain it involves a highly questionable use of stockholders' assets. As W. L. Chandler, of the Dodge Manufacturing Company, says: "Expense incurred in this way can only be justified on the grounds that more profit can be made

CHART III

THE ORGANIZATION OF AN INDUSTRIAL RELATIONS DEPARTMENT

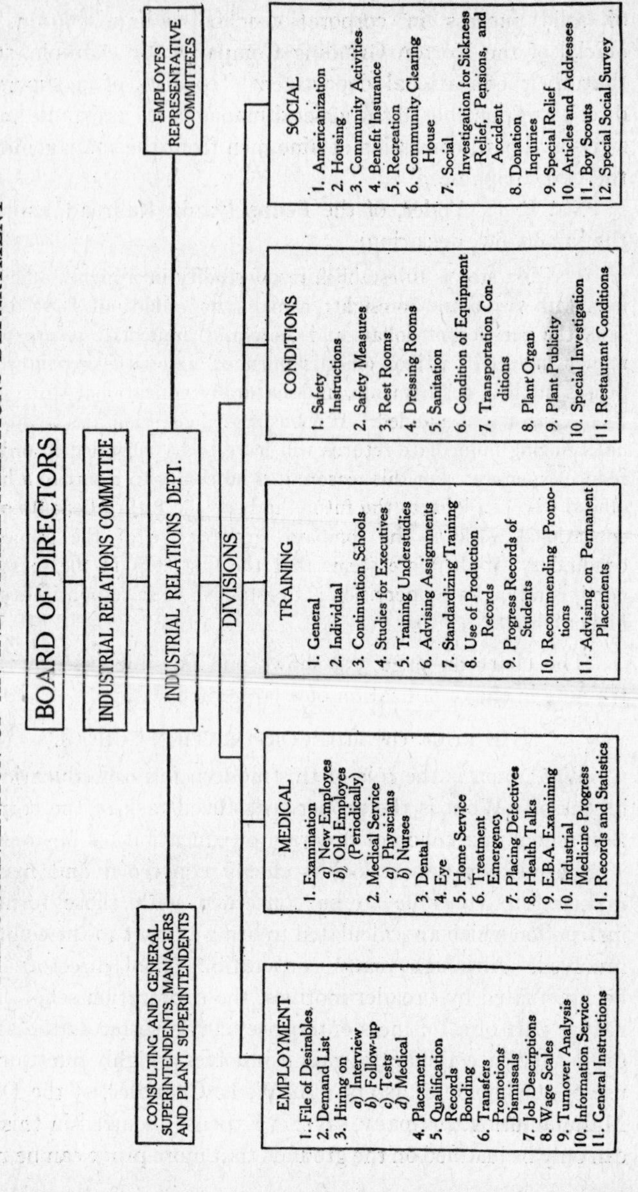

with the school than without it." Charles P. Steinmetz, the "Wizard" of the General Electric Company, expressed the same view in his presidential address at the Third Annual Convention of Corporation Schools. He said: "The limitation of the corporation activities in the educational and similar fields is that given by the limitation of the corporation purpose to earn dividends for its stockholders."

The profit motive as the spirit of the corporation school gives the cue to its possibilities and to its limitations.

1. The corporation school is, in its most organized form, more or less limited to large-scale industries. The overhead cost of the well-conducted school must be widely distributed to justify the undertaking. Indeed most of the members of the National Association of Corporation Schools have hundreds of employees. On the other hand there is large room for the development of corporation training by small-scale concerns through trade associations or similar arrangements. The American Institute of Banking referred to above is one excellent illustration of a very effective organization of this sort.

Moreover, the most important use of the corporation school lies in large-scale industries. It is there that the "general knowledge" of the employee most needs special "pointing." It is there that special guidance may mean most for advancement.

An additional reason for the affiliation of the corporation school and large-scale industry is that in such industries the investment in training is more likely to become a permanent asset of the company. Men are obviously less likely to leave when there is no place to go, and this is virtually the situation when the industry which has trained them is monopolistic or holds a dominating position in the field. Large industries, too, even where vigorous competition exists, are able to instil a loyalty and *esprit de corps*, a plant tradition, which holds men.

2. The corporation school, because of the profit motive, cannot be counted on to give "general education" or unbiased instruction regarding social institutions such as trade unions, governmental regulation, and tariffs; nor can it, because of the

uncertain loyalty of employees, be expected to make even its special training any broader than necessary.

The knowledge obtained from a general course in marketing is far more salable elsewhere than a course in "Our Sales Methods"; "Commercial Correspondence" is a more risky investment for Company A to make in an office-worker than instruction in "The Correspondence Forms of Company A."

This failure to give general training is no ground for criticizing the corporation school. It may be worth while to criticize the whole system of private enterprise but hardly to pick at such a detail.

3. Conversely to the above, the corporation school finds its chief rôle in teaching the detailed technique of particular businesses. "The corporation school," says the educational director of the Western Electric Company, "has come into existence because of the necessity for training young men and young women to know the details of how to perform the tasks peculiar to a particular business." In this rôle the corporation school can function to social advantage. It is a task which must be done; no other agency can do it with a comparable amount of social resources, in fact no other agency can, in some cases, do it at all.

4. Finally, and perhaps most significant of all, is the fact that, in broad ranges of industry, the corporation school *can be counted on* to give instruction in technique. This is gratifying not only because it will be done at less social cost than otherwise but because it rids other institutions of a burden in many cases too long assumed. It makes possible a much greater extension than has been common heretofore, either in the secondary school commercial course or in the collegiate school of business into the larger and more general phases of business and especially into the social aspects of enterprise, concerning which the corporation school cannot be trusted to give instruction even if it wishes to do so.

Mr. J. W. Dietz, whose remarks on corporation training are usually worth consideration, has placed the corporation school rather aptly in his statement:

Industry's point of view:

Train citizens. Let the public school do it.
Buy trained help. Let the other fellow do it.
Educate in business. It's our own job.

QUESTIONS FOR DISCUSSION

1. What is a corporation school? What is the National Association of Corporation Training?
2. What chief types of corporation schools may be distinguished? Try to have a working notion of what each of these types is.
3. Why should a company give an employee some days, weeks, months, or years of training while on pay?
4. The period of training given by the corporation and at the company's expense appears to increase as the preliminary education has been greater. Does this seem to be borne out by a study of the specific cases offered? Should not the reverse be true?
5. Corporations seem to have gone to great effort to make their schools successful. They have co-operated with public-school agencies, they have given evening courses, they have joined with one another into associations for education, they have even conducted correspondence courses for their employees. Give examples of the employment of each of these methods.
6. The trade-apprenticeship school reminds one of the old medieval apprenticeship. Examine the description of the school of the Lakeside Press. What similarities to medieval apprenticeship do you see in this school? What dissimilarities?
7. Is printing a trade that lends itself more readily to the apprenticeship type of training than some other occupations? Give examples.
8. What is the office-work school of a corporation? Could an office-work school be of any service to the graduate of a two-year high-school commercial course? of a four-year high-school commercial course?
9. What is Dietz's idea of the way in which a corporation school can train its correspondents? Would the same training be possible in a school?
10. Examine the description of the distribution course of the Ford Motor Company. What are the chief divisions of this course? Could not such a course be given in the secondary school? in a

college? Should such a course be given in the secondary school? in a college?

11. Apply the same queries asked above to the course outlined for the Eli-Lilly Company. If courses such as these should be given in schools, why not give courses that would have a specific application to every business establishment?
12. What are the unique features of the Curtis Publishing Company's sales school?
13. What is the retail sales school? Does it seem to you that retail selling is the proper subject to be taught in the high school, in the college, in the private business school, in the corporation school, or in all of them?
14. What are the chief duties of the education director of a corporation?
15. Draw up a statement that seems to you adequately to express the place of a corporation school in an organized scheme of education.

CHAPTER XIV

COLLEGIATE SCHOOLS OF BUSINESS

Collegiate schools of business in the United States have taken two forms. Although it is with only one of these forms that we are to concern ourselves to any extent, a word in passing should be said concerning the other. One type of collegiate school of business is the technical school, or institute of technology; the other may appropriately be called the collegiate school of commerce. Each of these types of school sprang more or less from the economic condition of the time which saw its beginning.

The capacity of the market to absorb goods has generally exceeded the ability of manufacturers to produce them. This at least was true from the introduction of power-driven machinery into English industry until the closing decades of the nineteenth century. Pressure of demand made it unnecessary for the business man to devote his time to searching out unformulated needs.[1]

Such pressure of demand, however, did put an emphasis on production. This emphasis upon production of manufactured goods furnished a proper atmosphere for the study of science, pure and applied, and consequently upon the growth of institutes of technology. In 1824 the Rensselaer Polytechnic Institute was founded, followed in 1847 by the Sheffield Scientific School at Yale, and in 1848 by the Lawrence Scientific School at Harvard. The really rapid growth of schools of applied science and engineering, however, came following the Civil War, when between 1870 and 1890 some twenty schools of first rank were established either as departments of universities or as separate institutions. In 1862 the Morrill Act brought the aid of public land grants to state colleges, giving special support to the teaching of agriculture and the mechanic arts. This act supple-

[1] A. W. Shaw, *An Approach to Business Problems*, p. 104. Harvard University Press, 1916.

mented by the so-called Second Morrill Act of 1890 is said to have been responsible for the establishment, by 1915, of sixty-seven institutions giving instruction to 69,000 students.

Leaving the institutes of technology with this brief statement, we find that a change in economic conditions may be thought of as responsible for the new interest in education of collegiate grade dealing with selling, advertising, traffic, and other social adjustments, rather than with the technique of production.

Only in recent years, when the development of production has potentially outstripped the available market and shifted the emphasis to distribution, has the manufacturer-merchant become a pioneer on the frontier of human desires and needs.

Today the progressive business man makes careful, intensive studies not merely of the consumer's recognized wants but of his tastes, his habits, his tendencies in all the common activities and relations of life. This he does in order to track down unconscious needs, to manufacture goods to satisfy them, to bring these products to the attention of the consumer in the most appealing ways, and finally to complete the cycle by transporting the goods to him in response to an expressed demand. His problem is chiefly one of adjustment. He must bend the materials and forces of nature to the end of human service. And, most difficult task of all, he must shape his making and selling policies alike to satisfy contradictory conditions and methods and to employ without waste the divergent and overlapping agencies through which present-day distribution is carried on.[1]

It is, then, the schools which have been founded to train men for working in these fields of "adjustment" in "making and shaping policies" that have come to be called collegiate schools of business, and it is with such schools that this chapter is concerned.

THE FIRST COLLEGIATE SCHOOL OF COMMERCE

The first institution in the United States to offer a professional training in business of collegiate grade was the Wharton School of Finance and Economy of the University of Penn-

[1] A. W. Shaw, *op. cit.*, p. 104.

sylvania. This school was founded in 1881 by Mr. Joseph Wharton, a wealthy citizen of Philadelphia. It was his desire that the school should provide facilities for "education in the principles underlying successful civil government" as well as "training suitable for those who intend to engage in business or to undertake the management of property."

At the time of its inception, the course was two years in length, requiring as prerequisite training two years in the general arts college course. Its curriculum consisted largely of political economy, political science, accounting, mercantile law, and practice. The student completing the course received a Bachelor's degree. Below is given the course of study offered by the Wharton School in the academic year 1881–82:[1]

Course of Study

SUB-JUNIOR YEAR

Social Science.—E. Peshine Smith's *Political Economy.* Thompson's *National Economy.* Johnston's *History of American Politics.*

Mercantile Practice.—Oral instruction in business procedure, in the management of trusts, and in the routine of banking.

English.—Chaucer (*The Canterbury Tales*). Spencer. Shakspere (Several Plays Illustrating the Growth of the Dramatist's Mind and Art.) Compositions and Declamations.

German.—Lessing's *Nathan der Weise. Der Mensch und die Natur.*

French.—Racine or Corneille.

Physics.—Mechanics, including Hydrostatics, Pneumatics and Sound.

Mineralogy.—General description of Minerals and Crystallography.

Latin (Elective with Drawing).—Smith's *Principia Latina,* Part 1. Caesar (*De Bello Gallico*).

Drawing (Elective with Latin).—Free-Hand Drawing, and Drawing from the Flat.

JUNIOR YEAR

Social Science.—History and Functions of Money. International Balance of Trade. Theory and Practice of Banking. The Credit System. Monetary Crises and Panics. The Stock and Bond Market.

[1] From a statement furnished by Emory R. Johnson, dean of the Wharton School.

Social Science. Municipal State and National Taxation. The Management of Revenue. Sinking Funds. Methods of Taxation, and Their Moral and Social Influence. (Direct and Indirect Taxes, Land Taxes, Taxes on Corporations, Internal Revenue, Taxes, and Duties on Imports.) The Relation of Wars and Military Systems, through Taxation, to National Industry. The Handling of Public Debts.

———. Industry, Commerce and Transportation. The National Necessity for a Balance of the Great Industries. National Self-Defence in the Development of the Industries.

———. Wage Questions. The Relations of Capital and Labor. Strikes and Lock Outs. Harmony and Discord.

Mental and Moral Science.—Atwater's *Logic.* Whewell's *Elements of Morality.*

English.—Compositions and Declamations.

Geology.—Elements of Geology. Descriptive and Determinative Mineralogy. Metallurgy.

Physics.—Heat and Light.

Latin.—Cicero's *Epistolae, De Senectute,* etc. (Long's edition). Virgil's *Georgics.*

German.—Schiller's *Wilhelm Tell.* Goethe's *Hermann and Dorothea.* Translations into German. Whitney's German Grammar.

French.—Molière.

SENIOR YEAR

Law.—Elementary Law. Mercantile Law (Law of Partnership. Law of Common Carrier. License Laws. Land Laws, etc., etc.). Constitutional Law of the United States and of the Commonwealth of Pennsylvania. The Rules of Order in Public and Corporation Meetings.

Social Science.—Lectures on Living Issues (Land, Labor, Monetary Questions in Their Popular Aspects, Socialism and Communism, Free Trade and Protections, Charity Organization, Popular and Industrial Education).

———. Mulford's *Nation.*

———. Original Research in the Theory and History of Economical Questions, under direction of the Professor.

History.—Lectures on Modern and Mediaeval History. Guizot's *History of Civilization in Europe.*

English.—Compositions and Declamations.

Physics.—Electricity. Practical and Astronomical Physics.

Astronomy.—Mathematical Astronomy.

NOTE.—Candidates who have passed through the Freshman and Sophomore Classes in either the Department of Arts or the Towne Scientific School, will be admitted as full students without examinations.

In the early days of the Wharton School there was the difficulty which might be expected from the assignment to the teaching of technical subjects of men who had been trained for academic work and who had neither interest nor experience in the specialized fields. In 1894 the program of the school was broadened, a more specialized faculty was introduced, and the number of years in the course was increased from two to four.[1] The bulletin for 1922 shows the following for the general course which is of interest by way of comparison with the earlier one:

COURSE REQUIREMENTS

FRESHMAN YEAR

(The following courses are required of all Freshmen.)

	Hours per Week
Physical Education	2
Composition	2
English Language (first term) / History of English Literature (second term)	2
Elementary Accounting	3
Business Law or General Inorganic Chemistry	3
Principles of Economics	3
Resources and Industries of the U.S.	3
Government	3

ADDITIONAL REQUIRED WORK

Before the end of the Junior year:

Two additional units of Political Science, or Economics, or two units of Sociology.

Three units of History.

One additional unit of Physical Education.

[1] Roswell McCrea, "The Work of the Wharton School of Finance and Commerce." *Journal of Political Economy*, XXI (1913), 111.

Before graduation:

Six units of foreign language (not elementary courses)
or
Three units of foreign language (not elementary courses) and three units of Science or Mathematics.
Two additional units of History.
One additional unit of Physical Education.
Two units of Senior Research work.

The satisfactory completion of a total of seventy units of work, in addition to Physical Education, is required for the degree. (A "unit" of work is the amount involved in attendance upon lectures or recitations one hour a week for one year, or upon laboratory work two hours a week for one year.)

These seventy units are distributed as follows:

Wharton School subjects	44
College subjects required	17
Free electives in either Wharton School or College subjects	9

Course Groupings

Prior to registration for the Sophomore year each student is required to elect one of the following groups of courses:

The General Course

SOPHOMORE YEAR

		Hours a Week
Physical Education		2
Composition (one term)		2
Nineteenth Century Novelists (one term)		
History or Foreign Language (see note)		3
Political Science, Economics, or Sociology		2
Money and Credit		3
Three of the following:		
Accounting 2 or 7.	Accounting	9
C.&T. 5.	Transportation	
Insurance 1 or 3.	Insurance	
G.&I. 7.	Manufacturing	
Electives		2–3

JUNIOR YEAR

	Hours a Week
Physical Education	2
Foreign Language	3
History	2–3
English—An advanced course (not included in Wharton units) (one term)	2
Nine units chosen from three of the following:	
Commerce and Transportation	9
Finance	
Insurance	
Geography and Industry	
Merchandising	
Business Law 2 or 3	
Electives, maximum 5 hours	5

SENIOR YEAR

	Hours a Week
Physical Education	2
Research	2
History or Foreign Language, according to the Uncompleted History or Language requirement at the end of Junior year (see note)	2–3
Public Finance (first term required; second term elective)	2
Three units chosen from the following:	
Commerce and Transportation	3
Geography and Industry	
Finance	
Merchandising	
Electives (minimum 3 hours)	3

NOTE.—Six units of advanced Foreign Language are required before graduation. Students are advised to take these in the Sophomore and Junior years, if possible. After completing three advanced units of such language the students may substitute a three-unit course in Science or Mathematics for the remaining three units of Language.

In January, 1898, the Regents of the University of California determined to establish a College of Commerce in that institution. Formal opening occurred in the fall term of that year. The four years' course consisted of about one-half of the type of the studies given in general college courses and of about one-half of courses in the fields of philosophy, law, politics, economics, geography, technology, mathematics. It was stated that "this college is intended to afford an opportunity for the scientific study of commerce in all its relations and for the higher education of business men and of the higher officers of the civil service."[1] In addition to the underlying courses a number of special ones in narrower fields were offered.

On October 1 of the same year, President Harper, of the University of Chicago, in his twenty-fifth quarterly statement said, "It is with a feeling of great satisfaction that I may announce the inauguration during the past quarter of the College of Commerce and Politics."[2] President Harper stated further that the inauguration of the College of Commerce at the University of Chicago was distinguished from similar undertakings elsewhere by the fact that the work "should be organized as a college and administered as such."

In 1900 Dartmouth College, New York University, and the University of Wisconsin opened schools of business. The next year such a school was organized at the University of Michigan. No other school gave what would now be considered collegiate business work until 1908. A number of state universities earlier than this put in "commercial courses." The catalogue of the University of the State of Missouri for 1897–98 states that instruction is given in correspondence, writing receipts, checks, notes, and drafts, and that a full course in stenography is provided for those students who wish to carry on this study. The University of South Dakota early offered courses in penmanship, commercial law, shorthand, typewriting, and office practice. Similar courses were common in western universities before 1900.

Schools of business in colleges and universities were founded most rapidly following 1910, there being scarcely a year since that time when one or more higher institutions of standing did not announce the inauguration of such a school. Between

[1] U.S. Bureau of Education, *Report of Commissioner*, II (1897–98), 2443.

[2] *Ibid.*, p. 2444.

1900 and 1918 a number of "conferences" were held by delegates of universities having schools of business. On November 13, 1919, at Harvard University, there was held the first program meeting of the Association of Collegiate Schools of Business.[1] Prior to this meeting the schools of fifteen of the leading universities had associated themselves as charter members. The membership now numbers twenty-three schools (May 1, 1922).

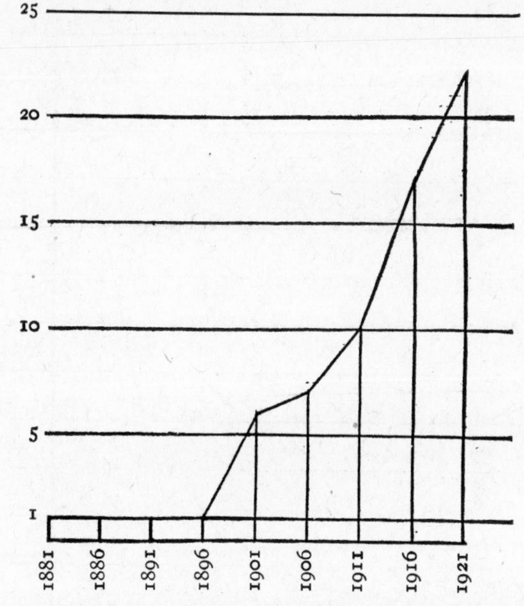

FIG. 27.—Increase in number of collegiate schools of business* from 1881 to 1921.

* Yale University, which discontinued its course in Business Administration in 1920–21, is not included.

The number of schools of business founded in various years is shown in Figure 4, on page 15, and need not be repeated here. The increase in numbers of schools and of students and the relation which the number of students bears to the total col-

[1] The organization meeting was held at the University Club of Chicago, June 16 and 17, 1916.

legiate undergraduates are presented, however. A period of twenty-five years includes the life of all of the collegiate schools of business excepting the Wharton School.

Figure 27 shows the increase in number of collegiate schools of business and makes clear the impetus which came in the development of such schools after 1910.

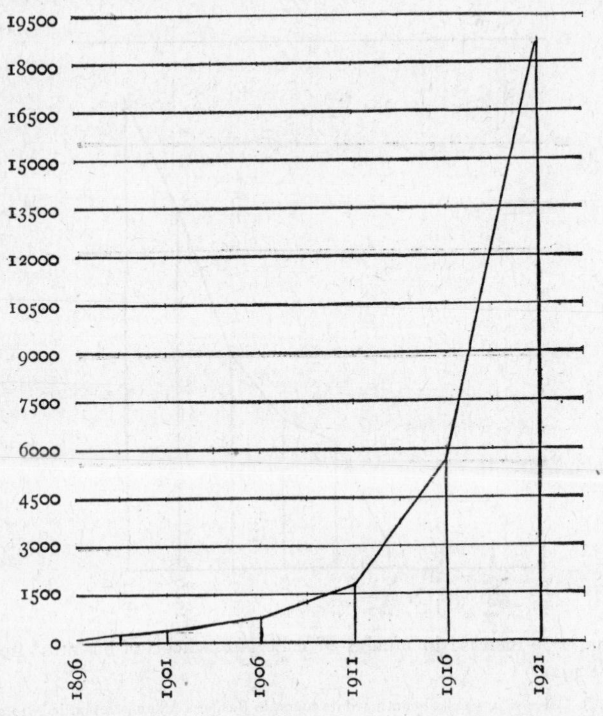

FIG. 28.—Increase in number of undergraduate students (men and women) in day courses of collegiate schools of business from 1896 to 1921.

In the data on which the diagrams are based, only institutions which are members of the National Association of Collegiate Schools of Business are included. There are other collegiate schools of business which, on a basis of quality, have equal right to inclusion, but an excluding line drawn on anything but an arbitrary basis would be difficult and irritating.

Figure 28 shows the increase in number of undergraduate students in day courses of collegiate schools of business for the years indicated. In making this diagram pre-commerce students were included in those schools where such control was

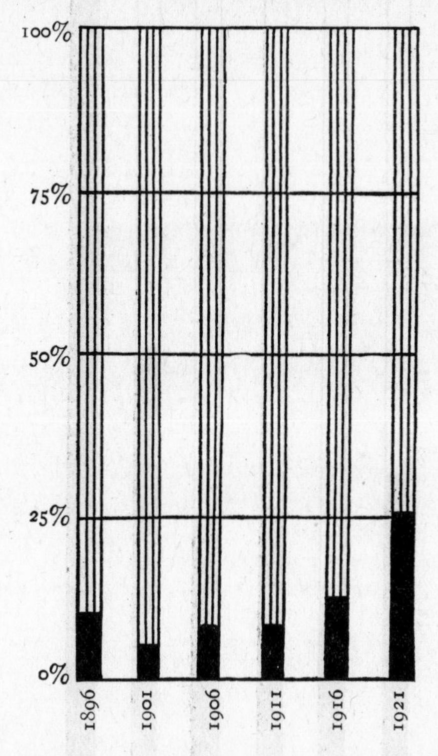

FIG. 29.—Ratio for the indicated years between undergraduate students in collegiate schools of business and other undergraduates in the institutions maintaining such schools.

exercised over them as to make them, to all practical purposes, members of the collegiate school. Government students are not included. In this diagram again only members of the National Association of Collegiate Schools of Business are

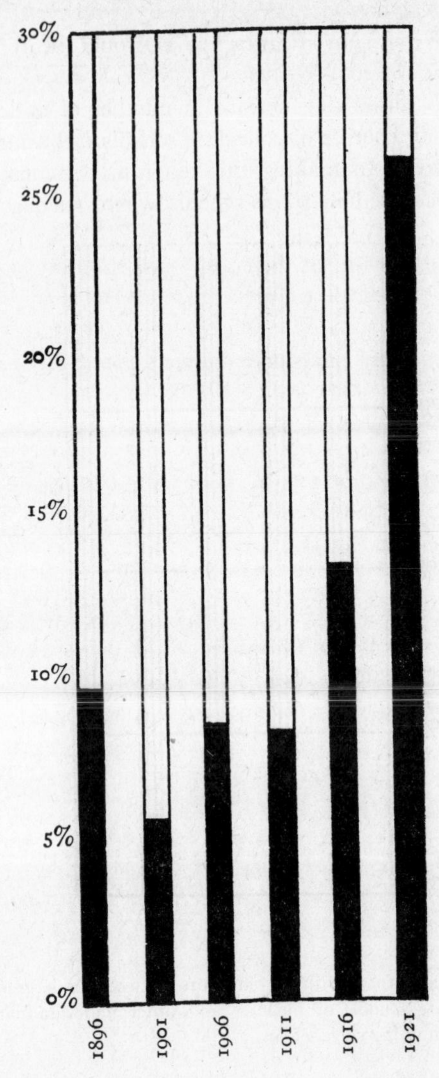

FIG. 29*A*.—Variations for the indicated years in the relation between business students and other undergraduates in universities maintaining such schools.

considered. New York University, Harvard, and Yale are not included. The first because it proved impossible to secure figures differentiating day from evening schools except at the present time, the second because its strictly graduate quality seemed to make the figures incomparable, and the last because Yale has abandoned its so-called school of business administration.

Figure 29 shows for the indicated years the relation between the number of students in collegiate schools of business and the number of all other undergraduate students in the same universities. The same exceptions made concerning Figure 28 apply to Figures 29 and 29*A*. Figure 29*A* is constructed to emphasize the variations in the relation between business students and other undergraduates in the universities considered. By limiting the chart to the lower 30 per cent, the variations are more obvious than in Figure 29.

IDEALS UNDERLYING COLLEGIATE SCHOOLS OF BUSINESS

Those responsible for directing the leading schools of commerce have, ever since the movement gathered momentum, conceived the functions of these schools in broad terms. There prevails the idea that it is the duty of such schools to liberalize as well as to train. More than this, there is the persistent notion that there must come from collegiate business schools a better culture and an extension of culture into realms of life where it is now too little known. "All who are concerned, through investigation or instruction, with the present movement for placing new departments of industrial activity upon a scientific basis, in the interest of greater efficiency, and of more just and liberal ideals, should appreciate the high calling whereunto they are called."[1] This statement made in 1913 was but an echo of that made nearly twenty years ago when at a conference of educators and business men called at the University of

[1] Edward D. Jones, "Some Propositions Concerning University Instruction in Business Administration," *Journal of Political Economy*, XXI (1913), 194.

Michigan to consider the purposes of higher commercial education, Professor William A. Scott said:[1]

There is another aspect of this question which must not be overlooked. How can a university best impress its ideals upon society? By cutting itself off from the most active departments of social life, by surrounding the young people placed in its charge with an atmosphere entirely different from that of the world in which they must live, or by opening wide its doors to all classes of students who are fitted to enter, and by striving to give them every possible assistance in the preparation of themselves for the specific careers they expect to follow? This latter course compels university professors to make a careful study of the actual life about them, to classify the phenomena of the actual world, and to reduce them to a scientific form. It gives them an opportunity to discover how high social, moral and religious ideals can be introduced into the life of society, and to impress upon the young people placed under their charge the importance of those ideals, and the dangers to which they will be exposed in the careers they propose to enter. For my part, I cannot understand how an unprejudiced student of the relations between civilization and education can possibly desire the universities to hold themselves aloof from the pulsing life of the present day. It seems to me that the movement which has resulted in the establishment of technical schools of all grades in connection with our universities is one of the most hopeful and encouraging of our time. To me it means that the power of our universities is increasing, that they are strengthening rather than loosening their grip upon the people and the country, that the cause of culture is safe, and that the highest educational ideals have a better chance of survival than ever before in our history. The refusal of our universities to establish schools of commerce and other technical schools, which belong to the college grade of development, I should deprecate as a great misfortune. It would mean a relative increase in the power and influence of institutions established for private gain and permeated by a narrow, selfish spirit, and a rapid diminution in the interest which young men and the most active and influential elements of society now feel in our colleges and universities. I believe that the highest interests of

[1] Adapted from William A. Scott, "The Place of Commercial Studies in the College or University Curriculum," *Publications of the Michigan Science Association*, V (1902–4), 53–54.

society can be trusted with safety to the faculties and governing boards of our college and universities.

Such liberal sentiments still find favor with those persons concerned with determining the policies of collegiate schools of business. In attempting to outline the function of a school of business in a university in 1920, Dean Hotchkiss expressed these views:[1]

A collegiate school of business is assumed in this discussion to be a school that has its setting in a college or university. The fact of such a setting carries certain implications which necessarily must influence our discussion. . . . . These ideas may be indicated by the words "public responsibility," "educational sequence," "scientific content," "professional aim," "vision."

Public responsibility.—Collegiate education, whether general or professional, and whether supported by the state, or by private endowment, is a public function, and it owes its first duty to the public. Schools of business are in no different situation in this regard from schools of law, medicine, or engineering. Their first duty is a function of the national life.

Educational sequence.—Relationship to an educational system means that education for business is not a thing by itself; it is something to be articulated with the framework of higher education; it must begin somewhere and end somewhere; it must be a part of a system. Doubtless the business curriculum will have some influence, possibly a large influence, on the system; and we need to use this influence to make the system more nearly what we think it should be; at any given time, however, we shall have to fit our curriculum into the system as we find it.

Scientific content.— . . . . In order to have proper scientific content a business curriculum must be so organized as to carry the student through basic analytical processes in which the fundamental principles of business organization and management will be set forth. On the other hand it is clear that the task of developing analytical power cannot proceed with great efficiency unless our efforts are put forth on really live material. It is not then a question of discipline rather than information, but a question of discipline

[1] Adapted from Willard E. Hotchkiss, "The Basic Elements and Their Proper Balance in the Curriculum of a Collegiate Business School," *Journal of Political Economy*, XXVIII (1920), 89–91.

through information. This means, I think, that our curriculum should be so organized that the basic facts of business will be introduced in an orderly and systematic way as subject-matter for analysis and not as matters of pure informational interest. . . . .

Professional aim.—Analysis of business data may have a purely research aim. Professional training is directed toward activity. Before there can be orderly and well-considered business activity the results of analysis must be brought together into working plans for dispatching business, for exercising control, and for achieving definite business results. . . . . Roughly stated, the professional purpose of the collegiate business school is to give the foundation training for managers, business experts, and all those whose function it is to develop and execute working plans in business.

Vision.—The subject-matter of education is drawn from the past, but education itself must look to the future. This is peculiarly true of education for business. . . . . Obviously the effort to build a curriculum on prophecy involves some danger. If we project ourselves so far into the future that we lose contact with the present we are likely to substitute speculation for fact and leave our course floating in air. But a greater danger than this is the danger of standing still or looking backward. The presence of experimental courses, courses which carry the curriculum beyond the present established frontiers, is perhaps the most tangible indication of vision and the surest guaranty of preventing a course of study from getting behind the times.

A somewhat more concrete conception of the social utility of a collegiate school of business may be made. Such schools can train for management. That is, they can provide men able to correlate the work of the innumerable specialists of our society. As long as we make use of specialization this is vital, and the usefulness of institutions which can produce such correlators will be unquestioned.

CLASSES OF SCHOOLS

Not every collegiate school of business has been able to put into practical form such broad and general ideals as have been recited above. Some have not been in a position to apply them. The curricula of the latter schools is often largely a collection of business subjects adapted to the immediate practical needs of the students. One should hesitate, however, to criticize such schools unduly. In large cities, especially in evening courses, such curricula render a unique and valuable service. Almost every phase of the curriculum problem of these schools is different from that of the school offering a full-time course to undergraduates who expect to work forward to a degree.

Even among the full-time day schools, however, there is still much to be done in the way of curriculum organization. It is not difficult to point out instances where "courses dealing with business" rather than "balanced curriculum" are offered. On the other hand some outstanding instances of a philosophy for building a curriculum are to be found. One statement of such a philosophy is that made by H. S. Person as follows:[1]

During the more than fifteen years of our efforts at the Tuck School we have been searching for the elements of a curriculum which are basic in the sense that they relate to elements in business which are universal in all business. We have come to believe that the differences between businesses which are ordinarily noted—that one manufactures or distributes shoes and another sugar; that one fashions or deals in tangible commodities and another offers services—are superficial from the educational point of view. Attention to these differences is essential but too much should not be made of them. A curriculum, the elements of which are determined by a consideration of these superficial differences, is likely to develop limitations in the graduate rather than give him professional freedom and power. Have you ever considered the fact that it is an exceptional student who knows until the time of graduation what business he is going to enter, and that the businesses most students enter are determined largely by the opportunities presented at the last moment; also that five years after graduation the majority of graduates are no longer in the businesses they entered at graduation? These are significant facts. The inevitable conclusion is that the object of training for business should be the development in the individual of

[1] Adapted from discussion by H. S. Person of Willard E. Hotchkiss, "The Basic Elements and Their Proper Balance in the Curriculum of a Collegiate Business School," *Journal of Political Economy*, XXVIII (1920), 109–12.

A CHART OF BUSINESS ACTIVITIES

Zone	Level	Organization
ZONE I Determination of larger business policies	Administration	Stockholders Directors President
		GENERAL MANAGER
ZONE II Determination of operating policies and plans Specific requirements Progress	Management	Executive Staff Requirements Control Progress Finance and Accts. Design Works Management Personnel Sales
		Planning Room
ZONE III Administrative and shop and other routine operations	Operation	Foremen Clerks Workers Clerks

universal and transferable professional business ability. That alone will give him freedom and power and make him master of his career.

If we can find the elements which are common to all business, we have made a start toward determining what the profession demands as the basic elements in our curricula. I shall take the liberty of suggesting diagrammatically a method of approach to the determination of the common elements. Let us draw in skeleton form a typical functional organization chart (p. 381). It may apply in principle to a manufacturing plant, a department store, a railroad, a firm of lawyers, a hospital—any organization for purposive collective activity. Upon this skeleton organization chart we superimpose horizontal lines which divide the activities of the organization into broad functional zones. These zones also hold for any business. Now we have a start, for we observe that every business demands in the large three kinds of professional skill: the ability to determine large governing policy (administrative or entrepreneur policy); the ability to determine operating policy and to control operations (management); the ability to carry out operating policy (routine operations). While the ambition of the individual is to become, through education, training, and experience, a master successively in Zones I, II, and III, there is no presumption that the elements of our curricula should be determined by giving equal weight to the requirements of these zones. It seems to me that general education, experience, and the professional training of the school of business have respectively a definite relation to the development of skill in some one of these zones more than in another.

With Zone I (the zone of routine operations), in which the graduates of our schools begin their careers, I believe "experience" is most concerned. Speaking broadly, and not without some reservation, (e.g., accounting, technique of foreign trade, etc.), I do not believe our schools should attempt to teach the routine of any particular business.

Another example of an underlying idea and one upon which an extended experiment in curriculum-building is being carried on, is that to be found in the School of Commerce and Administration of the University of Chicago.[1]

[1] This statement is adapted from the Preface to L. C. Marshall, *Business Administration*, pp. vii–ix. University of Chicago Press, 1921. A some-

. . . . The business executive administers his business under conditions imposed by his environment, both physical and social. The student should accordingly have an understanding of the physical environment. This justifies attention to the earth sciences. He should also have an understanding of the social environment and must accordingly give attention to civics, law, economics, social psychology, and other branches of the social sciences. His knowledge of environment should not be too abstract in character. It should be given practical content, and should be closely related to his knowledge of the internal problems of management. This may be accomplished through a range of courses dealing with business administration wherein the student may become acquainted with such matters as the measuring aids of control, the communicating aids of control, organization policies and methods; the manager's relation to production, to labor, to finance, to technology, to risk-bearing, to the market, to social control, etc. Business is, after all, a pecuniarily organized scheme of gratifying human wants, and, properly understood, falls little short of being as broad, as inclusive, as life itself in its motives, aspirations, and social obligations. It falls little short of being as broad as all science in its technique. Training for the task of the business administrator must have breadth and depth comparable with those of the task.

Stating the matter in another way, the modern business administrator is essentially a solver of business problems—problems of business policy, of organization, and of operation. These problems, great in number and broad in scope, divide themselves into certain type groups, and in each type group there are certain classes of obstacles to be overcome, as well as certain aids, or materials of solution.

If these problems are arranged (1) to show the significance of the organizing and administrative, or control, activities of the modern responsible manager, and (2) to indicate appropriate fields of training, the diagram on opposite page (which disregards much overlapping and interacting) results.

---

what extended discussion of this matter is to be found in L. C. Marshall, "A Balanced Curriculum in Business Education," *Journal of Political Economy*, XXV (January, 1917), 84.

BASIC ELEMENTS OF THE BUSINESS CURRICULUM

CONTROL
1. Communicating aids of control, for example
   a) English
   b) Foreign languages
2. Measuring aids of control, for example
   a) Mathematics
   b) Statistics and accounting
3. Standards and practices of control
   a) Psychology
   b) Organization policies and methods

Of problems of adjustment to physical environment
- a) The earth sciences
- b) The manager's relationship to these

Of problems of technology
- a) Physics through mechanics, basic, and other sciences as appropriate
- b) The manager's administration of production

Of problems of finance
- a) The financial organization of society
- b) The manager's administration of finance

Of problems connected with the market
- a) Market functions and market structure
- b) The manager's administration of marketing (including purchasing and traffic)

Of problems of risk and risk-bearing
- a) The risk aspects of modern industrial society
- b) The manager's administration of risk-bearing

Of problems of personnel
- a) The position of the worker in modern industrial society
- b) The manager's administration of personnel

Of problems of adjustment to social environment
- a) The historical background
- b) The socio-economic institutional life
- c) Business law and government

LENGTH OF COURSES

Collegiate schools of business have made three fairly clearly distinguishable arrangements in terms of length and school years. First may be mentioned the two-year collegiate school of business. This type in turn falls into two classes. Wisconsin and Minnesota are good examples of one class. They each give a two-year professional course in business during the Junior and Senior years of college. Although the business course proper does not begin until the Junior year, those students who are planning to take the business course follow a pre-business course during their Freshmen and Sophomore years. To a considerable degree the school of business indicates the subjects which shall be taken in these pre-commerce years. It is therefore a two-year course with a considerable influence over the two preceding years. The University of Pittsburgh, on the other hand, has a two-year course given also for Juniors and Seniors which recognizes no such term as pre-commerce students. The previous training of the students is a matter of no concern at Pittsburgh and the present administration stands definitely for this two-year course as distinguished from the course based on two years of "guidance."

The case for a rather sharp dividing line between the general training and the professional training has thus been put:[1]

It seems to us that technical commercial courses and liberal academic courses must be so related in a curriculum as to best develop two capacities in every physical man,—the *man*, in the loftiest sense of the word, and the business man in the special sense of the word; or to express it differently, to develop a man who looked at on one side, is a broad minded man interested in business, and looked at on the other side, is a business man who is broad minded.

We believe that the training of the man should precede the training of the business man and that the result can be best accomplished by having a period of education organized primarily for the first and followed by a period organized primarily to accomplish the other result.

[1] Adapted from H. S. Person, "Remarks Concerning the Amos Tuck School of Dartmouth College," *Publications of the Michigan Science Association*, V (1902–4), 60.

A second arrangement is the four-year course. The present program at the Wharton School outlines such a four-year undergraduate course. The School of Commerce and Administration of the University of Chicago is another example of a definite four-year course which is declared to offer undergraduate professional training. In both of these schools, as in other typical four-year courses, the student can find a desirable amount of work beyond his four years, although such work is not requisite to his degree. The advantages of this type of organization are presented in the following statement.[1]

The undergraduate-graduate school of business administration exercises control of the student's curriculum for a period of from four to seven years. The minimum four years carry the student to the bachelor's degree, the maximum seven years should carry him to the doctorate.

The advantages of this type of organization may be stated thus:

1. The control of the entire undergraduate curriculum makes it possible to arrange an orderly course of study which will (*a*) correct deficiencies of secondary education, (*b*) give the student an awareness of the great fields of human activity, and (*c*) systematically develop a knowledge of business in terms of its great functions. The plain truth is that the Arts college has largely broken down in the American educational system, and the college of business administration needs to control the entire four years of its students in order to guarantee an education that is really liberal, and not merely loose. That the college of business administration may abuse this trust, if it conceives its task narrowly, only serves to emphasize its opportunity.

2. Business education is so new and has before it so many problems, that it seems likely to gain by having the student under its own faculty for as long a period as is reasonably possible. Experimentation and comparative study will thus be facilitated. Among these problems may be cited the necessity of securing a proper background (discussed above), field or contact work, the development of instructional material in terms of basic functions, and the technique of instruction. These problems are all so large that a strong case may be made for having control of the student's course a sufficient time to make comparative studies.

[1] This statement was prepared by L. C. Marshall, Dean of the School of Commerce and Administration, The University of Chicago.

3. Control of the entering Freshman gives a much needed point of contact with secondary education. There is no question that the junior high school movement is working a revolution in that field and that it is entirely possible that the final outcome will force a complete overhauling of the college work. Students are already presenting for college admission, credits for work taken in the eighth and even in the seventh grade. It is quite possible that matters may proceed to the stage where college graduation requirements will be stated in terms of achievements from the time of the seventh grade. The School of Commerce and Administration of the University of Chicago has, indeed, already adopted such a curriculum as an alternative curriculum. It can readily be seen that a college of business administration which sincerely believes in broad education may well covet contact with secondary education, and may save one or two years of educational waste if it makes this contact wisely.

4. Precisely the same kind of argument may be made for contact with graduate work. If it be true, as I think it is, that careful planning of a liberal business education from the seventh grade on through college will, with incidental gains in liberal education, carry the Bachelor in business administration as far as a second-year graduate student is now carried, it is clear that our graduate work can be made to assume a new dignity and importance. Too many of our courses today are courses for graduate students rather than graduate courses. The school which has control of the whole undergraduate-graduate curriculum is in a strategic position for fruitful work in remedying this situation. The doctorate (presumably taken by those intending to teach in this field) can in such an institution involve very mature work.

A third period of possible training is represented in the graduate school of business. The Graduate School of Business at Harvard University is the outstanding example of such a school. The course at Harvard is two years in length. The Graduate School of the University of Pennsylvania includes a special course in business administration for graduates of accredited colleges and universities. Graduates of the Wharton School who in the opinion of the authorities have had undergraduate courses equivalent to the first year of this special graduate course are admitted to the second year of the course and are eligible to the degree of Master of Business Administration after one, instead of two, years of satisfactory resident work. Dean Wallace Donham, of the Graduate School of Harvard University, thus states what appears to him to be the function of a graduate school of commerce.[1]

My idea of the functions of a graduate school of business are based, of course, upon the problem as I have seen it in my three years in the Harvard Graduate School of Business Administration.

The aim of a graduate school of business should be to train men for future executive positions and train teachers of business, particularly for the undergraduate collegiate schools. I am firmly convinced from my business experience that it is necessary in training men for executive positions to give them a broad background, and I still more firmly believe this since coming in contact with the men in the school.

I do not feel that a graduate school of business should attempt to train specialists, in fact a school cannot give the technique of a particular job necessary to prepare specialists nearly as well as the industry itself can give it.

A graduate school should assume the responsibility to help the individual choose the type of business for which he is best suited. From our experience a majority of the men who come to the business school know only that they want to enter business, with little or no knowledge of the demands of different industries within business. To do this the Harvard Business School gives, first, a series of discussions for the first-year men in the school under the general heading, "Business School Methods and the Choice of the Study Group." The second group is given toward the end of the year for second-year men under the general heading, "Individual's Introduction to Business."

The first of these groups of lectures considers the relation of the individual to the business school and also includes a group of lectures on the general organization of business and specialized business careers, intended to help in the understanding of particular courses and to assist the individual in choosing the study group in which he shall concentrate his work in the school. The second group of lectures, given toward the end of the second year, is intended to bring to the attention of the beginner in business some of the more important phases in his relation to the organization into which he may go when

[1] A statement prepared by Dean Wallace Donham.

he leaves school. Particular emphasis is placed on the problems arising out of the personal attitude of the individual to his job and to the man or the institution which employs him.

In the actual instruction it seems to us that we have three definite things to give. The first of these is content of the particular courses of study and study groups in the school. This content is more and more resolving itself down to definite principles of instruction. It is necessary in a graduate curriculum to give the content of all of the basic subjects of business, that is, production, distribution, finance, and control. In many ways more important than content, however, is the method by which this content is given. Toward this end we are developing the case system of instruction by which means we are training the men to analyze business situations and to solve the type of problem than an executive in business has to solve. A third item of instruction is to give to the individual an understanding of the economic background of business. This phase of the instruction I believe is becoming very important. When a man undertakes a job after completing the courses in the graduate school, he should be able to interpret to his firm and to his particular job not only the basic facts or economic principles, but also should be able to apply the information which the economists and economic services are preparing for his use.

THE STAGE OF BUSINESS-EDUCATION DEVELOPMENT

The attempt to undertake graduate work in a collegiate school of business raises pointedly the question of how far business education has developed. One aspect which graduate work has taken up to the present time is to emphasize the study of certain specialities. Courses can be given in particular fields such as transportation, brokerage, insurance, or the administration of trust estates. Such a list of occupational courses could be multiplied almost endlessly, and it would be far from the truth to say that such courses are valueless. In regard to basic material, however, there is at least a fair doubt if there is any material of graduate grade which is of distinctly business character. It is perhaps a fair doubt if the first year, even of the Harvard Graduate School, has anything particularly new in content or viewpoint to offer the graduate of the four-year course of any of the better collegiate schools of business. Such a school can offer a useful opportunity for problem study on a somewhat more elaborate scale than is usual in undergraduate work. Obviously, too, the mere continuation of problem work is an extremely valuable undertaking even for the student who has had a thoroughgoing undergraduate business course. Most of all, however, such courses are useful to the liberal-arts or technical graduate who has not specialized in business.

The lack of thoroughly advanced material for schools of business is a fact of which leading business-school administrators are well aware. This lack is part and parcel of the development of the movement. When one realizes that the collegiate school of business began only a few years ago, almost without organized material, the amount which has been accomplished is more remarkable than the fact that much remains yet to be done. The men interested in collegiate schools of business have been too busy in laying the foundations for their work, to go far in the preparation of advanced material.

Now that much of the preliminary material has been organized, there is growing the feeling that a great deal of it is after all frankly elementary in character. This belief suggests an opportunity to the collegiate schools of business. If a considerable part of this elementary work could, with wisdom, be unloaded upon the secondary schools, the time for more advanced work would be made available in the undergraduate course, and the energies of the men now engaged in these more elementary courses could be freed and centered upon the preparation and organization of an advanced type of material.

Stimulating a movement in this direction is the thought that the secondary-school curriculum would be greatly enriched by an infusion of more social-science material and especially of material dealing with those social relations found in business activities. A definite step in the direction of such a program as that just suggested is the report of a commission appointed by the Association of Collegiate Schools of Business.[1]

[1] *Journal of Political Economy*, XXX (1922), 1–55. Published also under the title, *Social Studies in Secondary Schools*. University of Chicago Press, 1922.

This commission was authorized to undertake a study of the correlation of secondary and collegiate education. Interestingly enough, this report presented a review of the social studies in secondary schools and proposed a program of social studies for the junior high school, stating the belief that the junior high school was the "strategic point" for an attack at the present time.

The commission then proceeded to outline a proposed reorganization of social studies in the secondary schools which it believes will open a way to weld the whole structure of business education into a coherent whole.

There remains, therefore, a great deal of work to be done before the collegiate school of business will have found itself and will be offering to students work of a strictly collegiate character and courses upon which study of really graduate quality can be built.

There will no doubt be eventually, also, a considerable broadening of the present viewpoint of collegiate business education. At present, even where clearly planned curricula are to be found, they center largely around the technique of business administration and claim their justification in the attempt to train organizers and correlators in a régime of specialization. At best, however, one has the feeling that there is an appearance of business statesmanship in but few of the courses of the collegiate schools of business. Perhaps this is a matter of no concern. Perhaps it is meaningless language. Perhaps it is harking back to the canons of political economy. The collegiate school of business has justified itself if it has improved production and organization, and perhaps it cannot do more. The field of the collegiate school of business may be limited to improvement in technique and in organization. If this is the limit, however, it is unfortunate. It will be regrettable if the collegiate school of business cannot develop a corps of business men capable of guiding society. It will be regrettable if the collegiate school of business cannot place clearly before its students the underlying assumptions of a business world; if it cannot bring its students to see that captains of industry are as much needed properly to place business and to limit it, as they are to employ it and exercise it. Only with some such objective can the study of business in any sense apply to itself the notion of a profession. Law, which we think of as formerly a profession of this sort, has in large measure become a business. To make a profession of business, starting as we do with a heritage of individual attitudes and a tradition of free enterprise, will require of the directors of business education vision as well as courage and ability. But such is the challenge which we in collegiate schools of business face. It is that challenge which we must accept or drop all claims that business education can be liberal.

QUESTIONS FOR DISCUSSION

1. Forms of education may be said to spring from the economic situation. In what way is the collegiate technical or engineering school an example of this? In what way is the collegiate school of business an example?
2. Although institutions may arise to fill needs, accident and personalities are important in determining the exact times when institutions begin and the forms which they take. Does the early history of collegiate schools of business illustrate this fact?
3. How would you account for the fact that a number of state schools and other schools of collegiate grade organized courses of the business-college type in the period before 1900?
4. How would you account for the growth in collegiate schools of business from 1906 to 1921?
5. Does it appear that the great increase of students in collegiate schools of business from 1910 on is due to a new interest in business training, or to a new interest in collegiate training in general, or both?
6. "The functions of collegiate schools of business have been thought of from the beginning in broad and liberal terms." Is there evidence of this? If it is true, how would you account for it?
7. What was the belief expressed by Dean Scott concerning the cultural possibilities of schools of commerce? What were Dean Hotchkiss' views of specific duties of a collegiate school of business?

8. What do you understand to be meant by the statement that collegiate schools of business can provide men able to correlate the work of the innumerable specialists of our society?
9. Examine carefully Person's chart of business activities. Apply this analysis to some manufacturing business with which you are familiar, giving specific illustrations of certain tasks that would be done in each zone. Do the same for a mercantile business. Can you do the same for an educational institution?
10. "The business executive administers his business under the conditions imposed by his environment, both physical and social." Give examples which illustrate this statement.
11. Work through the "basic elements of the business curriculum" outlined by Marshall. Give an illustration of each of the types of problems mentioned.
12. What do you understand by the phrases, communicating aids of control, measuring aids of control, standards and practices of control?
13. Would a survey of the fields outlined in the list of the "basic elements" give a student a comprehensive view of the tasks of management? Do you believe that detailed study of each of these fields would give him some ability in the tasks of management?
14. Is there any value in the effort to make outlines or analyses such as those suggested by Person and Marshall? What value, if any?
15. No fundamental conclusion has yet been reached as to the proper length of a collegiate school of business course. Such courses vary with the beliefs of the organizers as to the amount of time which should be given for general training. Does this seem to you true? If so, illustrate.
16. Would it be possible to have a graduate school of business which gave elementary business work?
17. What would seem to you should be the ultimate tasks which schools of business of collegiate grade should attempt to accomplish?
18. What is meant by the statement, "Training is needed to teach where to place business"?
19. Can education for business be liberal education?

CHAPTER XV

THE TYPICAL HIGH-SCHOOL COMMERCIAL COURSE

In considering high-school commercial courses it will be useful to break up our study into several parts. First, we shall examine the typical high-school commerce course, the underlying institution, as it exists generally throughout the country. This first view will give us a useful general picture, but it will not give us a complete picture of high-school commerical courses. There are continual and important disturbances on the surface of this underlying mass. In some instances experiments are being proposed, in other cases experiments are on trial, and in still others they have been carried far enough to justify approval or rejection.

We shall, therefore, consider in later chapters what may be called certain modern extensions of the high-school commercial course. Some of these extensions are the more or less direct outgrowth of the commercial course in high schools. In other cases they are merely the adaptation to a new use of older institutions. These modern extensions include the high school of commerce, postgraduate commercial courses, evening commercial courses, and co-operative commercial courses.

In this chapter, however, we shall concern ourselves only with the general and typical high-school commercial course. It should be said, also, that in this chapter we shall make chiefly a descriptive study. This may serve as a basis of fact for Chapter XXI, in which we consider high-school commercial curriculum reform.

THE IMPORTANCE OF THE HIGH-SCHOOL COMMERCIAL COURSE

Enough has been said in Chapter X concerning the beginnings of commercial work in secondary schools to make unnecessary any historical statement in this place. So also the opening chapter of this volume in depicting the growth and position of business education gave in considerable detail the statistics relating to high-school students in commercial courses. It may be well to remind ourselves, however, that the number of high-school commercial students increased from slightly over 15,000 to over 278,000, an increase of more than 1,700 per cent, in the twenty-five years between 1893 and 1918.[1] Many of the large city high schools have between 30 and 40 per cent of their students in commercial courses. A considerable percentage of schools have between 40 and 50 per cent in this work. Furthermore, it is well to remember that some twenty cities have large high schools of commerce in which all of the students are taking commercial courses. Once one sees clearly the implications of these statistics and recalls the fact that it is to the secondary school that we are at present looking for a somewhat liberal training for large numbers, the significant position of the commercial course in secondary schools becomes apparent.

To gather the data upon which this chapter is based a questionnaire was sent to each high school, excepting high schools of commerce, which was listed in the report of the Commissioner of Education as having over 200 pupils in commercial courses.[2] There were 192 such schools. In addition to these, thirty-three questionnaires were sent to high schools having between 150 and 200 students in commercial work.

One hundred and thirty-six questionnaires, received from twenty-six of the thirty-six states included in the Commissioner's report, were returned in time to be included in the tabulations which were made.

THE LENGTH OF COMMERCIAL COURSES

One hundred and twenty-six schools reported that a four-year commercial course is offered. This is 90 per cent of the 136 that reported. Forty-five schools, 32.3 per cent, reported that a

[1] The latest date for which accurate figures are available.

[2] This questionnaire was the basis of a monograph by the author entitled *A Survey of Commercial Education in the Public High Schools of the United States*. "Supplementary Educational Monographs," Vol. II, No. 5. Published by the University of Chicago, 1919. This chapter, due to the courtesy of the publisher, the School of Education of the University of Chicago, is in considerable measure an adaptation of certain parts of that publication.

four-year course and a short course were given, and eleven schools, 8 per cent, reported a short course only. Fifty-six schools, 41.19 per cent, reported short courses. The term "short course" is used here to indicate any commercial course of less than four years, but it should be observed that there have developed in secondary commercial work short courses of two very distinct types. The first, which is by far the more common, is the course of one, two, or three years which usually, though not always, terminates in securing for the student some definite diploma or certificate, and which is designed purely to meet the demands of those students who wish to be rapidly qualified for clerical positions.

The second type of short course is commonly called the postgraduate short course. It is, as the term implies, a course that is offered essentially to students who have completed their high-school work. The Dorchester High School of Boston, Massachusetts, the East Orange High School of East Orange, New Jersey, the Madison High School of Madison, Wisconsin, all reported a short course of this type. Since the questionnaires were returned the city of Chicago has established several postgraduate short commercial courses in different sections of the city. Chicago's experience as well as that of others of these schools is discussed in Chapter XX.

LENGTH OF THE SHORT COURSE

Fifty-six schools, 41.1 per cent of those reporting, indicated that a short course was offered. The length of these short

TABLE XXXII

LENGTHS OF SHORT COURSES IN COMMERCIAL WORK IN 56 SCHOOLS*

Schools Reporting	Length of Courses			
	3 Years	2½ Years	2 Years	1 Year
No. of schools reporting...	16	1	35	8
Percentage of total.......	28.5	1.8	62.5	14.2

* Some schools report several short courses of different lengths.

courses varies from one to three years. The two-year course is the most popular of the short courses. Thirty-five, 62.5 per cent of the fifty-six schools reporting short courses, reported two-year courses. Table XXXII shows the variation in length of the short courses.

REQUIREMENTS OF COMMERCIAL TECHNICAL SUBJECTS

The questionnaire asked for a list of subjects required of students in the commercial course. In the tabulations the subjects were grouped according to a classification which will be explained as each group is discussed. The first classification considered included the technical subjects. This term is used to include the courses which train primarily in technical skill. The tabulations here presented refer only to the four-year course. No effort is made to summarize the technical subjects required in short courses. Stenography, typewriting, and bookkeeping predominate in the short course. These studies are usually arranged in the way that will best fit the length of the course, and they generally occupy all the time that is available. Under such circumstances it is obvious that a tabulation showing the variation in organization would indicate chiefly the varying length of the courses themselves. English—sometimes business English—penmanship, commercial arithmetic, and an elementary science are not infrequently included.[1] Usually, however, the curricula are prima facie clerk schools, masquerading under the deluding name of business courses.

The technical requirements of the four-year course are set forth in Table XXXIII.[2] Inasmuch as commercial education in American public schools had its beginning in bookkeeping, which was shortly followed by typewriting and stenography, it might seem reasonable to believe that all matters relating to these subjects would be fairly well standardized. As a matter of fact, the table shows that there is considerable lack of uniformity regarding all of them. In the teaching of bookkeeping, for instance, the reports show that the courses range from one-half year to four years. Two years is clearly the most common period to

[1] See Table XVI for non-technical subjects in short courses.

[2] In considering the variations in length of courses it should be remembered that the number of hours a week is a variable. The degree of variability was not brought out.

devote to bookkeeping. Nearly one-half of the 121 schools reporting, 49.5 per cent, have fixed upon two years as the requisite time. The remaining 50 per cent vary widely. Fourteen schools, or 11.5 per cent, reported that one year is given to bookkeeping. Nearly as many, 10.8 per cent of the schools reporting, have one and one-half-year courses, while a surprisingly large number, 14 per cent, utilize three years in the

TABLE XXXIII

LENGTH OF TIME REQUIRED FOR TECHNICAL SUBJECTS IN FOUR-YEAR COMMERCIAL COURSES IN PUBLIC HIGH SCHOOLS

Years Required	Bookkeeping		Typewriting		Stenography		Commercial Arithmetic	
	Schools Requiring (of 121 Reporting)		Schools Requiring (of 112 Reporting)		Schools Requiring (of 116 Reporting)		Schools Requiring (of 114 Reporting)	
	Number	Percentage	Number	Percentage	Number	Percentage	Number	Percentage
1/3	......	......	......	......	......	......	1	0.8
1/2	4	3.3	1	0.9	1	0.8	35	30.7
3/4	......	......	......	......	......	......	1	0.8
1	13	11.5	15	13.4	9	7.7	72	63.1
1 1/2	13	10.8	6	5.4	5	4.3	3	2.6
1 3/4	1	0.83	......	......	......	......	......	......
2	60	49.5	54	48.2	80	68.9	2	1.7
2 1/2	7	5.7	9	8.0	7	6.0	......	......
3	17	14.0	22	19.6	11	9.4	......	......
3 1/2	1	0.83	1	0.9	1	0.8	......	......
4	4	3.3	4	3.6	2	1.7	......	......

teaching of bookkeeping. Four schools, or 3.3 per cent, spread their course over four years, and an equal number require only one-half year.

In typewriting, the lack of uniformity is not quite so pronounced. Of the 112 reporting schools, 48.2 per cent have fixed upon two years for their typewriting course. In this work, however, as in bookkeeping, courses vary from one-half year to four years. Of the schools reporting, 13.4 per cent require a one-year course, 5.4 per cent require one and one-half years, 8 per cent do the work in two and one-half years, 19.6 per cent have a three-year course, and 3.6 per cent have a four-year course.

In stenography more emphasis has been put upon the two-year period than in bookkeeping, although the two-year course has apparently not been so generally adopted as in typewriting. Of 116 schools reporting, 68.9 per cent give two years to stenography, 7.7 per cent give their work in one year, 6 per cent in two and one-half years, 9.4 per cent require three years, and 1.7 per cent require four years of training.

A total of 114 schools reported concerning the length of time required in commercial arithmetic. Of these, seventy-two, 63.1 per cent, give a one-year course. The half-year course is also popular and is used in 30.7 per cent of the reporting schools. Only two schools reported courses in commercial arithmetic extending over a two-year period. Three schools reported a requirement of one and one-half years.

The lack of uniformity which exists in the length of courses in these technical subjects, where one naturally expects a considerable degree of standardization, is indicative of the uncertainty that seems to pervade commercial education in high schools. There is some reason, however, to believe that the two-year courses in bookkeeping, stenography, and typewriting have been emphasized for administrative reasons. Our study has shown that business colleges throughout the country give much more intensive courses in these technical subjects, and, so far as the technical training is concerned, these colleges appear to turn out a product quite equal to that which the public high school produces. There is nothing to indicate that the same work could not be accomplished in the same manner in high schools. Furthermore, and perhaps more to the point, there is nothing to indicate that a careful study has been made to determine the length of time necessary for the acquirement of proficiency in these technical subjects. It is common conversation among school people that technical courses fit well into a two-year plan, yet the reports indicate that many schools believe that they can be fitted into other plans. Noticeably lacking is a standard time for technical courses, based on careful experiment in teaching the subjects referred to.

NON-TECHNICAL SUBJECTS IN THE SHORT COURSE

In a consideration of non-technical subjects, it appears advisable to discuss English separately. One hesitates to classify it as a technical subject, and yet it can hardly be grouped with the distinctly non-technical work. Of the fifty-six schools reporting short courses, forty-five gave data on the English requirements in these courses. These data are given in Table XXXIV. This report indicates that English is a subject which has secured a place even in courses so largely given to narrow utilitarian uses as the short commercial courses. A comparison of this table with Table XXXII reveals some interesting facts. Table XXXII indicates that 28.5 per cent of the schools giving short courses have three-year courses. Table XXXIV shows

TABLE XXXIV

ENGLISH REQUIREMENTS OF THE SHORT COURSE

(45 Schools Reporting)

3 YEARS		2 YEARS		1 YEAR	
Number Schools	Percentage	Number Schools	Percentage	Number Schools	Percentage
11	24.4	33	73.3	1	2.2

that almost the same percentage, 24.4 per cent, require three years of English. Of the schools reporting short courses, 62.5 per cent give two-year courses. Of the short courses reported, 73.3 per cent require two years of English. Evidently English is usually a required subject throughout the short course.

OTHER NON-TECHNICAL SUBJECTS IN THE SHORT COURSE

A consideration of the non-technical subjects other than English in the short course brings out the lamentable paucity of general training which is given in these short business courses and the very limited vision of the world with which their graduates enter business. In Table XXXV the non-technical subjects have for convenience been thrown into three groups. Subjects commonly classified as science are grouped together. A second class is arbitrarily called "Social-Business Subjects." These subjects are grouped separately because they include those general subjects which deal with the social forces which surround the business man and which are sometimes taught under the direction of commercial departments. The third group is termed the "General Academic Subjects," and into it are put all subjects not enumerated in the first two groups.

An examination of Table XXXV shows clearly that the short courses are not planned to do much else than train along technical lines. Of the fifty-six schools reporting short courses, approximately 75 per cent require something in the way of science, but only twenty-four, 42 per cent, require at least one social-business subject, and only thirteen, 22.7 per cent, require at least one general academic subject. A closer examination of Table XXXV, however, reveals the infrequency with which any comprehensive demands are made in the fields of general training. Science has apparently made some small claim. Commercial geography, which in this discussion is classed as science, is required more universally than any other subject, and yet it is required in the commercial short courses in but twenty-three cases, 40 per cent of those reporting. Hygiene or physiology, doubtless owing to state law in many cases, is required in twelve of the short courses, 21 per cent of those reporting. Four schools, 7.1 per cent of those reporting, require physiography. A single school requires general science; one other requires physics or chemistry, and two schools require biology. This represents the meager claim which science has been able to make in the short courses, and yet its hold is more substantial than that of any other group of subjects. If we refer to the social-business subjects grouped in Table XXXV, we find that courses of such decidedly business flavor as economics, industrial history, and history of commerce have won almost no recognition. The last two of these are required in two instances, slightly less than

TABLE XXXV

NON-TECHNICAL SUBJECTS REQUIRED IN THE SHORT COURSES, ENGLISH EXCEPTED (56 Schools Reporting)

SCIENCE

Commercial Geography*		Hygiene or Physiology		Physiography		General Science		Biology		Physics or Chemistry		Total Schools Requiring Science	
No. of Schools Requiring	Percentage	No. of Schools Requiring	Percentage	No. of Schools Requiring	Percentage	No. of Schools Requiring	Percentage	No. of Schools Requiring	Percentage	No. of Schools Requiring	Percentage	Number	Percentage
23	40	12	21	4	7.1	1	1.7	2	4	1	1.7	43	76

SOCIAL-BUSINESS SUBJECTS

Industrial History*		History of Commerce		Economics†		Civics†		Commercial Law		Local Industry		Total Schools Requiring	
No. of Schools Requiring	Percentage	No. of Schools Requiring	Percentage	No. of Schools Requiring	Percentage	No. of Schools Requiring	Percentage	No. of Schools Requiring	Percentage	No. of Schools Requiring	Percentage	Number	Percentage
2	4	2	4	1	1.7	7	12	10	18	2	4	24	42

GENERAL ACADEMIC

United States History		Medieval and Modern History		English History		Algebra		Geometry		Modern Language‡		Total Schools Requiring	
No. of Schools Requiring	Percentage	No. of Schools Requiring	Percentage	No. of Schools Requiring	Percentage	No. of Schools Requiring	Percentage	No. of Schools Requiring	Percentage	No. of Schools Requiring	Percentage	Number	Percentage
4	7.1	1	1.7	1	1.7	1	1.7	1	1.7	5	8.5	13	22.7

* In five other cases commercial geography and industrial history were made optional.
† In one other case civics and economics were optional.
‡ In one other case optional with algebra or history.

4 per cent of the schools reporting. Economics is reported as required by only one school, 1.7 per cent of those reporting. Commercial law has a somewhat stronger position, inasmuch as ten schools, 18 per cent, require this subject. Civics is made a requirement in the short course by 7 schools, 12 per cent, and "local industry" is a requirement in two schools, 4 per cent of those reporting.

The general academic subjects are hardly noticed by the formulators of short commercial courses. Four of these schools, 7.1 per cent, require United States history, and five, 8.5 per cent, make some modern-language requirement. Modern and medieval history, English history, algebra, and geometry have, respectively, established places as required subjects in only one school.

THE ENGLISH REQUIREMENTS OF THE FOUR-YEAR COURSE

An examination of the English requirements in the four-year course leads to conclusions similar to those at which one arrives from the study of English in the short courses. Whatever objection against other academic subjects may be advanced

TABLE XXXVI

NUMBER OF YEARS OF ENGLISH REQUIRED IN THE FOUR-YEAR COMMERCIAL COURSE

(115 Schools Reporting)

4 Years		3½ Years		3 Years		2 Years		1 Year	
Number Schools	Percentage	Number Schools	Percentage	Number Schools	Percentage	Number Schools	Percentage	Number Schools	Percentage
86	74.7	6	5.2	18	15.6	4	3.4	1	0.8

by the utilitarian organizers of commercial curricula, it is clear that the need of English is admitted. A total of 115 schools reported on the English requirements in the four-year commercial course, and these reports are summarized in Table XXXVI. An examination of this table shows that approximately three-fourths of these schools have a requirement of four years of

English. Slightly over 15 per cent require three years of English. But a single school, 0.8 per cent, limits the requirements in English to one year, and only four of the 115 schools reporting 3.4 per cent, limit their English requirements to two years. The table shows that 94.5 per cent of the 115 schools require three years or more of English in the four-year commercial course.

OTHER NON-TECHNICAL SUBJECTS IN THE FOUR-YEAR COURSE

Table XXXVII, which presents data gathered concerning the non-technical subjects in the four-year course (English excepted), needs a word or two of introductory explanation. It will be noted that subjects have been classified in three groups: (*a*) "Subjects Dealing with Physical Environment"; (*b*) "Subjects Dealing Directly with Social Environment of Business"; (*c*) "Other Subjects."

Speaking broadly, these three divisions are intended to represent science, social-business subjects (such as those considered in Table XXXV), and the general academic subjects, typically mathematics, language, and history. These headings are used because the first two signify a business point of view from which these non-technical subjects may be regarded. In our study of what business is we have seen that an individual business enterprise must make an adjustment to the complex social relationship of which it is a part. Such social institutions as the market, finanical structures, laws, and business associations combine with a multitude of other mechanisms to make an intricate social environment for a business undertaking. Certain subjects in the curriculum, such as economics, commercial law, civics, and industrial history, are an aid in making the student aware of this social environment and in enabling him to adjust himself to it more effectively.

In the same way the individual business enterprise deals with the facts of physical science and utilizes them constantly in the conduct of its affairs. Some knowledge of this physical environment to which the individual business enterprise must make an adjustment is gained through the study of various sciences.

Students in science and geography have an opportunity to gain something which may be useful in making an adjustment to physical environment.

Nothing need be said in explanation of the column labeled "Other Subjects." They are, as has been suggested, typically mathematics, language, and history.

TABLE XXXVII

SCHOOLS OFFERING AND REQUIRING NON-TECHNICAL SUBJECTS IN THE FOUR-YEAR COMMERCIAL COURSE, ENGLISH EXCEPTED

(136 Schools Reporting)

Of Total Number of Schools Reporting	Subjects Dealing with Physical Environment (Science)		Subjects Dealing Directly with Social Environment of Business (Social Business)		Other Subjects (General Academic)	
	Number	Percentage	Number	Percentage	Number	Percentage
Schools offering to four-year commercial students (136 reporting)..	114	83.0	125	91.1	105	77.2
Schools requiring in first and second years (136 reporting)...........	93*	61.7	30†	22.0	80	59.0
Schools requiring in third and fourth years (123 reporting)...........	10	8.0	106	86.1	62‡	50.4

* In 63 instances this was commercial geography only.

† The distribution in the first and second years among the subjects considered in this group was as follows:

Industrial history	10 schools	Commercial law	9 schools
Economics	4 schools	History of commerce	4 schools
Civics	10 schools	Local industries	3 schools

‡ In 29 cases United States history, or United States history and civics, was the sole requirement.

An examination of Table XXXVII is, at first view, quite heartening to those who hope to see a broader type of education pervading commercial courses. The first column indicates that 114, 83 per cent, of the schools replying to the questionnaire, offer to commercial students courses dealing with physical environment; 125, 91.1 per cent, offer courses dealing with the social environment; while 105, 77.2 per cent, offer some general academic studies. A more careful analysis, however, shows that there is no certainty that these subjects will be taken by commercial students. The requirements in these lines of work are noticeably less than the offerings. The requirements have been divided into those which fall in the first and second years and those which fall in the third and fourth years. In the first and second years ninety-three schools, 61 per cent, make some science requirement of commercial students. This is more gratifying before one realizes that in more than two-thirds of the cases reporting science requirements, commercial geography is the only science required. In the first and second years only thirty schools, 22 per cent, require commercial students to take courses dealing with the social environment in which business is conducted. These requirements, as the footnote indicates, are scattered and varied. The significance of these meager requirements in the first and second years is emphasized when one's attention is called to the large number of students in the four-year courses who do not remain in school beyond the second year. The report of the Commissioner of Education for 1916 regarding the number and percentage of students in each year of high-school courses shows that the condition obtained which is set forth in Table XXXVIII.[1]

TABLE XXXVIII

NUMBER AND PERCENTAGE OF STUDENTS IN EACH YEAR OF PUBLIC HIGH-SCHOOL COURSES IN SCHOOLS REPORTING, 1914–15

FIRST YEAR		SECOND YEAR		THIRD YEAR		FOURTH YEAR	
Number	Percentage	Number	Percentage	Number	Percentage	Number	Percentage
543,206	40.86	354,705	26.69	245,380	18.46	185,873	13.99

There are many reasons for believing that in commercial courses the percentage of students who leave during the first and second years is somewhat higher than the averages quoted in Table XXXVIII, yet this table indicates that more than 67

[1] *Report of the Commissioner of Education, for the Year Ended June 30, 1916*, II, 448.

per cent of the high-school students leave without beginning their third year's work.

In the third and fourth years, as indicated in Table XXXVII, science is required in ten schools, 8 per cent of those reporting. The studies in the social-business group, however, obtain a noticeable prominence in the third and fourth years. Of the schools reporting, 106, 86.1 per cent, require one or more of the social-business group of studies. In few cases is there much plan or organization shown in these requirements, but it is at least satisfactory to notice that there is a keen realization of the need of this type of work for business students. Apparently the tendency is to crowd this work into the last two years at the expense of science in this period and at the expense of the first and second years. Science, on the other hand, has its strongest—almost its only—hold in the first two years.

An examination of the general subjects required in the four-year commercial course shows that commercial work and academic training have not established intimate relations. In the first two years 59 per cent of the reporting schools make some requirements, and in the last two years 50 per cent require commercial students to take some general subject or subjects. Usually, however, these requirements are limited, as is shown in the case of the third and the fourth years, in which United States history or United States history and civics is the sole general academic requirement in twenty-nine of the sixty-two schools that require some general academic work.

SOME CONCLUSIONS FROM THE PRECEDING DATA

Three conclusions are inevitable from a review of the data which we have been considering. The first of these conclusions is that the high-school commercial course is still dominated by heredity. It is still in the grip of its inheritance from the business colleges from which it so largely sprang. Brought into the secondary-school world to compete with private commercial education, fathered in its beginnings almost entirely by the graduates of business colleges, finding its ideals largely in an imitation of its competitors, the high-school commercial course has in great measure remained as it began—a technical training course, giving instruction in mechanical routine. In performing this function it has been encouraged by business men and business conditions. We have surveyed some of the characteristics of business growth and change which during the past fifty years have been conducive to the persistence of this type of training. The developing aspects of modern business have kept in the minds of business managers the need of clerical performance at the same time that increasing size, risk, and complexity have made industrial and commercial undertakings increasingly forbidding, if not impossible, to a great number of persons. These conditions have increased the inherent tendency of the high-school commercial course to imitate the business college.

The second conclusion derived from these data, and one that is akin to the first, is that the commercial course has never clearly allied itself with the traditional purposes of American high schools. There has been an attachment, but not a coalescence. The traditional courses of the high school have been organized into various groups under various heads, but always—poor as the accomplishment may have been—the high-school function has been conceived as one of socialization. In this aim the high-school commercial course has not liberally participated. Bound by its traditions and encouraged by circumstances, it has adhered to its narrow utilitarian ends.

The third conclusion follows from the second. The possibilities of the high-school commercial course, either as a utilitarian, or as a social course, have not been perceived, or, if they have been perceived, that perception has not been expressed by an adequate organization of work.

THE SOCIAL-BUSINESS SUBJECTS IN THE CONTEMPORARY HIGH-SCHOOL COMMERCIAL COURSE

As has been stated in Chapter X, late years have seen appearing in the high school certain new subjects dealing with social relations. Business has not formulated its feeling of its social relations. Producers talk broadly of the market, the financial situation, the administration's attitude, bad times, labor conditions, booms, business risks, and the public without always distinguishing between these factors or analyzing them in relation to one another. Neither has the secondary educator yet analyzed the social complex of which each business is a part, but has met this vague and general demand of business with general courses in economics, industrial history, histories of commerce, commercial geography, business writing, commercial law, and sometimes commercial organization.

These subjects that have more recently come into the high school have not all found place in the commercial department.[1] One inquiry of the questionnaire dealt with a number of these social-business subjects without regard to the claims of various departments. The effort was made to determine how far they are made effective in presenting to the student a reasonably comprehensive view of the social significance of business and the social implications of the technical work in any business enterprise.

The selected group of social-business subjects considered were:

Industrial history	Commercial law
History of commerce	Salesmanship
Economics	Advertising
Commercial geography	Commercial organization

Business English

The questions asked concerning these subjects were designed to learn: (*a*) the number and percentage of schools teaching these subjects; (*b*) the lengths of courses offered; (*c*) to what extent courses are required and in what years; (*d*) in what year courses are elective or required; (*e*) by what department courses are directed; (*f*) by teachers of what other subjects the courses are taught; (*g*) difficulties and problems in the work; (*h*) texts used; (*i*) purposes and methods employed. This last question was asked only concerning salesmanship, advertising, business English, and commercial organization.

[1] An argument, not uncommonly violent, rages in the high schools as to whether commercial English belongs to the English department or to the commercial department.

Not particularly related to the general purpose of this question, but intended to bring out the extent to which certain new courses are taught, a tenth subdivision was included in this question. This asked merely whether any work in office appliances, banking, and commercial designing was given.

To summarize the replies to these questions required that at least eight answers be noted and tabulated for each of nine questions for the 136 schools that replied. The summaries are set forth in the tables that follow.

REQUIREMENTS AND ELECTIVES IN SOCIAL-BUSINESS SUBJECTS

Table XXXIX presents the requirements and electives in this group of studies as they were reported by the schools to which the questionnaires were sent. A moment's study of this

TABLE XXXIX

REQUIREMENTS AND ELECTIVES IN A SELECTED GROUP OF SOCIAL-BUSINESS SUBJECTS

Subject	Number Reporting	Percentage of the Reporting Schools	Requiring		Elective	
			Number	Percentage of Those Offering	Number	Percentage of Those Offering
Industrial history	43	31.6	31	72	12	28
History of commerce	31	22	25	80.6	6	19.3
Economics	82	61	49	59.7	33	40.2
Commercial geography	119	87.3	94	78.9	25	21
Commercial law	118	86.8	90	76.2	28	23.7
Business English	73	53.6	64	87.6	9	12.3
Salesmanship	40	29.4	15	37.5	25	62.5
Advertising	24	18.3	8	33.3	16	66.6
Commercial organization	11	8.08	4	36.3	7	63.7

table reveals the fact that some of these subjects are much more widely taught than are others. Commercial geography and commercial law are far in the lead. Of the reporting schools, 87.3 per cent and 86.8 per cent, respectively, indicated that these courses were given. Economics ranks next in popularity. Sixty-one per cent of the reporting schools indicated that this subject is given. Business English is reported in slightly over 50 per cent of the reporting schools. Industrial history and salesmanship are each taught in about 30 per cent of the high schools reporting, history of commerce in 22 per cent, advertising in 18 per cent, commercial organization in 8 per cent.

Schools which offer these selected subjects by no means universally require them, although in those studies which are more commonly offered the percentage of requirement is high. The history of commerce, commercial geography, commercial law, and business English are all required in more than three-quarters of the schools where they are offered. Industrial history is required in 72 per cent of the schools which offer it. Next is economics, which is required in 59 per cent of the schools reporting it. Commercial organization, advertising, and salesmanship are, respectively, demanded of the pupil in slightly more than one-third of the schools which offer these subjects.[1]

VARIETY IN LENGTH OF COURSES

That the content of these social-business subjects is far from standardized and varies greatly in the various high schools is indicated by a study of the lengths of courses reported. The variations in some of the subjects are almost bewildering. Advertising, for example, is taught in courses of the following lengths: two years, one year, one-half year, one-third year, one-quarter year, and one-tenth year. The half-year course has apparently found more favor than any other length of course. In 54 per cent of the schools reporting, this is the preferred length of course. The other courses vary from 16 per cent of the reporting schools to 4 per cent of them. An examination of Table XL, in which the variation in lengths of courses is indicated, shows that advertising is no exception.

Business English, for instance, in 9 per cent of the cases reported, is taught for four years; in 6 per cent of the cases reported, for three years; and in 23 per cent of the cases, for two years. Twenty-seven per cent of the schools which reported teach the subject in a one-year course, while 31 per cent give a half-year's work.

The length of salesmanship courses is almost as varied. Two schools reported a course two years in length. From this

[1] The availability of good text is no doubt an important factor in determining the extent of these courses. They are also more difficult to give in small schools.

extreme the courses are reported shorter by gradations to quarter-year courses which are offered by four schools, 10 per cent of those giving work in salesmanship.

TABLE XL

LENGTHS OF COURSES OF A SELECTED GROUP OF SOCIAL-BUSINESS SUBJECTS

Subject	Length of Course in Years	Schools Offering Courses of Each Length	
		Number	Percentage of Those Reporting
Industrial history (44 schools reporting)	2	1	2.2
	1½	1	2.2
	1	21	47.7
	½	21	47.7
History of commerce (31 schools reporting)	1½	1	3.2
	1	9	29
	½	21	67.7
Economics (84 schools reporting)	1	22	26.1
	½	61	73.8
	1/10	1	1.1
Commercial geography (119 schools reporting)	2	1	0.8
	1	56	47
	½	62	52.1
Commercial law (116 schools reporting)	1	29	25
	½	87	75
Business English (76 schools reporting)	4	7	9.2
	3	5	6.5
	2	18	23.7
	1½	1	1.3
	1	21	27.5
	½	24	31.5
Salesmanship (40 schools reporting)	2	2	5
	1	10	25
	½	23	57.5
	⅓	1	2.5
	¼	4	10
Advertising (24 schools reporting)	2	2	8.3
	1	4	16.6
	½	13	54.1
	¼	3	12.5
	⅓	1	4.1
	1/10	1	4.1
Commercial organization (10 schools reporting)	1	3	30
	½	6	60
	⅓	1	10

In subjects where textbooks are available there is a less noticeable variation in the lengths of the courses which are given. Industrial history was reported once as a two-year course; it was reported once as a year-and-a-half course, while twenty-one schools require it as one-year and half-year courses, respectively. The history of commerce is reported in one instance as given for a year and a half, though it has quite generally settled into a year's or a half-year's work.

Commercial law, economics, and commercial geography have apparently reached a stage of quite uniform practice. In 75 per cent of the reporting schools commercial law is a half-year course, and in 25 per cent it is a one-year course. In 73.8 per cent of the reported cases economics is given for a half-year. In one instance, 1.1 per cent of the reported cases, economics is reported as one-tenth of a year's work. In 26.1 per cent of the schools giving it economics is a one-year subject. Commercial organization, a very recent addition to high-school work, is reported by only ten schools. In these ten schools, however, the course has been organized as a half-year or a one-year study with only a single exception, in which it is reported as a course lasting one-third of a year.

As has been suggested in a preceding section, it is unjustifiable to conclude from the fact that the length of a course has become standardized that the proper length of time for giving that work has been ascertained by any clearly thought-out or scientific means. All too frequently convenience of organization with other work proves to be the final factor in determining the length of a course.

HOW SOCIAL-BUSINESS SUBJECTS ARE DIRECTED

It is said that an oriental who has been given a fortune will produce a palace and a harem, while an Englishman or a Yankee will turn the same material into a factory or a railroad. A child with a box of wet clay will make a mud pie, but with the same substance a sculptor produces a work of art. The principle holds good in teaching. The interests of pedagogues determine in no small degree the results which are produced with courses.

It is pertinent, therefore, to ask who directs the social-business subjects in the high school. Table XLI presents the data collected on this matter. It shows quite clearly that there is disagreement as to the departments to which these various subjects should belong.

Commercial law is directed by the commercial department in 92.3 per cent of the reported cases. Salesmanship is given to the commercial department in 91 per cent of the reporting schools.

TABLE XLI

METHODS OF DIRECTING SOCIAL-BUSINESS SUBJECTS

Subject	No. of Schools Reporting Method of Direction	Number and Percentage of Schools Reporting These Subjects Directed by:					
		Commercial Department		Other than Commercial Department		Combination of Commercial and Other Departments	
		Number	Percentage	Number	Percentage	Number	Percentage
Industrial history	33	12	36.3	18	54.5	3	9
History of commerce	23	15	62.2	7	30.4	1	4.3
Economics	66	24	36.3	39	59	3	4.5
Commercial geography	89	76	85.3	11	12.3	3	3.3
Commercial law	91	84	92.3	5	5.4	2	2.1
Business English	57	32	56.1	22	38.5	3	5.8
Salesmanship	34	31	91.1	2	5.8	1	2.9
Advertising	22	18	81.8	4	18.1	....	....
Commercial organization	9	8	88.8	1	11.1	....	....

Advertising, commercial organization, and commercial geography are each directed by the commercial department in more than 80 but less than 90 per cent of the cases where these subjects are given.

Industrial history which is thought of by many as a subject very intimately related to business is directed by some department other than the commercial in more than 54 per cent of the schools where it is taught. In only 36 per cent of such schools does the commercial department direct this work. The history of commerce (is it because the term "commerce" is in the subject?) fares somewhat better from the point of view of the commercial department. More than 62 per cent of the schools which reported this subject allow the commercial department to direct it. It is directed by other departments in slightly over 30 per cent of the cases reported.

One may well wonder how closely economics is related to practical matters in secondary schools when he observes that in 59 per cent of the schools where it is offered, it is taught by some department other than the commercial. In only slightly over a third of the instances where this subject appears does the commercial department direct its destiny. There is reason to believe, although there is no evidence in these statistics to support the theory, that economics and industrial history are both largely in the hands of history departments. These subjects, especially economics, were in the high-school curriculum before commercial work made its appearance. Because they were associated with the history department in those early days, disassociation has not taken place.

It is interesting to notice that in a considerable number of instances the social-business subjects are directed by a combination of the commercial department and other departments. Industrial history is thus treated in 9 per cent of the schools which reported it. Advertising and commercial organization are in no cases thus handled, but the history of commerce, economics, business English, salesmanship, commercial geography, and even commercial law have a dual direction occasionally indicated.

WHO TEACHES SOCIAL-BUSINESS SUBJECTS?

Of perhaps greater significance than the departments which direct courses is the teacher who teaches them. As the teachers' interests are bent, so will the course be inclined. Something regarding the teachers' interests can be gleaned from the group of subjects which they are teaching. What other subjects, then, are being taught by the teachers of social-business subjects? Table XLII gives in tabulated form a classification of teachers who present these subjects to students. In this table teachers have been grouped in three classes: teachers of commercial subjects only, teachers of other subjects only, and teachers of both commercial and other subjects. This table shows a situation quite similar to that indicated in Table XLI. Fifty per cent of the industrial history courses are taught by teachers of some department other than the commercial department. In 25 per cent of the instances named the teachers of the commercial department give this work. The history of commerce is taught by teachers of commercial subjects only, in 45 per cent of the schools which reported; by teachers of other subjects only, in the

TABLE XLII

NUMBER OF TEACHERS GIVING SELECTED GROUPS OF SOCIAL-BUSINESS SUBJECTS

Subject	No. of Schools Reporting Class of Teachers	Number and Percentage of Schools Reporting These Subjects Taught by Teachers of:					
		Commercial Subjects Only		Other Subjects Only		Both Commercial and Other Subjects	
		Number	Percentage	Number	Percentage	Number	Percentage
Industrial history....	28	7	25	14	50	7	25
History of commerce.	20	9	45	9	45	2	10
Economics..........	66	21	31.8	34	51.6	11	16.6
Commercial geography..........	94	58	61.7	22	23.4	14	14.9
Commercial law.....	91	65	71.4	12	13.1	14	15.3
Business English....	52	27	51.9	21	40.3	4	7.6
Salesmanship.......	25	19	76	5	20	1	4
Advertising.........	19	12	63.1	7	36.8	....	....
Commercial organization.............	7	6	85.7	....	....	1	14.2

same percentage of cases; and in 10 per cent of the reported cases by teachers of commercial subjects and other subjects as well. In the teaching of economics, as might be expected from our previous observations, teachers of other subjects than commercial predominate, having the course in their hands in 51 per cent of the instances given. Teachers of commercial subjects only, teach economics in 31 per cent of the schools where this work is taught. In 16 per cent of the cases an instructor with varied teaching interests handles the class. Commercial geography and commercial law are quite thoroughly in the hands of commercial teachers, these subjects being thus taught in 61 per cent and 71 per cent, respectively, of the reporting schools. In approximately 15 per cent of the reporting schools each subject is taught by teachers of both commercial and other subjects, leaving 23.4 per cent of the geography and 40 per cent of the commercial-law classes with teachers of other subjects only. The teaching staff of business English is rather evenly divided. Slightly over half the teachers of this subject are of the strictly commercial type. Forty per cent teach other subjects only, presumably English in most cases. Commercial organization is in no case reported as being entirely out of the hands of commercial teachers. In one instance the reply was made that a teacher who taught some other subjects as well as commercial subjects was giving the work. In all other instances commercial organization is in the hands of commercial teachers.

Salesmanship and advertising are not so generally taught by commercial teachers as is commercial organization. In only three-quarters of the schools giving the work is salesmanship guided by strictly commercial teachers, while advertising is in the hands of such teachers in less than two-thirds of the schools which teach the subjects.

CORRELATION OF SOCIAL-BUSINESS SUBJECTS WITH OTHER SUBJECTS

Anyone who has taught economics, commercial law, industrial history, commercial organization, salesmanship, history of industry, or commercial geography, or who has studied more than one of these subjects, knows the intimacy with which the subject-matter is interrelated. Universities in some instances make rather careful efforts to have these subjects taught in such a way that the interrelations may be as apparent as possible. Teachers of these courses are often asked to visit, if not to take, allied work. The Doctor's degree is not given until a sufficient sequence has been taken to insure a somewhat comprehensive point of view. Such measures, whether or not the teacher is aware of it, result in aiding the student to fuse into a unified intelligence the various separate courses.

How far is an effort made to correlate these social-business courses in the high school? A query attempting to gain information on this matter was included in the questionnaire. The tabulated results are shown in Table XLIII. Before that table is examined, however, attention should be called to the fact that the query regarding correlation was not answered in as many cases as might be hoped for. The returns seemed to indicate that the idea of correlating courses was unthought-of in a great many schools. Even in schools where a great variety

TABLE XLIII

SCHOOLS NOT REPORTING CORRELATION COMPARED WITH SCHOOLS WHICH MIGHT HAVE REPORTED CORRELATION

Subject	Number and Percentage of Schools Not Reporting Correlation		Total Number of Schools Which Might Have Reported Correlation
	Number	Percentage	
Industrial history	20	45.5	44
History of commerce	12	40	30
Economics	48	57.1	84
Commercial geography	69	57	121
Commercial law	76	63.3	120
Business English	41	52.5	78
Salesmanship	22	53.6	41
Advertising	5	20.4	24
Commercial organization	7	63.4	11

of social-business subjects were offered, the question regarding correlation of any of these subjects was sometimes passed by with no comment, either affirmative or negative. One would be almost justified in concluding that in a considerable number of the cases where no report was made regarding correlation, correlation was absent.

Table XLIII may be used in conjunction with Table XLIV. It indicates the number and percentage of schools which did not report correlation as contrasted with the total number which might have reported correlation of subjects. This table needs little interpretation. The more recent additions to the commercial curriculum, such as advertising, seem to have more frequent correlation than longer-established subjects, such as commercial law and economics. Advertising was reported to be correlated with other subjects in all but 20 per cent of the schools giving it. No report of correlation was made for commercial law in 63 per cent of the schools reporting on the question. No correlation was reported for economics in 57 per cent of the schools giving the work. It is unsafe to generalize from this, however, for commercial organization, which is still too new an addition to the curriculum to be taught in many

TABLE XLIV

CORRELATION OF A SELECTED GROUP OF SOCIAL-BUSINESS SUBJECTS WITH OTHER SUBJECTS

Subject	No. of Schools Reporting Correlation	Number and Percentage of Schools Reporting Correlation of Commercial Subjects with:					
		Commercial Subjects Only		Other Subjects Only		Commercial and Other Subjects	
		Number	Percentage	Number	Percentage	Number	Percentage
Industrial history	24	13	54.1	7	29.1	4	16.6
History of commerce	18	16	88.8	1	5.5	1	5.5
Economics	36	14	38.8	10	27.7	12	33.3
Commercial geography	52	28	53.8	13	25	11	21.1
Commercial law	44	32	72.7	5	11.3	7	15.9
Business English	37	25	67.5	5	13.5	7	18.9
Salesmanship	19	14	73.6	3	15.7	2	10.5
Advertising	19	12	63.1	5	26.3	2	10.5
Commercial organization	4	4	100	....	....	....	....

schools, is as isolated, apparently, as is commercial law. As in the case of the latter study, commercial organization is not reported as correlated in 63 per cent of the schools teaching it. Three possible types of correlation were indicated in the questionnaire: correlation with commercial subjects only; correlation with other subjects only; correlation with commercial and other subjects. In those schools where correlation is attempted there is a considerable variation of this sort of effort. In every instance reported there is more correlation with technical commercial subjects than with other subjects. Commercial organization was reported to be taught in correlation with commercial subjects only, in 100 per cent of the cases where correlation is tried. Commercial law was reported taught in correlation with commercial subjects only, in 72 per cent of the correlation instances, as compared with 11 per cent of cases in which it is correlated with other subjects only, and 15.9 per cent of the instances of reported correlation in which it is related both to commercial and to other subjects. History of commerce is correlated with technical commercial subjects in 88 per cent, with other subjects only, in 5.5 per cent, and with other subjects and commercial subjects in 5.5 per cent of the instances where any correlation is made. Salesmanship was reported correlated with commercial subjects only, in 73 per cent of the cases of correlation, with other subjects only, in 15.7 per cent, and with both classes of subjects in 10.5 per cent. Advertising, in 63.1 per cent of the cases, was reported correlated with commercial subjects only, in 26.3 per cent with other subjects only, and in 10.5 per cent with both commercial and other subjects. Business English is correlated with business subjects only, in 67.5 per cent of the schools that correlate it with other work. It is correlated in 13.5 per cent with other subjects only, and in 18.9 per cent with both classes of subjects.

Commercial geography, in 53.8 per cent of the instances given, is correlated with commercial work only, with other subjects only in 25 per cent of the cases reporting, and with commercial and other subjects in 21 per cent of the given instances. Correlation in economics, as might be expected from the fact that it is so frequently taught by non-commercial teachers, is even more varied in correlations than commercial geography. In 38 per cent of the cases given it is correlated with commercial subjects alone, in 27 per cent of the cases with other subjects only, and in exactly one-third of the given instances it is correlated with commercial and other subjects. The correlation attempted with industrial history is likewise varied. Fifty-four per cent of the reporting schools correlate this with nothing but commercial subjects; 29 per cent relate it to other subjects only, and 16 per cent combine it with commercial and other subjects.

Many of the high schools in reporting the correlation which they attempted gave specific instances of courses taught in combination. Several such reports of combinations are given below:

- Shorthand, Typewriting, Spelling, Office procedure, Business English
- Bookkeeping, Business arithmetic, Penmanship
- Economics, Civics
- Economics, Commercial law, Commercial organization
- Physical geography, Commercial geography
- Salesmanship, Advertising
- Commercial law, Oral English
- Shorthand dictation, Commercial law
- Business forms, Penmanship

THREE SPECIAL SUBJECTS

As was indicated at the beginning of this section, a question was asked to determine merely the extent to which office appliances, banking, and commercial designing are given in the secondary-school courses. Table XLV shows in tabulated

TABLE XLV

NUMBER AND PERCENTAGE OF SCHOOLS GIVING WORK IN THREE SPECIAL SUBJECTS

(133 schools made a report on the questions, among which this was included)

Subject	Number	Percentage
Office appliances	89	66.9
Banking	45	33.8
Commercial design	29	21.8

form the replies received. As it easily observable in Table XXVI, a considerable number of secondary schools have introduced courses in these subjects. Especially is the subject of office appliances widely taught. It is perhaps surprising to find work in banking given in a third of the secondary-school commercial courses, and perhaps as much so to see the position of commercial design.

SOME CONCLUSIONS FROM THE FOREGOING DATA

A number of general conclusions are justified from a review of the statistical material which has been presented thus far. First is the fact that the social-business subjects have found their way into the secondary schools to a very considerable degree. Nearly every subject which would be considered as important in a modern university school of commerce has found some place in a secondary-school curriculum. The subjects of this group which are most commonly offered are those which have longest been substantial parts of college and university courses.

A second general conclusion is that the requirements in this group of subjects are not as extensive as the offerings. Requirements are most extensive in those subjects which are most commonly given. There seems to be almost a direct ratio between the percentage of schools offering and the percentage of schools requiring these subjects. One may see this by contrasting commercial law, which is offered in 86 per cent of the reporting schools and required in 76 per cent of the schools where it is offered, with commercial organization, which is offered in only 9 per cent of the reporting schools and is required in only 36 per cent of the schools offering it. From these two conclusions one might draw the inference that although the social-business subjects are widely taught, the definite work accomplished by each of them is not well enough defined or understood to justify the organizers of curricula to build up and require a definite standardized group of studies which shall acquaint the pupil with his social-business world.

Another conclusion, and one which supports the preceding, is that the courses in the subjects here under review are not well enough defined to permit conclusions regarding the length of time which they should be taught. The variation in length of courses as they now exist in secondary schools, especially in the more recently introduced subjects, is evidence of this.

Social-business subjects, directed and taught as they are, sometimes by strictly commercially minded individuals and sometimes by persons of purely classical training, cannot be relied upon to present any definite body of knowledge or consistent point of view. The evidence would seem to show that no definite point of view has been determined and that the results which are obtained with these courses must be varied in the extreme.

The lack of clearly determined purposes and methods is further indicated by the limitations which are reported in correlation. All too many schools report no effort to correlate subjects having such intimate connection as salesmanship, commercial organization, and economics, or accounting, commercial law, and business organization.

The lack of correlation also suggests a great waste of time and effort from overlapping and duplication. The student who studies accounting with no knowledge of business organization must gain a meager view, indeed, of the function of that great science. If the function of accounting is presented in the class specifically devoted to that work, waste of time is certain unless it is closely related to the work done in business organization and commercial law. The same situation is true of commercial law, industrial history, economics, and civics. In each of these, as the texts commonly present the matter, the student comes in contact with such institutions as the Interstate Commerce Commission. Each book gives certain facts. Unless there is careful correlation, perhaps more careful than is conceivably possible with the present textbooks, there is much duplication. Unfortunately the duplication is not usually from such different points of view that the student's knowledge is greatly widened. Few, indeed, are the high-school graduates who think of the Interstate Commerce Commission or similar institutions in terms of function, or who could show the relation between such an organization and overhead costs of which they have learned only in accounting.

Some considerable correlation of work, however, exists, and the instances which are reported augur well for what may be expected in the future. Handicapped as he is by textbooks of narrow view, public demand of still more limited vision, utilitarian traditions, and more work than any person can do well, it is small wonder that the high-school teacher of social-business subjects has not effected the correlation and organization of work which might be desired.

Finally, the situation shows a need for aid. Aid is needed in the preparation of texts which, dealing with this complex material of the social-business world, shall so organize it that duplication can be largely eliminated. The material must also be organized to bring out the subtle interrelations of the elements involved so far as that is possible. The subject-matter must be of such a character that predetermined purposes can, in general, be reached.

Aid is also needed, and from the outside, for teachers. The insistent and too numerous duties of the high-school teacher will not allow him at first hand to effect the reorganization which is desirable. A point of view, a body of material, and even methods may, through the proper machinery, be conveyed to the high-school teaching force. It is only from those who are removed from the details, who "can go outside of the house to look at it," that such aid can best come.

POLICIES AND METHODS IN THE HIGH-SCHOOL COMMERCIAL WORK

Inquiries were made to gather data on certain policies and methods now employed in high-school commercial work. Table XLVI presents a tabulation of the answers concerning election of courses, requirements for boys and girls and general aims of the course.

A very general election of studies other than commercial requirements seems to prevail in the business courses of secondary schools. In only 18.5 per cent of the reporting schools are commercial students restricted in their electives, once their commercial requirements are satisfactorily met. In the other 81.5 per cent a free election of studies is allowed. These percentages are on the basis of 119 schools which reported on this particular question.

TABLE XLVI

PURPOSES AND POLICIES IN COMMERCIAL COURSES

NUMBER AND PERCENTAGE OF 119 REPORTING SCHOOLS WHICH:				NUMBER AND PERCENTAGE OF 112 REPORTING SCHOOLS WHICH:				NUMBER AND PERCENTAGE OF 116 REPORTING SCHOOLS WHICH:			
Allow General Election of Studies Other than Commercial Requirements		Restrict Election Aside from Commercial Requirements		Make Different Requirements for Boys and Girls		Make No Different Requirements for Boys and Girls		Attempt to Prepare Only for "Office Work"		Attempt to Fit for Office Work and Business Administration	
Number	Percentage	Number	Percentage	Number	Percentage	Number	Percentage	Number	Percentage	Number	Percentage
97	81.5	22	18.5	3	2.7	109	97.3	71	61.2	45	38.8

REQUIREMENTS FOR BOYS AND GIRLS

One hundred twelve schools reported on the question relating to the different requirements for boys and girls. One hundred nine of this number, 97.3 per cent, reported no different requirements for boys and girls. Two and seven-tenths per cent make some difference in requirements for the sexes. The significance of the situation is apparent when one compares the demands in business for boys with the demands made upon girls. The difference has been presented at some length in the chapters dealing with "What Business Says It Wants."

CERTAIN METHODS USED IN COMMERCIAL TEACHING

Table XLVII presents a tabulation of the replies received to queries concerning certain methods employed in teaching commercial subjects. As this table shows, nearly three-quarters of the reporting schools use lecturers from business life as a means of aiding in commercial work. Approximately two-thirds of the schools which replied to this query indicate the use of business publications.

TABLE XLVII

CERTAIN METHODS USED IN COMMERCIAL WORK

Lecturers from Business Life (110 Reporting)		Business Publications (104 Reporting)		Tests in Typewriting and Stenography Other than Teacher's Judgment (117 Schools Reporting)	
Number Schools Using	Percentage of Those Reporting	Number Schools Using	Percentage of Those Reporting	Number Schools Using	Percentage of Those Reporting
81	73.6	68	65.3	70	59.8

TESTS

The question of standardized measurements in all educational work is one of increasing importance. In response to the question concerning the use of tests other than the teacher's judgments, 59.8 per cent of the schools replying reported the use of tests. These replies gave indications that the tests employed are usually those furnished by textbook and machine companies, such as the Gregg shorthand tests and the Underwood tests in typewriting. So far as can be ascertained, scientific tests to measure progress in skill under standardized conditions have not been worked out and are not applied. As has been already intimated, no one has yet proved what the proper length of the typewriting and stenographic courses should be. Neither has the skill which should be acquired with definite hours of work been ascertained.

TEXTBOOKS IN THE SOCIAL-BUSINESS SUBJECTS

Evidence in plenty was given in the returned questionnaires to show that many of the textbooks now available for use in teaching social-business subjects in the secondary schools are not satisfactory. The authors of textbooks are frequently more mindful of their academic reputation with their colleagues than of the limited ability of high-school students and the limited opportunities and occupied energies of high-school teachers. The result is often a type of text which is likely to be somewhat authoritative upon the subject but unserviceable in its supposed mission.

The lack of proper texts is well appreciated as among the difficulties of high-school teachers and principals. In the reports received on "difficulties or problems in the work" such comments as the following are to be found:

"It is difficult to find a good text that is not too difficult for the second-year students."

"Lack of reference books."

"No suitable textbook exists."

It is interesting to observe that no school reported a difficulty with its commercial-law books. No great amount of criticism of existing texts was reported in connection with the difficulties in teaching advertising and business writing. In all other fields specific criticisms were frequent.[1]

OTHER REPORTED DIFFICULTIES IN SOCIAL-BUSINESS SUBJECTS

Better textbooks are not the only need in a reorganized program for teaching social-business subjects in the secondary schools. The crowded curriculum, the limited ability of young students, the lack of required prerequisites for certain courses, the attitude of the universities in the matter of admission requirements, as well as the limitations in library, laboratory, and museum equipment, are mentioned among the handicaps of teachers.

CONCLUSIONS

Electives for commercial students are, aside from the requirements of the commercial course, usually quite open and free. Is this to the advantage or disadvantage of the student? It may well be contended that the commercial student completing the technical work required of him may through the use of his free electives acquire a fairly broad training. There is no

[1] For a more elaborate discussion of this matter the reader is referred to the author's monograph, *A Survey of Commercial Education in the United States*, chap. iv. The business-English situation was given special attention in an article in the *English Journal*, November, 1918.

doubt that the opportunity of choosing subjects outside of his own field of work is often an advantage to the commercial student. But it is quite as likely that the free election so widely given works to the student's disadvantage. The miscellaneous and assorted fragments from which the student is permitted to choose offer no certainty of a well-balanced intellectual meal. There is reason to believe that much more satisfactory results could be obtained from a wisely directed scheme of requirements, having a predetermined object, and controlling in considerable measure the intellectual environment which surrounds the student. Free election of studies in the commercial course, as elsewhere, is quite consistent with our somewhat overworked policy of laissez faire. Under the influence of thinking in evolutionary terms laissez faire is, however, giving place to regulation, and under the influence of prescience in thought it is giving place to planning. More prescient elements are needed in training for business. But the real function of such elements can be accomplished only by definite requirements.

There is a need for different work for boys and girls. Almost no schools differentiate the courses for boys and girls or offer specialized training to meet the demands made upon boys. Yet a large number of schools agree, and their belief is borne out by other studies, that boys eventually perform quite a different function in business than falls to the lot of women.

A vision of the social significance of business has not been put before the high-school teaching staff. But little material to teach of business as a social activity has been prepared in form suitable for high-school use.

Finally, no secondary institution has organized really thoroughgoing courses clearly designed to train for business administration. The example has not been set, and in education, as elsewhere, progress is made through imitation quite as rapidly as it is induced by homilies.

The fact that a great many secondary commercial teachers use literature and speakers from the business world shows an interest in improvement even though such methods may have little value. In the use, or rather the lack of use, of standardized tests the directors of secondary business courses are not necessarily at fault. Real tests with a scientific basis are lacking, and it is a matter for some commendation that such tests as are available are used by more than half of the secondary schools. It is unfortunate, however, that satisfactory tests are not available and are not in use. There is little in the commercial course as at present organized to lead a child toward the fields of higher education. In addition, commercial graduates are, very commonly, not prepared for college. Universities will not accept, in many instances, the technical courses for college-entrance requirements. This last matter is only another of the ways in which the commercial student is given a faulty training. Lured frequently into a narrow technical course by the false caption "Training for Business," the student, youthful and impressionable, is given no view of the tremendous social significance of his work, and is turned out lacking the desire for more education or, having it, unqualified to proceed.

In the chapters immediately following we shall examine a series of plans that are in operation tending to extend or improve the typical high-school commercial course. In the final chapter curriculum reform in the high-school commercial course is considered.

QUESTIONS FOR DISCUSSION

1. What advantage can you see in studying the high-school commercial course under two phases: (*a*) typical course; (*b*) modern extensions?
2. What types of short courses were reported? Distinguish between these.
3. What variations in length exist in the short courses? How would you account for such variations?
4. What conclusions are justified from a study of the length of time required for technical subjects in four-year commercial courses?
5. How do you account for the fact that English is almost universally required through the commercial courses?
6. What conclusions do you reach from a study of the non-technical subjects in the short courses?
7. Explain what is meant by the heading used in classifying the non-technical subjects in the four-year course.

8. What conclusions do you reach from a study of the non-technical subjects in the four-year course?
9. Does it make any difference whether or not students are given any of the non-technical subjects in their commercial course?
10. Does it make any difference whether non-technical subjects come early or late in the commercial course?
11. What is your reaction toward the "conclusions" given on page 406?
12. Of the group of social-business subjects discussed, what ones have taken the most important hold in high-school courses?
13. What facts were brought out by the inquiry concerning the relation of requirements and offerings of social-business subjects?
14. Does the data given indicate that courses in social-business subjects have reached a point where they can be said to be a part of a well-considered and balanced program?
15. Is it pertinent to inquire what department and what type of teacher teaches the various social-business subjects? Is this inquiry given any pertinence by the unorganized condition of the material and the limitations of existing textbooks?
16. What do you understand to be the meaning of correlation of two subjects? Give an example of how a correlation at some one or more points might be effected in two subjects with which you are familiar.
17. What is your reaction toward the conclusions given on pages 421 and 422.
18. Is it your feeling that requirements as contrasted with election of studies in the commercial course should be increased or lessened?
19. How do you account for the fact that so few schools make any different requirements for boys and girls?
20. List the difficulties which stand in the way of thoroughgoing study of social-business subjects in the secondary-school commercial course.
21. What facts do you observe that seem to you to point toward improvement in secondary business education?
22. What would you think of a proposal to teach no technical subjects such as stenography and typewriting in the commercial course of the secondary school?
23. What would you think of a proposal to teach technical subjects only in the last year of the high-school commercial course?

CHAPTER XVI

THE HIGH SCHOOL OF COMMERCE

The rapid development of commercial courses in secondary schools led naturally enough to interest in high schools definitely devoted to business work.

The first high school of commerce connected with a system of schools and wholly supported by public funds was the Business High School of Washington, D.C. This school was established in 1890. The report of the Business High School for 1890–91 showed that 310 students were enrolled the first year, 160 boys and 150 girls. From 1892 throughout the decade, the superintendent of public schools of Philadelphia stood out for his advocation of the establishment of a commercial high school in that city. Brooklyn and New York, however, were the next cities to establish commercial high schools. High schools of commerce in these two cities were authorized at the same time. The Brooklyn High School was opened in 1899. The High School of Commerce of the City of New York was under construction from 1900 to 1901 and in 1902 reported 410 pupils.

Philadelphia was next, establishing the Commercial High School in 1897.[1] In 1906 the Boston School Committee "undertook the realization of such a school," and in the same year the Boston High School of Commerce was established.[2] Interest in specialized schools of commerce spread until there are now in the United States about twenty such schools. Nearly half of these have come into existence within the last five or six years.

PURPOSES UNDERLYING HIGH SCHOOLS OF COMMERCE

In attempting to arrive at the purpose and rôle of high schools of commerce, it is useful to look at some of the state-

[1] This school has since become known as the William Penn High School.

[2] These data were collected from reports of the superintendents of education of the cities concerned and from correspondence.

ments made by persons responsible for their organization and direction. The statements given below have been compiled from courses of study and other literature of business high schools in 1922.

City A

The distinctive purpose of the business high school is to give business training leading directly to self-support. Emphasis is laid upon the business arts: penmanship, spelling, commercial drawing, arithmetic, bookkeeping, accounting, shorthand, typewriting, and office methods. In the four-year course these are supplemented by studies leading to an understanding of modern industrial activities and relations.

City B

The object of the high school of commerce is to give boys and girls a sound preparation for commercial life. To accomplish this purpose the course provides instruction of two kinds: first, in general high-school subjects; second, instruction in high-school grade in the special subject, commerce. It is to be noted, however, that the general subjects are all taught with the constant view of preparing the student to use them in business life. In like manner all instruction in the school is made to serve the special vocational purpose for which the school exists.

City C

The high school of commerce is a training-school for those boys and girls who are desirous of fitting themselves for positions in the business world. The school prepares for stenographic, bookkeeping, and general office and store positions, giving the thorough and complete training which is demanded today of the beginning office worker.

One of the features of the school is its equipment of modern office machines and appliances, such as adding and calculating machines, bookkeeping machines, duplicators, dictating machines, filing equipment, etc. It is unusual nowadays to find an office without one or more of these special machines. Consequently it is essential to have acquaintance with and training on these modern devices if one wishes to be thoroughly prepared for office work.

The complete course is four years in length and fits the pupil for the best type of office positions. It is possible, however, to take a shorter course of three, or even two, years and receive valuable preparation. Particularly is this true in the case of pupils who are more mature than the average eighth-grade graduate.

City D

The high school offers a four years' course as a preparation for business. A general high-school education is combined with thorough training in penmanship, bookkeeping, shorthand, and typewriting.

The work in commercial lines is begun in the first year with special attention to business English, penmanship, and elementary bookkeeping. Bookkeeping may be continued throughout the four years, typewriting is begun the second year, shorthand the third. Other work, commercial and academic, is pursued at the same time.

Students who graduate are qualified as bookkeepers, salesmen, and stenographers and typists. The school aims, however, not only to train office and store workers, but also to fit for the manufacturing, mercantile, and general business life of the community.

City E

This pamphlet is designed to assist pupils and parents in making a choice of the courses of study as offered by the commercial high school.

There are two courses of study provided for pupils who expect to remain four years in the high school. These are listed as four-year diploma courses. For students who can remain two years there is provided the commercial certificate course. This course offers preparation for stenographic or bookkeeping work, also for steno-bookkeeping positions.

To obtain any adequate knowledge of the work done in high schools of commerce in the United States, a personal investigation is necessary. No report concerning the high schools of commerce is provided by the United States Bureau of Education, or any other general agency. In an effort to secure information relating to the courses given in these institutions, therefore, a questionnaire was used by the writer. The questionnaire was sent out at about the same time that the data presented in Chapter XV were gathered. Information was secured from all but two or three high schools of commerce in existence at that time. A number of new high schools of commerce have come into existence since, and some of the high schools of commerce have made rather radical changes in their programs. A careful effort has been made, however, to compare the courses of most of the newer high schools of commerce with the generalizations reached as a result of the survey, and also to compare the recent statements of courses of study with the ones submitted about four years ago. While there is an occasional sharp divergence, the comparison of the original material with the most recent information shows few important changes. It may be believed, therefore, that the statements made are reasonably valid.

LENGTH OF COURSES IN COMMERCIAL HIGH SCHOOLS

An examination of Table XLVIII shows that there is a considerable lack of uniformity in the length of time required in different commercial high schools for teaching technical subjects. The variation in the length of courses is not so great as

TABLE XLVIII

LENGTH OF TIME REQUIRED FOR TECHNICAL SUBJECTS IN COMMERCIAL HIGH SCHOOLS

(10 Schools Reporting)

Years Required	Bookkeeping		Typewriting		Stenography 9 Schools Reporting		Commercial Arithmetic		Penmanship	
	Number	Percentage	Number	Percentage	Number	Percentage	Number	Percentage	Number	Percentage
½	.....	.....	.....	.....	.....	.....	3	30	.....	.....
1	2	20	.....	.....	.....	.....	4	40	.....	.....
1½	.....	.....	2	20	.....	.....	2	20	.....	.....
2	4	40	3	30	5	55.5	1	10	.....	.....
2½	1	10	.....	.....	.....	.....	.....	.....	.....	.....
3	1	10	4	40	3	33.3	.....	.....	.....	.....
3½	1	10	.....	.....	.....	.....	.....	.....	.....	.....
4	1	10	1	10	1	11.1	.....	.....	.....	.....
Some time	.....	.....	.....	.....	.....	.....	.....	.....	8	80

that found in the commercial courses in general high schools, but it is sufficiently noticeable to indicate that matters of organization, habit, and imitation have been as important as well-considered judgment or sound standards in determining the length of courses.

Four of the ten schools reporting on this question give a two-year course in bookkeeping. Two of the ten limit the course to one year. Every conceivable variation between two and four years is to be found represented. One school gives a course of two and a half years in bookkeeping, one a course of three years, one of three and a half years, and one a course four years in length.

The distribution in length of courses is almost as great in typewriting. Not a single school reports teaching typewriting in less than one and one-half years. Two schools use that length of time; three, or 30 per cent of the total, require two years; four institutions spread typewriting over three years; while one of them requires four years of work in typewriting.

Stenography in high schools of commerce is likewise treated as a course which requires an extended period for its study. Nine schools only reported on stenography, and over 55 per cent of these required two years' work in this subject. Three schools, a third of those reporting, require that stenography be studied for three years, while one makes it a four-year subject.

Commercial arithmetic is not given as extended treatment in high schools of commerce as bookkeeping and stenography. One school gives two years of this work, two a year and one-half, four schools have a one-year course, and three schools cover the ground in one-half year.

Penmanship as a highly organized undertaking does not appear to enter the curricula of commercial high schools. Eight of the ten reporting schools stated that "some time" was given to this subject.

NON-TECHNICAL SUBJECTS IN COMMERCIAL HIGH SCHOOLS

As has been stated in connection with the commercial course in high schools, it seems advisable to discuss English as a non-technical subject in spite of the fact that it has certain technical aspects. Table XLIX shows that English has a value well recognized in high schools of commerce. Seventy per cent of the reporting schools require four years of this subject, one school requires three and one-half years, one other three years; a single school finds two years of English to be enough.

TABLE XLIX

NUMBER OF YEARS OF ENGLISH REQUIRED IN COMMERCIAL HIGH SCHOOLS (10 Schools Reporting)

4 Years		3½ Years		3 Years		2 Years	
Number Schools	Percentage	Number Schools	Percentage	Number Schools	Percentage	Number Schools	Percentage
7	70	1	10	1	10	1	10

CONSIDERATION OF SOCIAL-BUSINESS SUBJECTS

Certain subjects dealing with a combination of social and business factors have been selected for treatment in this discussion of commercial high schools in much the same manner

TABLE L

REQUIREMENTS AND ELECTIVES IN A SELECTED GROUP OF SOCIAL-BUSINESS SUBJECTS

Subject	Number Offering	Required		Elective	
		Number	Percentage of Those Offering	Number	Percentage of Those Offering
Industrial history	5	5	100	0	0
History of commerce	6	6	100	0	0
Economics	8	5	62.5	3	37.5
Commercial geography	10	8	80	2	20
Commercial law	9	7	77.7	2	22.2
Salesmanship	6	2	33.3	4	66.6
Advertising	2	1	50	1	50
Commercial organization	4	4	100	0	0
Business English	7	7	100	0	0

as they were treated in the discussion of the business course in high schools. The requirements and electives in this selected group of subjects, as they were reported by the high schools of commerce, are set forth in Table L.

An examination of this table will indicate that not a single one of this list of subjects has so well established itself as necessary for proper business training as to be required in all of the high schools of commerce replying to the questionnaire. Commercial geography is offered in all of the schools and commercial law in 90 per cent of them, but in two instances each of these subjects are made elective. Commercial organization, business English, industrial history, and history of commerce are the subjects which are required in every instance where they are reported as being offered; but, in the first case, only four schools offer the subject, while business English is offered in only seven schools, and industrial history and history of commerce are given in five and six schools respectively. Eight schools reported that economics is offered, and five of these require that the subject be taken. Salesmanship is required in one-third of the instances in which it is offered, and advertising in one out of the two instances reported.

The length of courses given in these subjects shows almost as little standardization as was noticed in the study of the technical courses. Industrial history extends over two years in one instance, in two cases is taught for a year, and in two cases for a year and a half. History of commerce is taught for a year in five out of the six schools reporting the subject. Economics is a three-year course in one school, a one-year course in four schools, and a half-year course in three schools. Five of the high schools of commerce require commercial geography for a year, in three instances it is a half-year course, in one instance a two-and-a-half-year course, and in one school it is reported as being three-fifths of a year in length. Commercial law has established itself as a one-semester course in more than half of the schools where it is given, five schools giving courses of that length. Three schools give the subject for a year, and one for two fifths of a year. Salesmanship is a one-year course in five out of the six cases, and a half-year course in the other instance. Advertising divides evenly between one-year and half-year courses. Commercial-organization courses vary from one-half year to two years, while courses in business English range from one-half year to four years.

TABLE LI

LENGTHS OF COURSES OF A SELECTED GROUP OF SOCIAL-BUSINESS SUBJECTS

Subject	Length of Course in Years	Schools Offering Courses of Each Length	
		Number	Percentage of Those Reporting
Industrial history (5 schools reporting)	2	1	20
	1	2	40
	½	2	40
History of commerce (6 schools reporting)	1	5	83.3
	½	1	16.6
Economics (8 schools reporting)	3	1	12.5
	1	4	50
	½	3	37.5
Commercial geography (10 schools reporting)	2½	1	10
	1	5	50
	3/5	1	10
	½	3	30
Commercial law (9 schools reporting)	1	3	33.3
	½	5	55.5
	2/5	1	11.1
Salesmanship (6 schools reporting)	1	5	83.3
	½	1	16.6
Advertising (2 schools reporting)	1	1	50
	½	1	50
Commercial organization (4 schools reporting)	2	1	25
	1	1	25
	½	2	50
Business English (8 schools reporting)	4	3	37.5
	2	1	12.5
	1	3	37.5
	½	1	12.5

If anything, this variation in length of courses in these subjects is more marked and striking in the high schools of commerce than it is in commercial courses in high schools. If not actually more varied, it is striking that there should be so much variation in what is supposed to be the leading type of institution in the field of secondary education, and especially that such variety should be found when the total number of instances examined is so small.

CORRELATION OF COURSES

The same consideration is given correlation here as was given to it in the preceding chapter. The data are perhaps less significant because the number of schools considered is so much smaller. Roughly, half of the schools which might have reported correlation of the social-business subjects with other social subjects or with technical or academic subjects did not so report. Table LII presents the percentage of schools not

TABLE LII

SCHOOLS NOT REPORTING CORRELATION COMPARED WITH SCHOOLS WHICH MIGHT HAVE REPORTED CORRELATION

Subject	Schools Not Reporting Correlation		Total Number of Schools Which Might Have Reported Correlation
	Number	Percentage	
Industrial history	1	20	5
History of commerce	4	66.6	6
Economics	3	37.5	8
Commercial geography	5	50	10
Commercial law	4	44.4	9
Salesmanship	3	50	6
Advertising	1	50	2
Commercial organization	2	50	4
Business English	4	50	8

reporting correlation compared with the schools which might have reported correlation in these subjects.

Table LIII presents in somewhat detailed form the number of schools reporting correlation of each of the selected social-business subjects with commercial subjects only, other subjects only, and with commercial and other subjects. The amount of data is somewhat too small to make general observations of great value. It is interesting, however, to observe what a variety of attempts are made. In so far as this may represent the different interests of different instructors, it should probably be considered as a hopeful sign. In so far as it is an indication of a lack of clear planning and a lack of definite

TABLE LIII

CORRELATION OF A SELECTED GROUP OF SOCIAL-BUSINESS SUBJECTS WITH OTHER SUBJECTS

Subject	Number of Schools Reporting Correlation	Number and Percentage of Schools Reporting Correlation of Commercial Subjects					
		With Commercial Subjects Only		With Other Subjects Only		With Commercial and Other Subjects	
		Number	Percentage	Number	Percentage	Number	Percentage
Industrial history....	4	2	50	0	0	2	50
History of commerce.	2	1	50	1	50	....	....
Economics..........	5	1	20	2	40	2	40
Commercial geography..............	5	3	60	1	20	1	20
Commercial law.....	5	4	80	....	....	1	20
Salesmanship.......	3	1	33.3	2	66.6	....	....
Advertising.........	1	1	100	....	....	....	....
Commercial organization............	2	2	100	....	....	....	....
Business English ...	4	2	50	....	....	2	50

standards it is a less satisfactory showing. The specific types of correlation reported are not greatly different from those already shown in the discussion of the commercial course in the high school (p. 416).

SOME CURRENT COURSES

Three courses as now given in the high schools of commerce are presented as illustrative of the present work in such schools. The first is the 1922 program of the High School of Commerce of Washington, D.C. This, it will be remembered, is the oldest of the high schools of commerce of the country, and indicates the point at which this school has arrived since 1890. This outline is taken from a printed course of study of the school.

HIGH SCHOOL OF COMMERCE, WASHINGTON, D.C.

COURSE OF STUDY, 1922

FIRST YEAR

First Semester	Recs. per Week	Credits per Sem.	*Second Semester*	Recs. per Week	Credits per Sem.
*Bookkeeping or †Shorthand	5	1	Bookkeeping or Shorthand	5	1
Business Arithmetic	5	1	Physical Geography	5	1
English	5	1	*English*	5	1
Typewriting	5	½	Typewriting	5	½
Drawing	5	½	Penmanship	5	½
Physical Training	1	⅛	*Physical Training*	1	⅛
Physical Training	3	¼	Physical Training	3	¼
Military Drill	3	¼	Military Drill	3	¼

SECOND YEAR

Third Semester	Recs. per Week	Credits per Sem.	*Fourth Semester*	Recs. per Week	Credits per Sem.
*Bookkeeping or Shorthand	5	1	Bookkeeping or Shorthand	5	1
†Bookkeeping or Business Arithmetic	5	1	Bookkeeping or Business Arithmetic	5	1
Commercial Geography	5	1	*Commercial Law*	5	1
English	5	1	*English*	5	1
Typewriting	5	½	Typewriting	5	½
Physical Training	1	⅛	*Physical Training*	1	⅛
Physical Training	3	¼	Physical Training	3	¼
Military Drill	3	¼	Military Drill	3	¼

* Pupils who elect Bookkeeping in the first year must continue it in the second.

†Pupils who elect Shorthand in the first year must take Bookkeeping instead of Arithmetic in the second.

Pupils who obtain seventeen credits in the first year will be awarded the school certificate.

THIRD YEAR			FOURTH YEAR		
Fifth and Sixth Semesters	Recs. per Week	Credits per Sem.	*Seventh and Eighth Semesters*	Recs. per Week	Credits per Sem
English	5	1	*English*	5	1
Biology or *Physics*	5	1	*American History* and *Commercial Problems*	5	1
Accounting and Finance	5	1	Business Organization	5	1
Algebra	5	1	Geometry	5	1
General and Commercial History	5	1	Office Training and Shorthand	5	1
Spanish	5	1	Typewriting	5	½
Shorthand	5	1	Spanish	5	1
Typewriting	5	½	Chemistry	5	1
Physical Training	1	⅛	*Physical Training*	1	⅛
Physical Training	3	¼	Physical Training	3	¼
Military Drill	3	¼	Military Drill	3	¼

Pupils who obtain thirty-four credits will be awarded the school diploma.

Subjects italicized are prescribed.

Spanish, Algebra, and Geometry should be elected by pupils who intend to pursue a college course.

Pupils must take either Accounting and Finance in the third year or Business Organization in the fourth year.

A second course of study here shown is given to illustrate the work offered in a fairly new school of commerce and one in which the two-year, three-year, and four-year business courses are all given.

WILKINS HIGH SCHOOL OF COMMERCE, DETROIT, MICHIGAN

COURSE OF STUDY

TWO YEAR SHORTHAND COURSE

First Year

First Semester	Recitations per Week	*Second Semester*	Recitations per Week
Arithmetic I	5	Arithmetic II	5
English I	5	Bookkeeping II	10
Commercial Geography	5	English II	5
Penmanship and Bookkeeping	10	Penmanship II	5
Typewriting I	5	Shorthand I	5
		Typewriting II	5

Second Year

First Semester	Recitations per Week	Second Semester	Recitations per Week
General Science	5	Applied English	5
Economics	5	English IV	5
English III	5	Shorthand III	5
Shorthand II	5	Shorthand IV	5
Salesmanship	5	Typewriting IV, V	10
Typewriting III	5		

THREE YEAR BOOKKEEPING AND SHORTHAND COURSE

The first year will be the same as in the two year shorthand course.

Second Year

First Semester	Recitations per Week	Second Semester	Recitations per Week
Bookkeeping III	10	Bookkeeping IV	10
English III	5	English IV	5
General Science	5	Mathematics I	5
Shorthand II	5	Shorthand III	5
Typewriting III	5	Typewriting IV	5

Third Year

First Semester	Recitations per Week	Second Semester	Recitations per Week
Mathematics II	5	American History	5
Economics	5	Applied English	5
English V	5	Commercial Law	5
Salesmanship	5	Shorthand V	5
Shorthand IV	5	Typewriting VI	5
Typewriting V	5		

FOUR YEAR BUSINESS COURSE

The first two years will be the same as in the three year course except that the student enrolling for a regular four year business course will not begin shorthand until the second year. An elective subject may be taken in place of shorthand the second semester.

Third Year

First Semester	Recitations per Week	Second Semester	Recitations per Week
Mathematics II	5	American History	5
English V	5	Commercial Law	5
Salesmanship	5	English VI	5
Shorthand III	5	Shorthand IV	5
Typewriting V	5	Typewriting VI	5

Fourth Year

First Semester	Recitations per Week	*Second Semester*	Recitations per Week
Chemistry or Physics I	10	Applied English.......	5
Economics...........	5	Chemistry or Physics II	10
English VII..........	5	Industrial History.....	5
Shorthand V.........	5	Shorthand VI.........	5
Typewriting VII......	5	Typewriting VIII.....	5

THE HAAREN HIGH SCHOOL OF NEW YORK

One of the most recently established high schools of commerce is the Haaren High School of Manhattan, New York.

TABLE LIV

HAAREN HIGH SCHOOL FOUR-YEAR COMMERCIAL COURSE—ACCOUNTING

Term	1	2	3	4	5	6	7	8	
Required	30	25	14	14	13	23	23	13	15 units required
Elective	....	....	....	....	....	....	....	....	3 units elective
Total	....	....	....	....	....	....	....	....	18 units to graduate
English	5	5	5	5	5	5	5	5	
Music	1	1	1	1	....	....	....	....	
Drawing	2	2	....	....	....	....	....	....	
Physical training	3	3	3	3	3	3	3	3	
Typewriting	4	4	....	....	....	....	....	....	
Civics	5	....	....	....	....	....	....	....	
New York industries	....	5*	....	....	....	....	....	....	(One-half unit of New York industries or economic geography required)
Economic geography	....	....	5*	5*	....	....	....	....	
Commercial law	....	....	....	....	....	5	....	....	
Business procedure	....	....	....	....	....	....	5	....	
Economics	....	....	....	....	....	....	5	....	
Current economic problems	....	....	....	....	....	....	....	5	
Accounting	5	5	5	5	5	5	5*	5*	
General science or household arts	5	5	....	....	....	....	....	....	
American history	....	....	....	....	....	5	5	....	
Commercial mathematics	....	5*	5*	5*	5*	....	....	....	(One unit of commercial mathematics required)
Modern languages	....	5*	5*	5*	5*	5*	5*	5*	
Modern European history	....	....	....	5*	5*	....	....	....	
Chemistry	....	....	5*	5*	....	....	....	....	
Physics	....	....	....	5*	5*	....	....	....	
Commercial art	....	....	5*	5*	5*	5*	5*	5*	
Statistics	....	....	....	....	5*	5*	....	....	
Mathematics of investment	....	....	....	....	....	....	5*	5*	
Materials of commerce	....	....	....	....	5*	5*	....	....	
Salesmanship	....	....	....	....	....	....	5*	5*	
Household arts	....	....	5*	5*	....	....	....	....	

NOTE.—If a modern language is offered for credit toward graduation, not less than two units will be accepted.

* Elective.

(Some industrial courses are also offered.) This school was opened in September, 1920. "The work at the Haaren High

TABLE LV

HAAREN HIGH SCHOOL FOUR-YEAR COMMERCIAL COURSE—SUMMARY

	ACCOUNTING	SECRETARIAL	SALESMANSHIP	FOREIGN TRADE
	Required Units			
English	4	4	4	4
American history	1	1	1	1
Civics	½	½	½	½
Physical training	...	...	...	...
Drawing and music	1½	1½	1½	1½
Economics and economic geography	1½	1½	1½	2
Typewriting	½	1	½	½
Stenography	0	2	0	0
Law and business procedure	1	0	0	0
Commercial mathematics	1	0	0	1
General science or household arts	1	1	1	1
Chemistry or physics	0	0	1	0
Merchandising and salesmanship	0	0	3	0
Office practice and management	0	½	0	0
Secretarial studies	0	½	0	0
Accounting	3	1	1	1
Foreign exchange and foreign transaction procedure	0	0	0	1
Total required	15	14½	15	13½
	Elective Units			
Modern language	3	3½	3	4
Chemistry	1	1	1	1
Physics	1	1	1	1
Accounting	½ or 1	½ or 1	½ or 1	½ or 1
Stenography	0	0	2	2
Modern European history	1	1	1	1
Economic geography	½ or 1	½ or 1	½ or 1	½
Commercial art	3	3	3	3
Household arts	1	1	1	1
Commercial mathematics	0	1	1	0
Merchandising and salesmanship	1	1	0	1
Typewriting	0	0	½	½
Materials of commerce	1	1	0	1
Mathematics of investment	1	1	1	1
Statistics	1	1	1	1
Commercial law and business procedure	0	½ or 1	½ or 1	½ or 1

18 units required for graduation

School will differ from that in other high schools only in the fact that we are allowed to send our students out for practical experience in the business world on the alternate week plan."[1]

[1] A statement by R. Wesley Burnham, principal of Haaren High School, April, 1922.

The students in the Haaren High School are either elementary-school graduates, junior high school graduates, or transfers from different grades in the high schools. Commercial work is offered in secretarial and accounting fields, in salesmanship, and in foreign trade. The registration in February, 1922, in these courses was 900.

To illustrate the courses in the Haaren High School, the outline of the four-year commercial course is given in a summarized form. The four-year commercial course in accounting is also given as a detailed illustration of one of these courses.

AN EVALUATION OF THE HIGH SCHOOL OF COMMERCE

As an educational institution the high school of commerce has been something of a disappointment to observers and perhaps to its own administrators as well. From the statements which preceded the establishment of the earlier high schools of commerce, there is every reason to believe that there was hope that through such schools there might come into being a broader and deeper type of business education than had grown up in the secondary schools or business colleges. This view was expressed at the time of the construction of the High School of Commerce of the City of New York by G. W. Wharton:

> Its purpose is to be, not a business college, as that term is commonly understood, but an institution which will fit young men for managerial and other higher positions requiring expert knowledge in the world of trade, and to prepare them as far as possible for the consular service. The course insists strongly upon broad general training, with special emphasis on languages, beginning with English. In addition to this it will offer thorough courses in business methods, including accountancy as well as routine bookkeeping, special courses in foreign trade and exchange, insurance, brokerage, and other operations of a similar character.[1]

Again, if one examines the statements which precede the printed courses of study in modern high schools of commerce

[1] G. W. Wharton, *School Review*, XI (1903), 478.

(see p. 430), he finds advance notices of a rather strong character. But excepting in possibly a few instances the courses do not live up to these advance notices or to such optimistic expressions as that quoted above. The people who have been responsible for organizing high schools of commerce seem almost without exception to have been desirous of giving the students as much of the managerial viewpoint as possible and as much training of a managerial kind as they were able to supply. That they have failed for the most part has probably been due less to their wishes or efforts than to the lack of broadly trained teachers and the paucity of proper text material.

There are those who argue, however, that the high school of commerce is handicapped by its very nature. The contention is made that we have there a group of students, all of whose interests are centered upon a single objective and that as a result it is less easy for the broad socializing process which occurs in the general high school to take place. While the atmosphere of such a school, the argument runs, cannot be called professional, it is commercial and narrow. It is contended that the students in the high-school commercial course, in spite of the limitations of their subject-matter, the somewhat restricted viewpoint of textbooks, and their own special interests, do, through the mere general association and contact with a variety of students of varied interests, receive influences which are of great value to them in later years.

The high school of commerce, however, is an administrative unit which is more flexible for purposes of experiment than the commercial course in the secondary school. In some small degree it has met its responsibility as an educational laboratory. But it has not seized its opportunity or developed it fully. Unhampered by classical traditions, admittedly organized for the purpose of developing business education, the high school of commerce has the chance to play an important rôle in setting the pace for all secondary business education. Touched with the newer ideas concerning the meaning of education for business, and equipped with the texts which are appearing as a result of those ideas, the high school of commerce is likely yet to become an important influence in the improvement of business education and to fulfil the hopes of those who saw in it an educational agency of usefulness and progress.

QUESTIONS FOR DISCUSSION

1. Is it sensible to speak of the high school of commerce as an extension of the high-school commercial course?
2. Work over the statements of purposes and aims and make a list of the objectives stated for high schools of commerce. Indicate how many times each of these objectives is mentioned. On the basis of these data, what seem to be the outstanding aims of high schools of commerce?
3. From the data gathered as suggested above, do you conclude that the objectives of high schools of commerce are materially broader than the objectives of high-school commercial courses?
4. How do you account for the fact that there is such a diversity in the number of years required in high schools of commerce for such courses as bookkeeping, typewriting, stenography, and commercial arithmetic?
5. Does the examination of the data concerning social business subjects in the high school of commerce lead to the belief that the high school of commerce has progressed far beyond the high-school commercial course in the development and presentation of such subjects?
6. It is sometimes stated that the high school of commerce is the collegiate school of business of the people. Does it appear to you that this statement is justified? Is it any more true than to say that the high-school commercial course is the collegiate school of business of the people?
7. "The high school of commerce has been busy merely in taking care of its students. It has done little in experimenting with how *best* to take care of them." Do you feel that this statement is justified?
8. Everyone would agree that, where the number of cases concerned is few, conclusions drawn from the cases are likely to be inaccurate. Nevertheless in examining the courses of a selected group of social subjects, we find great variety shown among few schools concerned. Should you expect more variety or less, if the number of schools were larger?

9. Should you expect to find a more carefully worked-out correlation of subjects in high schools of commerce than in high-school commercial courses; do you feel that this is the case from examining the data presented?
10. Work over the courses offered by the high school of commerce of Washington, D.C.; of Detroit, Michigan. What features, if any, do you find which are strikingly different from those of the high-school commercial courses with which you are familiar?
11. Examine the course of Haaren High School of New York; in what way, if any, does this course differ from the high-school commercial courses with which you are familiar?
12. "The whole atmosphere of the high school of commerce is opposed to broadening and liberalizing commercial studies." What is the basis for this contention? Comment upon it.
13. "The high school of commerce has a more flexible unit than the high school course." Does this statement seem sound? If it is true, what ought the high school of commerce undertake to do for secondary business education?
14. Draw up a statement or series of statements which express your view of the place or rôle of the high school of commerce in an organized scheme of education for business.

CHAPTER XVII

THE CONTINUATION SCHOOL IN BUSINESS EDUCATION

Our interest in the continuation school centers in what it does in education for business. To secure a clear notion of what it does in that more limited field, however, it is necessary to see something of the continuation school in general. It may be well, therefore, to begin the study of the continuation school by getting clearly in mind the type of institution which it is, the kind of work which it undertakes to do, and the chief characteristics which it possesses. One definition is the following:[1]

Under the terms of the New York State Education Law a part-time or continuation school or class is a school or class for boys and girls between the ages of fourteen and eighteen years who are not high school graduates and who have discontinued attendance upon the regular full-time schools. Such a school or class provides instruction for not less than four and not more than eight hours a week for thirty-six weeks each year on regular school days between eight o'clock A.M. and five o'clock P.M. in subjects which are designed to increase the civic and vocational intelligence of the pupils.

A more clear notion of the continuation school, however, is to be found in the following catechism used by the Chicago Board of Education:[2]

THE CONTINUATION SCHOOL DEFINED

Q. What is a continuation school?

A. A part-time school for boys and girls between fourteen and sixteen years of age, who have left the full-time school to go to work.

[1] From *Bulletin No. 697* (November 1, 1919), p. 6. University of State of New York.

[2] From pamphlet on *Public Continuation Schools*, Board of Education, city of Chicago, January, 1922.

Q. By what authority are continuation schools established?

A. By a law of the Illinois Legislature passed in 1919.

Q. What is the most important provision of this law?

A. That all school districts, in which there are at least twenty minors eligible to continuation school, shall establish part-time classes.

Q. Between what ages do working boys and girls now go to continuation schools?

A. Between the ages of fourteen and sixteen.[1]

Q. Must all working boys and girls attend these schools?

A. Yes. Wherever such schools are open, working boys and girls between the ages of fourteen and sixteen must attend.

Q. What boys and girls need not go to continuation schools?

A. Those who go to full-time schools, and those who are graduates of a four-year high-school course.

Q. Must working boys and girls who are graduates of eighth grade go to continuation school?

A. Yes.

Q. Are working boys and girls who go to evening schools excused from attendance at continuation schools?

A. No.

Q. When are continuation schools in session?

A. The Chicago continuation schools are in session fifty weeks a year, being closed the two weeks immediately preceding Labor Day.

Q. What vacation is given to continuation school pupils?

A. Pupils are given their school vacation at the time they have their vacation from work.

Q. How many hours a week are pupils required to attend continuation school?

A. Eight hours a week. Employers may select any *one* of the following schedules:

Morning			Afternoon	
Mon.	8:00 to 12:00	and	Wed.	1:00 to 5:00
Tues.	8:00 to 12:00	and	Thurs.	1:00 to 5:00
Wed.	8:00 to 12:00	and	Fri.	1:00 to 5:00
Thurs.	8:00 to 12:00	and	Mon.	1:00 to 5:00
Fri.	8:00 to 12:00	and	Tues.	1:00 to 5:00

[1] During the spring of 1921 the Illinois Legislature raised the age limit to seventeen, effective 1923, and to eighteen, effective 1925.

Q. If boys or girls lose or quit their jobs, must they go to school?

A. Yes. They must go either to full-time school or to continuation school.

Q. What is required of continuation-school pupils who stay out of school?

A. They must make up all lost time, except time lost on account of illness.

Q. What will happen if the boys and girls do not attend regularly?

A. Their employment certificates will be taken away.

PURPOSE

Q. What is the purpose of the continuation schools?

A. To give working boys and girls, as nearly as possible, the opportunities enjoyed by their more fortunate brothers who remain in the full-time school.

Q. How is this attempted?

A. By providing day instruction and training that will promote their physical health, their general intelligence and their interest in the life of the community.

Q. Why is day instruction only provided?

A. Children cannot work all day and attend school at night without hazarding their physical health and their moral safety. They need their evenings for recreation, for rest and for general improvement.

Q. What is the nature of the instruction given?

A. We attempt to teach boys and girls how to use their working hours as well as their leisure time, laying special emphasis on outdoor exercise, wholesome recreation, hygienic, civic and vocational instruction.

Q. How is vocational instruction provided?

A. By improving the general intelligence of these young people, by giving them training in such vocational work as they need in their jobs, and by offering them opportunities to learn something of the theory and practice of some of the commoner trades and occupations.

Q. Do the continuation schools teach trades?

A. No. They are not trade schools. They aim to acquaint the children with the rudiments of several trades or occupations, helping the children to decide upon the kind of work for which they are best suited.

Q. Wherein do the purpose and methods of the continuation school differ from those of the full-time school?

A. The continuation school gives constant thought to both the present job and the possible future job of the boy and girl. The present job is the starting point for the vocational instruction. The possible future job serves as a goal.

Q. Why is the present job taken into consideration?

A. The present job is one of the vital interests of the working boy or girl. The job enables him to earn money. The training of the school must, therefore, lay some stress on the present job, while offering opportunities for exchanging it for a better one.

Q. Is vocational training regarded as the principal problem of the continuation school?

A. No. The greatest value of the continuation school is the opportunity afforded the working boy or girl to secure that general education and training that will fit them to fill their place in the community in which they live. The vocation is one of the elements to be taken into consideration.

THE NEED FOR CONTINUED EDUCATION

Everyone is somewhat familiar with the fact that pupils, boys especially, drop out of school in large numbers during their teens. Recently in New York the Military Training Commission had an opportunity to study the school histories of a very large number of boys. Their findings are so impressive concerning school mortality that they are quoted here:[1]

> The returns from 150,000 of these boys have been studied, in all sorts of groupings such as Greater New York, other large cities, small cities, large villages, small villages, rural sections, by nationalities, boys with fathers, boys without fathers, with mothers, without mothers, American boys, foreign boys, oldest boys, second oldest, third oldest, fourth oldest, fifth oldest and sixth oldest of both American and foreign birth, and it has been found that regardless of birth, family conditions and environments approximately 73,000, or 30 per cent, of these 245,000 boys leave school before fifteen, 172,000, or 70 per cent, before sixteen, and by the end of the sixteenth year less than 10 per cent, or 20,000, are still in school.

[1] Adapted by permission from Howard G. Burdge, *A Study of Employed Boys*, pp. 6–7. State of New York Military Training Commission, Bureau of Vocational Training, 1921.

About 61,000, or 25 per cent, drop out on or before completing the seventh grade, 132,000, or 50 per cent, on or before completing the eighth grade, and 220,000, or 90 per cent, before completing the first year of the high school. Investigations made by the Inter-Church World Movement show that boys desert the Sunday schools at these same ages and the leaders in the Boy Scouts of America report that most boys drop out of the Scout troops before reaching sixteen.

This study shows that these boys are thoroughly averse to further schooling and that compulsory part-time continuation-school and night-school work will be practically valueless unless we can awaken in these boys an interest in further education. They must be convinced that by completing certain definite and practical short courses they can increase their earning capacity and secure promotion. To accomplish this is the task of boy welfare organizations as well as of the schools. The major part of the future training and education of these boys will be secured through business and social contacts, but this must be supplemented by carefully selected and well planned short continuation-school courses which are attractive to boys because of their practical value.

Clearly it is not the belief of this commission that the continuation school is a tool ready made to take care of this appalling school mortality. It is rather to be thought of as one agency which by proper development may function usefully. The need for continued education of some sort suggested in this quotation should, however, be kept in mind in considering the evening school as well as here.

THE DEVELOPMENT OF CONTINUATION SCHOOLS

The continuation school as a definite, clearly defined institution seems to have had its beginning in Germany. It appeared not as a vocational school, but as a school giving supplementary education of a general, religious, or moral character. Although beginning somewhat earlier, continuation schools became important after 1800, when certain of the German states began to give them financial support and to make them to a degree compulsory. In these early schools the time for continuation was usually evenings and Sundays and the instruction given was limited.

The introduction of the factory system into Germany was accompanied by an increase in the number of continuation schools and the growth of an additional amount of vocational work. Later when some degree of suffrage was introduced in the German Empire, the continuation schools were looked to for more training in civic and economic matters. In the time during which these changes were taking place compulsory attendance became more common. Equipment and buildings were improved, and the hours of instruction were increased and were placed on week days and in daytime more commonly than before.[1]

The development of continuation schools in the United States is a comparatively recent movement. In 1910 Ohio passed the first of the state laws definitely concerned with continuation schools, the enactment of which is often referred to as the beginning of continuation schools in the United States. About the same time the founder of the Munich continuation-school system, Dr. George Kirchensteiner, toured the country in the interests of the continuation-school movement. Dr. Kirchensteiner's influence was increased by the prestige then popularly attached to Germany's "efficiency" methods.[2]

As a result of Dr. Kirchensteiner's visit, the leaders of the movement for industrial education in this country came to understand the real nature of the continuation school and many of them became enthusiastic advocates of it. From this time on, the continuation school movement gained ground with every year. Prior to the passage of the Smith-Hughes Act in 1917, seven states (Ohio, Wisconsin,[3] New York, New Jersey, Massachusetts, Indiana and

[1] For a further discussion of the continuation school in Germany see Edwin G. Cooley, "The Part Time School—Its Genesis and Permanent Place," *School and Home Education*, Vol. XXXV (October, 1915), No. 2, p. 41.

[2] This statement is adapted by permission from Paul H. Douglas, *American Apprenticeship and Industrial Education*, pp. 252–55, 261–62. "Columbia University Studies." Longmans, Green & Co., 1921.

[3] In 1921, the Wisconsin Legislature made an extension of the continuation-school requirements, making the law perhaps the most advanced of any in the United States. The law requires that "whenever any day vocational school shall be established in any town, village or city in this

Pennsylvania) had made some form of legislative provision for continuation schools and various systems were being put into effect. State legislation prior to the Smith-Hughes Act was based upon conflicting attitudes on the following two questions: (1) Whether or not the state should require attendance at the continuation schools. Wisconsin and Pennsylvania were the only states where the legislature made attendance compulsory for all. Massachusetts, New York, Ohio and Indiana had permissive mandatory laws by which the legislature empowered the local boards of education to require attendance. Experience was clearly showing, however, that the latter type of law was very ineffective in meeting the situation because of the reluctance of the local boards to impose any additional tax burden. Wisconsin and Pennsylvania, on the other hand, were demonstrating that state-wide compulsory continuation schools backed up by a system of state aid were the only effective means of educating the juvenile worker. (2) Whether or not the curriculum of the continuation schools should be narrowly vocational. The Indiana law permitted education only for the job at which the juvenile worker was employed and did not allow the trade preparation training or social subjects in the curriculum. Pennsylvania and Massachusetts, on the other hand, permitted a more diversified form of education and included civic and social subjects as well as the more strictly vocational.

---

state for minors, working under permit as now provided by law, every such child residing or employed within any town, village or city in which any such school is established, who has not completed four years of work above the eight elementary grades, and who is not in attendance at some other public, private or parochial school at least half time shall attend such school not less than half time in the daytime until the end of the school term quarter, semester or other division of the school year in which he is sixteen years of age, and after that eight hours a week until the end of the term, quarter, semester or other division of the school year in which he is eighteen years of age, for at least eight months in each year, and for such additional months or parts thereof as the other public schools in such city, town or village are in session in excess of eight during the regular school year, or the equivalent as may be determined by the local board of industrial education, and every employer shall allow all minor employees a reduction in hours of work of not less than the number of hours the minor is by law required to attend school. Whenever the working time and the class time coincide, such reduction in hours of work shall be allowed at the time when the classes which the minor is by law required to attend are held."—Author.

THE SMITH-HUGHES LAW

The second stage of continuation-school development in the United States occurred with the passage of the Smith-Hughes Act, approved Feburary 23, 1917. It was: "an act to provide for the promotion of vocational education; to provide for co-operation with the States in the promotion of such education in agriculture and the trades and industries; to provide for co-operation with the States in the preparation of teachers of vocational subjects; and to appropriate money and regulate its expenditure." Certain paragraphs of the law are worth quoting:[1]

Be it enacted by the Senate and House of Representatives of the United States of America in Congress assembled, That there is hereby annually appropriated, out of any money in the Treasury not otherwise appropriated, the sums provided in sections two, three, and four of this Act, to be paid to the respective States for the purpose of co-operating with the States in paying the salaries of teachers, supervisors, and directors of agricultural subjects, and teachers of trade, home economics, and industrial subjects, and in the preparation of teachers of agricultural, trade, industrial, and home economics subjects.

That a Federal Board for Vocational Education is hereby created, to consist of the Secretary of Agriculture, the Secretary of Commerce, the Secretary of Labor, the United States Commissioner of Education, and three citizens of the United States to be appointed by the President, by and with the advice and consent of the Senate. One of said three citizens shall be a representative of the manufacturing and commercial interests, one a representative of the agricultural interests and one a representative of labor.

The Smith-Hughes Act provided for co-operation between the federal government and the several states only through the acceptance of the federal act by the state legislature. It happened that the federal law was passed at a time when most of the state legislatures were in session. No less than thirty-

[1] Adapted by permission from Federal Board for Vocational Education, *Bulletin No. 1*, pp. 49, 51, 52. Washington: Government Printing Office, 1917.

nine of the states passed formal acts of acceptance in 1917, and either through such acceptance or through the governor's action every state in the union was qualified to participate in the distribution of federal money for the year ending June 30, 1918. By the close of the fiscal year 1918–19, every state had through a formal act of the legislature accepted the provisions of the Smith-Hughes Law. Three points had to be specifically covered by the state legislation under the provisions of the federal law. These are (1) the acceptance of the provisions of the federal act, (2) the creation or designation of a state board to administer the act, and (3) the appointment of the state treasurer as custodian of federal funds.[1]

In a few of the states the laws state specifically the conditions under which the vocational work is to be administered. In more, the actual administrative power is left to the state board for vocational education. In every state either the state board for vocational education or the state board of education is charged with the duty of formulating rules and regulations concerning the establishment of the compulsory part-time school.

The more essential provisions of the laws in the nineteen states which have enacted what may be called part-time compulsory-education laws is shown in the table on page 458.[2]

Practically every state requires that the schools or classes shall be held during the usual working hours of the minor; usually the laws state specifically that such classes shall be held between the hours of eight A.M. and five or six P.M. Some of the state directors favor the elimination of Saturday part-time classes, others believe that Saturday can be used advantageously for part-time work, especially in the larger cities.

It is certain that the attendance should be required during the working hours of the pupils. For example, when the state law allows a minor to work for forty-eight hours and the required part-time school attendance is eight hours, the number of hours in which a

[1] *Third Annual Report of the Federal Board for Vocational Education*, I, 13–21.

[2] This table is taken from *Bulletin 55*, pp. 8–9, 26–27. "Trade and Industrial Series," No. 14, Federal Board for Vocational Education.

minor may be legally employed should be automatically reduced to forty, the eight hours of attendance upon a part-time school being considered as a part of the time of the total forty-eight hours.

In this connection, it may be well to state that there is a practical unanimity of opinion that evening-school attendance should not be allowed as a substitute for attendance upon a day part-time

TABLE LVI

PROVISIONS OF PART-TIME COMPULSORY EDUCATION LAWS

State	Law in Effect	Minimum Number of Minors Required to Establish Classes	Age of Required Attendance	Hours of Required Attendance per Week	Length of School Year
Arizona	1919	15	14–16	5	150 hours
California	1920	12*	14–18	4	Same as public schools
Illinois	1921	20	14–18	8	Same as public schools
Iowa	1919	15	14–16	8	Same as public schools
Massachusetts	1920	200†	14–16	4	Same as public schools
Michigan	1920	50‡	14–18	8	Same as public schools
Missouri	1919	25	14–16	4	Same as public schools
Montana	1919	15	14–18	4	Same as public schools
Nebraska	1919	15	14–16	8	144 hours
Nevada	1919	15	14–18	4	Same as public schools
New Jersey	1920	20	14–16	6	36 weeks
New Mexico	1919	15	14–16	5	150 hours
New York	1920	20§	14–18	4–8	Same as public schools
Oklahoma	1919	20	16–18	....	144 hours
Oregon	1919	15‖	14–18	5	Same as public schools
Pennsylvania	1915	20	14–16	8	Same as public schools
Utah	1919	15	14–18	4	144 hours
Washington	1920	15¶	14–18	4	Same as public schools
Wisconsin	1911	(§)	14–17	8	8 months

* High-school districts having 50 or more pupils must establish part-time classes.

† Referendum law adopted by all towns affected except one.

‡ Establishment of schools is compulsory only in school districts having a population of 5,000 or more.

§ Establishment required only in cities of over 5,000 population.

‖ Attendance upon evening school may be substituted.

¶ Districts may organize schools upon written request of twenty-five residents.

school. Only one state of the Union requires attendance of fourteen to sixteen-year minors upon evening schools.

Several states, it may be noted, including Indiana, Kentucky, Ohio, Michigan, New York, and Massachusetts, have enacted permissive mandatory laws authorizing local districts to establish such schools, but relatively few communities in these states, Boston being notably one of these few, have taken advantage of the state laws. It may fairly be said, therefore, that legislation which has simply granted authority to local districts to establish part-time schools and to require attendance on them has not been very generally effective as a means of stimulating the establishment of such schools.

The importance of the Smith-Hughes Act to continuation schools grew out of the fact that the law particularly recognized the value of such schools. Section 11 of the law required:

That at least one-third of the sum appropriated to any State for the salaries of teachers of trade, home economics, and industrial subjects shall, if expended, be applied to part-time schools or classes for workers over fourteen years of age who have entered upon employment, and such subjects in a part-time school or class may mean any subject given to enlarge the civic or vocational intelligence of such workers over fourteen years of age who have entered upon employment, and such subjects in a part-time school or class may mean any subject given to enlarge the civic or vocational intelligence of such workers over fourteen and less than eighteen years of age; that such part-time schools or classes shall provide for not less than 144 hours of classroom instruction per year.

COMMERCIAL WORK UNDER THE SMITH-HUGHES LAW

The recommendations of the Commission on National Aid to Vocational Education, which led to the enactment of the Smith-Hughes Act, did not include a proposal for a subsidy for commercial education, and accordingly no such direct subsidy was given. The Commission did suggest, however, that the national government should give "substantial encouragement to commercial education." This suggestion was followed, and in Section 6 of the act the following is to be found:

It shall be the duty of the Federal Board for Vocational Education to make, or cause to have made, studies, investigations, and reports, with particular reference to their use in aiding the States in the establishment of vocational schools and classes and giving instruction in . . . . commerce and commercial pursuits. Such studies, investigations, and reports shall include . . . . commerce and commercial pursuits and requirements upon commercial workers. . . . .

When the Board deems it advisable such studies, investigations, and reports concerning commerce and commercial pursuits, for the purpose of commercial education, may be made in co-operation with or through the Department of Commerce.

The Federal Board created a Commercial Education Service at the same time that the other services of the Board were organized. It was the duty of this service to make the studies, investigations, and reports which were deemed necessary:

Within a year after the Board was organized it ruled that Federal money could be used in part-time schools and classes for the salaries of instructors in trade, home economics, industrial, commercial and general educational subjects. This resolution was to carry into effect the provision of Sec. 11 of the Act which specified that the subjects "in the part-time schools may mean any subject given to enlarge the civic and vocational intelligence," and obviously the commercial work could be regarded as enlarging either the civic or vocational intelligence.

The Board further ruled that part-time classes must be classes which divide the working day or school time between instruction and practical work in shop, factory, home, office, etc. As a result of these rulings the work of the Commercial Education Service has two phases: first, that of making studies, investigations and reports for the purpose of improving the quality of commercial education in every type of public school below college grade; second, that of administering and supervising the commercial work in the part-time schools.

The Board in defining the part-time school ruled that the definition means here not to separate the working day and school time into two equal parts but to apportion or distribute the total working day so that a portion of it is given to school instruction, or to apportion or distribute the total school time so that a portion of it is given to employment in shop, factory, home, or office, etc. Under this ruling what are known as co-operative high school classes in both retail selling and office practice were subsidized from Federal funds; that is part of the teacher's pay may be paid from Federal funds.

The state boards for vocational education submit to the Federal Board each year a state plan which outlines the work in vocational education which the state board proposes to carry on during the ensuing fiscal year. The decision as to whether the high school co-operative classes in commercial subjects will be subsidized or not, therefore, rests entirely with the state board. The Federal Board has ruled that the states may subsidize these classes but this does not mean that the states have to, and therefore the question of whether or not the high school co-operative classes in office work and retail selling in a particular state will be subsidized, rests entirely with the state board. It has not been the policy of the Commercial Education Service to press this matter in any state as it has not been considered advisable to have the state boards feel that they are under compulsion in any phase of vocational education which is optional under the rulings of the Board. In all the states which have compulsory part-time school laws, classes have been provided to meet the needs of children employed in stores and offices.[1]

SOME EXAMPLES OF CONTINUATION SCHOOLS

The continuation school does not exist to give training in commercial work alone. Examples therefore must necessarily include a description of the organization for other work as well as for instruction in commercial subjects. Such descriptions may be useful to those who are interested in the organization or direction of continuation schools; they are in any case more faithful portrayals of the facts than if the data concerning business teaching in continuation schools were isolated. The business training must usually be seen more or less as a setting of other studies. It may be well to begin with the description of a continuation school of general character. One such example can be found in Detroit.

In Detroit there has been a considerable re-working of educational work during the past year or two. One feature of the plan in this city is to keep the work for boys and girls entirely separate and to throw the students into groups around which separate courses can be built. Below is a statement of courses of study offered in the boys' continuation department of the Cass Technical High School of Detroit:[2]

[1] From materials distributed by the Commercial Service of the Federal Board for Vocational Education, March, 1922.

[2] From statement of courses of study submitted by Assistant Principal E. G. Allen.

Auto Mechanics I:

Chassis—Study and assembly of front and rear axles and transmissions. Three 45 minute periods.

Ignition—Study of fundamental principles of electricity, the study and assembly of generators and starting motors, distributors and batteries. Three 45 minute periods.

Auto Mechanics II:

Study of engines—different types of gas engines, carburetors, and vacuum forced speed gasoline systems, practical work in wiring up the electrical equipment.

Garage work—Actual repairing of all makes of cars.

Electrical Construction I:

Splicing, soldering, insulation, and bell wiring, work on different types of switches, open and receptacle work, and garage wiring.

Electrical Construction II:

Use of wood molding, rosette and drop cord work, snap switches for different circuits, metal molding, baseboard plugs, wiring of ordinary houses, safety switches, knife switches, and radio work.

Wood Shop:

Pattern making—Joinery, wood turning, coping down, split pattern, green sand core, and dry sand core, dry sand core box, vertical and horizontal types, balanced core, stop-off core, loose piece pattern, three-part pattern, built-up or segment pattern, and a master pattern.

Cabinet making—Typical types of joinery work; boys repair furniture and make new furniture.

Commercial:

Typewriting, office practice, business English, business arithmetic, economics.

Reservoir:

Into this group are placed all incoming students who have no definite aim or type of work they wish to follow, and boys who are subnormal and whom we are unable to place in the more advanced shop courses.

Mechanical Drawing:

The work in this course is divided into two sections: Students, upon entering, are placed in a sketching class and taught to letter and make sketches. As soon as one shows himself proficient in this class, he is put into a course which is the same as the Mechanical Drawing course in Cass High School.

Machine Shop:

Grinding and hardening of tools, chucking, centering—regular and irregular—facing, straight turning, shouldering, knurling, chuck wood, taper turning, taper boring, hand reaming, bevelling, and threading.

Freehand Sketching:

This is a special course offered on Saturday afternoons for boys who, we find, are talented in Freehand Sketching, and are desirous of doing some art work. As this is a very small group, we have to combine it with a small Mechanical Drawing class. The work done here is at the present time practically an experiment.

Printing:

The printing course consists of composition or type setting by hand, of press work and book binding. The boys here have practical experience in taking a job and carrying it through to completion. This work at the present time is offered only on Saturday, due to the crowded condition in this Department throughout the week.

Academic:

The academic subjects are carried on in connection with the different shop courses and the boys move throughout the eleven 45 minute periods a day as a group, and the work is so arranged as to bring as much bearing upon the shop work they are taking up as possible. The subjects offered are Mathematics, English, History, and Economics.

CONTINUATION SCHOOLS FOR GIRLS IN DETROIT

In planning vocational education of all types too little consideration has been given to special needs of girls. The immediate and temporary occupations which she shares in common with boys have been considered, but the more permanent vocation in which most women are employed has not been planned for with care. Some real thought appears to be given to this question in Detroit.[1]

[1] The following statement is adapted by permission from George F. Buxton, *Part-Time Education*, pp. 33-37. "Monographs on Vocational Education," 1921 Series, No. 2. Published by the Vocational Association of the Middle West.

The part-time continuation school for girls in Detroit has been, from its beginning, distinct from the same type of school for boys. The problems which it has presented have not been obscured or overshadowed by the easily solved problems of industrial education which continuation work for boys presents, as may be the case when the two types of work come under the same administration. Education of the young wage-earning girl is a twofold problem. Her initial wage-earning career is short and within a period of from three to ten years she enters upon her career of home-making. She must, therefore, be equipped for two vocations neither of which may be regarded as sufficiently permanent to warrant training for one to the exclusion of the other. . . . .

It is the girl of the adolescent age who comes to the part-time school when she is entering upon a new stage of her life. A new sense of her power is awakening, exhibited often by an attempt to throw off traditional control of home and school. She looks out upon a new world—spiritual, moral and mental, no less than practical and material. Her mind is most sensitive and most receptive at this age, and new capacities lie dormant but just ready for the awakening touch. She has left school to take her place in the world of production and trade because of conditions within the school which have not been adjustable to her individual desires or needs; or she is helping to bear the financial support of a large family; or she is endeavoring to meet her yearning for well-being expressing itself outwardly in a more elaborate wardrobe. Therefore, it becomes the purpose of the school to bring the girl to a realization of herself, to interpret to her the new world of life she is entering, to present her with opportunities for self knowledge, self appraisal, self expression, and self development.

The girl problem is inseparably bound up with the teacher problem. The right kind of a teacher is the most vital consideration in the success of a part-time school for girls. Her paramount interest must be in the individual. This must never be forgotten in her desire to perpetuate school traditions, or to teach a set lesson. She will study to understand the part-time school movement. She must believe in the school, its aims and its opportunities for young employed girls, and she must have faith in girls.

In the Detroit school, an average of about fifty girls each day form what is known as the "Mixed Group." They are the girls of lowest school attainment. The majority have finished the sixth grade, many were in the seventh at time of leaving school, and a few have left school at the termination of the compulsory school age while in grades below the sixth. The latter are subnormals—a class with which the school has not had to deal before this year.

The mixed group is divided into two classes, averaging twenty-five girls each. These girls seem to need, especially, civic and domestic intelligence, knowledge of health laws, and a general toning up of personal appearance and habits. Fifty per cent of their school day is occupied with home-making subjects—cooking, sewing, elementary home economics—and the remainder in English, arithmetic, spelling, civics, gymnasium and hygienic classes. The lessons in all academic subjects relate to the girl's life in her occupation and home, and every effort is made to have each lesson so practical that the girl may carry it directly into living. These fifteen and sixteen year old girls of seventh grade and below are very much retarded and belong to that large group of the youth of our country who rarely finish elementary school. Individually a few move out of this group to classes of higher grade girls from time to time during the school year. Those are the more promising ones who have been awakened probably by the close touch of a sympathetic and intelligent teacher. In the full-time school they were lost in the crowd.

This arrangement has revealed the value of one teacher over the many for this type of girl. They are her sole interest. She has visited their homes, and is devoted to their welfare. They are most difficult to keep in school regularly, yet the attendance of this group has shown a marked improvement.

Above this mixed group still less attention is paid to school grade, and greater effort is made to group girls according to occupations. There is the office group, the store group, the telephone group, and the home group. A girl from any one of these groups may be taking commercial studies as her desired vocational subject, but remains with her group for the classes that relate especially to her own job. The ungraded condition of these classes has been found quite satisfactory. An eighth grade girl will often do as well as a ninth when the class problems are vital and related to living. She will at least be following along the line of a real interest and gaining all she is capable of in the subject studied.

The problem presented by girls who are in employments that demand no special skill or training, and offer them no training for any permanent occupation has not been fully solved in the Detroit part-time school for girls. A vocational information class has been attempted for these girls. It includes girls from factories, laundries, and home girls. It offers an opportunity to emphasize the ethical principle of making good in any job, and at the same time endeavors to point the way to a more permanent vocation suited to individual capacities. These girls, from the simple automatic occupations, fit well into the home-making classes where manual skill is also required. To offset the dulling influence of automatic work for five days a week, there is the nature and folk dancing and recreational games in the gymnasium, the chorus work in the assembly, and the introduction to the world of good books in the English classes. Thus the young worker who stands all day taking marking pins out of clothes in family washes at the laundry, or turning men's hose right side out in the knitting mill, is directed into some wholesome self improving activities. The school needs especially to "tone up the minds, the bodies and the feelings" of this industrial group. But instruction that bears directly upon the work the girl is doing is quite beyond the ability of the school to provide because too many varieties of manual work are represented. Most of the jobs are learned in a day and skill and speed are acquired through the constant practice. Advancement comes to those who are fitted to do some manipulative task which requires a little more judgment or responsibility, or a little more physical strength, or willingness to perform disagreeable work.

COMMERCIAL CONTINUATION WORK IN TRENTON, NEW JERSEY

In Trenton, New Jersey, a good deal of effort has been spent to work out a sound plan of instruction in commercial subjects in the continuation school. The present system is thus described:[1]

1. *The compulsory New Jersey continuation school law.*—This law became effective July 1, 1920. Under the provisions of the law a continuation school must be established and maintained in every school district in which there are employed twenty or more children between the ages of fourteen and sixteen to whom age and schooling certificates have been granted in accordance with the child labor and compulsory attendance laws. Attendance of all these children (physically and mentally fit) is required for at least six

[1] This statement was prepared in May, 1922, by Paul S. Lomax, director of business education in Trenton.

hours a week for thirty-six weeks a year, or, if temporarily employed, for twenty hours a week during the period of unemployment. The time of attendance is on regular school days between eight o'clock in the morning and five o'clock in the afternoon.

2. *Maintenance and support.*—State aid is given continuation schools in the several districts to the amount of $400 to each teacher employed for a term of thirty-six weeks or more, or a proportionate amount based upon the ratio that the actual number of hours' service bears to 1080 hours. In addition, federal aid is granted when the requirements of the Federal Board for Vocational Education relative to class organization, equipment, purpose of instruction and qualifications of teachers are fulfilled.

3. *Organization of the Trenton continuation school.*—There are 850 pupils enrolled in the school in which ten teachers are employed. Of these students 125 are registered in commercial subjects, 400 in home economics and 325 in practical arts. In all three lines of work one-half of the day's session or three hours is given to the vocational subjects and the remaining three hours to work in related subjects, as English, physical training, arithmetic, hygiene and civics. The work in home economics consists of cooking, sewing and other home arts; in practical arts of wood-work, sheet metal work and electricity; and in commercial education of introductory business, penmanship and typewriting.

4. *Commercial subjects.*—The key subject of the commercial work is Introductory Business. The nature of the course is:

a) To study the organization and functions of local business enterprises, manufacturing, wholesaling, retailing, financial, commission, public utilities, etc., as viewed from the standpoint of junior workers who are employed in such businesses.

b) Within these organizations to study types of work which are performed by junior workers such as those who are enrolled in the continuation school classes. With reference to the junior occupations a study is made of the duties, essential personal qualifications required, general and special education needed, salaries paid, number employed, opportunities for advancement, promotional lines and educational opportunities available to facilitate promotion.

c) In connection with these types of junior employment to study the nature and use of the business papers which are involved.

d) To study and develop personal qualifications which make for success. Throughout all the work an effort is made to inculcate such virtues as industry, punctuality, initiative, courtesy and thrift.

The work is organized on the unit basis, by which is meant that from week to week particular junior business employments are studied. For example, the work for one week may be that of a stock record clerk in which there is included (*a*) such considerations as the importance of the clerkship to a business organization as a whole, the lines of promotion, the nature of the work performed; and (*b*) a study of the business papers which are used. Following the vocational work in the morning, this class in its related work in the afternoon makes a study of that arithmetic which is needed in connection with the stock records. In the morning the pupils have learned the nature and use of these records, and have gained a certain degree of skill in handling them. In the afternoon they are given problems in which are emphasized the arithmetic and other related subject matter which may be concerned. This procedure means that at the end of the day the pupil should have accomplished a definite unit of school work, and with that accomplishment there should go with the pupil to his employment a feeling of enthusiasm and progress which is ultimately shared by the business men themselves.

It will be observed that this work has both pre-vocational and vocational values in that in the one instance it enables the student to discover and gauge his interests, abilities and possibilities in his present or desired employment and in the other instance to acquire some degree of preparation which leads to improvement in his present employment, particularly if that happens to be commercial.[1]

Along with Introductory Business, courses are given in penmanship and typewriting. The penmanship I regard as essential in connection with the business practice work.

In typewriting we have two kinds of pupils enrolled: (*a*) that class of pupils who have had no knowledge of typewriting prior to enrollment in the continuation school and to whom, therefore, the work is preparatory, and (*b*) that class of pupils who have had typewriting before enrolling and to whom, therefore, the work is extension. For the first group I question very much if typewriting has sufficient value to warrant the time given to its study. The work can be given only once a week, and once a week over a period of thirty-six weeks is not sufficient in which to develop worth-while typewriting technique and skill. For the second group of pupils I believe that type-

[1] The two chief sources of material which are used in this course are *Junior Business Training* by F. G. Nichols and *Clerical Practice* by Anderson, Ross, and Staples.

writing is of real value if such pupils before enrolling have acquired a fair mastery of the typewriter keyboard. For such pupils there can be offered a very excellent course in typewriting technique and office practice, the latter to involve a maximum amount of typewriting in the handling of business correspondence and forms. The number in the second class of pupils is very small as compared with that in the first. Consequently, typewriting, with the one exception, is a subject, I believe, which has a very doubtful value in continuation school work. The course in Introductory Business, for example, will prove of far greater value both to junior workers and employers.

On a basis of three hours, as we have in Trenton, I would recommend the following commercial courses of study:

	Minutes
Elementary Business Organization	45
Study of Junior Business Employments	45
Penmanship	30
Junior Business Practice	60

COMMERCIAL CONTINUATION SCHOOLS IN CHICAGO

Commercial work in continuation schools in Chicago has been carried on both in centrally located classes and in the plants of large businesses. Its aims and methods are described as follows:[1]

In, Chicago before there was a Compulsory Continuation School Law, Commercial Continuation Schools were established by the Board of Education in the offices of Swift & Co., Wilson & Co., Morris & Co., Chicago Telephone Co., and a general Commercial Continuation School for employed young people in the central business district was opened in the McClurg Building.

Since the passing of the Compulsory Continuation School Law, whereby boys and girls between the ages of fourteen and sixteen must enroll in continuation schools for eight hours a week if not in the regular day schools, the enrollment has considerably increased and the entire Jones School building in the Central District has been turned over to the Commercial Continuation School.

Commercial classes have been opened in the Winchell Continuation School for girls, the South Division Continuation School for

[1] This statement of commercial work in Chicago continuation schools was prepared by Mr. William Bachrach, supervisor of commercial work in the high schools of Chicago.

boys and girls, and a class is soon to be begun in the Washburne Continuation School for boys.

From the beginning two viewpoints were kept in mind: to continue the general education of the student by offering courses in English, mathematics, civics, etc., and also to correlate the work with the present employment of the student to as great an extent as possible. This could be done very easily in the schools located at the packing houses. The actual problems arising in the accounting and correspondence departments are studied by the teacher and transferred to the school room, thereby adding great interest to what would ordinarily be dry routine work.

A new movement which was begun last year and which seems to be a very sensible one is to permit each student in the continuation school to try himself out in a ten weeks cycle of business training, shop work, household arts and science work, etc. In other words, we are coming to the point of view that it is not fair to the child to force him to crystallize his efforts in one line of endeavor until he has had some opportunity of trying himself out under the supervision of his teacher and principal. After the try-out cycle he is advised to specialize during the remainder of his continuation school course. The present thought also is to give shorter units of instruction, rather than small parts of large units, such as shorthand if the student has not had any instruction in it previously.

An effort has been made to break away as much as possible from the text and methods used in the regular high schools, and in some cases the teachers have compiled material more suitable to the conditions of the continuation schools.

A COMMERCIAL CONTINUATION SCHOOL IN A BUSINESS PLANT

Both the public-school system of Chicago and the concerns where the commercial continuation schools are in operation feel that there is much to be said for the location of a continuation school on the property of a business institution. The following material gives an impression of the commercial continuation school in the plant of Swift & Company, Chicago. It is to be remembered that although Swift & Company furnish the room and to some extent the equipment for this school, the public-school authorities furnish the teacher and direct the course of study. Incidentally, the pay for instruction comes in part from the federal government under the provisions of the Smith-Hughes Law.[1]

A. Aims:

1. To enable the boy or girl who has not completed the eighth grade to obtain the minimum essentials of the work given in the public grammar schools.
2. To enable the boy or girl who has an eighth-grade education to obtain an education equivalent to the Chicago two-year commercial high-school course.
3. To train the boy or girl for lines to which he or she is mentally and physically best adapted.
4. To recommend capable boys or girls for transfer or promotion when requested by department heads.
5. To train the boy or girl in that which is directly applicable to his or her future activities.

B. Selection of Subject-Matter:

1. Penmanship:

Special attention is given to the development of a rapid, legible hand. A definite effort is made to train the student in writing small legible figures, tabulating in ink, and filling in forms.

2. Arithmetic:

Footing, cross footing, balancing, check eleven, short cuts in multiplying, averaging, figuring per cents, prorating, distributing of overhead expenses, keeping bank accounts, payrolls, extending invoices, rendering statements of account, simple accounting, etc., are presented daily in both advanced and elementary sections.

3. English:

Much attention to spelling lists of words evolved from the company's correspondence; elementary word study. The business letter is not only studied in detail but original letters are composed in answer to practical business situations.

Errors in both written and oral English are corrected systematically.

[1] This statement is adapted from circulars published by Swift & Company. There are several such schools in Chicago. They exist, of course, elsewhere as well.

Advertising, year books, and other literature of the company are used consistently as material for spelling, reading, dictation exercises, and discussions.

Oral and written compositions receive regular attention. The subject-matter is based largely on the industry, but includes material from the daily newspaper; and such incidental material from commercial geography, civics, hygiene, and office practice as seems advisable.

4. Business organization:

Frequent lectures are given, by experts in their line, on departmental activities. These are followed by class work and reading assignments in our well equipped company library.

C. Methods of Teaching:

Textbooks are practically done away with, and definite, concrete lessons based on the office system and organization of the packing industry, worked out in mimeographed form, are the basis of most of the instruction. The office and packing industry are a laboratory; the three R's, as used in and useful to the packing industry, are the curriculum. The company furnishes rooms, equipment, supplies and pupils' time. This last element alone costs the company thousands of dollars yearly. Thus is the proper duty of the state to educate its young citizens maintained and carried into industry; at the same time, co-operation on the part of the particular industry furnishes the teachers with a vast mine of material which is most immediately useful to those pupils going into the industry in question and which, in all probability, never would find its way into any textbook.

This collaboration, in addition to the advantages named, is a good insurance against purely "vestibule school" instruction, which is liable to be found in private corporation schools.

Definite instruction in packing-house problems and methods is given by means of talks by the department heads and other executives supplemented by trips to the part of the plant concerned, and followed up later by oral and written composition exercises and arithmetic problems based on the particular department studied. It may be seen that this school has an advisory faculty which the most richly endowed university might be proud of.

D. Special Classes:

Girls under eighteen years of age are given instruction in typewriting and comptometer operation; another small group of girls trained in stenography in high school, but without business experience, are given a five months' finishing course in office practice and English. At the same time they do the regular work of a stenographer, though light volume only is expected of them.

E. Summary:

Our aim is not to make a mere machine out of the student, or to fit him for a blind-alley job. On the other hand we aim to fit him technically and give him a broader view of what business really is.

THE RÔLE OF THE CONTINUATION SCHOOL

If growth and interest during the past few years are indications, the continuation school is to play a great part in the vocational education of the future. What part it can best play needs careful thought. Undoubtedly it will for some time to come play a multiple rôle. The work which it can perform may be thought of as having three degrees of breadth: (1) the broadest possible cultural education, (2) the interpretation of the student's job so that its implications become more apparent and more full of meaning, and (3) a training in the performance of the job itself or in the technique of other jobs to which a transfer may be desired. It must be borne in mind, however, that one reason why the continuation school must give some notion of social relations and of the duties of a citizen to its present pupils is because instruction in such matters has been crowded out of the regular school courses by the pressure of technical training, or because the students have dropped school at an early age.

Let us assume, however, a rearrangement of work. In a state where a compulsory continuation-school law is operative, the student will necessarily, if the law is enforced, be under the direction of the school authorities until he is sixteen, seventeen, or eighteen years of age. Under these circumstances it seems likely that the number of students who drop out of the regular school work will be lessened. The two-year high-school commercial courses, for example, should prove less popular than they are at present, since the graduates of such courses, being too young to evade the continuation-school law, will find that their escape from school is but partial and their opportunity to earn very limited. The demand, therefore, for short cuts and ready-made education should lessen. Even if the demand does not lessen, the public-school authorities, having in mind their long period of control over the student, will do well to rearrange their objectives in most of the periods of school life.

Since the student is to stay in school longer, the need for early technical preparation disappears. In the grade school, and especially in the early years of the high school, we can no longer avoid doing our real educational duty of attempting to interpret the "Business of Living" for the student. The excuse that the student will be in school only a brief time, or that he must have a quick technical education to enable him to earn money, has little validity in a state where a compulsory part-time law is in force. When the early years of the secondary school are thus used for broad, general work, the part-time and continuation school will find, for pupils so trained, its own proper place is in dealing with certain techniques. On the basis of a broad foundation, a student may be related to this job, perhaps introduced to it, certainly improved in its performance, by the continuation school. But such introduction should come to require less of an interpretation of a job in its relation to social living. The meaning of our social life should have come earlier and the application of that knowledge to a specific task, once that task is comprehended, should follow naturally.

There should thus come to be left for the continuation school a narrower and more applied field of operations. This field, though narrow, will be varied. The work in such schools must be practical and will demand for its proper performance quite as careful planning, organization, and teaching, as are needed in any other type of school. There seems to be no doubt that the idea of short unit courses will persist. Materials for such courses must be prepared. There seems, too, good reason to believe that the continuation school and the corporation school will, to a considerable extent, join hands. In fact, there are instances already established where such schools are in part co-operative, in part continuation, and in part corporation institutions.

On the basis of a properly organized grade and secondary education, the continuation school can be an agency of great value. Its threat in the past has been in receiving pupils at too early an age, while they were without any proper basis of choice of vocation and without any notion of the social implications of various types of work. With a proper reorganization of the work in the grades and secondary school, however, this difficulty should be avoided, and the continuation school can play a rôle of increasing value in adjusting students to industry and in the improvement of specific vocational skills.

QUESTIONS FOR DISCUSSION

1. What is a continuation school?
2. May continuation schools be compulsory? not compulsory?
3. Taking the Chicago continuation school as an example, when are the schools in session? What are the requirements for pupils who go to continuation schools? Must eighth-grade graduates attend? Who need not go to continuation schools? Do continuation-school pupils have a vacation?
4. A continuation school is sometimes said to be a school for young people who have gone to work. Does this mean that an unemployed person of the designated ages is not required to attend continuation school?
5. The Illinois law provides that employment certificates will be withdrawn from those pupils whose attendance is irregular. Does this seem an adequate penalty? What weakness or strength do you discern in it?
6. Would it be as well to plan evening schools to do all the work now attempted by continuation schools?
7. From some source secure figures dealing with the same ideas as those presented by the survey of the New York Military Training Commission. On the basis of the data which you find, is it your conclusion that the New York figures overstate or understate the case?

8. The tradition of the continuation school is not that of a vocational school. Explain.
9. "State legislation, prior to the Smith-Hughes Law, was based upon conflicting attitudes." What were the matters of conflict?
10. What would you understand by the phrases "a mandatory continuation school law," "permissive continuation school law," and "permissive-mandatory continuation school law"?
11. What was the Smith-Hughes Act? What were the conditions under which the Smith-Hughes Law made federal money available for state aid in education?
12. What are the chief matters for which provision must be made in enacting a part-time compulsory-education law.
13. Just what was the significance of the Smith-Hughes Act to continuation schools?
14. How would you account for the fact that commercial education was less generously provided for under the Smith-Hughes Law than was industrial education?
15. It was only by liberal interpretation of the phrase "subjects given to enlarge the civic or vocational intelligence of workers" that commercial education was given attention under the Smith-Hughes Law. Explain.
16. "The Commercial Education Service has two phases." What are these two phases? What ruling was necessary to make it legal that co-operative high-school classes in retail-selling and office practice could be subsidized with federal funds?
17. Commercial work in continuation schools is incidental. Examples of such work must, therefore, be studied in a setting of general continuation-school organization. Is this statement true? Is it a natural outgrowth of the development of continuation schools?
18. Explain the course as outlined for the boys at Cass Technical High School of Detroit. Is this course essentially concerned with vocational activities or with the general broadening of the student's intelligence?
19. What are the features of the Detroit continuation school for girls? Why differentiate the schools for boys and girls? What are the chief vocations for girls? Is the problem of a girls' continuation school a more difficult one than the boys' continuation school?
20. What is the purpose of the "mixed group" in the girls' continuation school of Detroit?

21. What special problem is presented to continuation schools by pupils in employments that demand no special skill or training?
22. Examine the basis of commercial work in the Detroit continuation school. Prepare a list of comments on this work. These comments may be favorable or adverse, or they may elaborate on some of the ways in which this work can be done.
23. In Trenton the work is organized on a unit basis. What are Lomax' comments on the Trenton experience in teaching typewriting? Would you be inclined to extend the comment to any other subjects?
24. The directors of commercial continuation schools in Chicago think rather highly of the continuation schools which have been placed in business plants. What advantages are to be found in schools so located? Do such schools gain any advantage in teaching matters of general information or only in teaching those of immediate vocational concern? Do such schools appear to give a financial advantage to the public-school system? Do they give a financial advantage to the corporation as compared with the organization of a corporation school?
25. The statement is made concerning one continuation school in a business plant that the pupils' time alone "costs the company thousands of dollars annually." Is this a valid claim?
26. Work over the material describing the continuation school in the plant of Swift & Company, making a list of comments on the various divisions of the material presented.
27. Draw up a statement or series of statements which present what seems to you to be the proper place or rôle of the continuation school in the planned scheme of business education.

CHAPTER XVIII

CO-OPERATIVE BUSINESS COURSES

It is easy to confuse the co-operative plans of training which we are to discuss in this chapter with continuation schools or part-time schools as they are often called. The terms are used more or less interchangeably by many persons. Indeed in some instances there is official treatment of the two as practically identical. For example, under the rulings of the Federal Board for Vocational Education, "the decision as to whether the high-school co-operative classes in commercial subjects shall be subsidized or not" rests entirely with the state board. In case they are so subsidized, many would think they could properly be spoken of only as continuation schools. In many instances, however, no such subsidy is arranged, and, in fact, co-operative schools were in successful operation before the passage of the Smith-Hughes Law. In the case of co-operative schools, the school is the agency which operates and controls the scheme of education. The work is for regular students, while a continuation school is essentially for those persons who are no longer classified as regular students and whose interest in education is secondary rather than primary. The co-operative school course, then, is a device for aiding and improving the regular school instruction, while the continuation school is a means of continuing or supplementing an education which has been formally completed.

The co-operative idea, in American education at least, appears to have been begun in the work of Dean Herman L. Schneider, of the University of Cincinnati.

In the College of Engineering of the University of Cincinnati he first applied his much-imitated plan:[1]

[1] Adapted from the *University of Cincinnati Record*, Series I, Vol. XVII, No. 1, January, 1921. "Co-operative Courses, College of Engineering and Commerce, 1921–1922," pp. 10–13.

The College of Engineering of the University of Cincinnati originated in a professorship of civil engineering, which was established in 1874. In this year a complete four-year course was offered, leading to the degree of Civil Engineer. By 1905, instruction had been extended to include mechanical, chemical, and electrical engineering, and the enrollment in the several departments totaled 120 students.

In September, 1906, instruction on the co-operative plan was begun, and the first class of 27 co-operative students was admitted. The regular full-time theoretical courses were continued, with an enrollment of 107 students, but the co-operative course was offered as an alternative to those students of mechanical, chemical, and electrical engineering who wished to combine practical experience with their study of technical theory. Under the co-operative plan, a carefully co-ordinated schedule was arranged, whereby the student spent six years in alternate weeks of classroom instruction at the University and of practical work in the industries of Cincinnati. The co-operative class was divided into two sections, one of which was at the University while the other was at work in the shops, and vice versa. Unless by special arrangement, each student had an alternate, so that both the school and the shop were always full-manned. During the first year, the University co-operated with fifteen firms, including chiefly manufacturers of machine tools and of electrical equipment.

In September, 1909, a co-operative course in civil engineering was added to those in mechanical, electrical, and chemical engineering. The years from 1909–1910 to 1916–1917 witnessed a steady growth of the co-operative course in the four departments.

More significant than the number of firms are the variety of industries and the increased radius of operation. Typical of the firms added were rolling mills, structural iron works, a gas and electric company, and manufacturers of automobiles, elevators, engines, bicycles and motorcycles, cash registers, fire engines, printing machinery, paper-making machinery, adding machines, roofing, ink, and soap. The area covered by these industries included not only the city and suburbs of Cincinnati, but also Hamilton, Middletown, Dayton, Piqua, and Springfield, Ohio, and Richmond and Indianapolis, Indiana. During this period the time of the co-operative course was changed from six years of nine months each to five years of eleven months each, and the period of alternation was changed from one week to two.

In April, 1919, the College of Commerce was merged with the College of Engineering, and a reorganization of both courses was begun by committees of the two faculties. In the Department of Commerce, as in the engineering departments, the instruction is given on the co-operative plan. Under this arrangement, the student spends alternate two- or four-week periods at work in various business establishments in and near Cincinnati. During the first two years of the course, emphasis is placed on production, and the student obtains experience in one of the electrical, chemical, or mechanical manufacturing plants.

The last three years of the course are devoted to a study of the problems of financing and marketing. These terms must be interpreted broadly as including all the relationships involved in the conduct of business aside from the purely internal technical processes of production.

The city of Fitchburg, Massachusetts, furnishes an outstanding example of a public-school system which took over Dean Schneider's plan and made extensive use of it in connection with industrial education.[1]

The idea was not so rapidly absorbed in commercial work, although there are now numerous instances of its employment in public-school commercial courses. It has been applied perhaps most frequently in courses in retail selling, although it has been used often and extensively in office-work courses.

TYPES OF CO-OPERATIVE BUSINESS COURSES

Three clearly distinguishable plans are used in co-operative business courses. In one plan the pupils are allowed to go into commercial establishments on Saturdays and other holidays and after the regular school hours. A second plan may be called the "alternate-half-day" plan. Under this arrangement two pupils work in one establishment, one taking care of the duties of a position in the forenoon and the other in the afternoon. The second pupil attends school in the morning, the first in the afternoon. A third plan is the "alternate-week" plan. In this

[1] An interesting description of co-operation applied through an entire course is Arthur E. Morgan's "What Is College For?" in the *Atlantic Monthly* (May, 1922), pp. 642–50.

plan the school work is repeated alternate weeks for the two sets of pupils, the two groups alternating on the job.

CO-OPERATIVE COURSES IN RETAIL SELLING

The effort to carry on some form of co-operative high-school work in retail selling seems to have begun when Mrs. Lucinda W. Prince, now head of the Prince School of Education for Store Service of Boston, introduced courses in retail selling into the Boston high schools. Pupils were placed in stores on Saturday to get their store experience, or after school hours and on Saturdays. The courses proved popular, and the number of pupils increased rapidly, though it is claimed that there was a good deal of dissatisfaction because a great many of the girls who graduated left the field of retail selling. This caused merchants to complain that after they had put time and money into the work of training, the young people did not stay with them. This plan of Saturday and holiday work which gained some publicity as the "Boston plan" appears now to have been in part abandoned or at least supplemented by the alternate-week plan. This change is interesting in view of Boston's historic position in this movement and certain possible reasons for the loss of interest in salesmanship under the older scheme. These have been suggested.[1]

1. Pupils in a commercial course are devoting a large part of their time to preparing for office work. Upon graduation they are better prepared for this work and more interested in it than in the salesmanship.

2. The courses in salesmanship and merchandise, being new and somewhat experimental, were less rich in educational content than other courses and so did not command the respect of the pupils.

3. The store experience given in the rush of Saturday was both less valuable and less interesting, and more trying than when given under normal conditions.

[1] These reasons are adapted from *Bulletin of High Points*, IV, No. 2 (February, 1922), p. 4. Published by the Board of Education of the City of New York.

4. Saturday work for two years does not give a pupil enough experience to assure her a good position upon graduation, such a position, for instance, as that of a regular sales clerk in a good department, although for a pupil gifted with a desirable personality it may prove a sufficient apprenticeship.

5. If one adds to all this, the prejudice against store work among many of the parents and teachers, the opposition which any new movement has to overcome and the difficulty of obtaining satisfactory teachers for new subjects, it is not hard to see why salesmanship courses conducted on the Boston plan have made but little progress.

ESSENTIALS IN CO-OPERATIVE CLASSES

Four things seem to be essential for satisfactory co-operative commercial work. These are a well-planned course, trained teachers, proper agreements with business houses, and a capable co-ordinator. In considering the possibility of well-planned courses we can perhaps do no better than to examine several courses which are in operation in high schools.

The co-operative course at present in operation in Boston may be examined first.[1]

THE CO-OPERATIVE COURSE

The week-in and week-out plan of retail selling revolves around salesmanship, but it adds several other subjects. In this course, pupils are employed by the large stores. If they fail of employment, they must report to the high school for full time instruction. The stores keep a record of attendance and report the quality of the work done by the pupils who are routed through the stores according to the following schedule:

Marking	2 weeks
Examining	4 weeks
Stock work	2 weeks
Cashiering	4 weeks
Selling	8 weeks

Total 20 weeks in store

[1] This statement is adapted from Louis J. Fish, "Retail Selling in the Boston High Schools," *Current Affairs*, December 12, 1921.

Retail Selling Course as Authorized by the School Committee. Alternate Weeks in Stores and in School

TWO-YEAR COURSES[1]

Third Year

	Periods
Physical Training	2
English III (business)	5
History of Commerce	5
Physics or Chemistry (household)	5
Salesmanship (including store mathematics)	5
Drawing III (applied)	4
Co-operative Store Practice (or in school)	

Fourth Year

Physical Training	2
English IV (business)	5
American History and Citizenship	4
Salesmanship (with store mathematics)	5
Textiles	5
Commercial Law or Drawing IV (applied)	3 or 4
Co-operative Store Practice (or in school)	

ONE-YEAR COURSE[2]

Fourth Year

	Periods
Physical Training	2
English IV (business)	5
American History and Citizenship	4
Salesmanship (with store mathematics)	5
Textiles	5
Drawing IV (applied)	4
Co-operative Store Practice (or in school)	

Pupils taking this course are divided into two groups, one group to be in the store while the other group is in school—each group changing places alternate weeks, and the school work repeated alternate weeks.

[1] This course is authorized for the third and fourth years of a pupil's four-year course.

[2] This course is authorized for the fourth year only of the four-year course.

Two objects have been kept clearly in view in preparing these courses. First, the pupil must be thoroughly trained to do the tasks which fall to her lot as stock girl, examiner, marker, inspector, or salesperson. Most important of all, she must be trained in habits of promptness, neatness, and accuracy. Absolute honesty must be held up to her as a *sine qua non*. Second, the pupil must be given the foundation on which to build if she rises to an executive position in the store. Such a pupil may fairly be expected to rise out of the ranks in the course of a few years, and any training offered by the high school should take this into account.

The co-operative course in retail selling is given at the High School of Practical Arts to which any pupil in the Boston high schools may transfer.

CO-OPERATIVE COURSES IN NEW YORK

The Haaren High School of New York furnishes another very interesting example of co-operative work. The Haaren High School, it should be noted, is the co-operative high school for the city of New York. Co-operative courses are conducted only there, and pupils who wish to take co-operative courses go to Haaren rather than to other New York high schools. This concentration has obviously some administrative advantages. This notion of concentrating one type of work is similar to the idea of concentrating commercial work in specialized high schools. Certain facts concerning the work at Haaren follow.[1]

WHO MAY BE ADMITTED

1. A graduate of elementary school.
2. A graduate of an intermediate school.
3. Any student desiring to transfer from another high school.

Diploma given

Either school gives a regular high school diploma.

The four year commercial diploma is recognized by colleges offering advanced business courses.

The industrial diploma admits to certain technical schools such as the University of Cincinnati, Lowell School of Design, etc.

The courses do not prepare for an academic college.

Regents' examinations are not given.

[1] The data given is adapted from literature of the Haaren High School in March, 1922.

Courses offered

A secretarial course for pupils desiring training as stenographers and typists, including actual experience as such with business firms.

An accounting course training for business positions in this line of work or as preparatory work or university training. Actual practice with business firms is given.

A course in salesmanship including instruction in raw materials, processes of manufacture, and marketing of goods. During the course employment and adequate training in the actual selling of goods is furnished in the largest stores.

Industrial courses, where boys may enter technical, chemical or electrical occupations.

Employment work

Before pupils are sent out to work, a position is carefully investigated by a co-ordinator and must meet the requirements of the school in regard to surroundings, type of work, hours and compensation. Every effort is made to fit the pupil to the job. Misfits are changed from one position to another until the work for which they are best suited is found.

Although all outside work is under the supervision of the school, the pupil is subject to the same conditions of employment that he will have to face at graduation.

In the description of the co-operative courses in salesmanship, textiles, color, design, and advertising at the Haaren High School, the outlines are here very much abbreviated, and samples from the outline rather than the outline as a whole are introduced:[1]

The outlines in Salesmanship, Textiles, Non-Textiles, Color and Design, and Advertising which follow have been developed to meet the needs of the classes in these subjects at the Haaren High School. In order to grasp the full significance of these outlines one must understand that this school offers a four-year high-school course intended to fit boys and girls for selling, especially in the retail field. After the first year, pupils are placed on the week-in-week-out plan in various stores of the city. By this means practical experience under

[1] From an unsigned statement in *Bulletin of High Points*, III, No. 8 (October, 1921), pp. 9–19. Published by the Board of Education of the City of New York.

normal conditions goes hand in hand with school training. In the store, they are doing messenger work, packing, and stock work in the second year. In school, they are learning the importance of good stock-keeping and the best methods of caring for such merchandise as is commonly found in the stores of the city. By the third year of the school course most of the pupils are selling. In this year much training is given in selling, as the outline indicates.

Two objects have been kept clearly in view in preparing these outlines. First, the pupil must be thoroughly trained to do the tasks which fall to his lot as stock boy, packer, or salesman, with accuracy and intelligence. Second, the pupil must be given the foundation on which to build if he is to rise to an executive position in the store. Our intelligence tests indicate that the pupil who is able and willing to finish a four-year high-school course is above the average in mental ability. Such a person may fairly be expected to rise out of the ranks in the course of a few years and any training offered by the school should take this into account.

Second Term[1]

I. Stock keeping
  A. What is meant by a well-kept stock?
  B. Dead stock caused by:
II. Salesmanship
III. Salesmanship of merchandise
  A. Customer
  B. Sales clerk
  C. Talking points of merchandise
  D. The sale
  E. Much practice in selling by demonstration sales
IV. Use of telephone
V. Practice in writing and figuring sales checks

Third Term

I. Functions of the department store
  A. Buying goods
  B. Buying problems
  C. Selling
  D. Service to customers

[1] The first term deals with personality and to some extent with the relation of the individual to the organization.

II. Sales training
  A. Types of customers
  B. Answering objections
  C. Vocabulary work
  D. Sales dialogues prepared
  E. Practice in store mathematics discount

Fourth Term

I. History of retail selling
II. Different types of retail establishments
  A. Characteristics and special advantages and limitations of each of the following:
III. Wholesale selling
  A. Manufacturer and sales agents' expositions
  B. Manufacturers' selling department
  C. Manufacturers' agents
  D. Jobbers
  E. Traders and speculators
IV. Cost of production
  A. Manufacture
V. Factors determining the market price
VI. Cost of retailing
VII. Store mathematics. Problems based on the above
VIII. Training in selling for these different types of organizations

Fifth and Sixth Terms

I. Types of business organizations
  A. Retail
  B. Wholesale
II. Employment problems
  A. Employment blank. Content and purpose
  B. Interview. Analysis of the job
  C. Physical and mental tests
III. Welfare work in mercantile establishments
  A. Need for it
  B. Divisions
    1. Outside activities, recreational work
    2. Lunch room
    3. Health
    4. Mutual Benefit Association

IV. Educational departments
   A. Place of the educational department
   B. Content of courses
   C. Error systems
   D. Rating system
   E. Methods of paying sales people: Salary, bonus salary, and commission
   F. Manuals in mail-order houses, banks and stores
   G. Theory and practice of teaching
V. Merchandising
   A. Store advertising
   B. Mail-order department
   C. Adjustment department
   D. Correspondence department
   E. Comparison department
   F. Buying—department budget
   G. Selling—demonstration sales

Textiles

I. Acquaintance with materials in general. Samples of common materials, with which the students are familiar, are placed in their hands to be examined and unravelled. With the unravelling of the material an idea of warp and filling is introduced, and the consequent strength of finished materials
   A. Definition of textiles, woof or filling, picks, ends, selvedge, fiber, thread (yarn)
   B. Weaves.
   C. Staple fabrics. (Students are taught to use the pick glass to examine materials for weave, number of picks and ends and kind of material)
II. Acquaintance with woolen materials
   A. General characteristics
   B. Characteristics of wool fiber
   C. Causes of peculiarities in wool fiber
III. Carpets
   A. Kinds
   B. Uses for each
   C. Where manufactured
   D. History of carpet-making
IV. Acquaintance with silk
   A. Tests for silk

V. Acquaintance with cotton
VI. Acquaintance with linen
VII. Laces
  A. Real hand-made lace
  B. Imitation or machine-made

In addition to this study, the salesmanship course includes a similar study of books, stationery, leather goods, rubber goods, jewelry, cosmetics, toilet articles, notions, furniture, china, glass, and silverware.

THE ROCHESTER EXPERIENCE

Another example worth viewing is the experiment in Rochester, New York:[1]

The part-time commercial classes were actually started in Rochester in September, 1917, through co-operation with the Committee on Education at the Chamber of Commerce. In August the Chamber of Commerce sent out a circular letter to a large number of business offices. This letter described the proposed plan and suggested that the reader fill in and return an enclosed blank form for an interview with a representative of the Board of Education. The replies to these letters were very encouraging and the interviews which followed were even more gratifying. By September there had been listed all the positions for which there were students available.

A canvass in the schools had been made in June, so the approximate number of part-time students were known. Because there were only thirteen students registered for the work in East High and the same number registered in West High it was decided that one teacher going from one school to the other alternating weeks should handle both classes.

As the business man had been told the plan the position of the school was at this point much like that of an employment bureau. Here were the specifications and requirements of an existing job for which the school attempted to pick two students who seemed best suited both from the standpoint of education and personal qualifications to handle the work. Geographical conditions also had to be considered, as the students came from two high schools. The student

[1] Adapted from a statement received in March, 1922, from S. B. Carkin, director of business education, Rochester, N.Y.

had to do his own bargaining and finally make secure his own position. The school simply told him where to apply.

Before the student takes up his duties at the office he is given a sheet, "Suggestions to Students," which pictures the seriousness of business, as well as giving certain detailed suggestions. Each student on his return to school is required to have ready for the teacher a detailed weekly account of his business experience. This form shows the kind of work performed each day and the amount of time spent on each kind. It also shows the total hours spent on each type of work for the week. This weekly work report is transferred to a permanent record card which is kept on file to determine whether or not the student is receiving the proper variety of practice training. Since school credit is given for business experience it is desirable to know the progress of the student from the employer's viewpoint. The employer is asked to fill out monthly, or just before school reports are issued, a blank report form which is considered in making up the monthly grades of the student. The report of the employer is of a general nature and tends to show whether or not the student is making progress with the business man. Such qualifications as industry, punctuality, initiative, courtesy, and neatness appear on the report. A blank space is left after each qualification, where the employer may make suggestions. Some very interesting and helpful suggestions have been made by the business man.

One feature of the plan which is entirely different from that of most other cities is that the teacher of the class (that is the commercial teacher who has the regular part-time subjects) does the work of the so-called co-ordinator. The work of the co-ordinator is very important, but in some cities where it has been made a special work, separate from the teaching, much criticism has arisen concerning the cost. One argument in favor of the part-time teacher as the co-ordinator is that the work is done first hand. The teacher knows the student and after becoming acquainted with the co-operating firms is the natural medium, or go-between.

Up to the present only Seniors in the commercial course have been eligible for the part-time work. An attempt has been made to keep this plan before the other students in other departments as a goal toward which to work. This does not mean that students in other departments are barred from part-time work; it simply means that the Senior commercial students are trained for such office positions as this plan offers and they are therefore chosen. The subjects for this course are not necessarily exactly the same for every student. The required subjects are commercial English and correspondence, advertising, salesmanship and business organization, commercial law, one semester and economics the other and American history with civics. The electives are reporting principles, advanced bookkeeping, elocution and public speaking.

The school allows thirty credits for one school year for this business experience. This is equivalent to one full school subject and one-half. Only one-half the credits allowed full-time subjects are granted part-time subjects. While the actual school attendance is cut in half, it is felt that because of the quickened conception and interest of the student much more than half of the regular subject-matter is generally covered.

OFFICE WORK CO-OPERATION IN THE CINCINNATI HIGH SCHOOLS

A final example to be noticed is furnished by the Cincinnati high schools:[1]

This course is designed to give a thorough preparation for commercial work, and a broad general training in academic studies. It prepares directly for the occupations of stenographer and typist, bookkeeper, or any clerical office position, as well as for retail selling and commercial advertising.

The subjects required are English (four years), a foreign language (two years), mathematics (two years), history (one year), civics (two years), and the technical commercial subjects (four years), including bookkeeping, penmanship and applied art, stenography and typewriting and business practice, salesmanship and commercial advertising.

During the second half of the fourth year students may be employed during the afternoon in selected business houses.

The plan as carried out, in the main, is as follows: The program of studies for these pupils is so arranged that the technical studies, bookkeeping, shorthand and salesmanship, come in the afternoon and the academic studies in the morning. The pupils taking part in the plan are permitted to leave school at noon and report at the place of assignment for work. The pupil thus continues for a two week period, then another pupil is assigned to take his place. These two

[1] From statements of I. R. Garbutt and literature of the Cincinnati schools.

alternate then two weeks full time in school and two weeks part time in an office. By this plan the pupils can do the full amount of academic work required and at the same time gain valuable office experience.

At the end of each two week period a report is required from the employer of each pupil as to the efficiency of the work performed during that period. The pupil is given credit for this report on the class room teacher's record, rating Excellent 90 to 100, Very Good 80 to 90, Good 70 to 80. The employer is also given an opportunity on the report, to offer any suggestions that would better prepare the pupil for the work that he is undertaking. The pupil is paid for this work at the rate of seventy-five cents per each half day's service.

The plan has worked out fairly satisfactorily, the greatest difficulty being to place the pupils where they will get the kind of office practice that will be most beneficial to them.

Graduates of this course are admitted to the University of Cincinnati, provided applicants for admission to the College of Liberal Arts offer Mathematics I (Algebra) and Mathematics II (Plane Geometry) and three years of foreign language (two of which must be in one language), and applicants for admission to the College of Engineering and Commerce offer Solid Geometry.

A two-year salesmanship course, co-operative during both years, is offered for students who have completed the second year of any of the other courses. This course is intended especially to prepare for retail mercantile selling, and will also be a valuable preparation for other lines of salesmanship. The leading stores of the city have offered their assistance in this course, and students will be assigned to work in these stores during the afternoons and on Saturdays. For this work they will be paid the usual wages of the stores. This course does not prepare for college.

OTHER NECESSITIES IN SUCCESSFUL CO-OPERATION

The lack of properly trained teachers has apparently been a handicap to co-operative courses especially in retail selling. The Prince School of Salesmanship was for some time practically the only source from which such trained teachers could be drawn. In 1919, however, New York University opened a school to carry on this work. This school was, at least in its inception, in part supported by contributions of merchants who were interested in co-operative education.

Proper agreements with co-operating business houses have already been stated to be a requisite to good co-operative work. Forms used for agreements and reports are given below. The first is the agreement between stores and school department used in Boston. The second set of forms are the agreements and reports suggested by the Federal Board for Vocational Education.

AGREEMENT RELATIVE TO SALESMANSHIP COURSES[1]

In order that there may be a definite and understood policy governing the relations between the School Department of the City of Boston and various Boston retail stores, interested in securing as employees students enrolled in the salesmanship courses of the high schools, during their period of training and after graduation, the following agreement is entered into between the interested stores and the School Department:

(1) An advisory committee, representing the schools, the stores and the employees, to act upon any question arising in the course of administration of this plan, shall be immediately appointed upon the approval of this agreement. The representatives of the stores shall be nominated by the Governing Board of the Retail Trade Board, those of the schools by the School Department, and those of the employees by the members of the committee representing the stores and the schools. This committee will recommend from time to time such changes in the plan of operation as may appear advisable. No change shall be made in the plan of operation as affecting the stores until the advisory committee has notified the co-operating stores, and has called a meeting of these stores to discuss the proposed change if three or more stores believe that such a meeting is necessary.

(2) It is agreed that the stores approving this plan be given preference by the School Department in the assignment of services of students in training.

(3) So far as is practical students, upon entering the salesmanship courses, shall be definitely selected and engaged by the co-operating

[1] From Louis J. Fish, "Retail Selling in the Boston High Schools," *Current Affairs*, Boston High School, 1921.

stores, the student to be on the payroll of the store throughout the training course, subject to the store regulation, during days of employment, and subject to other conditions as may be specified in the agreement. Each student shall be sent to one or more of the stores with a card of introduction from the principal of the school, or from the School Department. The applicant will be interviewed personally by the superintendent or head of the employment department.

(4) The store shall furnish the School Department with regular reports as to the attendance and quality of work of students in training while in their employ. The students shall be subject to the same discipline as any other employee, and to discharge for cause on the same basis as any other employee, but it is understood that the School Department will be notified in the case of discipline or suspension, and prior to discharge, and that such actions may be considered by the advisory committee if it appears that they violate the spirit or intention of this approved plan.

(5) During the present year, so far as possible, students in training will be released for work in the stores on Saturdays and on Mondays from 12:00 o'clock noon. During the Christmas season students with an "A" grade will be released for three weeks prior to Christmas; those with a "B" grade for two weeks prior to Christmas; those with a "C" grade for one week prior to Christmas for the present year.

(6) The rate of compensation for students who are employed in the store shall be $10 per week during their first year of employment and $12 per week during their second year of employment.

(7) The stores agree that students in training in their employ shall be routed through the store, having training in the various lines of store work, including examining and cashiering, marking stock and selling work, in order that the student may have broad training and experience. Each co-operating store will submit a plan for this routing for the approval of the advisory committee.

(8) At the end of the course the student in training shall be given special consideration for regular employment, shall be credited for purposes of pay and promotion in the employing store with one year's experience, and in no case where the student is retained as a regular employee by the store that has employed the student during the training period shall the pay be less than the last rate paid during training.

(9) It is understood that the committee representing the stores and the School Department shall consider immediately the problem of undertaking publicity and other measures necessary to interest in the salesmanship courses the best available students.

Name of Firm ....
Signature ....
Date ....

FEDERAL BOARD FORMS

The following agreement and report forms are suggested by the Federal Board:[1]

CONTRACT FOR CO-OPERATIVE WORK

This Agreement, entered into this...... day of......, 19..., between......, party of the first part, and......, party of the second part, Provided as follows:

1. Party of the first part agrees to employ
   (*a*) Two or more students of the ...... high school on a co-operative basis beginning ......, 19...
   (*b*) To arrange for such students to work alternate weeks.
   (*c*) To pay a salary of $...... to each worker for the weeks actually spent in the office of such co-operating firm.
   (*d*) To rotate these workers in the various occupations of the office or store so as to insure an all-around experience.
   (*e*) To see that such workers are given the usual instruction given to beginners in such work.
   (*f*) To make a report on each such worker at least once a month on blanks furnished for the purpose.
   (*g*) To refrain from offering full-time employment to such workers before the expiration of the period covered by this agreement without the consent of the party of the second part.
   (*h*) To retain on a full-time basis one or both of such workers at the expiration of the period covered by this agreement, providing mutually satisfactory arrangements can be made by the parties concerned.
   (*i*) To attend occasional conferences as required for the discussion of important matters connected with co-operative educational work.

2. Party of the second part agrees
   (*a*) To consider the needs of the party of the first part in making assignments of students under this contract.
   (*b*) To co-operate in every way with the party of the first part to make this co-operative plan mutually advantageous.
   (*c*) To plan the courses pursued by such workers so as to aid them in the performance of their tasks from week to week.
   (*d*) To replace such workers with others when it seems best for all parties concerned providing additional student workers are available.
   (*e*) To attend conferences as required.

(Signed)..
Representative of the Company

(Signed)..
Co-ordinator or Instructor

[1] Adapted from Federal Board for Vocational Education, *Bulletin No. 34*, pp. 65–66. Commercial Series No. 3.

EMPLOYER'S REPORT ON CO-OPERATION OF STUDENTS

Name of student........................... Month ending...................
Name of firm..
By.... ....

If the student is above the average in any of the following, kindly note by using such terms as, "Good" or "Excellent." If the student is deficient, make a corresponding notation, in order that steps may be taken to remedy the trouble, if possible. Industry.. Punctuality..................................... Initiative... Judgment... Neatness.. Thoughtfulness............................... Courtesy.. Honesty... Other qualities...............................	Suggestions for benefit of students:

Remarks:

STUDENT'S REPORT

Report for week ending..........., 1919.
Name...
Employed by...
Dept...

Days absent from work (give dates and cause):

Kind of work and amount of time devoted to each.

Kinds of work	Mon.	Tues.	Wed.	Thur.	Fri.	Sat.	Total
....	....	....	....	....	....	....	....
....	....	....	....	....	....	....	....
....	....	....	....	....	....	....	....
....	....	....	....	....	....	....	....
....	....	....	....	....	....	....	....

Remarks on back.

PROGRESS AND EXPERIENCE RECORD

Summary of work—Co-operative plant
Name of student.............................. From.............., 191—
Employed by.................................... To................., 191—

Kind of work						
....	....	....	....	....	....	....
....	....	....	....	....	....	....
....	....	....	....	....	....	....
....	....	....	....	....	....	....
....	....	....	....	....	....	....

(The student's school record should be given on the reverse side of this card.)

NOTICE OF ASSIGNMENT TO CO-OPERATIVE POSITION

................., 19—

To..

....

You have been assigned to

....

....

....

for part-time work, in lieu of school work, alternate weeks, for the term beginning ....

Please report to............at the above address on Monday morning........1919, at — o'clock.

The salary agreed upon is $...... a week for the weeks you are actually employed.

The undersigned will co-operate with you to the end that your new work may be both pleasant and profitable.

____

Co-ordinator or Instructor

Perhaps more important than any other matter in successful co-operative undertakings is the work of the co-ordinator. It is the co-ordinator, as the term implies, who is finally responsible for what a course in co-operative education accomplishes. The first burden of making the courses, as well as the constant administration of the many difficult situations which arise, is likely to fall upon the co-ordinator. Miss Ellen L. Osgood, of the Haaren High School, who has met this difficult task with exceptional success, outlines the duties of the co-ordinator in the following way:[1]

1. Collect and organize teaching material necessary in new fields of education.

2. Bring to the school criticisms which come to us in connection with the performance of our pupils in business houses.

3. Interest business men in our proposition, make arrangements for the employment of our young people, select the boys and girls and send them out (this includes looking after working papers, keeping records, etc.), and after the young people are placed, following them up by observing them at work where possible, interviewing them in school and obtaining reports, both formal and informal, on their work. Out of these reports grows material for classroom work and subjects for personal interview.

4. Each co-ordinator teaches one class a day.

[1] From a statement prepared by Miss Osgood in April, 1922.

5. Co-ordinators should obtain much informative and valuable experience in fitting pupils with jobs which would enable them to do valuable vocational guidance work. It should also be possible for a co-ordinator to render his school a great service by collecting vocational guidance material and putting it at the service of the entire school.

The co-operative plan appears to be one of the most interesting of the newer developments in education for business. It offers an obvious opportunity for making an application of school theory and for learning in an actual commercial laboratory. It seems that where persons have fairly clearly settled upon their vocations, or at least upon the vocations with which they intend to ally themselves for some time after leaving school, the co-operative plan is invaluable. Imagine, for example, a student who is interested in selling. Careful students of salesmanship are increasingly inclined to the belief, which was so well brought out in the surveys (pages 198 to 201), that the most substantial factor in salesmanship is knowledge of the goods. Since an intimate knowledge of the goods especially in their commercial aspects and varieties can most economically be obtained by using a store as a laboratory, the co-operative scheme of training furnishes an economical method of procedure. On the other hand it seems quite possible that the co-operative idea may very easily be overdone. There may well be some doubt if students should be put into co-operative courses which train for so technical an undertaking as retail selling until the last six months or last year of their high-school course. (This statement of course need not apply to students who are certain they will not be in school beyond the first or second year.) It will be answered that it is impossible to teach young people all they should know about retail selling in one year. It seems quite likely, however, that if the first three years of a student's course have been properly used to give an understanding of business relationships and general business organization, with a proper study of accounting as an agency of control, that the specific application of this knowledge to retail selling or any other business will not be a matter requiring a great amount of time. It will also be asserted that the student who is interested in retail selling cannot learn enough of all products in one year. This is true, and it is one of the reasons why the course should be short. A student should not take time in school to learn enough of all products to be a salesman of all products. The most the high school should undertake should be to give him a background on which he can build more specific knowledge as he needs it, with perhaps specific knowledge enough of certain products, say furniture, *or* textiles, *or* books, *or* jewelry, to secure a position. The waste of giving a large group of people enough knowledge of all products to sell all of them well seems almost axiomatic.

A similar viewpoint is sound for co-operative office-work courses. An office is not a place to *teach principles*. It is a place to *teach the application* of principles to a particular office practice. The co-operative method, therefore, in office work should come late when the pupil is almost ready to take a job and should be used to make easy the connection between his underlying training and this job.

The proposal to place co-operative work late in the course neglects co-operation as a means of financing an education. But that consideration is outside this discussion. We are concerned here with *educational plans* only. The extent to which individuals should be publicly aided in securing education is no doubt an important matter. The extent to which the regular school should be organized to permit students to earn a living while in school, or the age at which pupils should be permitted to drop school in whole or in part (as is the case where the co-operative method is used to give the pupils a chance to earn) are important matters. But all of these matters are distinct from how best to arrange courses for *educational purposes*. They lie in the field of political science and legislation as related to education, not in the field of curriculum making.

The proper place of a high-school commercial co-operative course appears to be as an extension of a broad, basic, general course in business administration. It's only other proper rôle can perhaps be played as a special one- or two-year course for students who know definitely that they will be in school only for a short period of time. And in such an instance it is after all only a superstructure of technical work built on an assumption of general training and built unfortunately soon.

QUESTIONS FOR DISCUSSION

1. The terms continuation school and part-time school are, in most literature, used practically synonymously. How would you distinguish the co-operative course from the continuation school? What is the general philosophy behind such a plan as the co-operative course?
2. "Three clearly distinguishable plans are used in co-operative business courses." Distinguish carefully between these three. What advantage and disadvantage do you see in each of these? What matters of organization are essential for satisfactory co-operative commercial work?
3. Examine the co-operative course in retail selling as given in the Boston high schools. Consider whether this course covers the proper material for the technique of retail-sales work. Should a retail-sales person be taught subjects which are not included in this course? Should such a co-operative retail-sales course cover the last year, last two years, or more of the students' four years in high school?
4. What matters concerning salesmanship can be taught best through the actual selling process? What ones can better be taught without direct relation to the selling process?
5. Examine the co-operative selling courses of the Haaren High School. In connection with the outline of these courses consider the questions asked concerning the Boston course.
6. In Haaren considerable effort is made to specialize the courses. Is "Textiles" too broad a subject for a specialized course?
7. Contrast and compare the Boston, Haaren, and Rochester courses. What differences and similarities do you observe? What are the important matters in the organization of such a course?
8. Examine the plan of the co-operative office-work course in the Cincinnati high school. Does such a course raise issues not involved in the planning of a co-operative retail-selling course?
9. Go over the forms presented for use in co-operative work. Indicate where changes, if any, would need to be made in such forms if they were to be used in any school with which you are familiar.

10. What is the co-ordinator? What duties should the co-ordinator assume?
11. "The co-operative idea may easily be overdone." How, for example?
12. "Practice not principle can be taught in the office or shop. The co-operative course, therefore, is of value only when a large part of the training should be in practice." Would you agree or disagree?
13. Draw up a statement or series of statements that seem to you to express the proper place or rôle of co-operative courses in the plan scheme of business education.

CHAPTER XIX

EVENING-SCHOOL COMMERCIAL COURSES

While our chief interest in this study centers in the high-school evening courses in business work, it is necessary to an appreciation of that work to see something of the growth and significance of the evening-school movement, especially as it has been taken over by the public schools. The evening school in the United States is an old institution. The free public evening school is a much more recent undertaking. Still more recent is the extensive use of evening schools in business training.

The history of evening schools seems to fall roughly into three periods:[1] The earliest schools were private schools kept in the evening for pay. These early schools did not have a very large number of students, and they must not be compared with the private evening school of today which is ordinarily concerned with the presentation of technical courses. (Some considera-tion of these has been given in Chapters XII and XIV.) These early evening schools did, however, furnish an opportunity, to persons not otherwise provided for, to secure an elementary edu-cation. They familiarized people with the idea of evening study and attracted attention to the fact that many who were at work needed and desired more education.

A second phase of evening school work was that developed by benevolent societies for the benefit of the poor. From 1820 to 1840 or 1850 such schools were not uncommon. Some exam-ples were schools for slaves.

The third phase of evening-school work and the one in which we are most interested is represented by the free public evening schools established by the school authorities. Such schools were opened as early as 1681, when one was established in

[1] An extended study of the history of evening schools is to be found in Arthur J. Jones, *The Continuation School in the United States*, pp. 83–94. U.S. Bureau of Education, Bulletin No. 1, 1907, whole No. 367.

New York state. Numerous cities, however, are claimants for the distinction of having established the first night school in the United States. Most of these present the early half of the nineteenth century as the time of origin Louisville, Kentucky, appears to have organized such a school in 1834 and Cincinnati in 1840. In 1856 in Cincinnati there was opened what is probably the first free evening high school supported entirely by public funds. In 1866 such a free publicly supported high school was opened in New York City. This was the first public high school of any kind in New York City, the day high schools not being established until some years later.

Although the development of free public education offered in evening courses was much more tardy than was general public education, nevertheless, with the coming of the twentieth century, its extension was very rapid. The following comment of an educational journal in 1914 gives some impression of the rapidity in growth of this movement:[1]

> The press is filled with announcements of the tremendous sweep over the whole country of the night-school idea. The figures of attendance are almost incredible. Richmond, Virginia, enrols 4,000 students in 11 schools; Chicago has 35 schools with more than 25,000 attendance; St. Louis has 20,000 pupils in 22 schools; Milwaukee, 6,000 in 13 schools; Grand Rapids, Michigan, 4,000 students; Kansas City, 3,000; Minneapolis, 7,000; and hundreds of smaller cities report that their night-school facilities are taxed to the utmost. Every city reports a rapid increase in attendance, the figures from St. Louis being typical of the general 50 per cent increase: in 1912 there were 9,700 students in St. Louis night schools; in 1914, 20,000. Chicago has 8,000 more at the opening of the year than the total enrolment for last year. Three years ago, Richmond began with 43 pupils and two teachers; in six months there were 800 pupils and 18 teachers. The school grew only about 100 the second year, but during the third year a system of co-operation between school and employers increased the attendance to 4,000.
>
> The students who are thus attracted range in age from fourteen to sixty-five. There is no upper limit. By far the largest percentage

[1] Adapted by permission from Editorial Comment in *School Review*, XXII (December, 1914), 700–701.

are comparatively young men and women, roughly classified in three great groups: those who feel that they are handicapped by inadequate general education; foreigners who desire a command of English; and workers who wish to become more skilled in their occupations. The following data, collected from ten cities in Wisconsin, exclusive of Milwaukee, indicate pretty fairly the general distribution of night-school students:

Men, 6,887; women, 7,389; total number enrolled, 14,276; those leaving, 3,030; withdrawals, 443; returned to regular school, 17; enrolment at close of school, 6,791; average weekly attendance, 6,712. Enrolment by employment: bookkeepers, 336; stenographers, 379; laborers, 637; students, 208; housekeepers, 769; store clerks, 940; at home, 518; clerical work, 275; machinists, 469; carpenters, 124; factory workers, 1,796; electricians, 79; printers, 63; laundry workers, 33; helpers, 49; dressmakers, 127; telephone operators, 200; tailors, 17; milliners, 54; teamsters, 17; messengers, 14; plumbers and steam fitters, 11; candy-factory workers, 10; draftsmen, 121; molders, 49; painters, 35; blacksmiths, 27; cabinet-makers, 16; plasterers, 1; teachers, 290; pattern-makers, 18; waitresses, 426; librarians, 5; salesmen and women, 51; railroad employees, 29; delivery boys, 13; tinsmiths, 9; erectors, 13; typesetters, 3; storekeepers and business men, 197; domestics, 273; wood workers, 45; bakers, 9; rubber workers, 20; tanners, 41; farmers, 11; lumbermen, 31; nurses, 10; mechanics, 722; miscellaneous, 3,365; number of teachers, 328.

Perhaps in no better way than in the compilation of statistics can the present extent of public evening-school work be given. Table LVII, on page 505, though not all-inclusive, gives a fairly satisfactory presentation of the present enrolment and personnel in public night schools.

Just what evening-school enrolment means in one state is made clear in the quotation which follows. It is worth while to notice Mr. Fitzpatrick's statement that the evening school is almost the sole educational device for training the adult. In this respect evening schools differ from any other type of school considered, and this fact has an important bearing on the forms of work which they should offer.

The school is now serving the adult population largely through its evening classes. Adjustments are made in the day school for certain adults but this is largely an incidental service and affects comparatively few people. The extent and character of the service now rendered in the evening classes of the continuation school is shown in detail in the table on page 506.

An examination of this table indicates that the work of the evening school is largely given over to trade extension and trade preparatory work. The academic work given is apparently largely

TABLE LVII[1]

CURRENT ENROLMENT AND PERSONNEL IN PUBLIC NIGHT SCHOOLS

	Group I Cities of 100,000 Population and Over	Group II Cities of 30,000 to 100,000 Population	Group III Cities of 10,000 to 30,000 Population	Group IV Cities of 5,000 to 10,000 Population	Group V Cities of 2,500 to 5,000 Population	Preceding Groups Combined
Number of school systems reporting night schools	49	108	181	118	62	518
Teachers:						
Elementary schools	4,232	1,651	835	315	100	7,133
Secondary schools	4,288	1,082	633	171	46	6,220
Vocational schools	1,083	508	543	171	43	2,348
Other schools	142	107	89	25	13	376
Not distributed	495	7	....	....	....	502
Total men	4,957	1,469	926	284	85	7,721
Total women	5,283	1,886	1,174	398	117	8,858
Enrolment:						
Elementary schools	146,379	44,087	19,974	5,585	1,883	217,908
Secondary schools	201,717	36,919	19,663	4,053	1,031	263,383
Vocational schools	41,276	16,726	12,527	2,893	672	74,094
Other schools	3,892	3,265	2,029	500	237	9,923
Not distributed	19,892	213	....	....	....	20,105
Total boys	227,681	54,105	27,702	6,824	1,922	318,234
Total girls	185,475	47,105	26,491	6,207	1,901	267,179

intended for foreigners and for persons with very rudimentary educational training. These courses do not reveal any satisfaction of the general intellectual interests which must exist in the community. The civic interests are, also, not met. In a period when the women have been completely enfranchised it would seem that there should be in the vocational school evening classes immediate response to this opportunity for service.[2]

[1] Adapted by permission from *Statistics of City School Systems*, p. 9. U.S. Bureau of Education, Bulletin No. 24, 1919.

[2] The statement is adapted by permission from Edward A. Fitzpatrick, "Adult Education," *Wisconsin's Educational Horizon*, Vol. IV, No. 2, Part 2, pp. 9–10. State Board of Education, Madison, Wis., December, 1921.

TABLE LVIII

SCOPE OF WORK IN WISCONSIN EVENING SCHOOLS

Subject	No. of Schools	Men	Women	Total
Academic				
General—common branches course, reading, spelling	10	158	101	259
Citizenship	17	723	90	857
Civil service	2	120	55	175
Income tax	2	47	2	49
Language				
English				
General	18	844	321	1,165
Factory	1	28	28	56
Foreigners	15	798	250	1,081
French	10	45	124	169
Spanish	5	78	81	159
Mathematics (does not specify)	6	77	26	113
Algebra	2	22	......	22
Arithmetic	8	103	41	144
Business arithmetic	2	40	8	48
Shop mathematics	10	161	......	161
Trigonometry	1	8	......	8
Penmanship	8	69	84	177
Physiology	1	......	27	27
Spelling and penmanship	1	......	......	24
Science				
Chemistry	3	38	7	45
See also under Trade and Technical: Paper chemistry and pharmacy				
Social law	1	1	32	33
Commercial				
General (not described)	8	107	381	488
Accounting	6	112	71	203
Bookkeeping	31	566	675	1,356
Business English	8	121	126	247
Commercial law	2	31	7	50
Shorthand	31	274	1,948	2,418
Typewriting	28	527	2,091	2,700
Art				
Applied art	1	......	68	68
Architecture	2	137	1	138
Arts and crafts	3	1	68	76
China painting	2	......	38	38
Drawings	7	136	18	154
House decoration	5	12	127	184
Interior decoration	1	11	......	11
Needle art	1	......	102	102
Home Economics				
Cooking	28	3	932	935
Dietetics	2	......	62	62
Drafting patterns	1	......	10	10
Home nursing	6	......	87	87

TABLE LVIII—*Continued*

Subject	No. of Schools	Men	Women	Total
Home Economics				
House decoration	4	13	94	107
Knitting	1	......	74	74
Lace making	1	......	47	47
Sewing	35	......	3,179	3,179
Related Trade				
Blue print reading	3	79	......	79
Mechanical drawing	25	990	1	991
Slide rule	1	16	1	17
Trade and Technical				
Auto mechanics	17	1,120	48	1,168
Cabinet making	8	258	34	315
Carding	1	......	3	3
Concrete	1	17	......	17
Drafting	6	160	1	161
Electricity	9	320	......	320
Engineering principles	1	61	......	61
Estimating	1	21	......	21
Forging	3	116	......	116
Freight traffic	1	93	4	97
Gas engine	6	294	2	296
Heat treatment	1	33	......	33
Heating and ventilation	1	15	......	15
Machine shop	17	679	......	679
Massage	......	......	26	26
Millinery	19	......	936	936
Paper chemistry	1	17	1	18
Pattern making	2	48	......	48
Pharmacy	1	29	4	33
Printing	1	28	1	29
Salesmanship	2	36	7	43
Sheet metal	1	25	......	25
Shop (does not specify what)	1	......	......	63
Show card writing	2	41	5	46
Steam engine	1	92	......	92
Telegraphy	9	82	124	218
Trade analysis	8	......	......	8
Welding	1	20	......	20
Woodwork				
General	4	68	1	91
Carpentry	1	18	......	18
Cedar chests	1	2	12	14
Manual training	3	78	......	106
Roof framing	1	12	......	12
Miscellaneous				
First aid	1	......	23	23
Gymnasium and physical education	9	116	70	199
Music	3	37	111	173

A study of general figures, however, is likely to be very misleading. We are apt to gain the impression that the night school is a far more extensively used tool than is the case. It

TABLE LIX

ESTIMATED NUMBERS NOT ATTENDING SCHOOL

Age	Estimated Numbers Who Have Not Attended School in 1917–18		
	Total	Male	Female
14 years	370,000	190,000	180,000
15 years	620,000	320,000	300,000
16 years	1,040,000	530,000	510,000
17 years	1,360,000	690,000	670,000
18 years	1,630,000	820,000	810,000
19 years	1,800,000	890,000	910,000
20 years	1,920,000	950,000	970,000
Total	8,740,000	4,390,000	4,350,000

TABLE LX

A COMPARISON OF THOSE NOT IN SCHOOL AND THOSE GAINFULLY EMPLOYED

Age and Sex	Estimated Number in 1918	
	Gainfully Employed	Not in School
Both sexes		
14 to 20 years	7,130,000	8,740,000
14 and 15 years	1,210,000	990,000
16 to 20 years	5,920,000	7,750,000
Boys		
14 to 20 years	4,640,000	4,390,000
14 and 15 years	820,000	510,000
16 to 20 years	3,820,000	3,880,000
Girls		
14 to 20 years	2,490,000	4,350,000
14 and 15 years	390,000	480,000
16 to 20 years	2,100,000	3,870,000

has grown with rapidity, but the number of persons, even young persons to whom it could be usefully applied, is so vast that certainly not more than a tenth are reached. Dr. John Cummings has made the estimates shown above concerning the possible opportunity for evening schools and continuation schools.[1] He shows that between "eight and nine million boys and girls in the ages fourteen to twenty years have not attended any sort of school, public or private, day or evening," during the school year 1917–18.

Even more definite evidence on the limited reach of the evening school was furnished by the study of the New York Military Training Commission:[2]

The night-school enrolment of boys of these ages [sixteen, seventeen, and eighteen years] varies from 10 per cent in Greater New York to less than 5 per cent in the smaller cities and villages. Night

TABLE LXI

NIGHT SCHOOL SUMMARY FOR NEW YORK STATE

(Sixteen-, Seventeen-, and Eighteen-Year-Old Employed Boys)

Groups	Attendance in Percentage			Total Percentage
	Attends	Would Attend	Would Not Attend	
Greater New York	10.0	30.6	59.4	100.0
Cities over 25,000	10.2	21.5	68.3	100.0
Cities under 25,000	4.4	23.5	72.1	100.0
Villages over 5,000	3.0	37.5	59.5	100.0
Places under 5,000	1.0	53.5	45.5	100.0

schools, however, are not maintained in all the smaller cities and villages, which lowers the record for these groups. Where night schools are maintained between 20 and 30 per cent of the boys expressed a desire to attend. These desires were probably not very strong in most cases and it is quite likely were expressed in some instances to make a favorable impression on the teacher recording the answers. In general night schools are attended largely by men and older boys. Over 60 per cent do not wish to attend night school.

[1] Adapted from an article in the *Vocational Education Summary* of September, 1918.

[2] Adapted by permission from Howard G. Burdge, *A Study of Employed Boys*, pp. 181–83. State of New York Military Training Commission, Bureau of Vocational Training, 1921.

Although these answers were recorded by teachers to whom boys might be expected to give as favorable an answer as possible to this question, yet the majority of these boys were frank to state that they had no desire to attend night school. Personal interviews with some ten thousand of these boys made by the inspectors of the bureau making this survey disclosed this same attitude on the part of these boys toward any form of schooling which calls them back to schoolhouses, school books and school shops. Boys of these ages seem to have a feeling that schools are for "kids" while they are "men" and too old for such things. Until they experience a desire for further schooling, which a wise counselor might awaken, additional schooling will have to be compulsory and can well be likened to "forced feeding." . . . .

That there is a definite need for short unit courses was brought to light by the personal interviews with thousands of these boys made by the inspectors of this bureau in the course of the survey. Long, indefinite courses in arithmetic, mechanical drawing, auto mechanics and kindred subjects do not appeal to boys or for that matter to many men. A short course successfully covered is a great incentive to further effort, which cannot be said of long-drawn-out, indefinite courses in night schools or part-time schools.

The outstanding fact in regard to night-school attendance of boys of these ages is that the majority of them have no desire for further schooling. It is possible to create a desire for further schooling through proper guidance and counsel and the offering of popular short courses. . . . .

EXAMPLES OF EVENING SCHOOLS

The general plan of organization for public evening schools to secure the best possible results is not a wholly easy thing to devise. There are many difficulties in the way of successful night-school administration, and there are probably few fields in which public money can more easily be spent wastefully. There follow here a number of illustrations of evening schools in cities which have been working with the problem for some time. The results of their experience should be useful to anyone who is interested in a knowledge of how such schools are operated, or who may desire to organize or improve the organization of some school with which he is connected.

ST. LOUIS EVENING SCHOOLS[1]

Organization.—Evening school and extension courses are offered to persons whose employment prevents their attendance upon the regular day-school classes. The organization of such classes seeks to provide opportunity for school instruction at hours other than those of actual employment. The name "evening school" is used as a generic term, descriptive of the kind of school rather than the time of day when the classes are in session. Persons working in night shifts may be taught in classes held in the morning or afternoon.

The evening-school year is divided into three terms as follows:

First term: Registration nights, September 13, 14, 15, and 16 at all public high schools.

Registration: September 13 and 15 at elementary schools, continuing for thirteen weeks, closing December 15.

Second term: Beginning Monday, January 2, 1922, continuing for twelve weeks to and including March 23.

Third term: Beginning March 27 and continuing for eleven weeks to June 8, inclusive.

School sessions.—Each class group shall be taught two evenings per week only, as follows: Some groups taught on Monday and Wednesday evenings; other groups taught on Tuesday and Thursday evenings. Where necessary other groups may be organized for instruction on Friday and Saturday evenings.

The evening session in the elementary and high school shall begin at 7:20 and terminate at 9:30, the period from 7:20 to 7:30 to be devoted by the teachers to preparation, consultation with students, or individual help. The time from 7:30 to 9:30 shall be divided into two class periods of sixty minutes each, except for classes in cooking, auto-mechanics, and machine shop, which shall occupy the full two-hour session each night.

Public evening high schools are conducted on Monday, Tuesday, Wednesday, and Thursday evenings at all of the six high-school buildings.

Public evening elementary schools are conducted in these same high-school centers on the same evenings with length of term and nightly sessions as provided for the high schools. Evening elementary-school classes are conducted at some of the elementary-school centers also. Classes may be organized in other school build-

[1] Adapted from literature of the St. Louis Board of Education.

ings in connection with social-center activities when authorized by the Board of Education.

Students of all ages over fourteen, who are not attending the day schools, may attend the evening schools.

Students attending day schools are not eligible to attend either the high or elementary schools, except those students attending only four hours a week in part-time classes, or such students as may obtain permission from the Instruction Department.

Tuition for non-resident students: Non-resident students may be admitted to evening-school classes on payment of the tuition fee of $5.00 per term.

No charge for tuition or books: the public evening schools are free to all those who reside in St. Louis. This includes the use of all books and supplies without charge, except a deposit fee for the use of books.

When classes may be formed.—Twenty registrants shall be necessary for the formation of classes in both the elementary and high schools, except for classes in special subjects or for immigrants or illiterates. Such classes may be organized with a smaller registration subject to the approval of the superintendent of instruction. Classes may be divided if the average weekly attendance is thirty or more students.

When classes shall be discontinued.—Classes whose average monthly attendance falls below ten shall be combined with other classes or discontinued unless special permission to continue them is granted by superintendent.

Subjects taught in all evening high schools.—The high schools offer a wide selection in the choice of subjects. To those who are employed during the day they offer an excellent opportunity to broaden their education along lines required in their daily employment and fit them for greater responsibilities. To the earnest and ambitious worker they offer many opportunities to take up the study of those subjects in which he is interested.

Vocational classes: Short unit courses in Joinery, Pattern-Making, Foundry Practice, Machine Shop-Practice, Auto-Mechanics, Applied Electricity, Architectural and Mechanical Drawing, Commercial Art, Industrial Design, Trade Millinery and Trade Dressmaking, Interior Decoration.

Academic courses: Courses in Social Science, American History and Civics, Commercial Law, Social Economy, English and Literature, General Science.

Commercial classes: Practical courses in Bookkeeping, Shorthand, Typewriting, Office Practice, Salesmanship and Advertising, and Accounting.

Vocational home-making courses: Vocational home-making courses have for their aim the training of girls and women for the vocation of home-making as practiced by the wife and mother in the home. The following are suggested unit courses in home-making for this training:

A. Foods. Lessons in Cookery.
B. Hygiene and Home Nursing.
C. Making and Repairing Clothing.
D. Millinery
E. Home Planning and Home Furnishing.

Civics: All men and women should have a good general knowledge of the duties, rights, and privileges of American citizenship. Instruction in our form of government, city, state, and national, is fully covered in this course. This study is especially useful for men and women arriving at the voting age.

Modern languages: Spanish, French.

Gymnasium classes, chorus singing, orchestra, open forum, and debating clubs.

English and Civics for foreigners.

EVENING HIGH SCHOOLS IN BOSTON

The example given below, of the Boston evening high schools, may be studied as a rather complete statement of the administration of an extensive system of evening schools, and one in which the details of administration are presented. Certain features of the commercial work offered, with an outline of a sample course in advertising, are given:[1]

The evening high schools, which numbered five in 1910–11, are now nine in number. The growth of the evening high schools in number and influence has been accompanied by a distinct change in character. In 1910 the evening high schools, with the exception of the Central Evening High School, were changed from general high schools to commercial high schools. The Central Evening High

[1] Adapted from *Annual Report of the Superintendent, Boston Public Schools*, and from *A Provisional Course of Study for the Evening High Schools, Boston Public Schools*, pp. 6–12. (This material was submitted in April, 1922, as current.)

School offers both academic and commercial subjects. The number of pupils pursuing so-called cultural subjects is comparatively small, only 286 this year out of a total of 5,016, and questioning of these pupils on various occasions has disclosed the fact that most of them are taking academic subjects with a strictly vocational end in view. In other words, our evening high schools are today vocational schools, with the emphasis on commercial subjects. In 1916 the commercial character of these schools was further intensified and specialized commercial courses with definite requirements for graduation were authorized. In consequence of the changed character of the evening high schools the course of study was revised through the efforts of principals and teachers and was ready for distribution in printed form in September, 1917. The revised course of study offers pupils an opportunity to attempt specialized commercial courses with a view to receiving intensive training for particular types of commercial work. Among the specialized courses offered are the secretarial course, which emphasizes a mastery of phonography and typewriting; the accountancy course, which includes the principles and practices of advanced bookkeeping; the merchandising course, which includes principles of business organization, selling and service to customers; and the office practice course, which includes the principles and methods of adjusting one's self to modern business office conditions, and familiarity with the principles of filing systems and labor-saving machines and devices. Commercial Spanish was authorized as a subject in all evening high schools in 1917, and last year the subject of American government was likewise authorized.

SESSIONS

Sessions are held on Monday. Tuesday and Thursday evenings. They begin at half-past seven o'clock and close at half-past nine o'clock. The school rooms are opened and the teachers are present fifteen minutes before the time for the session to begin.

ADMISSION

Pupils are admitted to the evening high schools as follows:

(*a*) Residents of Boston who are graduates of Boston elementary day or evening schools, are over sixteen years of age and are not attending a public day school in the City of Boston.

(*b*) Residents of Boston who are graduates of schools of equal or higher grade than those mentioned in (*a*), are over sixteen years of age and are not attending a public day school in the City of Boston.

(*c*) Residents of Boston who have attended day high schools, are over sixteen years of age and are not attending a public day school in the City of Boston.

(*d*) Residents of Boston who are over sixteen years of age and who pass the entrance examinations.

(*e*) Non-residents of Boston who meet the admission requirements and pay the necessary tuition, one-half in advance and the remainder before January 1.

(*f*) No pupil will be admitted to an evening high school who is unable to attend at least two hours on two evenings each week except by permission of the director.

NOTE 1. Those included under (*a*), (*b*) and (*c*) are admitted without examination. Those included under (*d*) are required to pass an examination in reading, writing, English composition, and arithmetic. Admission examinations are held in the different high schools during the opening week of the term and at such other times as the principal of the school may determine.

NOTE 2. Pupils over fourteen years of age attending a public day school in the City of Boston are admitted to the evening high schools only by written permission on a form provided for the purpose and obtainable at the several schools.

ADVANCE PAYMENT

Each pupil who enters an evening high school is required to make an advance payment of one dollar ($1) at the time of his application for admission, for which he is given a receipt on a form provided for the purpose.

If at the end of the evening school term the pupil has complied with the regulations of the School Committee the amount of the advance payment will be refunded upon the surrender of his receipt. This receipt is not transferable and must be presented for the refund during the last week of the evening school term by the pupil named upon it.

ATTENDANCE

Any pupil who is absent from school for three consecutive evenings on which his attendance is due shall not be readmitted to his classes until his absence shall have been satisfactorily explained to the principal.

DIPLOMAS

Diplomas are granted for quality and quantity of work reported as follows:

(*a*) A diploma is awarded to pupils who have won twenty-four diploma points, which usually requires attendance at school on three evenings a week for four years.

(*b*) Diploma points cannot be granted more than once in the same subject.

(*c*) Not more than six diploma points can be earned in the same year.

(*d*) The twenty-four diploma points must include at least three points in English II.

(*e*) Pupils shall receive no credit unless they have been present at least two-thirds of all sessions held during the term, or at least three-fourths of all sessions held after January first.

(*f*) Pupils who have attended at least two-thirds of all sessions held during the term, or at least three-fourths of all sessions held after January first, may be granted advanced standing in subjects offered by the school under the following conditions:

1. A pupil may receive advanced standing in any subject authorized in the particular school at which he attends provided he presents satisfactory evidence that he has completed that subject in a school recognized and accredited as equivalent in rank. This evidence shall, in general, consist of duly signed certificates and may in the discretion of the principal be supplemented by examination.

2. A pupil may receive advanced standing in the work of the first or second year of a progressive subject authorized in the particular school at which he attends provided he presents satisfactory evidence of having studied the subject one year or more in school or in employment and provided he enters and satisfactorily completes a higher grade of the same subject and receives credit therefor. At the discretion of the principal pupils of sufficient maturity may be admitted to a higher grade and receive advanced standing under the above conditions.

3. Not more than eighteen points in advanced standing may be granted in any case, and not more than twelve points in advanced standing may be granted except in the case of a pupil who has satisfactorily completed three years in a Boston day high school of the same character as that of the particular school at which he attends.

4. Graduates of day high schools shall not receive advanced standing in subjects which have been credited towards day high school diplomas.

(*g*) Diplomas are granted in each of the following courses: Accountancy Course, Merchandising Course, Office Practice Course, Secretarial Course, General Commercial Course, General Academic Course.

A diploma in the Accountancy Course is awarded to pupils who have won three diploma points in Bookkeeping III and twenty-one diploma points in the following subjects: Bookkeeping I, II; Civil Service; Commerce and Industry; Commercial Arithmetic; Commercial Law; English I, II, III; Penmanship; Spanish I, II.

A diploma in the Merchandising Course is awarded to pupils who have won three diploma points in Merchandising and twenty-one diploma points in the following subjects: Advertising; Civil Service. Commerce and Industry; Commercial Arithmetic; Commercial Law; Economics; English I, II, III; Penmanship; Spanish I, II.

A diploma in the Office Practice Course is awarded to pupils who have won three diploma points in Office Practice and twenty-one diploma points in the following subjects: Bookkeeping I, II, II; Civil Service; Commercial Arithmetic; Commercial Law; Economics; English I, II, III; Penmanship; Phonography I, II, III; Spanish I, II; Typewriting I, II.

A diploma in the Secretarial Course is awarded to pupils who have won three diploma points in Phonography III and three diploma points in Typewriting II and eighteen diploma points in the following subjects: Advertising; Civil Service; Commercial Arithmetic; Commercial Law; English I, II, III; Penmanship; Phonography I, II; Spanish I, II; Typewriting I.

A diploma in the General Commercial Course is awarded to pupils unable to qualify for a diploma in the above-named courses who have won twenty-four diploma points in the subjects authorized in the evening commercial high schools.

A diploma in the General Academic Course is awarded to pupils unable to qualify for a diploma in the above-named courses who have won twenty-four diploma points in the subjects authorized in the Central Evening High School.

Not more than twelve points in the following subjects may be counted towards a diploma from any course; Algebra I; Bookkeeping I; Civil Service; Commercial Arithmetic; English I; French I; German I; Italian I; Latin I; Penmanship; Spanish I.

The subjects offered and the number of diploma points granted are shown in the following table:

EVENING HIGH SCHOOLS

Diploma Points

Subject	Points	Subject	Points
Advertising	*3	History II (English)	3
Algebra I	6	History III (United States)	3
Algebra II	6	Italian I (two hours)	6
Bookkeeping I	*3	Italian II (two hours)	6
Bookkeeping II	*3	Latin I	3
Bookkeeping III	*3	Latin I (two hours)	6
Chemistry I	3	Latin II (Caesar)	3
Chemistry II (two hours)	6	Latin III (Vergil)	3
Civil Government I	3	Literature I (American)	3
Civil Government II	3	Literature II (earlier English authors)	3
Civil Service	*3	Literature III (later English authors)	3
Civil Service (two hours)	*6	Lowell School Mathematics (two hours)	*6
Commerce and Industry	*3	Merchandising	*3
Commercial Arithmetic	*3	Office Practice	*3
Commercial Law	*3	Penmanship	*3
Economics	*3	Phonography I	*3
English I	*3	Phonography II	*3
English II	*3	Phonography III (speed)	*3
English III	*3	Physics I (two hours)	6
French I (two hours)	6	Physics II (two hours)	6
French II (two hours)	6	Spanish I (two hours)	*6
French III (two hours)	6	Spanish II (two hours)	*6
Geometry I (Plane)	3	Typewriting I	*3
Geometry II (solid)	3	Typewriting II	*3
German I (two hours)	6		
German II (two hours)	6		
German III (two hours)	6		
History I (Ancient)	3		

NOTE 1. Commercial evening high schools offer only such subjects as are marked with an asterisk.

NOTE 2. In case a class meets regularly less than three times each week or for a part of the year only, the number of diploma points will be diminished proportionately, but fractional parts of diploma points will be disregarded.

NOTE 3. Classes will be formed in subjects for which a reasonable number make application, and short unit courses will be conducted in subjects as are approved by the Director.

CERTIFICATES

At the end of each year pupils not receiving diplomas receive certificates of proficiency in each subject studied as follows:

(*a*) Provided their year's record has been satisfactory.

(*b*) Provided they have been in attendance upon at least two-thirds of all sessions held during the term, or at least three-fourths of all sessions held after January 1.

Certificates show the number of points credited toward a diploma.

OUTLINE OF A SAMPLE COURSE

Advertising

The aim of this course is to give pupils a practical knowledge of the underlying principles of advertising. The work should be made as concrete as possible, and the constant use of illustrative material is recommended.

It is suggested that pupils be advised to take Advertising in connection with Merchandising or with English III.

1. The place of advertising in business.
2. Purpose of advertising in business.
3. Analysis of goods.
4. Analysis of market.
5. Advertising mediums.
   (*a*) General periodicals.
   (*b*) Circulars, catalogues, sales letters.
   (*c*) House organs.
   (*d*) Novelties.
   (*e*) Educational lectures, demonstrations, moving pictures
   (*f*) Display of goods.
   (*g*) Outdoor advertising.
   (*h*) Dealers' aids.
6. Printing tools.
   (*a*) Type.
   (*b*) Stereotype.
   (*c*) Half tone.
   (*d*) Electrotype.
   (*e*) Two and three color process.
   (*f*) Lithograph.
   (*g*) Etchings.
   (*h*) Wood cuts.

7. Planning a campaign.
8. Measuring results.
9. The laws of attention applied to advertising.
   (*a*) Absence of counter-attractions.
   (*b*) Intensity of sensation.
   (*c*) Contrast.
   (*d*) Ease of comprehension.
   (*e*) Repetition.
   (*f*) Emotional appeal.
10. Appeals to senses and instincts ("Talking Points")—taste, hearing, smell, sight, touch, cleanliness, protection, luxury, health, family love, etc.
11. Classes of advertisements.
    (*a*) Argumentative, suggestive.
    (*b*) Classified, display.
    (*c*) Appeals to different classes.
    (*d*) Conversational.
    (*e*) Testimonial.
    (*f*) "You."
    (*g*) Possible combinations.

EVENING SCHOOL WORK IN WASHINGTON, D.C.

The evening-school situation in Washington is typical of that in a number of large cities. Courses of different types are offered in different schools. For example, in arts in a manual-training high school, in general subjects in general high schools, and in commercial subjects in the Business High School. Some of the features of the Business High Night School are thus described:[1]

The winter session of the business High Night School usually opens in late September and closes the last of June. The school is in session every evening from 7:30 to 9:30 o'clock, except Sundays and legal holidays.

There are no tuition fees or other charges. Pupils supply their own books, paper, etc.

Owing to the large number of pupils the school is organized into two groups. One group meets on Monday, Wednesday, and Friday

[1] The description is compiled from literature furnished by W. B. Patterson.

evenings and the other group meets on Tuesday, Thursday, and Saturday evenings. One group offers no advantage over the other.

Pupils should select the group they prefer and arrange to attend regularly for the three evenings each week.

There are two recitation periods each evening. Each period is one hour in length.

It is possible for a pupil to take two courses in either group.

The school has recently received more than 250 new typewriting machines, making a total of about 500 machines, and is now one of the best equipped night schools in the country.

New classes are started as demand requires, usually once a month.

Full high school credits are given for courses completed in the school.

The figures given below indicate the total number of hours in each subject pursued by students, a few taking one hour, a few three hours, but most of them two hours per night.

Stenography (Gregg and Pitman)	1420
Typewriting	685
English	400
Arithmetic	80
Bookkeeping	320
Bookkeeping machine	8
Rapid calculating machines	70
Accountancy	160
Commercial law	120
French	40
Spanish	140
Gymnasium	90

The last enrolment called for 499 men and 1406 women.

We give certificates of proficiency for satisfactory units of work but are planning to give night high school diplomas for a course of twenty-four semester hours of work, provided English and Civics have been included. Our courses are practically free as far as tuition is concerned.

THE ORGANIZATION OF EVENING SCHOOL WORK

The organization of evening work, as of any course, should be in terms of purposes. In so far, therefore, as the aims of night-school studies vary from those of day-school studies, there should be a variation in organization. Certain proposed principles for the organization of evening-school commercial courses are those given by one agency which has made a considerable study of the problem.[1]

Evening-school commercial courses should be regarded as vocational in the strictest sense of the term. They should be either extension or preparatory courses, and they should be organized with the exact needs of commercial workers definitely in mind.

By "extension" is meant that kind of training which will improve the worker in the performance of the tasks incident to his present employment and fit him for promotion in the same line. By "preparatory" is meant that kind of training which is designed to fit the student for a position different from the one he is now holding. Both types of training for commercial occupations may be included in evening-school courses.

So far as possible, each course should be so arranged as to provide complete training for all phases of the commercial occupation for which the course is designed and yet the whole course should be broken into units for the benefit of those who want specific intensive training for only one phase of the vocation. Thus, the complete course might extend over a period of one, two, or even three years, while each unit might be only ten weeks in length. Even shorter units would facilitate proper classification of those who register from time to time.

Having set up the above basic principles the next step is to determine what commercial vocations should be included in the list for which training is to be offered. The needs of the persons to be trained should be kept in mind in listing these vocations. Local conditions and requirements will be factors of prime importance.

With the occupations listed the next step will be to outline courses designed to give the needed training for each occupation. Careful study and research should precede the organization of such courses. If the unit course plan is followed, the complete course, which consists of a combination of units, would be considered as preparatory, while each single unit might well be regarded as extension training. For obvious reasons entirely separate courses for these two purposes will not be required.

[1] Adapted by permission from *Bulletin 34*, p. 37. Federal Board for Vocational Education.

There is helpful suggestion for persons interested in evening-school organization in the following very concrete statement of the difficulties found by one person who was concerned with such a school:[1]

We must bear in mind that the evening school of the present is primarily for the adult, and that of the future will be even more distinctively so. The evening school for the adult is here to stay. It is to be noted that at present attendance for by far the greater number is not compulsory, and this number is steadily growing larger. This is significant in considering regularity of attendance. For, granting the very best of motives on the part of the pupils, yet it is a matter of individual judgment as to which will yield the greater returns, for example, the two hours at the school or the evening at the lodge meeting, at home resting or doing some much-needed work.

But granting the desire on the part of the individual to be present a given evening, what are some of the conditions tending to make this frequently impossible? The kind of employment of the pupils represents one of the most common difficulties in the way of regular attendance. The following are actual cases which came within the experience of one evening-school teacher with a small class:

1. A plumber found it impossible to come when his work took him to a distant part of the city.

2. A laborer found work in a brickyard too far distant to permit him to come regularly.

3. A street-car motorman whose schedule had brought him to "the barn" at 6:40 was put on a schedule which brought him in at 7:40. He came to school for a while even though an hour late.

4. A grocer's clerk frequently could not get through with his work in time to come.

5. A pharmacist, a Hungarian trained in the *Gymnasium* and university of his home country, could come only alternate weeks, because of his working schedule. Aside from the matter in question but illustrating the interest and seriousness of purpose of foreigners learning English, it may be worth while to add that this man came alternate weeks a distance that required a car ride of over an hour for individual instruction, and later at even greater sacrifice took up

[1] Adapted by permission from Paul J. Kruse, "Some Problems of the Evening School," *School Review*, XXII (November, 1914), 595–97.

work at a university in the city preparatory to setting up as an assayer.

6. A waitress came when the hours of her work, frequently changed, made it possible for her to come.

Many men temporarily out of employment come in until they find employment again.

THE PLACE OF THE EVENING SCHOOL

Are we to conclude that the evening schools' function is essentially vocational? Many would so assert. It seems probable, indeed, that the evening school has a great opportunity in the giving of highly specialized short, unit, technical courses which will aid persons in the performance of the definite task with which they are concerned. It has an opportunity, also, in offering such courses for persons who can improve their situation through the acquisition of a technique. There can be no doubt that the prevalence of such opportunity would make it much more possible for the secondary and even the elementary schools to devote themselves more completely to the task for which they are best fitted. If high-school students were always sure that they could secure training in technical work, even if they did not get it during the two or four years which they spend in high school, it would be much easier for them to see why they should make the most of the high-school years in the study of basic subjects.

On the other hand, there will always be a demand in the evening schools for non-vocational work—work which will merely enrich vocational activities—and for work which can be taken largely for its recreative effect. Many persons whose occupations are fairly well fixed will find pleasure and growth in studies of a general nature. Whether society should, at public expense, provide for this form of consumption is, perhaps, a debatable question, the discussion of which would lead into fundamental issues of the purpose of social organization. That matter is, in any case, not a part of the more restricted question of the place of the night schools in education for business.

QUESTIONS FOR DISCUSSION

1. Are we justified in considering evening commercial work as a modern extension of the high-school commercial course?
2. "Evening commercial work, like commercial work in continuation schools, is only an incident to a broader development; it is the contribution of the commercial course to evening education." Does the foregoing seem to you a true statement? If it is true, what does it mean regarding the study of evening-school commercial work?
3. "Evening schools began with private evening schools operated for a profit." Has this been pretty generally the history of educational institutions? Can you cite instances where other schools have had the same origin?
4. Trace briefly the stages in the development of evening-school education.
5. How do you account for the rapid spread of the night-school idea, once it was well under way?
6. "The total number of persons in evening schools is impressive. It is less impressive when we consider the number which might be in such institutions." Comment.
7. The example of evening-school work in Wisconsin indicates that, in that state at least, evening schools are mostly concerned with giving what sort of service?
8. Examine the descriptions of evening schools in St. Louis, Boston, and Washington. Make a list of what seem to you the significant matters to be considered in the organization of such a school. Under each of these as headings, note the way in which they are handled in the evening schools of the three cities cited.
9. What points of merit or what disadvantages do you see in the evening-school commercial work in any of the three examples given?
10. List the difficulties which must be met in the organization of evening-school commercial courses. Opposite each of these difficulties set down any suggestions which you can for avoiding or overcoming them.
11. "Evening-school commercial courses should be regarded as vocational in the strictest sense of the term." What does the foregoing statement mean by vocational? Would you agree? If not, how would you definitely express the purpose of evening-school commercial courses?

12. The chance to do a broad educational type of business education in the high school depends largely on the chance which the student has to secure short, thorough technical courses in some of the extensions of the regular course, as in evening and continuation schools. Explain.
13. How can it be said to be debatable as to whether or not evening schools should give *general courses* for adults?
14. Draw up a statement or series of statements which seem to you to express the proper place of the evening school in all education.
15. Draw up a statement or series of statements expressing what seems to be to you the place or rôle of evening-school *commercial work* in an organized plan of education for business.

CHAPTER XX

POSTGRADUATE COMMERCIAL COURSES, SUPERVISION AND TEACHER TRAINING

In this chapter we shall give some consideration to a number of matters which are important in commercial education, although none of them have developed far enough or broadly enough to justify an extensive discussion. One of these, like the agencies we have just been considering, is an extension of the high-school commercial course. The others are extensions, perhaps, but cannot accurately be called teaching agencies. They are rather supplementary to the high-school commercial course and to all of the extensions which we have had under consideration.

THE POSTGRADUATE COMMERCIAL COURSE

The modern extension of the high-school commercial course to be considered in this chapter may be called the high-school postgraduate course, or the concentrated technical course. Although as yet not very extensively developed, such courses seem to have much promise. These courses are plans of operation which give the student an opportunity to secure training in technique such as stenography or typewriting during the last few months of the regular four-year course, or in a special five months' or year's course after graduation.

Such courses have been in operation in some schools for at least twenty years. In the Dorchester High School of Boston, for example, such a course in postgraduate form was established in 1902–3. The following statement summarizes the experience of Dorchester with this type of school.[1]

Our postgraduate course in commercial subjects is open only to high-school graduates who previously have not had commercial sub-

[1] A statement by W. L. Anderson, head of the commercial department, Dorchester High School, Boston, Mass.

jects. About half of the class are graduates of our own school, while many others come from public and private high schools. A few each year are college graduates. One year we had seven of these.

Since this is an intensified course for beginners, our own commercial-course graduates who for any reason desire to return to the school are cared for in a special fifth-year course. We probably have two or three people each year return for our postgraduate course after they have been in business or to other institutions. This means two or three out of sixty.

We do not find any trouble about the ready acquirement of skill at the average age of about twenty years for the whole class.

Uniformity of purpose is probably the most marked characteristic of the group, and this is the most important quality in any group in our schools.

There has grown up on the part of the teachers in courses other than commercial a tendency to advise able students to finish their general education before they specialize. This means that the average of intelligence of the class is very high, and this fact makes the product of the class well known and in demand by the business world.

The course began as an experiment in 1902–3 with three pupils, and therefore has been in operation some twenty years. It has grown steadily until now we have sixty or more persons in the class. For the past three years it has been divided into two sections. Being graduates, the pupils are permitted to take as many or as few subjects as they individually desire. The majority of the class take Phonography, Typewriting, Bookkeeping, and Commercial Law. In the Phonography, Typewriting, and Bookkeeping they have one lesson daily and cover in one year at least as much as is covered in two years in regular courses. This means that in shorthand they are beginners in September and in June can write as a class one hundred words per minute. Twenty-five of last year's class had good business positions before the close of school.

In the twenty years during which the class has been in operation, we have, simply as a side issue, trained and placed in high-school positions as commercial teachers some seventy-five young men and women. From this course more than 25 per cent of these have been college graduates.

In Madison the course has been open to Seniors and has been taken more extensively by Seniors than by graduates.

The course was established, however, to meet the needs of graduates who had not taken the commercial course.

A few years ago the Chicago public schools began an experiment with concentrated postgraduate courses. The experiment proved so satisfactory that the courses are now given in a number of high schools scattered over the city. A description of the work in some detail is given in the following statement:[1]

To meet a need which apparently was not being met, the supervisor of commercial work in the Chicago high schools introduced what he describes as an intensive five months' course in stenography, offered only to graduates of a four-year high-school course. This course was added to the high-school commercial curriculum in February, 1917, and was put into operation at that time in a single school, the Lucy Flower Technical High School for Girls. In June, 1917, a class of seven was certificated, and in February, 1918, a class of eleven finished the course.

So satisfactory were the results obtained that at the beginning of the February, 1918, semester this intensive five months' stenographic course was extended to five other Chicago high schools, namely: Austin, Lake View, Medill, Phillips, and Schurz. These schools represent geographical divisions of the city, and each is central to the other high schools in its part of town. At this writing there are 381 pupils enrolled in the six high schools offering this course. The Flower High School has an enrolment of seventy-one girls, all graduates of a four-year high-school course, and there is every prospect that the full quota will be certificated as stenographers in June.

It is common opinion that this course has been properly designated intensive. Exactly the same work in stenography and typewriting which is required in the two-year course is covered in this five months' course. The same standards are maintained for the successful completion of the work. For instance, a shorthand speed of one hundred words per minute and a typing speed of forty words per minute are the basis of certification in the two-year course, and, likewise, at least that standard must be attained to successfully complete the five months' course. The textbooks for this course

[1] A statement prepared by Margaret F. Babcock, in charge of the Commercial Continuation School, Chicago. September, 1921.

are those in use in the longer course, and the school day is the same—eight periods.

It is in the distribution of the daily periods, however, that the departure is made. In the first and second semesters of the longer course, one period daily is given to shorthand and one to typing. In the third and fourth semesters, one period daily is given to shorthand and one to typing, and a third period is variously distributed, sometimes to typing, sometimes to revision of previously typed matter, again to tests for speed in either shorthand or typing. In the five months' course, the entire day is given to shorthand and typing—three periods of class work in shorthand and three to typing, with two study periods placed to advantage. In the longer course two semesters are devoted to the mastery of the theory of shorthand and the technique of typing. The excellent work done at the Flower High school proves that this ground is covered successfully in six weeks when the course is given intensively as postgraduate work. This means fourteen of the twenty weeks may be devoted to practical stenographic drill to attain the facility and skill which give commercial value to this training.

Supplementary to the intensive work of the school day, the pupils report home work ranging from two to four hours daily. The students are encouraged to give all their time and energy to the work. It is made plain at the beginning of the course that it is not the place for coddling and that all are expected to qualify at the end of the semester. The Flower classes are conspicuously interested and even a casual observer feels the enthusiasm which pervades the work. The intensive character of the course, it appears, in no way dampens the ardor of the pupils.

As is usually the case where a capable progressive teacher directs stenographic work, this intensive course at Flower is expanded somewhat to take in training and drill in the office activities which are closely allied to stenography. Valuable training is being given in filing. The pupils have more or less intimate knowledge of alphabetical, numerical, geographical, and other filing methods. They are given some training in transcribing from dictating machines, and are also afforded some instruction in the use of the comptometer. Some attention is given to mimeography. It is hardly necessary to add that extensive training of this nature is not attempted though it is significant that a number of the pupils have availed themselves of the opportunity afforded in a nearby public evening school to secure further practice in the use of these various office machines. It is pointed out that practice of the kind is also available all the year round in the Public Continuation Commercial School.

Again, the matter of spelling, so completely interwoven in the stenographer's skill, is not neglected. Added to the spelling drill which is inescapable in the revision work, a period a week is given to spelling as such, even the old-fashioned but ever-effective spelldown being brought into play.

One can scarcely conceive a product of this training failing of immediate appreciation in the commercial world, and it is true that, with one exception, those who have finished the course at Flower are well placed at satisfactory beginning salaries. It is rather early to attempt a comparison of the rate of advancement as between these pupils and those who have taken only a two-year high-school course, though it is altogether to be expected that the contrast will be distinct.

A more recent development in postgraduate commercial courses in the Chicago secondary school system is the six months' secretarial course now offered in Commercial Continuation School. This course is open to graduates of a four-year high-school course. In addition to the shorthand and typewriting, short courses are given in accounting, letter-writing, commercial law, and filing. The aim is to equip for secretarial work of an exacting nature.

POSSIBILITIES IN THE CONCENTRATED COURSE

The postgraduate course is one which promises a great deal of opportunity for enriching the secondary-school commercial course. When the student has graduated or is about to do so he is much more likely to know the particular technique which he will need in the job which lies before him. The postgraduate concentrated course enables him to prepare for that kind of technique instead of giving him a variety of techniques which have no particular use. Moreover, it seems quite likely that a student acquires his technique more rapidly when it is thus given in concentrated form. Clearly there are limits to this. No one would allege that because five months may be better than two years in which to learn typewriting, that five days would be better than five months. As a matter of fact no careful study has yet been made of the learning curve in this field, and we are somewhat at sea as to what is the period of greatest increasing returns for the time spent. A third advantage which is not likely to be disputed is that the student comes to his new job with his technique freshly at hand. If he has taken stenography and typewriting in the first two years or second and third years, and has found his fourth year largely occupied with other subjects, there is plenty of chance to become inefficient in these techniques. Finally, and most important of all, is that the postponement of this technical work gives an opportunity for something of great value to be done for the student during the first three or possibly all four of the high-school years.

If the student is assured that he need not leave the public-school system without some technique which he can sell immediately, he will be much more willing to devote the early years of his high-school course to those studies which will be most valuable to him in the long run. The postgraduate or concentrated course offers such an opportunity. In addition it enables him to understand his technical training in relation to its uses in business, provided a proper knowledge of the meaning of business and the business organization has been given in the earlier years. When one adds to these considerations the fact that he is now more likely to know his job and the fact that he will go from this training directly to its practice, it seems that a strong case is made for courses of this type. It is doubtful if there is a single development in secondary work which could be used to greater advantage from the standpoint of the student than the postgraduate technical course or a technical course concentrated in the last semester or last year. Such work should of course not be limited to the students or graduates of commercial courses. In practice it has been found that the graduates of general courses often desire this work, and that there are many students who at the end of three years of general work wish to finish their high-school course with some technical subjects. Such courses should become much more common. The opportunities which they present should be given the most careful thought by everyone interested in broadening and improving secondary commercial education.

THE CITY SUPERVISOR OF COMMERCIAL WORK

Of the supplementary agencies to be discussed in this chapter, the city supervisor of commercial work may be considered first. Specialized supervisors for commercial work have not yet become very great in numbers, but the possible utility of such officers is attracting an increasing amount of attention. Special directors of manual training, music, drawing, and other subjects were numerous before commercial supervisors in the country numbered more than two or three. Even now the number of such supervisors is probably less than a dozen. An informal national organization has, however, been organized and at least one general meeting called to discuss the problems of city commercial directors. The duties of such a commercial director in a city school system have been thus described:[1]

The director should advise with the general superintendent in regard to the installation and supervision of commercial subjects and equipment. If there is no employment bureau maintained in a general employment department, he should establish and supervise such a bureau for graduates of the commercial department. He should advise with the superintendent with regard to the selection of textbooks and syllabi for commercial subjects. If he be wise, he will consult freely with his teachers and principals before making his recommendations. At all times, if he desires to be successful, he should remember that his supervision is horizontal and that the direct supervision of a school is in the hands of the principal. He should be very careful not to issue orders directly to teachers without consulting the principal who is immediately responsible for the success of his school. It is much more satisfactory to leave directions with a principal for the betterment of the commercial department in his school.

STATE SUPERVISION OF COMMERCIAL EDUCATION

A second form of direct supervision of commercial education which has developed within very recent years is state supervision by a special state officer. New York state was probably

[1] A statement by William Bachrach, supervisor of commercial work, Chicago public high schools. Mr. Bachrach, with a possible exception of Clay Slinker, of Des Moines, was the first commercial supervisor in the United States.

the first to create such an office, doing so in 1910. Idaho and Pennsylvania have now established similar offices. Such a supervisor has numerous opportunities to aid business education. One can conduct surveys as a basis for improving the training given students, formulate plans for state-wide programs of education, furnish informational and inspirational material to commercial teachers, carry on research upon which minimum standards of curriculum, teacher requirements, and equipment may be based. A supervisor can bring to legislative bodies the need for help in teacher-training and for proper certification laws for teachers of business subjects.

THE COMMERCIAL SERVICE OF THE FEDERAL BOARD

Enough concerning its work has been said at various points throughout this volume to make any discussion of the commercial service of the Federal Board for Vocational Education almost superfluous. It is worth while, however, to recall that it is an agency which can exercise an extensive influence. Several quotations in this volume are examples of the character of work already done by the board. For the making of broad surveys, for the collection and dissemination of data concerning business education experiments, and for stimulating general interest in the field, there is no other agency so well qualified, nor is there probably any single agency whose suggestions or proposals will be so kindly and so widely considered. This throws at once upon the commercial service of the Federal Board a great opportunity and a great responsibility.

COMMERCIAL TEACHER-TRAINING

Fundamental to any general growth in business education is proper teaching. Commercial teacher-training has in no way kept pace with teacher education in other fields. The following statement indicates the present status of teacher-training in commercial work.[1]

[1] This statement was prepared by May R. Freedman. It is in part based on data gathered by the Commercial Education Service of the Federal Board for Vocational Education, which through its chief, E. W. Barnhart,

Lack of clearly defined aims and widely varying standards of teaching requirements characterize the educational policies of the majority of states and cities. It is a testimony to the unexplored problems of providing adequately trained teachers for commercial courses that no study of the needs and possibilities of commercial teacher-training has been published up to the present time. The following conditions exist at present: (*a*) a policy of expediency, (*b*) lack of standardization in requirements and, (*c*) confusion as to what educational institution should assume the responsibility for preparing teachers.

Under the pressure of securing teachers, school authorities have turned to various sources. From business schools have been secured teachers thoroughly trained in shorthand, typewriting, sometimes bookkeeping and penmanship supported by a high-school education and possibly in addition a normal-school training. This group has served best under existing circumstances to teach the "technique" courses. From the business world have been obtained men and women with office or selling experience, whose knowledge of actual business, rather than their specific educational requirements, has been their qualification to teach commercial courses. Finally, a third source has been teachers of other subjects, who, because of the decrease in popularity of certain courses, as German and the classics, and the attractiveness of higher salaries offered to commercial teachers, have been willing to change their work. It is thus evident that the qualifications of commercial instructors vary greatly in respect to experience, educational training, and, as a result, outlook.

When uniformity is so utterly lacking in the methods of securing teachers, it is not to be expected that standardization of requirements is to be found. As a matter of fact, certain states and cities, where commercial education has assumed great importance, have developed regulations to be observed in selecting commercial teachers. But in many instances these have been set aside where their observation would prevent the procuring of a sufficient number to fill the school needs. Other states have not found it necessary to differentiate their requirements for commercial teachers from those for other teachers, or else have included them under the group called "Special." Certain cities, as Milwaukee, decide each case on its

has been making a series of investigations of teacher-training by means of questionnaires.

individual merits. The one generalization applicable to the country as a whole is that the requirements are moderate and where existing are often unobserved by individual cities.

With so urgent a need for offering means of preparing teachers for commercial work, various educational institutions have attempted to take over the task of training. The undertaking of the work by colleges and universities, normal schools, and special training schools accounts for the confusion that exists as to which of these is best equipped to do the work, and what should be the aim of the training offered. Universities give a more comprehensive training in the social sciences than normal schools, but they have just begun to organize teacher-training courses in this field. Normal schools are only beginning to broaden the nature of the courses to include something more than training in routine business procedure. A statement by F. G. Nichols, shortly before he left the Federal Board for Vocational Education, indicates the situation as he saw it:

"While more than thirty state normal schools profess to give courses for the training of commercial teachers, not more than six are really making a serious attempt to train such teachers for our public schools. In practically all of them except this small group of six[1] the commercial department is run more like a business college. The courses are open to those who desire training for office work as well as to those who desire to prepare for commercial teaching. The consequence is that the former group is much larger than the latter group, and the instruction is based upon the needs of office workers almost entirely. Furthermore, only a negligible number who complete the normal-school courses in commercial subjects ever become teachers; practically all of them accept business positions upon graduation."

Special schools for training teachers of selling and merchandising perform a limited service. The Prince School of Education for Store Service at Boston, Massachusetts, which is affiliated with Harvard University, is the leader of this work. The aim of these schools, however, is so highly specialized that they cannot be considered as an influential group of commercial-teacher-training agencies.

It may well be asked, following so unproductive an examination of the present possibilities of commercial teacher-training, what hope

[1] State Normal School at Salem, Mass.; State Normal School at Whitewater, Wis.; State Normal School at Plattsburg, New York; State Normal College at Trenton, N.J.; State Normal College at Albany, N.Y.; State Normal School at Willimantic, Conn.

exists for improvement. Two movements, while of modest proportions, indicate an enlightened attitude. A modification of the high-school curriculum is likely to occur through the general interest that has been aroused in the desirability of courses in the social sciences. A direct effort is being made by such groups as the National Association of Collegiate Schools of Business, the American Economic Association, and the committees of the National Education Association to improve the standards of the high-school curriculum. These efforts may very well influence the character of training given to secondary-school teachers. There is the possibility of shifting the emphasis from teachers of shorthand, typewriting, and bookkeeping, to teachers of industrial society and elementary economics, if not to socialize the entire viewpoint of instructors of commercial courses. In this connection the interest of the commercial advisers of high school in raising the requirements of teachers in their department may be another note of encouragement.

What other hope for commercial teacher-training exists is to be found in the introduction of courses on commercial education in universities. In the past there has been little correlation between business courses and educational courses. But there are appearing at present definite courses in commercial education which aim to present the development of commercial education, its relation to business, and the problems peculiar to this type of training. Such projects are significant particularly for the influence they may exert in stimulating a broader interest in commercial education and the suggestions they may give to other institutions to follow along similar lines. By giving a taste of the newer concept of commercial education to teachers attending summer sessions of universities, an appetite may be whetted which will be possible of satisfying only through the reorganization of the existing program of commercial teacher-training institutions.

FORMS OF TEACHER TRAINING NEEDED

There are at least five phases of teacher training that need development and that should be undertaken by schools that wish to work toward a well-rounded program of business-teaching education.

1. Commercial teachers have in the past approached their work with almost no understanding of its social significance and implications. They have seldom had an opportunity to

see the type of institution in which they worked in relation to other types. The result, frequently, has been a misconception of objectives or no thinking at all in terms of purposes. There is need, therefore, as the basis of teacher training, of a course concerned with the purposes and agencies of business education. On such an introductory course specialized courses can be soundly and intelligently built.

2. There is need of studies and courses in the technical subjects of business education. As has been pointed out in earlier sections, no one knows the best length of time in which to give courses in stenography, typewriting, machine operating, and similar techniques. No one knows with any certainty whether one age is better than another for such work.[1] Studies throwing light on these matters would be valuable for whatever agency could best give courses in the subjects concerned. Certain agencies, for example, the high school, which have spent too much time in such work, have more to gain than any other institutions if it can be shown that the advantage lies with giving these courses concentratedly.[2] Such a conclusion would open a large part of the high-school course for other work.

On such a basis courses in the technique of teaching the technical subjects would and should be developed. Even though the high schools were to give little of such work the

[1] In this connection George E. Freeland, "A Year's Study of the Daily Learning of Six Children" is interesting. Freeland, experimenting with pupils in the sixth grade and below, concluded that the older pupils learned most rapidly and retained the results best. He expressed the belief that class work below the fifth grade would be impossible but that so far as *subject-matter* is concerned typewriting could begin in that grade. This study may be found in the *Pedagogical Summary*, XXVIII (June, 1921), 97–115.

[2] Although a scientific study has not been made, the weight of evidence already leans well toward concentration and the late rather than the early years of adolescence. Experience with postgraduate courses is supported by business college history. The advantage the high-school graduate has had over the student from the business college has never been in mere technique. When the business college student has been a high-school graduate first, the advantage has been the other way. The moral is apparent that what is needed is more general training of a useful type.

normal schools could very properly train teachers who could function in business colleges, continuation schools, postgraduate courses and the like. This will be a form of practical training, which, on broader courses, can be usefully done by normal schools.

3. A third type of teacher training needed is instruction which will give candidates for commercial teaching a large amount of content material of the sort now available in the better collegiate schools of business. The material is that which makes clear the social setting of business and depicts the social structures in terms of which the business manager's work is conducted. Textbooks of a character which will be useful for high-school purposes must be developed but such books cannot yield their greatest service without the support of understanding teachers.

4. The material for presenting this new social science will be at best imperfect in its first forms and studies in the methods of teaching the ideas involved will be valuable. This will include not only classroom devices but possibilities of correlation with other subjects so that such courses may be made the core and the core only of a well-correlated, broadly inclusive curriculum.

QUESTIONS FOR DISCUSSION

1. What is the postgraduate commercial course or concentrated technical course?
2. Outline the matters which would need to be planned in installing such a course in any high school with which you are familiar.
3. Can such postgraduate or concentrated courses in technical subjects properly be given only to graduates of high-school commercial courses? Can they properly be given to all high-school graduates? Can they properly be given to all members of the Senior class in the commercial course? Can they properly be given earlier than the Senior year to students who could not long remain in school?
4. If all students in the commercial course were assured that they could secure thorough training in one or two technical subjects in not more than a year of postgraduate work, would many of them be interested in more general types of work while in high school?

5. If the high-school commercial course successfully gave in its Senior year adequate training in one or two technical subjects, what would be done with the students during the preceding three years? What would you suggest?
6. Outline what seem to you the advantages to a city of a supervisor of commercial education. Would it appear to you that a supervisor could properly undertake training of teachers?
7. Outline the duties which seem to you could be performed to advantage by the state supervisor of commercial education. Could such a supervisor properly be active in organizing teacher training?
8. What appear to be the general characteristics of the training generally required of commercial teachers?
9. Summarize the forces which seem to promise improved opportunity for commercial teachers' training.
10. What possibilities for assistance lie in the commercial service of the Federal Board for Vocational Education?
11. Examine each of the four possible phases of teacher training outlined at the conclusion of the chapter. Be prepared to discuss each.
12. Does it seem to you that the amount of commercial teacher training now available should be increased? If so, what agencies should offer it?

PART IV

HIGH-SCHOOL COMMERCIAL-CURRICULUM REFORM

CHAPTER XXI

A REVIEW OF PROPOSALS AND SOME CONCLUSIONS

In this section we are concerned with what should be done to make the best possible curriculum for the commercial course in a secondary school. If what should be done is more than what can be done immediately, we are also interested in knowing what can be done with materials existing at present.

This task breaks more or less logically into a double undertaking. It will be worth while, first, to examine the important proposals for improving the high-school commercial curriculum which have been made up to the present time, and to consider these in the light of the study which we have been making in this volume. Second, we must draw definite conclusions from our study and on the basis of those conclusions answer the questions, what should and what can be done with the high-school commercial course.

THE COMMITTEE OF NINE

We can recall from earlier chapters that the commercial course did not make a serious entrance into secondary schools until the latter part of the eighteen hundreds. It is natural enough, therefore, that we do not find a definite effort by secondary educators to outline the commercial course until after 1900. In July, 1901, at the Detroit meeting of the National Education Association a resolution was moved for the appointment of a Committee of Nine to report on commercial education in high schools. The course outlined by this Committee of Nine was presented in Boston, 1903. The curriculum proposed, together with certain statements of the Committee, were as follows:[1]

The course of study should be four years in length.

The paramount factor in shaping commercial courses in public schools should be the welfare of the student who goes directly from

[1] *Commercial Education in High Schools*, pp. 5–7. University of the State of New York, College Department, Bulletin 23, 1903.

the high school to his life work. It is expected, however, that such courses will provide a training of such a character as will fit the student completing them to enter the schools of commerce and industry now being established by many colleges and universities, as well as other modern courses in colleges and universities.

We believe that where possible separately organized commercial schools are advisable; but we realize that in the great majority of places the work must be given in regular public high schools as one of the several courses thereof.

COMMERCIAL COURSE FOR HIGH SCHOOLS

FIRST YEAR

First Half	Recitations a Week	*Second Half*	Recitations a Week
English	4	English	4
German, French, or Spanish	5	Same Language continued	5
Algebra	5	Algebra	5
Bookkeeping	3	General History to 800 A.D.	4
Drawing	3	Bookkeeping	3
Penmanship	3	Penmanship	2
Total	23	Total	23

SECOND YEAR

First Half		*Second Half*	
History of English Literature; Composition	3	History of English Literature, Commercial Correspondence	3
Modern Language continued	5	Modern Language continued	5
Commercial Arithmetic	5	English and European History	5
Study of Commercial Products or Local History and Industries	5	Commercial Geography	5
Bookkeeping	5	Typewriting	5
Total	23	Total	23

THIRD YEAR

First Half	Recitations a Week	*Second Half*	Recitations a Week
Rhetoric and Composition	3	Plane Geometry	5
United States History	5	Physics or Chemistry continued	5
Physics or Chemistry	5	Commercial Law	4
Bookkeeping and Office Practice	5	Political Economy	4
Foreign Language* continued or Second Modern Language or Shorthand and Typewriting	5	Election* of first half continued	5
Total	23	Total	23

FOURTH YEAR

First Half		*Second Half*	
English Literature, Themes and Parliamentary Practice	5	English continued	5
History of Commerce	5	Civil Government	5
15 periods to be selected from:		*15 periods to be selected from:*	
Language elected continued or shorthand and typewriting continued	5	Same election continued	5
Physics or Chemistry	5	Physics or Chemistry continued	5
Banking and Finance	5	Accounting, Organization and Auditing	5
Solid Geometry	5	Advanced Commercial Arithmetic and Applied arithmetic	5
Mechanical Drawing	5	Advertising, Study of Trade Journals, and Commercial English	5
		Office Work for Stenographers	5

* Those who do not desire to continue studying a foreign language or to take up shorthand may substitute one of the electives mentioned for the fourth year.

Commercial courses will include many subjects now taught in public high schools, though the methods of presentation in some cases may not be those best adapted to the needs of the business student. We realize that in most schools it will not be possible to organize separate classes in those subjects with methods specially modified to meet the wants of the commercial students. . . . .

On pages 544 and 545 is shown an outline of a four-year commercial high-school course. It is needless to say that it does not follow exactly the original plan submitted by any member of the Committee. Neither is it expected that it will suit every commercial teacher or public-school superintendent. It is hoped that it may be of service to all, in that it is suggestive. Allowances must be made for local conditions and the personal equation.

This report included an extensive supplement in which a careful discussion was given to particular subjects proposed in the outlined curriculum. Languages, sciences, history and commerce, mathematical subjects, and technical business studies were all the objects of detailed treatment.

The report was, as a matter of fact, an interesting document, especially in the amount of academic and social-science subjects proposed. In the first half of the first year, for example, there are fourteen recitation hours a week suggested for such subjects as compared with nine for technical subjects. In the second half of the first year the proportion is even greater—eighteen hours for general subjects as compared with five for technical work. A proportion comparable to this runs throughout the course. In the second year only five out of twenty-three hours are given over to technical subjects. In the third year five, or, if a student elected, ten out of a total of twenty-three are technical subjects in the first half. In the second half of the third year, eighteen of the twenty-three hours were necessarily to be general subjects and the entire twenty-three might be if the student so elected. Again in the fourth year it was made possible for the student entirely to avoid technical subjects, and to elect some such general studies of business as banking and finance, accounting, organization, and auditing, advertising, study of trade journals and commercial English.

It is worth while to compare the amount of general training which it would be possible for a student to acquire who pursued this course with the amount which can be obtained in the typical commercial course at the present time. It will be interesting also to compare it with some of the later proposals and to note the tendency for the inclusion of an increased amount of technical subjects and a decreased amount of general subjects. It is only when we come to view the more recent proposals for revising the commercial curriculum that we find so large an amount of general subject-matter suggested. The ultra-modern appearance of this course is probably due to different causes than those which now urge renewed emphasis on social-science and general subjects for business training. In 1903 the typical high school was the cultural high school. Its curriculum was in large part an imitation of the college curriculum. The general subjects enumerated were probably, therefore, thought of as similar to general subjects of the same nature given in colleges. The technical subjects had not, in 1903, dominated the cultural subjects simply because they were meeting with resistance from the established régime. This ultra-modern-looking course was, moreover, more ultra-modern in looks than in content. The modern emphasis on general studies in the high-school commercial course is based on something else than imitation of the college, and general studies are now proposed which are quite different from the general studies in the high schools of 1903.

The report of the Committee of Nine was made the subject of general discussion in the 1904 meeting of the National Education Association. Some of the comments made upon it were interesting. It was considered from the standpoint of the independent school of commerce by James J. Sheppard, of the New York High School of Commerce. Agreeing in general with the conclusions of the Committee, he expressed great interest in enriching the earlier years, especially the first year of the course. Superintendent Bertrand Parker, of the Rockford (Illinois) High School considered the course from the standpoint of the general high school. His objections to the proposed curriculum included "little faith in the plan which provides for recitations one, two, or three times per week"; a statement that "the study of American literature should run through the third year"; the belief that "the time allowed for each separate course [in history] should be doubled, and the history work be continuous throughout the four years." Superintendent Parker concluded his criticism with the following outline which he proposed as a modification of the course submitted by the Committee of Nine:

FIRST YEAR

First Half	*Second Half*
English	*English*
Algebra	*Algebra*
Modern Language	Modern Language
Ancient History	Ancient History
Penmanship	Commercial Arithmetic

SECOND YEAR

First Half	*Second Half*
English	*English*
Medieval and Modern History, English trend	*Medieval and Modern History, English trend*
Modern Language	Modern Language
Physiography	Physiography
Plane Geometry	Plane Geometry
Bookkeeping (double period)	Bookkeeping (double period)
	Stenography and Typewriting

THIRD YEAR

First Half	*Second Half*
American Literature and Composition	*American Literature and Composition*
United States History and Civics	*United States History and Civics*
Modern Language	Modern Language
Commercial Products	Commercial Geography
Physics	Physics
Office Practice (double period)	Accounting, Auditing, etc. (double period)
Stenography and Typewriting	Stenography and Typewriting

FOURTH YEAR

First Half	Second Half
English Literature and Composition	*English Literature and Composition*
History of Commerce	Political Economy
Modern Language	Modern Language
Commercial Law	Advertising, and Study of Trade Journals
Chemistry	Chemistry
Stenography and Typewriting	Stenography and Typewriting
Free-hand Drawing (double period)	Free-hand Drawing (double period)

NOTE.—The studies italicized are required.

An examination of this outline will show that while there is an increased amount of technical study required, it would be impossible for the student working through these courses to escape without a fair knowledge of the physical and social environment in which he lived, provided the subject-matter of the courses was appropriate to the titles.

A SECOND PROPOSAL OF THE NATIONAL EDUCATION ASSOCIATION

It was not until 1915 that the National Education Association made a second pronouncement upon the curriculum for commercial work in secondary schools. A scrutiny of the course then suggested shows at once what had been occurring in this field of educational work. The commercial course in high schools had "come into its own," and in that commercial course the technical subjects were now understood to be the important ones around which the course should be built.

The new proposals were presented at the National Education Association meeting at Oakland, California, with these words:[1]

> The Committee [the names of the Committee are stated in the original] have arranged, from the data at hand and obtained in response to questionnaires sent out, a proposed four-year high-school

[1] National Education Association, *Addresses and Proceedings*, Oakland, California, 1915, pp. 930–33.

course, with two schedules. One emphasizes accounting, and the other emphasizes stenography and typewriting, followed by a grouping of required subjects for several different vocational courses. Each course consists of carrying four subjects per semester during eight semesters of eighteen to twenty weeks, as shown in Table LXII.

TABLE LXII

	Course in Accounting	Course in Stenography
	Units	Units
Required of all students........	14	14
Required in vocational courses..	7	8
Electives........................	11	10
Total....................	32	32

NOTE.—A unit is a week's work of five daily forty-five-minute periods with an equal amount of home work carried during one semester of not less than eighteen weeks, or five daily ninety-minute periods of laboratory work without home assignment.

The subjects are grouped first around two main vocational subjects: (1) accounting, (2) stenography. But within each of these groups there will be one class of students who expect to make their major a life-work (Groups 1 and 4), and another class which selects it as a stepping-stone to some other occupation (Groups 2, 3, 5, and 6). Hence a system of grouping of the electives is recommended. It is recommended also that apprenticeship in stenography, salesmanship, or bookkeeping be encouraged and given one semester credit in Groups 1 and 4, providing the subject is taken under strict supervision of the instructor.

SUBJECTS REQUIRED IN BOTH COURSES

	Units
English	8
Bookkeeping	2
Penmanship	2
Commercial Arithmetic	1
Commercial Geography	1
	14

ADDITIONAL SUBJECTS REQUIRED IN THE ACCOUNTING COURSE

	Units
Bookkeeping	2
Economics	1
Salesmanship	1
Commercial Law	1
History and Civics	2
	7

ADDITIONAL SUBJECTS REQUIRED IN THE STENOGRAPHY COURSE

	Units
Stenography	4
Typewriting	4
	8

SUGGESTED ELECTIVE GROUPS

Group 1. Office Training for Accountants

	Units
Accounting	2
Advanced salesmanship	1
Advanced Economics	1
Apprenticeship in Bookkeeping or Salesmanship	1
Select	5
	10

Group 2. Mechanic Arts

	Units
Algebra II	2
Manual Training	4
Mechanical Drawing	2
Geometry	2
	10

Group 3. Agriculture

	Units
Chemistry	4
Agriculture	4
Botany and Zoölogy	2
	10

Group 4. Office Training for Stenographers

	Units
Advanced Stenography and Typewriting; Manifolding	2
Office Training	2
Apprenticeship in Stenography	1
Select	1
	6

Group 5. Domestic Science and Art

	Units
Domestic Science and Art	4
Drawing	1
Select	1
	6

Group 6. General Electives

	Units
Modern Languages	4
History	4
Science	2
Typewriting	4
	14

National Education Association Course

COMMERCIAL COURSE—EMPHASIZING ACCOUNTING

FIRST YEAR

First Semester		*Second Semester*	
English	5	English	5
Penmanship	5	Penmanship	5
*Elective	10	*Elective:	10
	20		20

†Manual Training	5	†Manual Training	5
†Domestic Science and Art	5	†Domestic Science and Art	5
Agriculture	5	Agriculture	5
Modern Language	5	Modern Language	5
Algebra	5	Algebra	5

SECOND YEAR

First Semester		*Second Semester*	
English	5	English	5
†Bookkeeping	5	†Bookkeeping	5
Commercial Arithmetic	5	Commercial Geography	5
*Elective:	5	*Elective:	5
	20		20

†Manual Training	5	†Manual Training	5
†Domestic Science and Art	5	†Domestic Science and Art	5
Agriculture	5	Agriculture	5
Modern Language	5	Modern Language	5
Plane Geometry	5	Plane Geometry	5

NOTE.—All general subjects are treated in relation to commerce so far as practicable. English includes public speaking.

* See suggested elective groups.

† Double periods.

THIRD YEAR

First Semester		*Second Semester*	
English	5	English	5
†Bookkeeping	5	†Bookkeeping	5
*Elective:	10	Commercial Law	5
	20	*Elective:	5
			20
Stenography 5		Stenography 5	
†Typewriting 5		†Typewriting 5	
Chemistry 5		Chemistry 5	
Physics 5		Physics 5	
History 5		History 5	

FOURTH YEAR

First Semester		*Second Semester*	
Business English	5	Business English	5
American History	5	Civics	5
Economics	5	Salesmanship	5
*Elective:	5	*Elective:	5
	20		20
Stenography 5		Stenography 5	
†Typewriting 5		†Typewriting 5	
†Bookkeeping 5		†Bookkeeping 5	
Office Training 5		Office Training 5	

COMMERCIAL COURSE—EMPHASIZING STENOGRAPHY

FIRST YEAR

First Semester		*Second Semester*	
English	5	English	5
Penmanship	5	Penmanship	5
*Elective:	10	*Elective:	10
	20		20
†Manual Training 5		†Manual Training 5	
†Domestic Science and Art 5		†Domestic Science and Art 5	
Modern Language 5		Modern Language 5	
Drawing 5		Drawing 5	

NOTE.—All general subjects are treated in relation to commerce so far as practicable. English includes public speaking.

* See suggested elective groups.

† Double periods.

SECOND YEAR

First Semester		*Second Semester*	
English	5	English	5
†Bookkeeping	5	†Bookkeeping	5
Commercial Arithmetic	5	Commercial Geography	5
*Elective:	5	*Elective:	5
	20		20
†Manual Training 5		†Manual Training 5	
†Domestic Science and Art 5		†Domestic Science and Art 5	
Modern Language 5		Modern Language 5	
Drawing 5		Drawing 5	

THIRD YEAR

First Semester		*Second Semester*	
English	5	English	5
Stenography	5	Stenography	5
†Typewriting	5	†Typewriting	5
*Elective:	5	*Elective:	5
	20		20
†Bookkeeping 5		†Bookkeeping 5	
†Domestic Science and Art 5		†Domestic Science and Art 5	
History 5		History 5	
General Elective 5		Commercial 5	

FOURTH YEAR

First Semester		*Second Semester*	
Business English	5	Business English	5
Stenography	5	Stenography	5
†Typewriting	5	†Typewriting	5
*Elective:	5	*Elective:	5
	20		20
Economics 5		Salesmanship 5	
Office Training 5		Office Training 5	
American History 5		Civics 5	
General Elective 5		Apprenticeship 5	

NOTE.—All general subjects are treated in relation to commerce so far as practicable. English includes public speaking.

* See suggested elective groups.

† Double periods.

In these courses, as has already been pointed out, it is the technical work which is emphasized, one of them being built with its emphasis on accounting, and the other with its emphasis on stenography. For those interested in making the commerce course something more than a clerk mill, this proposal of the National Education Association is more satisfactory than the courses actually given in a great many high schools. Its organizers show certainly an appreciation of the desirability of understanding as well as skill in business work. In the first year, for example, there is no technical subject other than penmanship required, in either the accounting or the stenographic courses. In the second year a somewhat larger amount of technical work is required, though in both this and the third year in the accounting course these requirements are rather limited. In the fourth year in the accounting course there is proposed a fairly extensive range of general subjects, including business English, American history, economics, civics, and salesmanship. None of these subjects are required in the fourth year of the stenographic course, although all of them are electives. Aside from the undue amount of emphasis which is placed on technical work in this program, its chief weakness is its lack of definite building toward anything in particular. It is largely a course of electives. These electives, it is true, are quite well selected, but so far as is indicated there is no thought of building a coherent program which will do certain definite things for the student. There does not lie behind this course any philosophy of business education, and there is no definite organization of work to give any philosophy reality.

An additional criticism of this course which will be made by all of those who believe that a notion of the organization of modern society should be a part of each citizen's equipment is the limited amount of social science in the lower years of the courses. If one believes that some idea of social structure is desirable, and at the same time recalls the small fraction of the pupils of the elementary school which reaches the fourth year, he can hardly find himself in disagreement with this criticism.

THE REPORT OF 1919

The most recent statement definitely on the subject of commercial-curriculum reform which has come from the National Education Association is the report called *Business Education in Secondary Schools*, published by the Bureau of Education in 1919.[1] One finds in the introductory pages of this report the very criticism leveled at the existing courses in business education which has been made in the discussion above: "Commercial work has hitherto not generally been organized as a curriculum devoted to a specific object. Instead, it has been a loosely formed group of elective studies to which were added a certain number of vague subjects, and as such it has failed to give the unity necessary in any really effective system of education."

Starting from this view of the deficiency of existing curricula and the proposals of the past, the report continues:

In a general way, commercial education up to the present has attempted to meet four distinct business needs:

First, and most definite of these, is the training of stenographers; and second, is the training of bookkeepers and clerks for general office work. These two functions have heretofore been regarded as the full obligation of commercial education.

Third, the need that business education has recently undertaken to meet, is the training for secretarial work of those who have had a broader fundamental education and who wish to take more responsible positions than to be merely stenographers. Stenography and typewriting are made elements in the training of secretaries, but to these are added numerous other professional studies, such as economics, commercial correspondence, business customs, and business law.

Fourth, the need that commercial education now seeks to supply is the demand for salesmen. This involves not only a training in the principles of salesmanship, meeting the public, making a sale, etc., but also a broader training in business, knowledge of merchandise, and the cultivation of taste.

Commercial education should have a much wider purpose than the training of stenographers and bookkeepers. Already the broadened commercial education has addressed itself to the task of training for service in the community, for participation in social life, and

[1] This report was published as *Bulletin, No. 55*, 1919.

for knowledge of, and ability to adapt one's self to, business as a whole. Such subjects as economics, business organization, advertising salesmanship, and store practice are relatively new, and yet in their entirety they make a new purpose of business education comparable with, if not more important than, stenography or bookkeeping. Young people trained for the broader and more professional aspects of commercial life have every prospect of finding for themselves highly useful places in business as they demonstrate their fitness for more responsible duties. In the suggested curriculum given below the attempt is made to realize these purposes.

SEVENTH YEAR

The work in this year should be practically the same as that of the other pupils in the school. It should include English, geography and history, arithmetic, physiology and hygiene, penmanship, physical education, household or industrial arts, drawing, and music. The work of this year may well include some "try-outs" projects or short unit courses designed to help in the choice of work for the following years. If such try-out courses are offered they should be taken by all students, or, at least, each student should have an opportunity to choose from a variety of such courses. Specializing is out of place in this year.

The try-out courses above suggested should serve two ends: first, to determine the interests, aptitudes, and capacities of pupils, and, second, to reveal to the pupils the major fields of academic and vocational interests. Only by such an arrangement as is here recommended can the pupil elect his curriculum intelligently. These try-out courses should at the same time have a content of assured educational value.

EIGHTH YEAR

	Periods*	
	Prepared	Unprepared
English (half the time devoted to practical English with emphasis on simple business English and letter forms)	5	....
U.S. history	5	....
Household or industrial arts	....	4
Business arithmetic	....	5
Elementary industrial and commercial geography	3	....
First lessons in business, including short daily drills in business writing	5	....
Total	18	9

* Length of periods to be approximately 45 to 50 minutes. The committee would call attention to the advantages of a longer school day with longer periods to include supervised study, and a reduced requirement for the preparation of lessons outside of school.

NINTH YEAR

	Periods*	
	Prepared	Unprepared
English	5	....
Community civics (5 periods one-half year)	2½	....
General science†	5	....
Commercial mathematics (5 periods one-half year)	2½	....
Elementary bookkeeping, business forms and business writing	....	10
Typewriting	....	5
Total	15	15

TENTH YEAR

Required		
English—Selected reading with oral and written composition	5	....
Bookkeeping, intermediate	5	....
Industrial and commercial geography, including local industries and commercial products		....
Electives (choose 1)‡		
Shorthand and typewriting	5	....
Science	5	....
History to the beginning of the eighteenth century	5	....
Modern language	5	....

* Length of periods to be approximately 45 to 50 minutes. The committee would call attention to the advantages of a longer school day with longer periods to include supervised study, and a reduced requirement for the preparation of lessons out of school.

† Conditions in some schools may warrant for some pupils the substitution of either household arts or a modern language.

‡ Additional electives which are available in the school and for which the pupils have special aptitude should be open to them. It is especially recommended that wherever well-organized courses in commercial or applied art are offered such courses be commended to commercial students who may have aptitude for them.

If shorthand is not elected, typewriting may be taken as an extra unprepared subject for 5 periods.

ELEVENTH AND TWELFTH YEARS

Beginning with the eleventh year the pupil's work should be more highly specialized in one of the three following fields: general business and bookkeeping; stenographic and presecretarial; or retail selling and store service. To make the suggestions under these heads more obvious the work for the eleventh and twelfth years is arranged in three type curriculums. These curriculums are each two years in length and include certain subjects which are common to all the curriculums. Naturally the studies common to the different curriculums will be taught jointly.

General business and bookkeeping curriculum

ELEVENTH YEAR

	Periods per Week
Required	
English—Selected reading with oral and written composition	5
Office practice	3
Bookkeeping, advanced	5
Electives (choose at least 2)	
Economic history since 1700	5
Science with industrial applications	5
Modern language	5

TWELFTH YEAR

Required	
Business English—theme writing, oral reports, and commercial correspondence	5
Advanced American history and citizenship	5
Commercial law (5 periods one-half year)	2½
Economics (5 periods one-half year)	2½
Advanced commercial arithmetic	2
Business organization, advertising, and salesmanship (or foreign language if begun earlier)	5

Stenographic and presecretarial curriculum

ELEVENTH YEAR

Required	
English—Selected reading with oral and written composition	5
Shorthand	5
Typewriting (transcripts)	2
Office practice	3
Electives (choose 1)	
Economic history since 1700	5
Home economics	5
Science with industrial applications	5

TWELFTH YEAR*

Business English—theme writing, oral reports, and commercial correspondence	5
Advanced American history and citizenship	5
Commercial law (5 periods one-half year)	2½
Economics (5 periods one-half year)	2½
Secretarial practice, including shorthand	5
Transcription and typewriting	4

* It is strongly urged that opportunity be found for part-time work during the twelfth year. For pupils who spend alternate weeks, or fortnights, in positions the total time available in school will of necessity be only one-half that given. For such pupils the distribution of their work while in school may well be as indicated for the twelfth year.

*Retail selling and store service curriculum**

ELEVENTH YEAR

	Periods per Week
Required	
English—Selected reading with oral and written composition	5
Salesmanship and merchandise	5
Electives (*choose 2*)	
Economic history since 1700	5
Science (with industrial applications)	5
Home economics	5

TWELFTH YEAR

Business English—theme writing, oral reports, and commercial correspondence	5
Advanced American history and citizenship	5
Salesmanship and retail store organization	5
Store practice and store mathematics	5

* It is essential that pupils following this curriculum have store experience. This is possible on the part-time arrangement suggested above, but additional opportunities will be found to get such experience from work on Saturdays, in evenings, on holidays, and during school vacations.

In presenting the curriculums above outlined. the committee cautions schools against attempting more than they can do creditably. Manifestly the small high school will not be able to differentiate in the threefold manner above suggested. The specialized type of high school or the large comprehensive high school will find the curriculums above suggested entirely feasible. The committee feels, however, that these suggestions are of value even to those administering commercial education in the small high school.

The proposals of this committee show a very definite change from what has preceded. In the first place, the amount of required work has been increased, in accordance with the notion that the achievement of a definite objective could only be accomplished by well-organized requirements. Second, there is the belief expressed that the commercial curriculum should do something more than train for technique. On page 22 of the report one finds this statement:

If commercial training is to secure and hold an honored place in education, it must not only provide for the needs of those who must enter business at an early age, but it must prepare the largest possible number of pupils for the competitive conditions of modern business. A conclusive argument for a commercial curriculum extending through the full secondary-school period is found in the fact that the necessary technical facility and a reasonable modicum of general intelligence can not be given earlier than the end of the twelfth school year. The committee urges that the rights of young people themselves forbid the introduction of a short course of the kind which attempts to fit them for service beyond the ability of the immature boy or girl, or which suggests leaving school before economic necessity, or other reasons, compel withdrawal. To give ill-prepared and immature boys and girls a highly specialized training without a background of intelligence and life interest, and to rush these young people into business at an early age, appears to the committee like exploiting children either to commercial greed of employers, or to the selfishness and shortsighted prejudices of their families. It should be pointed out here that the "needs of the community" can be best met by giving full regard to the rights of young people themselves.

This realization of the need for broader courses for students who contemplate business as an occupation is not so well expressed in the proposed curriculum itself as in the confession of faith of the committee. A study of the program outlined shows that it is still largely dominated by the notion of technical office work. No social science is required in the first three years of the high-school course, with the exception of community civics, five periods, one-half year, which is proposed for the first year. In the fourth year there is a requirement of American history, one-half year of commercial law, and one-half year of economics. Requirements of science are as meager. Nothing of science is required in the first three years, excepting general science in the Freshman year. It is hardly conceivable that these limited requirements can seriously be supposed to qualify one for intelligent participation in business.

One further comment which should be made on this proposed course is the fact that it recognizes certain new interests in commercial work. The third and fourth years are organized in two different ways: in one instance for a stenographic and presecretarial curriculum, and in the second instance for retail selling and store-service work. This is the first time that a general proposal for retail-store selling has appeared.

THE PROPOSALS OF THE FEDERAL BOARD

Published almost at the same time as the reorganization report which we have just considered was the important bulletin on commercial education of the Federal Board for Vocational Education. This bulletin is in many ways a supplement to the National Education Association report. Each document refers to the other as having such a relationship. In so far as the report pertains to the high-school commercial course, its most significant characteristic is its so-called unit plan. The reasoning which is behind this course and the unit plan were set forth at length by Mr. F. G. Nichols, at that time the assistant director for commercial education of the Federal Board. It will be worth while to look at this statement in some detail:[1]

In this paper I shall set forth the general basic principles upon which high school commercial courses should be organized; outline a course of study in accordance with these principles; and briefly explain how such a course may be made to function so as to safeguard the best interests of all concerned.

If commercial education is to play its legitimate part in the field of vocational training, it must be set up in terms of vocational occupations which shall include all vocations that have to do with the administrative and distributive phases of business as distinguished from the manual or productive ones which comprehend all industrial occupations.

In the light of this interpretation it is no longer possible to think of commercial courses in terms of bookkeeping and shorthand only. It is necessary to determine very definitely the vocational needs in each locality and to provide a type of training that will meet these needs most satisfactorily. Local surveys will be necessary if the needs peculiar to each locality are to be discovered and provided for. While in a general way commercial needs are more or less alike in different places, it is true that commercial development in any given community may be such as to call for specialized training that would not be needed in other communities.

[1] *Commercial Education*, pp. 17–29. National Society for Vocational Education, April, 1919; and *Commercial Education*, pp. 17–21. Federal Board for Vocational Education, Bulletin 34, June, 1919. The courses outlined are practically identical in both instances. The idea behind the course is expressed more fully in the first source.

An analysis of the commercial positions held by boys and girls in any city will reveal the fact that 80 per cent of the commercial workers are employed in occupations other than those most commonly provided for in commercial courses. Many of these positions are of a more or less technical character and can be held successfully only by those who have been trained for them. Such training may be secured through proper provision for it in local schools, or it may be obtained through experience on the job. The one essential thing is that it shall be obtained somewhere before any large measure of success can be achieved.

Another very important factor that must be given more weight in the organization of commercial work is the age factor of boys and girls who are available for this training. It has been common practice to provide the same kind of courses for students of varying ages regardless of their capacities to profit by them.

The time is ripe for a careful consideration of this whole matter. The capacities of boys and girls must be thoroughly understood. Those who are in the first year of the high school may be given a type of training designed to prepare them for such positions as they may hope to get and hold at that age. A slightly higher type of training may be offered in each of the succeeding years, but in no case should the training given be more advanced than is required for the occupations that are open to boys and girls of the ages usually found in the year in which such training is being offered.

For a great many years efforts have been made in one way or another to solve the problem of high school mortality, especially in the early years of the course. Commercial subjects have been added in the third and fourth years in the hope that students would remain to take them and thus complete their high school education. The only tangible effect of this program is to drive students into the private schools before they have reached the public school commercial course. A few places have offered a two-year course covering the first and second years of high school and consisting very largely of commercial subjects, in the hope that students might be held at least two years for high school training. This plan is offered as a sort of competition with the private commercial school. In a few instances a one-year course has been set up. The only result seems to be an increased attendance at private schools.

It seems to me that we must recognize the fact that there will continue to be a heavy school mortality at the end of the eighth year, ninth year and possibly the tenth year. We must also conclude that, since we have been unable to remedy this condition, it is incumbent upon us to prepare courses of study that will not only safeguard the interests of boys and girls who continue to the end of the usual high school program, but of those more numerous boys and girls who, for one reason or another, insist upon leaving school at the end of one of the earlier years. It is believed that what is referred to above as the one-year unit plan of organization will accomplish this result. The needs of boys and girls who complete the high school course and of those who leave at the end of one of the earlier years are not antagonistic to each other. In the preparation of our course of study, however, we recognize that the vocational needs of high school boys and girls differ radically as their ages and aptitudes differ. In other words, we must discover the positions in which boys and girls of the eighth school year age are employed; those in which students of the ninth school year usually find employment; those that are open to graduates of the tenth year; and the more highly specialized types of service for which high school graduates should be well qualified. Recognition of these varying needs calls for the organization of each year, beginning with the eighth, upon an independent unit basis with, however, connecting links that result in a unified course of study for those fortunate enough to complete all the units that go to make up the whole.

It should also be emphasized at this point that in addition to the local day school facilities for giving this kind of training, there should be available to those who drop out at the end of any unit, continuation school commercial courses for boys and girls up to the age of eighteen, and evening school courses for those above eighteen in which the training broken off in the day school may be resumed and completed.

In setting up a suggestive course of study the various types of school organizations have been kept in mind. In many cities the old eight-four plan still is used; in others, the six-six plan is being tried out; and in still others the six-three-three, or junior high school plan, has been established. The type of commercial course that I am suggesting is adaptable to all three forms of organization. In discussing this course briefly by years I shall number them consecutively, beginning with the seventh and ending with the twelfth. For convenience, the program will be divided into elementary and advanced courses.

JUNIOR HIGH SCHOOL COMMERCIAL COURSE

Such a course usually has its foundation in the seventh year, and while no special provision need be made for vocational training of boys and girls of the seventh school year age, it must be recognized that it is in this year that the choice of a course is made and the foundation for that course is laid. For this reason a seventh year outline is submitted, but it is not to be understood that highly specialized commercial training is necessary in this year.

At the end of the eighth year many boys and girls find it necessary to leave school and many others leave because of a desire to secure employment, or because of a dislike for school work. Therefore, it is necessary that we understand the positions that are open to such boys and girls. In a general way we may include the following among the occupations in which such boys and girls are employed: check and cash messenger; bundle clerk; shipping clerk; stock clerk; general clerical assistant; mail clerk; mimeograph operator, etc.

SEVENTH YEAR

Subjects	Hours per Week
English	5
Arithmetic (including rapid calculation)	4
Business Writing (20 minutes daily)	
Geography (largely place geography with commercial applications)	5
History, Commercial and Industrial	5
Physical Training	2
Physiology and Hygiene	1
Manual Training (boys)	4
Household Arts (girls)	4

EIGHTH YEAR

Subjects	Hours per Week
English	5
Business Arithmetic (including rapid calculation) (20 minutes daily)	5
Business Writing (20 minutes daily)	5
Commercial Geography (elementary character)	5
History and Citizenship	3
Typewriting	5
First Lessons in Business	5
Manual Training (boys)	4
Domestic Arts (girls)	4
Physical Training	2

NINTH YEAR

Subjects	Hours per Week
English (including simple business letter-writing)	5
Commercial Mathematics (unprepared)	5
Commercial I (including elementary bookkeeping, business practice, and business writing)	10
Typewriting (unprepared)	5
Science (including hygiene, etc.)	5
Physical training	2

Those who finish the ninth year will find it possible to secure positions as assistant bookkeepers, typists and general office workers—positions slightly in advance of those open to eighth year boys and girls.

It should be remembered that in each year's work an attempt is made to interest the student to such an extent as to induce him to remain in school for more advanced training. It has not been found necessary to eliminate fundamental academic training such as English, arithmetic, domestic art, physical training, history, geography and science, in order to prepare for the simple vocations for which he should be prepared. It is, therefore, quite possible for a student to cross over to almost any other course in the tenth year, if it seems best to do so. This is purely incidental, however, and has not influenced the organization of the course in any degree.

ADVANCED OR SENIOR HIGH SCHOOL COMMERCIAL COURSE

Those who remain for the tenth year in high school will find the following positions, among others, open to them: bookkeeping positions of a more advanced character than those of the routine type referred to as being open to graduates of the ninth year; filing positions in which considerable responsibility is placed upon those who have complete charge of the files; positions as mail clerks with full responsibility for receiving and distributing the incoming mail and preparing and dispatching outgoing mail; shorthand positions of a simple character for those who have elected this subject in the tenth year, and clerical work of a more advanced character, including machine work of different kinds. Shorthand positions referred to above will usually be the kind in which some other line of work is the important part of the requirement and the ability to do a small amount of easy shorthand work is desired.

Thus, it will be noted that up to the end of the tenth year the courses are the same for all students and afford the best basic training for the kind of service that can be performed by younger boys and girls. No differentiation is necessary up to this point because of the general character of the employment for which such students are justified in making preparation.

From the tenth year on, however, through the eleventh and twelfth years, a form of specialization ought to be made available. Students who have shown marked ability in English, use of words, spelling, shorthand and typewriting, and who have shown some of the characteristics that go to make a good secretary, may well be encouraged to specialize along this line. Such specialization will be especially advantageous for girls who desire to enter stenographic and secretarial positions.

Other students may show special aptitude for salesmanship. Such students may well be given an opportunity to specialize in an occupation that is rapidly developing along lines that will insure its place among the most desirable commercial occupations—retail selling. Others, especially boys, may be trained for outside selling.

Those who show special ability along accounting lines, or in general business administration, may be given a chance to prepare for accountancy and general business positions, including advertising, salesmanship and executive work.

In certain cities where foreign trade is important, those who are interested in this field should have an opportunity to specialize in it.

Therefore, the tenth, eleventh, and twelfth years are set up in the following form with the idea of affording such specialization as may be called for by certain well marked aptitudes:

TENTH YEAR

Required Subjects	Hours per Week
English	5
Commercial Geography (including physical geography, local industries and commercial products)	5
Commercial II (intermediate bookkeeping and business practice)	5
Elective (choose one)	
Shorthand (see note)	5
Foreign Language (preferably Spanish)	5
History	5
Typewriting (must be taken if shorthand is elected. May be taken as an extra subject without shorthand.) (Unprepared.)	5

NOTE.—If the student has decided definitely to choose the General Business or Retail Selling Course in the third year, Shorthand should not be elected. In case of doubt or in case the stenographic course is chosen, elect Shorthand.

ELEVENTH YEAR

General Business and Accounting		Stenographic, Secretarial, and Reporting		Retail Selling		Foreign Trade and Shipping	
Subjects	*Hours per Week	Subjects	Hours per Week	Subjects	Hours per Week	Subjects	Hours per Week
Required		*Required*		*Required*		*Required*	
English	5	English	5	English	5	English	5
Physics or Chemistry	7	Physics or Chemistry	7	Physics or Chemistry	7	Physics or Chemistry	7
Office Practice	3	Shorthand	5	Salesmanship and Merchandise	5	Document Technique of Foreign Trade	5
Advanced Bookkeeping	5	Typewriting (transcription 3 periods a week)					
		Office Practice	3				
Electives (Choose one)		*Electives* (Choose one)		*Electives* (Choose one)		*Electives* (Choose one)	
Foreign Language	5	History	5	History	5	History	5
History	5	Mathematics	5	Foreign Language	5	Foreign Language	5
		Domestic Science	5	Domestic Science	5		
				Manual Training	5		

* Not less than 40 minutes each.

TWELFTH YEAR

General Business and Accounting		Stenographic, Secretarial, and Reporting		Retail Selling		Foreign Trade and Shipping	
Subjects	Hours per Week	Subjects	Hours per Week	Subjects	Hours per Week	Subjects	Hours per Week
Commercial English (including business correspondence, public speaking, sales-talk, etc.	5	Commercial English (including business correspondence, public speaking, etc.)	5	Commercial English (including sales-talk, public speaking, and letter-writing)	5	Commercial English (including foreign commercial correspondence)	5
Advanced American History with Civics	5	Advanced American History with Civics	5	Advanced American History with Civics	5	Advanced American History with Civics	5
Commercial Law (1 sem.) / Economics (2 sem.) (bracketed)	5	Commercial Law / Economics (bracketed)	5	Salesmanship and Retail Store Organization	5	Advertising and Salesmanship; Business Organization and Management	5
Advertising, Salesmanship, and Business Organization	5	Secretarial Practice	5	Store Practice and Store Mathematics	5	Foreign Trade Sales Practice	5
Principles of Accounting	5	Office Experience — Alternate weeks is recommended.		Office Experience — Minimum 20 days and 30 Saturdays during Junior year, and minimum 40 school days and 30 Saturdays, evenings, and holidays Senior year with credit as for laboratory work. Alternate week arrangement if preferred.		Foreign Language (if begun earlier)	5
Office Experience—alternate weeks is recommended.						Experience in a business dealing with foreign trade either alternate weeks, or on some other basis as may be worked out by educational directors and employers.	

OFFICE OR STORE WORK

It will be noted that a part-time co-operative arrangement is suggested in connection with the twelfth year course outlined above. In retail selling, contact with the occupation may be provided to a limited extent in the eleventh year. This is desirable in view of the fact that a certain type of store service must be thoroughly understood before students are eligible to sell goods. The retail selling experience will be afforded in the twelfth year, the basis for this experience having been laid in the eleventh.

Finally, in the organization of commercial courses in any community, not only local occupational requirements should be kept in mind, but also the limitations of teaching force and equipment. The differentiation suggested for the eleventh and twelfth years should not be attempted in small high schools. However, the vocational principles suggested may well be given careful consideration in connection with the establishment of commerical courses in any high school where such training is offered. Know the needs of your students in the light of local business opportunities and meet those needs as fully as the financial support of the local school board will permit.

This proposed course coming as the official pronouncement of the Federal Board has had considerable influence on commercial work in the high schools in the United States. There are, without doubt, some things to be said in favor of this course. In the first place it has an objective basis. It is constructed upon the findings of the Federal Board's Survey of Commercial Occupations. Again, it recognizes the fact that students drop out of school and attempts to meet that difficulty. Moreover, it shows a realization that the training needed by boys is different from that needed by girls, and attempts an adjustment of studies accordingly.

There are, however, in this proposed course, certain weaknesses which to some appear fundamental. First, there should be expressed the belief that no survey of business requirements is alone an adequate basis upon which to determine a curriculum for the secondary commercial course. What business wants is important, but it is by no means the only matter of importance. What business is, is of quite as much significance, and our survey of what business is should be convincing evidence that there is needed in business education something much larger than is proposed in the offerings of the course under consideration. Nor does it follow that everything that is needed or wanted should be given by the *high school* business course. Indeed one of the interesting points brought out by the Federal Board's Junior Survey was the fact "That 80 per cent of the commercial workers are employed in occupations other than those most commonly provided for in commercial courses." This shows that to the extent that this 80 per cent of the commercial workers are succeeding in their occupations, they are doing so not because of any *high-school* training they may have had but in spite of it, thus proving that there are other agencies (chiefly training by ndustry itself, no doubt) competent to give the technical training satisfactorily. Furthermore, the board's program suggests the use of continuation school and evening school courses for those who drop out at the end of any unit "in which the training broken off in the day school may be resumed and completed." It is unfortunate that the board saw these institutions only as agencies for "resuming" education of the same sort as that planned in the high school. Such institutions should be thought of essentially as distinct agencies for a distinct specialized purpose. If a student *must* drop school before he is sixteen, seventeen, or eighteen, it is time, when he definitely decides to drop, to give him some definitely vocational courses. But there is no reason to give him any such courses before that time. And such courses should be definitely understood to be drop-out courses. For giving these vocational courses the public continuation school and evening schools, the corporation school, and other private schools must serve. But it is nonsensical to give the same type of work to those who are certain to go through, to those who *may* drop out, and to those who *have* dropped out. Yet this is what the board's proposal appears to be. The plan lacks a view of the various educational institutions functioning as specialists for specialized tasks.

Not only is practically all recognition of the broader requirements of business and the use of specialized agencies for specialized tasks omitted in the construction of the board's outline, but the whole social aspect of a publicly supported school in a democracy is likewise neglected. Vocation, immediate, is the keynote, and practically all else has yielded to the findings of immediate vocational requirements.

In consequence, if the board has its way, perhaps one-fourth of our school children who work in the seventh grade and above will go out to be citizens in this democracy with the following required formal instruction in the rights, duties, and obligations of citizenship.

Seventh year:	Commercial and industrial history	5 hours
Eighth year:	History and citizenship	3 hours
Ninth year:	Nothing	
Tenth year:	Nothing	
Eleventh year:	Nothing	
Twelfth year:	Advanced American history, with civics	5 hours
	Economics and commercial law	5 hours

The outlook that makes such a program possible holds forth little hope that the situation will be saved by the technical subjects being impregnated with social material, or by a wise use of electives.

It is not a sufficient answer to this criticism to say that the important thing is for the boys and girls to be able to make a living and that therefore everything must yield to the presentation of technical subjects. Such an answer beclouds the whole issue. May it not be that the technical subjects can be even better presented in connection with a presentation of the outstanding aspects of business activity and of our industrial society? If this is not possible, perhaps American democracy might better pay the price of assistance for longer continuance in school rather than pay the price of having masses of citizens unaware of how our society is put together. Even in the range of business activity, let us remember that productive capacity depends upon our business men having competence in social relationships as well as in technical matters. The program of the board savors too much of a plan for an educational system devoted primarily to the production of clerical help.[1]

[1] L. C. Marshall, "The Relation of the Collegiate School of Business to the Secondary School System," *Journal of Political Economy* (February, 1920), pp. 158–59.

A third particular in which the course outlined by the Federal Board is open to criticism is its acceptance of the idea that a course educating for business must be built largely out of the traditional commercial material. Such an acceptance obviously limits the resulting course most seriously and prevents it from becoming in the best sense a constructive program.

The fourth criticism which may be expressed is of the vocational unit idea itself when applied to a *secondary* commercial course. There is implicit in the vocational unit-course idea the belief that students are likely to be concluding their work with the conclusion of the unit of study. It is true enough that the school mortality is great at the conclusion of every year after the fifth or sixth grade, but it seems unfortunate to lend encouragement to that mortality by attempting to perfect the student at as many periods as possible with the technique necessary for immediate employment. With the desire to leave school apparently inherent, with as much of vocational flavor as possible given to his work, with his course at every period of his career pointed so that he can leave school and be equipped for the immediate job, the setting is perfectly calculated to make the school mortality high. The whole arrangement tends to indicate to the student that the school is to prepare him for a job, and that as soon as he is so prepared there is wisdom in leaving. It would be better vocational guidance to postpone all technically qualifying courses until the last year or two years of the high-school course. Nothing of a highly technical nature should be given in the regular high-school commercial course prior to the Junior year excepting such technique as will help the student *in his work as a student.*[1] The school situation should be so organized that everything makes it difficult rather than easy for the student to leave school; that everything indicates the value of remaining for those technical courses which can be obtained toward the end of the course; that everything during the early

[1] Typewriting and possibly stenography might be examples. The Federal Board's study seems to prove that they are next to useless after leaving school, however.

high-school years aids the student in securing knowledge of the situation in which he will apply his technique after he has acquired it.

Of course, it will be objected to such statements as the preceding that a course so arranged takes no account of those students who will quit school in spite of all the arranging and adjusting that can be done. It will be cried, "To postpone the technical work in the high school will mean an increase of students in the business colleges at the expense of commercial courses, and industry will be even more than now wearied with a flood of undertrained applicants." Let it be so. Once we recognize that the business colleges have in such work a legitimate field, we should throw about them such restrictions that they cannot sell false wares or any wares to those not qualified to use them. Controlled by these restrictions there is no reason why the business college should not give an immense part of the technical training for those students who will not go beyond the first or second year of high school. They can do it well and, although the incidence of the cost is different, the total cost to the community is doubtless less than when the work is performed in the secondary school. On the other hand, any family which can afford to keep its children in high school for two years cannot afford to have those two years wholly occupied with a narrow clerical training. That time is too precious to be thus spent. If technical training is omitted something else more valuable may be done, and the technical work may be easily obtained elsewhere. If technical work is given, the time is consumed and the more valuable thing cannot be obtained in any other institution. Nor is it sound to argue in terms of financial necessity for clerical courses in the public school, for any family which can afford to keep a child in the public school for two years can afford six or nine months of business college work.

So far as the complaints of industry concerning definite technique are concerned, there is likewise little cause to be disturbed. There is no reason why the secondary school should offer to each industry students competent to perform each detailed task. Given a sound foundation with, at most, broad types of technical training, industry through its own training-schools should assume the costs of special instruction. And those persons who most thoughtfully represent industry have over and over again laid down this principle. Here, again, the real costs to the community as a whole are far less than when a great number of people are trained in special techniques, many of which will not apply to special businesses, and when a number of the people so trained will never make any application of the techniques in any field. Any ordinary sense of social economy fixes the corporation school, sometimes supplemented by the public continuation, postgraduate, and evening schools, and sometimes by private schools as the proper agency for a large share of the technical work which many persons are anxious to place in the secondary school.

A CONSTRUCTIVE PROGRAM NEEDED

In many ways the most serious criticism of the Federal Board's proposal is the failure to outline a virile program to redeem the situation which its own survey revealed. The tragic joke on secondary educators, and rather a monumental one, uncovered by the Board's Survey, is the fact that after a great many years of impregnating the high-school commercial course with certain technical subjects, 80 per cent of the commercial workers are found to be in occupations other than those provided for in high-school commercial courses. The so-called vocational studies in the high-school commercial course are thus disclosed to be *not vocational courses* and *not anything else.* They have been merely "motion making."

With this situation made clear, largely as a result of the Federal Board's Survey, it becomes obvious that the old vocational courses in the high-school commercial curriculum must in large measure be abandoned. But this leaves a vacuum and the necessity of filling it. Unfortunately the Federal Board did not erect a substantial educational program with which to fill the space. Overlooking the fact that industry was already doing the technical training with formal or informal corporation schools, overlooking the fact that many private and public agencies were ready to supplement the corporation school, overlooking the fundamental purposes and duties of public education, nothing better was forthcoming than the proposal to fill up each of the precious high-school years with a juvenile study of the petty duties with which a boy or girl leaving school would be concerned for the first few months. By the board's own findings, these duties will be pertinent but a short time, for a new line of duties appropriate to each succeeding year of age is suggested in each of the one-year unit courses. The training for vocations is thus obviously directed toward the *immediate vocation only* with no serious consideration of the vocation of the many years to follow. It is vocational training for the first job, in no sense vocational training for a life in business.[1]

WHAT SHALL BE DONE WITH THE HIGH-SCHOOL BUSINESS COURSE?

The answer to What shall be done with the high-school commercial course? demands:

I. A clear recognition of certain basic facts

II. An answer to the question, What shall be the organization of the work to give a sense of social relationship?

III. A consideration of the technical work that must be given

Let us consider each of these matters in turn.

I. We need, first of all, a clear view of the following:

1. There are two great overlapping and interacting phases of business education. One of these is education in the perception of relationships; the other is training in technique.

2. The high-school commercial course is only one of a number of specialized educational institutions. It must not undertake to do all of the task of educating for business. To do so is to fail. This has been its weakness in the past. Its real task is to do as well as possible what other agencies cannot do better.

[1] The criticisms expressed above apply, obviously, to the course outlined by the board. That there is evidence at present of a somewhat changing view, see pages 159 and 160.

3. It is clear that there are many agencies which can give well a large part, if not all, of the technical training required. The corporation school, the business college, the continuation school, evening courses, co-operative courses, the postgraduate technical course, and the correspondence school, all perform in this field. These agencies are not qualified to give satisfactory training in *relationships* in any case. They need co-operation and encouragement, and in some cases they need control for the proper performance of *technical* training. In technical training, however, they each have an advantage over the high-school commercial course in that they function when the student is close to the job or actually employed in it. They can be used at almost any time; they can be readily shifted from one type of training to another. They are flexible, adaptable, and definite for varied and definite needs.

4. If we assume that *some* technical work must be done in the high school, there arises the question of proper division of time between such training and the studies dealing with social relationships. No amount of time is too long for the latter work. *The proper approach to this question is therefore* (a) *to determine the amount of technical work which must be done and which cannot be turned over to agencies other than the high school;* (b) *to determine the minimum time for the technical work which, as a result, must be given in the high school; finally,* (c) *to place that minimum period of time at the later part of the high-school commercial course. There is thus allowed all of the preceding period of high-school instruction for education in relationships.*

II. An answer to the question, What shall be the organization of the work to give a sense of social relationships? As a result of the analysis made above, this becomes the second question. *Any* arrangement of the social studies now existing in general high-school courses is better than the lack of such studies which has been typical of commercial courses. The high schools, however, have not worked out a method of giving social studies which offer the student a well-rounded view of the world in which he lives. A commission, following a rather extensive survey for the association of collegiate schools of business, reported as follows:[1]

A review of the pronouncements made up to the December, 1921, meetings by the leading organizations concerned with the presentation of social studies in our secondary schools of the academic type justifies the following comments:

a) The grip of history is strong. In the main, it seems to have been assumed that the historical study should be the chief instrumentality for giving our younger students an understanding of the structure of the present-day society.

b) This attitude has been challenged to some considerable extent in recent years by the community civics movement, and by the American Political Science Association and the American Sociological Society—so effectively challenged, indeed, that the historians themselves show signs that they appreciate that the monoply of history in secondary social studies is to be broken and that the history which remains in the curriculum is to be more definitely pointed toward understanding the society of today.

c) The report of the Subcommittee of the National Education Association on Social Studies in Secondary Education, more than any other report, displays a desire to make the student acquainted with the various aspects of the society in which he lives. But even that report blocks out a plan which is entirely inadequate. Notwithstanding its emphasis upon "community," "economic," and "vocational "civics, sufficient attention is not given to the economic aspects of modern society. The document shows the influence of the historian, the political scientist, and the sociologist, but not sufficiently that of the economist. In particular there is a haphazard and inadequate presentation of economic interests in the content of community civics. There is a good selection of scattered topics, but the student can scarcely secure a rounded, balanced view of our modern society. Quite aside from the poor balance in this program of social studies, it is inadequate in its senior high school presentation. The senior high school curriculum should bring to ripeness and maturity the earlier work, but this is not done.

The failure of secondary educators to organize existing social studies in a satisfactory way has suggested the necessity of

[1] Adapted by permission from Association of Collegiate Schools of Business, *Social Studies in Secondary Schools*, pp. 18–19. University of Chicago Press, 1922.

taking an entirely new view and perfecting a new arrangement of new material. Such undertakings have been stimulated by current movements in school organization.

Two recent proposals will be given some consideration here. They are both enterprising plans and both conceive the school program as a continuous project. The first of these is the program outlined by the commission of the collegiate schools of business. The work of this commission has more significance in view of the fact that it included a member from the Association of Secondary School Principals, one from the American Federation of Labor, and one who was an appointee of the National Industrial Conference Board.[1]

Enough has been said to make it reasonably clear, first, that the situation with respect to social studies is far from satisfactory in our educational institutions, second, that the whole matter is now under serious consideration and that modifications are practically certain to occur. But it is not merely the social studies which are in the melting-pot. Other studies are there also. There also will be found the whole scheme of organization of our American educational system.

.... For a variety of causes that system has taken a form which may be described as an end-to-end joining of an eight-year elementary school, a four-year secondary school, a four-year college course (frequently shortened when taken in connection with a professional course), and the professional school. For a variety of reasons this organization is under criticism, and has indeed been under ciriticism from the time of President Eliot's attacks upon it in the late eighties and early nineties. The outstanding aspects of that criticism for our purposes are these:

With the lengthening of the average period of school attendance per year, a six-year elementary course is sufficient. Its continuation as an eight-year program has meant an undue and ineffective inflation of the elementary subjects in order to occupy the time available. The result has been formalistic presentation of subjects, wasted time in the educational process, intellectual nausea on the part of its recipients, and wholesale desertion by the students in later years over

[1] The following statement is adapted from the Association of Collegiate Schools of Business, *Social Studies in Secondary Schools*, pp. 41–61. University of Chicago Press, 1922.

and above any amounts justified by the economic situation of the families concerned.

With the increasing complexity of our social organization, the increasing range of our intellectual pursuits, and the increasing intensity of modern life, the high schools—those colleges of the common people—have looked with longing eyes upon the seventh and eighth grades which are largely wasted under our present system, and in some cases have coveted the first two years of college work. The pressure of the high-school curriculum upon the time available in the ordinary four-year course is shown by the fact that the *average* high school in the territory of the North Central Association offers more than twice as many units of work as are required for graduation, and the larger schools offer from three to four times as many. School administrations, laboring under such pressure, are not likely to be patient with wasted opportunities in the earlier grades.

It is contended that an arrangement of work which terminated the elementary school at the end of six years, and followed that by a three-year junior high school, and then set up a three-year senior high school, would be more in accord with the psychological development of the child than is the present arrangement. While this is disputed territory, the Commission on the Reorganization of Secondary Education, appointed by the National Education Association, after a thorough investigation of the whole situation, definitely recommends the reorganization of the school system on the 6–3–3 basis.

The present arrangement is particularly under fire from the professional schools. They contend that both from the point of view of the welfare of the individual and from the point of view of society's interest in the case people should begin their professional training at least two years earlier. . . . .

European experience is also cited in criticism of our old scheme of organization. This requires no comment. It is true that our system stands alone.

As has been intimated, the first clear plea for a comprehensive reorganization was voiced by President Eliot in the late eighties and early nineties. Within the last ten years the movement has been given great impetus. In the form of the so-called 6–3–3 or 6–6 arrangement, it has been definitely recommended by the Commission of the National Education Association. It has been more or less assumed by the various educational committees which have reported in recent years; it is actually occurring with considerable rapidity in our various communities. In 1913, 13 per cent of the high schools of the North Central Association territory had taken on junior high schools; today over 25 per cent have assumed this form; and competent observers predict that the majority of the secondary schools of the country will be organized on this basis in the not far distant future.

True, in many cases this reorganization has been a mere administrative form, but this is not of the essence of the case. Properly understood, this so-called 6–3–3 or 6–6 arrangement or any other comparable plan means far more than the administrative device of taking two years away from one organization and bestowing them upon another. It contemplates the entire reorganization of the curriculum to the end that without loss of training (its advocates claim there will be a gain) two years of time may be saved and students may be carried by the end of the twelfth grade to approximately the position now reached by the end of the Sophomore year in college.[1]

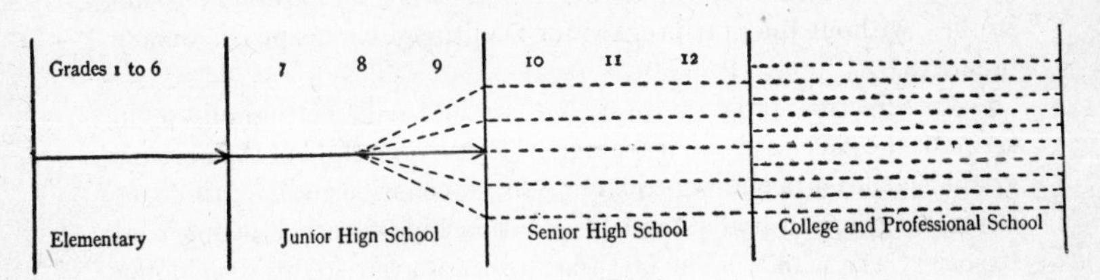

Clearly enough, the movement is on and is on vigorously. So far as we can now see, the educational system which will result may be crudely represented by the above diagram. A fairly coherent and unified system of training in fundamental processes in the elementary schools will be followed by the junior high school, in which it is at least desirable that the basic considerations shall be training in citizenship, with the beginnings of specialization occurring only in the later stages of that school. This will be followed by the senior high school in which, paralleled with the college preparatory course so called, will certainly go very considerable ranges of vocational training. The college and the professional school will receive the graduates of

[1] Preliminary experiments have already been conducted in this field with the result of saving one year of time, and experiments are well under way to bring about the saving of another year.

the senior high school, who will bring an equipment comparable with that possessed by the present Junior in college, if the reorganization works out successfully.

The Commission proposes a program of social studies for the junior high school which it believes to be more fundamental and far-reaching than the other proposals which have been made.

This Commission believes that the social studies should be the backbone of secondary education, with which all other studies and school activities should be closely articulated according to their contributions to the social objectives of education. Since each individual must be a citizen and as such must participate in group action, the social studies should be represented in each grade of education, and every pupil should have at least one unit of social study in every year of the school course.

The reorganization which is now in process in our educational system (which opens up the seventh and eighth grades for the introduction of new material) justifies a somewhat daring attempt to think through, as a coherent whole, our presentation of secondary social studies, without too much regard for traditional claims or customary practices.

An effective program of social studies will be organized in terms of the psychology of learning. The average child of the seventh grade is at least beginning to have a social consciousness. His mind is reaching out to understand his relationships to other people and to society as a whole. The fact that he is not aware of his developing attitude does not interfere with making use of this interest.

A SUMMARY VIEW OF THE PROPOSED JUNIOR HIGH SCHOOL PROGRAM IN SOCIAL STUDIES

. . . . . This summary view will present, in specific terms, only the work in social studies.

SEVENTH GRADE

1. Geographic bases of (physical environment with relation to) United States development
2. Social science survey (types of social organization)
   a) Simple industry and simple society
   b) The transforming effects of scientific knowledge
3. Other studies, correlated so far as may be practicable with the social-study material

EIGHTH GRADE

1. The opening of the world to the use of man
2. Vocational survey, the individual's place in our social organization (presented in functional terms so that it may contribute to an understanding of our type of social organization)
3. Other studies, correlated so far as may be practicable with the social-study material

NINTH GRADE

1. The history of the United States (presented with "citizenship material" occupying the center of attention)
2. Principles of social organization (economic, political, social)
3. Other studies, correlated so far as may be practicable with the social-study material
4. A general survey of business administration, elective

A DETAILED VIEW OF THE WORK OF THE SEVENTH GRADE

The work of this grade sets out consciously to "give our youth society and appreciation of what it means to live together in organized society, an appreciation of how we do live together, and an understanding of the conditions precedent to living together well." Its emphasis is upon the first and third of these propositions, without at all neglecting the second. The survey of types of social organization in simple societies emphasizes the first; the survey of the transforming effects of scientific knowledge, the work in geography, and the work in science emphasize the third. Of course, there is no intention of making a sharp differentiation in treatment.

The foregoing statement of purpose may be stated differently. The work of this grade seeks to sweep together, into a somewhat organic whole, the social-study work of the first six grades, and to take a further step in generalized thinking in the field.

The work in geographic bases of (physical environment with relation to) United States development is designed.

1. To bring into an organic whole the preceding work in history, civics, and geography in such a way as to
2. Show the importance of physical environment with respect to conditions precedent to living together well, and to
3. Prepare the way, in terms of principles, for the work of the next two grades, and to

4. Give the student who can go no farther a significant contribution to his "appreciation of how we live together and understanding of the conditions precedent to living together well."

The social-science survey of types of social organization is designed

1. To bring into an organic whole the preceding work in history, civics, and geography in such a way as to prepare the way, in terms of principles, for the work of the next two grades.
2. To lay a comparative basis for the later more careful survey of the evolutionary development of the functioning social structure.
3. To give the student who can go no farther a significant contribution to his "awareness of what it means to live together in organized society, appreciation of how we do live together and understanding of the conditions precedent to living together well."

The suggested method of presenting this social-science survey material is as follows:

1. Present a series of snapshots of simple types of social organization such as

   The life of Neolithic man
   The life of the Iroquois
   The life of nomads
   Life in a medieval manor
   Life in a medieval town
   Life in a modern secluded mountain district
   Life in a frontier mining camp

   in which the student can see how such matters as education, religion, health, social control, economic activities, etc. (these are only samples), were cared for and can begin to see wherein our ways of caring for such matters are different, if different.

   This comparative study should be directed toward bringing out certain concepts, of which the following may be taken as examples (they are only samples): self-sufficiency vs. interdependence; customary vs. competitive methods; non-exchange vs. exchange society; non-industrial vs. industrial society; the shifting emphasis in social control; the modern co-operation of specialists—all with the idea of leading the student to "generalize" his knowledge and with the further idea of preparing him for the study of "principles" in the ninth grade.
2. The latter part of the survey is to be devoted to showing the contribution of knowledge "to our living together well" and how that reacts upon the type of social organization. This should be

no mere threadbare account of the Industrial Revolution: it should be an account of the transforming effects of science on our ways of living together. Notice that the way has been prepared by the student's work in science, if science is offered in this grade.

A DETAILED VIEW OF THE WORK OF THE EIGHTH GRADE

There is presumably no need for a detailed statement of the general purpose of the work of this grade. It is obvious that, in addition to caring properly for those who must drop out at the end of the year, this grade must (*a*) begin to give many students a rational basis for selection of vocations and (*b*) continue the preparation for the more generalized social study of the ninth grade.

The work in "The Opening of the World to the Use of Man" is designed

1. To knit together and to build upon the social-science survey and geography of the preceding grade in such a way that the student will get as a part of his mental machinery—as tools of which he will make conscious use—concepts of change, development, and continuity.
2. In respect to factual background, to give the students some appreciation of the long, hard trail the human race has climbed; to let him see the emergence of Western civilization, its spread over the earth, and its contacts with other civilizations.
3. To give the student the "world-background" against which the history of his own country (ninth grade) may be seen in perspective and to make him "cosmopolitan" and "international" in a wholesome sense of those words.

The vocational survey (the individual's place in our social organization) is designed

1. To give the student an opportunity (upon which their experience has caused so many school men to insist) to think through in specific terms his own possible contribution to social living. Whether this results in his actually "choosing a vocation" matters little, if at all. Out of it, he should get a clearer notion of the qualities making for individual success in the process of social living.
2. To give this, however, not as a set of maxims and preachments and not as a set of "job analyses" but as a survey of the activities (emphasizing here economic activities without neglecting political and social considerations) which are carried on in *our* type of social organization, and

3. To do this in such a way that he will glimpse an economic organization in which activities are in terms of social purposes. By way of illustration. The student who sees the "undifferentiated" medieval trader split up as time goes on into transporter, insurer, financier, seller, etc., will have a different conception of the work of railroads, insurance companies, banks, etc., from the one he would have had after an unconnected "study of occupations." In other words, the vocational survey is designed to give the student a more thorough and specific conception of our social organization as it actually operates in our "living together."

A DETAILED VIEW OF THE WORK OF THE NINTH GRADE

Here, also, a detailed statement of general purpose may be omitted. Looking back over the junior high school curriculum, this year's work seeks to knit together the preceding work (*a*) in terms of principles, and (*b*) in terms of their application to citizenship in our own country. Looking forward to the work of the senior high school, this year's work seeks to pave the way for the more specialized presentation of the social sciences.

The work in the history of the United States (presented with "citizenship material" occupying the center of attention) is self-explanatory, if it is kept in mind that the ideal is that of bringing the social-science work of the preceding grades, as well as that of this ninth grade, to a focus in this account of the development of our own social living together. Such a statement indicates the kind of history which is to be presented.

The work in principles of social organization assumes that the student has been given sufficient factual background and has attained a sufficient maturity to enable him to view our social living in terms of principles rather than in terms of types or of practices. It asks the student to do, as a conscious matter, a most fundamental thing, namely, seek relationships on a scale which will give him an organic view of our social living. He is asked (so far as he may now be able) to formulate consciously the principles of social living which should guide him in later years. It is to be noticed in passing that no such opportunity now exists in any stage of our school curriculum. It is conceivable that the first draft of this will have to be in three parts: (1) economic organization, (2) political organization, (3) social organization not otherwise handled. But it is hoped and expected that it may be done not as three parts but as one unified whole.

While it forms no part of the basic material, the elective work (for those who plan to take the so-called commercial course) in Survey of Business Administration deserves passing notice. It should dovetail both with the vocational survey of the preceding grade and with the work in Principles of Social Organization of this grade. It should provide the sadly lacking unifying elements in the present miscellaneous collection of "commercial courses." It should be of distinct vocational service for the student who can go no farther, and it should pave the way for a higher standard of "commercial courses" in the senior high school.

A HINT OF THE PROGRAM OF THE SENIOR HIGH SCHOOL

The foregoing sets forth the material on which the Commission particularly covets discussion, but it is worth while to suggest something of its bearing upon the senior high school program. It is assumed that in each year of the senior high school, some social-study work will be required and that the work will be presented in more specialized (scientific ?) form than it was in the earlier grades.

The following statement gives merely a suggestion of possible courses in the field of economics and business. Perhaps it contains hints for other fields of study. The Commission believes that our larger high schools, at least, might in time offer considerable choice of courses in the fields that we now designate as political science, history, psychology, and sociology.

1. The financial organization of society and the manager's administration of finance.
2. The market organization of society and the manager's administration of market.
3. The position of the worker in our society and personnel administration.
4. The evolution of our economic society. (Note that this is vastly more than a "History of Commerce" and vastly more than the typical "Industrial History.")
5. Accounting (not merely as bookkeeping but also as an instrument of control in the hands of the executive).
6. Business law (as a manifestation of social control of business activities and as a facilitating aid of business).
7. Such technical courses as may be expedient. An illustration is shorthand and typewriting.
8. Theories of value and distribution.
9. Government and industry.

COMPARATIVE STATEMENT OF THREE PROPOSALS

	Seventh Grade	Eighth Grade	Ninth Grade	Tenth Grade	Eleventh Grade	Twelfth Grade
1. Committee on History and Education for Citizenship, American Historical Association	The world before 1607 and the beginnings of American history, including rise of Latin-American Republics	The world since 1607 viewed in relation to the evolution and expanding world-influence of the United States	Community and national activities or progress of civilization to about 1650	Progress toward world-democracy since 1650 (mainly European history emphasizing political aspects but seeking explanations in economic changes, inventions, discoveries, social regroupings, leadership, and thought)	United States history during national period studied in same spirit as that indicated for tenth grade	Social economic and political principles and problems
2. 1916 Report of Subcommittee on Social Studies in Secondary Education National Education Association Commission on Reorganization of Secondary Education	Geography (½ yr.), European history (½ yr.), in sequence or parallel Civics as phase of above, or segregated or both OR European history (1 yr.) Geography taught incidentally to history Civics as cited above	American history (½ yr.), Civics (½ yr.), in sequence or parallel Geography taught incidentally to above	Civics, state, national (½ yr.) Civics, economic and vocational (½ yr.) History in connection with above OR Civics, economic, and vocational (½ yr.), Economic History (½ yr.), in sequence or parallel	European history to approximately the end of the seventeenth century (1 yr.), including ancient, oriental, English, and American exploration European history (including English) since end of seventeenth century (1 or ½ yr.) American history since the seventeenth century (1 or ½ yr.) Problems of American Democracy (1 or ½ yr.)		
3. Commission of the Association of Collegiate Schools of Business and Committee of American Economic Association	Geographic bases of (physical environment in relation to) United States development Social-science survey (types of social organization) a) Simple industry and simple society b) Transforming effect of knowledge Other studies correlated	Opening of the world to the use of man The place of the individual in our society (vocational survey) Other studies correlated	The history of the United States Principles of social organization Other studies correlated	The presentation of social studies in more specialized form and more in accord with the traditional divisions of the social sciences than was suggested for the earlier grades. Availability of material, local organization of curricula, and vocational needs will all play a part in determining the selection of courses.		

THE NATIONAL COUNCIL OF EDUCATION PLAN

The second proposal, in many ways similar to the proposal of the Collegiate Schools, is "The Junior High School Program of Studies" outlined by a subcommittee of the National Council of Education.[1]

After emphasizing the importance of the junior high school movement and the experience which has been gained from the experiments from the junior high school, the committee states that the program of studies in the junior high school should be a resultant of several forces.[2]

It should be made up, in part, of a continuation of the elementary school curriculum, but a re-view of these courses, i.e., a new view through articulation of elementary and secondary courses; in part, a pre-view of secondary school courses of study, but a rearrangement of such courses in their "simpler aspects, deferring the refinements" to later senior high school grades; in part, a prevocational content from the industrial and commercial fields; and, finally, a liberal amount of social science materials and social and civic activities to the end of giving to the early adolescent a "self-conscious social adjustment." This transitional unit of the public-school system must preserve its contacts and become a composite product of the forces which precede and follow it.

At the same time the program of studies of the junior high school is a self-contained unit. The point of view of the elementary curriculum toward its pupils is en masse to the end that all may receive a usable knowledge of the common branches and a sympathetic understanding of the social and civic structure of our democratic society. Differentiation of pupils into groups, so far as program of studies is concerned, prevails in the senior high school to the end that individuals of each group may receive training in the types of work for which they have aptitudes.

Following this introductory statement the committee gives a more detailed view of what should be done in each of the periods of the junior high school.

[1] The chairman of this sub-committee is James M. Glass, Director of Junior High Schools in the Commonwealth of Pennsylvania. This material is used with his permission.

[2] The following is adapted from advance sheets distributed by the committee.

A. Adjustment. Low Seventh

A period of *adjustment* for the very young and immature adolescent of twelve years of age. He must be adjusted to a new school organization, and to a new type of school administration. It would seem wise, therefore, to subject him during the first semester to as little change as possible in his program of studies. Such change as is advisable should be restricted to the inevitable modification in the courses of study which are consequent to enlarged school facilities and departmentalization. There should be no change in the program of studies occasioned by the introduction of electives. In fact the tabulated report of the questionnaire[1] shows over 50 per cent vote in favor of postponing electives to the eighth year. Present practice gives little support to any seventh-year elective.

B. Exploration and Pre-view (Apperceptive Basis of Secondary Courses). High Seventh and Low Eighth

There should be a period of *exploration*, when there is a *pre-view* of the specialized secondary school courses which distinguishes one high-school curriculum from another, and when prevocational tryout is provided for drop-outs. This general introductory course offers opportunity for exploration of aptitude for the whole subject field and for a pre-view or apperceptive basis for the cross-sections of the subject. Properly, therefore, junior high school courses are designated as general mathematics, general science, world-history, and general social science, pre-vocational courses, junior business training, etc.

C. Provisional Choice of Electives. High Eighth

Following the period of exploration and pre-view there should be a period of *provisional choice* of electives. During this period facility of cross-over between electives should be promoted by every administrative device possible to the end of guaranteeing that evidence of unfitness for an elective will be followed by effecting a change of electives. In case this period of provisional choice does not extend beyond one semester, there would be justification for postponing promotion requirements in electives during this semester.

[1] Questionnaire in this quotation refers to one used in the investigations of the committee.—AUTHOR.

D. Stimulation. Ninth Year

Finally, in the accomplishment of the purpose of the junior high school, to serve as a transitional stage in the public school system, there must be a period of stimulation to facilitate transition to the senior high school. The ninth year of the junior high school is primarily for the purpose of making desirable in the estimation of each pupil advancement into the next higher type of school. The ninth year carries on the program selected after the experiment of the two previous grades. This stimulation is largely by the agency of the particular electives chosen during the periods of exploration and provisional choice.

This program has its center of interest in an effort to keep students in school. It is a course concerned with immediate educational guidance rather than with immediate vocational guidance or vocational training. The committee drawing the report realized fully that no program is adequate to retain all pupils. The committee states:

Yet there are several types of pupils who cannot be retained and who must inevitably become educational losses during or at the close of the junior high school period. These overaged, retarded, and mentally unfortunate groups are peculiarly the responsibility of the junior high school. The latter must therefore, unaided by the senior high school, offer special types of training to its own residuum of pupils for whom advancement is impossible or impracticable.

A. Particular Need for Training in Citizenship for Drop-Outs

Particularly for these groups should there be in the program of studies a liberal amount of social-science materials and especially social and civic activities so that principles of social co-operation and citizenship may be translated into conduct in the educational period which immediately precedes the entrance of the junior high school drop-outs into society and active citizenship.

If their civic-mindedness is not to be undermined by the blighting influence of becoming industrial misfits and consequently social and civic cynics, the junior high school must offer to these overaged and backward groups occupational training sufficient in extent to assure initial vocational placement. The junior high school can at least serve as a school of prevocational try-out and thereby replace, to an extent, the shifting from job to job in correcting industrial misfits during employment. If the junior high school can serve, even to a small degree with the limited facilities, in the prevention of industrial misfits and the consequent undermining of civic-mindedness, it will earn a degree of public confidence not possible through any other simple service.

B. Occupational Training for Drop-Outs

Therefore, the program of studies, as the resultant of several forces, includes a prevocational content partly for occupational placement in the industrial and commercial fields.

Vocational curricula in the junior high school, either of a commercial or industrial nature, should not represent a forced growth. They must represent the actual conditions as they exist when the *final* alternative of leaving school or choosing vocational training is reached. Whenever it is definitely determined by the guidance agencies of the school that this alternative is unavoidable, pupils should be transferred to these occupational courses, irrespective of grade classification. Grade organization must give way to a greater purpose, that of adaptability of program of studies tc individual need. Occupational courses are, therefore, matters almost wholly of individual adjustment. Arbitrary administrative regulations of promotion, classification, and organization should never be permitted to conflict with demonstrated individual needs. This statement does not set up an unsurmountable administrative difficulty; it is a direct contradiction of an unwarranted administrative practice which is frequently permitted to supersede individual justice to pupils. The junior high school program of studies must insist upon the adoption of this point of view, if it would promote equalization of educational opportunity.

C. Coaching Opportunities for Retardates

In addition to occupational training offered by commercial and industrial arts electives to some exceptional types of pupils, it is also desirable that the junior high school offer coaching opportunities to the retarded group who represent the preventable but inevitable proportion of non-promotions. This group includes those who, by lack of application, interest, or positive dislike for the restricted opportunities of a single curriculum, are able, in the light of intelligence tests, to maintain a creditable record of achievement. The fact that these preventable cases of subject failure have been shown to amount to as high as 60 to 75 per cent of all conditioned or non-promoted pupils is one evidence of the superior reliability of intelligence tests in measuring at least potential achievement. Study coach and opportunity classes or other type of coaching retarded pupils have been demonstrated to be very effective means of increasing the retentive power of the junior high school and of stabilizing subject promotion either by remedy or prevention of failure.

D. Acceleration and Enrichment for Super-normal

Still another special group for whom the junior high school program of studies should make provision is the high group. There is an affirmative vote of over 60 per cent in favor of acceleration. At the same time 72 per cent of the replies favor enrichment in the program of studies for the high group. There is, therefore, some difference of opinion as to whether it is not preferable, as one member of the general committee states it, "to prolong the period of education and enrich the program of studies for those who are able to do their work more easily, instead of putting a premium upon shortening the time spent in school." The writer of this report is of the opinion that acceleration should be restricted to the elementary school. However, another type of study coach organization may be organized for the super-normal group to effect acceleration where it has not already been achieved in the elementary grades; at the same time, this opportunity class organization for the high groups may be administered to provide extension course opportunities in an enriched program of studies. In Table LXIII (p. 594) the figures refer to hours required. The letters following figures refer to the interpretations given by committee in the notes which appear below. This is for a six-period day, sixty-minute period.

a) Including spelling and penmanship and one period a month for library instruction. One or two periods of time allotted to school activities could be used for spelling, penmanship, and library instruction. Until the school activities are fully in operation, it is desirable that this additional time for English be so used.

b) See Report of National Committee on Mathematical Requirements, Secondary School Circular No. 6, Bureau of Education, Washington. In the high eighth and ninth year, there is an option in mathematics, but no option of mathematics. Either general mathematics or the mathematics of the commercial curriculum are required of all groups.

c) U.S. history, or U.S. history and community civics.

d) Community civics, or U.S. history and community civics.

e) Elementary science and geography as a unit course, or science one period and geography three periods approximately.

f) Unit course, or science two periods and geography one period approximately.

TABLE LXIII

JUNIOR HIGH SCHOOL PROGRAM OF STUDIES

	Subject	Adjustment	Exploration and Pre-View		Provisional Choice	Stimulation
		Low Seventh	High Seventh	Low Eighth	High Eighth	Ninth
Prepared Work	**Required**					
	English	5*a*	4*a*	5*a*	4*a*	5
	General Mathematics or Commercial Mathematics	5*b*	5*b*	4	5*b*	5*b*
	Social Studies	4*c*	4*c*	3*d*	3*d*	4*h* or
	Science	4*e*	4	3	2*g*	(Gen. Sci.) 4*h* *y*
	Junior Business Training	....	....	3*n*	....	....
	Electives	....	....	....	4	4
	General Mathematics	....	....	....	5*b*	5*b*
	Foreign Languages	....	....	....	4*r*	5*s*
	Commercial Mathematics / Commercial Geography	....	....	....	4*t*	....
	Commercial Mathematics / Typewriting	....	....	....	....	5*v*
	Junior Business Training / Business Writing	....	....	....	5	....
	Bookkeeping / Business Writing	....	....	....	....	5*w*
	Industrial Arts / Agriculture / Home Economics	....	....	....	4*x*	....
Unprepared Work	**Required**					
	Industrial Arts					
	Agricultural Home Economics	2	2	2	2	2
	Music	1–I	1	1	1	1
	Art	1–II	1	1	1	1
	Guidance	1*m*	1	1	1	1
	Activities	5*o*	5	5	5	5

g) Elementary science introductory to general science of ninth year.

h) All pupils, except those electing commercial courses, required to take vocational and economic civics or general social science.

Commercial pupils required to take general science—their later commercial courses will contain much of economic civics. A minimum of science will be required in the academic curriculum of the senior high school; general science, therefore, should be postponed to the tenth year for the academic group. General social science should be required of all groups in the ninth year except as indicated for the commercial group.

i) Personal hygiene, gymnasium, directed games, etc.

j) General shop with progressive course of wood-working and metal working through three years. Agriculture optional with industrial arts for rural schools. Home economics, including sewing, cooking, textiles, laundry, millinery, dressmaking, dress and home design, and home training.

k) All boys for one term given an actual trade shop experience in a special trade type of shop equipment. The vocational side of practical arts stressed for one term for both girls and boys. Hence increase of time to three periods.

l) Additional time for fine arts may be provided by electing special work in school activities time, e.g., orchestra and chorus clubs, design and art clubs, musical or art appreciation clubs, etc.

m) Classroom instruction in educational or curriculum guidance—both educational and vocational information for pupils *prior* to choice of electives.

n) Elementary business practices and principles common to all life careers and a brief survey of commercial education and of junior commercial occupations.

o) Weekly periods for (1) home room period, (2) co-operative pupil government, (3) school assembly, (4) clubs, (5) faculty activities for professional study—a faculty esprit de corps for the co-operative solution of junior high school problems of both an administrative and instructional nature. Junior high school teachers must be trained through service; the most favorable conditions should be established. Until the school activities program is in full operation, part of the daily allotment of time for activities should be diverted to English, practical arts, fine arts, or other curricular requirement.

p) Other electives than those listed may be provided in the club activities, e.g., art, music, science, English, dramatic, practical arts, or social service clubs. The groups of electives indicate partially differentiated curricular. To facilitate cross-over between electives during this term, it is suggested that electives be made provisional, i.e., that promotion requirements in electives be deferred to the middle of the ninth year.

q) Partially differentiated curricula continued with twenty periods devoted to constants, fine and practical arts, and activities; and with ten periods devoted to electives. There are four major lines of curriculum choice provided this year, viz., the academic, the commercial, the scientific or technical, and the vocational.

r) Optional choice of Latin or one modern language. Small schools should restrict choice to one foreign language. Eight-year course introductory—vocabulary building, social life of people, etc. Earlier choice of a foreign language for pupils of high I.Q. is a program adjustment for each school. This earlier start of a foreign language should be an extension course opportunity in an enriched curriculum for special or accelerant groups.

s) First year high school course.

t) Two periods of each.

u) Ten minutes in junior business training, twenty minutes in business writing.

v) Forty minutes daily in typewriting, twenty minutes in commercial mathematics.

w) Forty minutes daily in bookkeeping, twenty minutes in business writing.

x) Four periods elective, plus the two periods required in constants of this term, give a total of six periods; five should be in special shops or advanced home training and one in drafting or design.

y) The third group of electives in the high eighth branches off into two curriculum choices in the ninth year, viz., first, the scientific or technical curriculum paralleling the academic in preparation for higher institutions, and second, the vocational or trade curriculum. In the former general science in the ninth year replaces the practical arts elective of the high eighth; but practical arts is still continued for this and all other non-vocational groups to the extent of two periods as a required subject.

z) Smith-Hughes curriculum organized as a ninth-year elective, but overage pupils should be transferred to this curriculum during seventh and eighth years, when *definitely* determined that alternatives of vocational curriculum or leaving school are unavoidable. All such transfers are problems of individual adjustment. The

4. Social Science—Industrial History, or History of Commerce first semester, and Economic Organization the second semester, or Economic Organization with a historical introduction throughout the year
5. Physical Education

FOURTH YEAR

1. English or Public Speaking
2. Social Science—Civics the first semester, and Commercial Law the second

3 and 4. Any two of the following, varying with the student's vocational interests at the time: Accounting; Stenography; Typewriting; Co-operative Office Work (this could well include some typewriting); Retail Selling, co-operative if possible; almost any elective studies for which the student has the prerequisites

5. Physical Education

This program, which was used with success in one high school some ten or twelve years ago, was based on the idea that living and business are processes of adjustment in a dual environment, social and physical. There is, therefore, throughout the four years a continuous study of existing materials which represent these two areas of contact. There is, moreover, an attempt to make the touch with these fields develop from the more generalized to the more particular. It will be noticed, for example, that the study of science moves from general science or a general study of earth structures to more special studies; social science study moves also from general history or a general study of institutions to social science study in more specialized forms. Industrial history was used as a background for economics. Government was studied after economics on the assumption that government's chief function is to assist in sustaining, guiding, and controlling the economic process. Finally came the brief study of law as the chief social device used by the social device of government. There was, as this indicates, something of viewpoint as well as content emphasized in the course and the constant emphasis of viewpoint was an important factor in the results.

The appearance of new material and definite indications of other work in prospect make it pertinent to suggest one further possible course. In nearly every way excepting the treatment of the social sciences it is similar to the course just outlined. In its treatment of the social sciences, however, there is a definite change. This work has been specialized into certain groups of subjects and organized with a definite plan in mind.

FIRST YEAR

1. English
2. General Mathematics or History or elective
3. Science—General or Physiography
4. Introduction to Business Studies—A survey which shows the need and sketches the history of social organization; business and government as methods of organizing and the types of vocations resulting
5. Physical Education

SECOND YEAR

1. English
2. General Mathematics or History or elective
3. Science—Geography, Commercial or of North America
4. Marketing in Our Society—First Semester
   Finance in Our Society—Second Semester
5. Physical Education

THIRD YEAR

1. English
2. Production Processes—Agricultural and Manufacturing—First Semester; Accounting as a Control—Second Semester
3. Physics or Chemistry or perhaps Psychology (Botany, Zoölogy, or Domestic Science may well be made optional for girls)
4. Political History or Economic History and Economic Organization or Economic Organization with a historical introduction throughout the year. Another option might be Psychology.
5. Physical Education

FOURTH YEAR

1. English or Business Communication or Public Speaking or a combination of these
2. Labor and Labor Problems or Civics the first semester and Commercial Law the second or Business and Government or Political History or Economic Organization might be given with options

3 and 4. Any two of the following, varying with the student's vocational interests at the time: Accounting; Stenography; Business Correspondence; Typewriting; Co-operative Office Work (this could well include some typewriting); Retail Selling, co-operative

if possible; almost any elective studies for which the student has the prerequisites

5. Physical Education

The problem with social science in the above course as always, is to give such a description and discussion of social phenomena as will interpret the life of which we are a part. This may be attempted in various ways; indeed, the present number of books treating social science in different ways is striking. All recognize more and more the interdependence of phenomena.

It would in some ways be desirable to study the whole complex at once, having in the first year a social science 1, in the second year a social science 2, and so on. But such a scheme has great practical difficulties. One of the greatest is to grade the material. Another is to find teachers who can work well through the whole range of material involved. In the plan outlined the whole complex has been broken into certain fields. The underlying thought appears to be that there is a large amount of data that can be intelligently organized under certain heads such as Marketing, Finance, Production, and Labor Problems, and which can at the same time be taught with adequate attention to relationships. Accounting is proposed as a study of the records used in effecting a general control and co-ordination of the work of marketing, finance, and production, studied earlier. Much of the record-keeping which is of importance to these fields alone can be taught directly in the courses dealing with them.

The course as a whole offers a considerable number of options and should be regarded as a statement of a plan to be used with a great deal of adaptation if necessary. It is, however, a scheme planned for students who are expected to "go through." In it certain subjects such as accounting are deliberately postponed until the time when it is believed they can be taught best.

It should be borne in mind in appraising the course that the work in marketing, finance, and production are thought of as chiefly descriptive. Many of the finer points in these studies would need to be omitted.

III. A consideration of the technical work that must be given. The third question which presses for solution in the secondary commercial course is what to do with the technical work. We are as yet largely uninformed as to the best methods, the proper amount of time, the proper periods for study and practice, in learning such subjects as stenography, typewriting, and machine operation. So long, then, as we think of the technical courses in terms of existing work, such as typewriting and stenography, studies of the technique of teaching are the chief need. But there is also need for studies to determine what technical courses should be given. It has been made fairly certain that stenography and typewriting have little sanction save from tradition. What should take their place or be given in addition in the high school? There is no wholly satisfactory answer, because such answers as we have are practically without exception merely statements of jobs which exist in business. It is hardly necessary to say again that the immediate vocational training for such jobs can better be given by industry or some auxiliary school agency than it can by a general high-school course. It is therefore an open question as to whether any technical courses in the narrow sense should ultimately be given in the general high-school course. The weight of evidence is in favor of the negative.

We can come to a satisfactory conclusion on this matter only by making a survey of business, not only to discover what jobs exist but to discover what ones of these jobs are not susceptible to economical training after employment. For specialized work it is as appropriate that a business furnish its own training as that it furnish its own light, space, equipment, or labor. (See also pages 311, 325, 357, 473, 498, 524, 531.)

A "LIBERAL" COMMERCIAL COURSE

We tend, then, toward a high-school commercial course from which the amount of technical work has been largely taken by other institutions better adapted to the task, and in which there has been introduced a large amount of new material. This new material, which in a general way may be designated as "social" and "scientific," must not be confused with the content of typical courses in history, civics, economics, and sociology, or with physics, chemistry, and botany. The new material must draw from all of these studies and from many others, but it must be organized in a new way and with a new view. The essence of the new view may be called functional. The student must early be shown that organized human living together is a process. In this process much occurs because of accident; much is unguided. But of certain ends, as, for example, the necessity of creating a certain amount of want-gratifying goods, we may be sure. Of other objectives we hold tentative if not final opinions. The highest human goal is to objectify living; to make us conscious of social process; to enable us to control the process of social life. To make the economic process clear, to objectify what business is and its function, merits, and deficiencies in the whole work of social life, becomes the principle upon which a curriculum of business education, publicly supported, must be framed. Sciences, financial institutions, industries, mercantile establishments, law, government, business—these are nothing but means to aid us in accomplishing our known or unrealized human aims. To see these and other human institutions as tools to be used and remade and used again is a proper goal of business education.

From such a knowledge comes at once an ability to understand the implications of technique, to use the institutions for business administrative purposes and an ability to remake them better to serve. Incidentally from such a knowledge there comes a view of purposes themselves which aids society in revision.

Such a course in business education, even if it were concluded by certain technical work, would bear little resemblance to existing courses in any department of high schools. If there can be organized a business course which will relate vocation to the varied phases of individual and social living and which will make clear the social meanings of a specialized society there will not only be a vastly improved training for business, but there will be created a general education more liberal and truly cultural than is now offered in the departments devoted to the achievement of those high goals.

QUESTIONS FOR DISCUSSION

1. Is there anything to be gained by a review of the efforts to revise the commercial curriculum?
2. What were the statements of principles laid down by the Committee of Nine concerning the commercial course in public schools? Do these principles convey to you a narrow or broad point of view concerning the course?
3. How would you characterize the course proposed by the Committee of Nine?
4. Indicate the amount of academic work, social-science work, and science work in each year of the proposed course.
5. How did the course offered by Superintendent Parker differ from the course outlined by the Committee of Nine?
6. Did the high-school commercial course become more or less technical between 1900 and 1915? How would you account for the change which occurred?
7. "Aside from the undue amount of emphasis placed on technical work, its chief weakness is its lack of definite building toward anything in particular." To which ones of the courses examined might this statement be applied?
8. To the extent that social sciences are offered in the first two courses proposed by the National Education Association, does it appear that they would give the student an adequate notion of the organization of modern society?
9. What were the criticisms of existing commercial work expressed by the National Education Association report for 1919? What were the statements of the committee reporting in 1919 concerning what the commercial course should do?
10. Examine the course outlined by the National Education Association committee reporting in 1919. How well do you feel that it achieves the purposes proposed by the committee?
11. How would you characterize the report proposed by the National Education Association in 1919?
12. The amount of requred work in the 1919 course is larger. Is this, in your mind, an advantage or the reverse?
13. The Federal Board's proposals made in 1919 conclude: "Know the needs of your students in the light of local business opportunities and meet those needs as fully as the financial support of the local school board will permit." Comment.

14. Why does the Federal Board begin to outline a commercial course beginning with the seventh year? How would you characterize the Federal Board's proposed program?
15. What is your reaction to the proposed differentiation and specialization in the last two years of the proposed course?
16. The course is criticized on the ground that "no survey of business requirements is alone sufficient basis upon which to determine the curriculum for a secondary course." Is this a justifiable criticism? If you believe this criticism justified, what else should be the basis for such a course?
17. "It does not follow that everything that is needed or wanted by business should be given by the regular commercial course." Would you agree or should the wants of business invariably be met by the high-school business course?
18. "The unit idea applied to the secondary commercial course is open to criticism." To what criticisms?
19. "Unit courses in the secondary school is the only plan which will save students from the business college." Does this statement, if true, justify unit courses?
20. The real costs to the community of giving technical training by means of the corporation school may be much less than the cost of giving such technical training in the high school. How is this possible? If it is possible, is it a reason for taking technical courses out of the high school?
21. The greatest gain in giving institutions other than the high school more of the required technical work lies in the fact that the high school is made available for work which cannot be done elsewhere. Explain.
22. "Any family which can afford to keep its children in high school for two years cannot afford to have those two years occupied merely with a narrow clerical training." Explain. Do you agree?
23. Outline the steps taken in answering the question, What should be done with the high-school commercial course? Why does the collegiate school of business program begin with the seventh grade? Contrast the proposals in this program with the proposals of the Federal Board. What are the outstanding differences? How would you characterize the program proposed by the collegiate schools of business commission?
24. Does the program outlined by the collegiate school of business commission offer a plan of courses that would enable a high-school student to comprehend what business is?

25. Does it seem to you that the collegiate commission has outlined material which, if simply presented, is beyond the comprehension of the high-school student?
26. Does it seem to you that the material outlined by the collegiate commission would, if covered, give a respectable vision of those fields in which a business man's problems lie?
27. Making decisions, exercising sound judgment, is largely a matter of being familiar with the facts about which judgments must be made. Would you agree? Would the statement apply to business judgments? If you do, consider question 26 again.
28. The plan of the National Council of Education, like that of the Collegiate Schools, emphasizes the importance of the junior high school. On what grounds?
29. The committee of the National Council says that the junior high school course should be a resultant of several forces. What forces?
30. Just what does the National Council Committee propose for "low seventh," "high seventh and low eighth," "high eighth," "ninth year"?
31. What do you understand by the "provisional choice of electives"?
32. "Vocational curricula in the junior high school should not represent a forced growth." Explain. Do you think vocational unit courses are such a forced growth?
33. "Vocational courses must represent conditions when the final alternative of leaving school or choosing vocational training is reached." Contrast this principle with the vocational unit course idea. Is there any reason why the same principle is not applicable through most of the senior high school?
34. Compare in as many respects as possible the treatment of vocational studies in the proposals of (1) the Federal Board, (2) the Collegiate School's Commission (3) the National Council's Committee.
35. Make similar comparisons for the treatment of social-business material.
36. Examine the course which is suggested, making use of existing materials. Would these courses be possible in any school with which you are familiar? To what extent would they accomplish the purposes proposed by the collegiate school's commission?
37. What is meant by saying that a properly organized commercial course would be more liberal and cultural than any course now given in any department of secondary schools?

CHAPTER XXII

A PLAN OF ORGANIZED SPECIALIZATION FOR A CITY SYSTEM

Suppose that we attempt to make an application of the conclusions reached in the foregoing chapters to a more or less idealized city situation. Two main conclusions (see pp. 576–82) from which we may derive principles have been reached:

1. Education for business has two outstanding objectives:
   a) To give an understanding of the relationships which result from specialization of business units; particularly to give an understanding of the adjustments to other related businesses which must be effected by any business man (chap. iv).
   b) To give a training in the specialized techniques which result from the high degree of specialization *within* business units (chap. v).
2. Institutions offering training in business have developed in great variety. Although almost all of them offer to undertake all the job, most of them actually train largely in technique. But some institutions are in a position where they can be used to train well in technique and *in that alone.* Examples are the corporation school, to a certain extent the business colleges and other private schools, the continuation school and, very importantly, the "post-grad" course and "drop out" courses of the high school. Other courses are in a position where they *can* be used to train in technique but where they *can also* be used to train in relationships.

The outstanding example of an institution which can give *either* type of training is the four-year high-school commercial course. But, since it is almost the only institution below the college level that can be effectively used to yield training in relationships it should be deliberately used for that purpose. The decision for such a use is further fortified by the fact that it is consistent with fundamental purposes of public education (chap. ix).

This means, then, a specialization of our educational institutions. The institutions are not in each case coincident with school buildings. For example, the "short commercial course," the "drop out" courses, the "four year commercial course," the "last year intensive or postgraduate intensive technical course," may all be given under the roof of one high school, but are distinct institutions in the sense in which the term is used here.

The required specialization of educational institutions will demand planning and organization. The directors of educational movements, however, are no strangers to such work. They have brought about the specialization of buildings and teachers now common in almost every school. They will anticipate a rearrangement of habits of thinking and will not hesitate to put old institutions to new uses.

A general program for a city (applicable in just this way perhaps to no specific city, but in general to all) might be charted in the following way:

OBJECTIVES OF EDUCATION FOR BUSINESS

Understanding of Relationships	Skill in a Specialized Technique
(The relationship of one business unit to others and of one task within a business to other tasks) (See chapters iv and v)	(This might be a broad technique such as stenography or it might be merely the skill to do well a single operation in a large firm's accounting system)
This job should be assigned to the four-year high-school commercial course. This institution should attempt to do this work if it does nothing else. At least the first three years must be devoted to it; much better all four. (For complete discussion of the high school's rôle see chapters xv and xxi)	This job should be assigned according to circumstances, to: A. Super schools 1. The business colleges and other private schools (for rôle, see pp. 311) 2. The Corporation school (for rôle, see pp. 357) 3. The continuation school (for rôle, see pp. 473) 4. Evening schools (for rôle see pp. 524) B. Technical courses for "drop outs." Technical courses of appropriate type for drop outs *at every level* of the high-school course should be created. See pp. 591–92. As a matter of fact many such courses already exist

If this plan were applied to a city system, the organization of work might be charted in this way:

FOUR-YEAR HIGH-SCHOOL COMMERCIAL COURSE[1]

Concerned, as far as business training is considered, with giving an understanding of the relationships of a business.

Purposes:

1. Aid in understanding use of technique.
2. Aid in workers' promotion through knowing functions of business.
3. Aid in possible entry into business management at a later date.
4. Aid in understanding of one's relations in a specialized business and a specialized world.

[1] The same course whether in general high schools or high schools of commerce. It is the *course* not the *building* that is specialized for the purpose. In one city where such an arrangement as the one here proposed is being considered, it has been suggested that the commercial high-school building shall be used to house the drop-out students and shall be frankly called "Technical School for Drop Out Students."

SUPER SCHOOLS

Corporation Schools
Private Schools
} These not part of the public school system—not subject to public school control.

Evening Schools
Continuation Schools

TECHNICAL COURSES FOR DROP OUTS

(See pp. 591–92)

Postgraduate Course—Technical subjects appropriate for high school graduates. (See pp. 527–72).

Fourth-Year Technical Courses—Technical subjects appropriate for students at this level. (The above two should be cooperative courses when they are retail selling or it is otherwise appropriate)

Third-Year Technical Courses. Subjects appropriate for students who must drop out at this level.

One- or two-year technical courses. Elementary technical subjects appropriate for students who must drop out without entering the general courses of high school or after one year of it. These courses can, of course, be differentiated for these two groups if thought desirable. The continuation school laws of many states, which require school attendance past this point, should make those courses decreasingly important.

Another chart showing the flow of students in such a system:

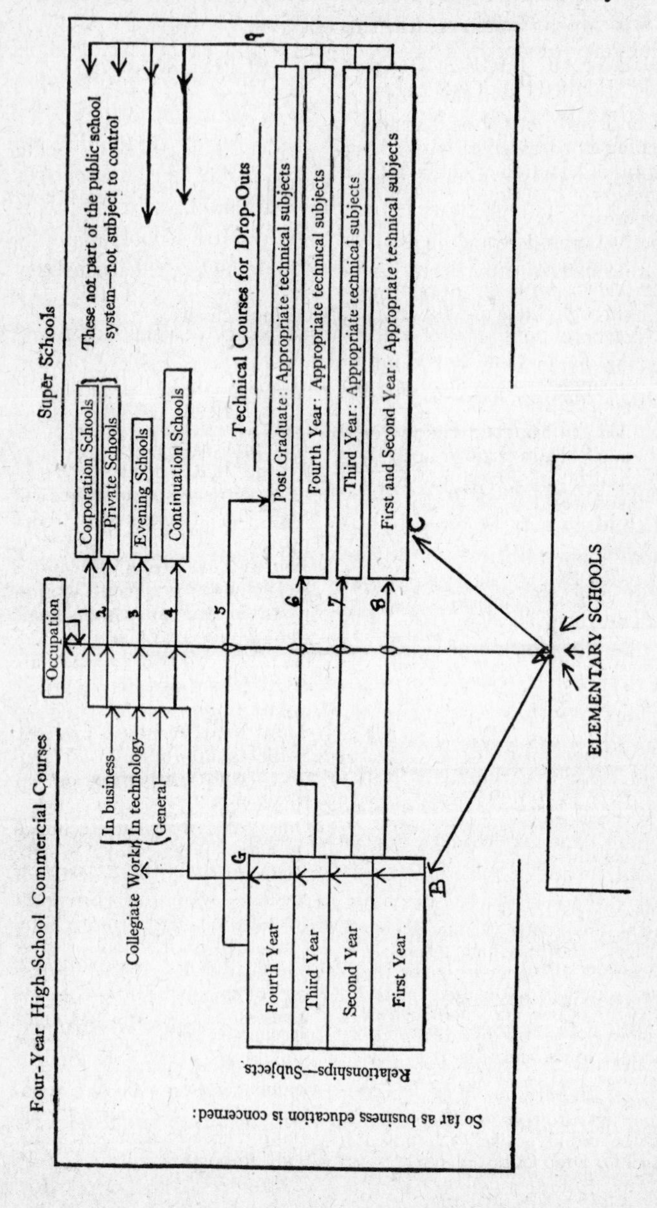

The chart above shows all the training travels which, with such a plan, might be mapped out for students leaving the elementary schools. They would leave the elementary schools at point A. If they were forced for any reason to abandon the educative process, and if they lived in a state where they were permitted by law to do so, they might travel directly toward occupation, committing themselves for the future, over routes 1, 2, 3, and 4 to what training they could get from schools in industry, business colleges, and other private schools or public evening and continuation schools. This would be the least desirable procedure from an educational standpoint.

A second possible direction of travel for those who abandoned the educative process at point A would be the right turn toward C to a one- or two-year technical course. The evidence is clear that such a course should not be typing and stenography as it has usually been (see chapter viii, especially pp. 148). It should be technical work of the sort these thirteen- to fifteen-year old children may be hired to do. The various types of "super-school" possibilities for further work after completing the technical course are still at hand. Route 9 is the channel.

The third chance (from point A again), the one encouraged by thoughtfulness and enforced by law in most states, is to the left, to point B, toward the high-school course. From B, where the four-year course, which is one of broad business study, begins, other alternatives are possible. The most obvious one of all is to go straight through the four years. From graduation, point G, college is open or the corporation school, private school, evening, and continuation school group are possibilities for special training. Or the graduate, over route 5, may reach a brief intensive course in vocational sharpening in the post-graduate technical course. Here, he should take the kind of technique—retail selling, stenography, or what not—appropriate to his age and education.

But if the student enters high school and cannot go through, the need for vocational skill is not neglected. It is provided in as brief and intensive a course as can be used to give the *vocational sharpening appropriate to his age and education at the level on which he definitely drops the educative process as such and prepares to enter industry.* This may be at the end of, or during any year. Routes 6, 7, and 8 show the way. Once through the technical course, he still may use some or all of the super schools to possible advantage. Route 9 is the outlet.

It may be well to say a word here in further explanation of the "drop-out" courses. They are really nothing but postgraduate technical courses *distributed for all.* We are no disturbed by the notion of technical courses for "drop outs" when they are called *postgraduate or two-year high-school courses.* We are in the habit of thinking of students dropping out of the *general educative process* at the eighth grade and at the end of high school. If we provide appropriate drop-out technical courses at *every level* of the high school, we shall not force those who fear they may not be able to go completely through high school to take the short commercial course, thus really dropping out at the end of the eighth grade. Much more important is the fact that we shall not be guilty of the preposterous waste proposed by some of making *every* child take a large amount of technical work *every* year as insurance against the chance that he *may* have to drop out. Consider saying to every child who enters the four-year commercial course, "You *may* drop out. At present you do not expect to, but you *may*, therefore, take a large amount of technical work so that if you do drop out, you will be prepared." At the beginning of each high-school year a similar statement is made to him. Thus he may go through the four years doing little but insuring himself against a possibility which he did not expect would happen and which, as a matter of fact, never did occur.

But suppose we do require a "safe" amount of technique in each year, and suppose the student does drop out, say at the end of the third year, as of course, many really do at the end of each year. We have, with such a plan, taken a large section of his time during each year to teach him technique fit only for a level at which he *did not quit school.* All those who do not quit are thus forced to take a large dose of insurance to cover those who drop out. Even if we assume that a third drop at the end of the first year, two-thirds have had their time at least partly occupied with the technique appropriate for fourteen-year olds. They will then, on the same principle, enter the second year learning (for protection) the technique appropriate to fifteen-year olds. A similar action will be repeated each year. Finally, if graduating or even advancing far in high school, they will leave behind them a good record of techniques learned but useless because they have outgrown them. And during the period their time will have been too much occupied to have learned much about relationshlps.

A far more economical use of time and resources is to put students who think they may be able to stay in school more than one year into a four-year course devoid of technique and protect those who find it necessary to drop out by having brief, intensive courses in technique ready for them when they must quit. These drop-out courses could give the technique at the level when it would *be used and then only*. Concerning vocational education it is doubtful if a more useful thought was ever expressed than that of James M. Glass, director of junior high schools in the Commonwealth of Pennsylvania, when he said:

> Vocational curricula in the junior high school, either of a commercial or industrial nature, should not represent a forced growth. They must represent the actual conditions as they exist when the *final* alternative of leaving school or choosing a vocation is reached. Whenever it is definitely determined by the guidance agencies of the school that this alternative is unavoidable, pupils should be transferred to these occupational courses irrespective of grade classification.

This principle is as applicable to senior high schools as to lower grades. It is a philosophy which must lie behind a plan of organized specialization of institutions directed toward the attainment of definite objectives.

INDEX

INDEX

PRINTED IN THE U.S.A